The Sociology of Work

For Richard, our *Sakura*

The Sociology of Work

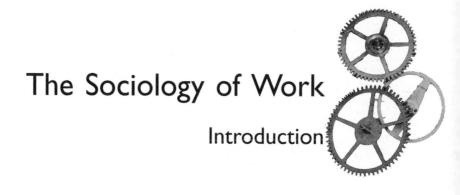

Introduction

Third Edition

Keith Grint

polity

First edition published 1991
Second edition published in 1998
This edition published in 2005 by Polity Press.

Reprinted 2006, 2007

Polity Press
65 Bridge Street
Cambridge CB2 1UR, UK

Polity Press
350 Main Street
Malden, MA 02148, USA

ISBN 978–0–7456–3249–0
ISBN 978–0–7456–3250–6 (pbk)

A catalogue record for this book is available from the British Library and has been applied for from the Library of Congress.

Typeset in 10 on 12pt Sabon
by Graphicraft Ltd, Hong Kong
Printed in Great Britain by MPG Books Ltd, Bodmin, Cornwall

This book is printed on acid-free paper.

Contents

List of Figures

List of Tables

Acknowledgements

This book was updated, rewritten and extended in 2003 and 2004 and I would like to express my gratitude to Sarah Dancy for her excellent editing skills and patience. I would like to thank Katy for keeping most of the trouble off the streets, Beki for keeping out of most of the shops, and Kris for keeping out of most of the pubs. I would also like to thank Sandra for her patience, her good humour, her skills on Excel, and much much more.

Preface

This book had its origins in the untimely death of Eric Batstone in 1987. Eric had been my doctoral supervisor from 1982 to 1985 at Nuffield College, Oxford, and I had hoped to combine our respective sets of lecture notes on industrial sociology and the sociology of work, which he taught at Oxford and I taught at Brunel. However, it soon became clear to me that it was an impossible task: although Eric remained the inspiration for this book, the work contained no direct input from his notes. Ten years on, and seven years after the publication of the first edition, I updated the text where appropriate, tried to make the material more accessible, and added a glossary; at the end of each chapter I added suggestions for further reading and possible exam or essay questions. I also took the opportunity to add a new chapter on the globalization of work – an issue that was still emerging in the early 1980s but has since become the flavour of the last decade of this century. An earlier version of it first appeared in Mike Haralambos's edition of *Developments in Sociology* (vol. 14, 1998).

In 2004 the text was again fully updated and I took the opportunity to reconstruct the final chapter by dividing it into two, one concerned with the state of contemporary employment and the other focused on globalization and the future of work.

Introduction

This book concerns work. Work occupies a substantial proportion of most people's lives and has often been taken as a symbol of personal value: work provides status, economic reward, a demonstration of religious faith and a means to realize self-potential. But work also embodies the opposite evaluations: labour can be back-breaking and mentally incapacitating; labour camps are punishment centres; work is a punishment for original sin and something which we would all rather avoid – something which was, to quote a woman munitions worker in the Second World War, 'the blank patch between one brief evening and the next' (Mass Observation, 1943: 43).

The ambiguous nature of work is a central theme running through this book. Rather than restricting the review to paid labour, and concentrating upon male factory workers as much as industrial or occupational sociology does, it considers work in a rather wider context, including unpaid domestic labour, which highlights the links between the sphere of employment and the domestic sphere, and which incorporates the notions of ethnicity and gender as well as class. Inevitably, an introductory text of this type can barely skim the surface of most of the debates here and I have not attempted to provide a comprehensive introduction to all forms of work in all varieties of society throughout all known periods of time. Instead, I have selected substantive fields that I consider significant and have attempted to illustrate these both with conventional material and with some rather less traditional. Since an underlying theme of the approach is the complexity and differences which exist at work, rather than the uniformities, the selection of substantive fields and source material is inevitably asymmetrical: it is, for example, because I dispute the allegedly archetypal significance of the male factory worker isolated from his domestic world that the book looks beyond him to female domestic workers, to eighteenth-century sailors and to twentieth-century women civil servants for the evidence. By definition, therefore, I miss out far more than I consider, but my intention is both to introduce the sociological world of work and to undermine some traditional myths, rather than to provide the definitive account of typical work – whatever that might involve.

Although introductory texts are, by their very nature, overviews of broad areas I do not think this means the book should avoid pursuing particular and explicit theoretical lines with regard to the current orthodoxies of the day. Each chapter has its own specific viewpoints to engage with but perhaps I should acknowledge an overriding engagement with four areas.

First is the denial of the superordinate position of class at the expense of gender, race and ethnicity, and the concomitant denial of the supremacy of the labour process separated from home and all else. The spheres of work, employment and home are all necessarily intertwined and to separate them as if they could exist independently is to misconceive the complex reality of work and misunderstand the significance of the relationships which it embodies. Moreover, to decant elements of social groups or individuals into categories like class, gender and ethnicity is to imply that individuals interpret the world through a single lens. If, on the other hand, individuals and the social groups they engage with are considered as heterogeneous constructs, for whom the world is perceived through a multifaceted lens, then we should concern ourselves with the fragmentation of work experience. Rather than puzzling over the 'failure' of the working class to develop a solidaristic political organization we might instead puzzle over why any collective organization exists and persists. In sum, what may appear to one person or analyst to be a self-evidently important social cleavage may not be interpreted as such by another.

The second issue is the polarization of organizational features into social and technical, with either the former or the latter being endowed with determinate qualities. Adopting the actor network approach, I argue that it is the mixture of human and non-human elements which generates significant resources, though how these 'alloys' are deployed is determined not by the content but by the interpretative actions of various agents within the network.

The third line I wish to pursue is that work is itself socially constructed and reconstructed. This implies that much of what we take for granted as inevitable or technically required or economically determined should be subjected to the most vigorous of critiques: if work is socially constructed then it is contingent and requires perpetual action by agents for its reproduction – it does not just happen but has to be brought off. Relatedly, whereas it is common to differentiate the moral economy of the pre-capitalist period from the market economy that displaced it, I argue that the moral and social aspects of work are still an essential component. To believe that contemporary employment is configured and constrained only by appeals to the rationality of market forces is to misconstrue the nature of work. If workers seek pay rises in line with inflation, rather than company profitability, or decry the disproportionate but performance-related increases of directors' salaries, then the market model can explain these only be asserting the irrationality of such workers; but if we retain the notion of work as a social and moral sphere, as well as a market sphere, then workers' actions become not irrational but rational from a different viewpoint. This does not mean that morality displaces market rationality and it would perhaps be more appropriate to consider the two as resources which different groups draw on to legitimate their particular campaigns at specific locations in space and time.

Fourth, and as an underlying feature of the above three issues, this book proceeds from the assumption that the world of work is one actively constructed through the interpretative acts of agents involved. Here, then, we should leave the world of 'objective' analysis, of certainty and predictability, and replace it with one constructed by indeterminacy, contingency and alternative viewpoints. What is important in attempting to explain the world of work is not what that world *is* but what those involved in it take it to be. In short, what counts as 'work', what counts as 'inevitable' and what counts as 'rational behaviour' does not lie within the object or the phenomenon itself but within the social relations and interpretative processes that sustain it.

Chapter 1 sets out to discuss this indeterminacy by establishing the enigmatic essence of work. It begins by noting the significance of any activity being labelled as work in so far as an evaluation may be placed upon such an activity. What appear to be identical activities very often embody widely contrasting norms of behaviour such that the same 'work' of individuals in war and peace may be either 'heroic' or 'bestial', depending on the social circumstances and relations under which they are undertaken. This equivocal feature of work is highlighted by focusing upon non-Western and historical approaches to work. It then moves on to consider the consequences of attempts to persuade workers that their efforts were either sanctioned by God or an essential element of their humanity or a necessary means to buy their way out of the hell they found themselves in. The chapter finishes by looking at informal work, particularly domestic labour and unemployment, through which the nature of work as a social construct is re-emphasized.

Chapter 2 explores the historical dimension of work in radically different societies. From Roman Britain to the Luddites to nineteenth-century textile factories and beyond I argue against any reduction of work to a single form and illuminate the moral economy of pre-capitalist work relations on land and at sea. Noting the occupational diversity that also typifies British industrial experience, I consider the redistribution of domestic labour and influence at home which accompanied the Industrial Revolution, and the consequential disappearance from visible paid employment by the majority of married women, especially the middle class, during the Victorian era. This is linked to the activities of the early trade unions which, in conjunction with the paternalistic concerns of the state, coerced women out of many areas of skilled employment and attempted to corral them within the home. Finally, I trace the rise of women's employment through the advance of clerical labour and the two world wars to a point where, despite patriarchal influence, the beginnings of wage equality at work were established.

Chapter 3 moves from the substantive field of historical work to the theoretical endeavours of the historical 'gang of three': Marx, Weber and Durkheim. While noting the limitations of such classical approaches, especially the gender-blind or patriarchal influences of all three, each has something in particular to offer our contemporary analysis of work though none individually nor all three together provide anything like a coherent account of work. They are, then, important but flawed foundation stones rather than the adumbrations that merely need to be fleshed out.

Chapter 4 switches from the historical to the contemporary and delves into the complex world of the modern organization and its multitude of competing

viewpoints and analyses. Running through most of the major alternative interpretations of organizations and underlining what I consider to be their major problems, I explore the possibilities offered by the most recent advances in related
areas: post-modernist theory and Actor Network theory. Drawing primarily on
the latter, I develop an analysis which demonstrates the difficulty of separating
human from non-human facets of organization and how such alloys of human
technology can be captured and deployed by various contending groups within
organizational settings.

From here the book moves on to review the three aspects of social stratification which I consider to be most important: class, in chapter 5, gender in
chapter 6, and race and ethnicity in chapter 7. I begin by considering the relative weight given to class rather than occupation and to income rather than
wealth, and pose some doubts as to any universal assumption about the role
of employment in accounting for life chances. I then move on to examine the
form of work activity most closely associated with class action – the strike.
Noting the essentially organized nature of such action, I throw doubt upon the
class orientation of most British strikes, though I emphasize the recalcitrance
that appears to typify many British workers. Finally, some time is spent examining the labour process debates, and I emphasize the problems of an approach
that systematically devalues all but the class issues and denies the necessary
links between the domestic and the non-domestic spheres of work.

This linkage is continued in chapter 6 on gender, patriarchy and trade unionism
which explains the various theoretical interpretations of gender inequalities and
poses an alternative in which individuals are reconstructed as composite and
heterogeneous embodiments of class, gender and ethnicity, rather than as discrete elements of each. Thus women and men do not experience work just through
their specific gender, nor just through their differential class, nor through their
ethnic group, but all three simultaneously. Using this model I examine the contemporary evidence of women at work, detailing the quest for equal pay, the
advances and retreats of professional women, and the part played by trade unions
in the subordination of women.

Chapter 7 considers the third of my three forms of social stratification, race
and ethnicity. It looks first at alternative theories of inequality and progress to
consider the wider issue of labour market influences. Again, the brief perusal
of the empirical evidence suggests that we cannot consider ethnic minorities as
a single group but reconceptualize them through the specificity of their ethnicity in conjunction with their class and gender. Following this, a number of
different aspects of the connections between ethnicity, race and the labour
market are covered, in particular the role of ethnic businesses, the value of anti-
discriminatory policies and legislation and the role of management, especially
in recruitment. Finally, the part played by trade unions in the persistence of
racism at work is assessed before reviewing the comparative experiences of
minorities in the USA and Britain.

Chapter 8 switches from the social to the technical aspects of work but only
in order to illustrate the problems of demarcating one from the other. Through
a review of the polarized arguments of technological and social determinists I
argue that both approaches misconstrue the nature of the relationship between

human and non-human elements at work: technology-less work systems are usually as unproductive as human-less technologies. Only when we conceive of the two features of work as intimately related in a creative 'alloy' of both can we begin to explain the nature of work properly. This is supplemented by a brief review of the two most recent attempts to propel the complex and uncertain world of work into a future of radical difference and stark simplicity: the 'post-Fordist' and the 'technocracy' debates. Maintaining a healthy scepticism of such revolutionary changes, on both theoretical and empirical grounds, I conclude that neither new nor old *universal* patterns of work exist: diversity rather than universality remains the norm, and part of the reason for this remains locked into the interpretative methods by which we come to know the world of work.

Chapter 9 concerns the nature of contemporary work. It begins by considering the state and status of jobs as the decline of manufacturing continues in the West, but then analyses arguments that suggest that the archetypal manufacturing job design – McDonaldization – is creeping into all areas of work. It then proceeds to consider the extent to which we are now living to work rather than working to live by analysing working hours and productivity. This then leads onto a discussion of the inequalities of work rewards and work experiences and it ends with a question: are workers today more likely to lead a Dog's Life or become Fat Cats?

Finally, in chapter 10, I consider the recent developments associated with the globalization of work, first by looking at whether we can model the future by looking at the past, then by setting out the context for globalization and the consequent debates about rising and declining levels of wealth and inequality. The last sections cover the anti-globalization debates and the persistence of a form of work that many people thought we had seen the last of in the nineteenth century: slavery.

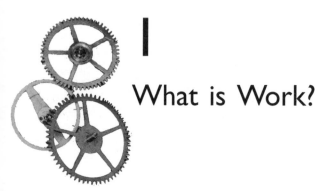

1

What is Work?

> Who first invented Work?
>
> Charles Lamb, letter to Barton

Introduction

This chapter demonstrates the difficulties of delineating the world of work from the sphere of non-work and argues that no unambiguous or objective definition of work is possible. **Work** tends to be an activity that transforms nature and is usually undertaken in social situations, but exactly what counts as work is dependent on the specific social circumstances under which such activities are undertaken and, critically, how these circumstances and activities are interpreted by those involved. Whether any particular activity is experienced as work or leisure or both or neither is intimately related to the temporal, spatial and cultural conditions in existence. This does not mean that the search for the meaning of work is the equivalent to the quest for the Holy Grail, nor that one person's definition of work is as influential as any other. Rather, it implies that we should consider the past and present definitions of work as symbols of cultures and especially as mirrors of power: if what counts as work is glorified or despised or gender-related, then the language and practice of work allows us to read embodied fragments of wider social power. For example, to be categorized as 'unemployed' today not only signifies the historically atypical creation of a formal division between the economy and the polity, employment and work, but also embodies the significance attached to one particular facet of contemporary Western social life. Unemployment is not a category that would be recognized outside a very limited slice of space and time; that it is today, and that the label is crucial to the status of the individual, tells us as much about the kind of society we inhabit as about the kind of individual stigmatized.

To illustrate the indexical nature of work, this chapter considers contemporary Western definitions of work and compares these to non-Western and historical forms before silhouetting radical critiques of, and contemporary orientations towards, work. It then moves on to a brief analysis of two substantive fields traditionally excluded from the study of work to illustrate the effects of such traditions: domestic work and unemployment.

Problems of definition

Labour and work

It is more than just a pedantic requirement that this chapter begins by trying to answer the most basic of questions: what is work? One of the ways of distinguishing between them is via Arendt's (1958) opposition between 'labour' and 'work': labour is bodily activity designed to ensure survival in which the results are consumed almost immediately; work is the activity undertaken with our hands which gives objectivity to the world. A major difficulty with Arendt's approach, however, is that in many industrial societies very little activity generates products for immediate consumption, whereas in some hunter-gatherer societies very little activity generates material artefacts that give objectivity to the world. Perhaps more conventionally, work has been imputed with transformative capacity – an activity which alters nature – while an occupation is something which locates individuals within some form of market (R. Brown, 1978: 56). Yet those who are unemployed, that is no longer within the labour market, very often consider themselves as retaining whatever notion of occupation they previously had, so that the status of occupation, perhaps, may be divorced from the practice of that occupation; but neither the status nor practice of an occupation are the *sine qua non* of work.

Work as objective

Is work, then, simply that which ensures individual and societal survival by engaging with nature? Certainly, all societies have to engage with nature to ensure their survival but are activities which are not essential to societal survival (e.g. writing sociology texts?) non-work? What is objectively essential to societal survival anyway, and is this the equivalent of individual survival? It is surely significant that the work of slaves, often derided as mere 'labour', may be critical for the survival of society yet simultaneously effect the exclusion from society of the very same slave and possibly result in her or his death. Moreover, if by work we embrace all social activities that are in some way transformative of nature, do we end up with a set of activities too broad to be of any value; if everything is work can anything be leisure or rest? Clearly, as Garfinkel (1984), Silverman (1970) and Giddens (1979) *inter alia* have maintained, since social reality has to be worked at – that is it has to be brought off by knowledgeable agents who sustain meaningful interchanges with each other – it could be asserted that every human activity is work, in which case the sociology of work ought to become the sociology of everything. Again, if everything is work then the label is significant in demonstrating the importance of human processes of interaction; but unless we wish to impose our sociological conception of work as all human activities on to the populace we wish to study, then we should beware of assuming that what we think of as work is objective: to impute our own meanings into the language and practices of others is precisely to miss out on the significance of the social aspect. It is because the meanings secreted within and expressed through work are so variant that our conventional model of work as paid employment should not be taken as 'normal' (see Joyce, 1987). After all, if language is indexical, as the ethnomethodologists and others maintain (Sharrock and Anderson, 1986: 42–3; Woolgar, 1988), then the word 'work' cannot have an objective and transcendent meaning. Rather, the language and discourse of work are symbolic representations through which meanings and social interests are constructed, mediated and deployed. In short, the meanings of work do not inhere within the practices of participants but are created, challenged, altered and sustained through the contending discourses: if particular forms of activity are represented through discourse as valued or valueless then the activities themselves take on such characteristics for those appropriating such a discourse. For example, whether one regards domestic activities as 'work' or 'leisure' or 'drudgery' or something else entirely does not depend upon the activities but how we read such activities through the appropriate lexicon. It is not that the activities remain the same but that our viewpoints are different: we can construct the activities only through the viewpoint. In effect, we do not 'see' the same activities.

Work, the economy and the state

The state often appears to have a definitive answer to the conundrum of meaning: the population is divided between those who are 'economically active' and those who 'economically inactive'. But the definition of activity here relates very closely to the formality of employment: if people are paying tax and insurance etc., they are working; if they are not they are not working. We might question whether such formality is the best way to define work when so many people, especially women with domestic responsibilities, appear by this definition to spend so long doing nothing. Equally significant, this model of work reflects the emergence of a viewpoint in which the economy gradually appears as the foundation stone of Western society and concomitantly the sphere of work assumes a discrete existence (Godelier, 1980). As Dumont (1977) has argued:

> The modern era has witnessed the emergence of a new mode of consid-eration of human phenomena, and the carving out of a separate domain, which are currently evoked for us by the words *economics, the economy* . . . It is conventional, and not too arbitrary, to take the publication by Adam Smith in 1776 . . . as the birth registration of the new category . . . the mercantilists of the seventeenth and eighteenth century mingled the phenomena we classify into *political* and *economic* . . . in the Indian civ-ilization, while the political had been distinguished from and subordinated to the religious, the economic was never conceptually detached from the political. (1977: 33–4)

This 'triumph of economic ideology' in eighteenth-century Western Europe not only attacked assumptions that citizens had social and political rights that stood outside and above the realm of the market place, it also embodies the state's desire to classify citizens first and foremost as economic rather than political agents. The evaluative connotations of this relationship are nicely captured in the convention that political demonstrations and marches may be acceptable 'providing they do not interfere with people's legitimate business'. In effect, eco-nomic action *qua* 'going to work' is normal, political action *qua* participating in a protest march is abnormal.

Work as employment

But does this dismemberment of social activities help or hinder us in the quest for the meaning of work? Even if we try to escape the definitional problem of 'work' and nestle in the blanket security of 'employment', the barbs of ambi-guity are wont to spring up through the cover: is the distinction between work and employment one of payment? – many activities can be subsumed under both labels. Is the distinction one based on formality? – a whole panoply of activities that are not conventionally considered as employment actually occur not so much 'under' the conventional economy but through it. In other words, although commentators like to categorize some activities as belonging to the informal or black economy rather than the official economy, it would appear that no clear-cut binary division exists. We have economically inspired activ-ity that occurs along a continuum rather than being situated in either one or another clearly marked category: formal and informal (Harding and Jenkins, 1989).

In general, most sociological accounts of 'work' actually concern themselves with paid employment; hence most sociology of work has actually been indus-trial sociology or the sociology of employment or the sociology of occupations. Industrial sociology, the sociology of employment and the sociology of occupations are wide and important fields of interest in and of themselves, but employment *qua* full-time wage labour through an occupation within an industrial setting has been a common phenomenon only in a very restricted window of space and time; i.e., the last two centuries of a minority of nations (R. Brown, 1988: 33). In fact, one might go further to agree with Moorhouse (1987: 237) that paid work in car factories has been 'elevated to an iconic status such that labour on the track or line became, somehow, the explicit or implicit model of what most modern work is like, or would soon be like'. This book, like the work of Moorhouse, is iconoclastic in intent; it does not reduce the sociology of work to industrial sociology or the sociology of occupations and employment but argues that they are all aspects of the sociology of work.

Work and non-work

In some senses work is the opposite of leisure: it is something we have to do, something we may prefer not to do and something we tend to get paid for. But we must also eat and drink without considering this as work; we usually have to go shopping but this is not conventionally recognized as work, though, as with much domestic labour for those undertaking it, such activities can be extremely arduous. Moreover, there are very few activities undertaken outside a pecuniary relationship which do not also occur inside one. Washing, ironing, breastfeeding, childminding, cooking and a myriad other such domestic activities all exist as unpaid and paid labour, though the correlation between paid labour and work normatively configured as 'valuable' or 'real' is not coincidental.

Nor can we distinguish between work and non-work on the basis of non-work being leisure: for some people playing sport is an occupation not a leisure activity while for others the enforced 'leisure' of unemployment turns the freedom of non-work into a nightmare of perceived worthlessness. Even for those who are employed it is not always clear how work and leisure can be separated. Loudon's review of work on South African farms suggests that for white farmers the social system requires the conflation of activities: 'Where sport and leisure activities are crucial factors in defining membership of a local community and also provide a setting for the informal exchange of ideas and information, farming as a way of life involves no clear separation between non-work and work' (Loudon, 1979: 129). Nearly two centuries earlier, the Quaker business community also managed to combine work and non-work into a seamless web of people and processes, for this 'group with the greatest overlap between kinship, friendship and religious community . . . often combined religious missions with commercial travelling' (Davidoff and Hall, 1987: 216).

In different segments of space and time the activities we may refer to as relaxations from work have been the difference between life and death: in contemporary Britain a failed crop of vegetables in the kitchen garden is a waste of time and effort but the equivalent failure in different parts of the world now or at earlier times in British history would be the end of time for the responsible gardener. Not that poor economic returns necessarily dissuade people from continuing particular forms of work. Crofting can hardly ever have been a route to economic prosperity and the rise of commercial agriculture has long since made it a marginal form of employment. Yet crofting continues because it is of great symbolic significance for those involved in it: it ensures 'the maintenance of a valued collective identity . . . through which men [*sic*] locate themselves in their cultural tradition' (Cohen, 1979: 250–1). That farming on a small scale may be considered as economically 'irrational' yet continue to involve many people is another demonstration of the incomplete dominance of economic ideology.

It is noticeable that we often avoid the term 'work' to describe activities involving children: workers, doctors, farmers and hairdressers may 'work' but parents just 'look after' children. In short, it is not just that the linguistic terms we use have some degree of ambiguity inherent to them, so that we cannot always distinguish between work and non-work; as Schwimmer (1979) reveals, for some people (in this case artists) the division is absurd. The very same term may also carry contrary meanings. 'Going to work' is one thing, having to work when you get there is a separate matter altogether. Work, then, in its physical features and its linguistic descriptions is socially constructed: there is no permanent or objective thing called work, there are aspects of social activities which we construe as work and this embodies social organization. The difference between work and non-work seldom lies within the actual activity itself and more generally inheres in the social context that supports the activity. By implication, therefore, what counts as work cannot be severed from the context within which it exists, and that context necessarily changes through space and time.

Working beyond the contemporary West

Clarification of what counts as work is often best achieved by pushing the boundaries of what we conventionally refer to as work to their most extreme forms. For example, Malinowski's (1984) account of the Trobriand Islanders is important in emphasizing two features: first, the irrelevance of monetary incentives in a cashless economy where social obligations to kin are the primary motive to engage in labour; and second, the seamless web which knits what we might recognize as work and leisure activities together in a social network of practices. For the islanders there is no separation between the work of gardening and the associated rituals – they are one and the same process:

> When the plants begin to grow a series of magical rites, parallel with the inaugural ones, is performed, in which the magician is supposed to give an impulse to the growth and development of the plant at each of its successive stages. Thus, one rite is performed to make the seed tuber sprout; another drives up the sprouting shoot; another lifts it out of the ground; yet another makes it twine around the support; then, with yet other rites, the leaves are made to bud, to open, to expand respectively. (Malinowski, quoted in Littler (ed.), 1985: 16)

Hunter-gatherers and work

Similarly, the work of Sahlins (1972) on some hunter-gatherer societies has demonstrated that the motivation to work, that is to fill up time with 'productive activities', is a distinctly contemporary Western idea, since for many hunter-gatherers 'work' ceases as soon as the minimum necessary activity has been achieved. More recently Woodburn (1980) has suggested that work-related activity is contingent on the nature of the subsistence system: most hunter-gatherers are indeed immediate consumers of the food obtained, though there are some, especially Australian Aborigines, where consumption is delayed and a consequentially more formal organizational system exists to distribute and control the food. The crucial point, though, is that abundance and scarcity of food and other resources do not appear to determine the form of social organization – whether hunter-gatherers are relatively sedentary and mobile, more or less formally organized, is ultimately the result of social constructions not environmental determination. One of the main problems with trying to assess the significance of work in hunter-gatherer societies is that many of them now exist only in the most marginal lands, pushed off the most productive land by the encroaching settlers. Thus although they may now have to work rather more hours than they would like in order to secure food supplies, it does seem that working hours are directly related to such concerns and not to any standardized hours of gainful activity.

Work in industrializing societies

Of course, many people in the so-called Third World today appear to have little option but to accommodate themselves to the newly industrializing order, and that means maximizing their potential income by extending the working day as long as possible. Just as many pre-industrial societies seem to have operated without a clear division between work and leisure, so too life in the huge 'informal sectors' of contemporary Third World cities often obliterates the division. However, the seamless web that knits work and non-work is more pervasive because of the absence of clear-cut non-pecuniary activities rather than the conflation of work and leisure. As Stalker argues: 'Work in this case is not so much what gives a meaning to life, more what makes life possible: a means of gleaning something, however slight, from a hostile environment. It has no beginning and no end. Working and eating and sleeping and childcare and everything else blend into one organic whole' (1986: 8). While the majority in Western industrial nations have or had fixed sites for employment and semi-permanent occupations and income, possibly between 20 and 70 per cent of the urban workforces in major Third World cities are informal, that is without fixed place of work, occupation or income (Rosenberg, 1986).

Some of the most poignant images of people caught in the transition between non-industrial and industrial societies are gleaned through the rhetoric of those without employment. Bourdieu's (1979) study of Algeria in 1960 high-lights the conflicts as 'old-fashioned peasant' becomes transformed into 'urban sub-proletarian' and, in the absence of employment, operates as a street trader. Given the relatively insignificant sums of money earned by such practices, Bourdieu argues that such practices

> borrow their justifications from the peasant morality of the past . . . the outward appearances of being occupied are the last resort against the ulti-mate degradation of the man who gets others to feed him . . . activity is identified with social function and is not measured by the product in kind (still less in money). . . . Those who find themselves in a position where it is impossible to get real work endeavour to fill the abyss between their unrealizable aspirations and the effective possibilities by performing work whose function is doubly symbolic in that it gives a fictitious satisfaction to the man who performs it while at the same time providing him with a justification in the eyes of others. (Bourdieu, 1979: 41–2)

Indeed, this concern for social obligation and the creation of self-respect, from what many might regard as the worst of all possible worlds, is also re-created in the rhetoric of the 'untouchable' road sweepers and lavatory cleaners of Benares (now Varanasi) for whom work provides both identity and material reward, and facilitates the reproduction of ritual and social obligations. Moreover:

> Sweepers associate their work of sweeping with a toughness that they admire in both men and women; with drinking and eating of 'hot' substances, meat and strong liquor. Linked with this is their belief that they are hot-blooded and highly-sexed. Both men and women lay great emphasis on honour and will in defence of it fight without much provocation. . . . The sweepers' sense of identity and self-esteem comes from their style of life rather than from their work . . . the meanings [they] attribute to that work are different from those attributed to it by the larger society. (Searle-Chatterjee, 1979: 284–5)

Images of Third World urban poverty are commonplace but why do people move in from the countryside to risk this form of marginality? The major reason appears to be to improve one's life chances: casual labourers in Delhi, for example, can work for 250 days a year – twice as many as are possible in a countryside already overcrowded (Stalker, 1986). Yet we should not assume that economic desire necessarily drives out all other issues of social life. As Lal (1989) has recently argued in the case of India, the explanation for problems related to limited economic growth may not be structural rigidities and labour market distortions derived from, among other things, the caste system, but may more simply be that even underemployed workers are not always willing to exchange leisure time for high money incomes. Similarly, Perlman's (1976) ana-lysis of informal workers in Rio de Janeiro and Bombay suggests that while almost half came to the city for financial reasons a similar proportion were driven by family or health reasons, though not by the attractions of the 'city lights'. Even for those towards the bottom of the material ladder the sphere of necessity, then, does not automatically invade and replace the sphere of freedom.

If some of the difficulties facing the urban poor of the Third World can be related to Western ideas of economic rationality, where do these original inter-pretations stem from? Some of the most enduring are from ancient Greece and many have their origins in the practices not of those undertaking the work – the view from below – but of those attempting to legitimize the view of those not engaged in it – the view from above.

Historical rhetorics of work: views from above and below

The language of work

In ancient Greek society the sphere of freedom is conventionally seen as being the opposite of the sphere of necessity, the labour of slaves being automatically associated with the latter. This did not mean that all forms of manual labour were regarded as loathsome but it did mean, first, that anyone who *had* to work at an occupation all the time was ignoble, and, second, that the essence of ennoblement lay in the realm of politics, a realm based on, but untarnished by, the labour of other, lesser mortals (Held, 1987). In fact, while the Hebrew word for work, *avodah*, has the same root as *eved*, meaning slave, the Greeks had no general word for 'work' but three particular ones: *ponos*, meaning painful activity; *ergon*, meaning task (military or agricultural); and *techne*, meaning technique. The sphere of necessity was complemented by the nature of depend-ence: if, as a craft worker, you were dependent on the whims of the customer, you were not considered to be engaged in truly creative activity. In fact, the element of originality imputed to skilled crafts actually declined as Greek society became more consumerist: the craft worker became the medium of the labour process not the originator (Godelier, 1980).

It is worth reflecting here on the sources of these ideas: many stem from individuals like Aristotle and Plato, whose distrust of democracy was insepar-able from their dislike of the labouring classes. For them, those who were depend-ent on others could not be free to engage in political debate, hence labour became conceived not as the foundation of the realm of politics, but as its underminer. Furthermore, Aristotle and Plato raged against democracy and labour *because* both individuals were unable to resist the democratic influence at the time. The pro-democratic forces were much more inclined to defend the status of labour – even if they left little in the way of literature to support their case (Wood, 1981). What the slaves would have had to say on the topic is even less certain. In Orwell's words:

> Civilizations founded on slavery have lasted for such periods as four thousand years [yet] the detail that frightens me is that those hundreds of millions of slaves on whose back civilization rested generation after generation have left behind them no record whatever. We do not even know their names. In the whole of Greek and Roman history, how many slaves' names are known to you? I can think of two. . . . One is Spartacus and the other is Epictetus. (1984: 232)

What passes for *the* Greek attitude to work, therefore, depends on which Greek you read and how you read the text.

The instability and metamorphosis in the nature of work represented in Greek literature is also contained in the couplets Labour/Work and *Mühe/Werke*, and captured in the development of the French words used to describe work. Indeed, it is striking how the words for work resonate with the twin images of forced labour and, to a lesser extent, free expression: *gagner* entered the language in the twelfth century from the Frankish word *waidajan*, meaning to pillage and search for food. Until the sixteenth century two words concerned work: *oevrer* was a work of art but derived from the Latin *operarus* meaning a man of pain or affliction; while *labourer*, to plough, came from the Latin *labor* or agricultural toil. These two words tended to be replaced by the single word *travailler*, to work, from the Latin *tripaliare*, meaning to torture using a *tripalium*, a three-pronged instrument (Godelier, 1980). The connection between work, pain and the absence of freedom is hardly coincidental.

Work and power

The position of slaves highlights another significant aspect of the human condition, for this most debased form of labour still contains a quintessential aspect of social relations often ignored in contemporary debates about work: the significance of resistance. Giddens (1979: 145–50) has argued that too many conceptualizations of power take a position in which the default category is one of zero-sum: the more A gains the more B loses, to the extent that many work relationships can be considered as ones of powerlessness on one side. Yet 'all power relations, or relations of autonomy and dependence, are reciprocal' (1979: 149). That is to say, despite enormous variations in power resources, individuals can make a difference; they are not coerced into a specific form of behaviour except in a remarkably small number of situations. Even suicide can be taken as an act of defiance rather than submission to external forces. The suicides in Alicante of defeated Republicans in the Spanish Civil War, so chillingly described by Saturnino Carod, a Saragossa trade union leader, are a valuable reminder of the ultimate rebellion: 'As he stood staring out to sea, the man next to him with a cigarette in his mouth slit his own throat and crumpled on the quay. Almost immediately, word came from the other end of the port that someone he knew had shot himself. Suicides spread like an epidemic . . .' (Fraser, 1979: 503).

But such extreme forms of consummate resistance should not divert attention away from the more mundane, yet probably more significant, forms of resistance enacted by those commonly regarded as powerless – slaves. Mary Prince, the first black slave to escape from slavery under British control and publish her memoirs, provides two distinct but important lessons for a study of work. First, her recognition of the situation of slavery as being socially constructed, and therefore subject to change as opposed to natural or inevitable, is one which she gradually comes to appreciate, not one she is born with. Thus for Mary her childhood as a slave 'was the happiest period of my life; for I was too young to understand rightly my condition as a slave, and too thought-less and full of spirits to look forward to the days of toil and sorrow' (Ferguson, 1987: 47). Second, even as a slave she manages to construct strategies of resist-ance that serve to restrain her owners' control and maintain her own dignity. Thus she manages to earn some money in the hope of buying her way to free-dom: 'When my master and mistress went from home . . . I took in washing and sold coffee and yams and other provisions to the captains of ships' (p. 71). And she also utilizes her knowledge of the different legal systems then operat-ing in the plantations; when her new owner in Bermuda begins to whip her just as her old owner in Turk's Island had, she repudiates his action: 'Sir, this is not Turk's Island' (p. 67). Her owner is typically abusive but appears to desist from the whipping. Ultimately, Mary's quest for freedom is linked by her owner to her indoctrination by the Moravian church, associated with Lutheran beliefs, but Christianity has not always played the role of the liberator from slavery and often interpreted work in a wide variety of ways.

Work and Christianity

Christianity originally had a jaundiced view of work: it was imposed upon humanity as a direct result of original sin and was a means, therefore, to avoid the temptations of the devil and the flesh, as well as a penance.

But spirituality, not work, was the true route to salvation for Christians, at least until Lutherans, and more particularly Calvinists, proposed that work, rather than prayer, could either save your soul or at least be taken as confirmation that your soul was already saved. It was this transformative period that is crit-ical both in the elevation of work itself, from a necessary chore to a moral duty, and, according to Weber (1978), in the augmentation of rational capit-alism (see chapter 3). Yet, as Weber made clear, the fragmentation of the Christian church also facilitated the unravelling of Christianity itself. If, as the Reformation ably demonstrated, there were divergent interpretations of God, then foundational belief in any omnipotent God was subject to severe doubt. As a result the certainties of life, as constructed by the priesthood, were replaced by the uncertainties of life: life itself became meaningless without any universally accepted form of religiously prescribed beliefs. If God was dead then humanity had to construct the meaning of life for itself. Furthermore, since an appeal to God could not resolve the clash between different ideals, the very meaning of life was now considered as subjective.

The later scepticism of intellectuals like Nietzsche and Weber to the search for the meaning of life seldom seemed to have concerned the manufacturers of the Victorian work ethic in Britain, many of whom explicitly linked the duty to work to religious incantations. As the contemporary economist J.R. McCulloch put it: 'the eternal law of Providence has decreed that wealth can only be secured by industry – that man must earn his bread by the sweat of his brow' (quoted in McClelland, 1987: 184). Samuel Smiles is probably the best-known early distributor of such ideas, based on his regurgitated religious maxim that 'Heaven helps those who help themselves'. The result, according to Mathias, was that 'The virtues of hard work – the gospel of work preached by Samuel Smiles – saving, thrift, sobriety became the new social imperatives dinned into the heads of the new working classes by their social betters by every known means of communication. They were enshrined in Nonconformist and evangelical doctrine' (1969: 208). What is particularly noteworthy here is that despite the popularity of this kind of rhetoric among certain sections of the middle class, neither the working class nor the aristocracy were universally enamoured of the sentiments. Even within the middle class the petty bourgeois and ascetic essence of Smiles never garnered total support. As Davidoff and Hall claim, at least until the middle of the nineteenth century, 'the thrusting individual entrepreneur whose only aim was profit maximization is rare in the local records' (1987: 215). At least one other middle-class Victorian crusade for work as a moral or religious duty existed, this time epitomized by Carlyle's phrase: 'blessed is he who has found work' (at least until you could afford to escape from banausic affairs (Musgrave, 1981: 62)). For Carlyle, the contemporary Victorian flight into the 'mechanical age' was a disastrous inversion of human potential, it turned work into drudgery against all rationality, for 'there is a perennial nobleness, and even sacredness, in Work . . . in idleness alone is there perpetual despair' (quoted in Clayre, 1977: 241). Or in Ruskin's equally evocative text:

> It is not that men are ill-fed, but that they have no pleasure in the work by which they make their bread, and therefore look to wealth as the only means of pleasure. . . . It is not, truly speaking, the labour that is divided; but the men: Divided into mere segments of men – broken into small fragments and crumbs of life. (quoted in Clayre, 1977: 260)

For Ruskin, Carlyle, Morris, Hobhouse and even J.S. Mill and Marx, work *should*, but self-evidently did not, provide the material base for the self-development of all. Indeed, even Carlyle rejected the 'mechanical age', not simply in terms of the impact of machinery upon individuals but also, and more particularly, because the period exuded a faith in machinery that was entirely misplaced and distorted the creative and 'dynamic' element of humanity (Carlyle, 1977). Work, for Carlyle then, was 'natural' in so far as it demonstrated the spiritual side of human nature.

Work and social class

The glorification of work, or the 'Gospel of Work' as Carlyle called it, found its physical apotheosis in the Great Exhibition of 1851, designed in part as 'an academy for teaching the nobility of labour' (Henry Mayhew, quoted in S. Brown and Clayre, 1978: 45), a symbolism not lost on an acerbic Marx who called it an exhibition where 'the world bourgeoisie . . . proudly places on show the deities it has fabricated' (quoted in Brown and Clayre, 1978: 46). Yet Marx was also fascinated by the incredible productivity and profusion of capitalism, and sought his own 'radical' gospel of work that paralleled the bourgeois version:

work was the medium through which humans realized their potential and created the cornucopia of communism.

In fact, establishing the effects of such doctrines, as opposed to their mere existence, is a difficult task. If the working class were so susceptible to the Victorian gospel of work, then reconciling the manifestations of discontent and poor productivity etc. poses some severe problems. Even at the height of the Victorian period, during which work arguably acquired a moral colour in harmony with the Smilesian (Briggs, 1955: 124–57), methodological and puritanical ethics of the time, work was infested with the sinews of class. Work, conceptualized as a moral responsibility, was still only really appropriated by the middle class and despised or ignored by the aristocracy and working class alike (Houghton, 1957). For the working class work appeared more akin to a material necessity than a duty, while for the aristocracy because work was not a material necessity it was relevant only in its exclusionary embodiment: if you had to work you were excluded from the aristocracy.

The apparent juxtaposition of the aristocracy and the working class in their disparagement of the Victorian work ethic should not blind us to the antipathy existing between the two: the aristocracy undoubtedly despised the manufacturers and 'grocers' but several socialist-inspired writers had also articulated a working-class hatred of 'the unproductive classes' (Saint-Simon) or 'the parasitical layers upon the broad backs of the proletariat' (Lenin). Work might be unremitting toil, and empty of the physical pleasures apparently represented, for example, in the painting of *Work* by Madox Brown, but this did not mean the aristocracy were admired for avoiding it. One of the reasons the aristocracy could avoid work was because in more Western industrial nations a very high division of labour was constructed, in which work became associated almost wholly with economic incentives and almost completely dissociated from the social relations that had entrammelled previous modes of work. Thus despite the critics from the radical left, the idle rich seldom came in for the same moral opprobrium as the idle poor. The idle rich had better things to do than work. As Veblen argued, the leisure class established an entire repertoire of behaviour that demonstrated their complete disdain for anything practical or useful (Veblen, 1899); an ethic that found great favour in the peculiarly British fascination for the cult of the amateur (Wiener, 1981; Roderick and Stephens, 1981; Elbaum and Lazonick, 1986).

While some historians have assumed that the work ethic impaled Victorian employers and employees alike (Best, 1979: 94–5), working-class autobiographical accounts suggest something wholly different. In the words of one such journeyman engineer, the surface layer of bustle and activity should not be mistaken for the 'inner life' of workshops where the first thing an apprentice learned was the skill of 'keeping nix':

> Keeping nix, consists in keeping a bright look-out for the approach of managers or foremen, so as to be able to give prompt and timely notice to men who may be skulking, or having a sly read or smoke, or who are engaged on 'corporation work' – that is, work of their own. (Wright, 1867/1967: 85)

This was certainly a work ethic but one which restricted, not promoted the activity of material production. Even when conditions were poor and incomes low, many members of the working class appeared to have more important things to do than work especially hard for somebody else's profits while accumulating marginal improvements of their own (Hobsbawm, 1964b). This should not be read as the incipient development of working-class socialism because, although such beliefs were present, there were also a large number of workers who appeared to accept the role of the market and the mutuality of labour and capital, albeit in a rather unequal and exploitive conjunction. As Charles Blake, secretary of the Tyne and Wear Chain Makers' Union, said in 1861:

> since the commencement of the present Union they had directed their attention to obtain the best wages the state of the market would allow, and to prevent employers obtaining an exorbitant profit out of their labour. Masters always had a right for a fair profit upon their capital invested, and remuneration also for their business capacity, but when trade was prosperous it was the business of workmen to see they enjoyed their share of that prosperity. (quoted in McClelland, 1987: 189)

Nevertheless, there is little evidence that, at least until very recently, work was anything other than something 'to be endured rather than enjoyed' (Burnett, 1974: 15). Writing in 1899 Allen Clarke wrote of Lancashire factory workers: 'Some few seek recreation in Sunday school work and prayer meetings, but these are the minority; the majority want stirring amusements, lively and intoxicating – something to make them forget' (quoted by McClelland, 1987: 205). As the late nineteenth-century music-hall songs revealed, work was an evil but there was no escape from it nor from the class system, both were simply facts of life. For all that socialists tried to generate some enthusiasm for an alternative social system it would always be the case, as Billy Bennett sang:

> it's the rich what gets the pleasure,
> It's the poor what gets the blame.
> (quoted in Jones, 1983: 229)

So where did such ethics that rejected the economic rationality of capitalism come from? Partly, of course, their origins lie in the conventions of pre-capitalist and pre-industrial society where work was structured by and festooned with the ribbons of social and normative convention – work was for social as much as material purpose. Partly, though considerably later, such ethics were forged through the pens of ideologues.

Radical approaches to work

Anarchists and work

Although Marxist- and socialist-inspired radicals tend to dominate the literature rejecting the Victorian gospel of work, there were other, especially anarchist, denunciations of the wage labour system, such as Kropotkin's inversion of the bourgeois gospel of work: 'let us begin by satisfying our needs of life, joy and freedom. And once all will have experienced this well-being we will set to work to demolish the last vestiges of the bourgeois regime, its morality derived from the account book, its philosophy of "debit" and "credit", its institutions of mine and thine' (Kropotkin, 1983: 107). There was also an outright rejection of the universal 'myth' of work as propagated by Lafargue in his *The Right to be Lazy* (to the considerable chagrin of his father-in-law, Marx) (Kumar, 1984: 11) and put rather more delicately by Russell in his *In Praise of Idleness* where he claimed that 'A great deal of harm is being done in the modern world by belief in the virtuousness of WORK . . . the road to happiness and prosperity lies in an organized diminution of work' (1984: 25).

Hegel on work

Yet the virtues of work were not simply a charade dreamed up by the bourgeoisie to increase still further the exploitation of the working class. From Locke's (1960: 329) theory of property, in which property could only be legitimated through its intermixing with human labour, to Hegel's discussion of the Master and Slave relationship in his *Phenomenology of Spirit*, with the concern for the significance of objectifying humanity in artefacts, and beyond to Marx's notion of 'species being', in which it only becomes possible for humans to realize their true potential through labour (*homo faber*), it had become accepted that the world of work was the central arena for social and individual development, as well as for the basic reproduction of material necessities and the satisfaction of immediate desires. In fact, Hegel's argument in his Jena lectures suggests that labour, like language, is significant in so far as it distances experience; it 'breaks the dictates of immediate perception . . . and immediate desire' (quoted in Giddens, 1982b: 150). Hegel, unlike Marx, was not concerned with the results of labour but only in the process of labour: it was not the material changes wrought in nature that interested Hegel but the fact that labour was essential to the production and reproduction of human consciousness. Thus in attempting to dominate nature, humanity realized its true self (Taylor, 1979: 50–1).

Marx on work

For Marx the material results of labour were significant in so far as they embodied uniquely human attributes: self-realization through work was at the heart of Marx's communist vision (Elster, 1985). Marx, while adopting Hegel's labour and interaction couplet, also subordinated the latter to the former, such that even though his empirical work paid due respect to the significance of human interaction, the theoretical primacy of labour and materialism ensured that interaction became perceived as derivative of, rather than irreducible to, labour. As a result, argues Habermas (1974), Marx saw social problems as technical problems and the ultimate aim of society as being **productivist**, based on an ever expanding technology of production rather than an ever expanding degree of participation and emancipation through 'communicative action' (see Giddens, 1982b).

Even Marx's primary target, economic liberalism in the guise of the utilitarians, could accept the significance of work, not in itself of course, but as a means to an end. Marx went so far as to call Adam Smith the 'Luther of political economy' because of his assertion that capital was not external to, but an expression of, the human subject (Avineri, 1968: 78). By trading off the necessary pain of work for the pleasures purchased with the material rewards, individuals could buy their way into self-realization. For Bentham, the moralistic essence of work, that is the assumption that work should provide a reward in and of itself, was rather bizarre, for the 'desire of labour *for the sake of labour, of labour considered in the character of an end,* without any view to anything else, is a sort of desire that seems scarcely to have a place in the human breast' (Bentham, 1977: 200–1). Adam Smith put it even more strongly, for work was actually a necessary evil, and individuals had to have some incentive to give up their leisure; that incentive was the material improvements secured through work. Thus a virtuous circle would emerge: since people could only realize their potential outside work, and since only through work could the material prerequisites for self-realization be obtained, individuals would create the very products that they would eventually consume in pursuit of self-realization. But the virtuous circle is a mirage: the utilitarian trade-off between pain and pleasure, between work and leisure, signally fails in so far as those with what are commonly regarded as the most interesting jobs also tend to have the greatest access to leisure, while those with the ostensibly worst jobs are often materially incapacitated by work to the extent that they cannot possibly purchase a compensatory level of leisure. Anyway, are people actually free to develop identities through leisure patterns that are dissociated from their occupational routines? Can those with what are experienced as the most demeaning and poorest paying jobs (and they do tend to go together) really buy their way to Nirvana?

For Marx, capitalism inverted the world of work and turned it against the workers, thereby not just preventing them from realizing themselves but actually developing a system through which work became the source of anti-humanism, the origin of alienation and exploitation. Like Marx, William Morris contrasted the possibilities raised by capitalism with its technical advances: it offered the chance of reducing mundane and tedious work as well as generating enormous advances in material prosperity, but his perception was of a reality where the environment was choked with poisons, where people became slaves to, not controllers of, machines, and where starvation and poverty still prevailed. While Marx's schema for the future of society counterposed an uneasy alliance between self-managed producer units and centrally co-ordinated social planning, the material wherewithal for the communist cornucopia was to be achieved through exploiting nature and eliminating scarcity. Towards the end of his life Marx argued that perhaps individuals could only realize their self-potential outside the realm of socially organized work (Rattansi, 1982). The anti-productivist drift of Marx's apparent volte-face in *Capital*, volume 3, is worth reproducing in full:

> The realm of freedom really begins only where labour determined by neces-
> sity and external expediency ends; it lies by its very nature beyond the
> sphere of material production proper. . . . The true realm of freedom, the
> development of human powers as an end in itself, begins beyond it, though
> it can only flourish with this realm of necessity as its basis. The reduc-
> tion of the working day is the basic prerequisite. (Marx, 1981: 959)

Nevertheless, the essence of the anti-capitalist alternative was a society which,
freed from the constraints imposed by private ownership and the profit motive,
would outproduce all previous societies. In practice this meant that the aim
of Lenin, Stalin and most other Marxist leaders was not to generate a society
that was more democratic than existed under capitalism, even though this may
still have been an ultimate aim; but a prerequisite to this was the provision of
a more productive society. Consequently, Marxism had a productivist kernel
underpinning its liberatory shell: the people would be freed from want through
technological advances; social progress meant material progress. It is not coincidental that one of the greatest advocates of Taylorism (see chapter 5) was
Lenin (1968c: 413–46) (cf. Nyland, 1987; Kossler and Muchic, 1990) nor that
what are experienced as the intrinsic satisfactions of work for the majority under
state socialism appear to be as minimal as they are under capitalism (Haraszti,
1977; cf. Burawoy, 1985; Burawoy and Lukács, 1989).

Morris on work

Morris, although an avowed socialist, would not have been impressed by Marx's
original productivist strategy but would have been very sympathetic to his later
reformulation. For Morris social progress had little to do with levels of material wealth and much to do with providing self-fulfilling work experiences, for:
'it is the nature of man [*sic*] . . . to take pleasure in his work [but] there is some
labour which is so far from being a blessing that it is a curse; that it would be
better for the community and for the worker if the latter were to fold his hands
and refuse to work' (1983: 35). Morris not only despised capitalism with its
degradation of work, he despised the results of capitalism: the degradation of
the workers' minds and bodies; the domestic servants who serviced the 'para-
sites' of society; the marketing departments; the creators and purchasers of 'articles of folly and luxury'; and the creators and consumers of 'inferior' goods. In
sum, Morris despised the entire ensemble of social classes: 'a class which does
not even pretend to work, a class which pretends to work but which produces
nothing, and a class which works, but is compelled by the other two classes
to do work which is often unproductive' (1983: 40). But what was Morris's
alternative, and what role did work play within it? As a foundational social
ethic Morris argued that 'No man [*sic*] would be tormented for the benefit of
another – nay, no one would be tormented for the benefit of society' (1983:
42). Note here that notwithstanding the progressive thrust of Morris's views,
his assumptions about the 'proper' role of women were hardly compatible with
this non-tormented society. Nor, despite his concern for the beauty of nature,

was he keen to work with it; rather his vision was replete with the 'conquering' of nature so popular with the rest of his more conventional Victorian colleagues. Nevertheless, Morris's vision of the future was distinct from the productivist world envisaged by capitalists and Marxists alike. Since all would be engaged in 'useful work', as opposed to 'useless toil' or idleness, the working day would be shorter, more varied and more harmonious than at present. The notion of variety is important because here Morris asserts that even skilled work can be alienating if it becomes the sole activity undertaken: just as soldering is commonly regarded as a skilled job and digging a hole is perceived to be less skilled, so soldering all day may be tedious while digging the garden twice a year can be pleasurable.

It is not just the content of the work which is critical, and it is axiomatic that there are limits to the amount of 'interesting' work any individual can cope with (Arneson, 1987) but the social relationships within which they occur are also crucial. Thus work for Morris should also be undertaken in decentralized units, in attractive surroundings where machinery would be used to minimize the duration of unpleasant but necessary labour. Work itself would then become the medium for self-realization. But what about the 'repulsive' work which even volunteers would hesitate to undertake? 'Well, then, let us see if the heavens will fall on us if we leave it undone, for it were better that they should. The produce of such work cannot be worth the price of it' (p. 55).

Gorz on work

This overt concern for the well-being of the individual producers, rather than the necessity of 'the system', is continued in the more contemporary writings of Gorz (1982, 1985, 1989). Gorz can best be described as an heretical Marxist: he accepts the humanist critique of capitalism developed by Marx but denies the **teleological** assumptions surrounding the role of the proletariat and the inevitability of socialism. He is also dismissive of the productivist essence of Marxism in a way very close to Morris. On the other hand, Gorz is more concerned than Morris to retain a 'necessary' degree of advanced technology and 'other-directed' or heteronomous work, since only such a structure can provide the level of material production to which we have now become accustomed, and without which the creation of a sphere of autonomous, or 'self-directed', work would be impractical. For Gorz, therefore, as for the later Marx and aspects of Morris's writings, self-realization, the fulfilment of potential, does not occur within conventional 'work' at all but is rather associated with what we might now call hobbies or leisure activities. We have to tread carefully here: if the argument is that heteronomous work *only* provides the material basis for the real work of identity construction which can only occur outside the sphere of heteronomous work, then the argument is simply over-generalized and hence suspect. Just because many people may find working on an assembly line alienating does not mean that everyone does; to accept this is to deny the significance of the social construction of work – its meaning is socially constructed, it does not inhere within the technology of the assembly line. Nor is it necessarily the case that a variety of craft-based activities can replace the degree of self-respect which employment appears to provide. Perhaps the clearest example of this is the experience of being unemployed, where the sudden provision of time, in and of itself, is often regarded as being as much a burden as an advantage. Nevertheless, the crucial point is that to privilege work over all other forms of human activity is simply to elevate one arbitrary action over another. As Arneson remarks in criticism of any work-dominated philosophy: 'If one has a vision of one monolithic good that society ought to pursue, then institutions ought to be organized so as to render society a crusade directed at this aim. The more one recognizes diversity in human good, the more one's perfectionism will in practice approximate to a preference-respecting policy' (1987: 533).

Contemporary Western orientations to work

The social construction of meaning

That work *has* been arbitrarily privileged over other forms of activity and discourse in contemporary Western societies has not led to any consensus about the meaning of work nor about the orientations that workers conventionally have about work. Dubin (1962) and Mannheim (1951) certainly appeared to take the utilitarian line that the absence of expectations of meaningful work was a demonstration of the acceptability of alienating work: if workers did not expect meaningful work then society had a green light to pursue the road to alienation, providing an adequate level of monetary reward could buy the necessary level of external compensation. But rather than assuming that manifestations of alienation can be taken as evidence of the impossibility of developing meaningful work it could well be argued that alienation at work only makes sense if we assume work ought to be non-alienating. Why should we experience work as alienating unless we expect it to be otherwise? (Sayers, 1988: 725–6). We do not have to accept Marx's prognosis of the ills of capitalism, nor assume that work is *the* central life activity, to accept that work is *a* central life activity that we have learned to expect more from than most of us tend to get. Nor should we assume that because workers may be instrumental about their work this is because they are inherently instrumental. In other words, although workers may appear to work primarily for extrinsic rewards (money etc.) rather than intrinsic rewards (job satisfaction), this is not foreordained. On the contrary, if the sociological approach to work tells us anything it is that our experiences are socially structured, not 'natural' or 'inevitable'.

Argyris (1964) attempted to resolve the enigma of the meaning of work by arguing that people want whatever it is that the job supplies in the greatest quantity: they rationalize their position *vis-à-vis* their job. But the meaning of work for any worker is not simply job-determined. Indeed, there is considerable evidence to suggest that the links between the domestic and the non-domestic spheres are critical: workers with heavy family responsibilities tend to be more concerned with extrinsic rewards (money and security) than those without. Workers with what have come to be regarded as the most intrinsically rewarding jobs value them for just this reason (Loscocco, 1989).

The whole issue of work orientations was put on a much firmer conceptual base by Lockwood's approach (1966), in which four types of worker are identified, each with a different outlook on society. Briefly, the middle-class employees perceived society in terms of a consensually graduated status hierarchy; the deferential workers had a very similar overall picture though they placed themselves lower in the hierarchy; the traditional proletarian configured society through a conflicts-driven class model; while the affluent or privatized workers envisaged society in terms of a desocialized structure divided on the basis of money. Such variations in imagery could be related, according to Lockwood, to the nature of the work situation and the community structure in which the different types of worker were located.

The affluent worker and orientation to work

Lockwood, in conjunction with Goldthorpe et al. (1968), set out to use the notion of affluent workers to test the **embourgeoisement thesis**, which suggested that as the working class acquired middle-class levels of income they also adopted middle-class social and political habits. Using prototypical affluent workers in Luton, they selected their sample of workers in terms of technology and as producers, as well as consumers, of affluence. As they noted: 'we wished to examine the effect on workers' attitudes and behaviour of different types of production system and our choice of firms was in fact made so that three major types – small batch, large batch and mass production, and process production – were represented' (1968: 4). The concept of '**orientation to work**' developed when the authors were unable to find significant differences in overall satisfaction according to the respondents' jobs. As they state:

> one very definite result emerges: that job satisfaction in terms of workers' experience of their immediate work tasks and roles cannot be associated in any direct way with job satisfaction in terms of workers' attachment to their present employment . . . the question of *satisfaction from* work cannot in the end be usefully considered except in relation to the more basic question of what we would term *orientation towards* work. Until one knows something of the way in which workers order their wants and expectations relative to their employment – until one knows what *meaning* work has for them – one is not in a position to understand what overall assessment of their job satisfaction may most appropriately be made in their case. (1968: 31–6)

Goldthorpe et al. go on to distinguish three types of orientation which broadly correspond to Lockwood's triple worker types. For the privatized worker with an instrumental orientation to employment the primary meaning of work is as a means to an end, work is 'labour' with ends external to the work situation;

these workers are therefore calculatively involved in the firm, they do not see work as a source of self-realization nor as a site for significant social relations but as a necessary arena for the improvement of non-work opportunities (1968: 38–9). The bureaucratic worker, typical perhaps of the middle-class employee, considers employment as a service to an organization, imbuing the relationship with moral elements which blur the distinction between work and non-work. The third type of orientation is solidaristic: work is seen as a group activity and, in the deferential type of situation, means moral involvement in the firm, while for the traditional proletarians – such as the miner – moral involvement is restricted to the mining community and involves a clear distinction between 'them' and 'us'; nevertheless there is little separation between work and non-work.

Even if we can identify a worker's orientation, what does this tell us about her or his behaviour? According to Goldthorpe et al., instrumentalism tended to be associated with a pecuniary interest not just to the firm but to work colleagues too. Yet, as they accept (1968: 76–7), this does not mean that such workers are inevitably moderate in their demands and behaviour. It could well be argued that such instrumentalism poses just as high a risk to management as does the more socially or politically inspired unionism, in so far as the primary relationship between employer and employee is money; no appeals to the interests of the firm or the nation are likely to dissuade such instrumental workers from taking whatever action they feel necessary to achieve their 'just' rewards. Thus very different orientations to work may generate apparently identical modes of behaviour.

Goldthorpe et al. assert that such instrumentalism reflects the choices made by such employees who have left what they regard as intrinsically interesting but poorly paid jobs for apparently intrinsically uninteresting but highly paid jobs. This does not mean that all workers, or even all workers in Goldthorpe et al.'s Luton sample, were uninterested in intrinsically satisfying work. It may mean that the choice is so limited that we have no way of assessing any third option. That is to say, because workers under certain contingent conditions work in what they regard as well-paid but boring jobs does not mean that they would not choose interesting jobs provided the economic rewards were satisfactory. Nor does it mean that jobs *are* intrinsically uninteresting – even if they are experienced as such.

The concept of orientation to work has been used widely since Goldthorpe et al.'s work: Cotgrove and Box (1970), for example, have adopted it with regard to the work of scientists, and Ingham (1970) in his comparison of small and large firms. However, the very notion of orientation to work has been subject to considerable debate. In particular, to what extent can one identify a clear and relatively stable set of worker priorities and expectations? Given the transient state of many workers, especially in the Luton sample, another aspect is critical: attitudes to work are not stable, they change as individuals change their status, their family situation, their age and their interpretation of the discourses imbricated around such categories. Indeed, a whole body of literature suggests that ideological viewpoints are inconsistent with regard to the distinctions between attitudes to general principles and particular events they become involved in, as well as being internally incongruous (Mann, 1970; Nichols and Armstrong,

1976; Held, 1984). An example is beautifully captured in the words of one Jock Kennan: 'Frankly, I hate work. Of course I could also say with equal truth that I love work; that it is a supremely interesting activity; that it is often fascinating; that I wish I didn't have to do it; that I wish I had a job at which I could earn a decent wage. That makes six subjective statements about work and all of them are true for me' (quoted in Fraser (ed.), 1968: 273).

This particular issue raises the related one concerning the origin of such orientations. Implicitly, Goldthorpe et al. develop their approach through an externally generated source of orientations: orientations appear to be autonomous of the working environment; they influence, but are not influenced by, what happens at work. Can it really be the case that orientations are affected by past work experiences but not present ones? Of course, it may be that over time the maturation of orientations leads to some degree of self-selectivity, such that workers end up in employment environments conducive to their orientations, but again this is not likely for all workers nor does it eliminate the significance of work experiences. As Brown (1973, 1974) has demonstrated, the initial movement of people into work can have very powerful influences upon the later orientations to work. Alternatively, it may be that orientations of instrumental workers *are* autonomous of the work situation *because* they are unconcerned by the working environment, while the orientations of non-instrumental workers are not autonomous.

The origins and significance of orientations of work

It is noticeable that most of the empirical studies are based on male workers and tend to assume that women are oriented towards the home rather than work. Such issues are discussed later in this chapter and more fully in chapter 6, but Dex's (1988) research implies two things worth bearing in mind when analysing orientations to work of men and women. First, the major differences in orientation can be explained through occupational differences rather than gender differences. Second, where gender differences appear more systematically, it is domestic responsibilities, and especially childcare, which are critical.

Where it does seem to be the case that work experiences have a direct impact upon orientations is in the long-term effects. Kornhauser (1965) has noted how older workers become fatalistic over time, learning to accept the delimited experiences as inevitable and adjusting their orientations in this direction – further evidence of the socially malleable and contingent nature of our interpretations of work. Argyris (1964) has examined the development of psychological methods to cope with the perceived frustration of work but it is not self-evident that workers always learn to accept their situation. Or, to put it more graphically, in the words of a bus driver: 'I was at the ripe age of twenty-five when I started with the London General Omnibus Company – I am now sixty-six years of age . . . If I were twenty-five years of age today, you could stick this job on the buses where a monkey is reputed to stick his nuts!' (Jones, quoted in Fraser (ed.), 1968: 217). Whatever the apparent orientations to work offered by workers, then, it is by no means clear that such attitudes operate independently of work:

if work *is* experienced as boring and alienating then it would be irrational to consider that it could be self-fulfilling. Such responses are not untypical and it appears common for American workers, at least, to blame themselves for their relatively low position in the social hierarchy which ultimately leads them to cultivate and sustain very low levels of expectation. If you do not expect much from work you will not be disappointed and may, in fact, remain 'happy' with your lot (Sennett and Cobb, 1977).

But if, as Anthony argues (1977), work is, and always has been, the most boring and mundane activity, why do so many other people appear to regard it with such high esteem? Does work exude a magic spell to enchant people? It certainly is the case that the question 'Are you happy at work?' embodies so many variant interpretations as to be almost worthless. Are people who answer 'yes' (and from Labriola's survey in 1931 to Jahoda's in 1979 the majority answer has been yes) happy with the skill content of their jobs or the responsibility they can exercise or the material reward or the social relationships, or the routines and the pride engendered through being employed; in particular, are people happy *in* jobs or *with* jobs? What has to be remembered, particularly by those looking at, rather than engaging in, apparently mundane manual labour is that no job is completely bereft of skill and many embody the potential for a measure of pride that exists independently of the requirements of employers. As I. Edwards (1983) so eloquently testifies, even shovelling is an art:

> A navvy, using his shield-shaped excavating shovel in a trench with a bad bottom, does wonders, but in a long time . . . and the corporation employee, lifting little bits in the street, would have died of fright had he seen our shovels. . . . Patsy slung the blade of the shovel towards the heap until it touched the edge, then followed up with both knees driving hard against the back of his hands to supply the power. A quick downward jerk of the wrist loaded the shovel, it was withdrawn slightly, swung backwards as the body straightened, then delivered over the shoulder into the skip with a graceful sway and twist of the trunk . . . the shovel and its motion seemed but an extension of those long arms [it] made shovelling an art to be studied and not merely a distasteful task for the unskilled. (1983: 85–6)

Correspondingly, the richness of life evoked by Roy's (1954, 1973), and later Burawoy's (1979) and Cavendish's (1982), ethnographic descriptions of factory life is a useful reminder of the creativity of people in what they regard as non-creative jobs, even if much of the creativity is expended in activity unrelated to productive activity. But it is worth reiterating here that the satisfactions gained by these people are generated *at* work without being directly related to any particular aspect *of* work, and without being produced independently of the non-work environment. As a Ford worker explained to Beynon, there is more to work than work:

> At the end of the shift we'd run for the clock. I don't know why we did . . . it just meant we had to wait on the bus. Well one day I run to the clock, grab for my coat and it's tied up in knots. It was Clarkey. He was

a strong bastard and he'd really tied it up tight. I couldn't move it. So the next day I took some boxes of those very small tacks into work. I made a tiny hole in the pocket of Clarkey's coat, tipped the tacks in and then gave the coat a shake. When he came to pick it up it was like a ton weight. (Beynon, 1975: 236)

Beyond the significance of orientations brought to work it is important to confirm the class-, race- and gender-based influences upon working experience. That is to say that the meaning of work may be structured by these kinds of categories more than it is by individual attitudes generated apparently auto-nomously. Much of these arguments form the basis for chapters 5, 6 and 7 but suffice it to say here that the vast majority of research carried out with regard to class divisions reproduces a very similar class-based level of work experience. In the USA, France and Britain and in the former Yugoslavia and Soviet Union it is the case that 'the lower we direct our attention within the occupational status scale, the more likely we are to find people deriving little conscious mean-ing from their work apart from the pay and security it offers' (Fox, 1976: 37). This does not mean that all manual employees all over the world have ident-ical experiences. After all, the decisive word in Fox's text is 'meaning'. Such meanings are not determined by the task nor the job nor the technology nor even the social structures. But then neither does this imply that meanings can be imputed to invariant tasks on an individual basis. It is not that individuals all read experiences in a different way but that some readings, especially but not exclusively those provided by superordinates, are endowed with a legitimacy and import that others are not.

What counts as work, therefore, and what we take as skilled or difficult or dirty work, is inherently unstable and ambiguous. It depends upon the social relations within which it is undertaken but it may also be a contested concept within those same relations. Work is more than employment but less than all forms of social activity; indeed, employment is a form of work but not all work is employment. Where the self-description of agents' activity implies that their activity is conceived by them as work, we should take note, but the point really is not whether this or that activity is actually work, but what such activities involve, whose interpretation of the activity carries the most weight, and why this should be the case.

In the remainder of this chapter I want to explore the nature of work fur-ther by focusing directly upon two areas which, under the conventional defini-tion of work *qua* paid labour, disappear from view: work in the informal economy, and especially domestic work; and non-work, or unemployment. The latter form of non-work is significant in so far as it highlights in stark form what work means to individuals and communities. Both these activities are often discounted in studies of work but they both act as powerful manifestations of the domi-nance of certain images of work. Moreover, they both signify an aspect of work which by convention is unconnected to work: the domestic sphere and the sphere of paid labour are intimately connected in a seamless web of relations. Indeed, unpaid domestic labour is an imperative element of paid labour because with-out the former the latter could not continue in its present form.

Domestic labour

Housework

Although domestic labour has conventionally been associated with unpaid home-work, or more appropriately 'housework', and has, therefore, been eliminated from most concerns about work until recently, it is worth noting that domestic labour also involves unpaid activities outside housework strictly defined, for example, shopping, gardening, fixing the plumbing, painting the walls, car maintenance, ferrying children to school, bearing and bringing up infants, organizing family recreation and entertainment etc. After all, who thinks having to watch endless Blue Peters, or worse, having to make all those wretched 'drawer sets' and 'gift boxes' out of battered shoe boxes without the proper glue and expensive shiny paper, does not count as hard work? Since almost every activity undertaken without payment in the home is also undertaken for money in the formal economy the distinction between work and non-work is seriously flawed.

The division is further eradicated by what Pahl (1984) calls 'household work strategies' through which the available labour within a household, rather than that available just to an individual, is the basis upon which work inside and outside the home, within and without the formal economy, is organized; however, Pahl's enthusiasm for the household approach seems to submerge all aspects of individualist strategies (cf. Moorhouse, 1987).

Some assessments of the links between the formal and the informal sector suggest that as people's time in one contracts it expands in the other. Thus, in general, such models assert that as women spend more time in formal employment they spend less time in the domestic sphere, and their male partners have a related and inverted correlation (Gershuny and Thomas, 1980; R. Rose, 1983). Others imply that the contraction of formal employment involves the reduction of the material resources to undertake informal work so that there is a joint contraction or expansion in both sectors depending on whether the individual is employed or not (Pahl, 1984).

Gender and domestic labour

Concomitantly, women's work outside the home has become circumscribed by their activities within it, resulting in the construction of occupational sex-typing (Cohn, 1985; Dex, 1985; cf. Grint, 1988). Thus employment opportunities for women have historically been restricted in the main to analogous domestic activities: cleaning, cooking, caring, teaching. Despite this relationship the primary positions in such occupations tend to be occupied by men. For example, chefs, consultants and head teachers are all involved in occupations associated with domestic activities but are nevertheless normally male reserves. Relatedly, many of the jobs undertaken by women have domestic reflections which lead employers to perceive them as less skilled than jobs undertaken by men which have no equivalent domestic associations (D. Taylor, 1988). Men are more involved in the care of the elderly than has hitherto been recognized, and Arber and Gilbert (1989) estimate that about 33 per cent of co-resident carers are men, but 75 per cent of these look after their spouses; they are not, therefore, heavily represented among those looking after parents or other elderly relations.

In short, we cannot erect an impervious division between domestic labour and formal employment because they are so intimately connected and inter-active. We do not have a division between work and home that is free from ideological nuances because the very model of work we operate with is a **patriarchal model.** It is not just that men tend to monopolize the privileged jobs and occupations; after all, there are token women in many positions of authority – so it cannot be the case that women are unable to succeed within the labour market. But the critical point is that this can only occur for indi-vidual and isolated cases if the patriarchal model of work is maintained. If employ-ment is automatically and inflexibly constructed around a five-day week from 9 to 5 then all those involved in such employment cannot look after sick chil-dren or relatives, nor can they take them to or pick them up from schools. Hence the problem of work is not simply a definitional one, nor even a norm-ative one, it is organizational in two senses: time and opportunity. First, unless we all decide to forego having children we either have to reorganize employ-ment hours to fit flexibly around children and domestic circumstances, and/or inaugurate multiple company and community crèches etc., or maintain the patri-archal status quo. Of course, altering working hours or organizing the provi-sion of crèches would probably not result in a sudden burst of enthusiasm for domestic work on the part of men, but it might be a first step towards the equal distribution of domestic work. Second, if women continue to remain prim-arily located within the worst-paying and least career-structured jobs, the end result is for most women to be without an adequate wage or occupational pen-sion; as a result the employment experiences of women have a direct bearing on their retirement experiences, dependent as they often are on meagre state pensions (Glendinning and Millar, 1988). Likewise, the significance of social networks for recruitment and promotion purposes, and the general predomin-ance of men in these, tends to delimit the opportunities for women's employ-ment and career development. But however important social networks are for promotional and occupational patterns, one has to beware of assuming that they are the primary route *into* employment: in 1988, for example, only 12 per cent of those seeking work actually used social networks as their primary method, 37 per cent used a job centre while 41 per cent used the newspapers or other form of advertisement (*Social Trends*, 1990: 81).

Naturally, not all women experience the same kind of restrictions: Victorian working-class women may have sought the kind of idyllic life allegedly consumed by middle-class women, with a houseful of servants and nothing but the garden-ing, bridge and dinner parties to organize, but few middle-class women probably languished in such a state of torpor (Davidoff and Hall, 1987: 388–96; Maynard, 1985) while many working-class women would have spent some time as a do-mestic servant themselves. It was not just that domestic work was regarded as unfit for men because it was low status; rather, women were regarded as inher-ently better suited to the creation of a domestic environment that was private, pure and moral, in sharp contrast to the public and immoral world of paid labour. Domestic work was, allegedly, a mirror image of the physically rough, dangerous and dirty world of the miner. Inevitably, class differences emerged through such gendered divisions of labour. In 1917 Elizabeth Stern, an American memoirist, recounted such class differences when visiting a school friend in a wealthier part of town:

> I could not believe that the woman who opened the door to my knock was my friend's mother. A woman in *white*! Why, mothers dressed in brown and black, I always knew. And this mother sang to us. She romped through the two steps with us . . . I had always thought that mothers never 'enjoyed', just worked. This strange mother opened a new window for me in the possibilities of women's lives. (quoted in Cowan, 1983: 170–1)

Seventy years later a variety of empirical studies still suggest that women consistently undertake more work than men, in terms of hours, whether they are employed outside the home as well or not. Thus, where women take on employment, although their domestic work contracts, their overall work level increases. With average weekly hours for male employees hovering around 44 (including overtime) and for full-time women around 37 hours (including one hour overtime) (*Social Trends*, 1988, 1990), the average hours of a full-time houseworker are between 57 (Walker and Woods, 1976; Berk and Berk, 1979) and 100 (Leghorn and Parker, 1981). The average hours of a full-time employed woman are over 70, with 33 hours spent on housework. By implication, those households with women in employment are making do with marginally more than half the time full-time houseworkers spend in maintaining the house: either the former live in veritable pigsties or we have cultural expectations of cleanliness that are remarkably consistent with Parkinson's, or perhaps more appropriately Parkindaughter's, law – domestic work expands to fill the time available. As Ehrenreich and English (1979) acknowledge, there is precious little evidence that such a high level of domestic cleanliness is necessary for health purposes, though there is some which suggests that such activities are damaging to women's health. The phrase 'a woman's work is never done' says more about women's domestic responsibilities than most books on the subject.

Alternatives to gendered domestic labour

Some feminists have argued that the solution to the problem of iniquitous work loads, and the exploitation it embodies, is to secure wages for housework, and several estimates suggest that the total costs would be staggering: almost half the West German and American GNP or a quarter of the Canadian GNP (Leghorn and Parker, 1981; Goldschmidt-Clermont, 1987; *New Internationalist*, 1988). In 1997 the British Office for National Statistics suggested that if domestic work was remunerated at the average hourly pay rate it would be worth £739 billion a year – 122 per cent of the current value of the economy (*The Guardian*, 7 October 1997). However, despite the propaganda value of such claims it is, as Gorz (1985) and Fairbairns (1988) argue, more an admission of defeat than a strategy for success since it confirms women's position within the household and acknowledges the failure to coerce or persuade men to undertake their share of domestic work.

There are counter-arguments which suggest that the sexual division of labour manifest in women's domestic responsibilities is not iniquitous at all but rather a mechanism to maximize the efficiency of the household unit. Just as specialization brings efficiency in conventional capitalist production so too, the argument goes, the specialization of partners in different spheres (who does what is not critical) is the most efficient way of allocating the labour available within a household (Becker, 1985). Yet, since housework is unending, and requires more in terms of organization than specialized knowledge, it would actually seem more efficient to minimize it by both partners being employed. Moreover, if women remain in employment (even part-time) then the detrimental consequences of a career break are minimized (Joshi, 1986). Even if specialization is marginally more efficient in economic terms, the cost to women's health, and via them to their children, throws doubt on the unambiguous advantages claimed for domestic specialization. In sum, the sexual division of labour in the domestic sphere appears to be both iniquitous and inefficient for the household (Owen, 1987).

Many women also tend to regard housework as intensely monotonous, yet shot through with moral attributes of cleanliness that they find difficult to ignore (Gale, 1985). For Suzanne Gail, 'Housewife': 'As I work, evangelical hymn-jingles from my carefully obliterated past well up in my mind. But I cannot achieve that degree of irony. It would be hubris, and the walls might fall in if I started chanting: "I'm H-A-P-P-Y" ' (Fraser, 1968: 144). Only cooking, shopping and childcare appear to have major benefits, though children can be both a source of disruption in themselves (as well as delight) and, at pre-school age particularly, have been associated with some mothers' mental ill-health and dependence on drugs of one sort or another (Gavron, 1968).

Despite the common assumption that some women's negative attitudes towards domestic work are very recent, research since the 1950s has suggested that such attitudes were relatively common even then. There has, though, been a slight shift away from the assumption that married women with children should not work among the younger generation of women (see Dex, 1988: 25–8). Nevertheless, Britain, in contrast to many major industrialized nations, has a particularly high proportion of women who prefer to stay at home (37 per cent) or perceive their work as 'just a job' rather than a career (30 per cent) (Bartos, 1989).

Even the domestic activities of fathers, as opposed to husbands or partners, appear to be restricted in degree and kind. The involvement of women in raising children is *in addition* to their houseworking responsibilities, whereas for fathers, child-raising activities are a *substitute* for housework (Maynard, 1985). Popular opinion would have us believe that households are far more egalitarian than they ever used to be, and there are arguments which assert that a form of equality does exist between men and women on a 'different but equal' basis, with the domestic jobs being gender-related (Edgell, 1980). But is there any empirical evidence for the claim, and is the division more like a gendered apartheid than an equitable division? In Oakley's (1974) research a mere 15 per cent of husbands participated in, or rather 'helped with', housework, with 25 per cent involved in childcare activities, though such help tended to be irregular and was perceived by men as a 'favour' to their wives rather than a responsibility of their own (Deem, 1985). One exception to this general norm is that men with children undertake more domestic work than men without children, primarily, it would seem, in order to facilitate their wives or partners' employment requirements (Dex, 1988). But the 'freeing' of time through male unemployment does not lead to any equivalent increase in domestic labour by men (Hartley, 1987). Nor has there been any rapid mushrooming of the New Man throughout the West. In the 1970s and 1980s American husbands extended their housework by an extra nine minutes a day on average, though even this appears to be considerably more than most Italian husbands (Taylor, 1988). The British experience (*Social Trends*, 1989) suggests that men undertake more domestic work than women in only one area – repairing household equipment. Overall women undertake 72 per cent of domestic tasks, while they are shared equally in just 22 per cent of the cases. Morris's (1990) Anglo-American study of domestic roles provides further evidence that patriarchy is alive, well and inertial. Men generally also tend to perceive the relationship between work and family to be unidirectional: where a conflict exists between family and work the normal response is to subordinate home to work; for women the opposite appears to hold in most cases (Deem, 1985: 43). Such attitudes coexist easily with those revealed by Dex (1988: 38–9) in which almost half of wives not working argued that their husbands' disapproval of working wives was a factor in their not seeking employment.

Gender-based inequalities are not inevitable, and Soviet-dominated societies long purveyed an ideology of egalitarianism. However, the reality was often one that 'allowed' women to undertake what were previously regarded as 'men's jobs' without ensuring that men undertook a concomitant degree of domestic work. One of the consequences of this has been a rejection of Western feminist attitudes among some women within the recently democratized Eastern European societies, and the generation of a 'return to the home movement':

> The communists said that in the first place a woman is a worker, then she should be active in political life, then in the third place have a family . . . add to this the time taken for shopping, then throw in the duties of childcare and housework and cooking, and it becomes understandable that women should now be wanting to slough off some of these burdens. (Redding and Leydon, 1990)

It should be remembered, however, that gender tends to interact with, rather than override, the significance of class. O'Brien's (1982) research suggests that working-class fathers perceive few contradictions between work and family, primarily because they see their role almost entirely in terms of 'the breadwinner' for whom practical activity, at least involving so called 'women's' jobs, stops once 'work' ceases. For middle-class fathers domestic responsibilities are considered as important but the demands of their professional jobs supposedly prevent them realizing much of their good intent.

Egalitarian households and 'free choice'

Hochschild (1989) suggests that even Western egalitarian households, where domestic and occupational responsibilities are initially divided equally, tend to subordinate the domestic to the occupational if both partners are professionals. For Moore Campbell (1988), such equality often prevails at first, but once babies arrive the typical response is for the conventional gendered division of labour to reappear or for the relationship to break up. There is an irony for many men, in that it is only because they are not responsible for domestic life that they can devote themselves full time to their careers – on the backs of their partners and behind the backs of their children. Thus, it would appear that the general occupational progression of women is dependent upon the displacement of men and the latters' engagement with domestic responsibilities (Dale, 1987).

We might wish to question just how much gendered choice is involved in the issue of domestic responsibilities; will professionals who stay home to look after sick children automatically lose out in the promotion race? Certainly many professionals who claim to support equal distribution of domestic activities end up by admitting that their employers or colleagues will not countenance such demonstrations of split loyalty (Hochschild, 1989). This very notion of split loyalty is a manifestation of the significance of work: paradoxically, for nations that pride themselves on the sanctity of the family, the idea that family commitments should take precedence over commitment to the work organization clings tenaciously to the banner of treason rather than the flag of reason. Even if corporations appear to subordinate family responsibilities to themselves, have many professionals attempted to reverse that assumption? Who chooses to engage in the promotion race anyway – are the spouses or partners of professional men consulted on the likely results, and do these spouses and partners have such a degree of choice in their own activities (J. Woolgar, 1989)? It may look as though professional men have no choice, but we have to be wary of the claim to external coercion; the fallacious self-denial of freedom and responsibility, or 'bad faith' as Sartre called it, has a long and not very pleasant history.

The case of cross-class families is interesting in so far as it tends to disrupt conventional assumptions and norms of behaviour. Sweden may not be representative of most European societies, let alone anywhere else, but it would appear here that working-class wives of working-class men are the most 'entrapped' in traditional gendered domestic roles, while middle-class wives of working-class men are the least likely to be similarly snared (Leiulfsrud and Woodward, 1987; see also G. Russell, 1983). This analysis also throws a rather abrasive spanner in the traditional class analysis pursued by Goldthorpe (1983, 1984b), since it questions the validity of ignoring the occupational position of women in the construction of stratification systems (Stanworth, 1984) (see chapter 6). If we continue to assume that families are the most appropriate means through which stratification systems should be analysed, we ignore the stratification that occurs *within* the family. This is not only with regard to the unequal division of domestic labour but also the inequalities of other resources, especially money. There is evidence that on the basis of total income, families which would otherwise be above the poverty line actually have those resources so maldis-tributed that women, and sometimes children, are below the line while men remain above it (Glendinning and Millar, 1988). Relatedly, although it is assumed that the break-up of a marriage tends to lead to the collective decline in mater-ial standards for all involved this need not necessarily occur. As Brannen and Wilson (1987) argue, although the total income entering a household may fall in proportion to the absence of the male adult, the pre-existing inequitous divisions within the family may be removed to the extent that family income levels may actually rise with the removal of a husband or male partner.

Domestic technology and freedom

It is another commonplace to assume that domestic technology has liberated women from housework. Certainly the pattern of work has changed from one where heavy and monotonous cleaning and washing was the major element to one where childcare, shopping, food preparation, cleaning and ironing are the prime elements. But as Schwartz Cowan's (1983) subtitle (*The Ironies of Household Technology*) reveals, the diffusion of household technology has done little or nothing to liberate houseworkers from the time spent in housework, even if it has limited the amount of heavy work. For example, the washing machine has not so much taken washing out of the realm of work but has ensured that we have clothes which are constantly clean. Similarly, the vacuum cleaner has not reduced the amount of time involved in cleaning the floors but led to even more time spent in ensuring ever cleaner floors; sophisticated cooking technologies and food preparation technologies lead not to the reduction in time spent preparing food but to more and more elaborate meals. In the event the time spent undertaking housework appears to rise or at least remain constant with the development of domestic technologies rather than decrease through them (Vanek, 1974).

In conclusion, I would just reaffirm the conviction that work is not simply restricted to paid labour but note also that the subordinate and gendered status of domestic labour and its popular classification as non-work is a valuable reminder of the significance of patriarchal ideology in the evaluation of work. As a central institution of society, work, and especially domestic work, embodies forms of power that spread far beyond the limits of the factory gate. A similar argument can be made for the inverse of domestic labour as unpaid work: paid inactivity as unemployment.

Unemployment

Domestic activities fall within the definition of work appropriated here, but unemployment is axiomatically more difficult to situate. In so far as being 'out of work' but 'available for work' implies the absence of any activity that might interfere with the search for work, it cannot be defined as work. But unemployment is still critical in several senses: it marks out the conventional Western boundary between work and non-work; it poses questions about the centrality of paid labour in contemporary society; it often has catastrophic consequences for the individual and household concerned; and its definition – as those seeking work and signed on for unemployment benefit – mirrors the state-supported ideology of work as a full-time non-domestic, and hence masculine, phenomenon. Unemployment is also important in the sense discussed throughout this chapter – that work *qua* activity may well continue even if employment does not.

Just as the definition and organization of employment is socially constructed, transient (see Deaton, 1983; and Marsh, 1988a) and often critical for the subordinate position of women at work and in the home, so too unemployment is dispersed unevenly between the able-bodied and the disabled, ethnic minorities and the white population, skilled and unskilled, and north and south of Britain. For example, the highest rates of unemployment tend to be found among those with no qualifications, from the working class, among those who are chronically sick or disabled, and whose ethnic background is Pakistani or Bangladeshi. Women, especially young married women, are more likely to be short-term unemployed than men, but men, notably older men, comprise the majority of the long-term unemployed (*Social Trends*, 1990). Regional variations are also noteworthy: Northern Ireland, the Western Isles, Strathclyde, Gwynedd, Mid Glamorgan, South Yorkshire and Cornwall are all well above the rest of the UK (*Employment Gazette*, March 1990).

Unemployment and households

Unemployment may also have considerable consequences for those who may not originally be unemployed. For example, there is a strong tendency for unemployment to run in families (White, 1983) to the extent that having the head of the household unemployed (irrespective of gender) effectively doubles the chances of the rest of the adult family being unemployed (Payne, 1987). The form of household is also significant for men in a rather different way to women: although women tend to leave employment during early child-rearing years, and their employment prospects are constrained by their domestic responsibilities, it is usually assumed that men operate independently of domestic responsibilities – though clearly dependent upon their partners' services. Yet unemployment also relates to marital status, with married men being significantly less likely to be unemployed than their single counterparts. This, it has been argued, probably reflects a number of facets of the domestic relationship: married men may have more incentive to seek or retain employment; they may be more conventionally oriented towards economic activity; and employers may prefer them since they believe them to be more constrained by the domestic commitments. In short, marriage appears to stabilize employment for men, though for young women the opposite appears to happen.

Unemployment also operates in reverse when marriages break down, such that unemployment among widowed, divorced and separated men is almost double that of married men (Payne, 1989). Indeed, since the first systematic studies of the unemployed in the 1930s the results have shown that for most individuals unemployment is consistently destructive, manifest in ill-health, despair and chronic lethargy – symptoms remarkably similar to those related to the loss of a friend or relation (Archer and Rhodes, 1987). Two of Sinfield's unemployed respondents bring this out quite acutely:

> It was very depressing and got worse the longer I was unemployed. It wasn't so much the money or the way I felt. It was degrading . . . when you are unemployed you are bored, frustrated, and worried, worried sick.

> My wife is right when she said it affects me as a *man*: it isn't the money so much as the feeling men have. (Sinfield, 1985: 194)

This does not mean that all households facing unemployment by one or more of the members react in a similar way. Far from it, because the reaction depends to a considerable extent on the numbers of unemployed involved, the stage in the life cycle of a family, the extent of their social networks within the local community (Clark, 1987), and the interpretation of the phenomena by those involved. It also depends on the interaction between a whole series of features conventionally derived from employment which are no longer available to the same extent for the unemployed, such as: the opportunities to use skill, for social contact, to control one's own environment, to achieve external goals, to accumulate money for all kinds of purposes, to acquire personal security and to maintain one's own status (Warr, 1987).

The social aspects of unemployment

The consequences of unemployment are also different depending on the class of the unemployed person. For example, Fineman (1983) suggests that the middle class suffer greater status collapse than the working class, given the former's greater personal involvement in work careers, and subsequent work in a different field or a different region may act disadvantageously towards them and their families. In the words of one 43-year-old redundant manager: 'I've been rejected for being over-qualified, underqualified, too old, not enough business experience, and too much experience! I've tried everything. . . . My wife can't get used to me being at home under her feet' (Fineman, 1987: 87). The working class, and especially the young working class, are more affected by the financial consequences (Warr, 1983). For many unemployed members of the working class in zones of high unemployment the experience of unemployment is tempered by the knowledge that perhaps as many as 50 per cent of their immediate neighbours are also unemployed. In these circumstances unemployment becomes a social condition as much as an individual problem. Nevertheless, the serious and deleterious consequences of unemployment should not be minimized: instances of suicide and particularly parasuicide have some correlations with patterns of unemployment (Ashton, 1986), and it would seem that much of the strain of maintaining a family intact during periods of unemployment is borne disproportionately by the mother (Hutson and Jenkins, 1989).

Despite the mass experience of the unemployed, however, even people who self-evidently have not priced themselves out of work, and who end up as redundant through massive plant closures unrelated to their own work efforts, appear to experience unemployment as an individual, not as a member of a social group. Such individualizing of what are, at heart, social problems runs against what Wright Mills (1970: 14–15) called 'the sociological imagination'. That is, the way in which 'the public issue of social structure' becomes perceived as 'the personal troubles of milieu'. In effect, a social problem is experienced as a personal problem and the responsibility for the issue is drawn off from the social structure and relocated within the apparent personal 'failings' of an individual, in this case a 22-year-old: 'Sometimes I feel like curling up in a corner. . . . The worst thing is when you write off and you hear nothing from them. When I was first unemployed, I had a little bit of hope, but not a lot now. If you think about it too much you crack up' (Buckland and MacGregor, 1987: 187). Irrespective of whether the unemployed perceive themselves to be responsible for their own plight, it would appear that the majority of employers do. Where the cause of unemployment is redundancy, rather than anything to do with the individual's conduct, there is still a widespread belief among employers that particular groups of individuals have been selected for redundancy because of their work records. Such employer hostility increases with the length of time an individual has been unemployed, and although many argue that the unemployed should lower their demands and seek work of any kind, the irony is that few employers are prepared to take on unemployed workers who do precisely this, assuming that anyone that desperate must have a personal problem or have no real interest in the particular job on offer (Crowley-Bainton, 1987). The other side of this picture is that management has indeed used redundancy not just to slim down the workforce but to remould it into a more malleable resource (Turnbull, 1988).

The impact of this non-sociological imagination is also critical to the response of people suffering the pressures of social problems. For example, if unemployment was experienced as the direct result of an inefficient or inhumane economic system then the unemployed and the employed might attempt to restructure the system. However, if unemployment is perceived as the fault of individuals (and there is considerable evidence to show that it usually is perceived in this way: cf. Sinfield, 1981), then little in the way of collective action against it is likely. After all, participation in any form of political activity is normally correlated with high levels of self-esteem and sufficient material resources to facilitate activity, not with the poverty and status disintegration that appears to be more common to the unemployed (Gallie, 1989). The disinclination of the unemployed in particular, and the labour movement in general, either in the 1930s (Croucher, 1986) or the 1980s (Forrester and Ward, 1986) to involve themselves in mass protests against unemployment is perhaps a good example of the way unemployment is experienced: it is both an individual event and, for the majority at least, probably an intermittent fate for many rather than a permanent state of affairs for a few (Marsh, 1988a). Were it otherwise the very heterogeneity and instability of the population of unemployed would act to disorganize any effective collective response; it is not coincidental that trade unions are usually strongest when their membership is permanently and securely employed in large factories, not transiently employed in isolated units. Nor is it likely that union members consider that they could affect the situation anyway – when collective bargaining is as decentralized as it is in Britain the likelihood of success of a single union's action against unemployment is strictly minimal. Deciding to forego a wage rise in one company is not going to resolve mass unemployment; for that co-ordinated mass action channelled through the TUC in conjunction with the government is essential: the history of British labour suggests that such events are unlikely in the extreme. In effect, concern for unemployment is organizationally dispersed away from conventional collective bargaining.

The politics of unemployment

Unemployment is not an inevitable consequence of organizational or economic systems; if it were, the gross international disparities highlighted by Therborn (1986) would not exist. Thus, for example, while Austria, Sweden, Norway, Japan and Switzerland managed to ride out the economic depression of the 1980s, other nations in similar economic positions, like Belgium, the Netherlands, Canada, Denmark and Britain, have literally been swamped by a veritable sea of unemployment. Disputing the assumptions that welfare systems generate unemployment, or that economic growth rates are correlated with unemployment, Therborn argues that it is the specific employment policy of each state that determines the level of unemployment. In effect, unemployment is socially or at least politically constructed, as are its effects: in Italy and France unemployment is primarily displaced on to women and the young, whereas in Britain unemployment, and particularly long-term unemployment, is almost wholly a male problem. In Austria and Switzerland it has been the policy of repatriating foreign workers which has enabled the apparent employment miracle to be brought off. Certainly technical development has not led inevitably to unemployment: Japan has the highest technological development and the lowest unemployment of the major nations. Nor does the contingent extraction of huge oil reserves necessarily soak up unemployment: the contrary experiences of Britain and Norway in this matter are useful reminders of the importance of practical policies to combat unemployment in place of market-driven spontaneous expansion. Sweden, on the other hand, has neither oil revenues nor rapid technological or economic expansion, yet in the 1970s and 1980s it did have a vigorous and successful anti-unemployment policy (Marsh, 1988a: 353–4).

Neither are the unemployment figures simply objective measures of the numbers of people who do not have paid employment. Again, what has to be stressed is the social construction of such data and thus their susceptibility to different interpretations and manipulations. For example, although the number officially unemployed in the UK in mid-1990 stood at around 1.5 million, a series of category and regulatory changes of the last decade appear to have removed 1 million from the register without them acquiring employment. About 750,000 of these are reputed to have been 'lost' through the government's Restart Programme which involved 6 million interviews with unemployed claimants, and which encouraged the unemployed into Employment Training or into a job (only 6000 appear to have gained a job as a result). Once these people returned to the unemployment register they were reclassified as new claimants rather than long-term unemployed. The upshot of such statistical and category massaging was the inexplicable 'loss' of 515,000 unemployed males between June 1985 and June 1988, without any concomitant rise in the employment figures. Most of these individuals appear to have been recategorized as disabled or the long-term sick (Harper, 1990). It is not only work which is socially constructed.

The experience of unemployment

Yet in industrial cultures, all of which are officially dedicated to some kind of work ethic, the experience of unemployment can be one of great personal shame and guilt, irrespective of the cause or political machinations behind the figures. The experience of mass unemployment between the wars generated several arguments about the importance of perceiving it as a process which changed through time for individuals. Initially, once the shock had worn off, unemployment was regarded as a temporary rest during which the stockpile of domestic jobs could be eliminated. There followed an active phase of searching for employment during which time optimism remained high, but this was gradually eroded so that after a period of six months individuals became fatalistic about their prospects, eventually treating unemployment as a way of life rather than a transient experience between jobs (Eisenberg and Lazarsfeld, 1938; Hill, 1978; Ashton, 1986). The long-term result of this, and the equivalent today, was often regarded as debilitating to the morale of the nation: eventually an entire generation of individuals would have lived without any experience of employment and would, consequently, be incapable of pursuing a 'normal' and 'responsible' life. Such fears appeared to melt rather rapidly with the onset of rearmament in the late 1930s, and we should remain similarly sceptical about the effects of long-term, rather than permanent, unemployment (see Jehoel-Gijsbers and Groot, 1989).

What do unemployed men do when not searching for work? The evidence suggests they are not engaged in domestic labour and many prefer to maintain appearances by being out of the house during conventional working hours. What little alteration there is in terms of domestic roles is limited to a small degree of 'role renegotiation' rather than a more radical 'role reversal'; some men may 'help' a little more but the majority do not (Hartley, 1987: 133). They also fail to appear as significant moonlighters; indeed, unemployment appears to rob the unemployed of the resources and will to undertake any kind of constructive activity. Assuredly, Jahoda's (1979) studies of the unemployed of Marienthal over a vast span of time, and the more recent research of Bostyn and Wright

(1987), imply that unemployment destroys the very structures that employment generates but that the employed take for granted – that is, the structures of time, routine, status and social networks. Given the excessive amount of time on their hands the unemployed ought not to be persistently late for interviews but they often are (cf. Miles, 1983); they ought to spend extra time on careful budgeting but they appear to lose interest in such details; they ought to have more time to undertake leisure activities but they seem to retreat from all such social interaction. Indeed, what interaction is undertaken very often compounds the problem by regenerating a local or vertical (within the same locale) network of relations with other unemployed people when the current evidence suggests that a wide or horizontal network of relations with employed people seems to offer the best chance for the unemployed to find employment (PSI, 1997; Perri 6, 1997). I will return to this division between vertical and horizontal developments in the final section on future work in the last chapter. Employment facilitates and unemployment tends to debilitate social routine and the rhythm of social life itself, but the exact nature of the impact of unemployment is a feature of the individuals themselves, rather than their collective position (Fryer and McKenna, 1987).

Work in itself may not be the means to self-realization, nor the means to achieve sufficient wealth to compensate for what may be experienced as the alienating consequences of work, but the effects of unemployment are a clear indication that work is a central social institution and an essential part of most people's lives.

Summary

This chapter has concerned the problematic and complex task of establishing the meaning of work by sketching in, and drawing upon, a wide range of tasks and activities that may not normally be associated with work conceived as paid employment in the contemporary West. In essence, work is a socially constructed phenomenon without fixed or universal meaning across space and time, but its meanings are delimited by the cultural forms in which it is practised. Some cultures do not distinguish between work and non-work; others distinguish between work and leisure; still others by reference to employment as a particular category of work. Generally, work might be any form of transformative activity, but what counts as work depends upon the social context within which that transformative activity occurs. The implication is that where particular activities are relegated to the category of work or non-work then it is these categories as well as the activities which should draw our attention. What some aristocratic and anti-democratic ancient Greeks despised because it was work, and hence for them the equivalent of slavery, others heralded as the foundation stone of (male) democracy. Where Christians and capitalists alike sought to inveigle the faithful and the working class with a metaphysical zeal for productive activity, anarchists and some socialists preached the gospel of laziness or of craft skills. Indeed, even the economy as a discrete category is a relatively recent social construction – a product of Western societies whose conventional epithet 'capitalist' is yet another reminder of the form of discourse within which we operate. That individuals come to be recognized as 'unemployed' rather than as 'mothers' or 'graduates' or 'gardeners' conveys a great deal about the significance allocated to formal employment as *the* distinguishing category of social life by the state. Similarly, the notion that domestic activities do not constitute conventional work or that certain people are 'just housewives', or that universal orientations to work can be derived from the experiences of male workers, connotes a culture shot through with patriarchal mores of work. The conventional adage may be 'one man's work is another man's leisure' but it might be more appropriately written as 'one man's leisure is another woman's work'. In effect, what counts as work cannot be read off from an objective analysis of specific activities because the meaning of work is not immanent to the activities; meanings are socially constructed and maintained, they are contingently present and permanently fragile. The answer, therefore, to Charles Lamb's question 'Who first invented Work?' might not be a name but another question: 'Who said the inventing of work had ceased?'

Exam/essay questions

1 What is work?
2 What isn't work?
3 Why are the definitions of work so important?
4 'Work isn't intrinsically satisfying or dissatisfying; work is what you make it.' Discuss.
5 Why do so many societies, past and present, regard the status of manual labour as subordinate to mental labour?
6 If manual labour is poorly regarded and rewarded, why are women discriminated against because they are not as strong as men?
7 'A great deal of harm is being done in the modern world by a belief in the virtuousness of WORK . . . the road to happiness and prosperity lies in an organized diminution of work' (Bertrand Russell). Discuss.
8 Is work the realm of self-realization or merely a method to achieve self-realization?
9 'Since work is organized along patriarchal principles the only way to ensure gendered equality is to abolish the conventional "working day".' Discuss.
10 The principal activities involved in being on holiday and being unemployed are similar – so why is the former so eagerly awaited and the latter so desperately avoided?

Further reading

One of the best single-author historical reviews of work is Applebaum's *The Concept of Work: Ancient, Medieval and Modern* (1992). A good collection of historical articles, but with a much narrower focus, is Joyce's *The Historical Meanings of Work* (1987). Pahl's edited collection, *On Work* (1988), is wider and more contemporary. Wallman provides a valuable collection of articles in *The Social Anthropology of Work* (1979), while Anthony's *The Ideology of Work* (1977) is a critical response to managerialist writings on the topic. Cowan's *More Work for Mother* (1983) is an innovative examination of the significance of technology for domestic work and women and, finally, Goldthorpe et al.'s two volumes of the *Affluent Worker* (1968–69) remain classics in their field, though obviously dated now.

2

Work in Historical Perspective

> I like work: it fascinates me. I can sit and look at it for hours.
> Jerome K. Jerome, *Three Men in a Boat*

Introduction

This chapter on the history of work refrains from attempting the impossible: to cover the history of work adequately is to cover a substantial section of all human history. Therefore, what it does is illuminate some significant features by reference to multiple examples. These examples are drawn from pre-industrial, agricultural, industrial and domestic sources, as well as some which do not fit into regular taxonomies. There is no attempt to cover a representative sample, nor to describe the 'typical' work experiences of history. Indeed, the argument is that such experiences are probably rare and we seldom have the knowledge to assess what might count as typical. Thus I have drawn from sources beyond the conventional focus of 'industrial' sociology to demonstrate the limited significance of what has become perceived as the archetypal 'worker': a male craft worker in pre-industrial periods or a male blue-collar factory worker in the industrial era. Since there are already several texts which focus predominantly on the historical experience of men at work (see, for example, Hobsbawm, 1964a, 1984; Fox, 1985) the bias of examples here tends to be towards women. This brief synopsis of work in historical perspective is designed to highlight several critical features. First, work is a social not an individual activity – even those who work on their own do so within a socially constructed network of relations. One implication of this is that such relations can alter the very meaning of work; in particular the process of industrialization in Britain witnessed a transformation from a moral to a market economy. Yet the transformation is not one where the market simply replaces morality but rather one where the market sits on top of the **moral economy**. To use a textile analogy, the moral economy underlies the market economy in the way that the batik process involves a waxen base to resist areas of surface colour. The result of a batik process may provide a sheen of surface colour but the pattern is affected by the form and extent of the wax underlay. Thus, the world of work remains one that cannot be adequately explained by reference to market forces and economic rationality alone: it is quintessentially a social phenomenon, a world of symbolic representations, meanings and interpretations rather than a world of self-evident objective facts. Second, the history of work buttresses the suggestion of the previous chapter that the very term 'work' is ambiguous and transient but this is not indicative of any pluralist notions of equality: it is important not just that disputes exist about the meaning of work but also that such disputes are often resolved in favour of the more powerful. Third, some patterns of work are ephemeral in the extreme while others are notoriously inertial. Fourth, the social inequalities of work manifest in gender, ethnic and class divisions long predate the rise of capitalism and therefore pose problems for theoretical viewpoints that root the generation of systematic inequalities solely in capitalism. Fifth, the image of work as separate from, and unrelated to, the home, and the associated predominance of male breadwinners, is both historically atypical and theoretically vacuous: home and the place of work have always been, and still are, intimately connected by a seamless web of social interdependence. Sixth, an appreciation of the history of work is crucial if we are not to assume that contemporary work is wholly the result of contemporary actors. What may appear irrational today, for example trade union demarcation disputes, may well reflect a pattern of work that was constructed to fulfil a real need at the time of origin, in this case the determination to remain employed by making each skill an essential part of the productive process.

In what follows I consider pre-industrial work, the transition from feudal to industrial forms of work, the significance of occupational changes, the rise of trade unions, the interventions of the state, the development of clerical labour, and the impact of the wars.

Pre-industrial work

Perhaps the major problem to be encountered in any historical review of work is the paucity of evidence about pre-industrial work and, by comparison, the enormous amount of data available for contemporary work. Even though we generally know very little about the working lives of the population in any epoch before the industrial one, as will be evident from the next few chapters, even the contemporary evidence is far from satisfactory. All that can be done is to adumbrate a skeleton of ideas and fragments of evidence rather than draw a series of definitive conclusions. Since the intention is to demonstrate the diversity of experience, as well as their social origins and forms of deployment through various discourses, such a skeletal approach should be sufficient.

If it is the case that contemporary hunter-gatherer societies are little changed from our own indigenous historical variants, then we can assume that the approach and forms of work considered in the previous chapter are appropriate. Hunter-gatherer societies are not normally encumbered by the kind of work ethics that require submission to socially constructed units of time of the 9 to 5 variety, nor do they divide up time into slices for work and recreation. Work and non-work are not so much merged together as irrelevant terms to describe the activity. Yet one of the major themes running through the approach has been to stress the continuities as well as the discontinuities across time. There is no doubt that changes occur all the time but these have to be contextualized adequately if we are to appreciate their relevance. Thus, we can only really talk about a decline in the work ethic or a rise in instrumental orientations to work if we know what existed previously, and not just a decade previously but perhaps a century or more. For example, in Britain the former Chancellor of the Exchequer, Nigel Lawson, noted in 1985 the common assumption amongst Conservatives that, as a direct result of post-war Labour policies, taxation rates had, for the first time ever, been pushed so high that they became economically damaging. Yet such concerns for work disincentives are not new: over 1,500 years earlier Priscus of Panium met a Greek merchant who preferred living free among his previous captors (Attila's Huns) rather than under the Roman Empire because, among other things, the taxes were lower (Salway, 1981: 457).

Roman Britain

Such financial calculations for work mobility in Roman Britain during the same era were no doubt irrelevant for the vast majority of the population involved. Most of them were primarily engaged in subsistence farming but there were also some specialized areas. For instance, Britain was renowned as a leading producer of agricultural commodities (cattle, hides and corn), as well as hunting dogs, timber, slaves and precious metals (Salway, 1981: 630–1). Nor should it be forgotten that the work of the Roman army and the economic viability of the Empire were intertwined in what Tacitus called the *pretium victoriae*: war was supposed to pay for itself, it was work not unlike any other in the underlying aim of securing a living, albeit through perfecting the art of killing.

The largest non-military industry for the major part of the Roman period seems to have been pig-iron, which Britain was self-sufficient in by the end of the first century AD. But what is significant about this is that a mere 1,500 craft workers would have been sufficient to provide the necessary labour: if iron production was the largest single industrial employer we can rest assured that the majority of the population not in the army were wholly agricultural in orientation and location (Salway, 1981: 639). That is not to say that everyone not engaged in killing people or moulding iron pigs spent all their time farming. On the contrary, a number of people were full-time potters, shopkeepers, smiths, metal and jewellery workers etc. Even the trusty British duffel coat made its first appearance under Roman rule as *byrrus Britannicus*.

Feudal Britain

Once the Roman army had gone, by the fifth century AD, Britain, like many areas of the old empire, was subject to the rapacious interests of external and internal military groups. One eventual socio-economic response to this was the system of feudalism which conjoined a method of agriculturally based production with a military protection racket. In return for resisting external threats to life and limb the military aristocracy secured the surplus from their peasants (North and Thomas, 1973; Anderson, 1974), yet such a system, although politically stable in the main, also reproduced economic and technical developments that tended to undermine, though not destroy, social and legal rigidities. In particular, the notion of property rights underwent some radical transformations, especially in Britain, which was somewhat distanced from the more ingrained Roman law of continental Europe. With the expansion of feudal agriculture into marginal lands, combined with fluctuating birth rates and natural catastrophes like the Black Death, the end result was declining productivity, a drastic economic squeeze on the nobility and an increasingly vociferous peasantry, eager to make the most of its new labour market strength despite its failure in revolt (Brown and Harrison, 1978: 48–71).

Early capitalism

As the social relations between serf and master were gradually eroded in favour of economic relations, manifest in the switch from the provision of labour to the provision of money rent, so too the personal forms of authority were depleted. In their place authority relations resurfaced at the level of the state, not at the level of the local noble: the absolutist state, complete with its power to dispense privileges to local trade groups and guilds of craft workers, was born and the age of feudalism was rapidly drawn to a close; the age of market capitalism was just beginning.

But at this stage, with technological innovations minimal, most industry as such was labour intensive and, with the single major exception of woollen cloth, England in the fifteenth century was economically retarded in comparison to its European neighbours. Indeed, the great economic success story of the European medieval world was Flanders, which had proved to be the single most important factor in the development of English commerce from the twelfth to the fourteenth century (Postan, 1972: 213–16). In England luxury textiles were still surpassed by those of Italy and the Low Countries; in mining and metals it was outproduced by the Germans and Swedes, and in many other things by all of these countries as well as France and Spain.

Mercantilism

By the sixteenth century the power of the English guilds had already been largely ceded to the state and by the eighteenth century many guilds had all but disappeared (Coleman, 1975: 19–22). The state's control of working arrangements was considerable: it acted through justices of the peace and through legislative controls to set wages and conditions and intervened extensively in a **mercantilist** fashion to protect and promote native industries. Thus to help the woollen industry and its workers there was a legal obligation to be buried in a woollen shroud, and the Statute of Artificers of 1563 demanded a seven-year apprenticeship for all clothiers. The state even restricted the size of enterprises in the woollen industry: by an Act of 1555 it was forbidden for country clothiers to own more than one loom; weavers could not own more than two. One of the clearest cases to demonstrate the social or normative rather than the inevitable or natural responses of the state to industrial considerations was the reaction to technical advances before the Industrial Revolution. Gig mills, devices to raise the nap on woven cloth before shearing, were banned in 1551 to protect jobs (Harvie, 1978: 15); over one and a half centuries later, in 1813, seventeen Luddites were hanged for their part in the rebellion against the new shearing technology which the state now presumed to be inevitable and necessary (R. Reid, 1986). The attempt to replace the 'moral economy' with the 'market economy' was a transition littered with similar, if less brutal, conflicts (Thompson, 1968).

It was not until the early eighteenth century, however, that the picture began to change dramatically as the state dismantled the legal restrictions on trade and industry, and English economic production began to outpace that of its continental neighbours (Coleman, 1975). Much of this seems to have come about through the dispersal of textiles away from the town-based guilds and into the rural-based putting-out system: the original greenfield sites. Yet despite the critical role played by the industrial textile workers, in terms of both generating wealth and the incipient trade union movement, the significance of the town-based craft workers should not be underestimated; for the coopers, masons, thatchers, carpenters and the like survived well into the nineteenth century and formed the productive core of town life in Britain and France (Sonenscher, 1989). However, their power rested squarely on controlling a static labour market; once product demand grew incessantly, as it did from the sixteenth century in England, the guilds slowly began to disintegrate, hastened by the rural developments in textiles and the shift in state sponsorship towards the Justices of the Peace and against the monopolistic guilds.

The transition from feudalism to proto-industrialization

In England the absolutist state was remarkably short lived. Having terminated the age of feudalism, it was itself subject to decline. In conjunction with the diminishing power of the crown was the associated decline of legal restrictions on trade and crafts. These lattice-like systems of property ownership and associated usufructs (rights to derive profit from land owned by someone else) were often grounded in common law and tradition but had been active inhibitors of private enterprise and capitalist market relationships (Landes, 1972). Not that the removal of such economic inhibitions had been achieved by an absolutist state. On the contrary, the British state, as a result of the Civil War and construction of a constitutional monarchy, was dominated by a landowning aristocracy not by any monarch. Moreover, this elite was directly involved in commercial activity; it transcended the distinction between landed and commercial interests rather than being swamped by the latter, and ultimately spawned an ideological system of values often regarded as instrumental in the degradation of manufacturing industry and the super-ordination of financial affairs (Wiener, 1981; Roderick and Stephens, 1981). But this did not mean that the political revolution of the seventeenth century resulted in a concomitant economic revolution; if anything the reverse is the case, for economic restructuring was noticeably absent (Hill, 1969: 240).

The putting-out system and decentralization

That said, economic and industrial stasis did not survive for long. One of its major underminers was the putting-out system, developed initially in thirteenth-century Flanders, but refined and expanded in England, where an abundant labour supply and the difficulty of making a living as an independent farmer or weaver ensured the growth of the first proletariat of industrial (i.e., textile) workers by the end of the eighteenth century. By then, for example, master clothiers, keen to rid themselves of legal regulations on their expanding businesses, and smaller entrepreneurs and journeymen under direct threat from the new factories, combined to demand a parliamentary inquiry into the woollen industry. Its report, in 1806, noted both the distinctions between the independent clothiers of Yorkshire and the putting-out system in the West Country, and that the latter system tended to undergo considerable bouts of unrest as technological innovation spread (Harvie, 1978). The network of medieval restrictions was much less significant for the relatively independent craft workers of Yorkshire, and Defoe, in his *Tour through the Whole Island of Great Britain* (1724–6), writes of Yorkshire in the early eighteenth century as a veritable Garden of Eden in its productivity and as a decentralized egalitarian idyll:

> this whole country, however mountainous, is yet infinitely full of people; these people are full of business; not a beggar not an idle person to be seen, except here and there in an alms house, where people ancient and

decrepit and past labour might perhaps be found; for it is observable, that the people here, however laborious, generally live to a great age, a certain testimony to the goodness and wholesomeness of the country. (quoted in R. Reid, 1986: 5–9)

In fact, although such descriptions undermine images of generalized pre-industrial poverty, the decentralization in Yorkshire did not lead to egalitarian work relations because, as Cole makes clear, most of the craft workers were small-scale capitalists rather than truly independent (cited by Landes, 1986: 605). Nevertheless, the point made by Hobsbawm is that such a decentralized industrial structure had profound consequences for the future development of the Industrial Revolution and the nature of workers' reactions to it: 'Such a form of business structure has the advantage of flexibility and lends itself readily to rapid initial expansion, but at later stages of industrial development, when the technical and economic advantages of planning and integration are far greater, develops considerable rigidities and inefficiencies' (1969: 65). This point is crucial because it reflects the fundamental significance of the historical dimension: the impact of the process of industrialization was such that it becomes very difficult to understand contemporary work patterns without some historical knowledge: today's ossified work practices and productivity inhibitors may simply be yesterday's radically innovative method for achieving productivity advances.

Class and community

It is also important to note that one of the most successful of the early trade unions developed in cotton where the very powerful, and male-dominated, skilled mule spinners organized both themselves, and ultimately the other cotton workers, to resist the might of the cotton masters. Whereas before the Industrial Revolution the social divisions between people were not channelled *primarily* along class-based employer/employee lines, they now tended to be. Whereas societal norms had been complex and pluralist they were now constrained by the increasing significance of a new breed of animal: capitalism (Hobsbawm, 1969: 66). As Thompson (1971) and A. Randall (1988) have argued, the work, life and protest of much of the eighteenth century is soaked with an over-arching concern, not with markets and issues of supply and demand, but with a 'moral economy' in which, however inegalitarian, relationships between social classes were at least reciprocal to some degree.

The moral framework of the combinations is well represented in the initiation ceremonies and oaths sworn by the Luddites and Tolpuddle Martyrs alike. Both groups were 'twisted in' rather than simply 'admitted' to membership. For each Luddite had to 'swear that I will use my utmost endeavour to punish with death any traitor or traitors who may rise up against us, though we should fly to the verge of existence' (quoted in R. Reid, 1986: 92). Each of the Tolpuddle Martyrs had to swear not to reveal the rules of the Union on pain of having their soul plunged into eternity (Marlow, 1985: 81). This moral undertone was not simply intended to deter reprobates from undermining the collectivity but also embodies a distinctive approach to working life: work was not simply an economic activity stripped of all non-pecuniary interests but a *social* activity circumscribed by custom and traditions that went far deeper than the cash nexus. Indeed, one of the reasons why the Luddites were initially so successful was that their fight was not one of skilled workers against unskilled, or even textile workers against textile machinery (much of which was not 'new' anyway); rather their conflict was, like the miners' strike some 170 years later, a strike involving a large proportion of the population of certain local communities (R. Reid, 1986; Berg, 1988a). The tenacity of such communities suggests that even now work remains imbued with a moral vigour consistently misunderstood or ignored by those whose analysis of work remains restricted to the operation of market forces alone. It was a struggle of one community against another and, as such, re-emphasizes a critical theme running throughout the book: work and the domestic sphere are intimately and irrevocably linked in a web that confounds all accounts which are ignorant of it. Work was, to put a gloss on it, a way of life; an end in itself not a means to an end. This point was not lost on Carlyle, for whom the whole process of industrialization had split society asunder, dissolving the critical moral fabric of the community, and for whom, as for Marx, the immediate future was one of foreboding.

Large-scale organizations

Yet not all employment during this transient stage towards industrialization was decentralized, home-based and ultimately threatened by technological development, even if much of it was. Mines, shipyards and mills had all been thriving non-domestic units from the Tudor and Stuart periods, although even if one or two units employed hundreds, most probably had little more than a handful. Indeed, even as late as 1851 the average productive unit still employed only about 8.5 employees: the apotheosis of early Victorian industrial Britain witnessed a nation of agricultural labourers, domestic servants and small workshops, not gigantic factories filled with thousands of clone-like workers (Hopkins, 1979; Burnett, 1990). A few mines in northern England operated with hundreds of miners but many just had a handful while some of the largest single productive units were not in the private sector at all but in the naval dockyards: by 1700 Chatham and Portsmouth employed more than 1,000 workers each (Coleman, 1975: 23–51). Work, then, before the dawn of the industrial factories and even well into it, was ultimately small scale, predicated on a social as well as an economic footing, and had few of the class-based antagonisms that were already being forged in the northern mills.

A useful place to assess any alleged pre-industrial homogeneity might be the largest and most expensive work unit in the Western world of the time, the eighteenth-century British Navy. Although the Civil Service employed 16,000 in 1759 the Navy had almost 85,000 officers and men (Rodger, 1986: 11,332).

Several critical aspects of this massive organization are pertinent to any assessment about pre-industrial work organizations. First, contrary to popular myth, officer or managerial control generally operated on the basis of persuasion not physical coercion. At a time when the civil land-based population had little regard for the control of the civil authorities it would seem appropriate that a similar absence of direct coercion was the norm at sea. This prescient form of participatory 'human resource management' extended to situations in which ship's captains would ask the crew whether they ought to engage the enemy or surrender:

> The *Penguin*, a twenty gun sloop, found herself chased by two French thirty-six gun frigates, which head-reached on her and ranged up on either side. Captain Harris summoned his officers and men and asked their advice whether to fight or not; they replied they would have taken on one thirty-six, but two was too much. So the *Penguin* struck her colours without firing a shot, and at the court martial Harris was honourably acquitted, as having done everything that a good officer could do. (Rodger, 1986: 237)

Ordinary seamen would also visit admirals in their homes to discuss personal grievances. This did not mean that anarchic confusion reigned supreme; quite the opposite, for the discipline of the British crews was an important factor in the victory over the less disciplined French Navy, and in terms of ensuring a particular proportion of the fleet was always at sea the mid-eighteenth century was more efficient than that operating during the Second World War (Rodger, 1986: 36, 229–37). Neither should we fall prey to the belief that sailors were disciplined through some patriotic duty; both sailors and shipwrights in the royal dockyard were quite prepared to strike or petition for improvements at the very moment of war (Rule, 1988: 5). Nor was it simply the case that shipboard life, with its inherent dangers and mutual dependence, ensured that discipline would not be a problem; since the merchant navy had an alarming number of mutinies and reports of brutality it would appear that the policy of the Admiralty, in conjunction with the protection of subordinates by the king's regulations, ensured peace usually prevailed. This is important because it is an early demonstration of the mutual advantages of bureaucratic regulation: it was not that the Navy was run by rule-bound officers, quite the opposite in many ways, but the existence of a backdrop of mutually advantageous rules deterred both officers and men from adopting the violent solutions to work-based problems that plagued the Merchant Navy and later, after considerable changes, the Royal Navy too.

Second, the typical ship's company was not divided cleanly along class lines (though these became much more prominent as the Industrial Revolution gathered pace into the nineteenth century); rather the divisions were multiple, based on different forms of hierarchies, and sustained by the groups themselves rather than being forced upon them by super-ordinate officers. For example, not only were the officers split between commissioned, warrant and petty, but all these were associated *with* the seamen but against a whole panoply of others including the marines, carpenters, gunners, cooks, servants and (male) children (Rodger, 1986: 15–29). There were one or two women who passed as men in

Navy, the most celebrated being William Prothero, a marine aboard the
ppriately named *Amazon*, but however relatively liberal the Navy was then
he extent that it commissioned a black sailor from Jamaica in 1782), it
not open its ranks to women.

Whatever else the pre-industrial world of work in Britain was like, it certainly does not appear to have been composed of a mass of skilled craft workers,
nor was it a world where employers or their agents always rode roughshod over
the interests of employees or labourers. Diversity and dependence are as useful
a summary of work in this period as solidarity and coercion; but the latter were
certainly to become more prominent as the industrialization, and especially the
development of factories in Britain, destabilized the occupational system and
with it the world of work.

Factories and technological change

Considerable controversy exists over the role of technology within industrial
development, particularly with regard to the rise and spread of factories. By
convention, from Adam Smith, Andrew Ure and Charles Babbage onwards, it
has been assumed that the organizational demands and economic rationality
of large-scale technology simply obliterated household production and replaced
it with gigantic factories. Whether the cause of technical development was
economic or social, or even whether it was autonomous, is secondary to the
reality of its alleged effects: the new powers of steam engines and mechanical
production required factory production, facilitated the division of labour and
thus demanded greater degrees of co-ordinative and controlling power on the
part of the capitalist factory owner. The hierarchy of control within factories,
then, was supposedly technically and organizationally inevitable; any other method
of organizing production would simply have been economically inefficient and
technically irrational.

This orthodoxy, which received support from Engels though less so from
Marx, has been subject to attack primarily from Marglin (1982). His argument
suggests that the origins of hierarchy within capitalist production lie not in the
extended division of labour engendered by technical developments but in the
desire for social control on the part of capitalists so that levels of exploitation
could be increased. Thus factories, which were, after all, established with the
kind of technology already in place in many domestic units, were constructed
to maximize control; they were not the inevitable results of technical change
nor were they the inexorable results of the search for simple efficiency. In effect,
capitalists divided up the labour process, beyond that concomitant with any
complex labour process, to fragment the workforce so that control over it was
facilitated. As a direct result this fragmentation provided capitalists with a formal,
and apparently technically required, role as integrator and co-ordinator. If
Marglin is right then, by implication, egalitarian and co-operative work organization is possible and hierarchies, beyond some form of co-ordination system,
are technically unnecessary.

One difficulty with Marglin's case is his assumption that capitalists needed to make a role for themselves. It is not self-evident why this should be so; after all, rentiers have been content to draw profits simply from their ownership of property without constructing an active role for themselves, so it is not clear why capitalists should feel obliged to do more than was required. Nor do they appear to have suffered from any crisis of legitimacy. A second issue relates to the irrelevance of capitalists: if their role was entirely specious why did workers not simply set up shop on their own without capitalists? Third, was the level of specialization really so unnecessary? If it was, then there is a difficulty in accounting for the connections between those, like Wedgwood, who extended the division of labour to the greatest possible degree and those, again like Wedgwood, who were the most efficient in terms of production costs (Landes, 1986).

However, if a radical division of labour was critical to efficient production in certain forms of production, this does not account for the transition to large numbers of factories. Since much domestic production adopted the latest techno-logical and organizational forms of production before the factories spread, we need to explain why a spectacularly efficient method of production based at home spawned a transition to factory organization. The answer is probably one on which even the protagonists of this particular debate would agree: domestic production of this form was *so* successful that it enabled workers to do less and less work for more and more money. As discussed in the previous chapter, there is no inherent human desire to acquire material wealth through work, instead there are culturally and temporally specific norms of human activ-ity. If technology facilitated greater levels of income for less effort, and if the cultural norm was to minimize human labour rather than maximize human reward, then technology could just as easily serve to restrict as to expand total production. The response of merchants and putting-out capitalists was clear: to make the most of the new techniques required central and hierarchic con-trol – workers had to be coerced to work when capitalists required them to, not when they felt like it.

Yet there appears to have been more to the success of the factory over domestic production than a concern for maximizing control. In that some production was housed in factories far sooner than others, and that some forms of manufacture remained stubbornly domesticated well into the nineteenth century, we should be wary of accepting that the issue is solely to do with control rather than control and other features. For example, it was seldom fea-sible to develop domestic production where the process required a large input of natural energy (as did iron), or the product was large (such as ship building), or the machinery very expensive etc. It is also clear that the technical innova-tions most associated with factory production were often aimed at circumventing the exclusive and, from the capitalists' point of view, profit-retarding skills of particular groups of workers.

Nor were the responses of the early nineteenth-century Luddites typical of the earlier period. When the Luddites rose against the machinery they did so because their very livelihoods were threatened by it and because certain of their skills could not be taken abroad. But Hargreaves's 'spinning jenny' (1767) and the 'water frame' (1768), initially at least, soaked up surplus labour rather than posed a threat to the existent workforce and enhanced or at least retained operatives' skills. Such technical advance was often marketed precisely as a means to generate work for the unemployed and underemployed, not as a method of dislodging recalcitrant workers, hence the limited resistance on the part of the workers to these early developments. The hybrid 'mule' (1779) was rather different because it was designed on a large scale which was deemed by its supporters as inappropriate for domestic adoption and because economic conditions had worsened by this time (Landes, 1986). Likewise, Roberts's 'self-acting mule' involved the degradation of skills and the elimination of labour and was consequently resisted, not just by Labour but also by many Tories shocked at the implications for the nation of such 'rationalizing' measures. For such patricians machinery was 'an insatiable Moloch [with a] heart of steel, jaws as wide as the grave, teeth of iron and claws of brass' (quoted in Berg, 1980: 265). The moral economy was not simply a dream of the working class but an element of reciprocal class relations. Similarly, technology was not axiomatically received as an embodiment of rationality by the middle and upper classes but interpreted in a variety of ways consonant with people's wider ideology.

Factory production, therefore, was not merely the result of capitalists' desire to carve themselves a role: they were probably more concerned with carving out a living than a role. Certain aspects of production were portrayed as more viable under factory regimes than situated within the domestic unit but the analysis of this development does not take place outside an arena of political life. After all, many domestic spinners and weavers soldiered on at their looms and wheels well after factories had made their product uncompetitive and their independent living precarious. For example, the handloom weavers' struggle for existence in the first quarter of the nineteenth century became increasingly difficult as wages fell (mechanization was not a major threat until around 1826), yet the number of handloom weavers actually continued to grow. As Mathias notes, it was not just economic need which maintained the family-based industry but also 'the cohesion of family employment [and] . . . the values of a whole way of life' (1969: 207). The point really is how different political interests were served by the rise of factory production: you do not have to be a capitalist to recognize that extending the division of labour can be a more efficient method of production – but who benefited from this extension and who suffered from it? Moreover, how did the beneficiaries manage to win out? Such a question requires more than a concern for issues of control over the labour process and more than an analysis of the putative technical superiority of certain kinds of machinery. It requires us to look at the seamless web that the victors managed to weave between themselves and the technical artefacts, between the domestic and the factory spheres of life, and between themselves and the politics of organizational life. We also need to explain why the resistance of the factory proletariat to the expansion of capitalism, so elegantly argued by Marx, appeared to be limited to trade unionism. A major reason is the apathetic nature of this same proletariat: its form and shape changed in conjunction with capitalist developments and a homogeneous class never emerged.

Occupational change

Diversity and domination

Although, as discussed in chapter 5, much has been made recently of the dis-aggregating consequences of capitalism, as a once homogeneous workforce of skilled craft workers is deskilled and degraded into a myriad of occupational specialisms and statuses, close attention to the pre-industrial historical evidence suggests that uniformity was noticeable mainly by its absence. We have always to be wary of any kind of data but occupational data before the nineteenth century are notoriously suspect. However, a glance at figure 1 should highlight the problems of reconstructing a homogeneous occupational structure.

Although the denials of homogeneity are probably safer to make than positive statements concerning the proportion of specific groups, it is noticeable that no occupational group accrues more than 25 per cent of the total at any period covering the century up until the beginnings of the Industrial Revolution, though a large margin of error must be accepted even here. Before the beginning of the Census in 1801 very little reliable evidence beyond local examples and parish registers exists, and up until 1831 the Census itself kept little occupational data. Lindhert's (1980) scrutiny of burial registers highlights the problem of identifying the occupations of women since they were mainly identified by their marital status, though it is clear that a large proportion of women worked at home producing saleable commodities, especially textiles. In line with the concern for the interpretative approach it should also be clear that different interpretations of 'significant categories' generate very heterogeneous models of the social and occupational structure. Since women recede from view in many of these early models a model based on gender would reveal the persistent and homogeneous domination of employment by men, rather than a fragmented social structure.

Lindhert's analysis suggests a generally stable occupational structure from the middle of the seventeenth to the middle of the eighteenth century with the exceptions of an expanding agricultural and manufacturing sector and a declining group of low-income dependants. In the second half of the eighteenth century, and the beginnings of Industrial Revolution proper, the occupational structure alters quite markedly: manufacturing, or rather textile manufacturing, mushrooms in size, with the numbers of men engaged tripling in fifty years, while the number of weavers doubles. Relatedly, building, mining, the professions and the armed forces all expand rapidly, while the numbers of unskilled rise only marginally and agricultural employment drops to the point where, very approximately, just over a third of the population are engaged in agriculture in some form by the beginning of the nineteenth century. What is particularly significant is the point that at no time can we really talk about the work experience of the majority of the categorized population as if such a homogeneous category existed. Of course, there are large groups with similar life experiences: handloom weavers or agricultural labourers or miners etc. Indeed, it could be argued that the wives of men in such categories probably had similar lives; but

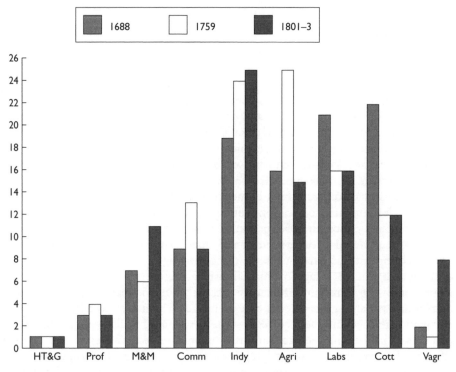

Key:
HT&G – High titles and gentlemen
Prof – Professions
M&M – Military and maritime
Comm – Commerce
Indy – Industry and building
Agri – Agriculture (freehold)
Labs – Labourers
Cott – Cottagers and paupers
Vagr – Vagrants
Note: There are significant problems with these data: domestic servants (mainly women) have been omitted; labourers are not distinguished by sector; women's occupations are rarely recorded; the figures reflect families rather than individuals.

Figure 1 Occupational structure of England and Wales: 1688, 1759, 1801–3 (%)
Source: Lindert and Williamson, 1982; Crafts, 1985

none of these groups ever approximates a majority of the population: diversity, not similarity, is probably a more appropriate universal term for describing their mode of existence.

Industry

The textile industry, with a million workers, was virtually the only one which, by the mid-nineteenth century, employed roughly equal numbers of men and women.

It was also the largest single industry involving widespread, and occasionally very large, factories. Indeed, with the exception of some iron and coal works, cotton was virtually the only industry that was mechanized and factory based relatively early (Hobsbawm, 1969: 72). Almost all of cotton spinning was mechanized and factory based by 1851, though weaving survived a little longer as a handloom operation. But however diverse the occupational structure of mid-nineteenth-century Britain, and however limited any specific occupation might be in size and distribution, it was still the case that industry figured largest, both in terms of overall size and, equally significant, in terms of influence. Not only was industry disproportionately important in terms of its provision towards the GNP but it was also critical in an indirect way: its absorption of labour from agriculture ensured the maintenance of a viable agricultural labour force, and its manifest success in the generation of a new middle class sustained the expansion of domestic service. The middle class was by no means insignificant in numbers: in London, even before the Industrial Revolution, the 'middle station' (as Defoe called them) comprised somewhere between 20 and 25 per cent of the total population (Earle, 1989).

The prototypical example of an industrial region was Lancashire, where despite the enormous importance of cotton and manufacturing the former declined through the second half of the nineteenth century while the latter was virtually static. In the country as a whole between 41 and 46 per cent of the population were employed in manufacturing, mining and industry between 1870 and 1914 but it was in directly related employment that the biggest growth occurred: in shipping, services, exporting, transport and finance (Mathias, 1969: 272–3).

Agriculture and rural work

It is important to note too that the decline of the more traditional, that is agriculturally based and home-located, lifestyle in Britain may not have been quite so rapid as has been previously assumed. It is common to argue that Britain's peasantry were virtually extinguished by the mid-nineteenth century (Hobsbawm and Rudé, 1973; Moore, 1967: 25–9), yet the problems of categorization in the Census obfuscate the probable persistence of the English peasant well into the nineteenth century. Even in 1851, although industrial occupations outnumbered agricultural ones, it is still the case that agricultural labour was the biggest single occupation, domestic service was the second largest and building the third. In fact, the population engaged in agriculture as labourers (1.75 million, of whom 0.25 million were women mainly employed as farm servants) had been growing, albeit slowly, throughout the nineteenth century. Yet at the same time there were four times as many industrial workers of various kinds as agricultural workers, though again only a quarter of the industrial workers were employed in mechanized (i.e., steam-driven) industry, including mining (Hopkins, 1979: 3). In short, no homogeneous factory proletariat existed and, furthermore, occupational divisions were seldom as clear cut as the Census data would suggest. Work for many people in the rural parts of Britain, then, and for much of the nineteenth century was still a matter of multiple rather than singular occupations.

For those in urban areas the typical place of employment was more likely to be a small workshop rather than a factory of any size. There were some very large industrial centres by the late nineteenth century: Swan Hunter's and Palmer's shipyards in north-east England both employed over 7,000 men (McClelland, 1987: 181). But many of the most successful manufacturing centres, rather than factories, were located in rural areas rather than urban centres; not because natural resources forced such dispersal but because social features encouraged it. That is, although we commonly consider the relocation of industry to 'greenfield sites' as a twentieth-century phenomenon, it has a long history. While the original guild organization in towns acted to inhibit greater levels of production through the guild members' influence over the labour and product markets, few such socially constructed barriers existed in rural areas. Here, wages were cheaper and restrictive practices fewer; and it was here that Britain generated the domestic forms of specialization that led the rest of the world at the end of the eighteenth century. As one contemporary put it: 'When Mr Arkwright established his works . . . he did not establish them where the people had been in the habits of spinning at all; but he established them at Cromford . . . where till that time the People [women and children] had been almost wholly unemployed, except in the washing of lead' (quoted in Landes, 1986: 608). Associated with the movements to greenfield sites, of course, are movements away from previously productive areas. This is significant in so far as many popular historical approaches tend to locate the growth of industry from a general agriculture base in the north. In reality, the rise of the manufacturing north had a long history of domestic-industrial production and brought with it the decline and collapse of similar industries in the south of Britain (Berg, 1988a).

Time, teams and punishments

At this time, in the late eighteenth and early nineteenth centuries, the working day was conventionally at least twelve hours long, even for children (of whom there were more than 50,000 officially employed full time in 1851 and still 22,000 as late as 1871; cf. DOE, 1971: table 102 note 7), and accidents and physical punishment a common hazard (Ayres, 1988). Perhaps few were as cruel as those suffered by one Robert Blencoe:

> I have seen the time when two hand-vices of a pound each, more or less, have been screwed to my ears at Lytton Mill, in Derbyshire. There are the scars remaining behind my ears. Then three or four of us at once have been hung on a cross beam above the machinery, hanging by our hands, without shirts or stockings. Mind, we were apprentices, without mother or father to take care of us. (quoted in Hopkins, 1979: 10–11)

Table I Selected distribution of the occupied (i.e., paid) British labour force (% of total males and females)

	1841		1871		1901		1921	
	M	F	M	F	M	F	M	F
Public administration	0.6	0.0	0.9	0.1	1.2	0.2	2.0	0.4
Armed forces	0.7	0.0	1.1	0.0	1.1	0.0	1.3	0.0
Professionals	1.6	0.7	1.7	1.3	2.1	2.0	2.1	2.3
Domestic servants	3.7	14.3	2.0	14.3	2.1	12.2	1.9	9.5
Commercial	1.4	0.0	1.8	0.0	3.7	0.5	4.7	3.0
Transport etc.	2.8	0.1	5.6	0.1	8.7	0.2	7.9	0.4
Agriculture and fishing	21.1	1.2	14.1	1.2	8.5	0.4	7.2	0.5
Mining	3.2	0.1	4.4	0.1	5.7	0.0	6.4	0.1
Metal manufacturing	5.7	0.2	7.4	0.4	9.1	0.5	11.0	0.9
Building	5.4	0.0	6.1	0.0	7.5	0.0	4.6	0.0
Other manufacturing	3.9	0.4	4.3	0.8	5.1	1.5	5.0	1.4
Textiles etc.	12.8	8.1	8.4	11.2	6.0	9.8	3.7	6.7
Food and drink	3.9	0.6	3.8	0.7	4.3	1.3	1.2	0.6
All others	6.9	0.6	8.0	0.2	5.8	0.5	11.6	3.6
Total occupied %	73.7	26.3	69.6	30.4	70.9	29.1	70.6	29.4
Number (million)	6.908		11.752		16.280		19.354	

Source: Reconstructed from DOE, *British Labour Statistics: Historical Abstract, 1886–1968*, tables 102 and 103

It should be remembered, however, that the long hours and miserable conditions of work in the first half of the nineteenth century were little different from those that existed in the previous century, or indeed in some places well into the twentieth century (Mathias, 1969: 203–4). Equally common, and soon to be eliminated, was the form of work group. Typically this was a small team, often family based, and clearly a derivation of pre-industrial work practices. Only in the cotton mills was team work unusual by the mid-nineteenth century (Landes, 1986), but via the Agricultural Act of 1867 the gang-based system of agricultural work (involving women and children supervised by a male overseer) was finally all but destroyed when it was declared illegal to employ women or children with men in a field gang. One of the major reasons for this, as in the related Factory Acts, was the desire on the part of the establishment to buttress the family as the normal social unit: married women and children were to have no place in the public world if it threatened the cohesion of the private world. By 1871 only 15 per cent of the working population of England and Wales were employed in agriculture, and by 1911 this had dropped by half to 7.6 per cent (Mathias, 1969: 263). Naturally, as the proportion of people able to supplement their wages through the produce of their own land diminished, so too did the number of workers and families who were not overwhelmingly proletarian in character. Also in decline was the number of people not subject to the discipline of the clock and free from what many experienced as the monotonous and putrefying conditions of many urban areas (Hobsbawm, 1969: 84–8; Engels, 1969a).

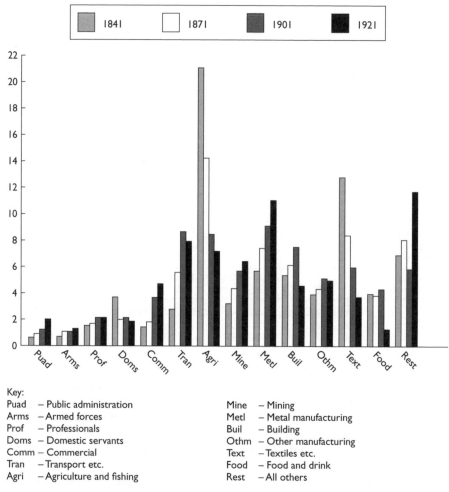

Key:
Puad – Public administration
Arms – Armed forces
Prof – Professionals
Doms – Domestic servants
Comm – Commercial
Tran – Transport etc.
Agri – Agriculture and fishing

Mine – Mining
Metl – Metal manufacturing
Buil – Building
Othm – Other manufacturing
Text – Textiles etc.
Food – Food and drink
Rest – All others

Figure 2 Male labour force, 1841–1921 (%)
Source: Table 1

Occupational change from 1850

As table 1 and figures 2 and 3 suggest, over the period from the middle of the nineteenth to the first quarter of the twentieth centuries, the occupational structure underwent some very radical alterations. Of particular note are the ways in which over two-thirds of women are virtually eliminated from the occupational tables except in so far as domestic service, textiles, and, towards the latter period, commercial employment are concerned. Also note the devastation of the agricultural and fishing populations: down by two-thirds over a mere eighty-year spell, accompanied by the 50 per cent reduction in the clothing and textile trade over the same period. Their places are taken by a much

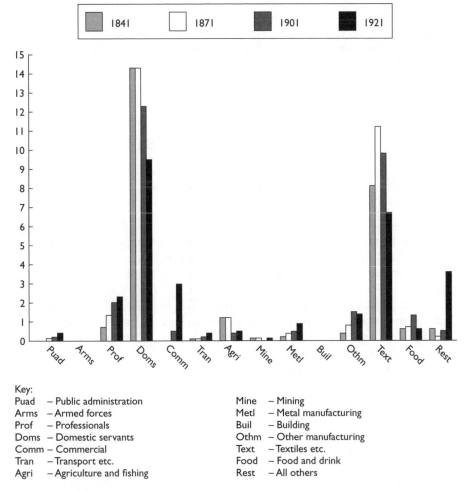

Key:
Puad – Public administration
Arms – Armed forces
Prof – Professionals
Doms – Domestic servants
Comm – Commercial
Tran – Transport etc.
Agri – Agriculture and fishing

Mine – Mining
Metl – Metal manufacturing
Buil – Building
Othm – Other manufacturing
Text – Textiles etc.
Food – Food and drink
Rest – All others

Figure 3 Female labour force, 1841–1921 (%)
Source: Table 1

wider variety of employment forms but especially commercial, transport and manufacturing of all kinds. Again, what is perhaps most significant here is the heterogeneous patterning which marks out the development of industrial capitalism in Britain, as more and more old occupations were systematically extirpated.

Furthermore, we should be wary of assuming that the experiences of textile or factory operatives were typical. As has already been stressed, typicality is a very dubious word to describe the experiences of the Industrial Revolution just because experiences were so very diverse. Thus, although the weavers of Lancashire did witness a very rapid transition in their lives from home workers to out-putting and eventually into the mechanized factory, other areas witnessed only gradual and incremental changes to the traditional pattern of work and life.

A case in point is the Birmingham tradition of small manufacturing workshops of the mid-eighteenth century which adapted to the new demands of industrial production with very little of the social or technical eruption that so bedevilled their northern neighbours (Hopkins, 1988). But such incremental change at the industrial level does not appear to have been the experience of the family and the home as the site of production.

Work, the family and gender

The gendered division of labour

If the Industrial Revolution had a differentiated effect upon occupations and regions in Britain, what impact did it have upon gender and the family? In particular, did the Industrial Revolution and the rise of industrial capitalism segregate home from work and allocate women to the former – the sphere of the private – and men to the latter – the public arena? Answers to this question are almost as various as the patterns of wages that have existed. There is some evidence that women undertook a much greater variety of jobs before, rather than after, the Industrial Revolution, though there were few areas where some degree of gender-related inequality or segregation did not exist. Certainly the evidence to base any overall assessment is limited but Middleton's (1988) perusal of bonded labour in the thirteenth century reflects the importance of gender for the allocation and reward of work with a disproportionate number of women undertaking the most menial, poorly paid and domestically related jobs. Although there appear to have been few travelling journey-women there were many female masons, carpenters and coopers – though most had faded from view by the sixteenth century (Leeson, 1980: 27). The activities of the craft guilds – the forerunners of trade unions – seem to have been exclusively male-oriented with increasingly severe restrictions on women's membership.

Yet we know remarkably little about work-related gender relations before the nineteenth century (Berg, 1988b: 67; Segalen, 1983) except that the distinctions drawn in the contemporary literature between domestic labour and paid work probably made little sense. Instead, it would appear that because the site of virtually all work was domestic and wage labour played a relatively small role until the nineteenth century, and because all members of the family participated in many forms of labour, work became an instrumental activity disconnected from its particular location. Thus gender-based patterns of work, and family located sites of work, are forms that predate capitalism: they are not the results of capitalist-induced social change (Middleton, 1988). As far as it is possible to tell, just as women were once employed alongside men as miners so they have traditionally undertaken a considerable share of all kinds of labour, even though a gendered division of labour has always existed. A typical example is brickmaking where by tradition women made the bricks, girls transported the clay and bricks, and boys fired them in the kilns (Hopkins, 1979: 7). That is not to say that all forms of work had equal status, or that men, women and children all undertook identical work. Rather, it would seem that a hierarchy of work did exist, with men at the apex, women in the centre and servants and children at the base.

Before the Industrial Revolution there were, of course, several forms of industry but most of them were intimately related to agricultural produce: milling, baking, distilling, textiles, wood-based produce etc. Moreover, such activities were seldom undertaken by particular crafts but tended to be executed by people whose main work was directly agricultural but due to the seasonal nature of such work undertook several different occupations. Equally, the first occupational identities that were distinct from the domestic sphere of collective activity appear to relate closely to men (Middleton, 1988: 28). However, although tasks within families did appear to be gender-related, the exact patterning of task allocation varied in time and space. It should also be remembered that patriarchal control over work is not restricted to sex segregation but encompasses the allocation of occupational statuses. Although male workers may construct innumerable strata within each occupation to provide exclusionary badges and labels, women's occupations tend to be provided with universal not variegated statuses: medical specialization may multiply in different fields and hierarchies, to the state where senior doctors lose their title to acquire the more prestigious consultants' Mr, or less commonly Mrs, but to many people all nurses – at whatever level of seniority and skill – are still 'just nurses' (Maynard, 1988).

The decline of family wages and the rise of the 'family wage'

Perhaps the clearest denial of any 'natural' form of the sexual division of labour is to note the atypicality of the male breadwinner status. For much of the industrial period since the end of the eighteenth century normative assumptions about the 'proper' role of men and women have regularly reproduced an ideology that perceives male workers to be the primary, if not the only, source of income for their families. Yet, just as the household was the site for a collective work effort so, before the Industrial Revolution, families were generally based upon multiple incomes, albeit of differential sizes. Nevertheless, it is the case that women, or more exactly married women, were systematically removed from the labour market after the initial phase of the Industrial Revolution. The exact timing of this fade from the labour market is itself disputed: Clark (1982) dates its origins in the seventeenth century, George (1965) places it roughly during the eighteenth century and argues that the early factory system proved beneficial to women, releasing them from the grossly exploitative domestic manufacturing system. Hill (1989) also places the change squarely in the eighteenth century but associates it with a decline in women's fortunes. Snell (1985) asserts that women in apprenticeships, later reserved for men, continued through to the middle of the nineteenth century, though it is by no means clear that female apprentices undertook the same kind of training as male apprentices. Skill, as Rule (1987: 107) notes, was usually configured (by men) as male property. Whatever the dating involved, the largest single form of employment for women for almost the entire period of the Industrial Revolution until the First World War was domestic service of one sort or another; initially as young unmarried farm servants living with a farm-owning family (Malcomson, 1988: 52), and later, from the beginning of the nineteenth century, as servants of the middle class (Beechey, 1986: 10). In 1911, the peak period of manual employment for men and women in Britain, and the high point for factory labour, there were more domestic servants (2,127,000) than miners (1,202,000) or the metal and engineering workers (1,795,000) (Stevenson, 1984: 183). In short, industrial capitalism not only witnessed the decline of agricultural work, most rural industry, multiple occupations and sources of income, but it facilitated the decline of the family as a collective work unit and polarized the work opportunities of men and women.

However, the polarization of opportunities did not necessarily mean the elimination of women from employment. On the contrary, the early phase of industrialization, manifest in the putting-out system, provided women with new opportunities for domestic industry, but only because of their cheap labour. Women who could work either from home or away from home in the new small factories often did so precisely because their income could be so much higher (Berg, 1985: 173). Even when the first spinning jennies were introduced towards the end of the eighteenth century, although many women were eventually made redundant through productivity advances, its initial small-scale development lent itself to cottage use, advancing rather than removing employment for some women. Only when the technology was introduced into the factories did women's wages fall in a more universal pattern. Indeed, in the Census of 1841 only 6 per cent of factory workers were women. This did not mean that such women were free from the exploitation commonly associated with this period; as James Leach, a Manchester operative, witnessed: 'We have repeatedly seen married females, in the last stages of pregnancy, slaving from morning till night beside the never tiring machines and when . . . they were obliged to sit down to take a moment's ease, and being seen by the manager, were fined sixpence for the offence' (quoted in Ayres, 1988: 8).

Gender and agricultural work

Agricultural work seems to have been an area where both technical advances and the genderized polarization of work opportunities marched in step throughout the eighteenth century, especially with the introduction of the corn scythe which gradually replaced the lighter sickle. Roberts (1979) links this to the physical superiority of male workers, though unless it is assumed that all men were stronger than all women we should expect fewer women scythers rather than none at all. What this suggests is that male representations of what women could or could not do were more successful than women's representations; whether all men were physically stronger than all women is not what matters – which group's rhetoric is deployed most effectively is what ultimately counts. Moreover, the shift towards more intensive cereal growing, the decline of common grazing land and the loss of peasant farms also squeezed a labour force that by the nineteenth century was actually beginning to expand rapidly, adding to the pressures for employment opportunities; the fact that this employment contraction was at the expense of women merely confirms not the physical strength of men but the political and organizational strength of patriarchy (Snell, 1985). That said, it still seems to be the case that many forms of labour were generally, if not uniquely, regarded as 'men's' or 'women's' work: men usually undertook the heaviest and what was perceived to be the most skilled work of ploughing, mowing and hedging; women looked after the garden, poultry, the dairy and most of the household duties. Occupational sex segregation, then, existed earlier than the Industrial Revolution and laid out a pattern that was reproduced and remoulded rather than shattered by the rise of industrial capitalism: the strong links between domestic responsibilities and employment were evident in seventeenth-century rural England, early nineteenth-century London (Alexander, 1976), and still abound today.

Respectable and unrespectable jobs

Whatever the rules and ruses developed by men to exclude women from the most preferential jobs, there were serious barriers to such strategies. As late as the middle of the nineteenth century the putative male breadwinners in Scottish manufacturing towns could often provide no more than between one-third and two-thirds of the family income (Holley, 1981). This wide disparity is important because it reflected the distinction between 'respectable' and 'unrespectable' families: those which included a skilled worker could survive on a single income providing it was consistently available and providing children could add supplementary income. But where the primary income generator was categorized as unskilled the family as a unit had no option but to engage as many of their members as possible, critically including the mother, in as many forms of employment as practical. The inability to survive without recourse to the earnings of married women denoted the badge of poverty in most parts of the country; for married women to *have* to work became less respectable as it became less common.

There were cases of women undertaking all jobs by convention executed by men, but they were atypical and more often than not related to the inheritance of an occupation or business through the death of a woman's husband or father; few women appear to have initiated occupations conventionally associated with men (Berg, 1988b: 83). It is perhaps not coincidental that where the laws of inheritance have been fashioned to ensure male predominance, the perceived threat and atypicality of women inheriting their husband's property appears to have been one of the factors associated with the accusation of witchcraft in late seventeenth-century New England (Karlsen, 1988). Equally patriarchal were the assumptions that jobs biologically restricted to women were the source of disease or evil; for example wet-nursing, which may have involved up to a quarter of all Parisian babies in the middle of the nineteenth century, was sometimes held responsible for spreading venereal disease (Fildes, 1988). There are several points in this historical development at which pecuniary and moralistic rationalizations of patriarchal interest are woven together in a seamless web to support not so much the interests of capital as the interests of men. But there are other times in which the thread of this patriarchal web is often spun into the adornments of trade unions.

The rise of trade unionism

The guilds

The origins of British trade unions lie in the original guild system, and the beginnings of British guilds can be traced back to the first century AD in the emergence of at least five *collegia* or associations, one of which was the *collegium fabrorum* (the guild of smiths) operating in Chichester (Salway, 1981: 659). Contrary to popular opinion, the first recorded instance of a strike was not among the Brigantian miners of what is now Yorkshire led by Arturus Scargillus but actually Hebrew brickmakers in Egypt in 1490 BC (Webb and Webb, 1919: 2). But the more recent development of guilds only really becomes confirmed in 1383, when the Corporation of the City of London prohibited them, though the prohibition seems to have been ineffective for a strike by the London guild of cordwainers is recorded five years later. By the eighteenth century guilds for all kinds of crafts which had been commonplace were in decline but it should be remembered that these were combinations of entrepreneurs and 'master' craft workers rather than manual workers (Webb and Webb, 1919: 14–16).

Early trade unions

The early British unions of the eighteenth century appear to have initiated a pattern of unionism still extremely influential today: they were craft-based, sectionalist, decentralized, highly democratic and successful (Fox, 1985). There are certainly several records of their vigorous defence of interests which included pitched battles with other groups of workers, and it is quite possible that their very success undermined the more radical political movements of the period (Dobson, 1980; Christie, 1984). As radical sentiments returned during the early nineteenth century it may be surmised that the suppression of unions was not a coincidental phenomenon. Yet despite their apparent illegality many unions, or combinations, particularly skilled ones, continued to operate with some degree of success faced by the kind of employers for whom pragmatic rather than ideo-logical hostility was the norm; where this failed, bargaining by riot sometimes succeeded (Hobsbawm, 1964a: 5–22). Certainly there was little unmediated con-nection between market position and employer response: labour and product market conditions were important, but seldom determined employers' responses to the early nineteenth-century unions. Indeed, many capitalists in the first half of the nineteenth century looked to the state for a resolution of their labour problems rather than attempting to stamp out or accommodate unions in their own factories. However, many capitalists simply refused to negotiate at all with unions, not so much because of the unions' radical claims, which were few any-way, but because of the symbolic power of such combinations. At a time when moral panics over subversion of the state were commonplace and when workers were wholly excluded from the democratic system, such as it was, many capit-alists appeared to have assumed that all unions, *qua* class organizations, were a fundamental and unequivocal threat to the status quo. Indeed, since those capitalists who did articulate a philosophical position generally appeared to assume a **paternalist** explanation of workers (as irrational and misled children) with-out recourse to paternalist policies (e.g., employer-built and -controlled housing and education etc.) it was self-evident to them that unions were not merely subversive but thoroughly irrational and transient. Not really until the mid-nineteenth century did employers begin to consider seriously the possibility of an accommodation with unions and a method of controlling the workforce that did not rest primarily upon physical coercion (Haynes, 1988). Even then, once the demands of trade unionists spread beyond the workplace to include elec-toral demands the greatest fears of the establishment resurfaced. In the words of Robert Lowe MP, speaking in the Commons in 1866:

> I shall not refer to the subject of strikes, but it is, I contend, impossible to believe that the same machinery which is at present brought into play in connection with strikes, would not be applied by the working classes for political purposes. Once give the men votes and the machinery is ready to launch those votes in one compact mass upon the institutions and prop-erty of the country. (quoted in Bagwell, 1974: 35)

But the state was seldom directly implicated in the control of trade unions. Despite the tyrannical implications of the Combination Acts of 1799 and 1800 it was still the case that, then as now, much of the initiation of proceedings against combinations had to begin with the employer and, just as today, the state began to distance itself from the regulation of wages, preferring to allow the market to determine due rewards. But the Acts were not simply confirmations of tradi-tion for they made combinations, rather than the activities of combinations, illegal, and, perhaps more significantly, the 1799 Act prescribed penalties not for specific occupations but for the class of 'workmen'. Social class, rather than occupational strata, now became an overt form of categorization, institution-alized in the new legal framework (Orth cited in Rule, 1988: 12). Equally significant was the repeal in 1813 and 1814 of the apprenticeship clauses of the Statute of Artificers (1563) which forbade journeymen's organizations from restricting the labour market via lengthy (e.g., seven-year) apprenticeships, and confirmed the revocation of wage-setting by justices of the peace. From then on the full force of the 'free' market was to prevail as the state withdrew from certain regulatory practices (Moher, 1988). In reality many journeymen's organizations retained their apprenticeship regulations, often by reconstructing them along more informal lines (Rule, 1987: 100; McClelland, 1987) but such tight worker control over labour was seldom achieved again (Leeson, 1980). The alteration in the rules of work was experienced by many workers, especially craft workers, as a violent and shameful assault upon their 'right' to exercise their skills. Skill was not just a means of carving out a living and a market niche, it was regarded as a 'property' from which, like other forms of property, certain rights and responsibilities accrued to the owner and were protected by the state. In the words of the watchmakers in 1817:

> the apprenticed artisans have collectively and individually, an unquestionable right to expect the most extended protection from the Legislature, in the quiet and exclusive use and enjoyment of their several and respective arts and trades, which the law has already conferred upon them as a property, as much as it has secured the property of the stock-holder in the public funds; and it is as clearly unjust to take away the whole of the ancient and established property and rights of any class of the community unless at the same time, the rights and property of the whole commonwealth should be dissolved, and parcelled out for the public good. (quoted in Rule, 1987: 105)

Not surprisingly, when these combinations of artisans were faced by the new legal restrictions, the technical innovations that threatened their very livelihood, and a steadily growing labour force desperate for work, disputes were common and violence not unknown, though much of it was directed against other workers rather than employers.

New model unionism

Despite the legitimation of restricted forms of trade unions after the repeal of the Combination Acts in 1824, the very impotence of individuals and most unions to resist the onslaught of capitalism in the first third of the nineteenth century seems to have ignited the movement towards a wider, more politically aware, alternative: Owenism and the Grand National Consolidated Trades Union (GNCTU) of 1834. Ultimately, the collapse of the GNCTU and the débâcle over the Tolpuddle Martyrs deflated the radical shift and inaugurated a movement towards more 'respectable' unionism, epitomized in the New Model Unionism of the Amalgamated Society of Engineers, formed in 1851. This respectability, however, did not imply submission to managerial control even if it did embody a vigorous hostility to the political intent of syndicalism or socialism. As Rule argues:

it is a fact of very great significance that British trade unionism has a long history which began before the era of the factory and the formation of the modern proletariat. . . . To its craft origins must be attributed British unionism's distaste for industrial unionism; its adherence to job demarcation and the closed shop and, not least, its willingness to contest the employers' right to manage in matters of recruitment, working practice and wage forms. For all that its distaste for 'foreign' socialism has seemed a matter for congratulation to some, the British trade union movement has, in important respects, been the least accommodating to the capitalist economy. (1988: 22/2)

It is also noticeable that unionism remained the preserve of skilled male workers in the main, and that exclusionary practices against women and unskilled men persisted and indeed strengthened throughout most of the nineteenth century: the generation of a homogeneous class-based labour movement was, with the exception of the early 1830s, never likely (Sykes, 1988; cf. Foster, 1974; Behagg, 1990).

Trade union consciousness

This heterogeneity should not be interpreted as providing support for individualism at work. Just because many British workers did not heed the call of the socialists does not mean that they fell for the opposite Victorian ethic of work (see chapter 1). The habit of taking 'St Monday' off work did not die with industrialization and such reinterpretations of time by employees persisted throughout the nineteenth century (and could well be argued to persist now), despite the alleged advance of the clock and employers' time as against the natural rhythms of pre-industrial work (Whipp, 1987; cf. Thompson, 1982). As Harry Pollitt recounted, at the turn of the century – when British shipbuilding productivity was superior to all others – the boilermakers' return to work after a holiday was highly contingent on a scientific experiment involving the eldest picking up a brick and declaring: ' "Now lads. If t'brick stops i' th'air, we start; if't brick comes down, we go whoam". I do not remember any occasion on which we did not go whoam' (quoted by McClelland, 1987: 197). It may have taken another thirty years for American consultants like Mayo to recognize the significance of social norms in restricting output (see chapter 4) but what Lenin called 'trade union consciousness' has a long history:

Self-seeking individuals who declined to observe the customs of the trade met with the sanctioning disapproval of their comrades. Offending compositors found their type had been mixed by the 'chapel ghost'. Deviant cabinet makers found the loss of their tools attributed to 'Mother Shorney'. . . . Liverpool shipwrights who took more than their share of work were 'drilled': that is, their fellows refused to work with them for a period of time thereby preventing them from working. (Rule, 1987: 112)

For the major part of this entire period what evidence we have suggests that male workers, and their collective organizations where they existed, were generally hostile to unskilled workers, to non-unionized workers, and to competing unions (McClelland, 1987). They were also antagonistic towards female workers, despite the history of women's participation in industrial action against exploitative capitalists and new technology (Berg, 1988b: 75–88).

Women and trade unions

The general hostility of trade unions to women was almost universal: the Mule Spinners' Union struck over women workers from 1810 and banned them from membership in 1829 (Berg, 1987: 80); the Amalgamated Cotton Spinners' Association, for example, admitted female members from 1837, but its predecessor – the Cotton Spinners' Union – had argued at the repeal of the Combination Acts in 1824 that women should not be allowed to take men's jobs because 90 per cent of women had only themselves to support, and to provide such jobs and money to women would mean that 'the reins of government are broken and the excited feelings of youth and inexperience let loose upon the world' (Hunt, 1981). This fear was echoed half a century later in 1875 when, at the newly fledged TUC, Henry Broadhurst noted that one of the functions of trade unionism was 'to bring about a condition . . . where wives and daughters would be in their proper sphere at home, instead of being dragged into competition for livelihood against the great and strong men of the world' (quoted in Turner, 1962: 185). The moral threat to patriarchal control seems to have been as important as the economic competition, and the two developments became entrammelled in the male spinners' vigorous and successful attempts to retain the most skilled and the supervisory positions within most textile factories for men (Walby, 1986a: 99–100).

This differentiation between the skilled and unskilled positions was influential later when technological advances in the shape of various forms of spinning mule began to threaten the employment of spinners: since the mules could not, initially at least, reproduce the more skilled aspects of spinning it was only the women representing the less skilled spinners who were under direct threat (Chapman, 1972). Spinning is a notable example because for the whole of the eighteenth century the textile industry was the largest form of manufacturing and it was dominated by women and children. By 1833, however, the workforce was split almost equally between adult males, adult females, juvenile males and juvenile females (Hammond and Hammond, 1949: vol. I, 36). Spinning, then, was an atypical industry in terms of the number of adult women employed and their location within factories, but spinning unions were not unusual in their patriarchal concerns: in the second half of the eighteenth century and the early nineteenth, women were forced out of work by the Spitalfield silk weavers, by journeymen bookbinders, by the Stockport Hatmakers, by the Mule Spinners' Union and by London tailors (Berg, 1988b: 68–77). By 1886 the results of this consistent onslaught against women were clear: only 1 per cent of women employees were unionized (Hunt, 1981); in comparison the male figure was approximately ten times this (Salamon, 1987: 559). In fact, the oldest durable union for women only appears to have been the Edinburgh Upholsterers Sewers Society, formed in 1872, though there were several earlier short-lived attempts, especially in the textile industry (Boston, 1987: 19), such as the West of Scotland Power Loom Female Weavers' Society, established in 1833 (Bagwell, 1974). By 1875 several small women-only unions flourished in London, including the Women Bookbinders, Upholsteresses, Shirt and Collar Makers and Dressmakers (Webb and Webb, 1919: 336), and in the same year Emma Paterson became the first woman delegate to the TUC. The real turning point for women, though, was probably signalled by the strike of women and girls at the Bryant and May match factory in London in 1888. Aided by Annie Besant, the strike garnered support from the unskilled workers, especially the Dockers and Gasworkers, who went on to admit women to membership. By 1914 women's union destiny had risen to 10 per cent while men's had climbed only to 23 per cent (ibid.).

Alternative communities

It is worth noting at this point that the forms of work-based resistance to capitalism and patriarchy were not restricted to activities undertaken *within* the orthodox system. Although not many alternative communities sprang up in the nineteenth century, there were some. These ranged from the barely disguised paternalism of Titus Salt's Saltaire community to Robert Owen's New Lanark (Morton, 1962), through to the more radical self-organizing communities such as Whiteway Colony in Gloucestershire. In the Whiteway Colony, for several decades from the end of the nineteenth century, an anarchist group provided not just a non-capitalist form of work community but one that attempted to pursue a non-patriarchal one too. It clearly had some success, ensuring that the women members undertook work which conventional society regarded as strictly male; however, it would appear that it was women's roles which expanded to encompass all activities while men's roles remained more or less static: women undertook men's jobs but seldom the other way round (Hardy, 1979: 201–2).

Yet, however implicated trade unions and trade unionists were in the employment-based discrimination against women, many of the most salient barriers to gender equality at work were erected not by unions but by the state.

State intervention and the Factory Acts

Men, women and children

If we can provide some sort of answer to the issue of *when* women, that is primarily married women, were segregated away from the labour market and restrained within the home this does not provide us with the definitive reason for such a development. Nor, indeed, is it the case that women became eco-nomically inactive just because their presence within the increasingly large-scale manufacturing industries was continually reduced (Pahl, 1984). Although it may seem more than coincidental that the rise of capitalism and the decline of women's employment opportunities occur with a remarkably parallel progression, in fact the progression is not parallel, nor is the connection self-evident. Since women tended to be cheaper than men to employ, it would seem more logical to assume that the new factories would be staffed by women and children, rather than men. Of course, many of them were until the various Factory Acts began to delimit the extent of women's and children's labour. In themselves, the legislat-ive restrictions on women's and children's labour embodied both progressive and regressive aspects: to prevent the gross exploitation of children and limit the hours of work was and is clearly a progressive move – as witnessed by the rage expressed by a reactionary employer's representative writing to Sir John Cam Hobhouse, who was responsible for introducing it:

> The first and immediate consequences of limiting the age of children employed, to 'under 9 years' will be to throw out of employment all that class of hands. This is perhaps the most cruel stroke to the poor man which could be inflicted . . . this threatened invasion of the rights of the parent over the child [is] an infringement of the liberty of the subject, and a direct violation of the homes of Englishmen. (quoted in Ward, 1970: 141–2)

Indeed, it is crucial to note just how innovative such legislative restrictions were, not so much in themselves, because state controls proliferated under the pre-industrial mercantilist economy, but rather in the protection of child labour. As George (1931: 132–3) argued, what was revolutionary about the factory system was that for the first time child labour came to be seen as inhumane; before this most children had worked at home as mini-adults with little public concern for their welfare. Some Tories in the Commons were shocked at the very sight of women and children labouring in factories, others were shocked merely because it occurred outside the home for the first time (Berg, 1980: 264). Again, this development should be seen as a reminder of the resilient moral economy: market forces alone would have stripped work from expensive men to cheap children and women but the moral economy that supported the patri-archal family was a critical resource in the demise of employment for married women and children.

The Factory Acts

Relatedly, the dawn of the factory age was not interpreted by all as one of dark satanic mills and therefore as a problem. It was also perceived not just as a method of acquiring a fortune for the owners but as a means of relieving unem-ployment, of improving desultory working-class moral habits, and of infusing some level of education (Gray, 1987). The factory presented inconsistent symbols of light and dark, solutions and problems – it was a very different beast for very different people, and it was an apathetic beast whose form altered as groups using particular forms of discourse sought to represent it in their own language, notably the moral economy versus the market economy. But even privileged modes of discourse do not always prevail. The first English Factory Acts, in 1802, 1819 and 1847, which restricted the hours of children and women, seem to have been ignored by many factory owners (Hammond and Hammond, 1949: 35), partly because so few inspectors were appointed to enforce them, and partly, perhaps, because so few adult women were actually covered by them. During the late nineteenth century most female employees were the daughters of agricultural labourers and were themselves domestic servants; a family-related pattern that long predated the rise of factory capitalism and was outside the scope of the first Acts. As Pahl put it: 'perhaps the best way to view women's employment in the nineteenth century is as the employment of *daughters* but not mothers' (1984: 64). As late as the 1920s about a quarter of all teenage girls were in residential domestic service (Ellison, 1989).

The restriction on women's labour simultaneously limited employer exploitation and ensured the predominance of male workers in the most skilled areas. Humphries (1988) insists that the interests of male workers were coterminous with those of working-class families since the elimination of women ensured the maintenance of a family wage for male breadwinners, rather than subsistence wages for all. Nevertheless, many families did not have breadwinners, many male workers did not have dependants, and a very large proportion of working-class families were still reliant upon multiple incomes (Harrison, 1984: 302), so this pro-class/family argument is dubious. It still does not explain why capitalists should acquiesce in the 'artificially' high wages for men, particularly when women were conventionally regarded as far less prone to trade unionism than men (Grint, 1988). After all, industrial capitalists were seldom philanthropists, so why should they concern themselves with the consequences of their action? Providing a labour force could be recruited, why limit profits by paying for men? Certainly there is evidence that families, rather than individuals, formed the basis of many work groups, especially in areas like the Potteries where the family provided the bridge between the world of work and the world of home: the mechanism for training, recruiting and disciplining (Whipp and Grieco, 1983). Barrett and McIntosh (1980) suggest that the moral qualms of bourgeois philanthropists, concerned with the potential disruption to family life initiated by working wives, in conjunction with the material and patriarchal interests of male workers, is a more powerful explanation of the success of the factory legislation – an argument further elaborated by Walby, who resurrects the significance of the Tory–Whig division (1986a: 108–34; cf. Gray, 1987). And it should not be assumed that all factory owners were divorced from the moral implications of their position: many were profit maximizers but many were intent simply on sustaining their position in society (Gray, 1987).

The limits of the law

Nevertheless, the instrumental alliance argument should not blind us to the limitations of the parliamentary aspect. First, the sparseness of the inspectorate meant that many factories were able to circumvent the law. This was not the only reason for the absence of prosecutions: although the Workshop Regulation Act of 1867 covered most domestic workshops, it did not cover those containing just a husband and wife. Moreover, even where women were illegally exploited by their husbands in larger workshops it was, as an inspector of 1889 put it: 'not usual to proceed against a man for overworking his wife' (Hopkins, 1979: 59–62, 105). Second, the impact of legislation on women was contingent on their activities before the legislation. In mining, for instance, although women were prohibited from underground work by the Mines Act of 1842 its impact was regionally dispersed: from then on men replaced women, boys and girls in areas like the east of Scotland where previously women had supplied a third of the adult labour (Ayres, 1988: 52–5), and monopolized the more lucrative jobs in the West Riding of Yorkshire, Cheshire, South Wales and some parts of Lancashire. But in other areas its impact was negligible: for example, women had not been employed in Lancashire east of Manchester for some time, and had been all but absent from the pits of north-east England since 1780 (Hammond and Hammond, 1949: vol. I, 39–40). Third, and crucially, female factory workers represented only a minority of female employees; small workshops were exempt from the legislation, as were all shop assistants, casual and unskilled workers, all home workers and, of course, all domestic servants (Best, 1979: 138). Fourth, even when prosecutions against owners were brought, the courts were keen to exploit all possible loopholes to facilitate the employer's escape from justice (Ayres, 1988: 46). What may have seemed a good example of various dualist theories, where the power of bourgeois philanthropy operated in conjunction with patriarchal trade unions, actually seems to be very limited because such a small proportion of women were covered by the Acts. This is significant because the focus on the import of the Factory Acts replicates the distorted lens of much conventional industrial sociology: factories were a minor part of the world of work in the middle of the nineteenth century, just as they are now, yet what happens within factories often seems to be taken as the model for all work experience.

Finally, it is worth reaffirming that patriarchal interests did not simply win out over the interests of capital. Women were forced out of many occupations both by the legislation and by male workers but there were many forms of employment where male interests were not sufficient to eject women and some forms of mechanization developed in conjunction with, rather than at the expense of, women (Berg, 1987: 88).

The legal inferiority of women

The Factory Acts are also significant in generating further doubts as to the coherence of capitalism and patriarchy. The liberal state had apparently ridden roughshod over industrial capitalism and, ostensibly, over its own philosophy of *laissez-faire*. Yet the factory legislation facilitated the legitimacy of the government and the factory system in the communities where it was designed to operate; it was 'an important symbol of "industrial legality" and reciprocity between employers and workers' (Gray, 1987: 177). *Laissez-faire* was qualified by patriarchy rather than removed by it. Although the legislation cut into the economic profits of industrial capital, it did so to prevent an abuse of *laissez-faire*. As Peel himself argued: 'it is not desirable that the state should interfere with the contracts of persons of ripe age and sound mind' (quoted in Taylor, 1972: 44). This underlines the inferior status of adult women as well as children, and rewrites rather than undermines the rules of *laissez-faire* (Perkin, 1969: 439). The legal inferiority of women was also manifest in the transference of all property to the husband upon marriage; a situation that included the sale of wives by their husbands which, though untypical, was not confined to the fictional pages of Hardy's *The Mayor of Casterbridge*. On the contrary, as late as 1840 newspapers could still be found recounting stories like the following: 'On Saturday week, a fellow named Gibbon sold his wife to a country fellow for 2s 0d. The latter was proud of his purchase, while the woman cried with joy at getting release from her master' (quoted in Hopkins, 1979: 203). Such gender-based legal inequality prevailed until the Woman's Property Act of 1882.

Even when women had been removed from the mines the intervention of the state often had unintended consequences and should remind us of the problem of reading historical change as the functional result of capitalist, or for that matter patriarchal, developments. For example, the Mines Act of 1860 provided for checkweighmen to alleviate the industrial unrest generated by suspicions of fraud by the mine owners. Yet the provision of these 'neutral' figures actually provided protection for a post which later came to be associated with the leaders of the miners' unions (Ayres, 1988: 51). Moreover, even though legal restrictions on women's employment facilitated patriarchal control over some sections of the labour force, the domination of employment by men had much more to do with the expansion of the engineering and metalworking industries, in conjunction with the growth of mining and transport systems etc., for it was in these areas that employment grew most rapidly in the second half of the nineteenth century (Harvie, 1978: 36).

In sum, the Factory and Mine Acts were passed not so much as a result of the interaction of the discrete forces of capitalism and patriarchy but by the internecine conflict of unholy alliances of groups within both comprising: men as workers, men as bourgeois philanthropists and men as Tory landowners etc. That is, not only is the alliance of forces a congealing and unstable mass but the individual components are themselves heterogeneous composites, not single elements (see chapter 6).

Occupational sex-segregation is considered in chapter 6 but it is important to note that discrimination against women also occurred within occupations that were not so strictly sex-segregated. One of the most important of these was clerical work, particularly within the largest single employer of clerical labour until after the Second World War, the British Post Office.

The state and the development of clerical labour

The Post Office was, in sharp contrast to the textile industry, one of the very few employers of self-allocated middle-class women. Women were first recruited into the Post Office through the nationalization of the telegraphic companies in 1870 and were employed throughout the organization except in the male-reserved areas of sorters and postmen (cf. Walby, 1986a: 150). Typically, men monopolized the most desirable positions and duties within clerical work generally and the Post Office in particular, but within the latter, the separation of men and women also necessitated distinctive career structures with consequential openings for women as superordinates over subordinate women. Some of the advantages of separate career structures for women were lost when gender-specific offices and departments were desegregated but this movement towards homogeneous conditions of service ultimately resulted first, in the termination of the marriage bar in 1946 and second, in the acquisition of equal pay by women in the Post Office main grades in 1961.

The reproduction and eventual overturning of pay inequality resulted from a rich and contingent concoction of influences, but broadly speaking it was male workers' opposition which inhibited equal pay, and their instrumental and rather deceitful 'support' for it (on the grounds that it would deter management from feminizing the labour force further) which removed the major obstacle. Walby (1986a: 154) argues that the hostility of male clerks was actually circumvented by employers channelling new female labour into new segregated sub-groups which did not threaten existing male areas. This argument may have some validity in the field of engineering but in the Civil Service and Post Office, the new all-female writing assistant was in fact both the only example and one comprising a minimal proportion of clerical employees. The fact is that after the 1926 General Strike débâcle for the labour movement, the management of the Post Office and the Civil Service was able to ride roughshod over the exclusivist interests of male workers; conflict was not avoided so much as met head on and overcome (Grint, 1986: 268–95).

Although equality of conditions or career potential is still not evident within the Post Office, equal pay for most major grades was a movement that began in 1919 and had achieved a considerable degree of success by 1961. This does not mean that male workers in the Post Office and Civil Service were the harbingers of the new egalitarian man, but it does imply three things: first, patriarchal interests are not omnipotent; second, labour market pressures can prove superior to such forces; and third, the state is not an unambiguous servant of capital or patriarchy but has a sufficient degree of autonomy to deflect – if not stop – the influence of both.

Underlying and shaping the state's complex position regarding women was a tightening labour market in which female clerical labour was increasingly difficult to recruit: between 1911 and 1951 female clerical workers increased sevenfold, and less than 5 per cent of this increase was due to the feminization of clerical labour, that is the displacement of male clerks by female clerks. An increase in the demand for clerical labour *per se*, which was filled by women, was the main explanation of the huge upsurge in female clerical labour (Joseph, 1983: 87); as the size of business enterprises grew and the division of labour intensified, white-collar labour became progressively more important (Abercrombie and Urry, 1983). Also, and very significantly, the state as an employer was influential in stimulating the expansion of white-collar labour, particularly in the first majority Labour administration after the Second World War, and in setting the standards required for all employers. In effect, its public presence and status as a public employer eventually exhausted its power to resist the limited flood tide of equality ninety years after women had first entered state employment in any substantial numbers (Grint, 1988). That most women have still not achieved the levels of wage equality acquired by women in the Post Office, Civil Service and teaching profession back in 1961 also underlines the importance of an employer that was not subject to the direct machinations of the competitive market, in so far as maximum profitability was not required. Yet it was subject to them in that to fulfil the political obligations of the government a tight labour market had to be eased apart by increasing labour rewards. Just as the respective genders seldom form cohesive fronts so too employers are internally differentiated.

Women, work and war

Dilution

Labour market pressures were also responsible for the greatest ever acceleration of wages and conditions of work for women – the experiences of the two world wars. On both occasions women in many of the nations involved (with notable exceptions such as Nazi Germany) were recruited to undertake all, or virtually all, the activities vacated by men at the front. On both occasions the state called women to undertake their patriotic duty in the munitions and armaments factories, on the farms and railways and in the shipyards. In Britain the dangers of military defeat were self-evident, the concerns of trade unions equally so: under the Treasury Agreement of 1915, the '**dilution** scheme' – which 'diluted' skilled jobs – and the later Munitions Act, the compromise between the major unions and the government, entailed women 'dilutees' taking what had previously been exclusively men's jobs only on condition that they were restricted to war work, paid the wages of skilled men and would be removed from their temporary positions at the termination of hostilities (Braybon, 1981). Very few women were recruited by male-based unions during the First World War, and although strikes were actually common throughout the period some of the largest were the direct result of infringements of the restrictions on dilutees. In the engineering and printing industry, and the Post Office, the evidence suggests that management was much more willing to concede to union threats based on the demands of male privilege than on demands based on class privilege (Walby, 1986a: 162; Grint, 1986: 437–62; Zeitlin, 1985: 216). That is, male privileges could be protected but rises in wages or increasing democracy were vigorously resisted. Yet even this statement is capable of two interpretations: either managers conspired with workers to keep women out, or class interests were more important than patriarchal ones.

The construction of identity and interests

In fact, neither of these is accurate: no patriarchal conspiracy was necessary because hostility to women at work was a normative convention, not a sinister secret, of most men; it was part of the male representation of the moral economy. Second, the comparison of class and patriarchal interests is illegitimate. Comparing a quantitative change in labour costs is not the equivalent of undermining a patriarchal system any more than it can be compared with ceding control to the workers. Thus a more realistic comparison would be just that, i.e., one where the prize and penalty is worker's control or patriarchal control. In short, union demands for taking over the factories, or even wage rises that threaten the survival of the factory, are obviously a direct threat to the preservation of management; but union demands for the continuation of male privileges are, for male managers, just an economic cost; for women employees the privileging of class over patriarchal interests is reversed. This implies not just that the hierarchy of influences is contingent upon the position of those affected (and therefore neither capitalism nor patriarchy can occupy an objectively superordinate position), but that the agents involved are not men or women first and capitalists or workers second (or vice versa) but male capitalists, female workers etc. The analysis therefore requires us to consider human agents as composite and heterogeneous entities, not unitary homogeneous entities, nor even entities with dualist features (see chapter 6).

Indeed, one can go further than this to say that **heterogeneous composites** rather than binary composites are likely. For example, in the Post Office case male managers who were likely to supervise women and men on the sorting office floor were often much more apprehensive about, and therefore hostile towards, women employees than their head office superiors whose interests lay in the financial benefits of feminizing the workforce. Concomitantly, the attitude of women depended not just on their gender but on their class and future prospects. Such prospects were themselves constrained by the official 'marriage bar' which forbade the employment of married women in the Civil Service from 1876 to 1946 (see Grint, 1988). Middle-class women, who perceived their future to lie in marriage, appeared concerned that they should give up work on marriage and 'retire' to the home. Working-class women supported the marriage bar because the associated marriage gratuity was their only chance to save enough capital to set up home. But for those women intent on remaining single and making the Post Office a career, the marriage bar sloughed off the great percentage of competitors for promotion. The marriage bar may have been a patriarchal institution but women interpreted it in several different ways and had their own reasons for supporting, or at least acquiescing to it (Grint, 1986). In sum, if we simply adopt gender- or class-based models of work then the contingent complexity of social relations becomes more opaque, not more transparent.

Women and work between wars

In Britain, at the end of the First World War, the returning men from the front and the economic decline effectively ensured the dispersal of women from areas of declining demand, such as engineering, shipbuilding and agriculture. Women had been particularly effective in farming where the Women's Land Army, in conjunction with the Corn Production Act of 1917 which guaranteed high prices and stable markets, had rescued farming from the oblivion to which it had fallen (and with it the agricultural unions: Pretty, 1989) since the last quarter of the nineteenth century (Pagnamenta and Overy, 1984: 195–6). The reversal of this long-term decline in agriculture, under pressure from foreign competition, did not survive the war; as James McIver remarks in *Akenfield*, when he arrived in East Anglia in 1932, 'what a scene we found . . . Dereliction' (Blythe, 1969: 316). Clerical work, however, remained relatively buoyant and the numbers almost static, especially in the south-east. Not that this reflected the eclipse of patriarchal concerns. Many attempts to extend the marriage bar were made, and they were particularly successful in the depressed textile industries of the north (Walby, 1986a: 180–1). The government also restructured its unemployment legislation to discourage women from seeking work, and Britain's leading trade unions were notably absent in the movement for equality that, ironically perhaps, began to gain ground during the inter-war period (Boston, 1987: 258–9). Nevertheless, two very significant achievements were made between the wars: in 1918 women over 30 with some property won the vote and in 1928 all women over 21 achieved suffrage on equal terms with men. Whether these compensated for the restriction of opportunities within the labour market is the subject of some dispute. Certainly the middle-class 'housewife' appears to have been the ideal which many women were encouraged to follow (Samuel, 1983a, b); and Roberts (1982) asserts that even working-class married women perceived their liberation to be away from, not towards, paid employment. Those married women who did undertake paid work often appeared to have little choice in the matter. This need not undermine attitudes concerned with the patriarchal advantages of restraining women within the home; it simply confirms the importance of ideological aspects and the flexibility of attitudes to work.

Women and the Second World War

During the Second World War women were once again drafted into previously 'male' occupations, although not immediately. When the war effort did require extra labour the government went beyond the confines of tradition to encourage married women into the factories by, among other things, providing a level of nurseries and crèches that, limited though it was, has never been achieved since. In fact, Britain's mobilization of its female workforce was unsurpassed by other nations, but the control over wages ceded to the trade unions through Bevin's insistence effectively ensured that the movement towards equal pay was stillborn; aided, no doubt, by a series of strikes against equal pay by men, the most infamous being at Rolls Royce, Glasgow, in 1943 (H.L. Smith, 1984). Equally, or rather unequally, the engineering unions went out of their way to inhibit the employment of women until they were reluctantly forced to accede to a reality not of their making or choice (Lewenhak, 1977).

The ambiguity surrounding the role of women in wartime was not limited to the engineering union. On the contrary, the government itself appeared caught between the need to mobilize all available labour for the war effort and yet simultaneously retain the conventions of family life. The immediate solution, which prevailed until 1941, was to call married women into the factories and on to the land but demand that they made their own provision for childminding. Even at the height of the war effort, in 1943, the government still only provided sufficient nursery places to accommodate one quarter of the children of women war workers. This difficulty, combined with the escalation of rationing and its associated phenomenon of queuing, pushed absenteeism so high that the government was eventually coerced into constructing a solution. It was typically minimal and based on self-help; women were encouraged to form 'neighbourhood shopping leagues' and granted unofficial leave to do their shopping. When this failed the government dreamed up another diversionary tactic – they readjusted the hours women were allowed to work to facilitate their double roles as mothers and employees (Summerfield, 1985).

Thus women entered the dawn of the post-war period much as they had entered the dawn of the Industrial Revolution; they took primary responsibility for domestic arrangements and undertook similar activities to men. The major differences were that most income-generating activities took place outside the home and women's occupational equality was generally perceived to be limited to the duration of hostilities. Also of significance, and perhaps an appropriate way to end this chapter on the history of work, the attitudes of the women working in wartime Britain are remarkably resemblant of many of the attitudes that have already been observed in the more contemporary period discussed in the previous chapter. Thus the *War Factory*, a Mass Observation study of the Second World War, reported a persistently low morale and complete lack of interest in anything connected to work despite its military significance and the nature of the threat facing the country. Work may have been indistinguishable from non-work for many hunter-gatherers; work may have been shot through with moral threads and traditional streamers for many pre-industrial and industrial workers; but for British women undertaking mundane but urgent assembly work in the 1940s work was not even primarily a means to an end, it was 'the blank patch between one brief evening and the next' (Mass Observation, 1943: 43). Eighty years earlier a favourite tale of the travelling journeymen of England was that relating to a workshop owned by one Davy Robinson. To ensure that his employees did not dawdle he prowled round his workshop 'shabbily dressed' and caught a new employee staring into space. ' "What are you looking for?" demanded Robinson. "Saturday night, you old varmint!" replied the man . . . Davy took to his heels and ran up to the shop, shouting out to his foreman, "Mills, Mills, here's a fellow looking for Saturday night, and it's only Thursday morning! Sack him! sack him!" ' (Wright, 1867/1967: 102).

Summary

Trying to summarize the experience of work over several millennia is one of my more difficult tasks. There is self-evidently so much material to cover that no text of conventional size would be able to deal adequately with the complexities of the situation. However, this chapter has been written on the assumption that some knowledge is preferable to complete ignorance, especially if to understand the present we have to situate it against the past, and it has tended to concentrate upon women to balance out the conventional preference for male history. The limited history that has been covered, focusing as it does on Britain until 1945, suggests that the complexity of the experience of work defies any simple assumptions about the significance of work or its relationships to non-work or its role in the development of modes of subordination and superordination. What perhaps can be salvaged from the past is not an objective model of what work has always been like, nor what it should be like, but rather a conclusion that illuminates the significance of the social. Work has been the medium of such a variety of forms and contents that its very diversity undermines universal propositions about work. While not wishing to argue that the history of work reveals an infinite anarchy of interpretations, such that work has been all things to all people, I would argue that work, like other institutions, is inherently and irreducibly constructed, interpreted and organized through social actions and social discourse. The implication of this is that no 'natural' form of work exists and no inevitable or necessary attitudes towards work are inscribed in the human psyche. The history of work suggests that the very meaning of work is something which has to be worked at; what is crucial is which individuals or groups or states secure the resources to have their own interpretation of work accepted as the legitimate interpretation. But control over the language of work does not ensure control over subordinates; the language of free markets and economic rationality may have gradually provided the dominant form of discourse through the process of industrialization but the prior moral economy of work remained to confound the capitalist visionaries. The pre-capitalist moral economy was not dismembered but overlain by the market economy where it served as a resource for all groups involved to legitimate their collective resistance and advance. Of course, whether such groups were successful or not is a separate issue: representing an issue as moral rather than economic does not guarantee that such representations are accepted. For example, many women and colonized peoples have resisted the representations of work made by men and colonizers, claiming the latter to be specious and unjustifiable; many such resisters found their cases 'not proved' and lived out their lives in poverty and slavery. Indeed, it is because of such historical acts and processes that contemporary work embodies lineages of the past: work today is not a prisoner of the past but it is a bruised descendant.

Exam/essay questions

1 To what extent did industrialization lead to the polarization of work experiences for men and women?
2 'In an age of *laissez-faire* capitalism the Factory Acts of nineteenth-century Britain are an inexplicable anomaly.' Discuss.
3 What part did technological change play in the rise of factories in Britain?

4 'The mercantilism of pre-industrial Britain was not a block on economic progress but a precondition of it.' Discuss.
5 Does the experience of mechanization and industrialization in the nineteenth century provide any clues as to the computerization of our own future?
6 'For the most part the employment of women in the nineteenth and early twentieth centuries in Britain was increasingly restricted to the employment of daughters.' Discuss.
7 The Combination Act virtually outlawed all trade union activity at the beginning of the nineteenth century but by the beginning of the twentieth century virtually every industry had experienced a growth in trade unionism – what accounts for the turnaround?
8 'The hostility of male trade unionists to women has been rooted not in patriarchal ideology but is instead simply a traditional restriction on entry to the labour market.' Discuss.
9 What role has the state played in the growth of sexual equality at work?
10 To what extent does the expansion of opportunities and rewards for women during the two world wars suggest that labour market restructuring, not collective action, is the most likely avenue for women to achieve equality?

Further reading

There are many good historical accounts worth reading but the ones I have found most useful are, first, two standard classic accounts of industrialization: Landes's *The Unbound Prometheus* (1972) and Mathias's *The First Industrial Nation* (1969). A valuable compilation of contemporary documents relating to the same period can be seen in Ward's two-volume set *The Factory System* (1970). Next, an excellent review of the significance of technology in the industrializing process is Berg's *The Machinery Question and the Making of Political Economy 1815–1848* (1980), and Gimpel's *The Medieval Machine* (1992), which has an earlier historical focus. A good introduction to comparative industrialization is Stearns's *The Industrial Revolution in World History* (1993), while Hobsbawm's polemical epics – *The Age of Revolution 1789–1848* (1962), *The Age of Capital 1848–1875* (1975), *The Age of Empire 1875–1914* (1987), and *The Age of Extremes 1914–1991* (1994) – provide a grand overview of the background of developments. A more local viewpoint on work during the industrial era can be gleaned from a wide variety of sources. Try Rodger's *The Wooden World* (1986), for a fascinating account of the British Navy in the eighteenth century; Malcomson's *Life and Labour in England 1700–1780* (1981) on the work at the dawn of industrialization; Thompson's *Lark Rise to Candleford* (1973), which describes rural life in the late nineteenth century Oxfordshire region; and, finally, Stewart's *Ramlin Rose* (1993), which brings us up to the mid-twentieth century aboard the 'working' canal boats of England.

3

Classical Approaches to Work: Marx, Weber and Durkheim

- Introduction
- Marx and capitalism
- Durkheim and industrial society
- Weber

- Summary
- Exam/essay questions
- Further reading

And the Gods of the Copybook Headings said: *if you don't work you die.*

Kipling, *The Gods of the Copybook Headings*

Introduction

This chapter considers the classical approaches to work through the ideas of the 'gang of three': Marx, Weber and Durkheim. Marx, Weber and Durkheim are usually portrayed, in both an academic and a political sense, as being situated at the three corners of a triangle: while Durkheim focused on, and sought to extend, social solidarity, integration and control, Marx concerned himself with social fragmentation, disintegration and conflict and Weber developed his theory of rationality and bureaucracy. Durkheim was of a social democratic orientation though he was seldom directly involved in politics except in the case of Dreyfus and in a more diffuse way as the supporter of the Third Republic against the vicissitudes of the French church and military. Marx, of course, was a revolutionary who railed against capitalism and actively promoted its overthrow. Weber, on the other hand, was a conservative liberal, anxious to preserve both the freedom of the individual and the sanctity of the German state, though his success as a sociologist was in sharp contrast to his failure as a politician. Both Marx and Durkheim adopted structural arguments that delimited the influence and impact of individuals upon society and social change. The structural approach of Durkheim was, in fact, far more rigid and consistent than that of Marx. Part of Durkheim's rigorous adherence to an anti-individualist methodology (as distinct from his support for ethical individualism) relates to his overarching concern to legitimate sociology as an academic discipline within French universities, in contrast to other social sciences, particularly psychology. For Marx, the issue of academic advancement was never pre-eminent and always subordinated to the needs of the proletarian revolution. Furthermore, Marx's arguments are neither simple nor coherent, and tensions between his early and late works, as well as between his theoretical and empirical texts, are discernible. Weber's individualist sociology was clearly demarcated from the approaches of Marx and Durkheim though, like the former, Weber's work does not form a coherent whole but is rather a collection of disparate, and sometimes incompatible, themes and ideas.

Marx and capitalism

Alienation

This is clearly not the place for a thorough review of the various interpretations of Marx (see Callinicos, 1983; Giddens, 1971; Kolakowski, 1978; Elster, 1985; Roemer (ed.), 1986) and the discussion will be limited to the essential features for our particular concerns.

One of the most significant distinctions between Marx and Durkheim lies in the former's disavowal of industrialization as the primary explanatory axis of society. Certainly, Marx considered industrial society to be both progressive in comparison to agrarian societies, and a necessary stage for the eventual triumph of human freedom, but the mainspring of this social formation was not the industrial process but its capitalist pattern. It is capitalism which is important because only capitalism, rather than industrialism, carries within it the seeds of its own destruction and the adumbration of what, to Marx at least, appeared to be the single viable non-exploitative alternative: communism.

Essentially, Marx's argument is that the human species is different from all other animal species, not because of its consciousness but because it alone produces its own means of subsistence (1970, 1975). This uniquely human attribute also provides the medium through which individuals can realize their true potential as humans: in short, the arena of productive activity, the world of work, incorporates the secret of human nature. But why does capitalism, rather than industrialism, deny humanity its quintessentiality, its 'species being'? Well, Marx is careful to distinguish between 'objectification' and 'alienation'. Objectification is the product of human labour on raw materials; it embodies the producer's creativity and yet remains separate from the producer. Thus some form of production is essential to humanity both in providing the material structure of social life and in facilitating the self-realization of individual potential. However, where the system of production is capitalist, that is where the means

Karl Marx, 1867. Photo: AKG London.

of production are owned by a minority, where the majority own only their labour power, and where production is for profit through a commodity market, the result is not objectification but alienation. Hence, the unique quality of human beings – their ability to produce their own means of existence, to actualize and realize their true, creative capacity through labour – is stultified and indeed inverted through capitalism.

Marx broke down the formulation of alienation into four conceptually discrete but empirically related spheres. The first facet of alienation is derived from the absence of control by the producer over the product. In the absence of control the product reduces, rather than expresses, the producer's humanity, and simultaneously sustains alienation by buttressing capitalism. The more workers expend themselves at work the weaker become their prospects of self-realization. Since products are designed and produced as profit maximizers, rather than for the satisfaction of human needs, capitalists are also alienated by capitalism but, since they gain materially from it, their alienation remains unconscious. The second aspect of alienation stems from the ever-increasing division of labour. This fragments the productive process into meaningless, and ostensibly unrelated, tasks such that the general orientation of labour to work is not one of creative liberation but instrumental and 'forced' labour. Note that for Marx this meaninglessness is an inherent feature of capitalism; for Durkheim the same meaninglessness is a transient phenomenon related to the pathological division of labour, not capitalism *per se*. The market economy and commodity exchange comprise the third facet of alienation, for they turn every productive group into competitors, setting individual against individual and reducing the social relations between people to economic exchanges of commodities. Finally, Marx asserts that the mindless repetition that typifies work under capitalism blurs the distinction between humanity and animality by destroying the creative content of production. In effect, objects designed for use by humans are transformed via the capitalist mode of production into commodities that dominate humans.

Labour necessity and freedom

It is clear from this argument that Marx would have had little time for the assertions of Durkheim concerning the importance of *extending* the division of labour; the problem for Marx was how to reintegrate disparate skills, not how to further differentiate between them. As he wrote in *The German Ideology*, the division of labour ensures that each

> has a particular exclusive sphere of activity, which is forced upon him and from which he cannot escape. He is a hunter, a fisherman, a herdsman, or a critical critic, and must remain so if he does not want to lose his means of livelihood; while in communist society . . . it [is] possible to hunt in the morning, fish in the afternoon, rear cattle in the evening, criticize after dinner, just as I have a mind to, without ever becoming hunter, fisherman, herdsman or critic. (1970: 54)

Paradoxically, towards the end of Marx's work, in the third volume of *Capital*, he reconsidered this whole issue and argued that rather than human self-realization being necessarily limited to the realm of labour (and hence the need for multi-skilled individuals), the realm of human freedom actually existed: 'beyond the sphere of material production' (1981: 959). In sum, while Marx's early criticisms of the capitalist division of labour are similar to Durkheim's interpretation of the pathological division of labour, Marx's early alternative is for the reintegration of skills, while Durkheim's is for the expansion of specialization in line with individuals' 'natural' propensities. However, while Durkheim's position remains at this level, Marx's entire approach is reconstructed in his later work through the assumption that the arena of labour is no longer the sphere of freedom but remains the **sphere of necessity**, even under communism; true freedom occurs outside, not inside, the realm of labour (cf. Rattansi, 1981; Gorz, 1982, 1985).

Unalienated production

Does this suggest Marx accepted that alienation would remain as an unfortunate but necessary aspect of work even under communism? This is difficult to say since Marx says so little about the future structure and form of communism, but there does seem to be an underlying contradiction within his criticism of alienation under capitalism. This does not concern the issue of operationalizing the concept of alienation: since, for Marx, alienation exists wherever capitalism exists, then the absence of empirical data concerning alienation is irrelevant. If alienation is not defined by the subjective experiences of workers but by the objective existence of capitalism, then the apparent satisfaction of workers at work is a manifestation of the depth of their alienation, not their freedom from it. In fact the concept is one unsuited to empirical investigation.

Beyond this issue, however, is the problem of whether unalienated production is feasible. It is already apparent that Marx changed his mind on the importance of the sphere of production for individual freedom but without specifying the reasons for this switch. One unarticulated difficulty with Marx's early assumptions about unalienated production is the tension that remains between a productive system democratically controlled by the producers and a social system democratically controlled by its citizens. Since there is no logical reason to suppose that the interests of producers and citizens exactly coincide, then the wishes of one or the other must prevail: society is either 'worker-controlled' or 'citizen-controlled', it is not self-evident how it can be both. Of course, some *degree* of both is plausible but Marx does not consider such a compromise and anyway this would necessarily imply that a degree of alienated activity remains. This is important because some Marxist approaches to the world of work embody a critical approach to capitalist methods that implicitly assume a utopian alternative. That is to say, that all the apparent or imputed ills of industrial society may be heaped upon its capitalist foundations when they may well be the effects of industrialized productive methods. This, of course, is precisely the issue dividing some of Marx's ideas from Durkheim's. It is also relevant to note here that contemporary green approaches to industrial society are seldom axiomatically compatible with Marxist approaches, and while Durkheim's attitude can hardly be considered green, given his enthusiasm for industrial growth, Marx does not fit easily in the founder's chair either (Spretnak and Capra, 1985).

Exploitation

If Marx's conceptualization of the alienating consequences of capitalism is both tension-ridden and at least partly flawed, his arguments within his later works, notably *Capital*, move from the field of philosophy to economics: from alienation to exploitation. What unites the early and late Marx is both the critical attacks upon capitalism, and, more importantly in this context, his focus upon the world of work as crucial to the explanation of social conflict and social change. It is crucial because *inter alia*: productive activity distinguishes humans from animals; it provides the medium for self-realization; under capitalism it distorts that very process; as a result of this distortion it generates social conflict; and, ultimately, it creates the means for the destruction of capitalism and the development of communist society – the revolutionary proletariat. What is significant in this for the sociology of work is not simply the focus upon work but the assertion of an inherent spawning of conflict between opposing interests and the concomitant requirement for methods of capitalist control.

How does Marx arrive at the conclusion that work in capitalist society is inherently conflictual and requires forms of industrial coercion? In brief, he begins by accepting Ricardo's (1951: chapter 1, section 1) argument that the exchange value of a product is determined by the quantity of labour necessary to produce it. An earlier argument by Locke (1960: 329) had similarly argued that property could only be legitimated through the intermixing of labour. However, neither Ricardo nor Locke confronted the possibility of exploitative wage labour because both argued that the rewards of wage labour were exactly equivalent to the value of labour added to the product. Where Marx differed was in his assumption that the very existence of the profitable employment of wage labour implied a disjunction between the exchange value of commodities and the exchange of labour for wages. Hence exploitation, the disequilibrium between work and wages, engendered by the relationship between employer and employee, must exist. Indeed, recognition of exploitation can only be evaded by assuming that the rewards of labour are exactly equivalent to the value of that labour added to the end product. Marx's position is that while it is labour that determines the exchange values of commodities, the exchange of labour for wages is not reciprocally balanced. In fact, what is exchanged is not labour at all, but labour *power*: the capacity to work. Thus while orthodox accounts regard labour as just one more commodity, and therefore encapsulated within simple exchange relations, Marx asserts three counter-points: first, labour is not just an inanimate commodity and cannot therefore be reduced to simple exchange relations; second, the commodity exchanged – labour power – is not the equivalent of that entering the labour process – labour; third, that the consumption of labour power does not take place within the sphere of circulation, or market, at a fair exchange, but within the sphere of production, the 'hidden abode of production', under conditions of gross inequality (1954: 172). This obscuring of exploitation made it appear 'natural and inevitable' while Marx regarded it as merely temporary and socially constructed.

The capitalist labour process

It was this 'hidden abode' that both distinguished capitalism from prior social formations and resulted in the conflicting and contradictory interests of employers and employees. Under feudalism the surplus produced by the peasantry was appropriated in kind by the ruling class: 'surplus labour' was visibly exploited. But under capitalism the surplus produced by the proletariat and appropriated by capitalists, 'surplus value', was invisible exploitation that occurred through the labour process itself. In effect, the difference between the workers' wages and the value of their productive activity provided the surplus value, which, when realized in commodity exchanges, became transformed into profits; since the exchange involved in wage labour was inequitable, the relationship between capital and labour was exploitative.

Four points are noteworthy from this analysis. First, despite its poor utility as a price theory (for it implies that inefficiently made commodities with considerable labour costs are exchanged at higher prices than those with lower labour costs), Marx's labour theory of value does have considerable merit in demonstrating that the relationship between exchanges, prices and values is not merely a quantitative economic one, but embodies social relations too. Second, because the capitalist only purchased the potential for labour, not a predefined quantity of products or effort, some mechanism of managerial control was essential in transforming labour power into labour. Third, because the wage labour relationship was inherently exploitative, the interests of labour and capital are considered to be necessarily antagonistic. Indeed, it is because the sphere of work generates exploitation not self-realization, and because this sphere is potentially the embodiment of all that is uniquely human, that Marx, and most Marxists, regard the exploitation based on class to be more important than exploitation based on gender or ethnic origin etc. – a point of considerable controversy. Fourth, Marx's analysis suggests that because capitalism is a system grounded in the imperatives of economic competition, the administrative machinery and policies of capital are determined by these market forces not by the individual wishes of capitalists: thus the motivations of individuals are irrelevant (1954: 555).

Using this framework Marx then distinguishes between three types of production: co-operation, manufacture and machinofacture. There is some doubt as to whether Marx considered these three within an evolutionary, or an analytic, typology but the controversy need not detain us here (Berg, 1980: 110; Friedman, 1977: 13, 19). Under co-operation a simple division of labour ensured a greater quantity of production and merely the 'formal subordination of labour'. That is, although labour was bound to work exclusively for capital, because it was excluded from ownership of the means of production and could not consume the commodities it produced, none the less it retained a degree of independent power. This power was founded upon the irreplaceable skill that provided the material base for labour's control of the labour process; capitalist control was therefore restricted to the economic sphere. While the technological apparatus of production remained relatively simple and static, any increase in exploitation invariably manifested itself in the guise of expanding 'absolute' surplus value – by lengthening the hours of work, for example. With 'manufacture' the beginnings of the 'detail labourer' appear, as the pre-existing 'natural', or social, division of labour into different trades is systematically extended such that each worker produces only a fraction of the total product. This stage also witnesses the growth of factories, as workers are brought together to facilitate the necessary reintegration of the specialized skills of the 'collective labourer' in the beginnings of the 'specifically capitalist mode of production' (Brighton Labour Process Group, 1977: 10). At this juncture machinery is introduced, initially within the parameters of 'manufacture' and ultimately this develops into 'machinofacture' and the 'real subordination of labour'. Under this, any remaining element of control by the workers over the labour process is dissolved, and they are collectively reduced to mere appendages of machines (Marx, 1954: part IV).

The reverberations of this development set the scene for Marx's subsequent analysis. First, deskilling becomes a universal phenomenon that simultaneously turns the workers into 'crippled monstrosities', cheapens labour, inhibits workers' upward mobility and homogenizes them as a class, uniting them in their exploitation by, and opposition towards, capitalism. Second, a wage hierarchy is established to fragment opposition to capitalism. This implies, paradoxically, that deskilling is not a comprehensive effect, and thus real subordination can never be achieved completely. This is inevitably the case since, as Marx argues elsewhere, coercive economic laws that force capitalists constantly to revolutionize the technology of production also require the development of new skills with their consequential leverage over the labour process (1954: 331–8). Third, technology facilitates the breaking of strikes, immunizes production from the problem of labour turnover, concentrates decision-making, and most importantly, the physical control of labour itself is no longer derived from any legal, moral or economic force alone but is actually inscribed upon the productive process itself. Fourth, because of the greater technical efficiency of new machinery, the labour time necessary to produce commodities is decreased through a rise in the production of 'relative surplus value'. And finally comes the 'creation of that monstrosity, an industrial reserve army kept in misery in order to be always at the disposal of capital' (1954: 457).

A particularly striking motif running through Marx's analysis here is that of autonomous technical development, where technology itself inaugurates various forms of social change and, in some senses, can be used as a measure of social development; a productivist outlook directly opposed to the contemporary green view but symmetrical with capitalist, social democratic and conventional Marxist, and especially Bolshevik, attitudes to economic growth (Anthony, 1977: 138–45; Sirianni, 1982: 245–60).

Freedom and despotism

It is also apparent that Marx appears confused over the role of management within advanced capitalist factories: at one point he considers them to be inherently authoritarian as they strain to retain control of an evermore belligerent workforce, yet since control is inscribed into the technology of production at this point it is difficult to see the necessity for such control strategies. This assumption of increasing despotism is not simply an empirical issue but actually manifests a political lacuna in Marx concerning the issue of 'freedom' in free wage labour. According to Marx this freedom is merely freedom to sell labour power and freedom from having anything else to sell; it is, therefore, a bourgeois sham. But, as Giddens (1981: 220–6) has argued, the freedom of free wage labour also implies that labour cannot be physically coerced into work and is thus free to organize resistance through trade unions etc. Of course, Marx recognized the existence and importance of trade unions and in his empirical works, such as the analysis of the British Factory Acts, was clearly aware that the alleged despotism of the factory was heavily circumscribed by forces other than those directly devolved from capital itself (1954: 264–80). Nevertheless, Marx does systematically underestimate the possibility that management may also need to organize consent as well as coercion (Burawoy, 1979: 27).

The reconceptualization of capitalist management as necessarily involved in consent construction also suggests that Marx's zero-sum theory of power is inadequate: while the interests of labour and capital are not coincident, the assumption that they are irreconcilably, and diametrically, antagonistic is misleading. Part of the explanation for the difficulty with Marx here lies at the level of analysis: while Marx's theory concerns the irreconcilable interests of social classes at a macro-level, this obscures the very real way in which, at the level of the enterprise, the interests of employees and employers may be very tightly intertwined. Marx's constant reassertion of the salience of class interests at the macro-level makes the theory particularly difficult to apply to discrete empirical cases (Tomlinson, 1982: 11–46).

Capitalism and class

This difficulty is exacerbated by Marx's dual theory of class. His concept of classes, which perceives them to be aggregates of individuals in the same relationship to the means of production, does not change: all owners of capital are capitalists, while those who own only their labour are proletarians. However, Marx does provide contradictory statements as to the historical development of the class structure: in *The Communist Manifesto* (Marx and Engels, 1968: 41–5) the class structure is polarizing; in the *Theories of Surplus Value* (1969: 573) the middle classes are expanding and consolidating their intermediate position. Exactly which of these theories is the one Marx would have preferred is difficult to say, for his work in this area effectively ended just as he was about to embark upon a major study of class. Nevertheless, it is appropriate to reiterate the point that Marx was not a reclusive academic but an active revolutionary, and the *Manifesto* was written as a polemical call to the barricades on the eve of the revolutions of 1848, not a scholarly text. Once the revolutions had failed Marx obviously had to reassess his assumptions and, in the light of more detailed empirical work, seemed to distance himself from the early claims to class polarization.

Rather more important than the nature of empirical trends is the radical breakthrough contained within Marx's theoretical approach to class. The innovative nature of Marx's theories actually lies not with the descriptive value of his analysis but with the causal explanation; in particular, Marx differentiates himself from the contemporary 'revenue' theories of class. These revenue theories took the levels and origin of income, and symbolic reward derived from the market, as the criteria for class construction, not the pattern of ownership of the means of production. But, argued Marx, this implied that the market itself was a pre-existing, natural, and therefore neutral, feature of society. For Marx, nothing could be further from the truth because the market itself was constructed upon the pre-existing relations of ownership and non-ownership of the means of production. It was not that the market had no impact upon the class structure but that the market was generated by a particular class structure. In turn, this meant that equality of opportunity in the market was not as significant as, and was actively undermined by, pre-market inequalities. Moreover, Marx's primary criticism of capitalism was not that it created an inegalitarian society; all societies would be inegalitarian to some extent. In the first phase of post-capitalist society, or socialism, Marx argued that rewards would have to relate to effort, not need; in the second, or communist, stage a form of positive discrimination would prevail where rewards were distributed according to need, not effort. Neither of these stages is inherently egalitarian. Rather, Marx's claim was that capitalism was inherently alienating and exploitative. Hence, to increase the level of rewards or even to provide equality of opportunity, does not, in itself, eradicate alienation or exploitation; thus a class structure of exploiters and exploited remains impervious to the manipulation of levels of material and symbolic reward. In political terms this meant that trade union actions to secure employment or boost wages and conditions did nothing to root out the cause of the proletariat's condition, it simply provided a temporary anaesthetic for the symptoms of spiritual degradation and material poverty.

This qualitative gulf separating the two major classes also explains the antagonistic, rather than simply competitive, relationship between them. This does not mean that mortal combat was a pervasive feature of the relationship, because although the system was inevitably exploitative, as already discussed, the system also obscured the reality of exploitation through the opaqueness of the labour process. Consequently, Marx distinguished between a class 'in itself', where the objective conditions generated a class, irrespective of the attitudes of the members, and a class 'for itself', where the objective conditions facilitated the creation of a conscious solidarity among a class in opposition to another class. Exactly how this revolutionary class consciousness is generated is the subject of considerable controversy (Giddens, 1973: 112–17), but basically Marx assumes that class consciousness corresponds to the stage of material production such that: 'it is not the consciousness of men that determines their being, but, on the contrary, their social being determines their consciousness' (1973a: 504). This can be interpreted to mean either that class consciousness is *determined* by material forces or that it is *constrained* by them. Either way it is still the case that Marx sees consciousness as being more influenced by social being than vice versa. This correspondence principle is, then, associated with the revolutionary activities of the proletariat, though the link between an ideology controlled by the ruling class, which facilitates the manipulation of the proletariat through false consciousness, and a revolutionary class of proletarians, free from the taint of capitalist ideology, is a leap of imagination as much as anything else, as Lukács (1971) and Lenin (1970) implicitly suggested by their own attempts to resolve the practicalities of revolutionary action. What neither Lukács nor Lenin does, of course, is to question the general theoretical approach of Marx: the primacy of economic relations. As a result, economic exploitation at the point of production is ensconced as the critical field for social analysis and political activity. In effect, class conflict predetermines all other forms of social conflict, in particular that based on gender, ethnic or national considerations. Concomitantly, the elimination of class conflict, in theory at least, simultaneously destroys the material base for these other social conflicts to the extent that the institutions necessary for mediating various forms of conflict are unnecessary. In political terms such an interpretation induces the 'end of politics': an apparent utopia that actually germinates the seeds of dictatorship (Held, 1987; Johnston, 1986; Polan, 1984).

The impact of Marx

In terms of the sociology of work the impact of Marx is considerable: his illumination of the essentially political nature of the employment relationship and the material base for industrial conflict still supplies one of the elementary building blocks for an analysis of employment. However, the exclusivist approach to economic exploitation at the point of production precludes, or at best subordinates, both analysis of the links between home and work, and forms of exploitation other than those based on class. In short, what Marx helped to do was stimulate the very idea of a sociological approach to work but delimit the scope to the sociology of the factory. Finally, following Merleau-Ponty, we should treat Marx as a classic: an intermediary we need if we are to progress beyond him. Even if we do reject his ideas we can only go beyond him *because of them*, rather than in spite of them.

Durkheim and industrial society

The division of labour

Emile Durkheim's contribution to the sociology of work is fundamentally derived from *The Division of Labour* and his discussion of '**anomie**'. Written as his doctoral thesis, at a time when sociology hardly existed in France, *The Division of Labour* grapples with the issue of social solidarity and cohesion during a time of rapid social and economic transition. In essence, Durkheim suggests that the popular assumptions of the time concerning the imminent collapse of social life, in response to the ever increasing division of labour and general urbanization of life, were not just exaggerated but actually wrong. Thus, although Tönnies claimed that modern society was disintegrating under the transition to industrial life, represented by the transition from *Gemeinschaft* or 'community' forms of society to *Gesellschaft* or 'societal' forms representing mere 'associations' where solidarity was disintegrating, Durkheim retorted that rather than being dismantled, solidarity was simply being reconstructed in a different form. Similarly, while Simmel (1971) asserted that the intensity

Emile Durkheim. Photo: Lauros-Giraudon.

of nervous stimulation in modern urban society was such that individuals would be forced to retreat into their own private worlds, Durkheim argued that modern industrial society actively freed people from isolation by inducing mutual dependence through the increasing division of labour.

Even Spencer, whose optimistic approach to social change through evolutionary development Durkheim would have partly accepted, failed to recognize the critical significance of the social nature of life. For Spencer the free reign of egoism and *laissez-faire* propagated, by means of natural selection, the best of all possible worlds, but for Durkheim only collective solidarity and morality could furnish the necessary foundations for individual freedom: ethical individualism, not psychological egoism, was the key to progress for Durkheim, and this key lay buried within the increasing division of labour. Of course, Durkheim recognized the difficulty of reconciling the apparent impending decline of moral order at the turn of the century; an atavistic response to the problems of change which he loosely labelled 'anomie': a situation where the prevailing morality disintegrated to leave an anarchy of selfishness, rather than a pluralism of difference. However, this was a temporary problem for the future and held out the prospect of combining individualism *and* social solidarity.

Mechanical and organic solidarity

In sharp contrast to what Durkheim perceived to be the reactionary viewpoints, he regarded pre-industrial social solidarity to be derived not from the liberatory aspects of any mythical independent yeomanry, but from the rather suffocating effects of uniformity of experience and thought. In such cultures individuals were integrated into society through the collective conscience, but that very integration was at the direct expense of individuality. This symmetry of life Durkheim called '**mechanical solidarity**' in contrast to the '**organic solidarity**' manifest in the contemporary individualism engendered under the increasing division of labour. There is, then, no necessary correlation between increased specialization and decreasing solidarity, though Durkheim maintained that 'abnormal' forms of the division of labour still persisted and brought with them problems for the production and reproduction of the necessary degrees of social solidarity. Of these abnormal forms two were particularly important: the 'anomic' and the 'forced' division of labour.

The anomic form referred to the meaninglessness of work: a transient form generated between the collapse of mechanical solidarity and the creation of organic solidarity. During this phase new norms of behaviour had yet to be diffused throughout society and were exacerbated by the apparent deskilling of work manifest in the factory system where workers were constrained to meaningless operations on products that they could hardly envisage and for consumers they would never know. As the norms of behaviour spread, and what Durkheim believed to be the unbridled anarchy of the free market dwindled under social regulation, the anomic division of labour would disappear. However, Durkheim also warned that mere construction of consensually grounded goals and meanings without the concomitant provision of opportunities to achieve such goals would extend the period under which anomie prevailed: an interpretation of industrial, and for that matter social, life which was to prove influential in the ideas of some of Britain's foremost scholars of the industrial scene over sixty years later (Fox and Flanders, 1969). Indeed, in the second edition of *The Division of Labour* (1902) Durkheim's optimism about the spontaneous generation of a normal division of labour had been replaced by his assumption that 'corporations', or occupational associations that bridged the gap between trade unions and employer associations, would form a prerequisite mediating institution between individuals and the state. This is important because Durkheim's suggestion is that without some form of institutionalized dispute resolution at work, anomie is likely to prevail.

The forced division of labour occurred when existing patterns of inequality failed to mirror what Durkheim took to be the normal or inevitable distribution of personal inequalities. Thus, the advantages of the normal division of labour would be found 'only if society is constituted in such a way that social inequalities exactly express natural inequalities' (1933: 377). Durkheim, then, was not an egalitarian but a supporter of meritocracy induced, among other things, by the eradication of personal inheritance. As he put it: 'there cannot be rich and poor at birth without there being unjust contracts' (1933: 384). His assumptions about 'natural' inequalities do have to be critically assessed:

he regarded industrial workers as more intelligent than farmers, and men as more intelligent than women, using the flimsiest of empirical evidence. He also assumed that the gender-based domestic division of labour was a good example of the social harmony generated when social inequalities were allowed to mirror 'natural' inequalities. Yet the 'naturally' affective functions of women and the 'naturally' intellectual functions of men also provided a case where Durkheim's own uncertainty about gender relations provoked the beginnings of a critique of patriarchy. For: 'Although by constitution women are predisposed to a life different from men . . . if these differences make possible the division of labour they do not necessitate it . . . for specialized activities to result they must be developed and organized' (1933: 264–5). In short, Durkheim suggests that only when 'predispositions' are buttressed by social organization do they become enacted.

Social regulation

Both meaninglessness and unjustifiable inequalities pose threats to the cohesion of contemporary society but few of the orthodox solutions to these issues satisfied Durkheim. The *laissez-faire* approach of free marketeers simply compounded the difficulties generated by both issues: inheritance was buttressed by liberal notions of individual freedom and the same philosophical position undermined any attempt to construct *social* norms that would regulate individual behaviour by providing regulated codes of conduct. In reality, argued Durkheim, such egotism posed a very grave threat to society since it stimulated individual desires and greed that were uncontrollable because they were inherently infinite. Only social regulation provided the resolution of social problems but this does not imply that Durkheim was favourably inclined towards Marx's ideas. Although a professed socialist, Durkheim considered the methodological assumptions of economic determination in Marxism to be overly restrictive, while Marx's solution to the crisis of capitalism was too dependent upon the state and yet paradoxically too limited in its concern for regulation. That is, he argued that, first, the state was too far removed from the everyday experience of individuals and hence mediating organizations or corporations would form the primary mode of social organization. Second, Marx's assumptions about the determining role of the economy prevented him from assessing the need for all institutions to be regulated, not just economic ones. It was, therefore, morally grounded and socially regulated institutions coupled with an ever widening division of labour that facilitated the development of individual skill which would ultimately create the future utopia: evolution not revolution; regulation not anarchy; solidarity through individualism and mutual dependence not conformity through uniformity.

Durkheim's contribution

It should be noted that Durkheim's critique of scholars and contemporary society, which he regarded as reactionary, was aimed not at the essence of capitalism but at industrialism. It was the case that Durkheim railed against the injustice of private inheritance and the inequities of unjustified inequalities but, although he died only a week after the Bolshevik revolution in Russia and had, therefore, no experience of state socialist states, he had little doubt that a revolutionary approach to social change, of the kind envisaged by Lenin and Marx, would fail to resolve the problems facing society. Certainly, Durkheim was no lover of capitalism but the transcendence of the ills of capitalist societies had to be through the forces unleashed by industrialization embodied in the division of labour, not through the political machinations of a minority of self-appointed, professional revolutionaries. Industrialization had spawned the promise of salvation and simultaneously generated some very unhealthy reactions, but the remedy lay in reconstructing the pattern of the original seed, not in the destruction of the soil. For Weber, however, as indeed for Marx, the original pattern displayed fault lines that boded ill for the future.

Weber

The third member of the founding 'gang of three' was Max Weber. His work is often assumed to be a dialogue with the ghost of Marx, though most of his dialogue was with contemporary Marxists rather than with the works of Marx himself – many of which were not published during Weber's lifetime. Weber's contribution to the sociology of work lies in several rather disparate fields: first, his theory of social stratification; second, his interpretative methodology; third, his arguments concerning the rise of rationality, the nature of bureaucracy and the form of bureaucratic control. In some sense all three substantive areas embrace criticisms of Marxist perspectives.

Class and stratification

It has also to be stated that there is much of common belief between Marx and Weber. In terms of Weber's approach to social stratification it is apparent that both accepted the significance of property ownership: it was for Weber the 'basic category' and determinant of class position. Yet, argued Weber, Marx was wrong to assume that the different components of stratification – in particular class, status and party – were necessarily coterminous when, in Weber's view, they were actually contingently related. This contingent aspect also extended to Weber's analysis of the relationship between class position and class consciousness. Rather than assuming that a proletariat without class consciousness must be suffering from the delusions of false consciousness, Weber asserted that the complex, multidimensional and cross-cutting nature of social stratification necessarily inhibited the acquisition of class consciousness. Much more likely was the creation of status groups with a degree of political or corporate consciousness that would thrust them to the forefront of political activity. This fragmented stratification system, in conjunction with the essentially subjective

Max Weber, c. 1900. Photo: AKG London.

nature of understanding, meant that the proletarian revolution predicted by Marx was extremely unlikely.

But what was the theoretical premise upon which Weber launched his critique of Marx? Well, it is closely associated with the revenue theories about which Marx was so disparaging: for Weber, a class existed when a number of individuals had a significant component of their life chances determined by their power within an economic order (1978: 302–7, 926–39). This indicates that classes are unambiguously economic and closely related to, if not identical with, market situations. Weber then goes on to distinguish between three types of class: property classes, commercial or acquisition classes, and social classes. Note here that, because Weber relates class to market situation, anyone without access to the market is restricted to a status group not a class; thus slaves, individuals with unpaid domestic duties, and even the long-term unemployed, are written out of Weber's class analysis and relocated within the status system. It is also evident that Weber provides no theoretical criteria for distinguishing between classes but simply assesses the general empirical distinctions of occupations; as such there can be no theoretical limit to the number of classes which exist, for there are as many classes as there are different occupations. The details of these groups need not detain us here but it is significant that Weber explicitly denies a link between property classes and political consciousness: property classes are, in this sense, non-dynamic. This is self-evidently counter to Marx's arguments and can hardly be considered as evidence of the importance Weber allegedly allocates to this 'basic category'.

Weber's third form of class, social class, is occupationally based and distinguishes between the Working Class of labour sellers; the Lower Middle Class of small shopkeepers etc.; the Intelligentsia with little property but technical qualifications; and, finally, the Privileged Class who owe their superordinate position to property ownership or education or both. Weber actually doubts whether many identical class situations exist but insists that all are derived from market situation. Thus, in the absence of materially resemblant situations, there is little possibility of collective class action. This is not to say that Weber refutes all possibility of class action but he does reject Marx's argument that seems to impute interests to social classes. In contrast, Weber asserts that the actual interests of specific classes must be studied empirically and this requires a distinction between two forms of social action: communal action, such as that undertaken by trade unions in defence of sacked colleagues, and societal action designed to reconstruct the general distribution of life chances, such as that manifested by socialist political parties. This distinction is significant because Weber locks the likelihood of social action to the transparency of the connections between the causes and the consequences of the class situation. Not only does a group have to be collectively aware of its unjust situation, but it also has to be in a position to resolve the perceived problem. For these reasons Weber believed that groups like trade unions in factories, where the physical constraints of production facilitated union organization, leadership and control, were best placed to demonstrate class-oriented social action.

Status

Nevertheless, Weber generally assumed that, outside periods of economic or political crisis, class action would be minimal. Instead, the norm would be action undertaken by status groups. Status, the distribution of social honour or social esteem, despite its tendency to correlate highly with class, was not determined by it, nor was the influence unidirectional. In fact, Weber argued that because markets were determined by impersonal forces, status considerations were of high value within capitalist societies. Usually status was determined by lifestyle, formal education, and hereditary or occupational prestige. Status groups were not identical with class groups but Weber believed that the greater homogeneity of status groups provided them with a stronger claim to social action. Furthermore, this homogeneity was actively reproduced by the exclusionary practices of members. A difficulty here is differentiating status from class: indeed, since the correlations between the two are usually so close it could well be argued that class provides the material wherewithal for the provision of status symbols. Thus status may not be as independent of class as Weber maintains. On the other hand, it would seem that in some circumstances status is more influential than, and independent of, class. For example, it may well be the case that membership of an ethnic minority or gender group is more influential for the determination of life chances than class position. In sum, it may be that in some circumstances class is more relevant as the explanatory variable, while in other circumstances status orientations are crucial.

Weber spends little time in analysing the position of women through the category of status group, even though it clearly lends itself to such an interpretation. In fact, like Marx and Durkheim, Weber was generally uninterested in women's subordinate position at work or in society generally. Although relatively liberal in his support for the political emancipation of women in Germany, Weber, like Durkheim, regarded them as 'naturally' fitted for domestic responsibilities and failed to link the patriarchal domination of employment organizations with the patriarchal construction of society. Such a lacuna necessarily leaves Weber's corpus of work, like that of Marx and Durkheim, significantly flawed.

Party

The final aspect of Weber's trilogy of power was the party. While classes fought over economic issues, and status groups contested the distribution of social honour, parties – which were oriented towards the acquisition of social power – operated at all levels and across all boundaries of class and status. The actual divisions between all three are notoriously slippery, though Weber implies that parties attempt to reconstruct the status quo, while class and status groups generally reflect the status quo.

Methodology

It is important to remember at this juncture that although Weber often wrote in terms of such collectivities as classes and status groups etc., he categorically denied the structural approach of both Marx and Durkheim, which seemed to him to relegate the role of the individual to the proverbial cog in a giant wheel. In contrast, Weber argued that all social collectivities and phenomena had to be reducible to their individual constituents: only individuals thought and acted; no group mind or behaviour existed above and beyond the sum of individuals' thoughts and actions. This assumption was critical because Weber's approach posits that individual interpretation was an inherent aspect of human knowledge. As such, sociology became a study of social collectivities explicable only through individual interpretation, and, moreover, a distinction had to be drawn between externally visible 'behaviour' and 'action' that required interpretation of intentions. Weber did not argue that intentions always led to specific outcomes but he did assert that identical forms of behaviour could be based upon divergent intentions. This 'interpretative method' or ***Verstehen*** was clearly different from the observational methods used by 'natural' science, primarily because sociologists, and social scientists more generally, faced a thinking subject whose subjective understanding was the secret to explaining action. Perhaps one of the clearest examples in this field is the distinction between wandering around town as a pleasurable experience during a vacation, and undertaking exactly the same 'behaviour' as an expression of boredom through unemployment. The difference between leisure and unemployment is difficult to explain at the level of observation and requires interpretative understanding for a more convincing analysis.

Inevitably this approach has its own difficulties. In particular the approach is conditional upon individuals being consciously aware of what they are doing. Interpretative understanding also depends upon a level of a priori understanding that Weber himself limits to a rather restricted vision of 'normality'. That is, Weber argues that sociologists can only interpret behaviour in so far as it is within the sociologists' sphere of normal action and behaviour. Quite where this leaves the anthropological approach to alien cultures is uncertain since to treat all aspects of culture as 'alien', that is requiring interpretation in the first instance, is something which Weber's method cannot accommodate.

Weber also distances himself from the more positivist approaches of Marx and Durkheim on the issue of external, objective reality. Durkheim, especially, laid great emphasis on the objective nature of external reality and its impact upon individuals but Weber, while accepting the existence of regularities in the social world, denied the presence of social 'laws'. Hence Weber's creation of the '**ideal type**': a theoretical abstraction, an artificial and one-sided extrapolation of important traits or characteristics that simultaneously suppresses unimportant traits. This ideal type was neither ideal nor typical. That is, it was not ideal in any evaluative sense, since Weber's argument seeks to extrapolate significant existing realities, rather than impose normative or projective forms. Indeed, Weber was very suspicious of those who sought to impose their own truth upon others since he regarded reality as ultimately meaningless, and thus no moral position could be scientifically accredited, though he was a staunch defender of liberalism and the interests of the German state. Nor was an ideal type typical because it did not represent any norm or average form but merely a one-sided exaggeration. Its use, then, was purely as a heuristic theoretical device to facilitate the measurement of reality and the comparison of empirical forms.

Capitalism and rationalization

Despite Weber's scepticism concerning any transcendent meaning to life or any historical patterns to it, he was convinced that contemporary society was increasingly grounded in the symbolic and material advance of rationality. What did he mean by this term? The principle physical manifestations took three related forms: capitalism, rational jurisprudence and bureaucracy. However, the essence of the concept consisted of three facets: secularization, calculability and the growth of ethics oriented to means, not ends. The rise of rationality meant, in short, the decline of magical interpretations and explanations of the world, and the gradual elimination of all mysteries, as science exploded more and more mythical assumptions. It also meant the replacement of 'affective' and 'traditional' action with 'rational' action: we no longer undertook activities because that was how things had always been done, nor because we had emotional reasons for doing it. Instead we did things because we calculated that the benefits outweighed the cost, or because we assessed the action as the most efficient way to achieve our goals. Human actions were also constrained by rational rules now. Not that they had previously been completely unconstrained but historically the rules guiding us had been religious or derived from the force of tradition. Now we obeyed rules because they appeared to be built upon rational principles and common sense, and the foremost example of this form of authority was, of course, bureaucracy.

Bureaucracy

Weber was clear that bureaucracies predated the rise of capitalism, notably in the 'patrimonial' bureaucracies of the Roman, Byzantine and Egyptian empires. But these were not structured around the rational principles of free contract, fixed salaries and delimited spheres of competence. Though Weber never formally defined bureaucracy he did provide an extensive analysis of the necessary principles of legitimacy, authority and selection. It is not essential here to repeat Weber's description of the principles at length (see Albrow, 1970: 40–5; Beetham, 1987; Pollitt, 1986), but the crucial elements involve: an abstract, legal code of conduct; individual spheres of competence structured within a hierarchy of offices; the non-ownership of offices; selection and promotion through qualifications and proven ability; and fixed salaries, with pension and security of tenure for all office holders (Weber, 1978: 217–21). The essential points of bureaucracy, then, are twofold. First, it was 'legal' in that it operated on the basis of procedures that could be adjudged correct or otherwise through resort to a body of rules by those subject to its authority. Second, it was 'rational' because it operated on the principles of expert knowledge and calculability.

It was upon these twin foundations that bureaucracy began its allegedly inexorable rise to power, though Weber limits the utility of bureaucracy to the requirement for legal rational administration rather than the desire for a universally efficient form of administration. In fact, Weber was by no means oblivious to the potential distortions likely to befall organizations administered through bureaucracies, particularly where red tape or sectional control undermined their rational hierarchical control in the interests of the whole. Yet a whole series of empirical case studies has suggested that the existence of rules does not determine their execution, nor are subordinates unaware of the value of utilizing rules to protect themselves from superordinates, either through control over upward flowing information or by failing to select appropriate rules in 'working to rule' (Merton, 1957: 50–4; Crozier, 1964: 187; Batstone, 1979: 262; Mitchell and Parris, 1983).

Clearly, then, Weberian bureaucracies are not simply the harbingers of top-down omnipotent control but, rather, they bring in their wake problems of control as well as enabling powers. In sum, bureaucratic control does not appear to be unambiguously effective. It is, however, not part of Weber's claim that the legitimation of authority through bureaucratic administration is, by itself, sufficient for the control of subordinates (cf. Littler, 1982: 37). Weber, like Marx, actually assumed that industrial control in market economies required an essential degree of economic need as well as normative acceptance of a work ethic and bureaucratic authority. The main reason for such a panoply of control measures lies in the expropriation of the workforce (including management in some circumstances) from ownership of the means of production. This expropriation is deemed necessary because individual control militates against co-ordinated social production, and because managerially controlled enterprises offer stricter controls over recruitment, discipline and investment (Weber, 1978: 130–7, 152). It has to be admitted, though, that Weber also accepts that the strongest incentive to work is individual ownership and control, though producer co-operatives avoid the contradictory interests that inhibit production in conventional capitalist enterprises.

The rise of capitalism

Weber's explanation for the rise of capitalism in the West is closely related to the generation of new modes of work incentive. As made clear in the previous chapter, work patterns tend to be governed by normatively inscribed human needs. Since human needs are socially constructed they are also transient and flexible; thus pre-capitalist working hours were often far more limited than those which currently exist. Weber claimed that the inauguration of a new attitude to work, the generation of cultural change in which work became a means of demonstrating godliness, was linked to the rise of Calvinism and that this cultural change was associated with the rise of rational capitalism itself. Capitalism, in some form, had probably always existed *qua* 'booty capitalism' practised by hundreds of invading armies etc., or in the form of 'pariah capitalism' in which an alien group provided financial assistance to those groups prevented from such activities by their cultural or religious beliefs. The early Christian outlawing of money lending and the proximity of Jewish money lenders to Christian businesses is one such example.

Rational capitalism, however, is associated with the Protestant arm of the Christian church, and Weber sought an explanation in the beliefs and actions of Calvinists in his work *The Protestant Ethic and the Spirit of Capitalism* (1976). With the Calvinist doctrine of predestination, manifest in the acquisition of a state of 'grace' by the chosen few, Weber argued that the orientation of Calvinists to work was quite different from their Catholic or non-Christian contemporaries. While Catholics, according to Weber, believed they could secure their place in heaven through, among other things, 'good works' on behalf of the poor on earth, Calvinists believed that their predestined future left them with no means of knowing or altering their ultimate destination. This uncertainty led Calvinists to search for signs of 'election' by God and to assume that worldly success could be taken as a manifestation of 'grace', though obviously not as a means of achieving 'grace'. However, although Calvinists were now persuaded that material success, including business enterprise, was something that should be pursued with all possible vigour, their ascetic lifestyles prevented them from consuming the results of material success. Thus Calvinists were coerced by their beliefs into reinvesting their profits rather than dissipating them in consumptive behaviour.

The result was the establishment of a group of people with radically new work ethics: they had to work, literally all hours that God sent, to demonstrate their state of grace but because they were forced to reinvest almost all their profits they very quickly became evermore successful capitalists. Of course, the development of rational capitalism had not been their intention; they intended to serve God but ended up serving Mammon. Indeed, Weber's thesis of rationalization is again brought into play as the very material success of capitalism gradually undermines the Calvinism, and eventually Christianity, which was associated with its birth. The word 'association' rather than 'cause' is significant here because it is not clear whether Weber's argument suggests that the cultural changes inspired by Calvinism were causally associated with the rise of capitalism or just contingently related through the 'elective affinity' between the two phenomena (Parkin, 1982). Either way, Weber's point is that the generation of rational capitalism, contrary to Marx, cannot be explained through wholly material and structural forces.

Inevitably, Weber's claims have been subject to considerable attack and equally determined defence (Marshall, 1982; Ray, 1987). First, his evidence of the actual behaviour of Calvinists is drawn primarily from the ideas of Baxter, a Calvinist preacher, rather than from an empirical investigation of Calvinist capitalists. Second, the earliest examples of rational capitalism are not restricted to Calvinist or even Protestant nations, with some Calvinist countries, such as Scotland, failing to 'take off' and some Catholic nations, such as Belgium and several Italian city-states, being among the market leaders. Third, it is not self-evident why Calvinists, faced with the salvation anxiety, should adopt material success as the manifestation of grace: charitable acts have a much stronger tradition in early Christianity than making money has. Fourth, the ascetic lifestyles of Calvinist capitalists face a significant problem because the system is dependent upon non-ascetic consumers. Either the only Calvinists who were ascetic were the capitalists, or large-scale trading with non-Calvinist nations must have sprung up to accommodate the flow of commodities. Indeed, this regional aspect is also important in highlighting the point that most of the successful early capitalist economies were geographically beyond easy control by the Catholic church (Mann, 1986).

The heritage of Weber

Whatever the problems of Weber's interpretation of the significance of cultural features for the generation of rational capitalism it remains a crucial work in its innovative approach and its suggestive interpretations of material change. For our purposes it appears to be a flawed but innovative account of the significance of interpretative sociology, the role of cultural factors and the development of work practices that continue to demand our contemporary concerns: why do people engage in such apparently irrational work patterns? If the work ethic does not exist how do we explain the almost compulsive work behaviour of some? Like Marx and Durkheim, Weber stands as a critical figure in the development of the sociology of work and his heritage of writings on rationalization, bureaucracy, and the significance of the individual as an interpretative actor whose actions often have unintended consequences, are a mainstay of contemporary approaches.

Summary

The three founders of the sociology of work all continue to have their contemporary adherents and detractors. Durkheim's moral concerns proved crucial to the development of work in mainstream industrial relations in the early 1970s and, as discussed in the previous chapter, the moral economy continues to pervade the market economy, making predictions about human action based on amoral, economically rational behaviour less than convincing. Perhaps where Durkheim has been most vigorously criticized has been in relation to the allegedly cohering effects of an extended division of labour. Neither Marx nor Weber nor the mainstream of managerial theories which are considered in the next chapter support Durkheim on this point: dependency does not generate mutual solidarity. For Marx, the division of labour generated the opposite social phenomenon: class conflict. Marx's fascination with class, conflict and the labour process formed the basis for the most popular new approach throughout much of industrial sociology from the late 1960s to the 1980s. However, although it spawned a complete school of thought in the labour process tradition (see chapter 5), its limitations became more evident as the approach attempted to explain all manner of social phenomena directly through the prism of class. Finally, Weber's theories of rationalization and bureaucracy have never been far from those analysing the trend towards larger and larger organizations or indeed from the apparent movement towards more flexible work organization patterns today. Again, however, Weber's over-rationalized approach underestimated the significance of destabilizing and sectional forces within work organizations. Had Weber adopted his own interpretative methodology more widely in his organizational studies, perhaps some of these shortfalls would have been attended to. Despite all these problems it is still the case that future research in the sociology of work will continue to adopt and adapt the ideas formulated by the 'gang of three', though probably not with the level of uncritical appreciation that has sometimes appeared in the past. In contemporary arguments there is much more concern for issues that none of these three considered crucial: the relationships between genders and ethnic groups; the significance of the links between the sphere of employment and the domestic sphere; and the role of social forces in the construction, as well as the deployment, of technology. Only a very thin slice of the classical approaches has been discussed here. Where, exactly, the ideas and values of these three founders of the debates appear today, and why a more disparate network of approaches has taken us beyond their original analyses, will be considered in the next four chapters.

Exam/essay questions

1 'It is not the consciousness of men that determines their being but, on the contrary, their social being determines their consciousness.' Is Marx right?
2 To what extent has the decline of communism undermined the utility of Marx's ideas?
3 'Marx's fixation with social class is as problematic as Durkheim's fixation with social facts.' Discuss.
4 Do Weber's ideas contradict or complement Marx's?
5 'The problem with Weber's idea of ideal types is that they become the model for the typical ideal. His discussion of bureaucracy is a case in point – bureaucracy is anything but ideal and, as a consequence, is no longer typical.' Discuss.
6 Compare Weber's and Durkheim's ideas on the division of labour.
7 'The relevance of the classical writers on the sociology of work is long gone.' Is it?
8 Durkheim and Marx discarded the individual in their explanations of society while Weber discarded all but the individual. Is it plausible to assume that an adequate sociological theory can be based on any of these approaches?
9 'The classical sociologists reduced work to employment, employment to men, and men to industrial workers.' To what extent is this an accurate representation of Marx, Weber and Durkheim?
10 Why was Weber so pessimistic about work when Durkheim and Marx were so optimistic?

Further reading

In terms of original works (which are often easier to read than subsequent interpretations), the following give a flavour of the 'gang of three'. Marx's *Communist Manifesto* (cf. Marx and Engels, 1968) is a classic example of polemical writing at its best, while his *German Ideology* (1970) is a much more sophisticated and analytic piece. Weber's *The Protestant Ethic and the Spirit of Capitalism* (1976) reveals his approach to empirical analysis, while his essay 'Politics as a Vocation' (in Weber, 1948) remains a powerful piece of committed writing. *The Division of Labour* (1933) is Durkheim's major contribution to the sociology of work, but his method is represented better by *Suicide* (1951).

Secondary accounts of the classics vary enormously and there are many from which to choose. I often think new students get a better insight by reading polemical approaches, and taking opposite sides of the fence on Marx are Callinicos's *The Revolutionary Ideas of Marx* (1983) and Conway's *A Farewell to Marx* (1987). For those seeking a more balanced approach, try McLellan's edited collection of his writings, *Karl Marx: His Life and Thought* (1974). Weber's *Protestant Ethic and the Spirit of Capitalism* (1976) is well covered in Marshall's *In Search of the Spirit of Capitalism* (1982), while a concise and lively introduction to his more general approach can be found in Parkin's *Max Weber* (1982). A similarly short introduction to Durkheim is Thompson's *Émile Durkheim* (1982), though Lukes's work of the same title (1973) is more subtle and substantial. Finally, a comparison of all three is provided by Giddens's excellent *Capitalism and Modern Social Theory* (1971).

4

Contemporary Theories of Work Organization

'Our sentence does not sound severe. Whatever commandment the condemned man has disobeyed is written upon his body by the Harrow.
This condemned man, for instance' – the officer indicated the man –
'will have written on his body: HONOUR THY SUPERIORS.'

Kafka, *In the Penal Settlement*

Introduction

Organizational approaches

Organizational theory is a discipline in itself with a consequentially huge corpus
of literature and research. A single chapter cannot hope to do justice to the
complexities of such debates and it will, therefore, seek to highlight some of
the major distinguishing themes.

The bewildering variety of organizational approaches often seems to obfuscate the explanations of organizational behaviour rather than clarify them.

Addressing such problems, some authors (e.g. Burrell and Morgan, 1979) have argued that each approach or paradigm should pursue its own path in splendid isolation. Only in this way will the messy effects of compromise be avoided, clear insights into organizations be achieved and, most critical of all for them, what they call 'radical organizational theory' be able to survive the imperialist intentions of others. Yet it is not self-evident that the greatest intellectual advances can be made by choosing to ignore the criticism of those from different viewpoints, and it would seem more likely that it is the clash between approaches, rather than the accretion of evidence from within discrete approaches, that will prove more heuristic.

A different procedure is suggested by Bernstein (1983) and supported by Reed (1985) in so far as a **pluralist** approach should be used which seeks to generate common ground, where possible, by reconciling differences through debate. This need not degenerate into a theoretical approach that lacks any form of critical edge and it does at least assert that an arena of commonality can ensure mutual enlightenment rather than isolated blindness. Unfortunately, Reed does not take us beyond a plea for pluralism so we are still unable to progress beyond a basic level of tolerance. Before embarking on the systematic analyses of the various approaches considered in this chapter, it is important to reconstruct the historical origins of the general substantive field of research: formal organizations.

Bureaucracy

Formal organizations, most of which are bureaucratic to some degree in that they are grounded in formal rules and a hierarchy of offices, are typically associated with problems of scale. In small organizations formal rules and a complex division of labour may be unnecessary. Thus, small-scale capitalist organizations were, and still are, often controlled by a single entrepreneur, and democratic or participatory organizations may be organized informally with rotating co-ordinators to avoid institutionalizing hierarchies of power. **Bureaucracy** may be avoided, then, for both economic and political reasons. However, once organizations expand beyond the point at which personal control or direct democracy is unproblematic, the general tendency has been to introduce some degree of bureaucratic control. This is not to say that democratic control of large organizations is impossible, as Michels (1949) claimed, but it is nevertheless notoriously difficult to develop properly and may require some degree of bureaucratization in order to ensure stability (Pollitt, 1986).

The relationship between the problems of scale and the advantages of bureaucracy usually ensured that the earliest forms of bureaucracy, as we have already noted in the previous chapter, emerged in either state-related organizations like the military, the Civil Service, state industries etc., or in religious organizations. In Germany, for example, an extended division of labour and its associated administrative hierarchy operated within monasteries and the sixteenth-century workhouses, developed to re-educate the criminals and beggars of the time (Kieser, 1989). In Britain the Civil Service, and particularly the Post Office, spawned the first large-scale non-military organization based on strictly demarcated offices, meritocratic career structures and rationalized systems of control. The preconditions for such a bureaucratic expansion are a necessary level of literacy which can provide recruits familiar with filing systems and accounts, a sophisticated money economy and an urbanized, and organizationally rich, society. Yet, as Stinchcombe (1965) has argued, even then the process of bureaucratization tends to be a two-stage affair. First, a bureaucratic administrative system of files and accounts is introduced and only after this is there a separation of ownership from immediate (day to day) organizational control. However, there is more to the growth of bureaucracy than determination by size alone: diversifications of products and services are also critical features, for the economic stimulus to diversification necessarily implies a diversified managerial and administrative structure (cf. Fletcher, 1973). Such linkages between diversification and bureaucratic growth have been well documented both in the USA (Chandler, 1962) and the UK (Channon, 1973). Perhaps the clearest examples of the ultimate result of such growth and diversification among work organizations are the multinational corporations (see chapter 9), and it is significant that these manage to create not just employment opportunities for the host nations and problems for national sovereignty (Held, 1989) but also manage to remain extremely centralized in terms of administrative control (see Lash and Urry (1987) and Harvey (1989) for a discussion of contemporary capitalist organizational trends at the national and international level).

Professions

Another aspect of the development of bureaucracies is the rise of the **professions**. It is important to remember here that organizational members may have interests in the expansion of their own profession or group which are independent of the assumed purposes of such organizations. Thus, for example, the classic arguments concerning the nature of the managerial revolution by Berle and Means (1968), Burnham (1962) and Dahrendorf (1959), in which a new profession of managers allegedly displaces the entrepreneurial capitalists of a previous era, are just one form of the professional 'capturing' of organizations (Scott, 1979; Johnson, 1972; Larson, 1977; Nichols, 1969; Reed, 1989). As Perkin (1989) has demonstrated, professionals in Britain approached the status of a fourth class through the period of the twentieth century, though their interests in corporatist administrations have fallen somewhat into disrepute after the Thatcher administration began to split public from private professions.

Mapping organizational theories

Organizational theories, despite their current diversity and proliferation, can, for the sake of understanding, be reduced to a position along two interlocking axes: the **determinist–interpretativist** axis and the **technocratic–critical** axis.

The former axis distinguishes between those approaches which stress the scientific and objective way in which organizations can be assessed, often relating specifically to underlying structural conditions and requirements (e.g., market imperatives, rational decision-making, efficiency etc.), from those approaches which focus on the indeterminate and contingent nature of reality, the significance of human interaction, the unintended consequences of human action, and the influence of interpretation. The technocratic–critical axis represents what may be called the political continuum. At one extreme, the **technocratic** pole, there are those approaches often developed by business consultants for whom organizational theories are essentially pragmatically oriented tools for the improvement of organizational efficiency. Within this framework the impact upon the lives of organizational members or the wider society is subsidiary at best, and irrelevant at worst, to the need to maximize profits and efficiency. At the other extreme, the critical pole, are radical explanations of organizations and behaviour within organizations for whom the social effects of the organization upon its members and the society within which it operates are more significant than the question of profits or efficiency. The **critical** side of this axis tends to encompass most conventional sociological approaches to organizations in that they are crucially premised upon explanatory accounts, rather than accounts which are primarily designed to improve or 'rationalize' organizations in some way. Of course, rationalizing organizations implies a high degree of knowledge surrounding the nature of organizations but this, in turn, begs the question of interests. In short, if 'improving' an organization requires mass redundancy, does this not rather suggest that improvement is defined solely in the interests of the owners and controllers rather than the entire body of employees or members? It is not necessary to label non-technocratic organizational theory 'radical organizational theory' as has become popular, since this implies that explanation is determined by political preferences. To admit to the inevitability of political bias is not the same as accepting that explanations may be accounted false simply by reference to their origins rather than their content. Thus, the knowledge that authoritarian control over organizational subordinates often generates counter-productive hostilities and conflicts does not require a radical viewpoint but rather a perusal of the experiences of such organizations.

What follows is another way of considering the relationships between various forms of organizational theory along the grid set out in figure 4. The interpretation of where the theories lie is clearly subject to dispute, nevertheless the claim is not that this is the best way of illustrating the types but that it is a heuristic way for our purposes. Since I have grave doubts about the validity of some of these claims, particularly those to 'scientific status', I have allocated them according to their professed claims, rather than their practices. Thus, for example, the human relations approach is located in the technocratic–determinist corner even though the interpretation here suggests that the practice of human relations approaches is far more contingent than its supporters claim. What is striking about the grid is the paucity of approaches that lie in the determinist–critical corner: if something is regarded as inevitable there is probably little incentive in generating an explanation or focusing upon organizational effects.

In what follows I consider the various facets of these theoretical approaches to organizations, attempting at the end to provide the outline of the Actor

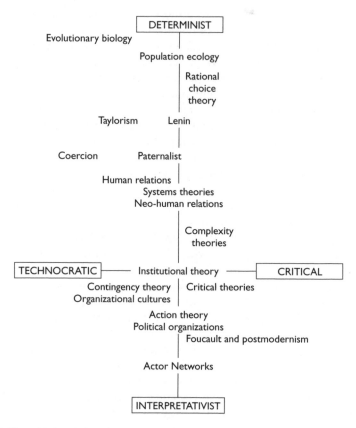

Figure 4 Organizational theories

Network approach, drawn from the sociology of science, which promises to circumvent some, at least, of the major problems in the preceding designs. In the first section I consider the earliest forms of organizational theory and practice in the modes of control attempted by the early factory capitalists: philanthropists and misanthropists alike.

Coercion

Historically speaking, most early (i.e., late eighteenth-century) British factory entrepreneurs did not seem unduly concerned about how their organization should be managed; provided it was profitable and the employees kept working there was little to be done in the way of improving the organization, let alone studying its workings. Not that things appear to have changed very quickly: in Houser's studies of American managers in 1924–5 very few had any information or apparent interest in what the employees thought of managers or how this might affect productivity (Jacoby, 1988). However, where labour problems erupted in the early factories there tended to be two rather different responses: coercion – the most common reaction; and paternalism.

Since one of the primary objects of constructing factories was to improve discipline through observation many owners attempted to construct a system of self-coercion; as Chadwick noted, the whole factory system was designed to maximize the effects of an internal network of social controls: 'the young are under the inspection of the old; the children are in many instances under the inspection of their parents, and all under the inspection of the whole body of workers, and under the inspection of the employer' (Chadwick, 1842). Thus control via detailed observation and regulation was already becoming common (cf. Joyce, 1980) in the mid-nineteenth century, though attempts by the first factory capitalists to impose control over the labour process in the eighteenth century were met with considerable, and initally successful, resistance by the factory operatives (Malcomson, 1981). Some factory owners altered the factory clocks to extract even more sweated labour from their exploited workforce and then sacked anyone caught with a watch for presuming 'to know too much about the science of horology' (Miles, 1850). Many of those who professed to be paternalists often appeared to wash their hands of activities occurring within their own factories and mines. As the *Reports from Commissioners Enquiring into Children's Employment* (1843) suggests: 'there is not one in fifty mine owners who cared about the housing and education or the moral condition of their employees' (quoted in D. Roberts, 1979: 183). Yet it was often some of the most successful capitalists who were keenest to enforce strict disciplinary codes, banning late time-keeping, drinking, swearing and mere talking. As Pollard (1965) argues, the vast majority of the earliest capitalists, faced with horrendous problems of control, and saturated with the belief that the labouring class were beyond moral improvement, let alone moral incentives, tended to resort to the traditional methods of coercion (fines, beatings or dismissal) or an occasional and very atypical reward. 'Rule 11' of one Manchester factory summed up this coercive approach: 'If any hand in the mill is seen talking to another, whistling or singing, [he] will be fined sixpence' (quoted in Ayres, 1988: 8). Some 'masters', such as Robert Blincoe's were undoubtedly sadistic: 'we beat only the lesser, up to thirteen or fourteen . . . we use a strap' (quoted in Pollard, 1965: 219). The factory owners were not alone in treating their employees harshly. John Bolling, a cotton-master, resisted such beatings but still had trouble with children running away from work: 'The other day there were three children run away; the mother of one of them brought him back and asked us to beat him; that I could not permit; she asked us to take him again; at last I consented, and she beat him' (quoted in Pollard, 1965: 219). Other control methods included piece work which accounted for almost half the payment systems of cotton mill workers in 1833, and which suggests that the traditional concern of labourers to earn just enough to provide for their customary level of subsistence was already breaking down.

Paternalism

The other kind of response to labour problems (the paternalist), was to assume that perhaps the workers were human after all and might actually respond better to a rather more gentle form of persuasion. As Josiah Wedgwood admitted: 'Our men have been at play four times this week, it being Burslem Wakes. I have roughed and smoothed them over, and promised them a long Xmass, but I know it is all in vain, for wakes must be observed though the world was to end with them' (quoted in Pollard, 1965: 214). Yet even Robert Owen's great experiment in paternalist organization, Harmony Hall, was premised on detailed control of members' behaviour, dress and furniture (Hardy, 1979: 54). This concern for detail was not dissimilar to the 'silent monitors' used in his New Lanark factory where workers had their previous day's work rate translated into a coloured mark and displayed above their machine. Similarly, the other paternalist capitalists, such as Crowley, Wedgwood, Marshall et al., all attempted to reconstruct the morality of the new working classes by delimiting the availability of drink, free time and self-indulgence (Pollard, 1965: 213–31).

Both coercive and paternalist responses were technocratic in the sense that the intention was to raise productivity not consider whether factory capitalism was an inherently problematic method of organizing production. But the paternalists were, nevertheless, critical of the brutal methods often used to coerce workers, not just because such methods bordered on the immoral but also because they seemed counter-productive. Both methods also sit within the determinist side of the vertical axis: both implied that through the correct application of specific forms of encouragement or violence, productivity could be maintained or increased. The possibility that organizations were inherently unstable social forms, for which no permanent or scientific strategy of control existed, did not figure high in these approaches.

Exactly why the first century of the Industrial Revolution had produced such a phenomenal growth in industrial organization and such a dearth of organizational theory is difficult to say. Pollard's (1965: 292–301) argument is probably as accurate as anyone's: first, the major problems facing capitalist organizations in this early period were perceived as external not internal. Obviously, worker discipline and organizational structures were obstacles to success, but the crucial issues as far as the capitalist entrepreneurs were concerned were often considered more significant, such as whether a road could be built to move the products or whether the labour supply would continue etc. Second, organizations were dominated by individual entrepreneurs and owner managers for whom the thought of delegating responsibility to a 'professional' manager was probably anathema. Third, the dominant ideology among organizational controllers was, for the most part, one that imbued labour with a sullen recalcitrance such that the 'solution' to organizational problems was obvious: more control, discipline and coercion, even if it had to be legally constrained; more importantly, more machinery to embody the mechanical discipline that was regarded as so much more effective than personal control.

Three-quarters of a century after the government commissioners were complaining about the level of employer indifference to the well-being of their employees, little seems to have changed with the exception, perhaps, of the Quaker employers, Rowntree, Cadbury and Lever, who argued vociferously for a direct connection between employee welfare and company prosperity. Their paternalist intent strayed well beyond concern for training and health within factories and moved into provision of entire communities like Cadbury's Bournville and Rowntree's New Earswick at York, the latter still very much a model Quaker village in the significant absence of pubs. Such major organizational innovations were not intended to ensure that the workers' places in heaven were secured but to maximize productivity through humanitarian and moralizing strategies of control. As such, they can be regarded as technocratic and deterministic in that they believed human nature and the capitalist system determined the best form of organization. Such examples of direct employer intervention over the entire lives of their employees were rare. What were increasingly visible, however, were moves in this direction by the state, first in terms of compulsory education. Later, after the débâcle of the Anglo-Boer War (1899–1902), during which time over a third of the recruits were rejected as medically unfit, and in conjuction with Booth's and Rowntree's poverty reports and the muscle flexing of the labour movement, further advances were made by the state towards the provision of improved health, welfare and later insurance (Hopkins, 1979).

The interests of the state in the mechanisms of organizational efficiency accelerated under the direct stimulus of the First World War, as the provision of manpower and munitions for the front forced the government to intervene directly in the management of industrial organizations. One result of this was the Industrial Fatigue Research Board, set up to investigate and promote mechanisms of efficiency at work, including the utility of rest, working hours, ventilation and lighting systems. By the end of the war, and under the guidance of Myers, the orthodox explanation for worker (mis)behaviour had switched from a physiological to a psychological causal analysis. Just as Taylor had argued that jobs and individuals should be matched, so too Myers, then heading the National Institute of Industrial Psychology, argued for vocational guidance to facilitate the individual requirements of specific workers and particular jobs. Moreover, where problems still manifested themselves, the cause was likely to be the disharmony between the personality of the workers and the work situation in which they found themselves (Rose, 1989). Myers, then, believed that work provided more than economic rewards and, in particular, it provided the means through which individual instincts could be gratified. Where work organizations were not constructed to provide such facilities, or worse, where they compounded otherwise minor mental or emotional instability, seriously maladjusted workers would result (Rose, 1989). This approach was yet another in the technocratic mould: the problem was not really how you explain organizations or whether organizational life was inherently damaging to health but how organizations could be made to operate more efficiently.

Taylor's approach (see chapter 5) conceived of personal health as identical with organizational efficiency. When Taylor began to develop his approach to incentive schemes and the wider issues of scientific management at the end of the nineteenth century, there were several rather distinctive facets that set it apart from the earlier modes of control. First, rather than assuming that all employees were universally similar, Taylor argued that individuals were differentially endowed and therefore, in the interests of efficiency, jobs and workers should be matched in terms of necessary skills and intelligence required. Second,

Taylor advanced the claim of control through expertise rather than property rights. It was the case that engineering had already begun to make claims towards a professional status in Britain in the first half of the nineteenth century but even here the movement was minimal and, outside of engineering, although well-defined groups of managers existed there was no managerial profession as such (Pollard, 1965: 159–88).

Lenin

The impact of Taylorism upon capitalist organizations is the subject of much dispute (see chapter 5), but one of its greatest admirers was Lenin. This may seem paradoxical in the light of the latter's political critique of capitalism but there are several points to remember. First, like Taylor, Lenin sought a 'scientific' solution to the problems of production and argued that Taylor's objective methods could be separated from his political ends. Second, Lenin's aim was not to develop a network of interacting autonomous units of production controlled by their own workforces but to institute a centrally controlled system of production that would unleash the potential hitherto inhibited by the capitalist quest for profits. Thus productivity was essential to the Bolshevik utopia because only when a cornucopia of production had been achieved would the conflicts generated by shortages be abolished. Hence, nothing that inhibited the drive to industrialize and outproduce the capitalists could be tolerated – including workers who still clamoured for 'outmoded' independent trade unions: since capitalism had been abolished, with the elimination of private property, all resistance to the 'Workers' State' must be counter-revolutionary. Lenin's approach to organizations, then, reproduces many of the assumptions of Taylor but in a new framework. Organizations are not essentially political bodies embodying conflicting interests but merely neutral mechanisms for achieving the consensually agreed goal – greater levels of production for the benefit of all. Thus Lenin sits uneasily midway along the technocratic–critical axis and halfway into the determinist camp. He was axiomatically critical of all capitalist organizations but argued that the problem lay in the issue of ownership not control: once the capitalists had been removed then rational organizations of the type avowed by Taylor could equally well serve the communist state.

Lenin's position is, to say the least, ambiguous. His arguments in *State and Revolution* suggest that organizational control would rest with local soviets but in almost all his other work control is restricted to the Bolshevik Party 'on behalf of' the working class. His admiration for the technocratic essence of Taylorism was clear:

> The Taylor system, the last word of capitalism in this respect, like all capitalist progress, is a combination of the refined brutality of bourgeois exploitation and a number of the greatest scientific achievements in the field of analysing mechanical motions during work. . . . We must organize in Russia the study and teaching of the Taylor system. (Lenin, 1968c: 413–14)

Rational organization for Lenin, then, was not a matter of interpretation any more than Marxism was a partial viewpoint – both represented the truth and both represented the only permanent solution to the contemporary organizational problems of capitalism. Given Lenin's previous insistence on the ineradicably capitalist nature of the state (1968b), and the need to dismantle it completely, his assumption about the neutrality of work organizations is astonishingly naive, and a disaster for the future direction of the Soviet state.

The Soviet experiment in atheist government was heading back down the road of the time and motion expert, having expropriated the capitalists and therefore apparently solved the problem of the alienated worker. Across the Bering Strait American capitalists were heading in a rather different direction towards the same goal: the maladjusted worker was about to make another appearance, this time not in a solo part in a psychological drama written by Myers, nor in a collective polemic directed by Lenin, but as part of small and irrational team production. Human relations and the social group were about to be written into the folklore of industrial and organizational sociology.

Human relations

Although, as we shall see in the next chapter, Taylorism faced stiff opposition from workers, managers and the American state, the movement towards a more scientific assessment of organizations in the USA did continue in particular enterprises, though without the kind of national research centre as provided by the National Institute of Industrial Psychology in Britain. One of the more enlightened businesses interested in experimental research was the Western Electric Company's Hawthorne plant at Chicago (Roethlisberger and Dickson, 1939), where 29,000 employees, representing sixty nationalities, produced telephone equipment for the Bell system. There is some doubt over exactly who was responsible for the research, and the part played by Mayo, but this has only marginal significance for our purposes (Rose, 1975: cf. J.H. Smith, 1987). What is more important is to note that although the motivational models eventually developed from the Taylorist and human relations schools were very different, the former being *homo economicus*, as opposed to the latter's *homo gregarious* (and Marx's *homo faber*), the technical features of Taylorism did not necessarily contradict the social implications of human relations; they were both technocratic in orientation with the human relations approach being more critical only in so far as it rejected Taylorist models of organizational efficiency: social interaction not money was the primary motivator at work.

There were obviously some tensions between them, besides the different motivational theories, and one was whether to facilitate or outlaw social groups, but the two were not diametrically opposed. It could be argued that the two models are linked in a more direct way, in so far as the results of Taylor's extension of the division of labour and its consequential destruction of 'inherent' interest for workers left the human relations approach to pick up the pieces and compensate for the loss of alleged intrinsic job interest with social stimulation. In this vein Sievers (1984) argues that motivation becomes an issue only when meaning is eliminated from jobs. There are three related problems with this. First, it still poses a romantic notion of work; that is, that at some indeterminate time all jobs had intrinsic interest. Second, it also misdirects attention wholly on to the job itself, when the situation within which the job is executed is also important in defining the nature of that intrinsic interest. Third, activities do not have 'intrinsic' interests in the sense that they can be objectively assessed in isolation from the person undertaking the job: job 'interests' are what the worker derives through interaction with materials etc., they do not sit 'within' materials waiting to be released. Thus it is the interaction and the interpretation of that interaction which should be considered in establishing forms of job interest. To take an example, building a television may be experienced as intrinsically interesting or inherently tedious but which of these is the case depends not upon the task of building but the interpretation of the builder and the persuasive powers of those attempting to make the task appear interesting or tedious.

Such interpretative concerns were not regarded as problems for the Hawthorne researchers, and the initial experiments, begun in 1924 in conjunction with the National Research Council of the National Academy of Sciences, assessed the conditions of work, monotony and fatigue, particularly in response to lighting variations. However, the results appeared so mystifying that Roethlisberger, from Harvard Graduate School of Business Administration, in association with Mayo (also from Harvard), and Dickson from the Hawthorne Employee Relations Department, set up a series of further experiments that were to take until 1932 to complete.

The 'illumination experiments' suggested that 'efficiency increased more or less continuously . . . but not as a sole function of illumination' (Roethlisberger and Dickson, 1939: 14–15). Indeed, the lighting of one group was systematically lowered such that only when the workers could not actually see what they were doing did the productivity rate stop rising and begin to fall. Finally, the lighting system was left stable while electricians merely pretended to increase or decrease the lighting. Although the workers praised the 'brighter' lighting, and complained when it got 'darker', no actual change took place and productivity remained stable. The conclusion which the department came to was basically one of perplexity, at which point they called in the Harvard academics. Over the next few years the experiments changed from lighting to include, among other things, variations in work rates, rest pauses, payment methods and hours. The Relay Assembly Test Room experiments involved selected groups of six women and their variations in output were charted by a single observer. Once again, productivity increases were recorded that bore markedly little connection to specific forms of variation in inputs. Two other experimental groups were inaugurated but these were discontinued after conflict developed both within the groups and between them and the rest of the workforce.

Ignoring the problematic results of these two latter groups, and the forced removal of two of the original six women in the first 'successful' group, one conclusion is of great significance: the work group was responding not to variations in conditions etc., but to the very fact of being treated as an experimental group with consequential high status. Moreover, they actually appeared to be reacting in the way they thought they were supposed to react: what became known as the 'Hawthorne Effect'. Although Roethlisberger and colleagues played this down (1939: 526–31), it was very significant for the time and motion studies then developing under Taylor's scientific management because it implied that observation of workers would not necessarily provide an accurate account of what normally happened. Instead, the very act of observation would alter the activity being measured, a human version of Heisenberg's Uncertainty Principle. Hence, although the human relations school considered themselves to be within what has been termed the deterministic axis, their 'science' of measuring human behaviour actually appeared much more like a game of estimation.

Clearly, not every group could be so treated but the major conclusion of the research team themselves was to be more significant in the resolution of organizational problems: the experience of working in a closely knit social group was, in itself, a direct boost to productivity. Second, although officially just an observer, the recorder had become a 'surrogate supervisor' acting on behalf of the work group. The implication of this was that supervisors would play a crucial role in mediating between the demands of the company and the desires of the worker group. Third, and relatedly, the productivity increases provided evidence of the 'latent energy' which work groups normally withheld through what the team called their 'non-logical sentiments' but which could only be released through the right kind of management. Fourth, despite the radical implications of the assessment there were many issues that remained problematic. In particular, did solidaristic work groups necessarily cohere in the pursuit of objectives that the company found acceptable? or did the troublesome elements in the experiments suggest that group solidarity was, if not inherently problematic as Taylor argued, at the very least a double-edged sword? For all the claims of 'social integration', what the human relations school was really talking about was 'social engineering': another form of technocratic theory and practice.

The first practical response of the company was to investigate in more detail the nature of company morale and the role of supervision, since this seemed to be a critical feature of sustaining efficiency. Consequently, the next stage of the experiments involved interviewing some 1,600 employees over the winter of 1928–9. The results suggested that the research programme itself was having beneficial effects on the morale of the employees, and the interview schedule was expanded to include 10,300 employees in 1929 and 21,126 in 1932. Subsequently, the general economic collapse led to massive redundancies and the interview programme was wound down. Nevertheless, the data, which in 1929 alone included 40,000 comments, was utilized in a series of supervisory training schemes. Employees' complaints were also channelled back to the appropriate department and the researchers spoke of the cathartic effects of employee interviews. As the report noted: 'it was thought that many adverse attitudes had been improved by these emotional "abreactions" which the interviews afforded' (Roethlisberger and Dickson, 1939: 228). Yet the interview schedule was not regarded as a success, and one of the reasons may well be that it highlighted a strong link between attitudes to work and the wider social attachments outside the plant, especially the early socialization of individuals, which the company was powerless to affect. Here, then, we can perceive an incipient critical approach to organizations but one which was ultimately stillborn: the employment situation cannot be analysed solely by reference to itself – the links between the domestic and the employment situation are crucial.

The final stage in the research programme was aimed at a detailed investigation of a small group, using anthropological methods to try and ascertain the 'more subtle and spontaneous aspects of the employees' social organization' (p. 376). This involved a group of fourteen men being closely observed for six months between 1931 and 1932. No environmental conditions were altered in this Bank Wiring Observation Room experiment but a rather complicated group bonus scheme was introduced. In the event the group appeared to limit their production to their group interpretation of 'a good day's work': 'the bogey'. This social norm did not just restrict the maximum output but ensured a minimum output too, as well as involving the fiddling of output records to maintain the norm. Where such norms were threatened, enforcement was usually restricted to verbal encouragement or threat: one of the inspectors who insisted on accurate recordings of work left after being threatened with 'a punch in the nose'.

In fact, one of the issues that became clarified later was that few of the workers really understood the group incentive scheme. The report concluded that the men were operating along non-logical sentiments and that, however problematic this was for increasing organizational efficiency, it clearly demonstrated the significance of the informal organization of work. Equally significant, the research had revealed the power of the 'logic of sentiments' as opposed to the 'logics of cost and efficiency'. Workers were stimulated by sentiments such as 'fairness' and the 'right to work', while managers and supervisors were more likely to be more concerned with the 'logics of cost and efficiency' because of their 'particular concrete situation' (p. 565). Management's, and particularly personnel managers', skill lay in channelling the logic of sentiments so that it paralleled, rather than contradicted, the logic of cost and efficiency. It was Mayo, rather than Roethlisberger and Dickson, who interpreted this in Durkheimian fashion as the call of the isolated individual to be bound into the collective; to replace the traditional bonds of community, now disrupted by the ever-increasing division of labour, with the new sinews of socially manipulated work groups. The integration of the individual through her or his subordination to the group, controlled and facilitated by expert managers, was the way forward. More alarmingly, Mayo linked the non-logical sentiments of the mass into a blend of elitist social engineering in a way that mirrored some of the fascist ideas then sprouting in Italy and Germany. Conformity to elite-inspired norms was the normal path for the mass of non-rational subordinates in organizations who would only become anxious if left to decide for themselves. In short, although the attitudes of the workers appeared unpredictable, this merely made the task of the manager more concerned with rooting out such contingencies and ensuring the direction of organizations could be determined by expert managers. Conflict and disharmony were not examples of inherently conflictual situations but of maladjustment; as Nik Rose argues: 'The minutiae of the human soul

. . . had emerged as a new domain for management . . . management could represent its authority as neutral, rational and in the workers' interest' (1989: 71–2). Ironically, it is dubious whether management actually needed to: the worldwide inter-war depression, and in Britain the catastrophe of the General Strike, probably ensured that few employees were willing to question too closely the legitimacy of their bosses' claims to authority on the basis of expertise.

In America the pattern of counselling set up in Hawthorne and repeated elsewhere eventually led to a massive government intervention to sustain employee morale. By 1945 over 20 per cent of American psychologists were engaged directly in such efforts (Jacoby, 1988: 78). However, the end of the war left the new school of human relations experts to pick up the pieces just where they had fallen before the war.

Neo-human relations

With the cessation of hostilities some of the ideas relating to the significance of social cohesion and the processes of the unconscious were fused in a new model of human relations on both sides of the Atlantic: by 1954 over 40 per cent of large US companies had introduced mass attitude surveys of their employees (though by 1981 this had barely changed to 45 per cent). Even General Motors was caught up in the enthusiasm: in 1947 it introduced a competition among its employees for the best essay in response to the question: 'My Job and Why I like it.' Most of the surveys were conducted without union knowledge or approval (Jacoby, 1988: 79–84). One branch of this eventually surfaced as sociotechnical systems from the psychoanalytic interests of the Tavistock Institute of Human Relations, which is discussed in chapter 8. The other branch, and the one more directly derived from the technocratic pragmatic of Mayo et al., began by rejecting the simplistic models of human social behaviour drawn by the early Human Relations studies. The human model now moved from *homo gregarious* to *homo actualis* (Managerialist): self-actualization, courtesy of the management, was the new order of the day, but the day remained technocratically organized and the arguments retained the air of a scientifically determined model rather than a sketch drawn around the interpretative actions of humans.

As McGregor, one of the leading lights of the neo-human relations school, concluded on the activities of the inter-war period: 'during this period the human side of enterprise has become a major preoccupation of management. The lot of the industrial employee . . . has improved to a degree which can hardly have been imagined by his counterpart of the 1920s . . . *but it has done all these things without changing its fundamental theory of management*' (1984: 325) (original emphasis). McGregor's complaint was not that management had simply been technocratic or instrumental in its adoption of humanistic policies. On the contrary, his concern was that many of the humanistic schemes, like 'permissive management', 'industrial democracy' and organizational 'peace' were simply unworkable; they were pendulum reactions to the previously autocratic methods of control. Neither worked, but human relations had established one possible alternative organizing principle to overt coercion: integration through self-actualization. Moreover, 'the model of the successful manager in our culture is a masculine one. He is not feminine; he is not soft or yielding or dependent or intuitive in the womanly sense. The very expression of emotion is widely viewed as a feminine weakness that would interfere with effective business processes' (McGregor, quoted in Basoux, 1987). The current vogue for intuitive thought and 'responsive' management, heralded by the likes of Peters and Waterman which I discuss below, could not be a better example of an apparent managerial inversion that leaves the technocratic status perfectly intact.

McGregor argued that traditionally firms were organized along what he termed Theory X principles: first, that most people had an inherent dislike of work; second, because of this, coercion of some variety was necessary to ensure compliance at work; third, most people preferred to be controlled than to have autonomy. This drew loosely on Maslow's (1943) motivational theory, which asserted that a hierarchy of needs existed with the physical needs at the base, moving through safety, love, esteem and ultimately self-actualization. In essence, McGregor asserted that Theory X neglected the dynamic nature of human needs, for as economic rewards satisfied material needs, so other, higher, needs were ignited and a concomitantly higher form of motivation was necessary. Thus, motivation becomes increasingly difficult because Theory X firms have no provision for coping with the new, higher needs of contemporary workers. McGregor argues, paradoxically, that the very success of capitalist management in the provision of high living standards undermined the only motivator it had consistently used: when nobody starved any more the provision of wages, in itself, was of little motivational value. But this is to assume that, at a given level, material demands stop rising, and also that universal human needs exist rather than, as discussed in chapter 1, needs which are socially and culturally constructed and hence transient.

The problem, as far as McGregor sees it, has a parallel with the pattern of human socialization. Adopting Argyris's (1957) notions of child/adult responsibilities, he notes that whereas individual development is premised upon the gradual accretion of responsibilities, organizations adopting Theory X principles provide only the very limited responsibilities associated with childhood: the result is childish behaviour by adult employees frustrated at their treatment by the employers.

Theory Y attempts to resolve these motivational and behavioural problems by generating a radically different set of basic assumptions: first, work is not disliked by everyone; second, coercion is not the only motivator; third, it is possible to provide organizational goals that fulfil the highest motivator – self-actualization; fourth, responsible behaviour is a result of trust, and the avoidance of responsibility is a reaction to experiences that deny responsibility; fifth, creativity is widely dispersed throughout the population, even if few jobs require it (McGregor, 1984: 326–7). McGregor concludes that management's task is to develop 'integrating' organizational procedures through which individuals can realize themselves through achieving organizational goals, that is the goals as specified by management. It is significant, then, that McGregor's schema is axiomatically technocratic; it is little more than sophisticated social engineering. The concern is not with creating a society in which individuals can realize themselves but with redeveloping managerial strategies, such that the latent energies so dear to human relations approaches can be directed more accurately towards managerially defined goals. Only if employees' goals coincide with managerial goals can they legitimately be pursued within the context of the organization.

Equally technocratic, and also mildly deterministic, are the ideas of another of the neo-human relations school, Herzberg (1966). His argument is similarly locked into motivational theories and reworks the problems of hierarchy of motivation into a dualism: hygiene and motivational factors. Hygiene factors, like the conditions, material rewards and security of work, are negative motivators in so far as their absence decreases productivity while their presence is merely the precondition for higher productivity. This has to be achieved through the positive motivation factors, which are symbolic and psychological rather than material, like status, advancement, intrinsic job interest etc. It is not clear why a dissatisfying job content should not be considered an element of the hygiene side, since this appears elsewhere to decrease levels of productivity (Lawler, 1973). In short, the new human relations may appear to have been sculpted from the clay of self-actualization rather than the old model of group relations but the original mould was still struck in technocratic bronze. Self-realization was only thought viable via the managerial route to organizational success.

What were the effects of this reworking of human relations? After all, although the general concern for social underpinnings and motivational complexities of work were irredeemably technocratic and managerialist in origin and orientation, the ideas might have been suggestive enough to introduce in and of themselves. The point that work cannot eliminate underlying contradictions of interest, and therefore can never be totally harmonious, should not have worried hardheaded personnel managers eager for a long-term solution to the problem of worker motivation. So what happened? Again, we have to make a clear distinction between developments within organizational theory and the common experiences of organizations: while academics and consultants battled away with their pens and clients, the reality of organizational life took a rather different turn. The apparently terminal crisis facing British industry at the time these works were published in the 1960s, wracked as it appeared to be by unofficial industrial action and declining efficiency, tended to smother the search for radical, let alone ostensibly humanist, personnel strategies. Batstone (1988a: 60–4) makes clear that although British personnel managers developed from the oppositional poles of welfare work and conventional management, by the time the neo-human relations material was available, the technocratic or orthodox management proxy role had already won out over the softer welfare approach. British management was then, as it had always been and predominantly still is, relatively unconcerned by labour relations or personnel issues that affect organizations: finance and fire fighting seem to be the twin pillars of interests (Batstone, 1988a: 64–71).

In many ways this may seem counter-productive to organizational efficiency but the hard-nosed British approach may be very practical. After all, despite claims to the contrary (Blumberg, 1968), there is precious little unambiguous evidence of a direct link between job satisfaction and work performance (Kelly, 1982), even if there is some for a link between dissatisfaction, absenteeism and labour turnover (Lawler, 1973). Moreover, it may be that managerial concern for ensuring harmonious social relations at work actually inhibits the time available for work concerned with improving products, acquiring customers and suchlike (Zaleznik, 1989). As Drucker noted 40 years ago: 'the main function and purpose of the enterprise is the production of goods, not the governance of men. Its governmental authority over men must always be subordinated to its economic performance and responsibility' (Drucker, 1951: 81). It should be noted, however, that many of the neo-human relations approaches may be more viable in the USA, where the limited nature of public health care and welfare makes in-house schemes more attractive to employees than they would be in Britain (Sloan et al., 1987). Yet it remains an irony in both countries that despite a succession of analyses that fail to establish this causal link between morale and productivity, most managers, most of the time, appear to believe there is one (Jacoby, 1988: 88). It is this kind of faith that aided the generation of a new form of 'organizational fundamentalism': organizational culture.

Organizational cultures

The assumption that management is merely the pursuit of rationality implies that rational choice, or as management gurus prefer to call it, strategic planning, is the solution to organizational problems. Yet the necessarily interpretative, contingent and discontinuous nature of business life makes such strategic planning today – and its progenitor, Fayol's functional structure and planning – utopian ideals. As Mintzberg has suggested, 'we have no techniques for predicting discontinuities, we can only extrapolate' (1989). Such extrapolations can become less contingent, according to the faithful of the organizational culture school, if we are able to analyse the culture and ensure it corresponds to organizational strategy. In short, organizations work best where members' and organizations' beliefs, actions and goals are mutually compatible.

A primary extrapolation from the work of this culturalist approach is derived from Durkheimian concerns for organizational solidarity through ideological consensus and from Mayo's postulations on the intimate links between the emotional needs of individuals and the organizational need for integration. Typically the approach is interpretative to the extent that organizations are free to interpret and develop a specific form of culture, though it should be noted that many of the 'best seller' approaches to the culture of success tend to assume that senior management's articulation of their company culture is identical with the actual culture itself – assuming that only one culture exists (Carroll, 1983; Alvesson, 1987). In fact one of the basic problems with this entire approach lies in its technocratic design: it is intended not so much to explain what the contemporary culture of an organization *is* but what it *should be*. Thus it operates along a pragmatic, if not a utopian, line of operation: changing the organization in a direction designed to facilitate efficiency rather than accounting for the current form of culture and assessing its significance. This is also problematic in that it may well persuade managers to act *as if* the preferred cultural attributes already existed, such that the acting out of a cultural myth becomes the organizational reality. Unless we really believe that all organizations claiming to be excellent are just that, then we should be wary of many such culturalist approaches. The current trend in which corporations formalize their cultures through explicit statements, which members are supposed to read and inwardly digest, implies that such formulations *create* cultures as much as *reflect* already existing ones (cf. Lorsch, 1986; Hassard and Sharifi, 1989).

A less manipulative approach to the significance of organizational cultures is provided by Handy (1985). He distinguishes between four types: power, role, task-based and person. Power cultures are symbolized by a concentric ring or web where key individuals radiate power from the centre and rely upon trust not rules for their control over the organization. Role cultures are typically to be found in bureaucracies; they exude rationality, specialization, procedures and rule following. Task cultures are primarily job- or project-oriented, represented by matrix organizations where flexibility and decentralized control prevails. Finally, person cultures exist where the individual is the focus of the organization, and Handy argues that while this exists within families, communes and small groups its significance is limited within conventional business organizations. Precisely how these various cultures evolve is related to the interrelationship between six major influencing factors: history and ownership, size, technology, goals and objectives, the environment, and the people. Generally speaking, Handy argues that the larger an organization, the more routine its environment, and the more interdependent and expensive its technology, the more likely it will be to adopt a role culture. Where the technology and environment changes rapidly and where the goals of the organization are rapid growth, then a power or task-based culture will tend to predominate. The result is that 'different cultures call for differing psychological contracts, and that certain types of people will be happy and successful in one culture but not in another' (Handy, 1985: 204). Culture then becomes the glue holding an organization together; it is the Durkheimian social cement without which no social group can exist.

However, rather than taking culture as the glue holding the organization together, it might be more appropriate to regard it as the result of social action. That is, culture does not cause people in organizations to act in specific ways, rather culture is generated by certain individuals defining some forms of action as representative of the 'official' organizational culture. A consideration of two of Handy's cultural types will suffice for my purposes here: role culture and power culture.

Power culture exists where organizational power/control is in the hands of an individual or a small elite: in Handy's phrase 'This culture depends on a central power source, with rays of power and influence spreading out from that central figure' (1985: 189). In short, a leader's power causes others to act. Yet when such a leader does 'exert power' it is subordinate others, not the leader, who engage in action. If the subordinates do not act then the leader has no power; only as a *consequence* of subordinate actions can leaders be deemed to have power. Thus power is a consequence of action, rather than a cause of action. This shift from the 'principle' of power to the 'practice' of power, as

Latour (1986) calls it, also implies that subordinate action occurs only through the interpretation of self-advantage by the subordinate. In turn, it is likely that the command of the leader will become distorted through what Latour calls the 'translation' process: not only are leaders dependent upon their subordinates but a subordinate's translation of the edict may well prove to be a distortion of the leader's intention. The implication of this for Handy's power culture model is that rather than the rays of power spreading out from the centre to the periphery in a determinate and unmediated fashion they are both highly contingent and the subject of constant interpretation and renegotiation. Such a revision enables us to cope rather better, for example, with some of the radical changes in the recent political history of Europe. The position of East European communist leaders and their structures of power did not change dramatically between 1988 and 1989 but the willingness of the subordinate population to obey them certainly did: their former power was a consequence of the populations' subordination not a cause of it.

The second of Handy's types, role culture, is epitomized by rule-based action – a bureaucracy. In theory, once we know the rule the action is determined by it. But again, this implies that the culture explains the organization. However, rules are inherently ambiguous: there can never be enough rules to cover every contingency nor are rules self-explanatory – we need rules to explain which rule to apply and to interpret the meaning of each rule *ad infinitum*. It is for just this reason that 'working to rule' – which should mean working as effectively as possible – leads to the development of grossly inefficient working practices. Rules, then, may be conceived of not as determinants of action but as *post hoc* rationalizations, as resources to justify action already taken. Again, the implications of this interpretative approach are profoundly disturbing to any assumption that role cultures provide for rule-bound behaviour.

This does not mean that analysing culture is an unimportant aspect of organizational theory, though it could be argued that the entire technocratic approach is of greater importance as a manifestation of dominant culture than any inter-organizational differences which may appear to exist (Alvesson, 1987: 213). Analysing the sellers of cultural excellence also provides insights into organizations and organizational consultants; but believing what organizational consultants claim, without assessing their empirical evidence, is tantamount to establishing a new school of organizational thought: what might be called the HLS (Hook, Line and Sinker) outlook. Relatedly, we should acknowledge the implication of adopting organizational myths as a symbol of corporate culture. As Bowles (1989) argues, such organizational myths embody attempts to generate an organizational belief system not too distant from those previously erected by religious groups: the myth of the corporate executive who subordinates everything to the greater good of the corporation acts both to inspire resemblant behaviour and to inculcate a body of executives whose allegiance is close to that of religious disciples. It may well be that few blue- or white-collar workers are drawn into the same level of 'dependence', despite (or perhaps because of) the best efforts of corporate managers to instil enthusiasm through company songs and collective company physical jerks, but the allegiance or pragmatic acquiescence of these groups may be acquired through other means. Just as dominant ideologies are crucial for the dominant, not the dominated groups (Abercrombie et al., 1980), so too the proselytizing essence of corporate enculturers is aimed primarily at corporate controllers not employees.

Critical theories

At the critical pole of the technocratic–critical continuum, towards the opposite end to the organizational cultures school discussed above, lie a collection of theories labelled critical theories. Whereas the organizational culture approach tends to assume that efficiency and rationality are uncontestable concepts that are axiomatically linked to the pursuit of a managerially inspired culture, the critical approach denies the rationality of the entire framework of capitalism. Much of the original work was undertaken by Marcuse (1964, 1969), and his starting point was one which situates capitalism itself as a form of 'technological rationality'. Technological rationality represents an instrumental and technologically determined approach to life and nature; all human problems are perceived as reducible to technological solutions with the result that what little debate exists focuses not on the ends of human society but the means to achieve a pre-given, normative end: the expansion of capitalism. Thought, under advanced capitalism, then, becomes one-dimensional, that is non-critical: it takes for granted that we should organize social institutions such as work in a way calculated to exploit, rather than nurture, natural resources; it takes for granted that there is no alternative to the status quo: organizations are, therefore, perceived to be 'naturally' hierarchical and authoritarian. Moreover, the system becomes self-reproducing in so far as it swamps all potential criticism in a sea of commodities: the 'good life' can be measured in the ownership of an ever-increasing supply of material goods, not an ever-increasing degree of self-actualization and democratic control over society.

Habermas (1970, 1971), the other major theorist within this approach, argues that human activity can be differentiated into 'purposive rational' action or work, and 'symbolic interaction' or 'communicative action'. The former is concerned, among other things, with material production which is based upon technical rules, while the latter is concerned with social and cultural life governed by socially constructed norms. According to Habermas the two different systems of thought become conflated to the extent that the critical aspects of symbolic interaction become subsumed under the purposive-rational systems. In other words, and translating these ideas very loosely, the critical aspects of organizational theory become suppressed by the technocratic aspects.

Neither Habermas nor Marcuse was overtly concerned with analysing individual organizations *per se*, and much of the recent work most directly related to this form of approach has been undertaken by Burrell and Morgan (1979), Clegg and Dunkerley (1980), Alvesson (1987) and Alvesson and Willmott (1992). Perhaps the most useful summary can be constructed from the model provided by Alvesson in his chapter 'Six Theses for a Critical Organization Theory' (1987).

First, there is a permanent source of tension in organizations between two contrasting rationalities: technological rationality seeks to maximize resources and minimize shortages; its opposite (which Alvesson calls 'practical reason') seeks to maximize freedom and minimize repression. Second, the dominance of technological rationality over the operational process corresponds to the interests of the predominant social strata. Third, technological rationality involves an ideology that systematically distorts the reality generated by itself. Fourth, an organizational practice which corresponds to the mental make-up of humans as well as to the interests of the majority must break with the supremacy of technological rationality. Fifth, business organizations etc. are instruments for reproducing technological rationality which, in turn, they depend on. Sixth, the functioning of organizations must be comprehended within the compass of that rationality which dominates the given historical and social context.

Several features of this list call for comment. The first point is accurate in so far as a tension does exist between differing rationalities. However, it is questionable whether just two rationalities are involved here. There is a considerable amount of empirical evidence to suggest that many people operate with multiple and internally conflicting rationalities such that the Manichaean 'either or' model of Alvesson may be a useful way of posing the extreme opposites but should not be taken to represent the two oppositional empirical norms (Mann, 1970; Held, 1984). Second, the correspondence between technological rationality and the dominant social strata should be seen as something which needs to be permanently reproduced, a contingent issue, rather than something which is itself taken for granted. That is not to say that the technological rationality of the dominant social group is permanently threatened but it is the case, for example, that the recent popularity of green issues poses a considerable threat to them. Third, the distorting effects of the ideology of technological rationality are undoubtedly influential but do not appear all-encompassing. If they were, then green politics would never emerge and the very idea of critical organization theory would have been stillborn. Fourth, claims about the mental make-up of humans and the unarticulated interests of the majority should always be treated with considerable caution. If, as argued in chapter 1, the needs of humans are socially constructed rather than innate dispositions, then such claims cannot be justified. Indeed, such claims are, like Marcuse's critique, a direct mirror image of the technocratic arguments: managerialists would have us believe that the interests of all society are exactly equivalent to theirs; some critical theorists would have us believe that our interests are being misrepresented by the managerialists – but not by critical theorists.

In sum, the critical theorists' criticisms of technocratic theories highlight the distortions and misrepresentations of human interest as reducible to the interests of managers. But equally problematic are the attempts by some critical theorists, and for that matter all other attempts, to impose or impute a set of universal interests upon humanity.

Systems theories

Around six years before Marcuse was to decry the absence of critical thought and the suppression of conflict in capitalist society, Dunlop was attempting to ensure that the fledgling discipline of industrial relations strenuously avoided any mention of the conflictual approach which he perceived to be rampant in industrial sociology at the time. It is ironic that while some of the critical theorists also decried the movement towards systems or holistic models of society, one of their number, Habermas, was himself to adopt and adapt systems theory to his own radical ends.

It has long been a tradition within many fields of study to explain phenomena through 'analysis', that is breaking up the whole into discrete elements for the purposes of clearer argument. One particularly successful movement in the opposite direction – towards a synthetic all-embracing theory – was 'systems theory'. Although elements of such an approach have been around from the beginning of the twentieth century, the first systematic approach was that of Bertalanffy in a series of articles in the 1950s and 1960s (1981). However, the more conventional route of systems theory into the sociology of work and organizations has been, paradoxically, via the work of Dunlop (1958). Dunlop adopted the Parsonian convention that rule-bound behaviour was the key explanatory category, and that these rules encompassed all major actors within the industrial relations system: unions, management and government. In turn, these groups are locked together by a normative consensus which, among other things (technology and markets), assumes that power analysis is beyond the scope of industrial relations theory (Roche, 1986). As Roche makes clear, not only is the removal of power a debilitating elision, but there is no reason why rule-making cannot exist outside a normative consensus. Indeed, it could well be argued that the reverse applies since a consensus implies that rules are less necessary, at least in any overt or coercive form, while disagreements may require precisely such a form of constraint via rules if the disputes are not to lead to serious conflict.

Systems theory asserts that it is the relationships and interactions between elements which explain the behaviour of the whole. Indeed, the systems approach is not only technocratic in its denial of conflicting ideologies and material interests but also deterministic in its pursuit of the correct prediction of behaviour through an analysis of organizational rules. Closed systems, such as central heating systems, are virtually internally self-regulating, and all the elements are mutually dependent. Open systems, however, are necessarily dependent upon the wider environment with which they interact. Hence, open systems are less stable than closed systems even though an explanation of the behaviour of the whole is still dependent upon the relationships between the sub-systems. For example, the behaviour of an organization is not wholly dependent upon the character of the director or the movements of the markets but on the way all the elements of the system interact with each other and in relation to the external environment.

Systems theorists, in their pursuit of holistic explanations, have often tended to mirror the conservative emphasis of evolutionary theories which highlight the significance of organizations and individuals reacting to, rather than actively constructing, their environment. That is, if organizations are merely reactive to changes in environments then they have little capacity to change radically in any proactive stance: they cannot change themselves except in so far as environmental change demands specific and functional forms of evolutionary change. However, not only is the evolutionary, environmental and functional emphasis misplaced – because social institutions can actually generate their own environments or at least change them as well as being changed by them – it is also inherently flawed because functionalism inverts the logic of cause and effect by assuming that effects lead to causes (see Giddens, 1977; Craib, 1984). In fact, the conservative label is not necessarily deserved. Even if most systems approaches have been concerned to explain how disequilibriums need to be resolved in favour of organizational equilibrium there are several writers whose interests lie in a much more radical development. Thus the works of Habermas (1970), Wallerstein (1974, 1979) and Baumgartner, Burns and DeVille (1979) can all be categorized as radical systems theorists.

Four forms of criticism tend to be mounted against systems theory. First, it reifies organizations. That is, it imputes animate needs to inanimate objects. To assert that an organization needs to find an equilibrium implies that organizations have needs. But organizations are merely legal institutions, they have no existence beyond their human members whose relationships bind an organization into existence. Thus, when we talk of organizations 'needing' something we really mean that some or all of the human elements of an organization need it. Furthermore, we usually mean that the human actors in control of the organization, the ones who articulate and represent allegedly organizational needs, are the ones whose needs are really being demonstrated.

The second and related criticism of systems theory concerns the nature of organizational stability. Even if we accept a degree of dynamism into the equilibrium it is still doubtful whether most organizations are stable across time. A mere reference to the British economy in the 1980s and 1990s would suggest that given the manufacturing collapse of the 1979–82 period, the stock market seesaws of October 1987 and 1989, and the record levels of bankruptcies, new businesses and mergers, the last label to describe the system as a whole, or the individual system elements, would be 'stable'.

Third, systems theories, at least within the organizational field, tend to take an ahistorical line. That is to say, they take for granted the prior development of systems and sub-systems to the extent that historical imbalances of power between groups, for example, are irrelevant to explaining their contemporary relations. This is akin to arguing that the present position of women in work organizations has nothing to do with their historically generated subordination. Obviously, not all systems theorists are guilty of this misunderstanding of the significance of history (Wallerstein's (1974, 1979) world systems theory being soaked in historical argument) but many of the pragmatic accounts are.

Fourth, the essential thrust of systems analysis is towards the development of integration and consensus. The explanation of disintegration and dissensus, therefore, requires some form of pathological or dysfunctional argument. Yet, as we shall discover below, it may be that disintegration and dissensus are the norm rather than atypical; for humans may thrive not on uniformity but disunity. If this is the case then the whole foundation stone of conventional, that is conservative, systems theory is subject to a terminal form of cancer (Cooper, 1986).

Systems theory, then, at least in its traditional conservative form, represents an approach that appears to be inherently deterministic and generally, though not wholly, technocratic. On the other hand the assumption that the links between ostensibly unrelated phenomena and institutions need to be assessed, that such a system may be inherently unstable, that it has a history, that little consensus exists, and that rules are resources for, not determinants of, action, all have some role in the development of Actor Networks which are discussed later. The idea of an interlocking system is not inherently flawed but the practical adoption of such an idea within conventional systems theory is. It was from just this latter kind of complaint that contingency theory developed.

Contingency theory

Contingency theory has probably proved to be the most influential of all organizational theories – at least until the organizational culture approach hit the bookstores. Its origins lie in the work of Burns and Stalker (1961), Lawrence and Lorsch (1967), and the Aston Studies (Pugh and Hickson, 1976). It was overtly technocratic in approach and attempted to reduce the infinity of information implied in the systems approach down to a manageable level. It did this by focusing upon a delimited number of specific management problems, such as the management structure, the issue of leadership, organizational bottlenecks etc. Such problems and their appropriate solutions were regarded as contingent upon a small number of variables.

There was not, at least according to contingency theorists, a 'single best way' to resolve organizational problems but then neither did management have the freedom to do whatever it liked. The label 'contingency' does not imply an increasing level of freedom for actors, based upon the significance of the interpretative act, but actually seeks to eliminate such 'freedom'. In the words of Greenwood et al.:

> Contingency theory rests upon the assumption that organizational characteristics have to be shaped to meet situational circumstances. The extent to which any organization secures a 'goodness of fit' between situational characteristics and structural characteristics will determine the level of organizational performance. (quoted in Lee and Lawrence, 1985: 38–9)

Where the contingency approach is most vulnerable to criticism, and why it sits very close to the determinist line, is in its construction of independent variables. This is most clearly shown in Woodward's (1958) account of organizational performance among manufacturing plants in the south-east of England. Woodward argued that although some degree of contingency existed, in so far as managers could choose between different forms of organizational structure, only those who chose the most 'appropriate' structure – as determined by the technology of production – were likely to be successful. Thus contingency does not really relate to unrestricted choice nor to the level of uncertainty. In fact, the argument is one which attempts to remove contingency by specifying the conditions under which the success of particular organizations can be determined. Similarly, Lawrence's and Lorsch's (1967) argument focuses on the way the internal structure of a manufacturing organization is determined by the level of contingency which exists in the product market: the higher the level of product market uncertainty the greater the need for a flexible, or 'differentiated' internal structure.

However, the most meticulous contingency study, and the one which best illustrates its problems, is the Aston approach of Pugh and Hickson (1976). This study distinguished between a sequence of independent variables – such as the pattern of ownership and control, the size, goals, technology, location, resources and level of interdependence with other organizations – and a series of dependent variables. These included the division of labour, level of bureaucratization, the extent of the formalization of communications, and the centralization and shape of the power structure. The relationship between the independent and the dependent variables was analysed through a stream of (mainly) quantitative data which suggested that size, technology and location were the three most significant factors affecting organizational performance. Yet, for all the effort and claimed 'objectivity' of this approach it is not self-evident that the choice of variables was objectively well founded, nor what exactly the statistical correlations were supposed to mean (Lee and Lawrence, 1985: 47).

The critical issue here is the meaning of 'contingency': although the label is used freely, it would appear that the element of contingency is directly related to – in fact determined by – variables which are independent of the organization. Thus it would seem that environmental factors actually determine the nature of the organization; albeit the specific organizational structure is contingent upon the exact mix of environmental influences. In short, human actors appear to play little part in much contingency theory (cf. Donaldson, 1985b). It was for this reason that some academics began to explore the value of an analysis that rescued the subjective and active side of organizations from the clutches of the determinists; this was to be the action approach.

Action theory

While systems theorists attempted to model some of their ideas on the natural sciences, and especially the deterministic engineering model which has adopted the systems approach most fully (Open Systems Group, 1981), other organizational sociologists were moving sharply in the opposite direction: towards a model where contingency, not determinism, was the 'default' category. In practice, action theory tended to remain in the province of sociology while contingency theory sprouted among the organizational behaviourists and the business schools.

One of the most notable attempts to develop such an alternative in the sociology discipline was Silverman's (1970) pursuit of an action theory drawn from the combined works of Weber, Schutz and Berger. Silverman argued that the social sciences were different orders of subject matter and thus, although the approach of both should be rigorous, their methods would be necessarily dissimilar. In particular, sociology was concerned with understanding rather than observing behaviour – the distinction being critical in so far as it is meanings which define social reality rather than social reality being self-evident through observation. Such meanings were, in themselves, liable to degenerate and therefore required constant reaffirmation in everyday actions. Thus, social reality did not just happen but had to be made to happen. The implication of this was that through social interaction people could modify and possibly even transform social meanings, and therefore any explanation of human action had to take into account the meanings which those involved assigned to their actions. For example, whether failure to obey a superordinate's command was a manifestation of worker militancy, misunderstanding or just the beginnings of deafness depended not so much on what bosses or researchers 'saw' happen but what the worker involved meant by her or his action. Of course, misunderstanding of the meaning of action was also possible, so that the ultimate result of the interaction may not have been willed by any of the participants.

Roy's ethnographic approach to work is a classic landmark in this form of sociological investigation, and it is his factory-based 'banana time' (1973) which most clearly demonstrates the way social reality is constructed and interpreted by the actors involved. In particular, Roy himself demonstrates the significance of interpretation rather than simply observation since, initially at least, the actions of his work colleagues appear completely spontaneous, irrational and bizarre. Each day Roy witnessed one of his workmates (Ike) steal another's (Sammy's) banana:

> Each morning after making the snatch, Ike would call out, 'Banana time!' and proceed to down his prize while Sammy made futile protests . . . he never did get to eat his banana but kept bringing one for his lunch. At first this daily theft startled and amazed me. Then I grew to look forward to the daily seizure and the verbal interaction which followed. (Roy, 1973: 211)

Only when he understands what the behaviour means to the workers, how they make sense of their lives through their actions and routines which structure the working day, and how they interpret the world, is Roy able to provide a satisfactory explanation of group interaction.

A further implication of the creative essence of such an approach is that social relations between superordinates and subordinates are not simply explained through the powerlessness of the latter. Since almost all aspects of social relations are necessarily reciprocal there are few situations where individuals can categorically be said to be powerless (Giddens, 1982a: 197–200). Obviously, where one individual is tied hand and foot and about to be physically exterminated by another, the former is powerless; yet, as argued in chapter 2, even slaves have some element of power because their relations with slave owners are not determined by the apparently objective situation. If slaves can sometimes manipulate situations to their advantage then we can be sure that subordinates in rational (i.e., rule-bound) organizations have access to many more power resources. This is not to say that a pattern of pluralist equality prevails in most work organizations, the point is merely that subordinates are not powerless. Perhaps the best example of how individuals in an apparently hopeless situation can carve out some measure of autonomy is Goffman's analysis of patients' behaviour in mental institutions (1961), an image more popularly revealed in Jack Nicholson's portrayal of a mental patient in the film *One Flew over the Cuckoo's Nest*. The nature of this unofficial bargain between subordinate and superordinate is also captured in the model of 'negotiated order' developed by Strauss et al. (1963), in which apparently intransitive structures of social life are actually the contingent subject of constant renegotiation. Here, then, actors' perceptions and their negotiations actively shape the social structure.

It could be argued that Strauss's approach is too restrictive in its assertion of the role of negotiations, rather than too expansive. That is, once limits are placed on the elements within the organization which are subject to negotiation then the crucial consequence of human interpretation is diminished. For example, while Strauss might want to limit the negotiated features of a hospital organization to the interactions of the humans involved, the interpretative approach would want to include the technical forms as well. For example, the technical limits of beds per ward or the technically determined capacities of various forms of medical technology are taken for granted by Strauss, but the interpretative approach would subject both these to the critical influence of human interpretation: what counts as the maximum ratio of beds per ward? and what forms of rhetoric have persuaded actors that such a ratio is the maximum viable? who decides that specific machines can only be operated in particular ways since other ways may be equally viable?

Population ecology theory

Population ecologists hold, in their most extreme form, that the interpretative framework of action theory is irrelevant because selection not adaptation is the mechanism for distinguishing between successful and unsuccessful organizations. If an organization has the requisite fit between environment and organization then it will survive; if it does not it will die through the survival of the fittest. This quasi-Darwinian (quasi because organizations are often 'taken over' by or merge with others rather than simply die) rebuff to the adaptive contingency theorists does not focus upon individual organizations, let alone individuals, because its interests and models are rooted in populations of organizations. Here organizations do not adapt to changed conditions, they die and are replaced by other organizations that are better aligned with the requirements of the environment. Thus death not change is critical because organizations rarely, if ever, change sufficiently enough to remain alive under changing conditions. Instead, new organizations spring up to replace the old as novel market niches are created by the maelstrom of dynamic change. This, it is argued, explains the enormous cull that regularly occurs as organizations fall in thousands, only to be replaced by others wishing to take their chance in the great 'selection'.

Moreover, because organizations cannot evolve fast enough to remain alive, each new organization has a limited life span. As long as the environment remains stable the new organization may survive, but once the environment changes the very structures and procedures designed for survival under a particular form of environment hinder the possibility of the organization surviving. This, then, sits at the deterministic end of the spectrum because people have virtually no role to play, either in interpreting the world or acting upon it.

Evolutionary biology

While population ecology models take the species or group as the focus, and ecological fitness as the explanation for change and survival, evolutionary biologists are more concerned with individuals and 'hard-wired' behaviour as the causal feature. There are precedents for this biological account of behaviour and organization – Aristotle divided the world into those with a natural propensity to be slaves and those whose natural inheritance propelled them to being slave-owners. Irrespective of the atypicality of this view, the point is that our behaviour – allegedly – is driven both by our evolutionary adaptations from the Stone Age and by our genes; hence this approach sits right at the apex of the determinist axis and on the technocratic side in so far as it implies that inequalities of all kinds are probably hard-wired and therefore irremovable. In effect, we should understand and work with the constraints rather than pretending they do not exist.

The most radical version of this approach relates to the 'hard-wiring' model of evolutionary psychology that has its origins in the socio-biology ideas of E.O. Wilson (1975) in which almost all aspects of human behaviour could be traced back to natural selection and genes. In this perspective, human behaviour is something that has remained unchanged in its causal features for between 100,000 and 600,000 years.

This genetic make-up tends to propel 'alpha-males' – those men with high levels of testosterone – into positions of leadership where, if successful, they then generate high levels of serotonin, a hormone associated with happiness. The subsequent forms of natural selection eliminate all but the strongest, or rather all but the most appropriate for leadership positions (Nicholson, 2000: 97–125). As Nicholson (2000: 1) puts it: 'We may have taken ourselves out of the Stone Age but we haven't taken the Stone Age out of ourselves.'

This approach has strong connections to the 'selfish gene' ideas of Richard Dawkins (1976), for whom people are 'robot vehicles' designed to maximize the chances of passing on genes. In other words, it isn't our own survival that is critical, because that is a conscious choice; rather, it is the unconscious controls of our genes which merely use our bodies as temporary homes in their greater journey through time, though, since only cells can reproduce, the notion of gene reproduction doesn't make much sense (Dover, 2000: 51). Dawkins has further suggested that we might profitably understand the transmission of cultures on a similar basis – but this time as 'memes' rather than genes. Memes are units of imitation – an abbreviation of Dawkins's own neologism 'mimemes', itself patterned on the units of speech described as 'phonemes' by linguists. Thus if we want to explain the development and reproduction of novel ideas in organizations, we might profitably consider them as 'memes' – units of culture that reproduce themselves *through* us, rather than us reproducing them *for* us. In effect, the development of Business Process Re-engineering (BPR) or Total Quality Management (TQM) or any other management 'fad' can be explained best by reversing the causation: our role is just to pass on the genes and the memes, not to ensure our own success, which is merely a means to their success.

However, beyond the problem of defining a meme as a fixed unit, it is clear that cultural transmission often involves intentional distortion, so that people and organizations do not simply replicate an idea but transform it to the point where no possible 'replication' can be said to have occurred (Midgley, 2000). In short, BPR or TQM are not simply reproduced through us but are changed each time they are reproduced because their interpretation and our intent tend to change.

We are left with an interesting case of a theory as a model of itself. In theory, since evolution all but stopped several thousand years ago, and since behaviour is hard-wired and overwhelmingly caused by natural selection working through genes, there really is not much that can be done about organizational life: it is as it is because that's the way it has to be. However, rather like many similar theoretical approaches that claim an imperialist monopoly of the truth and that generate 'disciples' rather than 'supporters', the viability of evolutionary psychology replicates that which it most resembles: a religion whose adherents remain unshaken by theoretical doubts or empirical counter-evidence because belief is ultimately rooted in faith not rational analysis. Badcock (2000) provides one of the few 'critical' appreciations, while Rose and Rose (2000) have gathered together a polemical rejection of the entire approach.

Rational choice theory

Rational choice, or rational choice theory, is firmly rooted in economics and has at its core a set of beliefs about human action that lock it into rational behaviour: we all act on the basis of a cost/benefit analysis and this can be modelled to become the basis for a predictive science. Gary Becker was one of the first economists to take the core ideas and apply them to criminal activity, the family and the domestic division of labour (see chapter 7) and John Elster (1986) has attempted to marry rational choice theory to Marxism.

It is not necessary within the general approach to argue that individuals have particular psychological states that cause them to act rationally, only that the models work simply by *assuming* that individuals act rationally. By 'rationally', the approach usually implies 'economically rational', in the sense that some form of exchange is involved: time for money, status for responsibility and so on – and as long the individual believes that their rewards outweigh their costs, then they will probably engage in the transaction, whatever it is. The value of both reward and effort or punishment is measured by the utility it has for that individual, which may vary but can still be modelled mathematically; indeed, contemporary rational choice theories are increasingly econometric in form.

Whatever the technical skills of this approach, it tends to be adopted by managers in a corrupted form that reduces everything to the assumption that managers are rational and can predict with incredible skill how employees will react to various motivational developments and strategies. All too often such approaches fail, but they tend to be written off as examples of poor deployment of the theory rather than seen as evidence of fundamental flaws in the theory.

Generally speaking, critics of rational choice theory have tended to focus on the problem of explaining altruistic behaviour and the social structures that emanate from it. For example, why should individuals join trade unions when they can free-ride the benefits (collective bargaining) without incurring the costs (union fees and political labelling)? It may be possible to argue that joining is perceived as rational on the basis of a long-term rational benefit (for instance, legal protection in the event of a disciplinary problem) rather than simply rooted in short-term rational analysis. Or it could be, as Olson (1965) suggests, that locally provided advantages are critical (active and supportive shop stewards and so on); thus the source and power of social 'norms' rest in their *outcomes* not in their *origins*.

However, critics remain unpersuaded that the complexities of human behaviour can be reduced to mathematic models – if for no other reason than that they so often fail to predict what will happen in complex human interactions. Moreover, experiments by Falk et al. (2003) suggest that self-oriented behaviour has significant limits. In their first experiment, two people are required to share £100, but one (A) will decide who gets what. It is then up to the other (B) to either accept their 'share' or reject the entire package; if the latter course is chosen, then 'A' is deprived of his or her share too. Since even £1 is better than nothing, it would be economically rational for B to accept whatever A offers, but the results of the experiment suggests that when B's share drops below £25, B usually punishes A by refusing to participate at all. This, interestingly enough, is a rational experiment demonstrating that not all human behaviour is rational!

Related experiments in public good confirm the suspicion that there is a lot more to behaviour than economic rationality, and that people are willing to punish selfish behaviour even if it causes them harm too (for related papers see <http://ideas.repec.org/e/pfe29.html>. Rather like evolutionary psychology, rational choice theory tends to generate imperialist ambitions simply because both approaches imply that no other approaches are necessary to explain behaviour at work, or anywhere else for that matter. For those with a sceptical view, an incisive critique is provided by Fevre (2003).

Complexity theories

Complexity theories – and there are several variants – essentially imply a radical change in traditional organizations. Sometimes the onset of complexity theories is related to the arrival of an era in business that is significantly more complicated and time-dependent than ever before: we have never been this busy before and time has never been in such short supply. But this is to suggest that business life in the twenty-first century is more complex, more global and operates at greater velocity than ever before. Yet if we consider the Second World War, it should be self-evident that the world was just as, if not more, globally interdependent, and organizations more complex then than now.

Complexity theories deny the viability of any mechanical laws with universal and predictable application to social organizations: organizations are not machines but living organisms. In some ways, this is hardly a novel perspective – Herbert Spencer's nineteenth-century organic analogy and his (not Darwin's) notion of the 'survival of the fittest' predates this by a long way. But the essence of the contemporary analogy is that self-organization, or local interaction, generates patterns – and thus no blue-print is necessary. In other words, while the traditional understanding of management is that of designing and executing predictable patterns – or plans – it now appears that such plans are both unnecessary and counter-productive. This is primarily because non-linear dynamics effectively inhibit the attainment of any such plans: you may plan to achieve something radical and substantive in your organization, but the chances of your achieving something that exactly matches the plan are negligible. Even holding everything constant, rather than trying to change things radically, is well-nigh impossible: organizational stability cannot be secured by imposing order on disorder because the interactions between the parts of an organization effectively undermine any attempt to impose order from above or from the centre. This is why small things at work are so important: it is the small things – the interactions between individuals, small groups and things – that change the way organizations work, that, indeed, make organizations work.

The earliest forays into complexity often hinged around chaos theory – a most unfortunate name, since chaos theory does not imply 'chaotic', i.e. disorderly, activity, but rather that the turbulent nature of complex systems were both unpredictable and have a multiplier effect. Hence Gleick's well-rehearsed words: 'a butterfly stirring the air in Peking today can transform storm systems next month in New York' (1988: 8). Chaos theory suggests that the behaviour of a system can be modelled by deterministic but non-linear equations; that is, by *attractors*: these are global patterns/boundaries that are displayed by a system and take a number of forms:

- *Point attractors*: which have a stable equilibrium state – such as a pendulum stopping;
- *Periodic attractors*: which have a stable equilibrium between two values – such as a pendulum swinging;
- *Torus attractors*: which embody free movement in confined spaces – such as ants on a doughnut; and the most common of all;
- *Strange attractors*: wherein rhythmic variations over time generate more complex positions than point or periodic attractors but nevertheless construct recognizable but irregular patterns – such as the weather.

Chaos theory, then, is rooted in deterministic laws that generate indeterminist results and, as a consequence, is unable to explain novelty – except through the destruction of a strange attractor that normally prevents such a move. This also explains why complexity theories sit at the centre of the determinist/interpretativist axis – because they are perceived as both determinist and interpretativist. The unpredictability at the heart of chaos theory also implies that 'leading change' is a virtual impossibility. In sum, it provides a useful metaphor but it ignores the non-deterministic nature of human interactions (c.f. Holland, 1998).

Chaos theory, however, does have some important arguments to make about the way organizations work. First, anything might matter – even the smallest event or decision by the lowliest employee can generate radical changes. Second, only the immediate future is predictable, but stable patterns exist that may undermine or support change. This has consequences for planning, for there can be no possibility of achieving any long-term plan – indeed, any reliance on long-term strategies can only mean that the organization is run by infallible or omnipotent leaders – who do not, in reality, exist.

One of the most radical managerial adoptions of this kind of approach to planning has been taken by SightSavers, a £20 million, 250-employee British eye charity. Until Adrian Poffley's intervention as Finance Director, SightSavers's annual budget involved 15,000 numbers in a two-inch thick manual and it took six months to plan. The problem was that this great level of detail not only took so much effort but also, apart from giving the charity answers to such questions as 'How many pencils existed in Ghana in the second week in February?', it was of marginal relevance. Much more important was what was happening on the ground in terms of war, famine, flood and resources. With a budget of so little relevance to what was actually happening, SightSavers decided to abandon the quest altogether and opt for a rolling twelve-month forecast that tracked where the charity was going, and not where the budget said it should be going. The switch allowed the board to concentrate on strategic issues, such as charity work, fundraising and support, and allowed the twenty operating units in developing countries to get on with their work and to operate on the basis of knowing that funding would be guaranteed for twenty-four months. As Poffley says: 'We're at last running the organization around its needs as a business, not for the accounting cycle' (quoted in Caulkin, 2003b: 9).

But for us the most important development of complexity theories is complex adaptive systems (CAS). Perhaps the most popular variant of CAS is what Reynolds originally termed 'boids' or 'simple rules' (see <http://www.red3d.com/cwr/boids/>). In trying to explain how birds flock or fish swim in shoals, it is apparent that perfect symmetry is almost always achieved – the creatures seem to know which way to turn and at what speed. Reynolds suggested that CAS consist of large numbers of agents each behaving according to its own principles of local interaction. In other words, no individual determines the whole or group movement. To achieve co-ordinated symmetry under these conditions, so-called 'simple rules' were derived. For example, to explain birds flocking, only three rules were required:

1 *Separation*: maintain a minimum of distance from other objects, including other boids.
2 *Alignment*: match velocities with neighbouring boids.
3 *Cohesion*: move towards the perceived centre of a mass of boids in the neighbourhood.

The importance for studying work in organizations is that these boids seemed to operate as leaderless groups simply by obeying three simple rules. Perhaps all leaders have to do is develop similar simple rules – or perhaps leaders are unnecessary because these simple rules can generate successful organizations in and through themselves. However, what simple rules cannot do is stimulate change.

Now the implication of this is that complex behaviour need not have a complex explanation and it may be possible to rethink the link between the two and replace all the complex manuals that bureaucracies employ with a few simple rules: maybe. But perhaps a more important issue is to recognize the importance of local interactions. After all, humans do not operate as birds in flocks or fish in shoals or molecules in test tubes. It is the case that complex behaviour such as walking along a pavement and avoiding other pedestrians could be reduced to a few rules ('avoid walking into others'; 'keep at a similar pace to others moving in your direction'; 'don't stop suddenly'; 'walk behind someone going in your direction', etc.), but this may not be enough to succeed in a complex arena and it doesn't explain the generation of novelty, whereas it may be that novelty arises spontaneously from local interaction – but only if sufficient diversity pre-exists there.

The final element of CAS for us to consider is 'fitness landscape'. This suggests not just that no level playing field exists upon which competitors compete, but that the very state of the field depends upon the acts of the players/competitors. Thus, where 'peaks' represent maximum 'fit' between the organization and the environment, and 'troughs' represent the minimum 'fit', because the field constantly moves as competitors alter their positions, so too must you keep moving. In fact, this 'field' is more akin to a water-bed than a field and the implication is that the field cannot be planned or predicted because it is the result of multiple actors, and a consequence of their actions. Even if we can establish causality, there is a subsequent problem in terms of providing prescriptive advice to organizations on the basis of complexity theories: if events are the consequence of multiple causation, then the construction of a 'winning strategy' is probably impossible because once a strategy is deployed, a counter-strategy is often developed to inhibit the achievement of the original strategy.

There is a child's game called 'Scissor, Paper, Stone', which embodies this lesson in beautiful simplicity. In 'Scissor, Paper, Stone', the winner of each round cannot be predicted because it depends on the relationship between the two 'hands': a hand that mimics a 'stone' beats a hand that mimics 'scissors' because the stone crushes the scissors; but 'stone' loses to 'paper' because the paper wraps around the stone, and 'scissors' beats 'paper' because they cut paper. Where two hands mimic the same item at the same time, a 'draw' is declared. The simplicity of this game should not allow us to ignore its critical lesson for organizational strategy: it is relative in both space and time. A hand that mimics the same item consecutively may not win because, second time round, your opponent may have changed his or her hand. If your strategy to beat your competitors is rooted in driving down prices – and if they do the same – you may have a price war that benefits neither side. But if your opposition moves to a strategy grounded in a niche quality market, then you may both prosper. If you devise a military strategy that seeks to knock out your enemy by bringing their main force to battle, your success will depend upon them not disengaging and adopting guerrilla tactics. In effect, you cannot construct a 'winning' strategy in isolation because its utility is dependent on the strategy deployed by your opposition. There is, therefore, no objectively correct strategy for a particular situation – as contingency theory implies – because the situation is likely to be in permanent flux as both sides adopt and adapt to what they perceive the opposition to be doing.

Political organizational theories

If population ecology and evolutionary biology models imply that we can make no difference to the way our organizations are run, while rational choice models suggest that what occurs is similarly inevitable (but for different reasons), the complexity theories deny that we can plan where we end up. However, that ability to predetermine direction and steer organizations is the essence of what we might call 'political organizational' approaches, which are themselves rather disparate. One strand took off under the auspices of Child's (1972) 'strategic choice' model in which the elite or dominant coalitions of managers took positive *action* to ensure their interests prevailed over all others. Lee and Lawrence (1985) draw upon the essentially political nature of organizational life, its innate contingency and the value of various strategies of influence to go well beyond Child. However, it would seem that in their desire to escape from the determinism of other models there is little room left for any analysis of the relationships between these human actors and the material and technological systems with which they interact. Thus power networks are restricted to social networks, rather than networks of human and non-human 'actors' (Lee and Lawrence, 1985: 143–4).

Probably the clearest account of a political model is that enunciated by Salaman (1979, 1984), though the original ideas are closely associated with Fox (1971, 1974, 1976). Salaman argues that the labour process orthodoxy, which held sway over much of academic industrial sociology for over a decade (see chapter 5), distorts the reality of work by focusing upon class to the exclusion of the more pervasive and significant aspects of work structuring: social relations. Social relations do not exclude class relations but the opposite often tends to hold, such that Marxist accounts of work organizations are partial. In its place Salaman argues that a model comprising the following should be adopted.

First, organizations should be deemed political organizations: they are structured by power relations. The implication of this is twofold: class relations are just one form, albeit an important one, of power relations and we should therefore seek out other forms, such as gender or ethnic relations etc., which may prove to be as important as, if not more significant than, class relations.

The establishment of workplace relations is therefore an empirical question rather than a theoretical one, though it is taken for granted that such workplace relations will be patterned. It also denies the managerialist approach which suggests that organizations are neutral instruments for universally agreed purposes. On the contrary, organizations embody and actively reproduce the forms of social inequality that prevail in the wider society.

Second, organizations are not free-floating bodies but locked into a wider, and again political, environment. Thus whatever goes on within organizations has to be explained partly as a reflection of the organization's environment. This means that we need to go beyond Marxist explanations that reduce causes to the structural requirements of capitalism and look at the complexities of organizational life rather than the simplicities. This does not mean that we should ignore the essentiality of capitalism, but this thirst for profit, while important in any account of organizations, is not sufficient in itself. Indeed, for those public organizations ostensibly beyond the conventional market imperatives a whole sequence of problems may arise that demonstrate the difficulties of assuming the issues are wholly capitalist in origin (Seglow, 1983; Batstone et al., 1984).

Third, Salaman argues for the significance of identity and the part played by organizational life in the construction of both personal and group identity. Frequently this is intimately connected to the patterning of differentiation discussed above, for the development of identity may often be forged negatively through the exclusion of others rather than positively through the creation of personal or group characteristics. Again, like the work of Lee and Lawrence (1985), a major issue with this neo-Weberian approach is the extent to which it encompasses the seamless web of relationships, not between human actors but between human actors, material and technological artefacts. The significance of human actors appears to have been rescued only to leave them bereft of a critical aspect of their character and influence: technology. Before we explore this, however, we need to develop the approach to organizational life represented by Foucault and post-modernism.

Foucault and post-modernism

Foucault's approach locates him firmly against much of the organizational approach discussed so far. While the writings of the classical school of organizations, such as Fayol, Urwick and Taylor, their human relation opponents, and even their radical critics like Habermas, tended to see organizations as the actual or potential epitome of human rationality, Foucault and the rest of the post-modernist tradition (e.g. Lyotard and Derrida etc.) regard organizations as more akin to defensive reactions against inherently destabilizing forces (Cooper and Burrell, 1988). Thus, where modernists perceive history as the gradual promotion of progress, reason and rationality, post-modernists perceive no such progressive intent or reality. In terms of the axes of determinism and interpretativism the post-modern tradition is firmly towards the end of the interpretativist pole.

The organization, and particularly the modern corporation, embodies for the opposing camps a useful example of opposition. For modernists the rationality of organization, complete with computer-aided decision-making, speaks to the future enlightenment of the world. But to post-modernists the very same organization threatens humanity with totalizing control derived not only from its spreading tentacles of material and ideological control but from the nature of its legitimacy. That is to say, the modern organization's claim to legitimacy rests in its claims to represent rationality and future progress. Naturally, not all modernists are of the same faith: Habermas's ideals are to return human organizations to the consensually constructed control of their human participants, whereas Bell's are much more limited to the development of rational organization. But where they both meet is in the belief that reason can promote human progress.

Another feature of differentiation between the two camps lies in the conservative modernist assumption that organizations tend towards certainty, stability and consensus; the post-modern assumption is that instability, uncertainty and dissensus are the norm. The latter is particularly important for organizational analysis for it implies that differentiation is not merely a contingent reaction to a specific mode of organizational life but a necessary feature of social relations. Accordingly, difference is, as Nietzsche argued, not one feature of social relations but the active force underlying them.

The uncertainty of social life is taken further by Derrida (1973, 1978) in that organizations are construed not as mechanisms to advance human control but processes to hide the very uncertainty we live in. This suggests that while labour process theorists are locked into an assessment of managerial control mechanisms, the post-modernist approach denies the plausibility of any group being 'in control'. To be in control presumes a rational intent and means to effect such intent but neither of these can exist within the post-modernist approach. In short, post-modernists start from the assumption that organizations are the results of reactive processes, attempts to delimit the disaggregating reality of everyday existence. The very uncertainty and fragility of social life becomes a stimulus to construct reality-distancing mechanisms: organizations are façades constructed not to advance human control but to obscure the reality that we have no control. In turn, this reproduction of the practices that sustain the precarious, but taken for granted, nature of the world ultimately prevents us from recognizing the nature of the social world (Knights, 1989). Since some (post-modernist) people are self-evidently not taken in by this mirage (otherwise they could not describe it as such), the modernist alchemy must be less powerful than either side claims.

Language is another critical medium of distinction between modernist and post-modernist approaches: for the former, language is usually regarded as the neutral carrier of information – a transparent mechanism for carrying the meaning of an organization. For the post-modernist, and particularly Derrida, language does not carry the meaning so much as provide the means by which meaning can be imposed upon or constructed into an organization. Meaning, then, does not reside in an organization and await the researchers' 'discovery' but is something the researcher imputes to an organization. Hence Derrida's concern that research should endeavour to 'deconstruct' what are taken for truths by demonstrating the essential ambivalence of language and therefore, in this instance, of organizations. By implication, writing, or in Latour and Woolgar's (1979) approach an 'inscription device', should be regarded as a means by which control may be formalized: the wall chart of organizational hierarchies is not a description of reality but an attempt to create the same (see Cooper, 1989).

Foucault's (1977, 1979; Sheridan, 1980) relevance to organizational theory lies in several related spheres. First, he argues that contemporary society is, and therefore presumably contemporary organizations are, maintained not by any consensus nor by the overt coercion of the state's judicial system but rather by the covert systems of bodily surveillance and discipline which are built into the framework of organizations. Thus, like prisoners, workers must always be visible to their controllers and the minutiae of daily life is legitimately ordered and observed from above and written up, not into personal details but into bureaucratic case notes. Subjectivity is systematically shredded by the organization, and a model of normality is reconstituted from the elements; anyone deviating from this model is the subject of further dissection by society's human scientists – the self-appointed judges of normality.

Foucault's major importance here lies in the notions of power articulated by his network model. Power is a semi-stable network of alliances but for Foucault the centre of concern is the human subject rather than the organization. Subjects are constructed by power but do not 'have' power. Power, then, is not the property of any individual or group, still less can it be discovered lurking in structures. While traditional theories of power, for Foucault, suggest that its origins lie in the state, its direction of flow is downwards against subordinates, and its essence is negative, he argues that this is to misunderstand the power-soaked nature of all social life and its constitutive force. Power, then, should be configured as a relation between subjects: the micro-physics of everyday life. It is 'capillary power'; it is exercised '*within* the social body, rather than *above* it' (Sheridan, 1980: 39). Not all subjects are equal within the network of power relations which defines them. On the contrary, the resources of power are unequally distributed and this inequality is often buttressed by the strategies employed by resource-rich subjects.

This does not mean that subordinates are helplessly caught in the web of power for the very indeterminacy of social life suggests that resistance and dissensus are ever present. Yet, for Foucault, the demonstration of resistance is merely a functional facilitator of greater subsequent discipline: only if resistance constantly tests the deployment of discipline can discipline be improved and secured (Burrell, 1988). Moreover, although all organizations are not akin to prisons, as Foucault suggests with his image of society as an extended Panopticon, it is still the case, Burrell argues, that as individuals we are never free of some form of organization. In this sense our lives are lived out within an incarcerated world that, with the ever-increasing expansion of computer networks and electronic surveillance, promises to claw tighter at the lineaments of the subject. This 'disciplinary power', which subjugates specific individuals (prisoners, workers, etc.), is distinguishable both from 'bio-power', in so far as the latter focuses upon the general population and subjugates it through the mechanisms of normalization such as sexual norms, and from prior forms of sovereign power. Thus during the eighteenth century the (French) state shifted its method of control from one of absolute terror, based in physical torture, to disciplinary power, based in prison-grounded regimes of institutional routine and the development of normative schemas of deviance. But the diffusion of power from the sovereign was not a strategic development as much as the result of other power centres developing their own forms of discipline. Factories, churches, schools, hospitals were all imbricated in the construction of 'normal' behaviour patterns that served to discipline the population and it is worth pointing out that if the disciplining effects of one, say education, facilitated the control of factory proletarians this was not, according to Foucault, because the factories needed such additional resources. Indeed, Foucault's argument is that the disciplinary method has its origin not in the pecuniary hands of capitalist factory owners but in the disciplinary hands of prison and asylum controllers.

Much of Foucault's and the other post-modernist writers' approach is fruitful in the different light it sheds on organizations. In particular, the contingent nature of organizations and notion of power as a web within which all are held, are useful counter-thrusts to the determinist and technocratic approaches of many managerialist and, indeed, orthodox Marxist approaches. However, there is a tendency to eliminate the superordinates in the desire to paint a picture of society like a prison in which even the prison authorities are entangled by, rather than in some semblance of control over, the web of power relations. To argue that prisoners' resistance is merely functional to the development of greater disciplinary powers is also unnecessarily determinist: the history of prisons – as the 1980s and 1990s in Britain were ample witness – is not one of ever-decreasing prisoner resistance as each eruption merely facilitates its own elimination. Foucault might have regarded the spate of prison riots in Britain in previous years as functionally necessary to eliminate further resistance of that kind; the £60 million rebuild of Strangeways prison after the 1990 riot suggests otherwise.

Actor networks

While conventional social network approaches might explain the length of the Strangeways' disturbance through an analysis of the characters involved, it seems clear that the materials and technology involved (physical barricades, food supplies, and strategic control over the roof) are critical elements too. The actor network model (Callon, 1986; Latour, 1988; and Law, 1988), which is principally aimed at explaining the development and stabilization of forms of technology, is particularly useful in this and other organizational contexts. Fundamentally, the approach suggests that power depends upon the construction and maintenance of a network of actors; crucially, and contrary to the implications of Clegg's (1989: 202–7, 225) otherwise useful review, these networks involve both human and non-human 'actors'. Perhaps 'elements' rather than 'actors' might be considered a better description here since it avoids the reification implied by non-human actors. But the approach is constructed on the premise that we should avoid the conventional distinctions between human and non-human elements and should talk instead of the 'heterogeneous entities that constitute a network' (Bijker et al., 1987: 11). That is, we should consider the unity of human and non-human actors in terms of a seamless web as Hughes (1979) calls it or 'heterogeneous engineering' in Law's (1986) case. The implication of this is that organizations should not be perceived as, or explained through, the activities of humans alone but through the alliances of human and non-human actors. These non-human actors may, for example, take the form of technology or material facets of institutions – buildings etc. For instance, it would be erroneous to consider the antics of a maniacal driver in terms of the driver or the car, or even the driver as a discrete unit and the car as a discrete unit. Rather, we should note the imperceptible network that links the two together: only when the driver is one *with* the car does the maniacal driver really exist.

When we consider the force of this approach with regard to organizational issues we have to seek out the alliance or networks that initiate and maintain the superordination of individuals or groups over others. Moreover, we should remember that many actors that are locked into networks exist outside the particular organization. For example, managerial networks rely not just upon the expertise of fellow managers and the control over material resources within the enterprise, but also the resources of the legal system (the police, the courts, the prisons etc.) and the domestic supports which are invisibly meshed into the organization's disciplinary mechanisms. Similarly, those scientists allegedly isolated from the rest of the world in their quest for knowledge are actually highly dependent upon a large array of supportive networks outside the laboratory (Latour, 1987: 145–76).

It is now possible to see the power of reification: where actor networks manage to construct a system that incorporates not just non-human actors but actually makes them appear independent of social aspects then the entire network becomes stronger. To clarify this point, it is not that the transport system or social inequality are both inevitable or that they can be explained as wholly technological or social phenomena. Rather, they are constructed through networks but they gain in obduracy if they can be made to appear natural or inevitable: once reified they resist attempts to deconstruct them (Woolgar, 1990). Skilled workers, therefore, maintain their position through networks that include union organization, control over specific forms of skill and machinery, and restrictions on recruitment etc. Relatedly, the network that binds women into employment is notoriously fragile and is constantly undermined by the state's refusal to establish universal crèche facilities and paid leave for family illness etc.

The means by which such networks are constructed is divided into 'moments' whereby allies are recruited in such a way that the solution to their own problems only appears viable through the network, and the point at which the network itself becomes differentiated from others through the mobilization and categorization of members. In Latour's (1986) terms, organizational power does not emanate from the leader(s) at the centre in a diffused mode but is the result of subordinates' translative action (see above). Hence we can shift analysis away from the problem of subordinate resistance to the problem of subordinate compliance. This shift from the 'principles of power' to the 'practices of power' is an essential aspect of the actor network model and operates as a valuable caution against those determinist accounts that explain organizations by concentrating on the formal organizational model itself rather than on the interpretative practices of humans in association with non-humans.

What should equally be stressed here is the fragile and transient nature of such networks and, implicitly therefore, the constant need for the network to be reproduced. Networks do not maintain themselves, even though a viable method of extending the time span of a network is to inscribe it in material form. For example, Latour (1988) notes how the radical Paris government built its subway bridges too small to allow the coaches of the private railroad companies to pass through, thereby ossifying its contingent political control into a concrete embodiment. As Latour concludes:

> They shifted their alliance from legal or contractual ones, to stones, earth and concrete. What was easily reversible in 1900 became less and less reversible as the subway network grew. The engineers of the railway company now took these thousands of tunnels built by the subway company as destiny and as an irreversible technical constraint. (1988: 36–7).

Institutional theory

The final theoretical approach sits at the fulcrum of the model because, its adherents suggest, institutional theory mirrors the fashion of the day – and since fashion changes so do the theories (Meyer and Rowan, 1977; Scott and Meyer, 1994). Institutional theory suggests that organizational decision-makers, especially under conditions of uncertainty, are forced into taking action that resembles the lead taken by others in the field. For instance, if – after a substantial research programme – a leading car producer adopted self-organized teams, rather than a conventional assembly line, to build vehicles, then its competitors may well assume that teams are more efficient than assembly lines. If they were not then why would a respected company like this adopt such a production system?

Under this approach the normative influences upon individuals are too great for most to resist – not only does it seem rational to copy a field leader but the possibility that the mimicry is undertaken for normative reasons rather than rational ones is itself denied. The power of normative influence is often difficult to establish for that very reason – they are normative.

Perhaps we should also consider the way each apparently novel approach renders an account of the problem and solution that sets up sympathetic 'resonances' with related developments. That is, the way it captures the *Zeitgeist*, or 'spirit of the times'.

There are precedents for this in the popularity of previous managerial philosophies (see Rose, 1990). For example, Taylorism and Fordism can be understood in relation to the contemporary development of social statistics: the rise of the eugenics movement in the USA and its attempted legitimation through scientific measures of IQ (Kamin, 1977; Karier, 1976a, 1976b), the high point of pre-1914 beliefs in the efficacy of scientific rationality – soon to be radic-ally disturbed by the events of 1914–18 (Pick, 1993); in light of the changes in disciplinary and temporal schemas adopted originally in armies and prisons (Foucault, 1979); and, of course, in the development of assembly line system, or rather disassembly line system, in the Chicago slaughterhouses, then 'pro-cessing' 200,000 hogs a day (Pick, 1993: 180). One might want to go further here and suggest that the kind of mechanical tactics adopted by the British Army, at the battle of the Somme in 1916, for example (Ellis, 1993), are precise rep-licas of the scientific management displaced from the factory to the killing fields of Flanders. Relatedly, the human relations reaction to Taylorism and Fordism can be read as a shift from the 'rational individual' to the 'irrational group' as the development of communism and fascism appeared to be explicable only through an assumption about the fundamentally irrational needs of people to belong to groups and to construct their group identity through the destruction of 'the other'. The defeat of fascism and the arrival of the Cold War sub-sequently provided fertile ground for the reconstruction of neo-human relations in the form of democratic individualism; the 'evil empire' was neither of these, and, particularly in the UK (Donovan Commission, 1968), the informal group, so long propounded by the human relations school, appeared to be the cause of the problem of economic malaise, not the solution. This time the alternative was written in the language of Lewin's democratic leadership, or McGregor's Theory Y version of responsible employees, and Maslow's and Herzberg's quest for self-fulfilment through work. Finally we can posit the arrival of the 'cultures of excellence' approach where the limits of modernism and Fordism are per-ceived as the stimulus to change. Re-engineering, from this point of view, is the summation of this development which has itself been tightly linked to the wider political movement towards the enterprise culture and the individual customer and against collectivism and state control of any kind (see Du Gay and Salaman, 1992; Du Gay, 1996).

Summary

This chapter has covered a large number of approaches to, and points of view on, organizations. In adopting a particular form of differentiating between the various theories through the organizational grid, the chapter has highlighted the twin axes, technocratic–critical and determinist–interpretative, which are a heuristic way of structuring the various possibilities. One axis concerns the degree to which the theories take the status quo for granted as self-evidently the best way to organize society. At one end of this pole, the technocratic end, lie prag-matic, business-oriented approaches which seek to confirm, reproduce and improve the 'efficiency' of contemporary work organizations. At the other, crit-ical, end of the pole are theories which focus not on the pragmatics of organ-izational improvement but on the explanatory analysis of organizations: the questions concern the ways by which organizations cohere and work, not whether this or that method might improve organizational performance. The other axis distinguished between determinist and interpretative approaches. The deter-minist approach implies that certain socio-economic or material structures or independent variables determine organizational form, at least in the long term: organizations may exist in opposition to the 'requirements' of their environment or variables but those that do not restructure in accordance with such forces are likely to wither. At the opposite end of this pole lie the interpretative approaches which deny, at their most radical, the determining influence of either social or technical aspects. For these approaches the significance of human and non-human components lies not in any imputed capabilities but in their construction via the interpretative processes of actors and the generation of persuasive representations of organizations.

Exam/essay questions

1 Do we need theory to explain the way organizations work?
2 Do post-modern approaches to organization offer any real advantage over modernist accounts?
3 'Theory is good – but it doesn't stop things from existing.' Discuss.
4 Do organizations have interests?
5 'The history of organizational theory is one of ever-increasing rationality and predictive accuracy.' Discuss.
6 Compare and contrast any two theories of work organization.
7 'The trouble with organizational theories is that they cannot be falsified and are, therefore, neither scientific nor useful.' Discuss.
8 Is there a 'one best way' to organize work?
9 'Since people are unpredictable it makes sense to assume that organizations are also unpredictable.' Discuss.
10 To what extent is work organization necessarily hierarchical?

Further reading

There are several good texts on organizational theory and one of the best, now nearly twenty years old, is Burrell's and Morgan's *Sociological Paradigms and Organizational Analysis* (1979). A contemporary competitor to this is Clegg's and Dunkerley's *Organization, Class and Control* (1980). Morgan has also written an excellent study adopting metaphors as a way of understanding organizations in his *Organizations* (1996 edition). For students without any background in the literature two clear introductory texts are: Hatch's *Organization Theory* (1997) and Sheldrake's *Management Theory* (1996). The link between sociology and economics is covered in Farkas's and England's edited collection, *Industries, Firms and Jobs* (1994). Finally, four very different reviews are: the critical theory viewpoint in Alvesson's and Willmott's collection, *Critical Management Studies* (1992); Westwood and Clegg's *Debating Organizations* (2003); Donaldson's positivist *American Anti-management Theories of Organizations* (1985); and, finally, the post-modern collections edited by Boje et al. *Postmodern Management and Organization Theory* (1996) and Reed's and Hughes's *Rethinking Organization* (1992).

5

Class, Industrial Conflict and the Labour Process

- ■ Introduction
- ■ Theoretical approaches to class
- ■ Class, trade unions and revolution
- ■ British trade unions and labourism
- ■ Class and industrial action

- ■ Accounting for industrial action
- ■ Marx, Taylorism and the capitalist labour process
- ■ Braverman and the labour process
- ■ Summary
- ■ Exam/essay questions
- ■ Further reading

Work is the curse of the drinking classes.

H. Pearson, *Life of Oscar Wilde*

Introduction

This chapter assesses the merits and problems of contemporary accounts of three closely related facets of work: class, industrial conflict and the labour process. It argues that although class is a critical issue it is not the only one, nor is there any unmediated connection between class position and class action: gender, ethnic and occupational divisions, mediated by the interpretative processes of individual and social interaction, ensure that heterogeneity not homogeneity is the historically constructed norm at the level of social groups and individuals. This does not mean that society comprises a mass of unrelated and discrete individuals, rather it implies that where cohesive groups exist they have to be produced and reproduced by their members – they are not inevitable products of material divisions. Relatedly, individuals can be considered as heterogeneous composites: they are not, for example, women, and black, and working class – as if these three facets exist independently of each other – but black, working-class women whose life chances are affected by these multiple and fused categories (this heterogeneous model is discussed more fully in the following chapter). Since, however, such patterns are socially and historically constructed they are neither natural nor inevitable – but they are typical. The significance of class is highlighted by the discussion of industrial action which considers the relationships between class and strikes and between the domestic and employment spheres. Finally the ghost of Braverman is raised within the labour process debate, which embodies one of the most popular class-based analyses of work, but it is raised in order to bury it properly, rather than to praise it.

Theoretical approaches to class

While many Marxists and radicals have concentrated almost wholly upon the theoretical intricacies of the labour process and attempted to consider recent changes in work in terms of the labour process concepts of deskilling and degradation etc., others have pursued the more conventional sociological questions concerning the nature and patterning of inequalities and the relationship between work, employment and social stratification. The analysis of class and social stratification has spawned entire libraries of sociological work in themselves but there is no attempt to regurgitate this here (see Giddens, 1973; Goldthorpe et al., 1980; Goldthorpe and Payne, 1986; Martin, 1987; Abercrombie et al., 1988; Heath, 1981). Rather, the necessary empirical data will just be adumbrated to draw out some significant links between the major forms of class inequality and work. Inequalities associated primarily with gender or race are considered in the following two chapters.

For most Marxists, class is defined so widely in direct relationship to ownership or non-ownership of the means of production, and encompasses so many widely variant occupational groups (to say nothing of the gender and ethnic divisions), that the relationship between class structure and class action tends to be either transparent or completely obscured. When it is the former the class appears to take action as a result of its objective position *vis-à-vis* the capitalists; when the latter occurs, through the ideological chicanery of the bourgeois media and superstructural apparatus, the class allegedly lapses into inaction or intra-class hostility. The possibility that occupational divisions may form the material basis for competing interests within the working class, or that the relations are actually very complex and opaque, or that the existence of exploitative relations do not, in and of themselves, imply any corresponding level or form of political or class consciousness, appears of marginal significance to this general approach. Yet if the evidence of working-class politics generally is anything to go by, the effects of the labour process are not simply homogenizing and radicalizing in many circumstances but are often fragmentary in material and ideological terms. Under this more complex approach to the nature of class and the labour process it becomes possible to accommodate otherwise incongruent manifestations of '**false consciousness**', such as the alliances of farm workers and landowners against industrial interests (Howkins, 1985: 130–53). Furthermore, where the relationship between employer and employee is not directly one of capitalist and proletariat, as in the state sector, the implicit correspondence between class position and class consciousness is even more problematic.

The retreat from the complexities thrown up in any attempt to relate objective class position to subjective class consciousness led Poulantzas (1978) to argue that only the direct producers of surplus value are proletarians, that is, only propertyless producers; white-collar workers are relegated to the realms of the petty bourgeoisie. But while this may delimit the extent of apparently false consciousness, it does so only by marginalizing the majority of the working class itself. Wright (1978, 1985) argues that while Marx's dichotomous model is inadequate, Poulantzas's approach takes the problem even deeper. Wright's solution to the problem of why occupational groups appear to have so little relationship to the class structure is to develop a model of 'unambiguously' bourgeois and proletarian classes separated by several ambiguous or contradictory classes based on different modes of exploitation. Briefly, Wright argues that individuals may occupy exploitative positions if they have ownership of capital assets or they control organizational assets or they possess the requisite skills and credentials that allow them to exploit those without such characteristics. Yet this still presumes that the working class, however defined, has an imputed real interest determined by its class location. Such 'real' interests are confounded by the point raised above that the labour process does not just generate homogenizing experiences and interests and is unlikely, therefore, to provide the foundations for universally collective real interests, let alone an alternative social system. Again, the claim is not that the labour process does not generate specific collective material grievances and power resources to resolve some of them, but that it does not generate *universal* effects upon, nor provide for the *universal* interests of, the working class.

The limitations of Weber's stratification model, with its potentially unlimited patterning of class and its dislocation from the 'situated market', have already been noted in chapter 2. The market in capitalism is not the sole origin of inequalities but both an effect and medium of property inequalities that are independent of the market. But it is the case that Weber's differentiated approach to stratification facilitates the introduction of variables such as gender and race as independently constructive of social structure, rather than as derivative of class as the orthodox Marxist position presumes.

One of the most significant attempts to go beyond the limitations of both Marxist and Weberian approaches to stratification has been the theory of **structuration** developed by Giddens (1973, 1984) (see also Cohen, 1989, and Held and Thompson, 1989). Giddens attempts to explain how 'economic relationships become translated into non-economic social structures' (1973: 105). He distinguishes between two forms of class structuration: 'mediate', which form the links between the market and the structured system of market relations, and 'proximate', the immediate, localized factors that affect and shape class formation. The distribution of mobility chances is a primary example of the mediate interventions which either hinder or facilitate the 'reproduction of common life experiences over generations' (Giddens, 1973: 105). Such mobility chances are greatly influenced by 'market capacity' of which Giddens discusses three types: ownership of the means of production; possession of educational or technical qualifications; and the possession of manual labour. Three sources of proximate structuration are significant: the division of labour within the enterprise; the accompanying authority relations; and the influence of distributive groups (such as housing location). This complex of mediate and proximate structuration factors advances a class structure that is itself internally differentiated along systematic patterns, though not in direct response to each and every form of inequality. Thus, class or stratification structures require empirical analysis and cannot be read off from particular sets of economic conditions, either of ownership or authority relations. For example, it is evident that the authority relations within state socialist factories were, and where they persist probably still are, very close to those in operation within some areas of contemporary European or North American societies, yet the patterns of property ownership are very dissimilar.

Class, trade unions and revolution

Classically, trade unions have operated as representatives of working-class employees against their employers. Yet since the late 1970s, trade union density has dropped in many places. Recent evidence in the UK suggests that a 'representation gap' (Nolan, 2000: 3) is increasing, whereby the majority of employees are not represented by any trade union and have their wages and conditions settled directly by their employer. In fact in the UK in 2001, 60 per cent of public sector workers remained unionized, while only 19 per cent of private sector workers were members. This actually represents a slight increase on the post-war low of 7.15 million reached in 1998, but it is still 5 million down on the peak of 1979. In 2003 British trade unions represented 29 per cent of all employees – 7 million people, compared to 12 million in 1980. Nevertheless, since 1997 two-thirds of unions have grown in size and even some of those companies that have resisted trade unions for many years have begun to recognize them: for example, Boots, American Airlines and Kwik-Fit in 2003 (Pandya, 2003: 20).

Perhaps more significantly, there are now more white-collar workers in unions (30 per cent) than blue-collar workers (29 per cent), and there are still more white members (30 per cent) than black and Asian members (24 per cent), though black women have the highest density (33 per cent). Yet unions continue to work in favour of equality with unionized firms demonstrating the lowest differentials between men and women and between black, Asian and white workers (Walker, 2001: 19, citing data from David Metcalfe). In the USA, such 'command and control' systems remain very powerful: more than 17 million Americans are employed solely to supervise the work of others. Yet trade unions still manage to make their mark: in 2001 two strikes in Los Angeles resulted in success. The first was the Screen Actors' Guild and the American Federation of Television and Radio Artists, who won a moderate 3.5 per cent pay increase. The second, rather more significantly, was a 25 per cent increase won by the office cleaners and janitors, primarily composed of poor Hispanics (Campbell, 2001b: 20). Nonetheless the role of trade unions has always been controversial, not just amongst those of the political right but also those of the political left.

It is certainly the case that few writers have claimed a specifically hallowed place for trade unions and their members in the struggle against capitalism, except perhaps the anarcho-syndicalists around the first quarter of this century (Hinton, 1973; Holton, 1976; Miller, 1984; Joll, 1979; Sirianni, 1982; Spriano, 1975; Gluckstein, 1985). Marx was initially convinced that trade unions would be able to resist capitalists and boost the wages and conditions of their members. But this would merely be attacking the symptoms of the capitalist malaise and would do nothing to surmount capitalism itself. The issue was not one of inequality, then, but exploitation and alienation that only the elimination of capitalism could resolve. However, once the trade unionists realized this, Marx assumed they would channel their energies away from the industrial battle and towards the political war through revolutionary parties.

Engels (1969b), after Marx's death, became more and more pessimistic about such a scenario and, on the basis of the British experience, argued that the workers had themselves become bourgeois. They, or at least the aristocracy of labour (the most skilled, rewarded and organized section), now had a direct interest in the maintenance of the capitalist system having been bought off by the profits of imperialism. Lenin pushed this argument to its furthest point, denying the possibility of trade unionists ever achieving class, that is socialist, consciousness unless it was brought to them by radical intellectuals from the bourgeoisie (1970, 1978). Others have taken the opposite stand with regard to the aristocracy of labour, believing it to be the most radical rather than the most reactionary (Pelling, 1968; Gray, 1981; Geary, 1984; Bonnell, 1984; cf. Hobsbawm, 1964a; Foster, 1974). But it is not just leftists that have denied the possibility of radical trade unions, for writers of variant political persuasions have said more or less the same (Webb and Webb, 1920; Flanders, 1965; Lane, 1974; Currie, 1979; and Gorz, 1982). Even the most sympathetic writers prefer to discuss the political intentions of trade unions in terms of ambiguous support of, and opposition to, the status quo (Hyman, 1971: 50–3; Anderson, 1977).

Kelly (1988) argued that trade unions still embody the potential for radical politics. This reaffirmation of Marx's original sanguine belief in trade unions is premised on three assumptions: first, workers' material interests are incompatible with those of capitalism; second, class mobilization is only likely in response to these interests; and third, the pursuit of these interests may, in itself, facilitate the development of socialism. Kelly is right to assume that the interests of capitalists and workers do not coincide, in so far as the former are responsible for, but not usually concerned with, exploitation, unemployment and alienation. But this does not mean that workers have an objective class interest in socialism because it is not self-evident how universal class-based objective interests can be established or legitimated, and because it is not clear exactly what socialism actually comprises. In the absence of an effective, efficient and liberatory theoretical model of the socialist alternative (let alone a working model) such arguments assume that the problems of one regime necessarily imply support for another; they do not. But Kelly is right to reject the mechanical interpretations of class consciousness. It is indeed the case that consciousness exhibits both long periods of somnambulance and brief episodes of radicalism, and therefore Kelly's support for Luxemburg's thesis is accurate: there are cases when economistic strikes flow over into political battles, when strictly militant action is transformed into radical action, albeit often unintentionally. But, as Kelly himself notes, such actions are rare in themselves (see Harman, 1982: 147–51), they tend to be significant only within general crises rather than being significant in and of themselves, and the two examples he chooses (Italy 1922 and Chile 1973) illustrate a real problem: if the mass of the population is working class and their interests are served by socialism, then something other than popular support will be necessary to carry through a radical transition to socialism. Indeed, Kelly undermines his own belief in mass support when he ends with a quote from Fox who notes that: 'if successful revolutions depended on mass understanding . . . the world would have seen few indeed' (Fox, 1985: 122, quoted in Kelly, 1988: 304). Or, as Mann put it: 'perhaps a genuine Leninist dictatorship of the proletariat *is* the only revolutionary way out of the impasse . . . a coup d'etat carried out during a period of social confusion in the name of the proletariat or – and this is more likely – a Fascist coup to forestall the latter eventuality' (Mann, 1973a: 73).

British trade unions and labourism

It may well be rather less exciting than revolutionary action but it is nevertheless the case that '**labourism**' – the pursuit of reforms within the existing forms and methods of parliamentary government and conventional collective bargaining – appears to be the overwhelming form of working-class response to capitalism, at least in Britain, so far. Labourism has already spawned a literature of its own (see: Fox, 1985; Saville, 1973; Kynaston, 1976; Hobsbawm, 1984; Kendall, 1969; Miliband, 1972; Cronin, 1984; and Hinton, 1983), and only the skeleton of the argument will be provided here. Briefly, then, labourism is explained through four interrelated spheres.

First, the patterning of actual, if discontinuous, rises in real living standards for the majority of the British working class, at least after the middle of the nineteenth century, undermined the logic of revolutionary collective action. In effect, the very success of trade unions displaced the concern for control over the productive and political process towards one enclosed by the economistic rewards that capitalism could more readily accommodate. Concomitantly, it could be argued that revolutionary unions, at least those in non-revolutionary situations, are manifestations of weakness not strength (Crouch, 1982: 137–8). The only major exception to this general pattern was just after the First World War, but living standards never fell as sharply in Britain as they did in other European nations where social unrest reached a scale not witnessed since the upheavals of 1848 (Geary, 1984: 134–78; Gallie, 1983: 224–51; Sirianni, 1982: 311–56).

The second factor is the occupational heterogeneity of the British working class that was mentioned above. Of course, such a fragmented pattern is not unique to Britain, and this goes some way to explaining the general absence of revolutionary actions by the working classes of capitalist nations, but perhaps the most notable point is exemplified by reference to the difference between British and Russian history. At the point of gravest economic and political tension (roughly 1917–21 in many capitalist states) the Russian working class was relatively small, faced with a situation that was deteriorating very rapidly and showed no prospect of improving, and free from the institutionalized structures of conventional reformist political parties and trade unions. Such organizations existed but, given the autocratic history of tsarism, they had never developed as in Britain nor was it clear how such reformism could possibly solve the crisis. Thus without the 'disadvantages of advancement', to invert Veblen's phrase, the Russian working class constructed industrial, rather than craft, unions which generated support for class policies not sectarian policies (S. Smith, 1981). In contrast, Britain, and to a lesser extent Germany, had already constructed a system of trade unionism based on craft and led by reformists (Fox, 1985). It was not that such leadership betrayed the masses so much as that this form of trade unionism was interpreted by those involved as the more appropriate in the circumstances of their initial development; it then enwrapped itself in the carapaces of institutional privilege to develop the social rigidities so well analysed by Olson (1982). As Gramsci argues, against the paranoiac implications of Trotsky's permanent betrayal thesis (which suggested that all labour defeats could ultimately be placed at the door of class traitors among the leadership), trade unions are constructed through, and reflective of, capitalism. The world of trade unions and the world of employment are not automatically conducive to class solidarity and are more likely to feed the sectionalist and sectarian ideologies upon which capitalism is founded. The road from sectionalist to class politics is necessarily elusive not self-evident; whilst trade unions *may* be socialist subjectively they are objectively capitalist (Gramsci, 1978: 76). This does not mean that trade unions axiomatically operate against the interests of their own weakest members, even if they may act against the interests of other workers and other capitalists. On the contrary, because the very nature of bargaining conventionally assumes a 'collective' format, unions often enact the 'sword of justice' whereby the weakest member is protected by the combined strength of the mass. For example, although the differential between skilled and unskilled workers has hardly changed in a century (reflecting to some degree the reproduction of the differential by unions), there is evidence that where unions operate, narrower sex, race and occupational differentials persist (Metcalfe, 1989). Of course, unions are not alone in maintaining the level of inequality: in 1889, when 'reliable' earnings figures were first published in Britain, the top fifth of the workforce received 43 per cent more than the national average while the bottom fifth received 31 per cent less. A century later the top fifth were 15 per cent *better off* in relative terms while the bottom fifth were 15 per cent *worse off* in relative terms (Horrie, 1989).

Third, while the leaders of the Russian trade unions and political parties were generally radical, if not revolutionary, the leaders of both the British trade unions and the Labour Party which grew out of the trade unions were generally reformist and, initially at least, of liberal rather than socialist persuasion. As such, the birthmarks of the unions upon the fledgling Labour Party remained etched indelibly upon the carcass of the mature movement. There were challenges to labourism, such as syndicalism, guild socialism and the Communist Party but they remained marginalized by the pre-existing power and success of the labourist position (Martin, 1969; Grint, 1986; Taylor, 1982; Kitching, 1983; Tomlinson, 1982).

None the less, there is no necessary connection between reformist trade union leaders and oligarchical control, nor between radical leaders and democratic control. As Zeitlin (1982) has argued, trade union bureaucracies are often defined so that radical local leaderships are outside the boundary wall and in some mysterious way perfectly aligned with the 'real' interests of the membership – which are seldom those pursued by the national leadership. Yet there is precious little evidence that, irrespective of the representative nature of the national leadership, local radicals are perfectly in tune with their members. Rather than having a division between the bureaucracy and the rank and file (led or at least represented by the radical local leaders) it is more appropriate to consider the division to be between (at least) two elites: a radical local elite and a reformist national elite. Moreover, if the actions of the rank and file are studied closely it is just as likely that they are as conservative and sectionalist as their leaders are alleged to be. If the masses are constantly betrayed or misled by their leaders one wonders not only how they could be so stupid as to re-elect them, but also how the future worker- or citizen-controlled decentralized society can be left safely in the hands of such a manipulable mass. The alternative is to assume, not that leaders are trustworthy and faithful to the ideals of the members, but that those who stray too far from the straight and narrow either lose support or members.

Fourth, and finally, labourism's success relates to the activities of the state. It should become clear from the discussion of the labour process below that conflict is generated at the point of production through the contrasting and conflicting interests of individuals and groups. Most of these conflicts become manifest as economistic desires of one form or another but the resolution of these conflicts in 'political' or 'economic' arenas, and through radical or reformist methods, depends to a large degree upon the presence or absence of collective bargaining. That is to say, where conflicts generated at the point of production can be resolved at the point of production through the bargaining of unions and employers, the conflict tends to remain contained and a disjunction is erected between industrial and political actions. By and large this is how British industrial relations have been constructed, with the activities of the state normally remaining in the background. This does not mean that collective bargaining operates autonomously of political interests nor does it exist within the arena of equal parties so beloved of pluralists, but it does mean that conflicts can be dispersed before they build into political movements with serious implications for the legitimacy of the state. This has been particularly significant with regard to the antecedent industrialization of Britain which provided for a generally buoyant economy and hence facilitated the buying-off, rather than the suppression, of working-class discontent through the raising of living standards. In contrast, where 'legitimate' collective bargaining has not been possible, either through state action or inaction, for example in France until relatively recently or pre-Weimar Germany, Francoist Spain, tsarist Russia or communist Poland, the result has often been the adoption of more radical and political strategies. Thus, just as democracy has often resulted from a realization by the authorities of the consequences of denying a legitimate voice to the population, so too trade unionism has often been tolerated by employers and the state for equally instrumental reasons (see Rustow, 1970; Therborn, 1977). But the legitimation or toleration of class-based trade unions by the state and employers, while it may have diverted pressure away from direct political challenges to capitalism or the state, has not ensured the creation of a quiescent workforce: industrial conflict is as much an inescapable element of work as collective forms of worker organization.

Class and industrial action

Class conflict *qua* industrial action has been the focus of a considerable amount of debate within the sociology of work (Hyman, 1972; Batstone et al., 1978; Durcan et al., 1983; Shorter and Tilly, 1974; Cronin, 1979; Gouldner, 1954; Eldridge, 1968; Edwards, 1981; Batstone, 1985; Jackson, 1987). However, almost all of this has been concentrated upon industrial action *qua* strikes; the number of studies about absenteeism, sabotage, working to rule etc. – that is, 'cut price' industrial action as Flanders (1970: 112) called it – is small in comparison (cf. Hudson, 1970; Brown, 1977; Batstone et al., 1977; Dubois, 1979; Edwards and Scullion, 1982). In itself this is an inversion of the probable occurrence of strikes and non-strike action: less than a third of manufacturing plants typically experience strike action by manual workers in any two-year period yet almost half may suffer some other form of industrial action (usually an overtime ban or work to rule) (Brown, 1981: 81).

Strikes, according to the Department of Employment – the central institution for the collation of strike data in Britain – are defined as: all stoppages of work due to industrial disputes involving ten or more workers and lasting for at least one day. Where the aggregate days lost exceed a hundred working days a strike is included in the data even if it fails to count under the preceding criteria. Whether this measure is an accurate reflection of strikes in British industry is difficult to say. Brown (1981) estimates that since Britain has historically been particularly affected by short and small-scale stoppages, especially in manufacturing industry, as many as half the actual strikes may be missed. It is, however, more conventional to assume that the statistics cover around 66 per cent of the total numbers of strikes and 95 per cent of the days lost. The disparity really relates to the ease with which long stoppages are recorded and the difficulty of accounting for the lightning strikes that appear to persist in particular industries, for example car manufacturing.

Most of Britain's strikes have tended to be unofficial, though since the Thatcher government's legislative changes there has been a swing towards official strikes. The swing back to unofficial action on the London Underground, British Rail and London buses in 1989 (Beavis, 1989; Kemp, 1989) was just one attempt in a long history of industrial action that seeks to circumvent what the strikers perceive to be restrictive legal controls. The unofficial element is significant in so far as two countries may have identical strike data but the one where 'lightning' unofficial strikes are most prominent may suffer the greatest economic damage. The Donovan Commission (1968) was broadly in agreement with this short strike/high damage analysis, though Turner (1969) suggested that the impact of short strikes tended to be limited to the enterprise directly affected, while long strikes had far-reaching consequences for industry as a whole. Since then there have been important changes in the occupational sources of strike action with the heavy manufacturing industries being replaced by more white-collar and service sector strikes. The Donovan Commission is also important in so far as it highlighted the '**British disease**' with the number of working days lost per year hovering around 4 million. The disease promptly developed even more symptoms with 1979 accumulating 29 million days lost and the miners' strike of 1984 itself resulting in 22 million days lost. However, by 1991 it had begun to look as if the 'disease' had run its course – and with it an excuse for Britain's relative economic decline. The raw data are reproduced in table 2.

Table 2 British strike statistics (annual averages), 1895–2002

Year	No. of Stoppages	Workers involved	Working days lost	No. of trade unionists	Trade union density (%)
1895–9	777		7,470,000	1,701,000	11
1900–4	484		2,888,000	2,004,000	12
1905–9	445		4,204,000	2,336,000	14
1910–14	932	993,250	16,120,000	3,480,000	20
1915–19	890	1,060,600	10,378,000	5,792,000	32
1920–4	857	1,061,000	30,277,000	6,316,000	35
1925–9	393	472,000	13,207,000	5,062,000	27
1930–4	412	289,000	3,980,000	4,578,000	24
1935–9	863	359,000	1,938,000	5,671,000	29
1940–4	1491	499,000	1,813,000	7,581,000	38
1945–9	1881	507,000	2,235,000	8,901,000	43
1950–4	1701	584,000	1,903,000	9,500,000	45
1955–9	2530	742,000	4,602,000	9,722,000	44
1960–4	2512	1,499,000	3,180,000	10,010,000	44
1965–9	2380	1,213,000	3,920,000	10,291,000	44
1970–4	2884	1,567,000	14,039,000	11,380,000	49
1975–9	2310	1,658,000	11,663,000	12,763,000	53
1980–4	1363	1,297,000	10,487,000	11,775,000	50
1985–9	890	783,000	3,939,000	10,611,000	46
1990–4	334	223,000	824,000	8,169,000	36
1995–9	213	180,000	495,000	7,454,000	31
2000–2	184	435,000	782,000	7,416,000	29

Source: H. Pelling, 1976; Bain and Price, 1980; Salamon, 1987; Jackson, 1977; *Employment Gazette* (various)

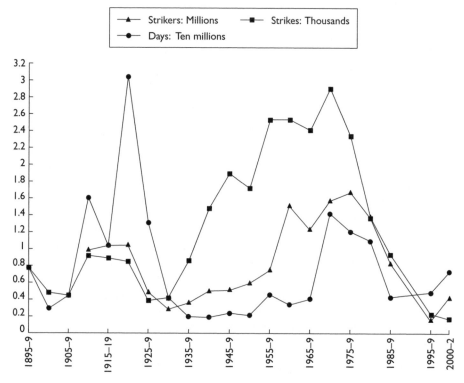

Figure 5 UK strikes, 1895–1996: number of strikers (millions), strikes (thousands), days lost (ten millions)
Source: Table 2

To make interpretation of this data a little easier, figure 5 compares the number of strikes, the numbers of strikers and the number of days lost for the entire period. Two points are worth highlighting. First, the decline in the number of strikes and days lost predates the Thatcher administration and may not, therefore, be a direct and simple consequence of the latter's actions. Second, strike indicators tend to correlate with general economic activity, rather than political administrations. Indeed, when the data for international comparisons are procured it would seem that, with the exceptions of Denmark, Finland and New Zealand, all the major Western societies have witnessed parallel declines in strike activity (Brown and Wadhwani, 1990). This is graphically illustrated in figure 6.

It is important to note here that the strike data concern internal features not external effects. Even when the media consider the impact of strikes in terms of 'lost production' it is not always an accurate assessment since much production can actually be 'saved' through overtime or higher subsequent productivity etc. Strikes are also more significant where they affect other production. For example, a strike in a manufacturing plant operating within 'just in time' procedures, where stock levels are minimal, can be more effective and affective than where the more conventional 'just in case' procedure operates and stocks include high levels of reserves – just in case a shortage occurs.

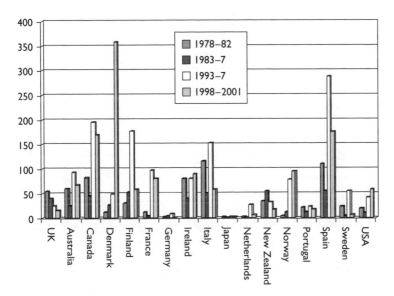

Figure 6 National comparison of strikes, selected years (days lost per 1,000 employees, by country)
Source: Brown and Wadhwani, 1990, and *Labour Market Trends*, April 2003: 182.

Perhaps more important is the disproportionate influence strikes seem to have on the media rather than in industry itself. For example, as Durcan et al. note, production lost through strikes is negligible compared with total production (about 0.25 per cent) (1983: 426), with the time lost through unemployment (about 6 per cent) (1983: 404) and, at least in Australia, compared with industrial accidents (Dabscheck and Niland, 1981). Indeed, even when strikes apparently reached their nadir, in 1987, it is still the case that for every three days lost through strikes there are two hundred lost through absenteeism (Cornelius, 1987). Physical illness is a significant factor: in 1988 there were 46 million days lost through back problems alone: almost twice as many as lost in the miners' strike (NBPA, 1989). It might also serve as a useful illustration to know that the average employee was involved in less than three hours of strikes in each year of the 1980s. In the 1970s the average was four hours a year; whereas the 1960s, the origin of the British disease, involved an average of three hours. Only the second and third decades of this century have involved more action per employee, with the 1920s marking the peak at one day's strike per year. Whichever decade is chosen the actual period spent on strike by the average British employee is minimal.

Exactly where these strikes tend to occur and what causes them are represented in figure 7. Three aspects are critical: first, the variability of the strike pattern; second, the domination of different sectors – thus in 1993 and 2001 it was mining, energy and water that dominated, whereas in 1996 and 2002 it was services; third, manufacturing workers seldom dominate the strike data. Figure 8 provides a different view on the UK strike data. This time the official cause is highlighted, and while redundancy dominated at the beginning of the

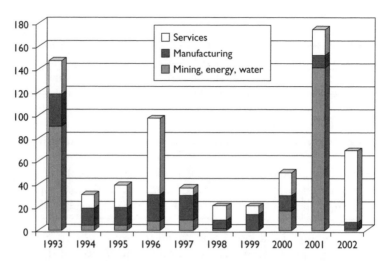

Figure 7 Working days lost by employment category (UK), 1993–2002
Source: *Labour Market Trends*, June 2003

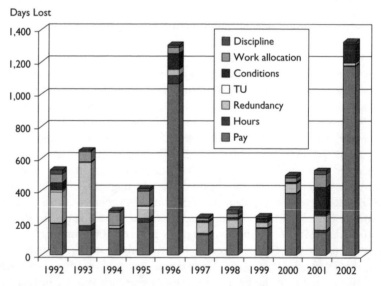

Figure 8 Working days lost by main cause (UK), 1992–2002
Source: *Labour Market Trends*, June 2003

1990s, almost all the rest of the time it is pay that relates to strikes. I say 'relates' rather than 'causes' because very often disputes are resolved by a pay deal even if they are not necessarily caused by a problem of pay. For example, a disciplinary dispute may start when managers are perceived to be acting 'tyrannically' by the employees. But since it is infinitely easier to resolve such a dispute with a pay rise rather than a deal to limit the powers of management, many disputes end up being 'paid off'.

It was for these kinds of reason, amongst many others, that labour and social democratic governments in particular have striven to introduce processes that defuse disputes before they arise. For example, the Information and Consultation Directive means that from March 2005 all employees in companies with more than 50 employees have the right to be informed and consulted – through their elected representatives – on matters affecting their jobs and future employment prospects. Similarly, by 2003 the TUC's Partnership Institute had facilitated the construction of 74 partnership agreements between trade unions and employers that attempted to forge more constructive relationships. Despite criticism that these 'blur' the boundaries between employee and employer and are merely a more sophisticated form of management control, the agreements do seem to inhibit redundancies, shorten working hours and enhance pay (Pandya, 2003: 20). Nevertheless, it is worth pondering on the London Underground strike that disrupted the system at the end of June 2004. The strike, originally aligned with a national rail strike, was called to protest against the cutting of the rail workers' pension schemes, and came after the number of strikes reached an all-time low in the previous year (133) and in the face of successful action to defend pensions by the strongest of all unions – what Denny et al. (2004: 26) called the AUENED (Amalgamated Union of Executive and Non-Executive Directors). If, as chapter 9 suggests, the bosses can promote themselves at the expense of shareholders and employees, it is little wonder that rail workers try to imitate their goal if not their methods.

It is also worth considering the extent to which trade unions act as merely a conduit for workplace grievances, rather than the cause of them. For example, as figure 9 suggests, if we compare strike data with the number of individual

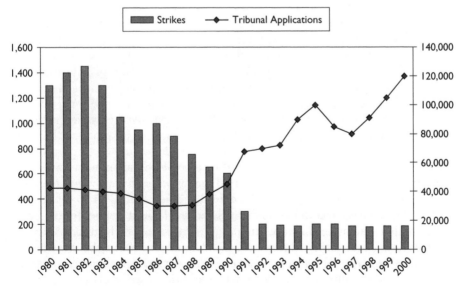

Figure 9 Strikes and industrial tribunal applications (UK), 1980–2000
Source: Reconstructed from Burkitt, 2001: 17

applications to industrial tribunals, there is at least some inverse relationship between them. In other words, it may be that the collective disputes at the root of the 1970s' strikes have merely been displaced into individual disputes in the 1980s and 1990s. This hypothesis is also supported by the growth of personnel help services – for instance, in 2003 Acas received 750,000 telephone calls for help, split evenly between employers and individual employees (Caulkin, 2004).

Relatedly, it is not the case that strikes are axiomatically indicative of union strength. Some clearly are, but several strikes have been concerned with last-ditch defences rather than in pursuit of an expanding orbit of control or reward. Hence the absence of strikes may well be a demonstration of union strength not weakness. For example, Swedish unions have low levels of strikes but relatively high levels of material reward and influence over management. Similarly, there are few strikes among workers within small plants, but this represents the common weakness of labour in such situations not their strength or satisfaction (Rainnie, 1989). Relatedly, despite the decline in the number of strikes in Britain since 1979, real wages have kept ahead of inflation and productivity, with the pay of unionized plants possibly being boosted by between 8 per cent (Jowell et al., 1989) and 10 per cent (Metcalfe, 1989) in Britain, 4 per cent in Switzerland and 26 per cent in the USA. Of course, some of this pay inflation is a consequence of skill shortages, especially in the south-east of England, but nevertheless a union movement that had ostensibly been tamed should not have been in a position to secure inflationary wage rises, nor required the further legislative constraints in 1990. It is also true that during periods where product market competition is intensifying many manufacturing firms are not in a position to risk all by the pursuit of macho management policies; a reason, no doubt, for the relatively minimal use of such Thatcherite policies outside the public sector (Batstone, 1988a).

The British strike data are limited to industrial disputes; political strikes are excluded from the data, though precisely what counts as a political strike is unclear (Hain, 1986). For example, the 1974 strike by dockers for May Day to be declared a public holiday was included as an industrial dispute while the AUEW strike against the sequestration of its funds by the Industrial Relations Court in the same year was excluded as a political strike. In fact, three one-day strikes in 1971 against the Industrial Relations Bill involved twice as many strikers as were eventually included in the strike statistics for that year but they were discounted as political strikes (Silver, 1973). It could well be argued that strikes for higher wages during a period of incomes policy are action against the state and therefore political, as indeed might be all strikes within the Civil Service. Similarly, all strikes could be considered as political in so far as they embody aspects of power that are inherently political, albeit not necessarily party political. For example, Batstone et al.'s (1978) analysis of strike situations suggests that part of the motivation for strike action lies in the struggle for control between employers and employees. Where managers are perceived to be acting beyond the limit of their legitimate authority a strike becomes political because it concerns authority relations, but this need not develop into either party- or class-based politics. Rather, such conflict concerns **factory politics**, a dispute about control over the labour process which is as likely to be sectional as universal in origin and effect.

The collection and definitions of strikes are very varied across time and space. In Britain the three main indices are the number of stoppages, the number of workers involved, and the number of working days lost. Most of the data are obtained through the voluntary self-reporting of action by employers, while in Germany employers are legally obliged to report the number of days lost. However, the German statistics do not record the number of strikes and the Americans have recently altered their criteria for a strike from at least six strikers involved to at least 1,000 strikers involved. It is estimated that this order of redefinition will remove 96 per cent of the actions previously regarded as strikes, an action which makes them of 'little analytic value' according to Edwards (1983a), though the more recent re-analysis by Garen and Krislov (1988) is markedly more optimistic about the utility of the new data. Other problems for the comparison of data include the absence of a threshold for inclusion in the French, Italian and Belgian statistics as well as the changes that occur in the definitions over time. This obviously poses considerable difficulties but, providing the definitions remain the same over the time period in question, significant trends between countries across time can still be compared.

Predictions of strike rates, as manifestations of wider social conflicts, have varied widely, from Marx's assumptions about the ever-increasing intensity of industrial conflict within capitalism to Kerr et al.'s (1960) polar opposite position, whereby the capitalist and communist worlds converged and industrial relations became institutionalized and civilized. A further possibility is Dahrendorf's (1959) hybrid theory in which conflicts based on class are replaced by conflicts grounded in authority. None of these prescriptive views appears to have been realized: there may well be patterns within strikes but they are seldom unilinear. The actual study of strikes has been as varied as the patterns: some have pursued a single strike while others have analysed broad comparative trends. Within both forms of study the focus has often ranged between the causes of strikes, the process of strike mobilization and variations in the propensity to strike. In short, the topic is enormous, but one of the most important aspects to bear in mind when considering strikes is the historical patterning that tends to occur, often in conjunction with business cycles and other related political developments.

Accounting for industrial action

The disorganization model

The first thing to consider is attempts to explain *why* strikes occur. It is common to delineate three variant explanations: social disorganization or breakdown; frustration and communication; and conflicting or contradictory interests. The disorganization model is often linked to long-term trends and individual case studies: industrialization leads, in a pattern derived from Durkheimian principles, initially to the breakdown of consensus, although the institution-alization of collective bargaining ultimately rebuilds the consensus (Kerr et al., 1960). Alternatively, the structure, technology or management patterns are radic-ally altered, leading to some form of temporary moral disequilibrium (Gouldner, 1954; Warner and Low, 1947). An immediate question for the disorganization theories is: 'Can they account for the disorganized environments that do not lead to strikes?' For example, in the Warner and Low case the observed dis-organization at work had been preceded by a long-term community and indus-trial disorganization so that it is not self-evident what sparked off the specific conflict.

The frustration model

The second strike model relates to frustration and problematic communications. Quite often these accounts minimize the explanations of the strikers involved and seek out what they regard as the more compelling reasons, such as the extent of effective channels of communications to diffuse work-based frustra-tion (Scott and Homans, 1947). The frustration model implicitly embodies an unmediated connection between frustration and action, yet it seems much more likely that between frustration and action lies a critical variable – organization (Shorter and Tilly, 1974: 338). In fact, Shorter and Tilly reproduce the same structural approach they criticize in Scott and Homans, arguing that wage demands are not so much the causes of strikes as the symptoms of deeper problems. Yet if wage demands are not causal variables one then has to explain why so many strikers appear to be so easily misled while their academic interpreters alone are capable of establishing their true motivations. This does not mean either that dissatisfaction with wages is sufficient to generate a strike nor that all strikes are about wages. If, as suggested in chapter 2, the moral economy continues to pervade work then many so-called 'economically irrational' strikes are being analysed through the wrong approach: moral principles are not lost in work.

There is, in fact, considerable controversy as to whether strikes over wages are actually economically rational in so far as the wages lost through striking are seldom made up by any increases gained through a successful strike. Skeels (1971) argues that strikes are *initiated* through decisions that are economically rational but they may continue beyond the point at which they become 'self-financing'; though since one can never be sure what would have happened if strike action had not occurred (i.e., wages may have dropped dramatically), scepticism of such economic analyses should remain. On the other hand, strikes can impose severe financial penalties upon strikers right from the very beginning of their action (Gennard, 1977; Durcan and McCarthy, 1974). What-ever issue or issues the strike concerns, the way in which they become legitimated as justifications for strike activity appears to depend crucially upon the action of particular members of the workplace organization (Batstone et al., 1978), and inevitably entails some aspect of the wage-effort or reward-deprivation bargain (Baldamus, 1961). The implication of this is that the strike situation is seldom static and is generally subject to negotiation and redefinition. This does not mean that strike situations are completely random: although variations between and within industries do occur it is nevertheless the case that different industries appear to be associated with different forms of industrial conflict (Knowles, 1952).

The conflict model

The third approach identified is in terms of conflicting or contradictory interests. These arguments tend to derive from Marxist analyses of economic exploitation and alienation, but the wage-effort model of Baldamus is equally relevant: since the labour contract seldom specifies the exact amount of effort required for a particular wage it is in the interests of employers to maximize the effort of employees and in the interest of employees to minimize effort. Yet neither model can explain the timing or vigour of particular strikes: if the interests of workers and managers are permanently opposed why do strikes break out only occasionally? One could resort to the conventional Marxist default category of false consciousness, but aside from the implicit arrogance of this explanation, which sometimes reserves true knowledge for the educated elite of Marxist intellectuals, it is not clear whether all strikes that do break out are manifestations of 'true' consciousness, nor why they break out at all. This is not to dispute the attempts by the state and management to distort the picture of reality presented to the workers but it does deny the unfailing success of this ruse.

Organizational models

While all three 'universal' models are unsatisfactory, other studies have striven to demonstrate the value of organizational facilities to the generation of strikes, and the process by which the institutionalization of industrial relations leads to a decline in strike rates. One of the classic arguments in this vein is that of Kerr and Siegel (1954), who attempted to explain the inter-industry propensities to strike that were common across a number of countries. The focus of their explanation lay in terms of the most strike-prone industries being those in which workers constituted an 'isolated mass'. High strike proneness, they argued, was associated with single industry communities, little occupational differentiation, geographical or social isolation from the wider society, and group cohesion. These factors were seen to influence the disposition of workers to strike and their ability to strike. Strikes were interpreted as 'colonial revolts' in so far as they were attacks upon authority far removed from the workplace, and operated as substitutes for occupational and social mobility as well as the general build-up of social tensions. However, such groups could strike only because of their group cohesion and, relatedly, their isolation from broader social pressures.

The Kerr and Siegel hypothesis has been subjected to numerous criticisms, not least that the empirical evidence does not fit their theory (Shorter and Tilly, 1974; Edwards, 1978, 1981; Jackson, 1977, 1987). But the important point here is that they bring into account an organizational variable – a necessary mediation between dissatisfaction at work and strike action. Shorter and Tilly (1974) have also pursued this institutional theme with regard to French strikes, arguing that union strength is a necessary precondition of strike action, though it must be said that the causal direction may well be the other way around. That is, as in so much of social science, the correlation between two forms of activities does not specify the direction of the causal relationship. In this instance it could be argued that strikes lead to union strength rather than vice versa.

The withering away of strikes

This kind of approach is extended by the institutionalization of conflict argument of Ross and Hartmann (1960), in which the organizational development of unions and collective bargaining leads to a decrease, nay the 'withering away', of strikes. They identify four broad patterns of strike activity. The first of these is the Northern European (mark 1) pattern, covering countries like the UK and West Germany. Here strikes involve few members and last only a relatively short period of time. The Northern European (mark 2), or Scandinavian, model reveals minimal member involvement but long-lasting strikes, while the Mediterranean-Asian pattern (France, Italy, Japan and Australia) has the opposite, that is to say high levels of involvement by members but short strikes. Finally, the North American pattern has fairly high levels of involvement in long strikes. Ross and Hartmann attempt to explain these patterns by looking at the configurations of variables rather than single variables in isolation. These variables include first, the stability of the labour movement, in terms of its age and membership, both of which serve to reduce conflict; the longer a union has been in existence the more likely it is to have established a *modus vivendi* with the employers, and the more likely it is to have secured the interests of its members. The second variable focuses upon leadership conflicts in the labour movement, in terms of factionalism and rival unions on the one hand and strength of the communist groups on the other. Both weaken central leadership, and therefore the less united a union movement is the more likely it is to promote conflict. Third, the status of union management relations, manifested by the degree of acceptance of unions by employers and the consolidation of bargaining structures, reduces conflict; the more egalitarian the union/employer relationship the less likely are strikes. Fourth, strikes are reduced where the Labour Party is a potent force, and particularly where it is in office, since it can achieve workers' aims through political means, thereby reducing the potential resource implications for workers and buttressing the Labour Party. And finally, conflict may be reduced where the state actively intervenes in industrial relations and has its own dispute-resolution policies to minimize industrial disruption. Where all five features were present, Ross and Hartman argued that strikes would 'wither away'.

Perhaps the first point to make is that the analysis was developed between 1948 and 1956 and since then conditions in many places have altered radically on several occasions. In short, a central enigma still remains: do strong unions become strong through striking and are their current resources so strong that striking becomes unnecessary?

Power resources models

For Shorter and Tilly's (1974) French study the issue is crucially one of control over power resources, and this control is regarded as a precondition of collective action. Thus conflict is most likely when control over such power resources becomes subject to movement, i.e., when opportunities arise and when the organizational 'latticework' is sufficient to transform individual perceptions of opportunity into collective action, and in particular into working-class action.

Cronin's (1979) approach reintroduces workers' expectations linked to the patterning of **economic 'long waves'**, but although his analysis appears to explain certain periods of strike explosions it cannot explain others. Korpi and Shalev (1979, 1980) attempt to fill this sort of partial analysis by arguing that the shifts in the distribution of power affect not only the chances of successful industrial action but also the assessment of rewards. Yet, because there is a lag in the relationship between the distribution of power and its effects on aspirations there may well be periods when power resources do not match aspirations and strikes may either fail or fail to materialize. Furthermore, the results of any conflict themselves often lead to the institutionalization of class conflict in collective bargaining and working-class political parties; thus as the labour movement grows it tends to transfer interest away from the industrial scene to the political. This approach fixes attention upon the level of working-class mobilization (defined as the level of unionization and support for left political parties) and the degree of control it has over government. Hence, in Norway and Sweden the labour movement has achieved a high level of mobilization and relatively stable political control and the result is low levels of industrial action. In contrast, Britain has a high level of labour mobilization but only sporadic political control with the consequence that conflict is high. France also has a high strike rate because of the limited influence of the left in the political sphere. In sum, where social democratic governments achieve power, and most decisively where they implement social democratic policies that favour the working class, strike levels will fall.

The superficial similarities with the Ross and Hartmann approach are, of course, striking, though Korpi and Shalev are keen to note their distancing from any structural approach: for them the structures of power resources etc. merely provide the preconditions or potential for certain forms of action and limit the viability of others. However, to explain why certain actions occur requires an analysis of the actions of individuals and groups who must mobilize the resources and turn the potential into reality. Equally relevant, one should acknowledge the import of wider economic preconditions for strike action: if the material resources for some form of compromise simply do not exist then strike action is unlikely to occur and even less likely to succeed where it does occur. Korpi and Shalev certainly seem to assume that wherever strike action does occur it implicitly embodies the political unity of the working class, and they consequently fail to consider the possibility discussed earlier that the labour process itself generates disunity as well as unity among the workers. In particular, one might note here that the institutional features of industrial relations, notably the forms of collective bargaining, may themselves be influential in determining the success of class-oriented union policies: where bargaining is decentralized it is enormously difficult to construct and reproduce a co-ordinated wage policy that protects the interests of the weakest as against those of the strongest.

The institutional model

The most institutional argument remains that of Clegg (1976) who claims, from his analysis of six countries, that strike patterns can be explained primarily by reference to differences in the nature of collective bargaining. For Clegg, plant bargaining leads to large numbers of official strikes while regional or industry-wide bargaining leads to a smaller number of strikes but a larger number of strikers. Where a sophisticated disputes procedure exists, such as in Sweden as opposed to France, then the number of strikes is likely to be lower. Similarly, the limited number of disputes in West Germany can be associated with the labour courts and work councils which act as institutional defusers of industrial conflict. Nevertheless, the critical aspect for Clegg is the level of bargaining, and where decentralized bargaining occurs, inter-union rivalry and unofficial action are most likely.

There are clearly limits to Clegg's argument and he acknowledges several of these. First, to focus the research upon the influence of collective bargaining structures begs the question of their origin: is it the level of bargaining which is significant or the forces that spawned the particular level and form of bargaining? Second, the data are drawn only from countries with collective bargaining but many others do not have this, even if they do have trade unions. To what extent, then, can his arguments be extrapolated? Third, his data may explain long-term trends but there are considerable difficulties in accounting for short-term variations. Fourth, as several studies have suggested, the very act of changing the form of collective bargaining may in itself have no impact upon the overall levels of industrial action (Edwards and Scullion, 1982), and may actually stimulate unrest through the disequilibrium introduced (Hyman, 1972). This is clearly evident in the explosion of strikes that usually accompanies the termination of an incomes policy or, as the National Power Loading Agreement (NPLA) of the miners showed, displacing the locus of collective bargaining may simply shift the level of conflict in parallel with the level of the bargaining: in this instance from a multiplicity of short pit level strikes to infrequent but very damaging national stoppages in association with the move from pit level bargaining to national bargaining. Thus, in 1956, ten years before the NPLA, almost 80 per cent of all strikes in Britain were in coal mining. Four years after the agreement, in 1970, a mere 4 per cent of strikes were in mining (Allen, 1981: 90). Yet this movement did not, ultimately, undermine the expressions of conflict in the mining industry but merely served to redirect them into the national explosions in the mines in 1972, 1974 and notably in 1984. As Krieger concludes: 'for the first time the interests of the face worker and of the miner working elsewhere below ground were linked, since all their wage rates were covered by a single comprehensive agreement' (1984: 269). In itself the preponderance of miners' strikes in the statistics at both the unofficial and the official end of the spectrum, from the lightning walk-out to the 358 days of the last national stoppage, should alert us to the problem of using such aggregated strike data as clear indicators of industrial passivity or unrest in the wider economic environment. Until very recently the strike picture has been dominated by five industrial areas: mining, the docks, shipbuilding, car manufacturing, and iron and steel. In 1979 over half of the days lost were derived from a strike by engineering workers; in 1980 the national steel strike accounted for three-quarters of the days lost; whereas the miners' strike of 1984–5 was responsible for 83 per cent and 63 per cent of the days lost in the respective years (*Employment Gazette*, July 1988: 374). All of these have either suffered a slimming down that approximates industrial anorexia and/or a lengthy strike followed by relative passivity. Yet in 1987, over two years after the collapse of the national miners' strike, 30 per cent of the total number of stoppages were still associated with the mining industry. More significantly still, 10 per cent occurred in the fields of public administration and education and a further 10 per cent in communication industries (*Employment Gazette*, July 1988). Although some major industries and their unions were clearly devastated during the 1980s, other, newer industries and unions have sprung up to fill the gap.

Similarly, it has to be accepted that even where models of strike explanation appear to account for activity within certain periods of time this does not imply the universal utility of any model across space and time; the level of political and economic contingency is simply too high for any universal model to cope (Davies, 1979; Edwards, 1983b). Nor is there any unmediated connection between patterns of union strength and strike activity: as the power workers have consistently demonstrated, unions in strategic positions of power do not have to strike to persuade management to provide relatively high incomes. In fact, it is Clegg's later work (1979: 274–7) which establishes a further particular link between decentralized bargaining and wildly fluctuating incomes in strike-prone industries, though as Edwards (1983b: 223–4) points out, such material frustrations do not in and of themselves lead to high strike rates; for that a strong union organization must exist. But strong unions are themselves dependent upon a cohesive community that exists beyond the bounds of the factory gates or the mine. Not only have strikes tended historically to relate to communities where the domestic/work boundary is ambiguous, such as pit and fishing villages, but even the longest mass strike in British history, the miners' strike of 1984–5, was critically reliant upon the action of autonomous women's groups in sustaining the communities through their collective ideal.

The asymmetric model

In Batstone's (1985) analysis, it seems more appropriate to assume that strike rates rise with the following features. First, an asymmetrical relationship between the union and its bargaining structure; that is, where the organizational strength and the bargaining institutions do not coincide. Second, where the political left is disunited such that there can be little prospect of a left government gaining and holding power, and introducing pro-labour policies. Third, where the union is in a monopoly position so that its action will not lead to an immediate loss of membership elsewhere. Fourth, where there is a wide degree of variation between blue- and white-collar workers, between men and women, and between workers and managers. Yet although these macro-level analyses are important they seldom explain the way the structural limitation and opportunities they illuminate become realized or missed by those involved on the shop floor. In short, are strikes generated purely by socially structured conditions or do social actors play a significant part in bringing them off?

Strikes as social processes

One of the major problems with answering this question relates to the way strikes have become symbolic of heroic resistance by the labouring masses against the exploitative forces of capital on the one hand, and the greedy and political machinations of an unrepresentative, extremist and bullying minority on the other hand. The former analysis usually considers strikes as spontaneously constructed manifestations of structural inequalities and exploitation. The latter analysis disavows the structural approach altogether and focuses almost wholly upon the personalities and personal whims of the strikers, and particularly the strike leaders who appear to have a charismatic appeal capable of inducing blind obedience from otherwise rational workers (see Turner, 1963; Hyman, 1972: 106–39). Yet the purely individualist approach cannot explain the frequency and social patterning of strikes, while the strictly structural approach systematically fails to explain why similar structural conditions produce dissimilar strike results.

An attempt to trace the process by which the potential for strike action becomes realized is made by Batstone et al. (1978). The viewpoint here is one in which the organization of strike action is considered as an active social process in which the unsystematic discontent of the rank and file is channelled and controlled by certain of the shop stewards. This channelling and articulation of grievances is developed through 'systems of argument' or **'vocabularies of motive'**, to use Wright Mills's phrase, and the study illustrates the way the 'leader' shop stewards actively mould shop-floor opinion, and are courted by management because of their leadership abilities. This moulding process, however, is intimately related to the direct experiences and perceptions of the workers involved; opinion can be moulded but it is seldom successfully manufactured *de novo*. Other 'populist' shop stewards are mere mouthpieces of the rank and file, subject to their capricious changes and thus generally limited in their influence with workers or managers, among other things because they lack the influential network of social relationships which sustain the 'leader' stewards in power. This is not to say that 'leader' stewards lead their members continually into conflictual situations; unless these bring positive results on every occasion such a strategy would soon prove self-defeating. Nor is this to suggest that the rank and file are infinitely manipulable, they are clearly not; the refusal of strikers to return to work despite the request of their stewards and the refusal of workers to accede to the advice for a strike by stewards are clear demonstrations of the limits of leadership in such inevitably contingent situations. It is because work relationships are permanently renegotiated, at least to some extent, that strikes are necessarily difficult to predict. Thus even allegedly structural features/determinants of work are themselves open to renegotiation, as the reconstruction of union organization in the wake of the unofficial strike at Pilkingtons demonstrated (Lane and Roberts, 1971). Nevertheless, given the necessary preconditioning organization underlying the vast majority of strikes it is questionable whether many spontaneous strikes are actually unorganized (Batsone et al., 1978: 222).

As Batstone et al. conclude:

> Structural factors may foster conditions which make strikes easier, but at the same time strikes and other forms of collective bargaining, along with many other factors, may change those factors. Moreover the nature of worker organization may change quite rapidly while the process of mobilization for strike action is by no means a certain one. . . . An understanding of the phenomenon of strikes may start from an awareness of the subordination of the worker, but it has to go further and recognize the complex historical interplay between structure and consciousness as mediated by organizational processes. (1978: 223)

Now it is clear that no direct correlation between union organization and industrial militancy prevails: some of the strongest unions in organizational and strategic terms have a record that displays none of the strike actions commonly associated with powerful groups (for example the electricity supply industries). Organization, therefore, provides the means to develop militant strategies but also a level of institutionalization that may either negate the necessity for strike action or actually demobilize the membership.

The institutionalization of conflict

The debate over the value of a reformist strategy within trade unions has been long and relatively acrimonious (Pfeffer, 1979; Herding, 1972; Hyman,

1989: 149–65; Kelly, 1988: 147–83; McIlroy, 1988: 127–57; Batstone, 1988a: 72–119) in a way not dissimilar to the equivalent argument within the realms of socialist strategies (Turner, 1986; Jacques and Mulhearn, 1981; Buick and Crump, 1986; Coates and Johnston, 1983). In essence, trade union organization, in association with the institutionalization of conflict expressed through collective bargaining and shop stewards' organizations, legitimates the expression of conflict but simultaneously constrains its expression through agreed channels. Thus unions achieve a stake in the system's survival both because of the substantive benefits accrued and through the legitimacy afforded to it. Such institutionalization for radicals inevitably degenerates into bureaucracy with the Michelsian consequences of **oligarchical control** replacing representative democracy. Certainly the recent period has seen the development of management-sponsored shop steward organizations, often at the expense of the full-time union officials, but the evidence for their 'betrayal' of rank and file interests is sketchy and it is not self-evident why the rank and file would allow their interests to be supplanted by such renegades. It is much more likely that most 'institutionalization' of industrial relations can be explained through the mutual recognition of, and desire for, some form of incomplete but necessary accommodation between labour and capital rather than through union sell-outs or quiescence. Because the accommodation is incomplete, in terms of procedural and substantive features, no permanent consensus can prevail. Indeed, the very agreement itself provides for yet further disagreements in so far as rules and regulations appertaining to agreements are seldom self-explanatory. It is, as Mann (1973a) has noted, pragmatic acquiescence not ideological accommodation that explains the development of collective bargaining. It is also a precondition of pragmatic acquiescence that the material basis for this is reproduced: without a permanent, if erratic, rise in living standards the primary mechanism for workers' 'allegiance' to their employer would surely wither and the labour process become the locus of ever-greater levels of industrial conflict. But is the labour process as critical to the sociology of work as Braverman and labour process theorists maintain?

Marx, Taylorism and the capitalist labour process

Much of the contemporary interest of Marxists and radicals in the issues of labour and industrial control is derived in some way from the seminal work of Braverman: *Labor and Monopoly Capital*, written in 1974. Braverman reopened a concern of Marx that the critical area for explaining social conflict and control was the **labour process** itself: the place where commodities were constructed and developed by mixing human labour with raw materials. It was the exploitative and alienating essence of the labour process under capitalism which made the system inherently flawed for Marx, and thus necessitated its complete destruction through revolutionary action. With the failure of such action in Russia to bring about the communist utopia, and more particularly the failure of revolutionary action in Western Europe, Western Marxists, especially those

in the Frankfurt school of critical theory, began to explore the issues of capitalist culture and ideology in an attempt to account for these failures (Jay, 1973;
Held, 1980). More orthodox Marxists, however, remained wedded to the notion
of economic determinism – the inevitable working out of economic contradictions within capitalism which would eventually lead to communism irrespective of the activities of social actors *qua* revolutionaries (McLellan, 1980). Neither
of these two alternative assessments of the situation required attention to the
point of production, and Marxist interest in work and employment itself generally waned. There were, of course, radicals working in the area of work, for
example C. Wright Mill's 1951 study of white-collar workers in the USA, and
several historical studies with radical origins (Cole and Postgate, 1938) but the
overwhelming proportion of studies of contemporary work bore little affiliation
to any form of radicalism let alone Marxism, and were perhaps closer to the
liberal managerialist position adopted, and indeed epitomized, by Kerr et al.'s
Industrialism and Industrial Man (1960).

Braverman himself saw his work as developing the expansion of Marxist
theory in the field of capitalist economic development, particularly that undertaken by Sweezy (1942) and Baran and Sweezy (1966). While they had concentrated on macro-economic 'laws' of accumulation etc., Braverman wanted
to bring the focus closer to the shop floor to what he considered as the
structurally determined imperatives of managerial control, its effects upon
the workers themselves, and the dynamic and immanent process of deskilling
and degradation that he believed underlay the progression towards monopoly
capitalism. Braverman's initial challenge to the claims of what he regarded as
capitalism's apologists was to refute the simple connection between broad changes
in the occupational structure and an increase in individual skill levels. For Braverman all such developments have to be situated against the actual content of
the jobs in question, rather than their occupational labelling, and the background
of the nineteenth-century craft worker who combined a wide range of knowledge and skills so that levels of individual discretion, autonomy and control
were high. For the capitalist the problem of work is the problem of managerial control: how can managers ensure the maximum degree of effort for the
minimum amount of reward? The solution to the problem, as perceived by Braverman following Taylor, is through extending the division of labour, separating
the conception of work from its execution, and deskilling the workforce. This
will, in theory at least, provide not only for higher levels of productivity and
cheaper labour, but also for more compliant labour. Thus the labour process
itself becomes divorced from the skills of the labourer and, therefore, from the
control of the labourer.

Such a managerial philosophy Braverman saw most clearly in the ideas of
F.W. Taylor. When Taylor began work in the USA at the turn of the century,
subcontracting was still the predominant form of labour organization, though
most firms appear to have been relatively indifferent to the methods of labour
control (see chapters 2 and 4). However, the increasing competition, and the
developments in trade unionism at the time, pushed some into searching for
alternative methods of control. In Britain one route, taken most conspicuously
by the Quaker chocolate manufacturers Cadbury and Rowntree, was a system

benevolent paternalism but others preferred a more direct method of labour control, and it was this which Taylor provided. Having worked as a labourer, clerk and machinist himself, Taylor was well aware of the problems of production at the level of the shop floor and argued that three specific reasons were evident: first, management lacked the knowledge to maximize production – their ignorance left them at the mercy of workers' wisdom; second, the workers themselves had a rationale for restricting output – the real fear of underpayment or redundancy; third, the existing payment system lacked a sufficiently sophisticated incentive scheme. Taylor castigated management, not the workforce, for these problems and insisted that they drop their conventional 'rule of thumb' schemes and appropriate his 'scientific management' techniques. These involved several discrete changes, especially technical improvements to the machinery, but more significantly they concerned the extension of the division of labour to the extent that each task was fragmented into its smallest constituent units which would be timed and measured. A piece-rate system that was individually not collectively organized (to avoid encouraging collective action and trade unions) was also essential, and this must involve accelerating rewards and punishment as the (high) targets were under- or over-shot. The jobs would be deskilled, both to further facilitate the employment of cheaper labour and to eliminate the restrictive practices then employed by employees on the basis of their monopoly over knowledge. Some of these restrictive practices, or 'natural soldiering' as Taylor called them, were related to what he regarded as the laziness inherent to human nature and could not therefore be completely eliminated. It could, however, be contained by the provision of economic incentives – the primary stimulus to work as far as Taylor was concerned. But 'systematic soldiering', i.e., that which was 'artificially' constructed and maintained by collective action, resulted from the poor supervision and problematic incentive systems that actually discouraged maximum efficiency.

Taylor's approach, like his overall philosophy, was deeply imbued with pretensions to a scientific status, and most systematic experiments were undertaken with an immigrant called Schmidt, whom Taylor believed to have the mentality of an ox, though since Schmidt was also engaged at the time in building his own house, there must have been some remarkable oxen in the States at this time. Through the close monitoring of Schmidt's work practices in shovelling pig-iron, including rest times, operating methods etc., Taylor managed to persuade Schmidt to increase his productivity by 400 per cent, in exchange for a wage increase of 40 per cent. *Homo economicus* had arrived: by the adoption of science Taylor had demonstrated the essence of his policy: 'there is no question that when the work to be done is at all complicated a good organization with a poor plant will give better results than at the best plant with a poor organization' (1903: 62). Taylor's method, then, was not so much technical as organizational and psychological: scientific management involved both an organizational and mental revolution. The barriers between worker and employer would be broken down by demonstrating that through applying his scientific principles work would become more efficient and therefore all would benefit in the increasing levels of material rewards. Of course, since the method was scientific there could be no bargaining involved; worker resistance to management may have been rational when management was irrational but under the new scheme all would gain so all resistance was irrational. The system, however, was not constructed to provide satisfying work for all; work was about the acquisition of material rewards not individual or social satisfaction, and the way to maximize rewards for all involved was to increase the division of labour (in management too), match the ability of the worker to that required by the job, use the cheapest form of labour, and adopt intensive training methods (Noble, 1974: 276).

In fact, until 1911 most of Taylor's practical work was carried out within union-free or weakly unionized plants, while the American Federation of Labour (AFL) initiated its anti-scientific management campaign. Within weeks of its first major implementation, in the state-owned arsenal at Watertown, a strike broke out, and, following a full investigation by a House of Representatives Special Committee in which widespread malpractices and arbitrary rather than scientific applications were uncovered, Taylorist methods were banned from all arsenals, Navy yards and, from 1916 to 1949, from all government-funded operations (Noble, 1974: 272; cf. Nyland, 1987).

Taylor's unpopularity was not limited to the unions and US government: despite Taylor's previous position as president of the American Society of Mechanical Engineers (in 1906) they refused to publish his *Principles of Scientific Management* on the grounds that it was not scientific. Supporters of the general movement towards a more scientific approach to management attempted to compensate for several of his most blatant errors. Chipman argued that worker consent to any development was as crucial as the scheme itself; Gantt emphasized the error of punishing low performance through Taylor's differential piece system and the need to rely on rewards in the light of the 'human factor' at work – a movement taken further and more successfully by Frank Gilbreth, and more importantly by Lillian Gilbreth, in their fusion of industrial psychology and scientific management. For Taylor it was enough that he had demonstrated the rationality of his system to the workers; for Lillian Gilbreth managers had to persuade workers that the system was rational, not simply impose it. Frank Gilbreth was more influential in reorienting scientific management towards the labour unions in a positive light. Indeed, once Taylor was dead, and with the unions involved in the war effort, a rapprochement between the AFL and the scientific management school was eventually constructed during the 1920s. By this time Taylorism had been overshadowed by the rise of corporate liberal management: human engineering not mechanical engineering was the result (Noble, 1974: 276–8).

In sum Taylorism, despite the assumptions of Braverman, had only a limited influence upon the USA. The surveys by Nadworny (1955), Nelson (1974), Ozanne (1979) and Goldman and Van Houten (1980) can demonstrate only minimal involvement outside the areas where Taylorism was outlawed; and Littler's (1982: 179–85) attempt to argue that Bedauxism, as a derivative of Taylorism, was influential, and therefore we should not dismiss Taylor, has very limited empirical support (see below). Outside the USA Taylorism was adopted wholeheartedly by Lenin (Traub, 1978), though even here the might of the Soviet state under Stalin failed in its attempt to achieve complete mastery of the labour process (Andrle, 1989; Kossler and Muchic, 1990; cf. Nyland, 1987). The position of Japan is very ambiguous. According to Dore (1973), Taylor's time and motion ideas were introduced in the period around the First World War, though his individual incentive scheme was ignored and the contradiction between an extended division of labour and the traditional Japanese distrust of delimited skills clearly inhibited a complete Taylorist revolution and many early Taylorist schemes were abandoned in the inter-war period (Littler, 1982: 156–8). Nakase (1979) claims that scientific management did not really enter Japan until 1927, and while its influence was limited within Japanese companies because of the different ideologies, several American-owned companies introduced it wholesale quite successfully. These were, however, to fall victim to Japanese fascism in the run up to the Second World War. Perhaps the most significant points are raised by Daito: 'we have not been able to identify any firm which adopted the Taylor system in its complete form' (1979: 248), and a major problem is that anything concerned with 'efficiency' was called 'scientific management'. Given the conflation of terms here it would seem that Taylorism, at least in its total form as a unique and discrete managerial strategy, rather than just one more form of an increasingly rationalized approach to management, had very limited application anywhere.

Braverman and the labour process

Whatever the limits of Taylorism in practice, it did not stop Braverman from developing a theoretical critique of capitalist labour processes based directly on Taylor's ideas. Once in the public arena Braverman's 'labour process' approach enrolled many Marxist and radical sociologists, and the new viewpoint rapidly approached *de rigueur* status for any self-respecting non-conservative academic. This section considers the essence and entrails of the labour process.

Taylorism, for Braverman (1974), comprised three 'principles'. First, 'the dissociation of the labor process from the skills of the workers' (p. 113); second, 'the separation of conception from execution' (p. 114); and third, the managerial 'use of this monopoly over knowledge to control each step of the labor process and its mode of execution' (p. 119). As Braverman notes: 'the separation of hand and brain is the most decisive single step in the division of labor taken by the capitalist mode of production'. Braverman was primarily concerned with the objective conditions of work, though he makes some acknowledgement of the way in which workers are induced to accept their degradation. In particular he notes how more fulfilling ways of working are progressively eroded and relatively high wages and consumer-oriented lifestyles dissuaded workers from seeking alternatives to monopoly capitalism. In this process of dehumanization, science and technology play their roles as servants of capital, replacing human labour, and deskilling that labour which is left, while management becomes the receptacle of the displaced knowledge and skill. The implication of this is that management itself is restructured through capitalism: it becomes not only strengthened but also stratified. Simultaneously, the process generates new service industries staffed by even lower waged and less skilled workers than operated within the previous manufacturing sectors. Hence, office work and retailing both become areas subject to the rationalizing mayhem of scientific management in Braverman's vision. Such a vision involves wresting control from the direct producers or operatives and re-establishing it, after the labour process has been fragmented and reaggregated, under the co-ordinative control of management, much of which is inscribed with a mechanical mode, for: 'machinery offers to management the opportunity to do by wholly mechanical means, that which it had previously attempted to do by organizational and disciplinary means' (Braverman, 1974: 195). An additional effect of this new control mode is the growth of white-collar staff to maintain and analyse the increased level of data produced by the fragmentation of the labour process. But Braverman makes clear that the new black-coated or clerical worker is vastly different from the old clerk. In contradiction to Lockwood's (1958) claim, Braverman argues that contemporary clerical labour has been proletarianized, and, moreover, that management is subject to the same onslaught from the 'Babbage principle'. In sum, Marx's prognostication on the proletarianization and homogenization of the class structure (Marx, 1968: 35–46) is validated by the universal deskilling which, Braverman argues, underpins the evolution of the capitalist labour process.

But how accurate is this vision? In the years since its publication *Monopoly Capital* has received a veritable avalanche of criticism from radicals and non-radicals alike (Wood (ed.), 1982; Watson, 1986; Buchanan and Huczynski, 1985), and a whole variety of critical issues has emerged.

First, to what extent does Braverman's account of the deskilling imperative rest upon an illusory base of nineteenth-century craft work as typical? It has to be said that Braverman is far from unique in his romantic notion of the early and pre-capitalist labourer as highly skilled (Wright Mills, 1951: 220; Anthony, 1977: 113–45; Sirianni, 1982: 245–60; Pahl, 1984) but this does not prevent this notion from being erroneous, for the majority of the population work was never in the rustic craft tradition espoused by the idealists (Cutler, 1978; Elger, 1982; Harrison, 1984). Nor is his concentration on skill and specialization unique: from the late nineteenth century these had been the topics of considerable dispute (More, 1980; Gramsci, 1971). In fact, most authorities on the subject after Adam Smith, irrespective of political sympathy, have accepted the logic of deskilling as both a means to cheapen labour, and as a means of wresting control from the workforce to concentrate it within management (cf. Cole, 1955: 28), though it is far from obvious that any universal deskilling has taken place through the period of industrial capitalism (Form, 1987). Even if many jobs have been deskilled it is by no means self-evident that the experience of work being controlled through a bureaucratic mechanism or even through a machine is necessarily more degrading than control transmitted through autocratic management.

Second, to assume that work has been deskilled requires some formal definition of skill. For Braverman, skill is the equivalent of 'craft mastery' (1974: 443) but the implication of this is that skill comprises solely technical components which can be objectively evaluated and observed. Yet skill is socially constructed and therefore a contingent phenomenon. For example, clerical work was originally regarded as highly skilled because of the limited levels of literacy (though one must beware of romanticizing about this too; see Anderson, 1976); today clerical work is merely one form of labour, rather than the pinnacle of non-managerial occupations. Alternatively, some occupations managed to retain their skilled status despite the progress of time. For example, working in the printing industry, up until the 1980s at least, has always been regarded as a skilled occupation; even mere machine watchers were paid as skilled employees. The ability of the work group to negotiate and retain the label of skill, independently of any ostensibly technically defined job content, must, then, be considered (Turner, 1962; Lee, 1982). Indeed, when occupations are labelled skilled it is not always clear whether this refers to the whole range of tasks involved in a job or just the most difficult or even the prerequisite levels of training laid down. Since trade unions have often used control over the labour market as a mechanism for protecting their own position it has been common to extend the length of training in apprentices way beyond that normally required by the particular activities undertaken as a mature worker. Thus skill should not simply be regarded as a mechanism for resisting management but also as a means by which intra-class differentials can be advanced or buttressed (Taylor, 1982; Penn, 1982; Selbourne, 1985).

The level of discretion is not an objective measure of skill either, despite Jacques's (1967: 96) arguments, because discretion is itself context-dependent not context-free. For example, it may be that machinists have close supervision and therefore low levels of discretion and perhaps low levels of skill (and the associations between gender and skill are clear indications of the social construction of skill (Cavendish, 1982; Phillips and Taylor, 1980)), but post and milk deliverers have negligible supervision and thus high levels of discretion without any related boost in skill levels. Nor will reliance upon the number of rules provide a satisfactory measure of skill (Crompton and Jones, 1982: 59): pilots have more rules to follow than cleaners, and cleaners have more than artists, but there does not appear to be a concrete link between the number of rules and the level of skill involved.

We also need to be aware of the cross-national variations that undermine the significance of concentrating purely upon the point of production. For instance, British unions tend to be relatively powerful in influencing issues very directly related to the labour process itself, but relatively weak over the more general social aspects of employment, such as levels of employment, employee participation in strategic decision-making etc. The opposite tends to occur within the Scandinavian countries, Austria, Belgium and the Netherlands (Batstone, 1988b: 222). This distinction suggests further qualifications of the labour process approach. Where the approach implies that control over the labour process is directly related to the power resources utilized by labour, it is clear that resources involved in the disruption of production are merely one form of resource, the two most notable other variants being the scarcity value of particular forms of skill in the labour market (Kelly, 1985) and the ability of workers to influence the wider political process (Grint, 1986; Batstone et al., 1984).

The third problem with Braverman's analysis is that though this expansion of the work relations arena is important it does not imply any correlation between employee control or influence and *class* strategies of control. While many labour process accounts appear to assume an axiomatic link between resistance *to* employers and the advance of class interests, the two are separate. The point here is that a very powerful form of worker control over the labour process implies nothing about what that control is used for. It may well be that it advances or protects the interests of those particular workers, but advancing the interests of one group of workers may be at the expense, not of capitalists, but of other, less organized, workers. Indeed, it may well be that a very powerful system of control is erected by a union leadership not to expropriate the capitalists but rather to disinherit the lay members and ensure the reproduction of union 'dictatorship'; the National Union of Seamen in the 1920s is a good example of such a misnomer as 'worker-control' (Marsh and Ryan, 1989).

The fourth critical issue is that if Braverman, and for that matter Taylor, is right about the persistent deskilling of labour, then the process should lead to a homogenous population of deskilled proletarians. In reality the opposite seems closer to the truth, with ever more divisions within the working class and a persistent tendency to heterogeneity. This heterogeneity has also been accompanied (see above) by a general shrinkage in the size of the manual labour force and an increase in the proportion of professional or service classes. Notwithstanding the concern for the definition of skill it would seem that a persistent and general deskilling of the labour force is not supported by the data on the occupational structure itself, nor by such data as the responses of a survey on class which reported that 96 per cent thought the skill content of their job had remained stable or increased (Marshall et al., 1988).

Fifth, are Braverman's data reliable? Unfortunately not; Braverman seems to have assumed that Taylor's schema was widely adopted without resistance, such that the reorganization of the work process appears to be the result of the conscious design of management rather than the effect of multiple and contentious social relations between different groups. Even the most obvious aspect of Taylorism, work study, is currently practised by only half the work establishments considered in a range of recent surveys of Britain and they are even less common in foreign-owned companies operating in Britain (Batstone, 1988a: 193–4). Thus Braverman falls into the same delusion that befell Taylor: that there is only one best way to organize capitalist production efficiently. For Taylor this best way is simply that derived from the application of scientific principles; for Braverman it is rather the most effective way of managing alienated labour. But a single best way, however defined, could only exist if all managements were homogeneous, faced common problems, interpreted them as such, and encountered no resistance from an undifferentiated working class. None of these provisos appears to be accurate.

Within the Marxist camp Friedman most effectively disposes of the single strategy myth with his development of a continuum between 'responsible autonomy', where workers are allowed 'leeway . . . to adapt to changing situations in a manner beneficial to the firm' (1977: 78), and the more Taylorist 'direct control'. Yet this is hardly different from the development by Fox (1974) of the 'high trust/discretion–low trust/discretion' managerial strategies, nor do strategies based on notions like 'responsible autonomy' adequately distinguish between the individual control of craft workers and the collective control issued through trade unions; both may involve responsible autonomy but they are clearly not identical. Such strategies indeed are common to the whole plethora of human relations alternatives to direct control: McGregor's (1960) Theory Y; Ouchi's (1981) Theory Z; Argyris's (1964) 'self-actualizing' strategies etc. (see chapter 4). Nor is it self-evident in which direction the causal line runs; that is whether high levels of discretion operate because managers trust employees or because the strength of the employees or their particular job prevents management invoking low discretion control mechanisms (Roche, 1983).

Sixth, Braverman rightly takes Bell to task for taking Taylor's word that the arc of the swing of poor Schmidt's shovel could be scientifically adjusted when the weight was 92 lb (Braverman, 1974: 106). Yet Braverman does exactly the same when he moves beyond his own area of experience into clerical labour. Quoting from 'A Guide to Office Clerical Times Standards' (p. 321) Braverman implies that the times taken to open drawers (centre drawer 0.026 seconds, side drawer 0.014 seconds) etc. are significant developments in the scientific management of clerical work. But how many employers are in a position to determine this? Anyway, even if they are, does this mean the drawer opening times are significant? It seems more likely that such regulations are closer to the 'mock bureaucracies' described by Gouldner (1954), and still present today in the large-scale bureaucracies such as the Post Office where times and methods for opening letter boxes etc. exist but are routinely ignored. In short, what many labour process approaches ignore is the critical role played by the interpretative processes of agents: as considered in the previous chapter, whether such rules are deployed or not depends on who interprets them and how they are interpreted.

Such apparently trivial issues are actually symptomatic of an important fixation that both Braverman and many other labour process theorists have with the very nature of employment in capitalist society. Whether the drawer opening times are a valuable aid to management depends on their utility not in facilitating control but in promoting profit. Capitalism as a system of production does not thrive on the minutiae of control, *contra* Foucault, because control has an economic cost. If an office is to be based upon the supervised opening of drawers the number of supervisors will be almost equal to the number of clerical workers. In short, such a 'perfect' control system would be financially unviable. It may well be that workers and their unions are overtly concerned with the issues of control because they are the bearers of the effects. But for employers, control is secondary, and because it is derivative the crucial issue becomes whether control systems are facilitative or inhibitory of profits. As the Donovan Commission, and several authors since (Batstone et al., 1984; Jacobs et al., 1978; Marsh, 1982; Rose and Jones, 1985) have noted, labour relations are rarely considered in strategic decision-making by boards of directors and are more usually the responsibility of subordinate level managers (1968: 41–4). Therefore, the issue must be whether control promotes or undermines profits. If it is the latter then some other method of ensuring productive activity must be constructed. This may even involve areas completely outside the particular point of production, for example asset stripping or investing in fine art or playing the market or whatever.

Paradoxically, as Kusterer (1978) has argued, the devaluation of labour regulation in British management often leads to the workers being able to control the labour process specifically because management is not particularly interested in this field. It may even be that a managerial strategy needs to embody both greater levels of coercive control for some employees and greater levels of accommodation for others simultaneously. Where technical developments promote key workers to points of strategic control over an integrated production process, while others become peripheral to it, managers may need to develop internally contradictory policies in an attempt to balance the relative influence of strategically placed workers. This more complex strategy is further compounded by delineating the different interests that management has within the labour process: while senior executives may be concerned with profits, line management is more likely to be responsible for, and therefore most interested in, ensuring production schedules are adhered to – even if this involves ignoring the rules constructed to maintain control or profits.

Not only, then, does the labour process approach tend to impute a uniformity to the workers, but an invariant strategy and interest is thrust upon management too: their foremost concern is allegedly controlling a recalcitrant workforce. Thus technology becomes a means not for advancing competitive advantage, or resolving productive quality problems etc., but for controlling the workers. This may be commonplace to industrial sociologists but it appears to be closer to fiction for many practising managers themselves (Blackburn and Mann, 1979; Northcott and Rogers, 1982; Batstone et al., 1987). Of course, as Bruland (1982) and Wallace (1978) have demonstrated, technology has been used as a method for wresting the control of the production process away from the workforce, but the point is that technology is not *just* a control mechanism, and even when it is intended as such this does not imply either that capitalism is the victor of the struggle, or alternatively that the working class is the victor. It may well be that sections of the workforce, especially white, male, skilled workers, are more likely than any other working-class group to retain at least some semblance of autonomy (Lazonick, 1979).

This universalist essence of the labour process theorists reappears between the wars in the guise of Bedauxism, a form of neo-Taylorism that allegedly swept to prominence so that 250 firms had adopted it by 1939, making it 'the most common system of managerial control in Britain' (Littler, 1982: 114–15), a claim apparently accepted by many commentators (e.g. Gospel, 1983: 102; Lash and Urry, 1987: 180–1). Yet in the absence of any quantitative data beyond the simple number of firms, and given that Littler includes only two of the largest fifty at the time (Hannah, 1983: 101–3, 190–1), one should remain sceptical of the impact of Bedauxism. Certainly the largest single employer of the period, the Post Office, made no significant attempt to adopt Taylorist or Bedauxist policies (Grint, 1986: 298–304), and it is more likely that the (in)significance of Taylorism is demonstrated by Littler's attention to the minimal evidence available (Zeitlin, 1983: 371).

Burawoy's (1979) account of the labour process does go some way in rescuing the Marxist approach by emphasizing the way consent is generated by
management in its attempt to increase productivity and through the wider social
system beyond the factory gates, and also by noting the ways in which workers
play games with and against management. Yet the different strategies of control
by both managers and workers cannot really be explained within the restricted
perspective of class politics, and it is by no means clear that playing games is
the quintessence of capital-labour relations either. Edwards (1979) makes another
attempt to expand the labour process debate by distinguishing between three
phases of capitalist control: simple or hierarchical control, technical control
and bureaucratic control. All three are allegedly the result of worker resistance.
Simple control is prevalent during the first competitive phase of capitalism, but
the capricious nature of such personal systems of authority stimulated wide-
scale resistance and control was therefore inscribed into the machinery of production through technical control. Eventually this allowed groups of workers
to control the entire production process and hence the switch to a depersonalized
system of bureaucratic control complete with hierarchies, rules and careers. Note
that not only does the historical evidence not support Edwards (Edwards and
Scullion, 1982; P. Thompson, 1984; Batstone et al., 1987), but the assumption
is still that 'work' actually means factory employment. Since large numbers of
employees have never worked with machines that they could be controlled
by, the theoretical significance of technical control must itself be questionable.
Paradoxically, Edwards seems to suggest that managerial strategies of control,
which are essential to obscure the exploitative nature of the labour process,
are themselves a direct response to the patterns and forms of worker resistance
rather than assuming that resistance may be one element in the desire for reconstruction. Quite why managers should feel the need to obscure a practice
which is hardly newsworthy is unclear. In short, Edwards's account swings the
pendulum away from Braverman's lacuna of resistance towards an analysis of
managerial strategies based wholly on resistance.

Just as this is inherently limited and delimiting, so too are the general
approaches towards technology within this theoretical tradition. This is considered elsewhere (see chapters 4 and 8), but it is worth reinforcing the point
in terms of the class analysis. For Marx and the labour process theorists
technology is quintessentially a class tool: a machine to oppress and exploit
the working class further. But the problem becomes visible when technology
appears not to deskill but to enskill, not to degrade but to enhance working
experience. It is not necessary to fall into the trap of assuming that all technology enskills and enhances to accept the point that some of it may do. The
question then becomes, how can this apparent event best be explained? For
Marxists it must be an aberration, forced upon capital for very specific and
atypical reasons; possibly concerning the unusual strength of working-class
resistance. But the problem is then one of accounting for the very large numbers of aberrations. When aberrations become typical it is time to reconsider
the explanation of aberrance and normality.

An alternative is to assume that what drives capitalists along is not the quest
for control over the working class but, once again, the desire for profits and the

necessity for competing against – not allying with – other capitalists. Thus, whether technology is responsible for deskilling or enskilling, degrading or enhancing is primarily the result of multiple conflicts between capitalists as well as between capitalists and workers, and producers and consumers. What the capitalist is coerced into doing, then, is stitching up alliances where possible and limiting the damage inflicted by foes where necessary. It is, as Latour (1988) has written, as if the contemporary capitalist has become the new Machiavellian Prince; the quest for this Prince is not control over labour through machinery because this is merely a single tactic among many in the greater quest for profit or power or whatever. Hence, because labour control is subordinate to, and a derivation of, the greater quest for money or profit it is quite logical to assume that on some occasions the capitalist will seek reduced overt control and enhanced working conditions – provided these facilitate the greater aim in the longer run. The problem, therefore, is not how to explain the atypicality and apparent irrationality of capitalists but to stop perceiving capitalist actions as if they must be explained through the prism of class control.

This brings us to a critical weakness in both Braverman's approach and most Marxist approaches. Unless it can be shown that the labour process is *the* most important arena for explaining social relations, and concomitantly that within the labour process class is the crucial variable, and hence all other social relations are derived from it, then such an approach can be only partly accurate. This does not mean that class is irrelevant or even subordinate to other forms of stratification such as race and gender, and some influential reconstructed approaches to the labour process have been made (Kelly, 1985; Knights et al., 1985; Knights and Willmott, 1988, 1989), though the more they move away from the restrictive concern with the labour process the less overtly Marxist they become. For example, work by Collinson (2002a,b, 2003), Alvesson and Willmott (2002) and Willmott (1997) has retained a radical edge whilst embracing a much more diverse political agenda. At the same time, much of the focus of this work has shifted from the labour process of factory workers to that of management (see, for instance, Alvesson and Willmott, 2003). Nor does it mean that class-conscious activity generated at the point of production is impossible: the delimited demonstration of such a phenomenon does not equate with its theoretical disposal to the dustbin of history (cf. Edwards, 1986). Moreover, the alternative approach means that the examination of social relations at the point of production, and their links with other areas of life (especially the domestic), should not be delimited by theoretical closure. As argued in the next chapter, exactly which aspect of stratification is the most important may not be determined other than through empirical examination. Furthermore, one needs to begin to specify not just the top-down constraints and facilities provided by socially structured conditions – such as race, gender and class etc. – but also the way these are aggregated at the level of the individual. That is to say, individuals are not simply, for example, female *and* white *and* working class but a consolidated, if dynamic unity of all three: a white, working-class female for whom her race, class and gender may be of differential significance given the particular situation she is in at the time and the associated interpretations of that situation. Thus the problem of determining the relative importance of class, gender and race necessarily involves examining the experiences as perceived by the individual as well as the material forms present (such as income level, career prospects etc.). Braverman's approach can accommodate neither of these aspects since it ignores the significance of subjective factors and presumes the superiority of class.

Summary

This chapter has sought to demonstrate the value and limits of adopting a class-based analysis of work. Although class is critical to any such analysis, to inscribe all forms of industrial action as class action, and all forms of managerial concern as class concerns, remains problematic. The point is not so much that class is merely a fragmentary aspect of individual and collective experience (albeit a large fragment), but that no single social dimension is sufficiently broad to encompass the complexity of social relations at work. What counts as a significant category of social relations at work is not determined by the material structures within which agents act because these structures are themselves the product of agents' interpretations and actions. Thus occupation, craft, family, ethnicity and gender shape different categories of work experience which tends to undermine the solidarity generated solely on class. As we shall consider in the following two chapters, just because employees have similar class backgrounds does not generate any automatic forms of class solidarity; it may well be that these working-class employees consider race or gender or religion or something else as the defining and distinguishing category at work. Similarly, it is a mistake to focus solely upon the labour process itself as if a single slice of work organization holds the key to the totality; it does not. Class control over the labour process is not the *sine qua non* of capitalism, profit is. And since there are many ways to make a profit there can be no automatic and unmediated connection between class interests and the organization of work. The degradation of labour is not an inevitable result of capitalist work methods because labour is not necessarily critical to the process. Indeed, whether labour is degraded, enskilled, made more autonomous or completely eliminated from production is contingent upon the successful accumulation of profit. Work in capitalist societies does tend to generate conflict given the wage-effort negotiations at the heart of the system, but how that conflict is mediated by the actors involved, and how the result is translated into the organizational forms of work, is not determined by any transcendental need to control the labour *process*. For capitalists and many managers the end product is more important than the process; for many employees the reverse may apply.

Exam/essay questions

1 Have we seen the end of the strike?
2 'The data on wealth and income suggest that employment is insignificant as a method of securing greater levels of equality.' Discuss.

3 In the past the sociology of work tends to have been restricted to the study of male industrial workers. What does the future research agenda look like and why?
4 Why have British trade unions traditionally avoided radical political action?
5 How can we best account for industrial action?
6 Why do we know so much about strikes and so little about other forms of industrial action?
7 Why did Marx think that industrial workers were so important? Was he right?
8 'Machinery offers to management the opportunity to do by wholly mechanical means that which it had previously attempted to do by organizational and disciplinary means.' Is Braverman right?
9 To what extent are managers concerned about control over labour?
10 How important is class in the explanation of industrial conflict?

Further reading

This area of the literature is covered by both the sociology of work and industrial relations and there is a vast choice of books. In terms of recent material, a good review of British aspects is Kessler and Bayliss, *Contemporary British Industrial Relations* (1994), while the European angle is well covered in Hyman and Ferner, *New Frontiers in European Industrial Relations* (1994), and a global view is offered in Belanger, Edwards and Haivers, *Workplace Industrial Relations and the Global Challenge* (1994). Currently the best historical overview of the development of US industrial relations is Jacques's *Manufacturing the Employee* (1996), while Fox's *History and Heritage* (1985) remains the best overview of British industrial relations history. For those seeking an understanding of the shop floor from a sociological view, I recommend Batstone et al.'s *Shop Stewards in Action* (1977) and *The Social Organization of Strikes* (1978).

6

Gender, Patriarchy and Trade Unions

- Introduction
- Theoretical viewpoints on women and work
- Women and paid labour: the contemporary evidence
- Labour market restructuring and professional women

- Women and trade unions
- Masculinity, domestic labour and violence
- Summary
- Exam/essay questions
- Further reading

And thy estimation shall be of the male from twenty years old even unto sixty years old, even thy estimation shall be fifty shekels of silver. . . . And if it be female, then thy estimation shall be thirty shekels.

Leviticus, 27: 3–4

Introduction

Gender inequality is nothing new. Both paid and unpaid forms of work have consistently exhibited patterns of inequality. One of the most persistent aspects of paid labour is that relating to gender-related inequality of rewards. Ignoring all the many problems involved in wage calculations which blur issues of skill, qualifications and hours etc., it is a sobering experience to consider the gendered wage differential. Studies of the sixteenth century calculate that, on average, women earned something between 52 per cent (Roberts, 1979) and 61 per cent (Kussmaul, 1981) of men's average earnings, hardly different from the prescribed differential set down in Leviticus. In 1913 the equivalent figure was 53 per cent (Grint, 1988) and the 1989 figure was about 67 per cent, with women's hourly earnings about 76 per cent of men's (Low Pay Unit, 1989; *Employment Gazette*, April 1990). By 1995 the latter figure had reached

79 per cent (*The Guardian*, 20 June 1995) and by 2000 it was 82 per cent (*Labour Market Trends*, 2003: 432).

This chapter considers the complex circumstances surrounding women at work by considering three related aspects: first, the various theoretical approaches; second, the post-war era (aspects of the pre-1945 period are discussed in chapter 2); and finally, the influence of trade unions. The approach is one that seeks to explore the various available viewpoints and then to use the one most heuristic to guide the necessarily brief review of the literature. The essence of the approach is one which perceives the position of women at work to be premised on three axial principles.

First, work patterns are necessarily related to their domestic responsibilities, so that the analysis of 'work' cannot occur in isolation from the analysis of the home–work link. Second, gender, although critical, is not uniquely important in explaining women's work patterns and experiences because individuals are heterogeneous composites: occupationally derived class and ethnicity are also relevant, as may be religion, age, nationality etc. In this particular text attention is restricted primarily to gender, class and ethnicity. Third, the experience of women is not one that can be read off from an 'objective' analysis of social categories but is quintessentially an interpretative process. These social categories influence but do not determine the experience of work. Indeed, what counts as a significant category is an interpretative and therefore contingent phenomenon.

Theoretical viewpoints on women and work

The invisibility of gender within the classical approaches has given way in recent years to a plethora of competing approaches. Although a multitude of positions exists, Walby's (1986a) categorization is the clearest and forms the basis of this review. In sequence, then, the discussion follows the following plan:

1 Classical approaches to women and work.
2 Gender as irrelevant.
3 Gender as secondary to or derived from class subordination.
4 Patriarchally derived subordination, where gender inequality relates primarily to gender relations.
5 Symbiotically derived subordination, where gender inequality relates to the seamless interleaving of capitalism and patriarchy – capitalist patriarchy.
6 Dualist subordination, where gender inequality relates to the discrete interaction between two autonomous spheres of capitalism and patriarchy.
7 Composite contingent subordination, where gender inequality is derived from the heterogeneous interleaving of gender, ethnicity and class but the connections and their particular influences are both contingently interpreted and constructed and tension-ridden.

In what follows the first six approaches are schematically presented and an alternative formulation, which seeks to overcome some of the main problems of the others, is developed. I then consider the heuristic utility of this alternative 'composite model' in an examination of historical and contemporary gender relations at work. In this instance most of the evidence relates to paid work and a majority applies to paid work outside the home. However, it will become apparent that the relationships between paid and unpaid labour, and between home and work, are so interlaced that the divisions are often merely for analytic purposes. Nevertheless, this chapter will focus, in the main, on paid labour outside the home. Unpaid domestic labour is discussed in chapter 2.

Classical approaches

As noted in chapter 3, the contributions of Marx, Weber and Durkheim to the examination of gender relations at work are less than useful in the main. Certainly they all seemed to assume that gender inequalities were omnipresent in all forms of society, though Marx's collaborator Engels had put forward an argument for the initial existence of a matriarchal society which was undermined by the differentiation between production and reproduction. As production – the sphere of men – began to provide surpluses, so it achieved predominance over reproduction – the sphere of women – and led to the creation of a whole panoply of institutions associated with patriarchal control: private property, social classes and the state. In theory, since **patriarchy** was derived from private property, and since working men's exploitation of their female partners was a reflection of their own exploited position within capitalism, the elimination of capitalism and private property would reintroduce sexual equality (Engels, 1968). Engels's anthropological evidence for matriarchy is dubious and the connection between capitalism and patriarchy much more complex than he makes out (Delmar, 1976). That is not to say that there never were any pre-capitalist societies controlled by women: Chinese empresses and Assyrian war queens were as real as Boadicea (Fraser, 1988) or Cleopatra, and certain Pict tribes operated with matrilineal inheritance and descent (Chadwick, 1970: 118). Even though the vast majority of contemporary societies have patriarchal lines of property control some have long traditions of matriarchal control over property, the Reang hill tribe of northeast India being a case in point (*The Guardian*, 25 May 1988). In northern Albania, near Tirana, some villages retain a feudal custom in which families whose male line no longer exists (often through the effects of blood feuds) are headed by women, known as 'avowed virgins', who act, dress, talk and are treated as men (*The Guardian*, 7 May 1996).

However sympathetic to certain aspects of the women's emancipation movement in Germany Weber may have been (1948: 26), he regarded the existence of patriarchal domination as 'normal' in the light of 'the normal superiority of the physical and intellectual energies of the male' (1978: 1007). If anything, Durkheim was even more reactionary, though somewhat ambiguous about gender relationships and the relative benefits of marriage to men and women (1933: 57–60; cf. 264–5). In short, the classical theorists have little of substance to add to the debate on gender at work.

Gender as irrelevant

The concentration upon men within sociology has, until very recently, been so common that it was seldom perceived to require an explanation; there is, as Marx argued, no greater power than when what is actually a sectional interest becomes represented and accepted as a universal interest, as common sense. There is some inconsistency within this rather heterogeneous group of approaches to gender, with some using individuals as the unit of study while others use the family, but it is only in conjunction with familially based analysis that theoretical justifications for the exclusion of gender are introduced. Both Goldthorpe (et al., 1980, 1983, 1984b) and Parkin (1972) argue that women's position is dependent upon the class situation of the family, which, in turn, is conditioned by the class position of the head of the family. Naturally, runs their argument, since the head of the family – i.e. the main breadwinner – is male, women's class position is determined by their husband's or partner's class. Of course, some women may have a higher social class than their partner, but they argue that this is unlikely to be a general rule. In fact, logically it cannot be a rule at all, for if a woman's class is determined by her partner's class then self-evidently the former cannot be different from the latter (Macrae, 1986; Walby, 1986a: 10). Goldthorpe's assessment (1984b) suggests that the determination of women's class position by their partners' (obviously single women have their own class) is a manifestation of sexism not within sociology but within society. Thus, he argues, it is because women's life changes *are* dependent upon their partners that sociologists should concentrate upon men.

There are several problems with this kind of approach. First, because it allocates women's class through the family it assumes that income distribution within the family is correlated with class: the higher the class of the male the higher the class of the female. But as pointed out in chapters 1 and 5, and as Brannen and Wilson (1987) and Gershuny (1983) have argued, male monopolization over economic resources makes a mockery of any assumed equality within the family, and it is therefore not possible to assume that women's class is identical with that of their male partners. Indeed, the differentiated control over resources is just one facet of a gendered inequality within the family that also encompasses several areas including domestic labour (see chapter 2) and especially domestic and sexual violence. In Britain only 10 per cent of convictions involve women (Bennett, 1996), only 5 per cent of convictions for violence are made against women (James, 1988), and while women are sometimes violent towards children (as are men), very few women are violent towards other adults – in sharp contrast to men (Rose, 1986: 166–8). It was not always thus: throughout history there have been many women who have breached the cultural stereotypes of their gender (Robinson, 2002). In eighteenth-century Portsmouth between 1696 and 1781, for instance, 2,891 women were charged with assault – that is, almost a third of all those charged with assault in the city, compared to the current proportion of between 10 and 15 per cent. During wartime the proportion of violence caused by women in Portsmouth increased to as much as 38 per cent (Warner, 2003: 13–15).

The actual extent of domestic violence inflicted on women by men is unknown, though a review of the evidence suggests that at least 500,000 women suffer in England and Wales alone (Home Office, 1989); on average about 150 people in the UK are killed by a current or former partner every year and one in four women and one in six men will suffer attack from their partner at some point in their lives (<http://www.homeoffice.gov.uk/crimpol/crimreduc/domviolence/>). Yet Britain has 200 times more sanctuary spaces for abandoned animals than women fleeing violent partners (*The Guardian*, 6 March 1996). That is not to say that social, or rather societal violence, as opposed to individual violence, does not sometimes alleviate the subordination of women. Societally organized violence, especially in wars of liberation or resistance to foreign oppressors, 'appears to promote citizenship for women more than any other single factor' (Turner, 1986: 71). Violence, then, can both destroy and subjugate women as well as facilitate their partial unshackling.

Second, it is not possible to allocate all class categories to women through male partners because many women are unmarried or do not live with a male partner. In 1994 22 per cent of all families were headed by single mothers – up from 6 per cent in 1971; single fathers comprise 2 per cent of the total (*Social Trends*, 1997). The proportion of traditional households in Great Britain (two adults with dependent children) reduced from around 33 per cent in 1971 to just over 20 per cent in 2003. Over the same period, the proportion of single-parent households with dependent children almost doubled, comprising about 5 per cent of households by 2003 (<http://www.statistics.gov.uk/statbase/Product.asp?vlnk=10942&image.x=17&image.y=6>). A further percentage have a different class from their male partners – or they would have if the criteria for class were individually based, not family based (Stanworth, 1984; Walby, 1986a; Macrae, 1986; Leiulfsrud and Woodward, 1987). Third, even the focus upon men as heads of households is inhibited by the exclusion of their female partners, for it assumes that such men are completely unaffected by the resources brought into the family by women. This is markedly influential where analyses of social mobility are made, for although much has been made of the relative mobility of the British 'working class' in the work of Goldthorpe et al. (1980), more recent analysis indicates that although many male workers have been upwardly mobile, many female workers may have suffered a consequential downward mobility (Abbott and Sapsford, 1988). Fourth, in contrast to the above, the emergence of dual-income families within homogamous (same-class) marriages may well polarize the experiences of middle- and working-class families. That is, although the rise of cross-class families is important they do not represent the norm. Within that norm almost half of all wives were economically active in 1981 compared with 42 per cent in 1971. But, and this is the crucial point, the disparity between the classes is constantly growing: taking the Registrar General's classification of social classes, wives of professional-class males (class 1) increased their activity rate by 11 per cent over the decade but wives of semi-skilled and unskilled males increased their activity rate by only 3 per cent. The life experiences of British working-class women and middle-class women, therefore, are undergoing qualitatively different, that is polarizing, changes (Bonney, 1988; Truman and Keating, 1988), though American data imply that some form of convergence may be occurring (Treas, 1987).

Finally, Lockwood (1986) has argued that gender cannot be regarded as an explanatory category, not because women derive their class from their male partners but because women do not form a cohesive collectivity, capable of pursuing gender-based issues. This severing of the gender line through alleged political and organizational incompetence not only misrepresents the actions of many women and their organizations over many years (Bouchier, 1983; Boston, 1987), but imbues class-based movements with a coherence they simply do not have. Ironically, despite Lockwood's Weberian approach, such a definition of class is much closer to the 'class for itself' label which Marx introduced as just *one* facet of a class movement.

Gender as secondary or derived subordination

One theoretical solution to the problems posed by a family-based analysis is to consider women both individually, through their occupational status, and collectively through their gender. This opens up a veritable Pandora's box, for women without paid employment, but who are not unemployed, appear to be in the same occupationally defined class. Such a class might well be extremely heterogeneous in terms of life chances, including female members of the 'idle rich' as well as the 'feckless poor', a combination that defies the conventions of stratification theory even if the patterns of life experience within the family *relative* to their male partners may be similar.

Alternatively, although the most orthodox of Marxists have ignored the gendered dimension to stratification some have regarded it as simply a by-product of class, and therefore of capitalism. Thus Edwards (1979), Braverman (1974) and Rubery (1980) all suggest, though in different ways, that gender plays a part in constraining the supply of labour but is not a central feature of segregation within work. Gender is also influential in so far as it is associated with capitalist strategies for control by 'divide and rule' (Stone, 1974).

A critical aspect of the controversy surrounds the question of exploitation: since domestic labour is not paid, the value it has lies in providing capitalism with a virtually free source of domestic servicing for its employees; capitalists exploit the domestic labour of women by providing wages for men that do not encompass the true costs of producing and reproducing the labour force. One branch of the argument asserts that women's domestic labour is productive in the sense that it is self-evidently labour; without it capitalism would not be viable, and anyway domestic and paid labour are so intertwined as to be mutually productive of value (Seccombe, 1974, 1975). Himmelweit and Mohun (1977) place the emphasis on the consumption undertaken by domestic labour rather than production; a point of some importance to Marxism since only productive labour is deemed to be constructive of value for only this form is exchanged directly with capital.

A second branch is taken by Engels, who argued that a major step outside the boundaries of domestic exploitation for women would come when more women entered the labour force directly through paid employment, but it has to be said that almost the whole of this debate among Marxists has been conducted within the confines of the class-exploitative nature of capitalism. That is, the issue of gender exploitation by men, and this includes both proletarian and bourgeois men, is either unimportant or relevant only in so far as it illuminates class-based exploitation. As Walby puts it: 'these writers face a serious inconsistency between asserting the derivative nature of women's oppression from capitalism, while recognizing the fact that this oppression pre-dates capitalism. It is illogical to suppose that a social system which arose after patriarchy could be deemed to create social inequalities which pre-date it' (1986a: 20).

A third position is pushed by Gorz whose rather heretical form of Marxism actually has strong resonances with Marx's critique of the commodification of all relations. The evisceration of social relations through the encroachment of economic relations was, according to Marx, an inevitable result of the market imperatives undergirding capitalism. Gorz's argument is that to suggest payment for domestic labour, as a solution to patriarchal and/or capitalist exploitation, is to substitute economic relations for social relations. Thus Gorz charges that although domestic labour is unpaid because it carries associations of servility and subordination to the economically oriented activities of paid labour, it is these associations that should be challenged, not the apparent 'problem' of uncommodified labour (see chapter 1).

A rather different approach, which explains gender exploitation through capitalism, is that associated with the diremption of the home from the central unit of family production through industrialization. Some of the historical evidence on this issue has already been covered above but the issue is theoretically as well as empirically important: the removal of women from paid labour enforces a level of economic dependence by women on men that would, in theory, serve to *exacerbate* patriarchal predominance in the home (Middleton, 1981), or as Zaretsky (1976) argues (though on the basis of inadequate information), to *instigate* patriarchal predominance in the home.

The final interpretation locks into an argument of Marx concerning women's role in the '**reserve army of labour**' (Braverman, 1974), that is the pool of unemployed workers who are essential to the smooth functioning of the capitalist economy by providing the extra labour necessary in booms and embodying the deterrent to wage rises and industrial conflict during slumps. Unfortunately, the evidence for this theory is very dubious, primarily because it suggests that men and women are interchangeable in the labour market when in fact the labour market is highly sex-segregated (Alexander, 1976; Beechey, 1986). The argument seems to suggest that the functional utility of women as a cheap, docile labour force explains the development of capitalism; but since patriarchy predates capitalism, and since the reserve army of labour cannot both predate capitalism and be caused by it, the argument appears to suffocate itself in contradictory logic (cf. Barrett, 1980).

Patriarchally derived subordination

The third approach to the explanation of gender inequality avers that capitalism is irrelevant, or at best subordinate, to the production and reproduction of male dominance. Since pre-capitalist and non-capitalist social formations manifest patriarchal control, the origins and perpetuating forces must lie in gender relations themselves. One of the earliest and most influential writers in this radical feminist genre is Firestone (1974). She argues that women's subordinate position is directly related to the biological differences between men and women, and, more specifically, to the debilitating consequences for women of sexual reproduction in its various facets: childbirth, pregnancy, breastfeeding, childcare and menstruation. Adopting Marx's **base-superstructure** schema she asserts that reproduction is the base from which everything else follows: hence, again like Marx, she denies the value of tinkering with the superstructure while the reproductive base remains untouched (cf. O'Brien, 1981). Rather, the link between women and reproduction must be severed by the pursuit of a biological solution: only by constructing a reproductive system that does not depend on women can patriarchal power be broken. It is, then, to 'artificial' reproduction that women must look for liberation. However, this really begs the question of technical control. If patriarchy is dependent upon the biological link and, because of this, in control of technical and biological advances, then it would be irrational for patriarchy to allow the development of its own suicide note. Moreover, Firestone's argument seems to slip from the biological aspects of reproduction to the socially constructed aspects of child-rearing etc., without much concern for the distinctions; while only women can have children, not all women do, nor does this require that only women are responsible for childcare. Indeed, since many men either do not marry or do not father children it is difficult to explain how these individuals necessarily gain directly from the reproductive activities of most women. Other writers have located the locus of patriarchal power in rape (Brownmiller, 1976) or pornography (Dworkin, 1981). But despite the importance of these two facets of patriarchy in its self-reproduction, it is not self-evident that either or both are the *principal* means for this. It seems unlikely that a society without pornography or rape would necessarily exhibit gender equality, even if it would be a considerably better place to live.

Part of the problem with theoretical evaluations of the superordinate position of patriarchy is the ahistoricism and universalism that often prevails. Not only are men presumed to have been dominant through all time and space but all men are engulfed in the same unidirectional subordination of all women, who in turn have identical experiences. It is also difficult to see how such an invariant and omnipotent system of oppression could be challenged, let alone dissipated. It is problems like this that have encouraged the dismissal of patriarchy as the only independent variable and a return to the possibility of uniting capitalism and patriarchy as symbiotically related twin pillars of gender oppression.

Symbiotically derived subordination: capitalist patriarchy

If patriarchy alone cannot fully explain gender subordination perhaps the solution is to draw the separate modes of exploitation together: capitalism exploits some women (and some men) economically; patriarchy exploits women politically and socially. This position, most thoroughly argued by Eisenstein (1979, 1984), implies that capitalism and patriarchy are mutually dependent and self-reinforcing. In certain circumstances this may well be true, but there are contradictory forces within both that undermine the alleged mutuality. For example, capitalism is actually composed of discrete capitals whose interests are often incompatible in the sphere of economic exploitation of women, and each discrete capital harbours an inherent antagonism to the requirements of all others: it may be in the interests of one capitalist to exploit his or her employees by providing the lowest possible wages but the consumption of commodities is dependent upon a high level of general income, not a parsimonious one. Furthermore, the interests of men are riven by their contending economic interests as employers and employees (Grint, 1988), and are in no sense universally and congruously patterned by their gender. Capitalist men do not have the same interests as working-class men, even with regard to women workers. The former may consider women as a source of cheap and compliant labour, and prefer them to men as employees; for precisely the same reason working-class men may seek to exclude women from the labour market altogether.

Dualist approaches: capitalism and patriarchy as autonomous

Given the incompatible aspects of capitalism and patriarchy the final attempt to resolve the problem of gender-based oppression and exploitation is to reunite the two systems in parallel. A variety of routes are proposed in this field: Mitchell (1975) locates ideological control within patriarchy and economic control within capitalism, though this dualism is again one without clear lines of friction between the two. Indeed, the reduction of capitalism to material control, and patriarchy to ideological control, misunderstands the interleaving of each with the other. Thus male workers often fear and resist the encroachment of women not just because they regard 'women's work' as demeaning but because it is perceived as a distinct threat to their material standards of reward (Grint, 1988).

Delphy's (1977) dualism reverts to the conventional Marxist materialist analysis for both spheres: the domestic and capitalist modes of production. Both modes are sites for the exploitation and subordination of women because it is theoretically vacuous to hive off domestic work as unproductive while retaining all work under capitalist exchange as productive. Whatever activities are currently undertaken by women at home as part of their domestic duties are, with very few exceptions, executed for monetary reward outside the home. Indeed, one estimate of the cost of domestic work puts the total annual figure for 'replacing a wife' in Britain at £19,292, in 1987 prices (the figure is calculated by an insurance group to facilitate 'Family Income Insurance': PLA, 1987: 10). It is, then, not the content of labour that makes it productive or unproductive but the social relations within which it is performed. Nevertheless, according to Delphy, it is the domestic mode which is critical since this prestructures the pattern of gender-related inequalities in the capitalist mode of production.

One of the difficulties with this is that the domestic exploitation of women as a class by men glosses over the gross inequalities between women: both 'idle rich' women and poverty-stricken working women are mutually exploited by their respective male partners. This is not to say that both may well be exploited, but it is to point out the greatly variant forms of exploitation that may exist. Furthermore, we need to be assured that households without men are either non-exploitative, or can isolate themselves from the power of patriarchy derived not from physical manifestations, *qua* men at home, but in its multifarious formations that exist irrespective of adult male presence. For example, the portrayal of women as subordinate in the media or in everyday life in the local neighbourhood or via male children, does not depend upon adult male presence for its viability. Nor do women need to live with a male partner to feel the effects of patriarchy at work. It is because there is no hermetic seal between home and work (unpaid and paid) that they continue to infect each other. If these opaque, and sometimes invisible, links between home and work are ignored, it becomes possible to argue that the under-representation of women amongst senior management has nothing to do with their over-representation at home. As Wolff puts it in her critique of organization theory that ignores the wider social context: 'we can see how long hours and inflexible working time militate against the employment of women with "two roles", but we cannot discuss the basic question of why women have two roles' (Wolff, 1977: 20). We also need to be clear about the exploitation of women by women in the domestic scene. Both white and black South African women may be exploited by men at home but black women servants are also exploited by their female white employers: as Orwell might have argued, under capitalist patriarchy all women are equal – but some are more equal than others.

While Delphy tends to stress the importance of the domestic mode, Hartmann's (1982) account inverts the hierarchy by highlighting the critical role of occupational sex-segregation. This patriarchal control of employment opportunities delimits the opportunities for women outside the home and therefore buttresses the ideological pressures on women to remain at home looking after children. One particular feature of this albeit contingent locking of patriarchy and capitalism is apparently demonstrated by the adoption of the family wage as a legitimate trade union principle for collective bargaining acceptable to male workers and capitalists alike. Nevertheless, it is not clear why capitalists should acquiesce to this demand since it keeps wages higher than they need be. Nor, of course, does it gel with claims that capitalism exploits women by *not* paying for domestic services provided by women. It may be that family wages provide an uneasy compromise by balancing the need for quiescent labour with the demands for cheap labour but there is little evidence that employers were anything but unwilling parties to this bargain (Grint, 1988).

The final version of dualism covered here is that of Walby (1986a). She retains the parallel aspects of patriarchy and mode of production but distinguishes between various aspects of patriarchal relations, such as domestic work, paid work, the state, male violence and sexuality, whose relative importance depends upon the nature of the link between patriarchy and the particular mode of production. Thus under capitalism it is paid work and the domestic division of labour which are critical, and they generate both a patriarchal, and essentially privatized, mode of production that exploits 'housewives' or domestic labourers, and a capitalist mode of production that exploits proletarians. These two are correlated through the delimiting of opportunities for women in paid work which effectively renders them economically dependent upon their male partner.

Reconstructing the theories: a composite contingency model

There is much to be said for Walby's suggestion (especially the more flexible approach developed in her *Theorizing Patriarchy*, 1990) because its contingent relationships between the different spheres of patriarchy can be used to explain the variations that exist in time and space; without this flexibility patriarchy becomes so inherently omnipotent as to be incapable of change within or between societies. Nevertheless, the model underlying many other approaches to gender inequality, appears to be, rather ironically, the nuclear family in which the primary breadwinner is a man in full-time employment. The implication of this conventional model (and its typicality is severely restricted in time and space with in the 1980s a mere 3 per cent fitting the single male breadwinner and full-time 'housewife and mother' 'ideal' in Britain and 7 per cent in the USA (BMRB, 1988; Kakabadse and McWilliam, 1987; Pahl (ed.), 1988: 12–15)) is that women who do not live with men are, by definition, less exploited than all those who do. This may be the empirical norm but it is not an axiomatic principle to be accepted a priori. Families or households where an egalitarian division of domestic labour exists between male and female partners may be atypical but their existence should warn us of the dangers of 'guilt by association'. That is to say that the blanket derivation of oppression by men, the concomitant location of oppression in all women, and the corresponding Manichaean distinction between exploiting employers and non-exploiting employees ought to be the subject of empirical investigation rather than theoretical generalization. Nor is it self-evident that the arena of paid work should be prioritized above that of domestic work: it is the case that the limited opportunities for paid work delimit women's freedom within the home but it also clear that women's domestic responsibilities prevent or deter them from seeking certain forms of paid work. It is the seamless web that knits home and 'work', unpaid and paid labour, that confounds the dualist models and the contingent position of individuals within the web.

In fact, while it may be useful for heuristic purposes to separate patriarchy and capitalism, three dangers remain: first, that of slipping from analytic distinctions to empirically discrete explanations; second, in subordinating forms of oppression which are not derived from capitalism or patriarchy; and third, in presuming that analytic models of oppression are the means by which most people understand the world. Hence, in facing empirical reality women do not necessarily confront 'men' or 'capitalists' but particular men who are heterogeneous or composite individuals or representative of such composites. They are white or black; and they are capitalists or supervisors or workers; and they are young or old; and where interpreted as significant they are Catholic or Protestant or Jewish or Muslim etc. Concomitantly, women do not form a homogeneous collective but experience work as middle-class or working-class women; as white or black, and within the ethnic minorities as black or Asian or Mexican etc.; the fact of gender similarity says little about the specific form of oppression or the contradictions between women from different class or ethnic backgrounds (Ramazanoglou, 1989). Indeed, what exist in work situations are individuals and groups whose primary characteristics embody (at least) three distinctive facets of the stratification structure: class, gender and ethnic origin. This is not to deny that other issues are potentially divisive, nor does it deny that non-capitalist societies may be patriarchal and racist but it is to state that social relations are inherently more complex than those implicit in dualist theories.

It is not a question of theoretically unravelling the triple threads that go to make up individuals and groups so that they can be better analysed separately because they only exist as heterogeneous composites. For heuristic purposes, it is important that the threads are identified and most research has followed one such thread at a time (hence the structure of this book), but to postulate discrete hierarchies of influence emanating from each thread is to misunderstand the distinction between the composite as a whole and the sum of its parts. An analytic model may provide a picture in triptych form: for example, of an individual as a worker, as black, and as a woman. But the life experiences of this individual are more likely to be refracted through the multiplex network or prism of these social forms: as a black-female-worker. In sum, the analysis, in this instance of women and work, should proceed from the assumption that patriarchy, racism and capitalism form not parallel modes of oppression but a contingent and discordant whole riddled with internal tensions and contradictions.

Perhaps a useful analogy to differentiate this model from dualist models that separate the threads is the distinction between interleaved metals and an alloy: bronze has properties which are distinct from the copper, tin and zinc or lead metals on which it is based. Where the analogy is limited is in the distinction between the tension-ridden and contingent social relationship and the static and stabilized relationship between the metals. This does not mean that there is no utility in considering race, class or gender separately: the material that can be marshalled to cover all these areas is immense, and much of it is constructed from viewpoints vastly different from this one, so the process of reconstruction in an introductory text of this sort is an inordinately complex task. And of course many social relationships do not involve all or any of the three aspects: relationships between white middle-class males may or may not involve aspects of gender, race and class: whether they do or not is a contingent aspect subject to empirical investigation. Since those areas where class and race are pre-eminent are covered elsewhere, the next section concentrates on the experiences of women in paid labour outside the home since 1945; unpaid domestic labour and home working are considered in chapter 1, pre-1945 work is covered in chapter 2. Furthermore, from a practical point of view analytic divisions have to be made if we are to avoid paralysing the reader with a morass of unstructured information. Ultimately, of course, to reproduce the divisions is to perpetuate conventions but neither the resources nor the research material to reconstruct the sociology of work afresh are yet available; this chapter can only point towards a future possibility for research. Readers interested in pursuing these debates should consider the following: Bradley et al. (2000); Grusky (2000) provides a useful collection of articles; Hakim's (1996) work contains a vigorous attack upon some mainstream feminist approaches; McCall (2001) relates the arguments to the US economy; Rees (2003) considers the role of 'competencies' in the progress of women at work.

Women and paid labour: the contemporary evidence

After the end of the Second World War the experience of women workers was quite different from those in 1919. First, no economic depression followed and, indeed, over two decades of uninterrupted economic growth spanned the period up until the early 1970s. As a result, the opportunities for women, married and single, did not suddenly disappear but rather continued to expand, so that in 2003 in the UK there were 15.2 million men working (54 per cent of the total) and 12.9 million women (46 per cent of the total). That represents an employment rate of 80 per cent for men and 70 per cent for women (<http://www.statistics.gov.uk/downloads/theme_labour/LMT_Jan04.pdf>). Second, and relatedly, the shifts in the economy towards the service sector with its resultant increase in demand for white-collar labour, actually forced some employers into providing unheard-of levels of equality between men and women, most notably in these areas of white-collar shortage (Grint, 1988). Third, the proportion of women working part time continued to increase (to 42 per cent in 2003 compared with 9 per cent of men: see <http://www.statistics.gov.uk/downloads/theme_labour/LMT_Nov03.pdf>), partly as a result of wartime experiences of women with domestic responsibilities and partly because it suited employers to use part-timers to soak up fluctuations in demand and yet avoid having to pay National Insurance contributions or involve themselves in the legal aspects of dismissing full-time employees etc. (Beechey, 1986: 28–9). Fourth, women began reappearing in the labour market after their children went to school so that a bimodal distribution was evident from the 1960s, in sharp contrast to the prior pre-1939 pattern (outside the wars themselves) where most women, but especially middle-class women, left the labour market permanently if and when they got married and had children.

Outside the limited areas where some degree of equality prevailed, levels and forms of segregation were and still are very common. The segregation of men and women into different occupations – horizontal segregation – is shown in figure 10. In fact, the relative crudity of the distinctions underestimates the degree of inequality in authority terms and some of the more detailed data are provided later (see also Hakim, 1979). At this point it is just worth noting a few points. First, there are no occupations, as classified here, that are exactly equal in gender composition. Second, the genders are distributed in a non-random way: women predominate in public administration, education, health, distribution, hotels and restaurants; men dominate manufacturing, transport and communications, construction, agriculture and fishing and energy; only banking, finance and insurance and other services are relatively equal in terms of gender distribution. Even when women acquire the necessary training in

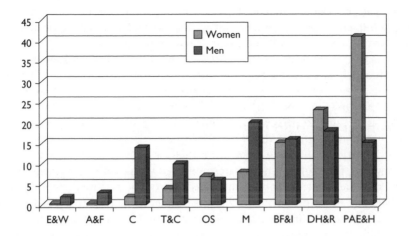

Key:
E&W   Energy and water
A&F   Agriculture and fishing
C   Construction
T&C   Transport and communications
OS   Other services
M   Manufacturing
BF&I   Banking, finance and insurance
DH&R   Distributions, hotels and restaurants
PAE&H   Public administration, education and health

Figure 10 Gender and occupation (UK), 2003 (millions)
Source: Reconstructed from *Labour Market Trends*, November 2003: 538

male-dominated occupations, such as construction, it is still difficult for them to acquire employment because of the informal male networks that dominate the occupation (Clarke et al., 2004). Thus there are, at most, 16,000 women construction workers in the UK, compared to more than 1.5 million men; fewer than 10,000 women plumbers, compared to almost 200,000 men; around 64,000 women engineers, compared to almost 750,000 million men; and around 150,000 women IT workers, compared to 834,000 men. Not surprisingly, there are fewer than 10,000 male childcare workers, compared to almost 300,000 female (Ward, 2004: 9). Third, and as a summation of the previous points, there are strong connections between occupations related to the domestic sphere and poorer pay.

Inequality prevails, then, both because of the jobs that women do but also because of the unequal pay they receive when they do similar jobs to men. Most recent reviews would suggest that unequal treatment within jobs, rather than unequal access to particular jobs, is the critical problem for women (Horrell, Rubery and Burchell, 1989), though as figure 9 (p. 165) implies, unequal access is itself commonplace.

British women have, for the most part, never comprised more than a quarter of employers, more than a fifth of managers and more than a tenth of higher professionals throughout the twentieth century. Where there has been a considerable expansion in both the absolute and relative numbers of female employees has been in the white-collar and service sector. Very roughly a quarter of all white-collar employees were women at the turn of the century whereas the equivalent figure towards its end is well over half.

One of the changes most often associated with the Industrial Revolution was the gradual eclipse of employment opportunities for married women. The 1851 Census in Britain records that 25 per cent of married women had an 'extraneous occupation' – a label perfectly in keeping with the subsequent Victorian ideology that came to perceive the woman's role as almost wholly encapsulated by the home and family (Alexander, 1976); and, despite the growing significance of factory labour for women from the last quarter of the nineteenth century onwards, the proportion of married women with paid employment dropped to under 10 per cent in the first three decades of the twentieth century before rising steadily to 22 per cent by 1951, just under 50 per cent by 1981 (Joseph, 1983: 6; Beechey, 1986: 13), and 54 per cent in 1989 (*Employment Gazette*, April 1990). Currently over 65 per cent of American mothers with children under 18 are employed (Meade-King, 1988), a midway point between Britain, where 48 per cent of mothers with children under 10 are employed (Martin and Roberts, 1984), and Sweden, where 82 per cent of mothers with children under school age are employed (Leiulfsrud and Woodward, 1987). Coincident with a rise in the proportion of married women within the labour force has been a rise in the number of employed women with sole responsibility for dependants. Although the conventional stereotyped male breadwinner may suggest that most men have dependants, in fact only 40 per cent of both men and women have them (Beechey, 1986: 9).

The increased rate of employment for married women generally is the most substantial single area of change in occupational activity since the beginning of this century. Generally speaking, since the Second World War, women have tended to adopt either a fragmented work career or a two-phase career with a substantial break of between five and fifteen years while they raise their children. Even when children become full-time pupils many women still structure their employment around their continuing domestic responsibilities so that school holidays and early finishing become an essential part of employment arrangements. In 1997 this division in responsibilities becomes partly visible in the proportions undertaking full-time and part-time labour. Including permanent and temporary workers together, approximately 21 per cent of the labour force are part-time women while only 4 per cent are part-time men. The data are reproduced in figure 11.

Married women, like the majority of all employees, tend, and indeed have always tended, to regard the monetary rewards of work as critical (Parker et al., 1967: 53; Roberts, 1985: 241–2; Burnett, 1984), though boredom at home and the need for company also figure prominently in the reasons given for taking up paid work (Hunt, 1968: 77). The pecuniary link is important not just because it delimits assumptions about women's work being for 'pin money' but also because economic rewards are themselves a manifestation of status. That is to say that money is both economically and socially essential, for it provides women with a large number of potential benefits: independent means, a higher familial standard of living, and higher social status etc. But,

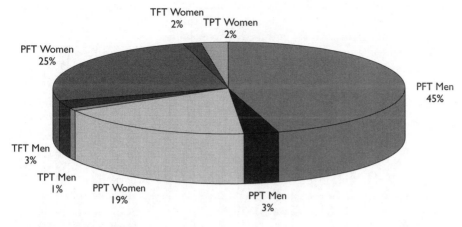

Key: PFT – Permanent full-time
     TFT – Temporary full-time
     PPT – Permanent part-time
     TPT – Temporary part-time

Figure 11 The flexible British labour market
Source: Labour Market Trends, April 1997

as we shall see, the experiences of women are not identical, for they are pre-structured through their position as single or with a partner, with or without dependent children, middle-class or working-class, black or white etc.

Equal pay

Of course, not all occupations are either sex-segregated or subject to unequal rewards. For example, the civil services of many countries, along with their associated public sector like education and health etc., often exhibit markedly egalitarian policies. Thus the British Post Office, Civil Service and teaching profession have relatively little in the way of official sexual discrimination, at least compared with the private sectors (Grint, 1988). On the contrary, all three have provided equal pay in certain areas for decades. That is not to say that equality was ever the primary intention behind the instigators of the policy, nor is it to suggest that these areas currently demonstrate an equality of distribution regarding positions of authority, career structures etc. Equal pay in the teaching profession, first mooted in the NUT referendum of 1919 and achieved by 1961, and a 60 per cent majority of the workforce being female, does not alter the fact that only 15 per cent of female primary school teachers are heads compared with 50 per cent of male primary teachers (NUT, 1988), even though women comprise 80 per cent of primary school teachers (De Lyon and Migniolo, 1989), a level of inequality which worsens with distance from London (MacLeod, 1996). The pattern of wage movements for the average full-time male and female employee between 1981 and 2003 is shown in

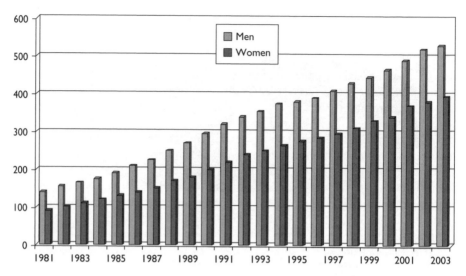

Figure 12 Average gross full-time weekly earnings in £ (UK), 1981–2003
Source: Reconstructed from *Labour Market Trends*, 2003: 602

figure 12. It should be clear just how stubborn the gap between men and women has been: both have been getting wealthier but the difference remains very reluctant to disappear.

Of equal relevance have been the activities of the state, in Britain most notably through the 1970 Equal Pay Act, the 1975 Sex Discrimination Act and the 1983 Equal Pay (Amendment) Regulations, and in the USA, for example, through the 1963 Equal Pay Act and 1964 Civil Rights Act. This earlier dating of the US Acts should not necessarily be taken to imply a greater concern for justice on the part of the American authorities: Frank Thompson, chairperson of the US House Select Subcommittee on the Equal Pay Bill is reputed to have filed documents relating to women under 'B' for 'Broads' (Randall, 1988), though the liberal ethos of Kennedy's era counteracted this to some extent.

Analyses of the effects of the two British Acts varies quite considerably. Gregory (1982) insists the effects were minimal, though Zabalza and Tzannatos (1985), Atkins (1986) and the Labour Research Department (1986), while noting the limited value of both Acts, suggest that some marginal advances were effected, and Marsh (1988b: 55) suggests that women's earnings were raised by about 5 per cent relative to men's to reach the plateau of 67 per cent that they have remained around since. In terms of the individuals who take their case to tribunals only between 1 per cent and 12 per cent were successful between 1985 and 1994 (*The Guardian*, 20 June 1995) and the actual process itself appears to be very stressful: only 11 per cent of applicants remained with their employers, and continued victimization is common. Given the economic rewards of a successful application (50 per cent of all awards are for less than £300 and 40 per cent of pay increases ordered were for less than £8 a week) it is small wonder that the tribunal option is so little used (Leonard, 1987). In fact, in

1995, of the 1,623 complaints about discrimination notified to the Equal Opportunity Commission, 823 came from men – the first time the majority have not been women. This is probably a consequence of two particular elements: first, the displacement of traditional 'male' jobs (mining and factory work) by 'female' jobs (clerical, nursing and retailing), and second, the increasing attempt by men to enter the latter arena (Freely, 1996; Boseley, 1996).

Also important at the time of the original Acts was the Social Contract negotiated between the TUC and the Labour Government between 1974 and 1977 which initially embodied an egalitarian incomes policy and facilitated the erosion of gender-based wage differentials (G. Thompson, 1984). It is noticeable that many ostensibly left-wing unions declined to appreciate the value of this to women and the low paid, and proffered instead 'a cult of militancy which assumed that the low paid would be rewarded by the efforts of the higher paid, without recognizing that this pattern would only reproduce the balance of relativities which were precisely the problem, when what women workers needed was a redistribution within the working class, as much as redistribution between classes' (Campbell, 1982b: 23). Hakim (1981) adds further support to the value of this period, noting a much greater decrease in segregation after the Act than would have been predictable on the basis of historical trends before it. Ultimately, the Equal Pay Act garnered support of one sort or another from many sections of the community, although the TUC had by this time recognized the growing importance of women as union members and begun to support the idea of equal pay for equal value while the CBI still preferred the idea of equal pay for equal work. The latter policy, enacted by the Act, enabled employers to maintain general patterns of gender-based inequality by ensuring that women did not undertake identical duties to men, or, where this proved impossible to maintain, introducing a token man to the 'women's' jobs. However, a series of tribunal cases in 1984 following the Equal Value Regulations (enacted in January 1984 to bring Britain in line with EEC legislation), and Julie Heyward's victory over Cammel Laird, began to undermine the conservative implications of the Act (Hadjifotiou, 1985). The case in favour of equal pay for **equal value** has recently taken a significant step forward with the sequence of judgements supporting Rene Pickstone. Ms Pickstone, a warehouse worker employed by Freemans' mail order company, whose case was supported by the Equal Opportunities Commission, claimed that work of her type was of equivalent value to that undertaken by male warehouse checkers despite the fact that a token male warehouse worker earned the same as his female colleagues. Under the 1970 Equal Pay Act such a case could not be made but the Appeal Court ruled, on 25 March 1987, that Article 119 of the Treaty of Rome and previous European Court rulings were applicable in Ms Pickstone's case, and the Appeal Court judgement was upheld by the Law Lords on 30 June 1988. Relatedly, in 1995 the House of Lords ruled in favour of 1,300 'dinner ladies' who had been dismissed by North Yorkshire County Council and immediately re-employed at lower pay to defeat an outside tender for the meals service. This followed a previous acceptance by the council that women's work was of equal value to the gardeners, road sweepers and refuse collectors who were overwhelmingly men (Clement, 1995).

Of course, securing the backing of the law is not the equivalent of remov-ing sex discrimination, and many forms of discrimination are beyond the grasp of legal recrimination. Even those within the law are encumbered by the com-plexities of due process. For example, since the Equal Pay Act was introduced over 3,800 cases have been taken up but only twelve have made it through the fifteen-stage procedure to claim equal pay (Wintour and Tirbutt, 1988). Sim-ilarly, the existence of an Equal Opportunities Policy, in and of itself, says little about the effect this may have upon the reality of gender discrimination (Hughes, 1989), and fewer than a third of British companies actually appear to have a written policy (Dickens, 1989: 169). Nevertheless, we should be clear that the limited utility of legal restraint upon employers and employees in purely material or economic terms has also to be supplemented by the symbolic value of legal support for equality and the illegality of certain forms of discrimina-tion (O'Donovan and Szyszczak, 1988). In November 1988, 310 Royal Ulster Constabulary women officers were awarded almost £1 million in damages between them in an out of court settlement in Belfast. The political embarrassment of acting illegally, to say nothing of the monetary costs involved, may act as a warning to other employers.

When the Equal Pay and Sex Discrimination Acts were passed by the Brit-ish government in 1975, under Barbara Castle's guidance, it was the 42nd attempt to achieve equal pay at work. Since then, many men have assumed that women have had it all their own way. Franks (1998) certainly doubts this, for rather than 'having it all' – that is, a career, a family and a life – many women have ended up 'having none of it' because they have taken on the con-straints of employment without being able to divest themselves of domestic responsibilities. Indeed, having taken the decision not to have children and to concentrate on their career, many 'career women' appear to be far more resent-ful than men of 'family-friendly' policies that discriminate in favour of parents (Bird, 2000: 5).

Hours, workers and class

Women are also divided by their involvement with paid labour, particularly regard-ing their status as full-time or part-time workers. Part-time work, in Britain particularly, is overwhelmingly a female experience with fewer than 8 per cent of men undertaking it: six times less than women (*Social Trends*, 1997). Such work tends to be less skilled and is also concentrated in the white-collar, ser-vice and smaller enterprises – all issues which tend to inhibit trade unions and which undermine the likelihood of women furthering their careers.

It is not sufficient to say that women are, in some vague way, exploited by the dual forces of capitalism and patriarchy because a minority of women *are* capitalists and therefore exploit other women and men; yet others have suf-ficient income or wealth to off-load the most menial tasks on to poorer or less qualified women. Another important element of this is manifested in the means by which men construct career paths for women such that poor rewards actively deter women from seeking careers; the result is a vicious circle of low levels of ambition, commitment and investment in human capital. This is particularly prevalent among working-class women, many of whom appear to consider pre-family work in factories and offices as a temporary phenomenon, a short intrusion prior to the 'real' career of marriage and motherhood (see Hakim, 1996 on a recent controversy on the 'real' preferences of women). Despite the fact that most women will spend three to four times as long in paid work than as a full-time home worker, the perception of paid work as temporary continues (Poilert, 1981; Porter, 1982). In contrast, Alban-Metcalfe and Nicholson's (1984) review of women managers suggests that women are just as committed and ambitious, but with a higher level of qualifications than the equivalently placed male manager.

One important distinction to note here is that of class: the overwhelmingly heteronomous content of many working-class women's jobs with minimal prospects of promotion contrasts sharply with middle-class women's jobs which can combine both greater levels of autonomous activity and career prospects. It is vital, therefore, to retain a grip on both class and gender aspects when considering the evidence of work. Relatedly, although the importance of ethnic divisions is discussed in the following chapter, it should not be taken for granted that women, while united by exploitation from patriarchy and capitalism, form a naturally cohesive unit. It is sufficient to note the sharp fragmentation of attitudes and opinions manifest in Cavendish's (1982) *Women on the Line* to undermine any utopian images of natural sisterhood. In sum, there is no experience which is typical; there are instead a delimited number of compound experiences.

Labour market restructuring and professional women

Since 1975, of course, the general picture of employment has changed quite considerably in Britain, most notably in terms of mass unemployment and shifts in economic and occupational structure away from the northern-based manufacturing industries towards the south-eastern service-based businesses. Walby (1986a: 222–30) suggests that although employers have tended to discriminate against women, the overall impact has actually been favourable to women, mainly because women have been over-represented in those industries least affected by the economic collapse; a point supported by the wider comparative study of Therborn (1986: 71–3) who suggests that there are links between gender and the patterns of unemployment but they are specific to each country rather than universal. Ironically, then, it has been the segregation of women away from 'men's work' that has protected many of them from the worst effects of the economic slump in Britain, and is currently providing greater opportunities for new employment than those available to, or rather appropriated by, men. Thus, women continue to be barely visible in engineering, particularly within the ranks of technical specialists or management, but also in the manual sectors (C. Smith, 1987: 78–9); whereas clerical work has come to be pre-eminently the area of female predominance with around 75 per cent of the total currently being women (Crompton and Jones, 1982; Routh, 1980; *Social Trends*, 1997).

The current data suggest that most of the projected rise in the workforce until 2006 will involve women (Duffy, 1997: 13). Indeed, in the five years between 1983 and 1988 an astonishing inversion of traditional job creation and destruction has been evident. Over that period almost 0.75 million new part-time jobs went to women with just over half a million full-time positions in addition. In contrast, part-time jobs held by men increased by just under 0.25 million while full-time jobs held by men decreased by 100,000 (Gapper, 1989). Yet not all women have managed to survive the collapse of manufacturing unscathed, and women from the ethnic minorities have borne the brunt in some areas. These women have often been unable to find alternative work of equivalent reward within ethnic businesses (Phizacklea, 1987), as the compound threads of capitalism, patriarchy and ethnicity operate in conjunction against them. It is apparent too that in some areas previously associated with the growth of women's employment, such as the financial sector, the introduction of new technology has begun to impinge upon this expansion and, in some circumstances, to reverse it (Mallier and Rosser, 1987).

A more pervasive presence within a particular occupation does not, of course, ensure a greater presence within the hierarchy. For example, British banks have been a major source of employment for women but a minor source of managerial opportunities. About 1 million women currently work for British clearing banks and comprise 60 per cent of the total staff. Yet in 1986 only 2.5 per cent of Lloyds managers were women, 2.7 per cent of the Midland, and 1.8 per cent at the National Westminster. The most progress in the 1980s was made at Barclays, with the relevant figure standing at 4.3 per cent. How can we account for this, albeit extremely modest, differential? Basically, Barclays discarded their previously discriminatory recruitment channels (GCSE-level entrance for girls, A-level entrance for boys) after the Equal Opportunities Commission threatened to investigate the company's recruiting strategy: just as the screening of recruits can delimit the opportunities available to individuals from the ethnic minorities so too are women discriminated against even before they are employed. Of course, where the proportion of women achieving the pre-requisite level of professional qualification is increasing, and the proportion of women finalists in the Institute of Banking examinations increased from 4 per cent in 1975 to 27 per cent in 1988 (Crompton, 1989; Crompton and Sanderson, 1986), then employers are discouraged from selective recruitment, even if it is not prevented. The most progress in the 1990s has been made by the National Westminster Bank, a member of the Opportunity 2000 group set up in 1991 to advance the position of women. In the first five years the proportion of managers who are women increased by 64 per cent. In fact Abbey National, another member, currently has women as two-thirds of its managers (Wylie and Papworth, 1996). The fact that some progress has been made here suggests that the inertia of tradition is not quite as immovable as many people suspect (Pagano, 1987), even if the cause may have more to do with labour market shortages than concern for implementing equal opportunities policies.

It has also to be remembered, however, that even the suspicion of immobility may be enough to render the attitudes of decision-makers, such as recruiters, impermeable to rational critique. As Pearn et al. (1987) argue, in respect of selection tests, even though such tests are not objective measures of ability the fact that recruiters *interpret* them as being objective ensures that they are used in this fashion, often to the detriment of prospective female employees. Career intentions and domestic arrangements are regular questions asked at interviews, but only of women; and the frequency of such events reflects the strength of stereotyping (Collinson, 1987). Some organizations, such as United Biscuits (Pizzaland, Wimpy *inter alia*), Marks and Spencer and John Lewis have even concerned themselves with the regularity of a woman's periods and, in some cases, the details of pregnancies; questions of dubious legality to say nothing of the questionable ethics involved (Macrae, 1988). Again, we have to be clear that such discrimination does not always occur. The study by Chiplin and Grieg (1986) of one Regional Health Authority in the National Health Service suggests that women are not discriminated against, at least not in the process of shortlisting candidates. But the occupational segregation was such that a non-gender-segregated service would require the reallocation of 70 per cent of the existing female employees. Women currently comprise 77 per cent of the NHS staff but only one in seven unit managers is a woman. Women do succeed in becoming managers but the majority do not stay within the service and over half of these leave for domestic reasons (Thayer, 1987).

This career break is crucial in explaining the relative absence of senior women managers in the NHS, for the 'golden pathway' to career success is essentially a male path determined by the requirement to be geographically mobile, and to enact a continuous commitment to the NHS, at least until the age of 30. Of course, many women leave to have children prior to this critical point and their domestic responsibilities often impair their geographical mobility; it certainly is not a case of men having superior qualifications, indeed the reality is the reverse. As a direct result the 'golden pathway' appears to be made with patriarchal bricks (Davies and Rosser, 1987).

That the pathway only appears gender-biased from the viewpoint of women is represented by a survey of men in the insurance industry. This indicated that almost half thought women were uninterested in a career – yet three-quarters of the women employed in the same industry said they considered career prospects to be crucial. The insurance industry may be more patriarchal than some but it is by no means unusual: a third of senior male managers from all areas of business in the UK also think that women are inherently unsuitable for managerial jobs (Meade-King, 1986). What is apparent is that male managers seem willing to employ women in subordinate positions but not where they provide future competition for themselves or their male managerial colleagues.

In the USA, women still represent only about 2 per cent of the senior corporate executives, but this is still twice the rate in the UK (Marshall, 1987). By 1996 there was still only one woman in charge of a FTSE 100 company (Wylie and Papworth, 1996). However, by 1998 one-third of British company directors were women (*The Observer*, 1 February). Thus although the golden pathways in the USA have some women on them they still tend to hit that all too familiar 'glass ceiling', composed of 'men only' translucent silicates; even those who pass through are wont to reappear within one of the 'triple P departments': purchasing, personnel and public relations (Meade-King, 1988). American women have also been notably successful in establishing their own businesses, currently owning 25 per cent of all US small businesses and starting new ones at five times the rate of men. They are equally well represented within the middle ranks of US corporations, compared with their European colleagues, though they are particularly poorly represented among the skilled blue-collar jobs. This higher level of discrimination within manual work is also evident within Britain where female trainees on skilled manual trades often find themselves shunted by their employers back into higher education on the completion of their training rather than taken on as qualified craft workers (YWCA, 1987). This particular problem was present within the British Youth Training Scheme of the 1980s, where segregated training into jobs conventionally associated with specific genders reinforced the barriers to women, with at least 75 per cent of those on the scheme undertaking sex-stereotyped jobs (Cockburn, 1986, 1987a and b). We should acknowledge that legislative control over discriminatory practices is not a precondition for success. For example, women in France do considerably better than their British counterparts yet France has little of the legislation in place which supposedly prevents discrimination (Dex and Walters, 1989). Here, then, cultural differences should be added to the composite model. In 1997, for instance, Britain was tenth in a review of sex inequality undertaken by the Council of Europe. In 1987 there were 41 women MPs in Britain and in 2000 there were 120, but the tripling of numbers still appears small compared to the number of male MPs, who represent over 80 per cent of the seats in the House of Commons. We might expect, as figure 13 shows, that Scandinavian countries have proportionately more women MPs than the UK, but so do China, Cuba and Argentina. In fact, New Zealand – the first country to enfranchise women – boasts a significantly better record than most countries: in 2001, a third of the MPs were women, the prime minister was a woman (Helen Clarke), as was the leader of the opposition (Jenny Shipley – the country's first woman prime minister); the attorney-general was also a woman (Margaret Wilson), and so was the chief justice (Sian Elias) (Barkham, 2001b: 8).

One of the most difficult aspects of this area of inequality is actually establishing the determinate explanations. For example, in 1984 there were only 93 women professors in Britain, accounting for barely 3 per cent of the total, and women comprise 31 per cent of contract researchers but only 7 per cent of tenured staff in 1988 (Bogdanor, 1990). By 1996 the proportion of professors who were women had increased to around 7 per cent (Major, 1996). Four years later the proportion had increased to 10 per cent (Ross, 2000) though, on average, male lecturers (70 per cent of the total) still earned over £1,500 more than female lecturers. There were some 'anomalies': the 59 female professors of nursing earn more than their male counterparts, but this is very unusual; on average, women veterinary professors earn £6,000 per year less than their male counterparts (Macleod, 2000: 14). Could this not be explained simply by the differing types of life pattern with women academics in part undermining

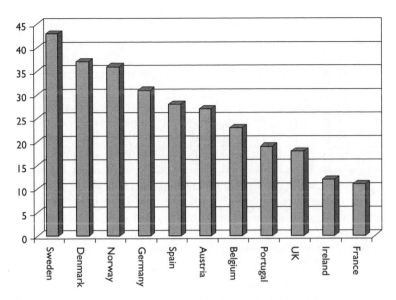

Figure 13 Percentage of female members of European parliaments, 2001
Source: Reconstructed from Russell, 2001: 19

their own promotions by career breaks etc? Well hardly: of the 202 young professors, that is those under 40, only 2 were women. Unless we assume that an inordinate number of women academics have career breaks this ratio seems capable only of a discriminatory explanation. Furthermore, if there were institutions where women did achieve proportionate levels of professorial posts then the 'normal' pattern of male dominance would no longer be able to rest secure in an argument grounded in the 'inevitable and universal' nature of male dominance. Since in 1989 Bristol University boasted just one woman professor but University College London had fifteen we can be legitimately sceptical as to the claims of disinterested appointments. The record of Scottish universities is even worse than the overall British record, with a mere 1.5 per cent of Scottish professors being women (Wojtas, 1989). An American rule of thumb, used by the US courts, is to assume discrimination exists if the success rate of women is less than 80 per cent of that obtained by men. In British universities the method clearly reveals discrimination: only 11 per cent of the total number of academics are women; of these only 17 per cent will be senior lecturers or above, compared with 42 per cent of men; in 2004 only 8 per cent of university vice-chancellors were women (Smithers, 2004: 7). As Donoghue (1988) notes: 'the women seem to be 10 to 15 years behind the men in terms of promotion'. Even egalitarian Sweden can only manage to achieve a miserly 7 per cent as the proportion of professors who are women (Wennerås and Wold, 1997). Overall, although women in the professions remain significantly underrepresented, there are some areas where progress has been made. For instance, according to an EOC poll in 2004, women comprised only 7 per cent of the senior judiciary, 7 per cent of senior police officers, 9 per cent of top business leaders

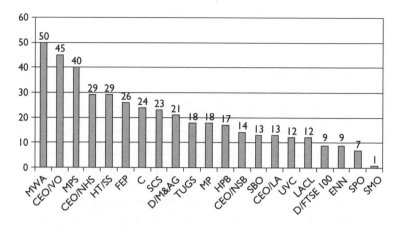

Key:

MWA	Members of the Welsh Assembly
CEO/VO	CEOs of voluntary organizations
MPS	Members of Scottish Parliament
CEO/NHS	CEOs of the National Health Services
HT/SS	Head teachers in secondary schools
FEP	FE college principals
C	Cabinet
SCS	Senior civil servants
D/M&AG	Directors of museums and art galleries
TUGS	Trade union general secretaries
MP	Members of Parliament
HPB	Heads of professional bodies
CEO/NSB	CEOs of national sports bodies
SBO	Small business owners
CEO/LA	Local authority CEOs
UVC	University vice-chancellors
LACL	Local authority council leaders
D/FTSE	Directors of FTSE 100
ENN	Editors of national newspapers
SPO	Senior police officers
SMO	Senior military officers

Figure 14 Average percentage of professional female leaders (UK), 2003

Source: Reconstructed from Equal Opportunity Commission, *Sex and Power: Who Runs Britain?* Available at <http://www.eoc.org.uk/EOCeng/EOCcs/PolicyAndCampaigns/whorunsbritain.pdf>

and 9 per cent of national newspaper editors. However, 23 per cent of the Civil Service top management and 36 per cent of public appointments were women and, as figure 14 suggests, from the British military officers (1 per cent) to members of the Welsh Assembly (50 per cent) there are wide variations in representation.

A depressingly familiar picture emerges from Spencer and Podmore's (1986) survey of the legal profession: more than 14 per cent of solicitors and barristers are women, representing around a fivefold increase since the mid-1950s but there are no female lords of appeal, only 3 per cent of high court judges are women (all in the Family Division) and a not too dissimilar percentage are circuit judges and recorders (Dyer, 1995). The reasons provided by male solicitors for either not recruiting women or not promoting them when they are recruited typically centre on the issue of child-rearing and career breaks. But the level of inequality extends beyond prospective career structures to include current reward levels. Research by the Fawcett Society in 2004 suggested that 'entrenched discrimination and prejudice' were responsible for the presence of just one woman judge in the House of Lords; moreover women comprised just 5 of 43 chief police constables, 18 of 42 chief officers of probation, 7 of 42 chief crown prosecutors, and 31 of 138 prison governors (Dustin, 2004: 5). In the late 1970s the Royal Commission on Legal Services discovered that the average income of female barristers was some 50–60 per cent of their identically qualified and employed male colleagues. The route between articled clerk and senior position is littered with impediments for women: some involve the channelling of women into specialities that offer low prestige and little prospect of advancement, such as matrimonial and family law; others relate to the social lives of this very small group of professionals which are exclusively constructed around forms of assumed male superiority, notably the macho image of tough, competitive and aggressive courtroom professionals and the all-male clubs where judges and barristers dine together. Yet underlying the gloom is another picture of increasingly embattled senior men confronted by young women undeterred by history or tradition. By 2003 in the UK, 57 per cent of law students enrolled with the Law Society were women, though still only just over 20 per cent of lawyers and 9 per cent of circuit judges were women. Concomitantly, according to the Law Society, more female students currently get 'good' degree (1 or 2:1) results than men and men achieve a disproportionately high number of third-class degrees. By 2004 even the top of the legal pyramid cracked when the first female law lord, Dame Brenda Hale, was appointed, though there were already women in the highest courts in the USA, Australia and New Zealand. In Canada, where the legal system was led by a female chief justice in 2004, three of the nine strong supreme court judges were women; the Court appointed its first woman supreme court judge in 1982 (Dyer, 2003). Progress at the top end of the occupational ladder may be slow but it is progress, and it goes beyond that achieved in skilled manual jobs.

The medical profession is more open to women than law, though this has not prevented the monopolization of key posts by men, nor has it staunched the apparent influence of the old-boy network in maintaining male control. Sponsorship by a patron is one method by which the existing elite reproduce themselves in their own image, most notably within certain specialities. Women comprise 20 per cent of GPs and 13 per cent of hospital consultants, but 98 per cent of general surgeons are men (Allen, 1988). At the level of Medical Laboratory Scientific Officers (MLSO), the advance of new technology has not loosened up the 'genderarchy', as Harvey (1987) calls it, but actually polarized the career prospects of men and women with the latter increasingly locked into the subordinate career structure. Of course, the 'old-boy network' goes far beyond the medical world and it is probably more significant in the fields of business and politics, particularly through the network of male-only or male-dominated private clubs (Rogers, 1988; Coe, 1992), another reason for casting our analytic net wider than necessary just to cover employment organizations.

In engineering, that most archetypal male occupation, there are even fewer women in senior posts than elsewhere (though even the Royal Navy began appointing women as captains of warships in 1998: *The Guardian*, 7 February 1998). In 1980 22 per cent of the engineering labour force were women, but they comprised only 5 per cent of the qualified engineers, 3 per cent of the managers (Radford, 1993), under 3 per cent of the scientists, technologists and technicians and 0.25 per cent of the fellows of engineering institutions (Cockburn, 1983b). A substantial part of the explanation for this lies in the cultural attributes of society and its ramifications for the differentiated educational provision at schools which deter girls from taking subjects that are considered male (technical drawing, maths, chemistry and physics etc.). But a less evident causal factor is the recruitment policies of engineering departments in further education establishments. As Newton (1986) remarks, selectors seemed to recruit only those women whom they considered to be androgenous, rather than overtly 'masculine' *or* 'feminine' applicants, either of which would have been perceived as a threat. It is this kind of discrimination which has led to the recent WISE (Women Into Science and Engineering) campaign, which has produced a measured degree of success, boosting the proportion of women on engineering degree courses from 7.8 per cent in 1984 to 10.5 per cent in 1987 (Boseley, 1987).

The evidence relating to the development of computer studies is equally revealing here, for although 25 per cent of the entrants to UK computer courses at universities were women in 1976, by 1987 the percentage had dropped to 15 per cent (Gerver, 1989; Grint and Woolgar, 1997). Since those schools which delayed the choice of subject specialization until late (primarily Scottish schools), and those which taught computer studies in single-sex classes, did better than the rest, we can assume that the stereotypical notions of 'appropriate' subjects at schools play a large part in dissuading girls and women from such topics, and thus in delimiting their occupational choices. Since it is also the case that female pupils in America, Singapore and France show little of the same kind of gendered lack of interest in computers we can also assume that there is something particularly disadvantageous within the English system: in particular that computers were introduced to English schools through maths departments headed by male teachers and within a system that demanded early specialization. In effect, computer technology became gendered through the process of educational induction. In 1990 the business sector revealed that just 8 per cent of British managers were women, but by 1999 this figure had risen to just under 20 per cent. However, the very top of the tree remains just as difficult to reach for women, who comprise a mere 3.6 per cent of directors. Only 2 (0.4 per cent) of the CEOs of the 'Fortune 500' companies are women and only 3.6 per cent of the top corporate officers in these companies are women (less than 1 per cent were women of colour). Nonetheless, it is possible to achieve more substantial change: nearly 15 per cent of the directors of the group of companies in Opportunity 2000 (supporters of a UK government-sponsored pro-equality initiative) were women in 1999 (<http://www.eurofound.eu.int/emire/UNITED%20KINGDOM/OPPORTUNITY2000-EN.html>; see also Caulkin, 1999: 12). In Norway, the government has demanded that 40 per cent of

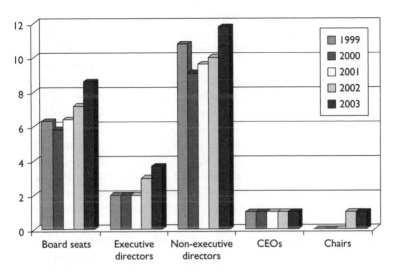

Figure 15 Percentage of women on the FTSE 100 boards, 1999–2003
Source: Reconstructed from Vinnicombe and Singh, 2003

Norwegian business board directors should be women. Indeed, there is a North–South divide on this issue, but it divides Europe not the UK: Norway, Finland and Sweden lead the field, with 19, 14 and 13 per cent of women directors respectively, while Italy trails bottom with just 2 per cent (the UK has 10 per cent and the average in the European top 200 companies and their 3,600 directorships is 8 per cent) (Maitland, 2004: 9). Globally, and in terms of managers not directors, Russian companies are the most likely to have female managers (89 per cent), followed closely by the Philippines (85 per cent) and the USA (75 per cent); at the bottom of the pile is Pakistan with just 27 per cent (Paton Walsh, 2004: 13).

In the FTSE 100 companies, the numbers of women on the board has increased from 79 in 1999 to 101 in 2003 but, as figure 15 demonstrates (based on research by Cranfield University), the numbers still comprise very small relative proportions and there was still only one woman CEO of a FTSE 100 company in 2004 (Marjori Scardino at Pearson) and only one female chair (Baroness Hogg at 3i). Even those who break through the 'glass ceiling' are likely to find another problem: the 'glass cliff' – that is, women are often promoted to very risky jobs where failure is likely. The reason relates to the correlations that link women directors to failing companies (Judge, 2003), but the causation seems to run in reverse; in other words, only when companies get into financial difficulties do they tend to 'risk' appointing women – hence women are faced with situations that are often more difficult than those of their male companions (Ryan and Haslam, 2004).

Yet if the professions seem to be opening up to women, it remains the case that the leisure activities of the professional class remain a significant bastion to gender equality. Of the 35 sports that currently comprise the Olympics, only one has a combined competition: equestrianism. Most attention tends to be focused on golf: two-thirds of complaints made to the British Equal Opportunities Commission in 1998 outside the work area related to golf clubs (Stuart, 1998: 2). The Sex Discrimination Act makes it unlawful to discriminate directly or indirectly on the grounds of a person's sex and marital status, or in recruitment, promotion, training and transfer, terms and conditions of employment and dismissal. However, there are several exemptions to this – for example, under section 29, private sports clubs are exempt from provisions of the Act (there are around 2,000 golf clubs in the UK), as are Working Men's social clubs (of which there are more than 3,000). Infamous excluders of women include the prestigious Royal and Ancient Golf Club at St Andrews, where, according to Chambers (1995), during a recent Ladies' British Open Amateur Championship a cloudburst forced all the women officials to huddle under umbrellas outside the clubhouse, from which they were banned. A man appeared from the clubhouse and the women assumed he had come to apologize for the exclusion and invite them inside to dry off, but instead he merely asked them to put down their umbrellas because they were obscuring the view of the men inside (quoted in Donegan, 2004: 6). New legislation to prohibit discrimination on grounds of sexual orientation, religion or belief is planned for 2004.

In the USA, the National Council of Women's Organizations also has trouble with golf: the prestigious Augusta National Golf Club – home of the appropriately named 'Masters' tournament every April, still has a 'No Girls Allowed' sign prominently displayed and refuses to allow women entry. The club only allowed African-American men in from 1990, but the campaign against its (legal) discrimination continues (Chambers, 1995; see also <http://www.augustadiscriminates.org/>). At the other extreme, the largest private employer in the USA in 2003, Wal-Mart, faces what may become the largest ever class suit in an alleged case of discrimination against its female employees, which may include 1.5 million women (women make up 70 per cent of Wal-Mart's employees but only 15 per cent of the management) (Campbell, 2003a: 20).

It remains illegal to pay women less than men for doing the same job, but in 2003 women working full-time earned, on average, £559 less per month than men (<http://www.eoc.org.uk/>). The British female–male pay gap, in 2003, stood at 18 per cent for full-time workers (equivalent to between £6,700 and £7,600 per annum depending on the figures used) and 39 per cent for part-time workers (of whom there are 5 million, almost all of whom are women) (Carvel, 2004a: 7). (The Fawcett Society, which has campaigned for equality for many years, suggests that the average British salaries in 2003 were £20,314 for women and £28,065 for men; see <http://www.fawcettsociety.org.uk/>.)

In 1979, the gap in Britain was 37 per cent. At the top end of the scale, more than 12 million people paid tax at the top rate (40 per cent) but only 500,000 of these were women. The long-term consequences of this inequality are significant: a middle-skilled childless woman, on average, receives £241,000 less than an equivalent male over a lifetime. Equally problematic, the consequence for women who devote their lives to raising a family rather than earning enough for a significant occupational pension is that 40 per cent of divorced British women over the age of 65 end up in poverty – poor enough to qualify for income support (Carvel, 2004b: 13).

That inequality stems from the five reasons that have prevailed for some time:

- job segregation;
- low value on caring work;
- part-time penalty;
- attitudes of male managers;
- underselling by women.

The last issue is of some import and much controversy: historically, for example, it has concerned the way female pupils at school have under-performed to save embarrassing their less intelligent or less dedicated boyfriends, but more recently it has been suggested that women are simply 'too nice'. In Wood's (2001) terms, women assume (and are conditioned to believe) that being popular, attractive, sociable and deferential wins them promotion, when in reality the latter is linked to getting the job done – which may not require such skills at all. Yet research in 2001 by the *Wall Street Journal Europe*, amongst European women business executives, suggested that few regard their gender as important at work and few regard childcare benefits as important (Finch, 2001b: 29). Perhaps this is because women at this level (75 per cent of whom were mothers) are able to afford their own private childcare arrangements.

An 'Equal Pay' government task force suggested in 2001 that between 25 and 50 per cent of British gender inequality – which at 18 per cent was the highest in Europe – is due to simple discrimination, though the vast majority of employers surveyed denied that they had a pay gap. As a result, the task force advised that a pay review should be undertaken in order to make the inequalities more transparent. And though women now outnumber and out-perform men at university, even by the age of 20 the average woman earns 10 per cent less than the average man (Carvel, 2001c: 10). More problematic, however, is the knowledge that pay in the public sector reflects not market demand but government policies. For example, the gap between the starting salaries of nurses and police officers has grown from 15 to 31 per cent, but that is despite the fact that the former group has a more significant labour shortage; the government has simply decided to pay the police proportionately more than the nurses (Garrett, 2001: 18).

In terms of which professional occupation is the most relatively advantageous to British women in general, the police and security forces offer the best deal – at 76 per cent of men's income in 2003. However, according to Doward (2003b: 13) the absolute salaries of the average woman in the finance sector (£24,457) still exceed that of the police and security sector (£23,070), even if the relative income is lower in finance (69 per cent). The Equal Opportunity Commission has slightly different data, putting women in the financial district of the City on an average of £23,500, while their male colleagues are on an average of £41,000; although that leaves women 41 per cent behind, the absolute rewards remain slightly higher in finance (Walsh, 2004: 2). Either way, the City is traditionally regarded as a bastion of patriarchy – in 2003 Cantor Fitzgerald paid a former employee £1 million in compensation for 'months of

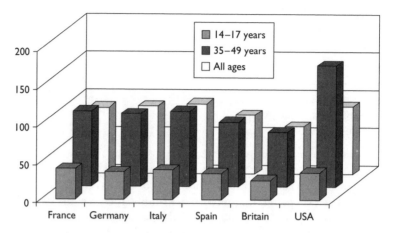

Figure 16 Women's pay as a percentage of men's at various ages, 2003
Source: Reconstructed from data in Doward and Reilly, 2003: 11

obscenities, threats and public humiliation' (Caulkin, 2004: 9). Witness also the tirade of chauvinist abuse suffered by Clara Furse who, in February 2001, became the first head of the London Stock Exchange in its 243-year history (<http://www.ananova.com/business/story/sm_751469.html?menu=>).

In comparative terms British women remain significantly worse off than many of their EU and American colleagues, as figure 16 suggests. What is important about the data here is not just that British women are so poorly paid relative to British men and relative to other women, but that the inequality is highest when women first start working as 14–17-year-olds and hardly recovers. Moreover, as the US figures suggest, American women actually earn more than their male colleagues at certain times (between 25 and 49), but that average is dragged down by the early and late inequalities. Nevertheless, the responsibility for the persistence of inequality also lies within the cultural confines of society, and this again is often related to age. Hence the most conservative groups tend to be older: in one survey in 2001, 80 per cent of 18–24-year-old British respondents *disagreed* with the statement: 'a man's job is to earn the money; a woman's . . . to look after the home and family' (quoted in Roberts, 2001: 6). On the other hand, as figure 17 suggests, simply in terms of the comparative proportion of managers who are women (the USA is excluded unfortunately), British women do relatively well – though whether the same measure is used in each country is very difficult to tell.

Although in 1970 women represented only 33 per cent of the British workforce (and earned 51 per cent of men's average wages), by 2000 they represented 50 per cent of the British workforce (and earned 72 per cent of men's average wages). Similarly, although in 1975 women represented just 35 per cent of British higher education students, by 2000 they represented 55 per cent of British higher education students (Roberts, 2001: 6–7). The implications of this figure are significant, not just for the debate of gender inequality at work but for inequality generally: women only won the right to matriculate at Oxford

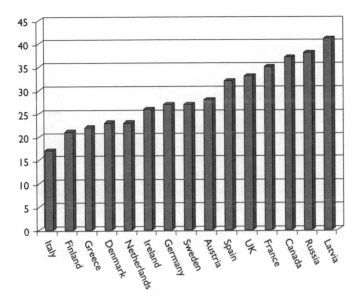

Figure 17 Women as a percentage of managers, late 1990s
Source: Reconstructed from data in *Guardian* 2, 31 March 2003: 9

University in 1920; eighty years later there were more women in the higher educational system than men and more of these achieved better degree results than their male counterparts. Thus one can either argue that women remain radically constrained by patriarchal forces within society, or one can argue that enormous progress has been made in a comparatively short space of time. Indeed, Judge and Cable (2004) have argued that an individual's height is more critical in explaining unequal rewards than is their gender; thus, an American man of five foot five inches is likely to be paid $5,000 (£3,000) less than his colleague of six foot; every extra inch adds $789 (£471).

Height notwithstanding, if the educational data imply that women are achieving equality, does this translate into women's attitudes to work? A survey of 5,000 working women in Britain, carried out for *Top Santé* magazine and Bupa in 2001, suggested that only 9 per cent of working women would continue with their careers full time if they could choose to do otherwise – but since we don't have any comparative figures for men we cannot really extrapolate from this. Yet 68 per cent of women also reported that they would enjoy work, if that was all they had to do. In other words, it is the conventional double-job, which lands women with the vast majority of domestic tasks, that undermines their ability to progress at 'work'. In fact, the proportion of both men and women who regarded themselves as 'satisfied' or 'very satisfied' with their careers dropped over the 1990s from 35 per cent to 20 per cent for men and from 51 per cent to 29 per cent for women. The majority of these people were most concerned by the increasing hours put in at work, which they insist they do because it is expected of them, rather than because they require the extra money (quoted in Branigan, 2001b: 11). The 'working all hours' culture of the British National Health Service was particularly singled out by women doctors as the primary explanation for the persistence of gender inequality in the medical profession. Although women made up 50 per cent of medical students in 1991, by 1999 they still only formed 17 per cent of consultants in medical specialities in hospitals. With training often persisting into a doctor's thirties, and with long hours a precondition for promotion, almost twice as many women as men have suggested that they would choose part-time contracts, even if this were to compromise their career prospects (Meikie, 2001: 9).

And, of course, if you are a woman and from an ethic minority, then your chances of promotion are doubly hampered. Fewer than 1 per cent of senior directors of nursing in the British NHS are from an ethnic minority, even though they comprise 8 per cent of the total number of nurses (Ahmed, 2001: 10). Similarly, although black doctors comprise 3.8 per cent of the workforce, only 2.1 per cent of the consultants' posts are held by black people (Carvel, 2001a: 1). The level of racism in the NHS is, according to a government report in 2001, extremely high. The 100,000 staff from the ethnic minorities have been 'abused by their patients, ostracised by their colleagues and sidelined by bosses' (quoted in Carvel, 2001b: 4). As one Nigerian trainee surgeon was allegedly informed by her white boss: 'You are not operating on bloody Nigerians now. These are my patients – they are normal human beings' (quoted in Carvel, 2001b: 4). A survey on ethnic minorities for the Runnymede Trust of the top FTSE 100 companies in 2000 produced a very similar result: only 55 companies replied and only 27 collected data on ethnic origins; of these, 5.4 per cent of their staff were from ethnic minorities (the UK total is 6.4 per cent), but only 3.2 per cent of junior and middle managers and 1 per cent of senior managers were from ethnic minorities (Spence, 2000: 24).

Some women, naturally, break the mould and succeed to the highest level: in 2001 Ruth Simmons became the first African-American in the USA to lead an ivy-league university (Brown University). And in 2001 in the UK Carol Galley, for example, was the highest paid woman in Britain, having sold the business she ran, Mercury Asset Management, to Merrill Lynch for £3.1 billion. She then continued to work for the latter, earning an estimated £20 million per annum (Collinson, 2001: 3). As an end-of-term report might put it on the acquisition of equality at work at the beginning of the twenty-first century: 'A very poor start, some good progress of late, but could still do a lot better.'

It is significant that much of the progress that women have made since the Second World War has been in the 1980s and 1990s: one manifestation of this is not just the growing numbers of women within higher education but the age range of female business executives compared with their male counterparts. In 1988 only 24 per cent of British male executives (broadly defined) were under 35, but over 55 per cent of women executives are this young. Similarly, although the percentage of women assistant secretaries in the British Civil Service remains at a mere 13 per cent this represents a doubling of the proportion since 1982 (Hencke, 1988). Yet the net increase of women in the six highest grades from 1985 to 1995 was one and there are still no women heading ministries (Bevins, 1995). By 2000, however, 20 per cent of the British government's top 3,000 civil servants were women. This figure includes a tripling in the number of permanent secretaries since 1989, but since in actual numbers this just meant an increase from one to three (out of a total of sixteen), it is a misleading statistic. Perhaps significantly, 50 per cent of new entrants to the Civil Service in 2000 were women. Progress in local government in England and Wales has been better: between 1991 and 1995 the percentage of women chief executives increased from 1.3 per cent to 4.9 per cent (Meikle, 1996). However, as we noted in chapter 2, it is the case that the current success of women professionals appears to be restricted, or at least related, to those who consciously decide not to have children. Certainly there is scant evidence that firms are rapidly coming to terms with the demographic changes to encourage women with families back to work (IMS, 1990). The future for women, then, is neither simply opening up generally nor reproducing the exclusions of old; rather, women are being asked to decide between one of two careers: home or work but not both. As Schwartz (1989) has argued, the structures and ideologies of work now force women to consider a twin-track future: 'career-primary' or 'career-family'.

For British women approaching the 'career-family' track, one important consideration is state provision. British maternity rights are the worst in Europe, as figure 18 suggests. Indeed, British rights are actually worse than those of women in Congo, Brazil, Peru, Angola, India and Bangladesh. However, there are no statutory rights to paid maternity leave in the USA or Australia, where only unpaid leave is available (Papworth, 2001: 10). It is also important to highlight the costs of childcare for those women with children intent on staying at work: research by the Daycare Trust suggested in 2004 that a nursery place in the UK costs almost 25 per cent of the average family's income (£134 a week) (see <http://www.daycaretrust.org.uk/mod.php?mod=userpage&menu =1001&page_id=7&PHPSESSID=06bb6b7477771e177e3386cb67883139>). This is critical in understanding the debate about women 'having it all'. On the one hand, some of the shifts in women's attitudes against a career seem to relate

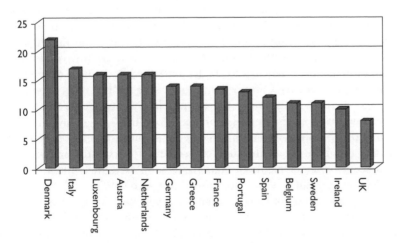

Figure 18 Maternity entitlements in Europe, 1999 (equivalent number of weeks on full pay)
Source: Reconstructed from Income Data Services, November 1999

to the difficulties they face in trying to balance the double responsibilities of home and work in a way that seldom imposes itself upon men. Men may believe themselves to have less choice in this area than women – few men choose to become 'househusbands' and thus feel themselves driven to accept the 'work-only' route – but the greater choice available to women has often resulted in their having neither a successful career nor an acceptable family life. The result has often been a polarization of opportunities: many of the most successful professional women end up without children (42 per cent of 'high salary' American women are childless and the proportion increases as the reward levels increase), either by design or default; while many younger women seem to be opting out of the employment career in the knowledge that it bears significant domestic costs. Hewlett (2003) suggests in her book *Baby Hunger* that since women's fertility rates drop by 50 per cent after the age of 35 and by 95 per cent after the age of 40, women are just going to have to accept that they cannot have it all and they must make a choice, and a choice relatively early in their careers. However, this is to ignore the potential role of the state in its tax regime and regulations about working hours that could – if it chose to do so – make it much more attractive for women to have children and a career (Ashley, 2002: 16).

As the demographic change gradually alters the ratio of young to old, the situation of one male-based institution that has suffered more than most in the last decade of economic restructuring will become ever more precarious: the trade unions.

Women and trade unions

As has already been implied, the position of trade unions on the employment of women and the achievement of equality is less than auspicious. Despite the traditional exclusionary practices of such organizations, which derive their influence through limiting access to employment, the trade unions certainly entered the era following the Second World War with an unenviable record of discrimination against women, and, as demonstrated in the next chapter, against ethnic minorities too. As Campbell succinctly put it: 'For most women, trade unions meet at the wrong time in the wrong place about the wrong things. For most trade unions, women are the wrong people in the wrong place at the wrong time going on about the wrong things' (1982b). But just as labour market conditions and the influence of the state coerced employers and trade unions alike to acquiesce to some elements of equality in the Post Office and Civil Service, so too the same pressures began mounting through the 1950s and into the 1960s. An increasing proportion of female labour (especially well-educated female labour), an increasing competition between unions for members (especially as manual work declined in importance), and the generation of a reinvigorated feminist political and industrial movement by women for women, all pushed the union movement into reluctant action. Indeed, it has been the historical lack of interest of unions in women that has furthered the survival of a vicious circle of union uninterest stimulating low female density thereby reinforcing the mutual ignorance and hostility of each to the other (Yeandle, 1984: 115–19).

Union density for women has only recently begun to approach the male equivalent. By 1978 the figure was still below 30 per cent but the rapid growth in women's employment facilitated a jump to the 1987 figure of 41 per cent, representing around 32 per cent of the total number of trade unionists. Union density rates are notoriously difficult to assess but the 1989 Labour Force Survey suggests that 39 per cent of all employees (including the unemployed) are members, encompassing 44 per cent of men and 33 per cent of women. Women, then, comprised 39 per cent of the current union membership (*Employment Gazette*, April 1990). According to the Labour Force Survey, by 1995 35 per cent of men and 30 per cent of women were unionized (MacErlean, 1996). Since almost 80 per cent of women tend to be employed within the non-manual sector rather than the manual sector, the discrepancy is more explicable in occupational rather than gender terms. Indeed, when the larger number of part-time workers are held constant the union density rates for men and women are roughly equivalent (Millward and Stevens, 1986: 54, 61–2; Horne, 1987: 78). However, by 2002, the trade union density for women was higher on both counts: amongst full-time employees, 33 per cent of women and 31 per cent of men were in unions, whereas for part-timers the equivalent figures were 23 per cent of women and 12 per cent of men. Yet despite the fact that over 38 per cent of TUC-affiliated union members are women only around 18 per cent of the delegates to the TUC are women (Trades Unions Congress, 1986).

Concomitantly, different occupations have very different levels of union density: the teaching unions recruit about 70 per cent of women members while unions in the retail sector recruit only 17 per cent of female employees.

Figure 19 shows trade union membership in Britain, in 1995, by gender and industry. In fact, the greatest variable is not between manual and non-manual work but between part-time and full-time work, and since women comprise the overwhelming number of part-time workers they are under-represented within the trade unions (Bruegel, 1983: 159–60; IRRU, 1984; TURU, 1986: 17). This under-representation is bolstered by the traditional difficulties trade unions face in recruiting part-time workers: they are more difficult to recruit because they are geographically dispersed and often work unsocial hours; and the unions have less incentive to recruit them because their turnover rates make membership records difficult to maintain and because unions have a history of hostility to part-timers. The inflexibility of trade unions is also relevant here, for few have proportionately reduced subscriptions for part-time members yet these are usually among the least affluent workers of all (Beechey and Perkins, 1987: 150–82). Such is the influence of skilled workers anyway that few unions are controlled by the less skilled and, since many part-timers are considered to be unskilled or at best semi-skilled, it is seldom that their interests prevail (Cockburn, 1987b). None the less, the switch away from full-time male employment in the manufacturing sector towards part-time female employment in the service sector is of some import to the unions, for membership has to follow job creation if the unions are to prosper. With the TGWU (Transport and General Workers' Union), NUT (National Union of Teachers) and CPSA (Civil and

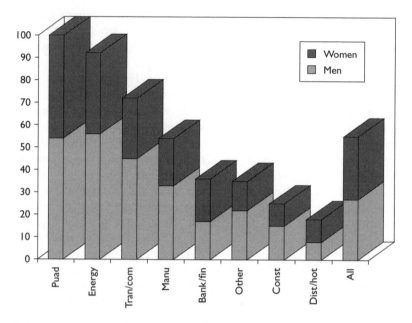

Key:
Puad — Public administration, education and health
Energy — Energy and water supply
Tran/com — Transport and communication
Manu — Manufacturing
Bank/fin — Banking, finance and insurance
Other — Other services
Const — Construction
Dist/hot — Distribution, hotels and restaurants
All — All industries

Figure 19 Trade union membership (%) by gender and industry, 1995
Source: Social Trends, 1997

Public Servants Association) all losing a third of their respective memberships between 1979 and 1986 (McIlroy, 1988: 29), hostility to part-timers represents organizational suicide.

Given the belief in the 1980s that at least 66 per cent of all new jobs in Britain in 1990–5 would be taken by women in part-time jobs, and that 90 per cent of the labour force growth over the 1990s would be from women (*Employment Gazette*, April 1989), it is a moot point whether the change of course for unions represented a change of heart or pure self-interest; it was possibly both, but probably the latter. Of course, the proliferation of policy statements and policies on women need not amount to any material gain but it is important to note that wage differentials based on sex are smaller within unionized enterprises than those without unions. However lethargic and un-interested unions may have been in the past they are at least beginning to have some impact upon the levels of gender-based inequalities (Metcalfe, 1989).

By 1984 the TUC had increased the number of women's seats on the General Council to six, it had published a 'Charter for Women' and ensured that every

Regional Council in England and Wales had a Women's Advisory Committee. Individual affiliated unions had also begun to make progress: the General, Municipal, and Boilermakers' Trade Union (GMBATU) had a national Equal Rights Advisory Committee, and an equal rights officer in each region by 1980; and many, though by no means all, unions had undertaken internal investigations of their treatment of women (Walby, 1986a: 212–30). That said, only five of the TUC's eighty-four affiliated unions had women general secretaries in 1990, and only one (GMBATU) has a quota system to promote the selection of women as Labour parliamentary candidates. The Manufacturing, Science and Finance Union (MSF) and the National Union of Public Employees (NUPE) have reserved seats on the executive for women. It may or may not be coincidental that the three most recent female general secretaries led unaffiliated 'associations': the Police Federation, the First Division of Civil Servants, and the Royal College of Nursing. The real disparity becomes evident when we move beyond the national leadership level: of the three thousand officials employed by the largest five unions only seventy-seven are women (Heery and Kelly, 1988), and overall the proportion of full-time officers (FTOs) who are women appears to be about 8 per cent (Heery and Kelly, 1989), though the increase in the number of women full-time officers is three times that of men in the last few years; a movement similar to that among professional women. Nevertheless, whether this increase is an effect of union policies or coincidental is a separate issue; although most women FTOs are within the largest unions this merely reflects the more universal connection between size and numbers of FTOs irrespective of gender. Certainly, John Edmonds was vigorously denounced at the GMBATU's 1987 conference when he suggested that 'first class women should replace second class men' (quoted in Gow, 1987), and the vast majority of the women FTOs in the Heery and Kelly survey reported that they had been discriminated against both by lay members and fellow male FTOs.

There is still a long way to go: a Labour Research review of the ten unions with the largest proportion of women members shows four unions increasing the number of full-time women officials but four other unions decreasing the number. Over half of these ten unions had fewer than 10 per cent of their full-time officer posts filled by women (Beavis, 1988). Heery and Kelly (1989) suggest from their review, however, that women FTOs are more likely to be within unions with a high proportion of women because this tends to lead to a pool of female activists and because there is a build-up of pressure from the rank and file for FTOs which reflects the membership. Women FTOs are also more in evidence in unions which appoint, rather than elect, to such positions, mainly because election is often contingent upon long service which, in turn, is something that not many women members can achieve given their domestic responsibilities and bi-modal working careers.

It is also worth noting the unintended consequences of government restrictions on unions since 1979. In particular, it would appear that one effect of the 1984 Trade Union Act, which required that all voting members of trade union executives be elected by secret individual ballot, has cut away some of the male predominance in branch and mass meetings and actually facilitated the rise of women within union executives. For example: the National Union of Taylor and Garment Workers now has eleven women out of a fourteen-strong executive; the Inland Revenue Staff Association now has seven women out of twenty-seven executive officers; and APEX and ASTMS (Association of Scientific, Technical and Managerial Staffs) have both recorded increases in the proportion of women executive members. All these changes occurred after the Act, and all four witnessed a rapid increase in the proportion of women voting (Hague, 1986).

However, the issue of expanding women's trade unionism is not simply a matter of economic restructuring providing more jobs for women than men (albeit part-time jobs), or of delimiting the effect of patriarchally dominated modes of organization. As Bain (1970) argues, some of the new patterns of work up until 1970 were the very areas which have also exhibited the greatest levels of bureaucratization, particularly in the public sector, and the similarity of conditions engineered by bureaucratization has always proved conducive to trade union development. Of course, the gradual reduction in the public sector in the last two decades has interrupted this post-war development, as indeed did the much more hostile attitude of the Conservative government itself towards the recognition of unions within its own boundaries. Equally important, since 1970 the number of large plants (employing more than a thousand workers) has fallen while the number of small plants (employing fewer than a hundred workers) has risen, so that the unions who traditionally recruit best within large plants have been doubly hit (Lash and Urry, 1987: 103–5).

The greater likelihood of men to be found within large organizations, and particularly those within export-oriented manufacturing plants, also partly explains the predominance of men within industrial conflicts. As Purcell (1984) demonstrates, the fact that most women do not appear to be militant trade unionists – defined as those regularly involved in industrial action – obfuscates the point that most men are not militant trade unionists either. It may be more appropriate, then, to assume that certain occupations, and indeed certain regions, rather than specific genders, are militantly oriented (cf. Parkin, 1967; Stead, 1987; Dolby, 1987; Walby, 1988).

This need not, of course, undermine the notion that women are not typically involved in militant activity. Women tend to be drawn to the caring professions, though again it may not be the gender of the carer here which is critical but the fact that the individual is in a caring profession whose professional code of conduct and powerful ethical commitment constrain industrial action. Nor is there any exigent connection between industrial involvement and radical consciousness. As Wajcman's (1983) review of the Fakenham women's co-operative concludes, despite the engagement of women with both capitalist economic forces and patriarchal 'co-operatives', the majority retained their conservative beliefs in the sphere of politics and the home. Fatalism, not radicalism or militancy, is the typical reaction of most people, irrespective of gender, to a situation that appears to be beyond the influence of human agents (Purcell, 1984; Cunnison, 1984).

Where you would expect women to be more involved in union activity and industrial action would be where women have returned to work once their children have started school. This return provides several sources of independence that might lead to union membership: an independent source of income; relative independence from children; and direct experience of power relations inherent at work. There is some evidence for this, though little for any direct decanting of resistance at work to supervisors, into resistance at home to men. Watts (1984) suggests that this barrier between industrial radicalism and domestic radicalism reflects the discrete patterning of the two areas of activity with the domestic mode subordinated to the industrial, but a different interpretation would be to substitute the term militancy for radicalism; militancy being concerned with the increased acquisition of economistic rewards within the existing socio-economic structure, radicalism concerned with the restructuring of the system itself. If we assume that women can be militant at work without being radical at home, not only does this provide a different viewpoint on the division of ideologies but it actually reflects the normal pattern of most work-based groups: many such groups have long been associated with all manner of economistic militancy, often in defence of privileges retained at the expense of the less well off; few such groups have ever been involved in the promotion of radical measures to restructure the industrial system itself (Grint, 1986: 106–26).

Another important aspect of the gradual increase in women's membership of the trade unions has been the success of the recruitment campaigns by unions themselves as they have struggled to stem the haemorrhaging of members through the collapse of the manufacturing sector. Partly, this has involved recognition of the problems of holding union meetings late at night, or in pubs; issues which reflect and reproduce the conventional patriarchal control over the night and most public arenas. But even the recognition of this kind of problem and the election of women to official positions in unions does not, in and of itself, secure equality; a women union official interviewed by Imray (Imray and Middleton, 1983) told how the 'chivalry' of male officials in driving her home or seeing her on the bus turned out to be a scheme by which the 'real' business of the branch could be conducted after she had left. It is not just a case of moving the location and timing of meetings, or even providing crèches. Part of the answer has to lie in re-educating the male membership to accept their share of the domestic responsibilities. It is of limited use just providing meetings at more convenient times if women are still held to be solely responsible for children and domestic chores; this not only leaves women with a double workload but ensures that any women with domestic responsibilities, paid employment and an active interest in union affairs has a triple workload (Central London Community Law Centre, 1987). Part of the answer also lies in the acceptance by men that real equality can only be achieved at their expense (Dale, 1987); not all power games are variable-sum ones.

Of course, very few men use whatever spare time they may have to attend their union's meetings anyway, and it has conventionally been understood that the figure for women must be lower. Little research has been undertaken in this area, and the levels of sex-segregated occupations always make comparisons difficult, though Harrison's (1979) survey of an ASTMS branch suggests that a higher proportion of women than men attended normal meetings. In many ways this is rather surprising given the conventions of unionism that clearly reflect male lifestyle. As Gill and Whitty argue: 'Without malice or design, but also without concern, men have shaped trade union life to suit those who have no childcare or other domestic responsibilities and on an expectation that every trade union activist has endless evening hours to devote to union work' (quoted in TURU, 1986: 24). Certainly the female FTOs of Heery and Kelly's sample were three times less likely to have children than the average. Once again, it is the links to the domestic sphere which crucially constrain women in the roles they can undertake. It is this form of discriminatory practice that accounts for one survey that showed over 50 per cent of the female labour force to be either uninterested in or actively hostile to trade unions (Martin and Roberts, 1980). Even where trade unions develop non-discriminatory policies this would not necessarily lead to any wide-scale change, at least not immediately; for as Beynon and Blackburn (1984) suggest, even if all the evidence negates all patriarchal assumptions about women in unions the effect of traditions and misinterpretations is to buttress the position of men. Thus, if men *think* that women make poor union members then they will do little to recruit or retain them; as a result women will comprise a small percentage of union members, thereby 'demonstrating' the apparent validity of the patriarchal attitude (Pollert, 1981).

Masculinity, domestic labour and violence

Often underlying some of the patriarchal assumptions about the superiority of men and their work are what appear to women at least rather thinly veiled strategies to protect male egos, though to men they may well seem invisible. Pollert's (1981) account of women factory operatives is a good example here for it reveals how women find security within their poorly paid jobs in part because their income level does not threaten their male partners' egos. Such low self-esteem, ironically premised upon the fragility of masculinity, merely reinforces the perception of work for many working-class women as an interruption between school and having a family, or as a place to secure 'extra' money and social friendship rather than a career in itself. Both of these may further undermine any assumption by women that trade unionism can play any important role in their lives. The analysis of girls at school supports the contention that females both consciously underplay their own abilities so as not to threaten the brittle egos of males (Sharpe, 1976; Horner, 1976) and consider the boredom of both school and employment sufficient to warrant a low level of interest in either. This throws a different light on the 1990s concern about the increasing polarization of school exam results as girls pull further and further ahead of boys in virtually all subjects (Sianne and Wilkinson, 1995; OFSTED, 1996; *Social Trends*, 1997). Correspondingly, the assumption that where jobs are short they should be reserved for men is not simply an assumption made by men; as some of the women in Pollert's (1981) study demonstrate, if they had to provide for their husbands or even earned more than them, many of the men would feel 'downgraded' and many of the women would suffer as a result. Even when male unemployment has left women's wages as the main source of income women still perceive their earning power to be auxiliary, rather than primary, within the household (Morris, 1987; Mintel, 1995), and, as suggested in chapter 1, there is little evidence of unemployed men using their 'free' time to take over domestic responsibilities from 'working' wives.

The issue of time is relevant in another sense, for a primary distinguishing feature between male and female employees is the differential use made of 'free' time: men conventionally negotiate a shortening of normal hours to maximize their overtime potential, women prefer to use the extra time at home. In itself, this does not establish autonomously chosen alternatives: it has become a commonplace to acknowledge that men endure, rather than support, their wives' employment activities, and then only on condition that they do not interfere with domestic arrangements (Martin and Roberts, 1984).

Men, it would seem, have remained impervious to debates, complaints or arguments about sharing domestic work. This should not be such a surprise: in the early days of the Russian Revolution the Bolsheviks opened up all kinds of jobs to Soviet women, but Soviet men remained steadfast in their tenacious grip on tradition. As a consequence, women did 'men's' and 'women's' jobs, but men just did their 'own'. In fact, British women still did 75 per cent of the domestic work (excluding childcare) in 2001 (18 hours per week compared to men's average of 6 hours per week), and women's focus remained on the routine and the internal jobs (cooking, cleaning and caring), while men continued to do non-routine and external tasks, especially repairs. On a daily basis, the average (over a lifetime) British man spends three hours watching TV or listening to the radio – 22 minutes more than the average woman; he spends 45 minutes a day on housework – 93 minutes less than she does; and he spends 13 minutes looking after his children – she spends 23 minutes more than he does. If we take couples who *currently* have children, the average man spends 45 minutes a day with his children, while the average woman spends just over 90 minutes a day. On the other hand, over a lifetime he spends 193 minutes a day in paid work, while she spends just 75 minutes. And the consequence of all these activities is that his average weekly wage is £247 while hers is just £119. The downside for men of this inequality is that they are more likely than women to commit suicide, drink heavily, have a major accident and a heart attack, and they live five years less – to 75 on average. Men also comprise 80 per cent of the criminal population and are three times more likely to be attacked by a stranger than a woman is (Office for National Statistics, 2001).

Generally, women with more education and better paying jobs do less domestic work than their poorer educated and paid colleagues, not because the wealthier ones can buy more domestic technology – since this does not make much difference in hours devoted to the house; it just makes the house cleaner (Cowan, 1983) – but because they have a more egalitarian attitude to domestic work. Their greater earning power also provides them with a stronger bargaining position (Man-yee Kan quoted in Vasager 2001).

The real point of value is to note the connection rather than the contradiction between these two apparently dichotomous attitudes to time. It is only because men 'underachieve' at home that they can take advantage of the extra time: the time is made available not by their employers nor by their union's efforts, but by their female partners shouldering most, if not all, of the domestic responsibilities. Thus the model of male work as full-time work, far from being separated from that of women, is intimately dependent upon it.

The issue is one that goes beyond unequal work loads and involves the importance of work and the family to men and women. Crehan (1986: 205–6) argues that many women do not just have obligations to their families, but their family life provides the central meaning of their lives. Crehan further asserts that this is not the case for men, but the evidence is restricted to women and comparative research tends to suggest that men and women both value family life higher than paid work (Feldberg and Glenn, 1984; Dex, 1985: 36–44). The point really is that men are not systematically faced with the dilemma of combining paid work and domestic responsibilities. As Crehan rightly concludes: 'being a conscientious parent and being a conscientious worker should not be competing options that individuals must choose between' (1986: 206).

A further twist in the tail of male egos must be the commensurability of masculinity with militancy. The world of work, in particular the world of male manual work, is one where the pursuit of proletarian maleness – aggression, domination and physical strength – is embodied in many notions of trade union power and working-class resistance. Perhaps the clearest demonstration of this, and the gulf between the prevailing cultures of men and women, is in Willis's (1977) descriptions of working-class boys at school preparing for working-class jobs in factories. It is essentially this preparation for work that carries with it the implicit degradation of women's work and women's worth and the double standards on sexual behaviour that are commonplace. Women also suffer from a more pervasive sexual harassment, that is 'behaviour of a sexual nature which is unwanted, unwelcome and unreciprocated and which might threaten job security or create a stressful or intimidating working environment' (WASH, 1987). The way such harassment is used to control women is another example of the opacity of privilege. That is the way that power often appears almost invisible to the those wielding it but self-evident to those suffering from it. Many men appear to deny their association with discriminatory practices, for such people sexual harassment is 'merely horseplay', and women have long been deterred from complaining about it in the sure knowledge that nothing will be done about an activity that will probably be considered by the (male) managers to be little more than 'fooling around' (Seddon, 1983). That sexual harassment is far from 'horseplay', and far from declining, is demonstrated in a survey of US students which revealed that 17 per cent of women were the victims of rape or attempted rape, and 7 per cent of men admitted committing rape or attempting to commit rape in the previous twelve months (*THES*, 9 September 1988).

Currently, the issue of sexual harassment at work is receiving a considerable amount of attention, both in its historical manifestations (Lambertz, 1985), and its contemporary forms (NALGO, 1981; Bularzik, 1978; Gordon, 1981; Hearn and Parkin, 1987; Rubinstein, 1989). The NALGO study is important in exposing the very high levels of harassment that exist; in their study of the Liverpool branch 25 per cent had experienced harassment at their current place of work and 50 per cent at some time in their working lives. Subsequently, several unions have initiated policy statements, including NALGO, NATFHE (National Association of Teachers in Further and Higher Education), ASTMS, CPSA and the National Union of Journalists (NUJ). Even trade union officers themselves appear to be widely involved in such activities: in Heery and Kelly's (1989) survey of 87 women FTOs, 51 per cent complained of sexual harassment from fellow male officers, only marginally less than had complained about harassment from the male rank and file.

Yet some progress is visible. Since the 1980s British women have been awarded damages by industrial tribunals when sexual harassment has forced them to resign and, for the first time, this has been interpreted as unfair dismissal (Equal Opportunities Commission, 1987). However, the most progressive policies derive from the USA, especially since May 1988 when a district court judge ruled that a female Securities and Exchange Commission attorney was victimized and discriminated against by a 'pervasive sexual atmosphere' in the regional office between 1979 and 1984. This judgement is important because the defendant was not directly involved but argued that the tradition of granting favours and privileges to women employees who consented to managers' sexual advances generated a 'hostile and offensive workplace'. Thus, not only was the complaint upheld against a practice that did not directly involve the defendant but it was upheld against the culture of the organization rather than specific individuals (Hambleton, 1988). In 1996 even overtly macho organizations like the Virginia Military Institute (VMI) appeared to be resigned to a more egalitarian future when it accepted a Supreme Court order to allow women to register for the first time. But for such women there is a price: the VMI authorities have ruled that women must have the same levels of fitness, the same uniforms and the same haircuts as men (*THES*, 1996). As in the USA so it is in Britain that one of the most significant examples of the remaining barriers to the equality are the armed forces (the British military is exempt from the 1975 Sex Discrimination Act). Women have been recruited into the British Army for many years and 7 per cent of the army's total of 109,000 in 1998 were women, but 14 per cent of the recruits were women. (This is far higher than the proportion of female firefighters in the UK in 2002: just 1 per cent; Turner, 2002: 5). By 2000 there were 17,000 women in the army, as it responded not so much to equal opportunities as to a dire shortage of recruits. Indeed, the proportion of soldiers going absent without leave (AWOL) doubled between 1996 and 2000 to 1.3 per cent, with many blaming bullying, an unreconstructed 'macho' culture, and poor quality recruits (Burke, 2001: 5).

Unlike several other armed forces (notably Germany, New Zealand and Canada), British women remain restricted to specific roles (76 per cent of the total) and are not permitted to bear arms in 'direct combat'. Thus in 2004 Brigadier Patricia Purves was the highest-ranking woman in the British Army and the highest-ranking woman in a post open to both sexes. In the RAF there were already women fighter pilots, and many women serve on Royal Naval warships – but not on submarines. In fact, women have comprised a significant element of the combat arms of other nations for some time: the Soviet armed forces involved many women as infantry, tank crews and fighter pilots in the

Second World War and in 2000 were already in combat positions within the US, Canadian, Norwegian, Dutch, German and Israeli armies (Burke, 2000a; Hartley-Brewer, 2000; Krechtig, 2001: 14).

Tests carried out by the British Army in 1999–2000 seemed to suggest that women performed as well as their male counterparts (Burke, 2000b), though training injuries appear to be far more common amongst women (Fox, 2001: 5), and in 2000 the drop-out rate for women (8 per cent) from army training courses remained significantly higher than for men (2.3 per cent) (Evans, 2001: 7). (In 2002 Captain Philippa Tattersall, the first woman to pass the 10-week all-arms commando course, was awarded the Green Beret, undertaking exactly the same course as her male colleagues. The Royal Marines 42-week commando course is a separate requirement for those wishing to join the combat rather than the support units: Wilson, 2002.) Yet contrary to popular opinion, there is evidence to suggest that many women are at least as aggressive as men (Grint, Katy, 2000) or perhaps even more aggressive. Grossman (1998), for example, suggests in his review that women on the battlefield are twice as likely to kill as their male colleagues because to have reached that position they already need to have 'proved' themselves far more than their male colleagues. On the other hand, Nancy Mace – who became the first woman to graduate in 1999 from the Citadel in South Carolina, the USA's toughest military college (Shannon Faulkner had enrolled earlier but dropped out after one week) – suggests that men can be very aggressive, at least in trying to keep women out (Mace and Ross, 2002).

In contrast, men in jobs more traditionally associated with women are even more visible by their general absence. For example, only 3 per cent of British nursery teachers and 17 per cent of primary school teachers are men.

Summary

This chapter has outlined some important contemporary theories that attempt to explain the position and experiences of women at work, and provided a review of the nature of contemporary gender relationships in capitalist society. Self-evidently it has done little more than skim the surface on any of these areas, but that is the nature of such an introductory text as this.

It is important that the major themes are represented here so that their significance is not obscured in the detail. Fundamentally, an analysis of gender at work requires some form of coherent theoretical viewpoint; a glance at data tables may enlighten you as to how many women are executives but it cannot tell you why this number is as it is, or whether it is capable of alteration. Of the theories discussed earlier I hold little faith in the value of those which ignore gender because the relationships between men and women are crucial in the construction of work ideologies, structures and experiences. Theories which retain either capitalism *or* patriarchy as uniquely critical are inevitably partial and simply cannot explain the gendered work variations that exist in time and space.

The symbiotic mutualism theory that presumes capitalist and patriarchal interests are congruent is similarly incapable of accounting for the tension-ridden relationship between these two; and dualist theories that hold the two separated as autonomous forces neglect the qualitative changes that occur when the two are conjoined. The contingent and heterogeneous compound model illustrated here allows the model to encompass the issues of race and ethnicity, and hinges the whole on a respect for the importance of contingency that does not surrender to some of the traditional contingency approaches where everything appears to explain everything. Although the social world of work is inordinately complex the variables of class, race and gender are significantly superordinate in the quest for explanation. Relationships at work are not constructed by the interaction of men and women, workers and bosses, blacks and whites, but by white male bosses, and by black female workers and by all the other possible permutations of this triangular social construct.

The two other significant points that should be drawn from the review of the evidence are the insoluble link between home and work, and the historical patterning of gender relationships. Ultimately, the model of a full-time, single-occupation, male breadwinner who worked outside the home and kept his family achieved pre-eminence in the dominant ideology. However, this model is historically atypical and surrounded by so many qualifications that its period of relevance is restricted to between the last third of the nineteenth century and the first third of the twentieth. Equally important, the model was one of a modal representation: there may have been more such male workers around during this period than any other single group, but they did not form an overwhelming majority of the working population. The current pattern of paid work, though still undertaken away from home, has some features reminiscent of previous eras, particularly multiple incomes, bi-modal employment for women and transient occupations. What also exists today is a permutation of a pattern of gender-differentiated work experiences, occupations and rewards that has prevailed for much longer than the era of industrial capitalism. Thus women are paid less, have less chance of promotion, are less likely to be owners of businesses, are usually found in unskilled or semi-skilled service jobs, and tend to combine paid work with unpaid domestic work. Women are also less likely to be in unions and almost non-existent within union hierarchies. On the other hand, labour market pressures and the force of women's self-organization and commitment to change have begun to restructure their collective experience: they are now less likely than men to be unemployed and more likely to be found in executive positions than before, though still unlikely to be found in skilled manual jobs, especially in the field of engineering. Both employers and trade unions are now seeking to recruit women as never before and, however unimpressive the histories of both these groups have been in their relationships with women, a small but perceptible shift in attitude is developing. Marx was wrong in assuming that history was on the side of the proletariat, history is far more contingently constructed than this; but historically rare opportunities for the advancement of women at work are beginning to appear – whether they mature is another matter.

Exam/essay questions

1 'A career or a family.' Must women choose one or is it possible to under-take both?
2 To what extent are women's careers the result of free choice?
3 'The sudden interest of trade unions in recruiting women merely represents self-interest, it does not demonstrate a sudden change of heart.' Discuss.
4 Which theory, if any, best explains the position of women at work in con-temporary Britain?
5 'The solution to gender inequality at work is gender equality at home.' Is it?
6 If women are generally more skilled, more flexible and paid less, why do employers employ men?
7 'The future for men, for trade unions and for the unskilled looks bleak; the future is female.' Discuss.
8 To what extent does gender condition the experience of women?
9 'The highest levels of discrimination are not among the professions but among blue-collar industrial workers.' Discuss.
10 Is there a way through the glass ceiling for women?

Further reading

For an historical overview of women in the twentieth century, try: Rowbotham's *A Century of Women: the History of Women in Britain and the US* (1997). A thorough account of various theoretical positions can be found in Walby's *Theorizing Patriarchy* (1990), while one of the most radical discussions is Haraway's *Simians, Cyborgs and Women* (1991). Closer to the world of work I would suggest the following: Cockburn's *In the Way of Women* (1991), Beechey's *Unequal Work* (1987), the volume edited by Crompton, Gallie and Pourcell titled *Changing Forms of Employment* (1996), and, finally, Rosener's *America's Competitive Secret: Utilizing Women as a Management Strategy* (1995).

7

Race, Ethnicity and Labour Markets: Recruitment and the Politics of Exclusion

- Introduction
- Race, racism and ethnicity
- Labour markets and racism
- Recruitment and racism
- Trade unions, workers and racial discrimination
- Summary
- Exam/essay questions
- Further reading

I have a dream that one day this nation will rise up, live out the true meaning of its creed: we hold these truths to be self-evident, that all men are created equal.

Martin Luther King, 27 August 1963

Introduction

This chapter provides an introduction to the debates on ethnicity, race and racism at work. It begins by examining the theoretical controversies surrounding the terms themselves and then analyses the classical model of labour markets – which suggest that skin colour, cultural origin and ethnic allegiance are irrelevant to success at work. The problems of this suggestion, and the assumption that all ethnic minorities can be placed in the same collective category 'black', are then discussed, along with various accounts for the patterning of rewards and recruitment. Finally, the experience of minority workers in trade unions in Britain and the USA is considered.

Race, racism and ethnicity

The problem of agency

One of the most important facets of the sociological approach to work relates to the underlying claim that work is a social not an individual activity. In a sense, no one is ever alone at work because of the social structures that under-pin, and prevail over, work activities. What appears a freely chosen individual activity may well reflect, at least in part, socially structured constraints and facil-itators which are, or appear to be, opaque in nature. For example, white middle-class men may take for granted that their professional career is wholly due to their individual efforts, yet the dearth of ethnic minority women in such careers suggests that the former are facilitated by social forces while the latter are inhibited by them. This relationship between the freedom of individuals to choose their own future and the socially constructed and sustained limitations and opportunities is a theme which runs through much of the sociology of work, and indeed the social sciences more generally. There are many ways of illus-trating this '**problem of agency**', though perhaps the three most important socially structured facilitators and constraints existing in contemporary capitalist soci-eties are those of class, gender and race. The first two are dealt with in the two previous chapters and therefore the concentration here is primarily, though not exclusively, on the issue of race and ethnicity at work.

Racism

Racism, as suggested in chapter 2, long predates capitalism and has always posed a problem for Marxist accounts: capitalism may be, and indeed has been, able to take advantage of divisions between the workforce on ethnic or racial lines but these divisions were not created by capitalism any more than sexism or patriarchy was. This is not the place to consider the intricacies of the current debates on race and ethnicity and readers unfamiliar with the general debates should consult one or more of the following: Rex (1970, 1986); Banton (1983, 1987); Miles (1982, 1989); Fryer (1984); Sivanandan (1982); Centre for Con-temporary Cultural Studies (1982); Brittan and Maynard (1984); Solomos (1989); Anthias and Yuval-Davis (1992); Gilroy (1987); and Modood (1997b). The term 'race' is infused with political force. Race has become such a pejorative label that many liberal and radically minded researchers have questioned its contin-ued use in social science. After all, since there is no 'scientific' proof that racial groups exist beyond skin colour and minor physical differences, to continue using the term is to fall into the trap of assuming they do exist and thus per-petuate the racism which many such writers disparage. After all, there are greater genetic variations between individuals of the same alleged 'race' than there are between the averages of different 'races' (Stringer and McKie, 1997). Even the term 'racism' is the subject of considerable debate, but adopting the conven-tional view – that **racism** involves any suggestion within which humans can be divided into discrete groups in order to legitimate inequality between these groups – physical differences exist within all societies. However, the paramount point is that some features are selected by certain powerful members of such societies as 'ethnically significant'. Conventionally, little attempt is made to ensure that the worst jobs and housing go to those of us with large ears or those who are bald or spotty, but in Europe and North America those with dark skins are often treated just as inequitably (except, of course, in the ironic practices of white racist sunbathers). Racism, therefore, 'categorizes the "other" as inherently different and typically inferior . . . and involves the disadvantageous treatment of the "other", whether intentionally or not' (Jenkins, 1988: 311). What this chapter does is to explain how this racism manifests itself in and at work.

Ethnicity

One way of approaching the delicate topic of race is to ignore it altogether and appropriate instead the term **'ethnicity'** since this refers to cultural rather than physical or allegedly 'natural' differences between groups. Ethnicity is also significant in so far as many groups are discriminated against because of their cultural attributes rather than their skin colour or apparent racial differences. For example, almost all countries have ethnic minorities within them which remain the butt of discriminatory 'jokes' yet they are often physically identical with the majority population. Of course, not all groups that are discriminated against are minorities – the clearest counter-example being South African blacks – but it is more typical within Western capitalist nations at least for the ethnic groups to be minority groups as well. But if the evidence for racial difference, as opposed to ethnic/cultural differences, is marginal at the very best, why persist in the use of such a term? Perhaps the clearest answer relates to the experiences of people who are discriminated against because of their alleged racial distinction: the fact that the distinctions are false does not prevent the discrimination, and ignoring the issue on the grounds of its non-scientific status has seldom proved a resolution to such problems. And since, in 1995, 79 per cent of the white population in Britain believed that racial prejudice still exists we must assume the problem remains (ICM, 1995).

Indeed, a European Union poll in 1997 revealed that roughly one-third of the British population admitted they were racist (including 8 per cent who said they were 'very racist') – though this figure remains far below that for France, Belgium and Austria where half admitted to being racist (*The Guardian*, 20 December 1997). Nor should the issue of race be reduced to that of ethnicity. As Rex observes: 'The attempt to assimilate racial to ethnic problems, therefore, often led to the interpretation of racial problems not as forms of conflict but as benign phenomena of difference' (1986: 19). That is to say, that racial relationships have been, with few exceptions, conflictual, whereas ethnic relations exhibit a much wider span of reactions from (atypically) mutual admiration to outright hostility. But just as race has a dubious claim to objective existence, so too ethnicity is a socially constructed, and therefore contested, subject. Thus both race and ethnicity may be better conceptualized as a resource which individuals and groups draw upon, and in so doing actively construct, rather than something which exists 'out there'. This does not imply that race is socially constructed only by superordinate groups and that this construct is applied to themselves and imposed upon subordinates, whereas ethnicity is self-constructed. Both constructs are socially constructed and capable of self-application or imposition from outside. Indeed, no categorical distinction can be made between them; rather it is the case that racial constructs are related *primarily* to physical features, while ethnic constructs are related *primarily* to cultural features like common forms of language, location, kinship and customs etc. (Geertz, 1963). In many cases the two will simply be indistinguishable in practice.

The relative importance of cultural aspects of ethnicity is manifest in the debates in the USA concerning the numbers of Native Americans in 2003. Many of the eighty separate Native American tribes challenged the 2000 Census, which established the numbers belonging to each tribe. Since the size of the tribe determines the level of federal support, there was a financial reason for reconsidering the tribal numbers, but it is also the case that claiming tribal identity has become a source of cultural pride which many people previously sought to hide. Exactly who can claim such an identity is itself determined more by cultural than by biological prerequisites. For instance, since the US Supreme Court ruled in 1978 that each tribe could define its own membership, the diversity of definitions has grown: the Cherokee nation demand that tribal members be descended from someone on the 1906 federal roll after the destruction of their reservation, while the Yakimas require at least one grandparent to be from the tribe. In 1910 just over a quarter of a million Americans were registered as Native American, and half of these were 'full bloods'. The 2000 Census suggested there were 2.5 million classified as 'wholly' Native American, and 1.6 million as 'part' Native American. Whatever the numbers, the point is to consider how the definition cannot simply be related to physical aspects of 'race' (Campbell, 2003b). Moreover, early work on the DNA analysis of 229 'black' men in the UK in 2003 suggested that 26 per cent had at least one 'white' male ancestor: in effect, many if not most of us would have great difficulty *disproving* a 'mixed' biological heritage, and, by implication, our identity is a social not a biological construct (McKie and Revill, 2003: 20).

Weber and exclusion

Weberian approaches to the general area are represented by reference to exclusionary mechanisms using status as a concept to include race and ethnicity. Just as small-scale social groups and coteries exist and reproduce themselves by excluding those without the necessary characteristics or possessions, so too racial or ethnic groups do the same, as do other social institutions such as trade unions or religious groups (Parkin, 1979). Groups are not restricted simply to rejecting the advances of outsiders, they may also attempt to invade the territory of those by whom they themselves are excluded. Trade unions, for example, may operate with two different forms of exclusionary practice, or 'dual closure': they may attempt **'usurpationary' action** against the employers and **'exclusionary' action** against minority workers. In principle, exclusionary practices by one group tend to be associated with a priori legitimation of 'inferiority' and 'superiority' by the state (Parkin, 1982: 102), though at the level of the enterprise this need not be so. For example, the exclusion of individuals on the basis of non-possession of familial links, as in the printing or dock trades for many years, has seldom been approved by the state as such, but none the less retains its significance. The opposite method by which groups attempt to wrest control *from* existing exclusivist groups, Parkin's 'usurpationary' strategy, is represented by the Italian cigar makers of Tampa discussed below. The exclusionary line is the one adopted by Gordon (1972), Rubery (1980), Lee (1980), and Craig et al. (1982), but two rather different mechanisms need delineating here: on the one hand there is the conventional market-oriented exclusionary strategy of most groups in positions of power who retain power by excluding the majority irrespective of their characteristics, cultural or social; on the other hand are policies of exclusion focused directly on specific groups, such as women and ethnic minorities (Grint, 1988). In the first case fall the sectionalist methods adopted by many trade unions (Currie, 1979), but most notably craft unions, in which work-based privileges depend upon control over the labour market. The archetypal exclusionary mechanism here is the demand for all labour to be apprenticed, hence 'skilled', and for the number and form of apprenticeships to be controlled by the unions. Printers embody this kind of exclusionary approach and have reaped the benefits of limiting the labour supply for generations in the form of relatively high salary levels (Sisson, 1975; Open University, 1976). Such control has also played a part in the downfall of the printing unions as their strategic influence simultaneously pushed labour costs ever higher, inhibited the adoption of new technology and, therefore, made such technology inevitably more attractive to employers. In the second case fall the activities of unions determined to preserve privileges not just *for* their members but *against* particular out groups, sometimes even those who are members of the same union (Grint, 1988).

Institutionalized racism

The major problem with some exclusionary approaches, and Parkin's approach in particular, is the implication that social life is no more than a network of exclusionary and usurpationary groups. Where Parkin rightly criticizes Marxists for neglecting the existence of non-class issues, he merely inverts the image and denies the existence of all but groups actively excluding others. As many radical critics of putative pluralist societies have demonstrated, to concentrate on what is actively fought over at the level of overt conflict ignores that which embodies inequality of resources but is not revealed in any specific activity (Giddens, 1982a; Lukes, 1974; Clegg, 1989). This is particularly important in explaining **institutionalized racism**: a group dominated by whites may not adopt overtly racist practices but if it simply recruits in its own image then what appear to be equal opportunities lead to unequal results (Rex, 1986: 108–18; Miles, 1989: 84–7). For example, the British police requirements for male recruits to be at least 5 foot 8 inches has indirectly discriminated against British Asians who tend to be rather shorter than British whites. The recent removal of this height requirement thus removes the institutionalized racism. Similarly, the British armed forces' requirements for all service personnel to wear protective helmets in combat zones effectively debars British Sikhs from joining the 200,000 existing forces – despite the fact that almost 200,000 Sikhs were killed or wounded fighting for Britain in two world wars. Few British trade unions, or indeed less progressive institu-tions, operate with overt exclusionary policies based on race or ethnicity yet the empirical evidence suggests that many are racist. Whether the racism is a reflection of members or institutional practices and policies is a separate issue (see for example, Virdee and Grint, 1994).

Marxism and racism

As discussed in chapter 4, the conventional Marxist approach to social stratification is to subordinate aspects such as gender, race and ethnicity to class: the former are derivative of, and therefore subordinate to, the latter. It follows that once class societies are abandoned in favour of socialist and classless societies, sexism and racism will wither spontaneously. The experience of non-capitalist societies, ancient and modern, suggest that nothing of the sort is likely and that discrimination based on gender and race or ethnicity, while it may not be completely autonomous of that derived from social class, is unlikely to disintegrate with the removal of class discrimination. That is not to say that the legitimations of discrimination are constant across time. For example, neither Greek nor Roman slavery was grounded in an ideology of *racial* inferiority. Rather they were both culturally legitimated: free people with political rights (i.e., men) were culturally distinct from the 'barbarians' they enslaved. In turn, this meant that even barbarians, black or white, could become cultured and hence attain equivalent status as the free citizens of Rome or most of the ancient Greek city-states (Snowden, 1983). Skin colour as a sign of status, therefore, is a more recent phenomenon associated more directly with the expansion of European powers into Africa and Asia from the fifteenth century, and before this through the development of general hostility between the Islamic and Christian worlds from the twelfth century (Daniel, 1975). Indeed, Hall (1992) argues that a European identity was itself partly constructed in and through the apparent differences between the Old World and the New World which became manifest in the European explorations of the Americas in the fifteenth and sixteenth centuries. Even the slavery system of the West Indies and America operated within an ideological defence of enslavement that sought to justify it rather than simply take it for granted (Curtin, 1972). After all, had not the 'father' of British liberal thought, John Locke, argued in his 1690 *Essay Concerning Human Understanding* that 'A Negro is not a Man' (see Segal, 1995)? For example, Africans were deigned particularly suited to work in tropical conditions, in contrast to Europeans; and since the Europeans regarded themselves as culturally superior to Africans, the capture of slaves was sometimes represented as a form of liberation for the slaves from the cultural depravities of their homeland (Barker, 1978; Miles, 1989).

This historical dimension is also important in situating the post-1945 immigrations against previous movements. Since one of the features of capitalism that distinguish it from slavery and prior modes of production is the formal freeing of labour it is likely that emigration and immigration take on a high level of significance. As such we should beware of linking immigration into Britain *per se* with immigration from the post-war Caribbean and Asian immigration (see Miles, 1990). That the language of immigration still conflates the phenomenon, and persists in labelling ethnic minority Britons as 'immigrants', illustrates the power of certain forms of discourse over others.

Since many ethnic minorities in contemporary Britain still do not occupy positions of equality with the white population it then becomes necessary to consider how various theories explain the persistence of divisions and inequalities. Marxist accounts like that of Castles and Kosack (1973) imply that the divisions between white and minority workers are representations of a transient hostility derived from competition within the labour market. Over time, the interests of minority and white workers will be perceived as converging and thus white working-class racism will disappear. The critical problem for such accounts lies in the assumption that the temporal dimension is the explanatory variable: workers of different races have to *learn* to combine and, over time, eventually they will do so. It may well be that experience is a significant educative medium, which in itself undermines any deterministic connection between social position and political activity, but the assumption of an inevitable and evolutionary progression, to a point where class interests prevail over racial interests, is premised on very shaky foundations; *when* do these interests coincide and what exactly are the mechanisms that deny the possibility of greater polarization between racial and ethnic groups rather than greater integration?

Making sense of racism

Marxist accounts often assume that racism is related to distorted or false consciousness: since the interests of the working class, irrespective of race, ethnicity or gender, are constructed through their exploited position, any denial of universal class interests may be explained by reference to misunderstanding or capitalist propaganda designed to divide and rule the working class. Yet racism may form what Miles (1989: 79) calls a 'relatively coherent theory' in so far as it 'explains' the subordinate position of the white working class by reference to the activities of the minorities. What is important here is that an ideology can 'make sense' of the world as interpreted by certain members of the white working class. For example, the construction of the British Empire, and the concomitant destruction of indigenous African and Indian industries and political regimes, is explicable through a complex web of social, economic and especially military developments which the colonized did not have access to. But a simpler explanation, albeit an erroneous one, is that the Empire reflects the innate superiority of the white British 'race': the simple explanation makes sense of a complex phenomenon and serves to reproduce racism. The fact that this simpler explanation is empirically wrong does not prevent people from using it to make sense of the world (Miles, 1989: 80–1). Similarly, the fact that competition between different racial or ethnic groups in the labour market is severely limited by the different niches that each group tends to operate within does not debar individuals from explaining their racism by reference to assumed competition. It should be added further that racism cannot simply be related to the workplace since so many children, even as young as three and a half, have already recognized, adopted or rejected cultural attitudes concerning race and prejudice (Commission for Racial Equality, 1990). Nor are whites necessarily the most racist groups in the UK. In 1997 a survey for the Institute for Public Policy Research suggested that Asians and Jews were more concerned than non-Jewish whites about the prospect of a close relative marrying a person of Afro-Caribbean origin (IPPR, 1997).

It is assumed, then, that race or ethnicity is neither subordinate nor superordinate to class, nor indeed to gender. As argued in the previous chapter, the exact significance of any of the three major variables is an empirical question not one that can be settled a priori. Just because the existence and potential importance of ethnic minorities is acknowledged, it cannot be assumed that their ethnicity is the major influence or determinant of their particular position in the social structure or at work. The position of minority working-class women is not equivalent to minority middle-class men, nor is either of these two examples one which is permanent through space and time. For example, the number of middle-class minorities has grown quite rapidly in the last decade, especially in the USA; fifty years ago few minorities could have aspired to such a position. For example, between 1982 and 1994 the number of African-American households with an income above the national average ($35,000 in 1995) doubled to over 1 million. On the other hand, young (14–35) African-American men are more likely to be in jail than in college; one in three is either in prison, on probation or awaiting trial, one is murdered every hour (a mortality rate that exceeds that of US troops in the Second World War) and 38 per cent of prison executions are of such men (Walker, 1995). Even at college African Americans, who constitute 13 per cent of the population, account for only 2 per cent of the PhDs awarded and have the highest drop-out rate at 50 per cent (Edmonds, 1995).

The rest of this chapter concentrates on three areas which may be considered pre-eminent in the analysis of race and ethnicity at work. The first section considers the part of the labour market in the perpetuation and elimination of racial discrimination; the second concerns the role played by management in discriminatory recruitment and promotion; the third covers the actions and attitudes of trade unions and workers in Britain and the USA.

Labour markets and racism

Classical models

The notion of markets is, of course, central to the machinations of the capitalist economy. In the **neo-classical labour market model** wages are determined by the direct relationship between the supply and demand of labour. Employers' demands for labour are determined by its marginal productivity and employees' actions are grounded in an equivalent form of economic rationality: the trade-off between costs and benefits in any particular job (Wootton, 1995; Marsden, 1986: 19–24). Although most of the work in this area has conventionally been regarded as the preserve of economists, sociological interest has been increasing lately and, in fact, dates back to the rise of functionalist accounts of stratification. Davis and Moore (1945) first developed the approach which asserted that rewards were differentially distributed in order to attract the most capable individuals into the most demanding jobs: without considerable reward those most qualified would have little incentive to undertake the most responsible jobs. The theoretical difficulties of functionalism are not the prime consideration here (see Giddens, 1977) but it is important to note how such theoretical limitations undermine the utility of this approach to labour markets. For example, functionalist accounts are unable to provide any criteria for estimating rewards other than that which exactly replicates the status quo: since rewards are functionally distributed, the existing position must be functional. No mental acrobatics in comparing the social value of nurses or teachers with indolent members of the landed gentry or drug dealers are necessary to know that the relationship between worth and reward is less than transparent. Indeed, it is only necessary to demonstrate that the rewards due to identically qualified white men and minority women are divergent to know that the functionalist model simply does not operate as an adequate explanation.

Dual labour markets

So how do employers decide what to reward employees? What are the criteria used for assessing the relative merit of individuals? A review of the evidence by Blackburn and Mann suggests that:

> instead of using direct measures of ability, they [employers] use what the economic literature terms 'screening devices', that is, they assume that some readily observable characteristic [like race] can serve as an indicator of a certain degree of ability, and select according to that. The most common screening devices are race, sex, previous job history, age, marital status and [in countries where it is appropriate] years of schooling. (1979: 12–13)

This plurality of employment conditions, and its relationship to discrimination and exclusion, has been reduced to a rather starker binary system in several approaches of late, all bearing witness to the development of 'dual labour markets'. **Dual labour markets** are divided between primary and secondary sections. The primary labour market tends to be restricted to large, profitable and capital intensive industries and enterprises which are often unionized, exhibit internal labour market structures of promotion etc., and pay relatively high wages. These organizations are comparatively isolated from the competitive market. The secondary labour market has the reverse characteristics and tends to be related to those with low skills and to women and ethnic minorities, as well as involving much seasonal, part-time and temporary labour. The terms primary and secondary relate to ideal types rather than empirically discrete cases and within both are several tiers so that, for example, the upper tier of the primary labour market comprises professional and managerial jobs whose skills and expertise provide such individuals with considerable chances for inter-firm mobility. The lower tier of this primary labour market still provides better rewards and conditions than those generally available in the secondary market, but the skills and expertise tend to be firm-specific. Beyond these distinctions it is also the case that a number of secondary labour jobs will exist within the primary sector, such as the office cleaners of financial corporations in capital cities. Concomitantly, the directors of firms in the secondary market will probably receive rewards well in excess of those earned by the lower tier of the primary market. Nevertheless, these specific counter-examples confirm, rather than deny, the validity of the general rule.

The growth of this division has been the subject of a number of explanations. First, it may be related to economic concentration, with the more stable and prosperous enterprises controlling higher percentages of the product market and therefore requiring greater levels of staff stability. Second, it may be linked to technical developments and hence to capital intensive firms where investments in training and experience put premiums on worker loyalty: the so-called 'golden handcuffs'. The seminal works of Doeringer and Piore (1971) and Berger and Piore (1980) are very influential within this approach, arguing that the emergence of firm-specific skills led inexorably to a segmented market. It is worth reinforcing the point, however, that firm-specific skills not only distil the 'gold' for their bearers but enact the 'handcuffs' too, for such restricted skills operate as controlling mechanisms over their owners since they are, by definition, of limited value outside the firm to which they are specific (Brown, 1982). Third, as Garnsey et al. (1985) have argued, it seems to relate to the pursuit of sectional exclusion as work groups, including trade unions, have sought to protect and advance their own interests, if necessary at the expense of others. But even these explanations, and the model they represent, still have to incorporate the dynamic element of change, for in some countries, especially Italy, once stable primary markets have succumbed to the dispersal effects of peripheralization (Sabel, 1982).

Although ethnic minorities do gravitate towards the secondary labour market the dispersal effects tend to be less salient than those which differentiate between the genders. Of course not all minorities work in the secondary labour market. For example, many football players in the English Premier League are black – though there are claims that such players are still paid less than their white colleagues (Atkinson, 1997). In fact, ethnic minorities in Britain fare relatively well in comparison to some nations such as Switzerland, where guest workers account for 40 per cent of all factory workers; and in France, where the building trade, for example, is in some areas almost wholly staffed by immigrant workers (Castles and Kosack, 1973). It is, of course, possible to remain within the secondary market and yet derive a high level of earnings from it, though this typically means extremely long hours in rather unsavoury conditions, typically within textile mills or on assembly lines. There is, however, another important feature of secondary markets emphasized by Edwards (1979) among others: this is the very high level of insecurity, and in particular the disastrous impact that long-term unemployment can have upon individuals. Workers of ethnic minority origin have consistently suffered a disproportionately high level of unemployment, not merely since the rise of mass unemployment from the late 1970s but right through the 1970s, 1980s and 1990s (Brown, 1984; Modood, 1997b).

Disaggregating ethnic minorities

In 1945 there were approximately 30,000 non-whites in Britain; in 2000 there were approximately 3 million non-whites (Feldman, 2002: 23). In 2001, according to the Census, of the 57,104,000 people in Britain, 4,623,000 were from ethnic minorities, comprising 8 per cent of the total, and, as figure 20 reveals, the ethnic minorities are a very heterogeneous group, which poses a problem if we assume they can all be represented by the identity of 'black'. It is important here to note the differences which do exist between and within the ethnic minorities: to view them as disaggregated rather than aggregated. If the composite contingency model of stratification, which was introduced in the last chapter, is viable then considerable variation between individuals based on the specific and heterogeneous amalgam generated by the interrelationships

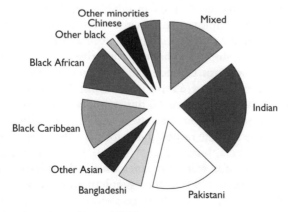

Figure 20 Ethnic minorities in Britain, 2001
Source: Census 2001, Office for National Statistics

between their class, race and gender should be apparent. Inevitably, the data for such an analysis is inadequate, in particular it is not possible to distinguish categories of class properly and for my purposes I have to rely on qualifications as a poor but necessary substitute; there are, after all, strong correlations between class and educational achievement (Halsey, 1986; Burgess, 1986; I. Reid, 1986) and between class, ethnicity and qualifications (Craft and Craft, 1983). A glance at the employment rates in 2001/2 in table 3 reveals some suggestive aspects.

Several points are worth raising here, in particular, the contrast between the employment rates of whites and ethnic minorities generally with regard to qualifications. For white men, overall, those without qualifications have an employment rate of just 58 per cent, compared to those with higher qualifications (A levels plus) who have an employment rate of 90 per cent. The same pattern holds for White women, at 48 per cent and 85 per cent respectively. For Pakistani women the figures are even more significant: only 7 per cent of Pakistani women without qualifications are employed while 64 per cent of those with higher qualifications are employed. The corresponding figures for Pakistani men are 53 and 82 per cent respectively. Similarly, Black African women without qualifications are significantly more prone to unemployment than Black African men. We can generalize from this table in two ways: first, qualifications make a huge difference to employment status irrespective of ethnic origin at the top end – the labour market is *relatively* disinterested in the ethnic origin of men with high qualifications, and although high qualifications help all women into employment, their ethnic origin and gender do matter more; second, the lower the qualifications, the more important become the gender and ethnic origin of the individual seeking employment.

Finally, it is important to note that where sample sizes are too small for statistical analysis the result is often the camouflaging of discrimination and inequality. Thus, minority women in particular tend to be omitted from labour market surveys, and consequently their situation at the bottom of the class, race and gender triangle tends to be underplayed if not completely ignored (Bruegel, 1989). Similarly there is considerable disparity between ethnic groups in terms of educational achievements, as represented in table 4 (p. 250), and this may be a pointer towards future employment success, even if the correlations between unemployment and qualifications may be tenuous at best.

In 2002 the groups gaining the highest collective scores, in terms of five or more 'good' GCSEs, were of Chinese (73 per cent) and Indian (64 per cent) origin. White children secured 51 per cent, while Bangladeshis achieved 45 per cent, Pakistani children secured 40 per cent along with black African children. The lowest scores (30 per cent) were achieved by children from Afro-Caribbean origins. Much of the responsibility for these disparities has been heaped upon schools and teachers, but, as Davey (2003: 4) points out, there are three unresolved problems. First, if teachers are responsible for driving *down* the scores of black children, it seems odd that they simultaneously drive *up* the scores of Chinese and Indian children. Second, since children spend only 15 per cent of their time in school, it seems odd that family background – and more especially peer-group pressure – are not taken into the equation. Third, if 70 per

Table 3 Employment rates by ethnic group, sex and highest qualification (UK), 2001–2 (%)

	Males				Females			
	Higher qualification	Other qualification	No qualifications	All aged 16–64	Higher qualification	Other qualification	No qualifications	All aged 16–59
White	90	82	58	80	85	72	48	71
Mixed	89	66	43	68	66	56	33	55
Asian								
Indian	91	67	60	73	80	56	36	58
Pakistani	82	60	53	61	64	29	7	24
Bangladeshi	76	53	51	55	—	27	—	17
Other Asian	83	64	46	67	80	46	—	52
Black								
Black Caribbean	85	68	50	67	84	63	45	65
Black African	79	56	31	61	75	48	15	49
Other Black	—	63	—	58	—	55	—	57
Chinese	84	57	68	66	74	47	38	54
Other	78	60	41	62	65	45	28	48
All ethnic groups	89	81	58	79	84	70	45	69

Source: Annual Local Area Labour Force Survey, Office for National Statistics

Table 4 Highest qualification held:[a] by sex and ethnic group (GB), 2003 (%)

	Degree or equivalent	Higher education qualification[b]	GCE A level or equivalent	GCSE grades A*–C or equivalent	Other qualification	No qualification	All
Males							
White	18	8	31	18	12	13	100
Mixed	14	7	21	22	17	17	100
Asian	20	6	17	11	24	20	100
Black	19	7	21	16	23	12	100
Chinese	29	4	19	9	28	10	100
Other ethnic group[c]	23	6	11	7	36	18	100
All	18	8	29	17	14	13	100
Females							
White	15	10	18	27	13	16	100
Mixed	21	9	17	21	15	17	100
Asian	14	6	13	17	25	24	100
Black	13	12	16	21	24	13	100
Chinese	26	9	14	10	30	11	100
Other ethnic group[c]	14	9	11	10	34	22	100
All	15	10	18	26	14	16	100

[a] Males aged 16 to 64, females aged 16 to 59
[b] Below degree level
[c] Includes those who did not state their ethnic group
Source: Department for Education and Skills, from the Labour Force Survey, 2003

cent of Afro-Caribbean children are 'failing' at school, what is it about the other 30 per cent that makes them succeed? The whole debate has a ring of the 'over-socialized man' (Wrong, 1961) about it: that is, the assumption that who or whatever is responsible for the parlous state of affairs, it cannot be the individual because they are constrained by social forces to the point where they have no power to control their own futures and should be regarded only as social aggregates. Moreover, as figure 21 below suggests, there is still no direct transition from qualifications at the age of 16 into full-time education beyond 16 because white participation rates in further education are the lowest of all ethnic groups. In effect, as Willis (1977) argued almost 30 years ago, pupils engage in actions that create cultures which, in turn, act against their educational interests. In effect, just as white working-class boys in the 1970s often recreated a white male 'factory' culture that inhibited their educational achievements, so too black working-class boys often tend to do the same 30 years later; thus to work hard at school is 'to sell out' and to 'act white' (Arnot, 2004: 6). Nevertheless, as figure 22 suggests, individuals are not discrete actors in the labour market but rather tend to be constrained and empowered by a variety of social influences, including ethnic origin. These figures relate to economic activity rather than employment, so they include self-employment. As

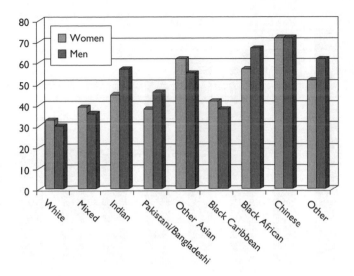

Figure 21 Percentage of 16–24-year-olds in full-time education by ethnic group and sex (UK), 2003
Source: Labour Market Trends, September 2003: 439

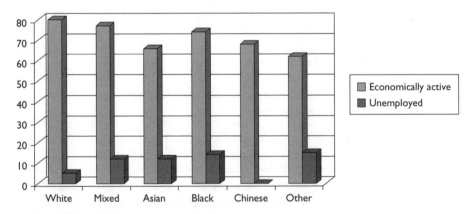

Figure 22 Economic activity by ethnic group (UK), 2003
Source: Labour Market Trends, December, 2003: 599

such, it is clear that the economic activity rate of the white population is the highest and the unemployment rate of the Chinese population is the lowest.

When we dig a little deeper into the relationship between occupation and ethnicity it becomes clear that some groups dominate particular occupations. For example, although whites clearly provide the vast majority of the labour force in absolute terms, figures 23 and 24 reveal first how whites are distributed across the occupational spectrum in absolute terms and then how the groups fit relative to each other in proportionate terms. (The data refer to England and Wales only.)

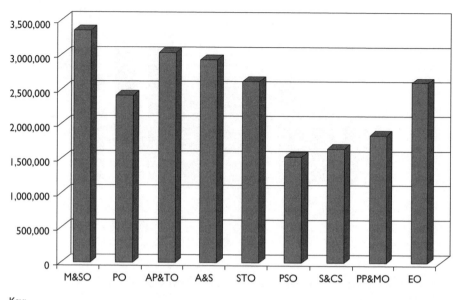

Key:
M&SO	Managers and senior officials
PO	Professional occupations
AP&TO	Associate professional and technical occupations
A&S	Administrative and secretarial
STO	Skilled trades occupations
PSO	Personal service occupations
S&CS	Sales and customer services
PP&MO	Process, plant and machine operatives
EO	Elementary occupations

Figure 23 Occupation and ethnicity: white, England and Wales, 2003
Source: 2001 Census. Reconstructed from Table S109

Taking into account that we are looking at the *pattern* of the lines rather than the absolute *level* of the lines in figure 24 to understand the proportionate level of occupations, and assuming – a large assumption – that the pattern of whites provides the template against which the ethnic minorities should be measured, several aspects are worth highlighting: first, while Asians are well represented at the 'top' of the occupation ladder on the left-hand side, they also appear in disproportionate numbers on the right-hand side, particularly amongst sales, operatives and elementary occupations. Second, the mixed group does well in management but not elsewhere. Third, blacks do poorly in terms of management, but are relatively well distributed in line with the pattern of whites elsewhere.

When we consider this data by gender, as in figures 25 and 26, white men are heavily over-represented in the managerial and skilled trades, a pattern almost mirrored in Asian men. For women, the most significant asymmetries occur with Asian women who are over-represented in the skilled trades and under-represented in personal services.

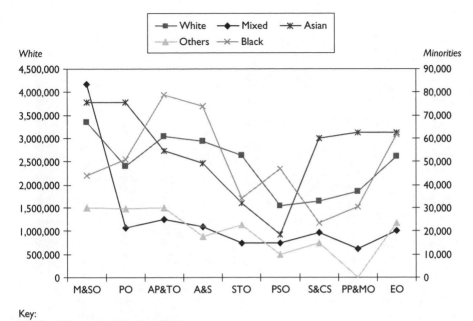

Figure 24 Occupation and ethnicity: England and Wales, 2003
Source: 2001 Census. Reconstructed from Table S109

Key:
M&SO   Managers and senior officials
PO   Professional occupations
AP&TO   Associate professional and technical occupations
A&S   Administrative and secretarial
STO   Skilled trades occupations
PSO   Personal service occupations
S&CS   Sales and customer services
PP&MO   Process, plant and machine operatives
EO   Elementary occupations

In short, neither ethnic origin nor class (manifest, admittedly weakly, in terms of qualifications) nor gender can predict employment status as independent variables. Only when these variables are reconstructed in a compound unity can we begin to make adequate sense of a very complex picture. Even then we need to go beyond the general level of social categories to that of interpretative influences to establish why identically qualified individuals might have very different experiences (see also Bruegel, 1989).

Internal and external labour markets

While these macro-level external market data are relatively transparent, many **internal labour market** constructs appear rather opaque in small and private enterprises, though they do become translucent within large-scale, and most notably public, bureaucracies. Thus, incremental pay scales, promotion by seniority, and internal recruitment to senior posts have long been the hallmark of

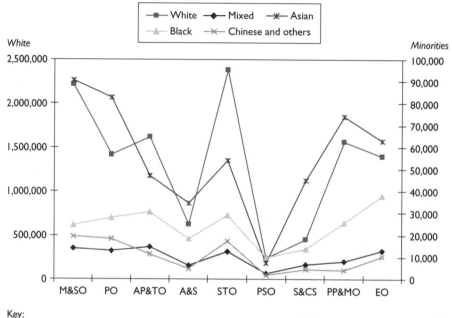

Key:
M&SO   Managers and senior officials
PO   Professional occupations
AP&TO   Associate professional and technical occupations
A&S   Administrative and secretarial
STO   Skilled trades occupations
PSO   Personal service occupations
S&CS   Sales and customer services
PP&MO   Process, plant and machine operatives
EO   Elementary occupations

Figure 25 Men, occupation and ethnicity: England and Wales, 2003
Source: 2001 Census. Reconstructed from Table S109

civil services generally (Weber, 1978), with the British Post Office and British Steel providing particularly 'ideal' types (Grint, 1986; Brannen et al., 1976; Batstone et al., 1983, 1984) long before Japanese companies became noted for adapting such regimes (Grint, 1993). Such 'open' systems have often been associated with greater equality simply because discrimination of any sort is rather harder to hide and easier to disclose.

Other, smaller, firms may also be reliant upon their internal labour market, and a classic case is described by Mann (1973a) where a relocating firm takes a large proportion of its workforce with it. So are internal labour markets more appropriate to large stable bureaucracies or to innovative small firms? There is a strong possibility that widely divergent explanations may exist: the internal labour market of the British Post Office developed through the historical importance of its nineteenth-century middle-class clerks, its initial requirement for literate, honest and therefore relatively well-rewarded employees, and the need to provide some form of long-term incentive for individual acquiescence and

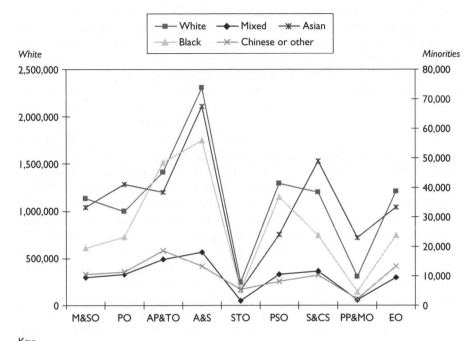

Key:
M&SO   Managers and senior officials
PO   Professional occupations
AP&TO   Associate professional and technical occupations
A&S   Administrative and secretarial
STO   Skilled trades occupations
PSO   Personal service occupations
S&CS   Sales and customer services
PP&MO   Process, plant and machine operatives
EO   Elementary occupations

Figure 26 Women, occupation and ethnicity: England and Wales, 2003
Source: 2001 Census. Reconstructed from Table S109

loyalty (Grint, 1986). On the other hand, and despite the contrary arguments of Gordon et al. (1982), the segmentation of the labour market is not a recent phenomenon nor do firms facing rapid technological changes always require long-term loyalty from their employees; indeed, one of the advantages of technological change for employers is that it may well reduce the compunction for firms to retain labour by reducing the training periods associated with technology (Berger and Piore, 1980).

But if some enterprises exhibit clearly defined boundaries between internal and **external labour markets** the same cannot be said for all of them. Using the more volatile engineering sector as an illustration, Robinson and Conboy (1970) note how the complex combination, if not confusion, of internal and external markets led to an anarchic wage structure. Freedman's (1984) analysis of US labour markets, on the other hand, concentrates the apparent morass into fourteen more or less coherent segments within which wages are contingently related to variables like size, workers' characteristics and forms of collective bargaining etc. Such apparent pluralism is directly challenged by radical labour market theories (e.g. Stone, 1974) which construe the market pattern as the premeditated outcome of a managerial strategy of control; labour exploitation is achieved through the ancient tactic of divide and rule. But it is not self-evident either why employers should discriminate against the relatively cheap labour of women and ethnic minorities in favour of white male, and therefore expensive, labour. A rather more sophisticated approach has been adopted by Gordon (1972), Lee (1980), Rubery (1980) and Craig et al. (1982). This group emphasizes the part played by strategic groups of workers themselves in rebutting the threat of deskilling, proletarianization and degradation, often at the expense of other less powerful groups. Even this reassessment of the radical conspiratorial approach is denied by the research of Blackburn and Mann (1979) into the labour market for unskilled male manual workers in Peterborough. For them the situation is simply too disorganized for groups to impose their own rational strategies upon the rest. Yet the limitations of the empirical focus, upon a group of unskilled (non-apprenticed) male employees that cannot be regarded as representative of the overall workforce, mean that the results of the study have to be treated with a degree of scepticism. Labour markets, then, are segmented in so far as women and minority groups (and the less skilled) tend to be at the receiving end of many discriminatory practices. Such discrimination is most transparent when immigrant or migrant labour is involved.

Migrant and immigrant labour

Piore's (1979) assessment of migrant workers suggests that underlying the apparent confusion of labour markets and most notably the market for migrant labour, where poor wages, conditions and security prevail, is an employers' strategy designed to circumvent a labour shortage. After all, immigration is seldom economically detrimental to the host nation. As Hawkins (1989) has pointed out, the doubling of Australian and Canadian populations through (selective) immigration over the last half century has boosted, not undermined, the wealth creation of these two countries and, because most immigrants tend to be adult and thus immediate potential employees, the host country avoids the social costs involved in their childhood and education. Indeed, there are few, if any, cases where immigration does act as an economic disadvantage to the host country, except perhaps in the very short term; the West German economic decline in 1961, exactly at the time of the Berlin Wall's construction, for example, can hardly be coincidental.

But why do migrant workers accept such terms of employment? Because, argues Piore, they are migrant workers and therefore have few employment rights, little industrial muscle, and even less intention of staying: they work to return home, not to create a new identity for themselves and, as such, approach work in an almost clinically instrumental fashion (Power and Hardman, 1978). Furthermore, what may be low-paying and subordinate jobs to indigenous workers in Britain, Germany or California may well be more attractive than their equivalent opportunities in Pakistan, Turkey or Mexico (Leggett, 1968; Braham, 1980). Piore also asserts that such radical discontinuities in the labour market, which were originally restricted to peripheral areas of the economy, have become increasingly important within the core area. But this implies that the immigrant workers consistently seek the worst kind of jobs available, rather than the best. What is missing here, then, is any concern for the discriminatory practices of the indigenous population who act to keep immigrant workers out of particular jobs. Relatedly, what is critical here is to explain not why immigrant workers accept such poor conditions and rewards but why ethnic minorities, who are citizens of the countries where they work, also suffer similar fates at work. The assessment of the two groups need not begin from radically dichotomous positions. After all, a major difficulty with the neo-classical approach is to assume that shifts in the patterns of labour supply and demand lead to equivalent movements in rewards levels. But the neo-classical approach assumes an inherent scarcity of labour, while in reality alternative sources of labour are often available: immigrant workers, 'full-time' houseworkers, 'retired' or juvenile workers can be, and historically often have been, sucked into the labour market during periods of labour shortage, so that wages of existing employees need not be driven up (Gorz, 1970; Bohning, 1972).

This employer-driven model of labour market control is also relevant to the assessment of power and intent within the labour market because the radical labour market theories not only underestimate the part played by sectionalism in generating internecine struggle within the working class, but they also tend to overestimate the degree of corporate interest underlying employers. Although capital has interests which directly contradict those of labour, the reality, as Marx noted, is one of many capitals not a united capital (Marx, 1973a: 414), and it might be added that it is also one of many parts of labour. Thus, as Garnsey et al. have made clear, in coping with economic uncertainties: 'Wherever possible, employers providing primary employment conditions attempt to pass the costs and burdens of uncertainty on to *smaller firms*' (1985: 21; my emphasis). However imperfect the market for labour may be, it is still market-driven, in part at least, by competitive forces of one sort or another. This dispersal of costs is expressly relevant to the way core firms employing indigenous workers tend to push the burden of recession and economic malaise on to those secondary or peripheral firms employing migrant or ethnic minority labour (Piore, 1979), a policy also prevalent within Japan, except that dispersal is contained within the indigenous workforce (Nishikawa, 1980; Hanami, 1979).

Despite the economic constraints operated by the labour market in immigration, the political spectre of 'waves' or 'floods' of economic migrants is common parlance for politicians and the mass media, who deploy such images at will. For example, as the EU was due to expand its boundaries in May 2004 the popular British papers were replete with scare stories of thousands of East Europeans just waiting to 'breach' the British dam wall. In the event, of the 24,000 foreigners who signed up for work in the UK by June 2004, only 8,000 arrived after 1 May (Ford, 2004: 6). The precise pattern of immigrant workers to the UK – as measured by the number of work permits issued – between 1946

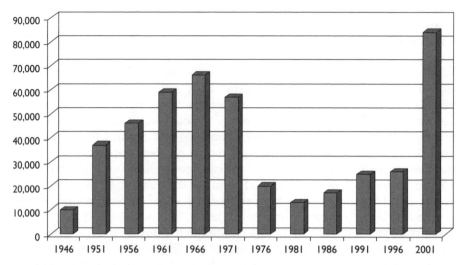

Figure 27 Work permits issued (UK), 1946–2001
Source: Labour Market Trends, November, 2003: 564

and 2001 is shown in figure 27 and it should be clear that the pattern relates very much to labour market demands of the host nation, coupled with political instability in the 'donor' nation. Contrary to some popular opinion, in 2002 the top three occupations where work permits were approved was not at the bottom of the occupational reward structure but the top: medicine (24 per cent), computing (17 per cent) and management (13 per cent) comprised the top three and over half the total. India (21 per cent), the USA (11 per cent) and South Africa (9 per cent) were the top sources for these. Indeed, somewhere around 35 per cent of all work permits are inter-company transfers rather than 'immigrants' seeking work (*Labour Market Trends*, November 2003: 563–69).

Rewarding labour

It should be clear at this point that although employers are in a competitive situation, and are therefore unlikely to collaborate with each other against general employee interests, this does not imply that delimited collaboration is impossible. Such collaboration may take one of several forms, from the mutual surveillance and avoidance of trade union militants through to corporate resistance to government policies via employers' organizations, but one form of co-operative endeavour recognizably reflecting labour market forces is the setting of minimum wages. Either through the medium of wages councils such as those which used to exist in Britain, or through mutual consent, firms in direct competition with one another have sometimes agreed to set minimum reward levels so as to remove labour costs from the competitive basket. Whether this provides long-term benefits to either employers or employees is difficult to say, but there is certainly some evidence that it makes firms internationally uncompetitive (Craig et al., 1982; see also chapter 9 below). Nevertheless, the removal of minimum wage agreements could prove catastrophic for those employees without the collective support of trade union organization to replace the safety net, and most at risk are the very same employees that appear to be discriminated against from all angles: women, immigrants and ethnic minorities.

Another link between women, immigrant and ethnic minority workers is the patterning of collective rewards. In neo-classical accounts *individuals* are rewarded for their skills but in reality very few employers reward their employees on such a basis and tend, instead, to adopt blanket payment schemes grounded in putative 'going rates'. There are, of course, exceptions to this, either through individual piece rates or in differential schemes where juniors undertaking identical work to seniors are paid considerably less (Grint, 1988), but such patterns are atypical at the moment despite the current trend for individual contracts. Rather more typical is the inertial element of wages which, despite rapid and substantial fluctuations in labour market conditions, tend to remain stable through time (Routh, 1980). This kind of stability poses similar difficulties for a related facet of the labour market in which particular groups are disproportionately funnelled into a narrow band of employment areas, thereby leading to an oversupply of local labour and consequently poor wages and conditions. This 'crowding hypothesis', originally based on the work of Fawcett (1918), Edgeworth (1922) and Robinson (1934), often assumes exclusionary action by male trade unionists. Chiplin and Sloane's (1974) analysis disputes the utility of the overall relationship between crowding and low earnings and it is more reasonable to assume, at least in the case of women, that there is little if any connection between the patterning of labour market fluctuations and the level of collective rewards (Routh, 1980: 123; Grint, 1988).

One attempt to recombine the importance of individual merit with collective reward has been that encapsulated by **human capital theory**. This seeks to explain differentials between employees on the basis of their variant levels of productivity. In turn, these levels are explained through the degree of investment in training and education. Empirical accounts of this imply that it has some relevance and may be able to explain up to two-thirds of the inequalities of reward between individuals (Mincer and Polachek, 1974; Polachek, 1975). When applied to the differential between minority and white workers, holding qualifications constant, it is patently inappropriate, not just because the wage differentials undermine the theory's relevance (Brown, 1984; *Employment Gazette*, December 1985), but because, as an inquiry into British medical schools suggests, the ability of individuals to achieve qualifications may be dependent upon the colour of their skin (Commission for Racial Equality, 1988b). In this case minority students were twice as likely to be refused places as white students (Smith, 1988). In the US human capital explanations can only account for one-sixth of the improvement in African-American women's improvements in reward since 1940 (King, 1995); labour market restructuring was far more important.

More recent general empirical approaches to wage inequalities have also produced a rather more widely dispersed wage structure (Sloan, 1980; Cohn, 1985) but they have still failed to account for different levels of investment in education and training. In short, it may be that some correlations exist between levels of qualifications and rewards (though even this is severely limited with regard to some ethnic minorities) but why do some groups, and especially women and ethnic minorities, appear to choose this approach and invest relatively little in their human capital?

The two most conventional explanations suggest that the choice is 'rational' in either economic or biological terms. Becker (1985) takes the first line, insisting that since it is economically rational for couples to divide up their labour, it makes sense for one to specialize in the domestic sphere; and since women earn less than men in the labour market, it therefore becomes rational for women to devote themselves to domestic labour. This, of course, fails to explain why the labour market itself is gender-biased. The biological case for the subordination of women is made most forcefully by Goldberg (1993) who suggests that physiological differences supported by hormonal differences lead men to become more assertive, more aggressive and more competitive than women. Hence men have a greater motivation to climb the organizational hierarchy than women. The problem lies in the generalization of these approaches: it *may* be that men are stronger, more aggressive and more competitive – *on average* – but that doesn't explain the systematic discrimination against women nor the success of some women (see the review by Hakim, 1996).

A partial explanation can be given for some women, in so far as they have fragmented and discontinuous careers during their child-rearing period (Crompton and Jones, 1982; Garnsey et al., 1985; Walby, 1986a). If such women intend to concentrate upon these activities then it may be that investment in education is considered secondary to their primary role of motherhood. This does not explain why women, rather than women and men, become full-time child-rearers, nor does it account for employer discrimination against women without children. Indeed, it self-evidently collapses before the cases where women have a higher level of human investment, but a lower level of reward, than men in comparative jobs (Grint, 1988). Nevertheless, since it is collectivities rather than individuals who tend to set the patterns of reward, there is some evidence that employers operate through stereotypical pictures that regard all women as potential career breakers and reward them disproportionately. Such indiscriminate analysis can also be used to explain why employers continue to reward ethnic minorities as if they were migrant workers (Arrow, 1972). That said, it still is not clear that the correlations between human investment, or assumed human investment, and reward are necessary correlations. That is to say, although women and ethnic minorities may have lower qualifications than men and whites (and it has already been suggested that this does not hold for all groups), since many jobs do not require anything like the levels of skill acquired through training it may well be that qualifications are simply a mechanism for exclusion rather than a necessary precondition for the execution of work-related tasks. As Blackburn and Mann's study of manual workers concludes: 'the *absolute* level of skill of all but the very highest jobs is – to say the least

– minimal. Eighty seven per cent of our workers exercise less skill at work than they would if they drove to work. Indeed, most of them expend more mental effort and resourcefulness in getting to work than in doing their jobs' (1979: 280). This artificial relationship between human capital and employment is nicely exposed during times of social crisis, such as war, when apparently unqualified women and juveniles have taken over the jobs of skilled men at the war front with little if any deleterious effect upon levels of efficiency and productivity (Pagnamenta and Overy, 1984; Grint, 1986: 309–10; Boston, 1987: 185–218).

Two ramifications flow from this. First, it reinforces the importance of an analysis of the social construction of rewards, rather than an analysis based upon some hypothetical neo-classical account of the labour market. Second, it focuses attention directly upon the way particular groups exploit their market position to promote their own collective interests, at the expense of other, less fortunate, groups if necessary.

The domestic and the employment spheres

It should not be assumed that the constraints under which individuals and col-lectivities operate are only those derived from economic or political or techno-logical sources outside the home. The exact nature of the link between domestic and wage labour is discussed elsewhere but it is important here to illuminate the difficulty of assuming either that the family operates autonomously from the world of employment or that the actions of agents within the family are somehow free of external constraints generated in and through the labour market. For example, although individuals may deny the ideological relevance of the nuclear family, complete with its mythical two children and full-time house-worker, it is extremely difficult to attempt to construct alternative lifestyles involv-ing a shared responsibility towards housework and child-rearing. Not only were 22 per cent of families in Britain headed by single parents in 1997 (a threefold increase since 1971) but, on average, single parents spent half the time with their children that couples did (Office of National Statistics, 1997). It is not difficult simply in the sense of resisting the dominant ideology, but in guaranteeing career advancement or material security for either partner, and therefore for the family as a whole, should housework be shared equally (Freedman, 1984: 59–61). Family ideologies are also important in explaining the restricted employment opportunities of some ethnic minority women. Moreover, it does seem to be the case that the influence of powerful domestic ideologies within some ethnic minor-ities can undermine what might otherwise be more radical shop-floor systems of resistance by women workers (Westwood and Bhachu, 1989). That is not to say that family relationships are inherently constraining upon the freedom of individuals to move within the labour market. On the contrary, there is much empirical evidence to suggest that social networks grounded in familial and ethnically oriented relationships can play a decisive role in opening up, as well as inhibiting, job opportunities.

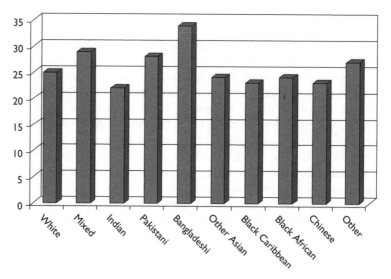

Figure 28 Self-employment and ethnicity (UK), 2003 (%)
Source: Labour Market Trends, December 2003

Ethnic enclaves

Ethnic enclaves are, of course, common in many industrial nations, especially those with large recently immigrant populations where initial language difficulties coupled with native hostility may well encourage new immigrants to seek employment within existing ethnic and family enclaves rather than within the wider labour market (Rimmer, 1972; Ward, 1985; Waldinger, 1985: 213–28; Evans, 1987). For some ethnic minorities the most viable market niche is self-employment in a small business. In Britain the East African Asian and Gujarati communities, in particular, have been remarkably successful in this avenue. In terms of self-employment, as figure 28 suggests, although there are no radical asymmetries in the ethnic patterning, it is the case that Bangladeshis lead the table in self-employment at 34 per cent of the total Bangladeshi population, whereas Indians and Chinese have the lowest proportions at 22 and 23 per cent respectively.

These figures hide a large gender differential: twice as many Indian men are self-employed as Indian women while the figure for self-employed Pakistani women is too small for a reliable estimate (cf. Huhne, 1988a; Foster, 1987; Brown 1984; *Social Trends,* 1989; Curran and Burrows, 1988). The proportion of self-employed Asian women is the same as the white proportion at 4 per cent. The Afro-Caribbean community, however, is markedly less involved in running the conventional stereotypical minority businesses like restaurants, corner shops and clothing ventures, though such stereotypes are very much part of the host mythology rather than an accurate reflection of the diversity of small businesses currently under minorities' control (Wilson and Stanworth, 1988; Ram and Jones, 1998). That said, it is still the case that ethnic minority manufacturing entrepreneurs are disproportionately small in number, and one of the explanations appears to be the racism which such individuals face (Centre for Employment Research, 1990).

A major reason often given for the paucity of Afro-Caribbean small businesses is the allegedly looser family ties which inhibit the initial accumulation of start-up capital, though it does seem that the exclusionary activities of the host society are more important in restricting the employment opportunities for minorities (Jones and McEvoy, 1986). Once a low level of business tradition develops, however, it appears to be self-fulfilling and very detrimental to those seeking to break out of the spiral. A survey of the London borough of Lambeth revealed that 74 per cent of black Britons with Caribbean roots were unsuccessful in gaining start-up capital from banks, while only 13 per cent of those with Asian roots and 6 per cent of native whites were similarly rejected (Smith, 1988). There are (at least) two ways of explaining this differentiation. Either black Britons are simply not economically effective or bank lenders *interpret* them as bad risks. Since the economic activity rate of this group is the highest of all minorities (and for black women it is higher than for white women), the prime responsibility appears to rest with the interpretative activities of discriminatory bank lenders.

Despite the common assumption that minority businesses all tend to be small, family-based enterprises, there is now some evidence of substantial growth in all areas of the economy; though it does seem that while new ventures are aided by family ties they can often only develop properly by disentangling themselves from the family to attract external expertise and capital (Wilson, 1987). Nevertheless, despite the utility of family networks, workers of ethnic minority origin have long provided a substantial part of the secondary labour market with concomitantly poor working conditions, rewards and security.

Anti-discriminatory practices

In theory, a free labour market should ensure the efficient allocation of resources such that the only discrimination extant would be that based on the positive projection of efficient employees. As Lewis naively asserts, regarding minority Britons: 'precisely because it is colour-blind, the free market is their friend' (quoted in Rushdie, 1988). Of course, the very existence of the British Race Relations Act (1976), which forbids discrimination on racial grounds (defined as colour, race, nationality or ethnic or national origins), and the similar American anti-discriminatory legislation from 1964 implies, among other things, that the operations of the 'free' market are systematically flawed. Not only do ethnic minorities find access to organizations difficult, but once inside they generally find themselves discriminated against for reasons that are social rather than economic in origin, and for criteria that include not just skin colour (Doeringer and Piore, 1971) but religious and political affiliation too. For example, the unemployment rate for Catholic workers in Northern Ireland is twice as high as that for Protestant workers (Hearst, 1988; Jenkins, 1988): a manifestation of the troubles in Northern Ireland that have prompted the British government to enact the Fair Employment policy to halt discrimination against Catholics. This carries penalties far more severe than those liable for discrimination on the grounds of race or gender, though this has yet to prove significant in undermining discriminatory practices.

Note, though, that discrimination can take many forms. Take, for example, the following advert that relates to the recruitment of a primary school teacher in Lancashire (a Church of England primary school) in 2004. Listed under 'Essential Requirements', and above 'Excellent Team Player', is this: 'Enjoy working within the strong Christian ethos of the school.' Listed under 'Desirable Requirements', and above 'Evidence of working in innovative ways', is: 'Faith reference from someone who can verify your commitment to supporting a Christian ethos, i.e., from your church or head teacher about your school activities.' Now, apart from the fact that all state schools in the UK are funded from public taxation that is drawn from people of all faiths and no faith (even Peter Vardy's King's Academy in Middlesbrough, which teaches Creationism – praised by Tony Blair during his visit there on 5 March 2004 after he had made a speech about the dangers of religious fundamentalism that very morning – relies on the state for 80 per cent of its funding: see Adams, 2004: 20–8) – so one might argue that these should not therefore support the teaching of one faith above all others – there is an issue about discrimination against teachers from different faiths or no faiths for jobs paid for by the public purse. This might be better illustrated by replacing the word 'Christian' with some other exclusionary category. For example, would we not object if a job requirement was 'Enjoy working within the strong able-bodied ethos of the school', or 'should have a reference from someone who can verify your commitment to support a white ethos'? Or if, amongst the criteria for getting your child into school, was one stating: 'Parents who are involved in the work and worship of garage music'? or 'Parents who are involved in the work and worship of another anti-abortion organization'? That these criteria seem outrageous is testimony to the power of social norms at work in work: being a committed Christian in such organizations appears not as an interesting personal choice but as a manifestation of normality that excludes all others. ('Community schools' have no religious affiliation, are paid for by general taxation and account for two-thirds of all children's education in England. Voluntary schools come in different forms but are all paid for primarily by general taxation and tend to be faith-based – that is, controlled by a church – and account for almost all the remaining one-third of children's education in England. The largest numbers – in declining order of numbers – are Church of England, Roman Catholic, Methodist, other Christian, Muslim, Sikh, others. See, <http://www.angelfire.com/nb/lt/docs/legal.htm>. In 2003, 7.5 per cent of the population attended church on a Sunday on average though 12 per cent were church members.)

Even those nations which maintain more general policies of positive discrimination or affirmative action (such as the USA) still exhibit considerable levels of discrimination, as of course do those which do not, such as the UK. The significance of the American system of legislative influence via the Supreme Court is indicative of what can be achieved. For example in 1990, New York's Police Commissioner, Benjamin Ward, was black; as was America's top military individual, Colin Powell, the Chair of the Joint Chiefs of Staff, and David Dinkins, the Mayor of New York. This does not mean that American minorities can expect equal treatment at work, far from it. Boston's (1988) review of the empirical evidence suggests that black workers are paid less but work longer hours than white workers across almost all areas of work and in all parts of the USA, though the wage differential is highest in the southern states. Yet some minority groups do seem to succeed within a potentially hostile host society. For example, Gibson's (1988) study of Punjabi Sikhs in America suggests that male, though not female, children, can and do succeed at school and in the labour market, especially in computer sciences and engineering.

However the paucity of such cases suggests their limited generalizability, and the wider view throws up a rather different conclusion: between 1970 and 1980 (a decade of affirmative action in the US educational system) the number of full-time black students enrolled in American colleges rose by almost 100 per cent, while their acquisition of professional, technical and managerial positions rose by 57 per cent between 1973 and 1982 (the comparative figure for the white population in the latter category was 38 per cent) (Macnicol, 1988). However, the material position of young unskilled urban blacks actually worsened during the same period, as the increased opportunities became monopolized by a new black middle class as the economic recession of the late 1970s and early 1980s took effect (Wilson, 1987). Moreover, the Civil Rights Act of 1964, the legal framework upon which the American '**affirmative action**' policies of equal opportunity are based, is now under direct threat from the new conservative majority on the US Supreme Court. Three times in 1989 the court upheld the position of white workers seeking to challenge the affirmative action policies for minorities, and the court ruled that the burden of proof in employment discrimination rests with the plaintiff rather than the employer (Walker, 1989).

Affirmative action policies have certainly had some effect. In 1970 just over 10 per cent of black US families had the equivalent of the US average family income. By 1994 (the last year the data are available) this proportion had doubled. However, the unravelling of affirmative action policies, most recently led by Ward Connerly, a black Californian, in getting proposition 209 passed (which forbids positive discrimination in appointment to state jobs or student selection) is already eating into the progress made in the USA. For example, in the University of Texas Law School, in 1996, 5.9 per cent of the students were black and 6.3 per cent Hispanic. But in 1997 these proportions had dropped to 0.7 per cent and 2.3 per cent respectively. Previously the Scholastic Assessment Test (SAT), which is used to secure admission to US higher education, was routinely set lower for African Americans and Hispanics to compensate for prior discrimination at school and in society generally. For some individuals like Connerly this compounds rather than compensates for the problem since it can be interpreted as implying that minorities secure places above better qualified whites – rather than implying that, given an equal playing field, the minorities would have outperformed the whites. In other words, the minorities in universities are the best minorities but still not the best Americans. But for others, such as Diana Soldana, president of the Chicano-Hispanic law students' association, the outlook is dire, as she says: 'It took us 30 years to get here, and it took them [US courts] 24 hours to dismantle any progress we have made' (quoted in Walker, 1997).

Yet there are clear limits to the potential regression on affirmative action. For instance, in 1994 Texaco settled a case of racial discrimination, brought by 1,400 black professional and middle managers, for $175 million over five years, after a group of senior (white) executives were taped discussing the destruction of incriminating documents that documented the discrimination at work. In 1996 an African-American employee of Brand Services was awarded $7.6 million for his experiences of discrimination, and several similar cases are pending. All of these have prompted US employers to tread carefully in this emotive area (Caudron, 1997). The temperature of this debate was clearly seen in April 2004 when the limits of multiculturalism as a strategic policy were debated by both Trevor Phillips, then Chair of the Commission for Racial Equality, and David Goodhart, then Editor of *Prospects* Magazine. (Goodhart's article is available at <http://www.prospect-magazine.co.uk/ArticleView.asp?link=yes&P_Article=12394>; Phillips's response is available at: <http://www.guardian.co.uk/comment/story/0,3604,1148847,00.html>; see also the debate in the *Guardian*, 26 February 2004.)

In short, labour-market-based racism appears to be a universal rather than British phenomenon in contemporary capitalist societies; from France (Linhart, 1981) to Australia (Kriegler, 1982) and the USA (Lash, 1984) it is as commonplace as it is pernicious. But to understand the process through which discrimination is produced and reproduced it is necessary to go beyond the labour market itself and examine several different aspects. Quite clearly, racism and discrimination are engendered and sustained by all manner of different societal forces, including the influence of the state and education (Coates, 1984: 155–91; Rex, 1986; Brittan and Maynard, 1984). But the limitations of space preclude a full analysis, and the next section concentrates upon an issue that is more axiomatically related to issues of work: recruitment.

Recruitment and racism

Grapevine recruitment

Among the clearest examples of the intimate links between home and work are the familially-based recruitment procedures, or **'grapevine recruitment'** (Grieco, 1987: 33) used by many firms. Grieco's evidence relates to working-class recruitment but the mechanisms, of first constructing a family-based 'vacancy chain' and then solidifying it into the 'capture of opportunity' by a family, are not restricted to class-based exclusionary measures. The implication of this is that even those groups who are not in 'objectively' powerful positions through their skills or control of apprenticeships etc. may still be able to influence the operation of the labour market. This familial base to the control over recruitment is control neither in class terms nor in gender terms but control in the interests of the family network. The ability of apparently weak market groups to intervene in their own future is well demonstrated in the case of Italian migrant labour in the cigar factories of Tampa. Mormino (1982) argues that despite being discriminated against, and notwithstanding the absence of cigar-making craft skills, Italian migrants managed to capture the cigar-making employment from the Hispanics. They did this by a minimalist strategy of secreting tobacco out from the factory, setting up self-help groups to acquire the necessary skills and, eventually, taking over the primary employment opportunities. Not only does this reveal the potential influence of out groups to transcend their weak market position but, equally important, it shows the limitations of assuming that work practices can be neatly decanted into either class antagonisms or gender antagonisms. It should be reaffirmed here, however, that the ethnic dimension is more powerful in the USA than in most European nations, though the experience of Turkish, Yugoslav or Irish workers etc. demonstrates that ethnic origin and identity is never an irrelevance. Thus, companies employing predominantly white workers, and those recruiting workers from the ethnic minorities, often tend to reproduce the dominant characteristics of their workforce by recruiting through existing family networks (Jenkins, 1985; Manwaring, 1984; Phizacklea, 1982; Brooks and Singh, 1979), and, originally at least, the isolation of language occasionally played some role in this exclusionary recruitment (Rimmer, 1972). It is not axiomatic, of course, that all individuals will make use of such familial networks to acquire employment. There is evidence of young Afro-Caribbean British workers refusing to accede to the utility of such networks since it implies reproducing the disadvantages suffered by their parents as immigrants. As black Britons their sights are set in line with white workers, not their parents, and as such the familial networks may appear to represent the very institutionalized racism they are trying to avoid (Dex, 1978–9; Jenkins and Parker, 1987). Here the structuring of work experiences through the filters of racism act to buttress the vicious circle of poor jobs, low living standards, and poor education leading back to poor jobs *ad infinitum* (Ashton, 1986; Braham et al. (eds), 1981).

This should not be taken to imply that grapevine recruitment is the most important method. Quantitative data on recruitment seldom provides sufficient evidence about how different ethnic groups seek employment but that which exists implies that the differences are only sometimes significant and even then seldom crucial. For example, 39 per cent of white and minority workers seek work through job centres and around 20 per cent of each via newspaper advertisements or direct to employers; however a higher proportion of whites (28 per cent) than minorities (22 per cent) use the situations vacant columns in newspapers, and more minorities (15 per cent) than whites (10 per cent) use personal contacts (*Employment Gazette*, March 1990). What these data do not tell us, of course, is what happens when different individuals have got past the approach stage and have applied to employers for employment. What role do managers play in perpetuating or undermining discrimination?

Managerial practice

If the recruitment procedure is designed to reproduce the ethnic homogeneity that already prevails there, then analysis of the gatekeeping role of management may well be irrelevant. Since very few private firms in Britain undertake ethnic monitoring it is also difficult to know just how widespread managerial racism really is; but the refusal of organizations to monitor their ethnic mix, on the grounds that everyone is equal, is akin to the problematic status of the neo-liberal market model: the point is that everyone does not *enter* the market as equal, nor does the market operate along meritocratic principles. Jenkins's (1985, 1988) research suggests that managers involved in the recruiting process have a hierarchy of criteria for acceptability. The primary criteria involve appearance, manner and attitude, and maturity. Secondary criteria relate to 'gut feeling', employment history and experience, the ability to fit in, age, speech style, literacy and marital status. Tertiary criteria concern references and English language competence. In several areas minority workers are likely to face discrimination: they are less likely to fit the stereotypical 'married, two kids and a mortgage' pattern that recruiters seem to seek; their accent may well be regarded by white recruiters as inferior to white speech patterns; and they are less likely to 'fit in' to the existing organization, given the prevailing work-group racism discussed above. In short, minority workers suffer the ignominies commonly associated with disparaging racial stereotypes. In many ways it seems that a large number of recruiters do not perceive themselves to be racist but prefer white workers on the grounds of expediency: the white workforce is racist, therefore, irrespective of their own liberal notions of 'fairness'; white recruiters fear the consequences of recruiting minority workers (Jenkins, 1985). Inevitably, the refusal to challenge assumed racism actually facilitates its reproduction; thus the self-proclaimed liberalism acts merely as a conduit for the perpetuation of racism.

Given the conventional recruitment procedures in many manufacturing firms – word of mouth and social networks – even overtly racist recruiters may never need to execute racial discrimination in any open manner because the method of recruitment preselects ethnic minorities out of the pool through employee screening: a method of some value to US companies too (Rees, 1966). This informal recruitment also implies that surveillance by state agencies is more difficult; even where identically qualified individuals are interviewed the emphasis placed upon the subjective assessment of the interviewer may ensure that the minority interviewee is not selected. A partial solution to this subjectivism is to formalize the procedure, and though this may be not the means to eliminate racial discrimination in the recruitment process, it is seen by Jenkins as a means by which its effects can be reduced (1985).

Ethnic origin and the professions

When we delve below the very general occupational categories, the significance of ethnic factors is reinforced. For example, although 8 per cent of the British population under 16 is from the ethnic minorities this category provides only 2 per cent of the nation's teachers. Moreover, minority teachers were over-represented in shortage areas, or outside mainstream teaching, and more were employed at the lower end of the salary scale than white teachers (Commission for Racial Equality [CRE], 1988a). Other professions are also likely to reproduce the existing imbalance of employees. There are, for example, no ethnic minorities among the top three grades of the British Civil Service, and within the top seven grades there are only 207 out of 18,644 (1 per cent). This is not because ethnic minorities have avoided work in the Civil Service; on the contrary about 4 per cent of the total are minorities (Indians, Pakistanis and Bangladeshis, and West Indians make up about 1 per cent each with a further 1 per cent for all other minorities), marginally higher than the proportion for the total working population (Hencke, 1989).

Another CRE investigation, this time into chartered accountancy, found that members of ethnic minorities were three and a half times less likely to be offered a job than white applicants, and the discriminatory practices occurred at all levels of the screening process (Commission for Racial Equality, 1987). There were in 1997, only two non-whites in the top four grades of the Civil Service and only 58 out of 3,000 formed the next grade (Travis, 1997). Relatedly, there are a mere 1.9 per cent of probation officers and 0.9 per cent of police officers who are minorities. Yet progress is being made in the UK: on 5 January 2004 Mike Fuller became the first black chief constable in the UK, as head of the Kent police. Fuller, who founded the Metropolitan Black Police Association in 1993, was born to unmarried Jamaican parents in south London and was brought up in a children's home in West Sussex. There were only five black cadets with him when he joined the Metropolitan Police in 1975; now there are more than 1,650 officers from various ethnic minorities (Cowan, 2004). Ironically, his appointment coincided with an official inquiry into allegations of racism by Scotland Yard (Muir, 2004: 8), and the removal of the head of a £20 million Metropolitan Police programme aimed at tackling racism – because of alleged racism (Thompson, 2004: 13).

Only 1 per cent of solicitors derive from the minorities and most of these work in the smaller law firms, and there are only two minority circuit judges (Dyer, 1988; NAPO, 1988; Home Affairs Committee, 1989). The situation has caused such embarrassment that the Bar Council, and indeed the Association of Graduate Careers Advisory Services, has called for recruiters to delete requests for photographs from applicants. In prisons, of 28,000 officers, only nine principal officers were black in 1997 and only six have made it to junior governor. There has never been a black governor of a British prison (Mills, 1997). In sharp contrast, at the receiving end of the law, 20 per cent of prisoners are from the minorities and racism appears to be an intrinsic part of the prison service according to an unpublished study completed for the Home Office in 1986 (BBC, 1988). Even prior to conviction it appears that minorities are twice as likely as whites to be imprisoned yet twice as likely to be acquitted too (*The Guardian*, 18 December 1989).

Job search

In terms of the general recruitment of non-university graduates it appears that a wide disparity exists between the 70 per cent of white graduates in employment twelve months after graduation compared with less than half the graduates from ethnic minorities (Brennan and McGeevor, 1987). In what Modood (1997b: 144) calls 'the ethnic penalty', a glass ceiling actively inhibits most ethnic minorities from achieving the highest positions – even though Chinese and African Asians are more likely than whites to be earning in excess of £500 per week. Yet the informality of network recruitment also operates to perpetuate the supply of labour for ethnic businesses, and to ensure that competitors are disadvantaged, as Kim (1981) has demonstrated with regard to Korean businesses in New York, and Light and Bonzicich (1988) *vis-à-vis* Korean entrepreneurial success in Los Angeles. Despite the under-representation of minorities in the professional sections of the public sector, it is still here, where recruitment is more often associated with advertising and bureaucratic procedures, that minority workers are generally more likely to receive a greater degree of equality of opportunity; though as the evidence cited above reveals, this may well be a long way short of equality of opportunity. Indeed, since it tends to be those jobs which cannot be filled by word of mouth that end up in the state employment services, and since some of these often tend to be the least attractive jobs, minority workers are provided with fewer and less attractive jobs to choose between. In addition, according to the Manpower Services Commission (MSC), almost half of the Afro-Caribbean people using job centres claimed to have suffered racial discrimination in the search for employment, while almost a quarter of Asian job seekers said the same. The Youth Training Scheme (YTS) has similar overall results: less than 1 per cent of those on YTS schemes were from the minorities in 1987 or 1988, though some companies, such as Dixons, Abbey National and Marks and Spencer were radically more responsive to the needs of minority youths than were most British companies (Sousa, 1988; Hyder, 1989). Similarly, while 69 per cent of all those leaving the YTS found employment, only half of the Afro-Caribbean and Asian youths did so (Manpower Services Commission, 1987).

It would seem that, under many conditions, it would be rational, that is in their own self-interests, for managers to construct a more formal and less prejudiced approach to recruitment. After all, if discrimination hinders the recruitment of the most qualified and suitable individual for the particular job then it must be against the interests of the company: not just morally but economically too. This is exactly the code of conduct spelled out in numerous Confederation of British Industry (CBI) (1970, 1981) reports. In fact, as Jewson and Mason (1986) point out, formality can actually provide the cover for more, rather than less, manipulation of the recruitment procedure. Concomitantly, reducing informal procedures may actually undermine some of the shop-floor patterns of trust between managers and workers. Since there can never be a sufficiently universal rulebook to cover all contingencies there clearly is a problem regarding the manipulation or misinterpretation of rules. However, the ordinarily superior record of public employment to private employment regarding ethnic minorities suggests that formality should not be cast aside because of its inevitable problems.

Racism in the community

Several studies have demonstrated the disadvantages associated by white employers with ethnic minorities in the recruiting world, but few more vividly than the experiments using fictitious matched pairs of identically qualified white and minority workers. The surveys of Daniel (1968), Jowell and Prescott-Clarke (1970), Smith (1977), the 1988 BBC documentary series based in Bristol and the 1997 BBC survey of the NHS reveal the high levels of racial discrimination that masquerade behind the often liberal façades at work and in the wider community. A BBC survey in 2004 involved CVs from six fictitious applications being sent to 50 employers, where the qualifications and experiences were identical but the names were constructed to represent two white candidates (Jenny Hughes and John Andrews), two black candidates (Abu Olasemi and Yinka Olatunde) and two Muslim candidates (Fatima Khan and Nasser Hanif). While 25 per cent of the white candidates were offered interviews, they were offered to only 13 per cent of the black candidates and to a mere 9 per cent of the Muslim candidates (see <http://news.bbc.co.uk/1/hi/business/3885213.stm>).

In 2000, a survey commissioned by the Department of Health suggested that half of frontline NHS staff from ethnic minorities had been subject to racial harassment by patients and the public in the previous year, and four years later the Royal College of Nursing published a survey showing that nurses from the ethnic minorities were twice as likely as their white colleagues to be underpaid. In the same year 8.4 per cent of the 1.3 million NHS staff were from ethnic minorities but they only accounted for 1 per cent of NHS CEOs. Sir John Blofeld's 2004 inquiry into the death of David 'Rocky' Bennett, a Jamaican-born Rastafarian who died while being forcibly restrained on a floor by four mental health nurses in 1998, concluded that institutional racism was a 'festering abscess' in the NHS (Carvel, 2004c: 6). Even the British Medical Association (BMA) has admitted that 'widespread discrimination' exists against doctors from ethnic minorities, against women doctors and against gay and disabled doctors (Carvel, 2004c: 7).

In some areas, at least until fairly recently, discriminatory policies were much more explicit, bordering on a system not dissimilar to South African apartheid; as a representative of one engineering firm put it, the firm had: 'a policy never to employ a coloured man in a position . . . where in the course of events he would rise to a position where he would give orders to a white man' (Wright, 1968: 75–6). Another method for taking advantage of ethnic differences is that of occupational segregation. This was particularly prevalent in the USA in the early part of this century, when employers both segregated and mixed different ethnic groups with the explicit intention of increasing or decreasing levels of hostility and competition between ethnic groups. The nearest equivalent practice in the UK has been that enacted by employers in Northern Ireland to set

Catholics against Protestants (Jenkins, 1988: 316–19). The undermining of any labour solidarity that appeared to be fostering union sympathies appears to have been a primary aim of this divide and rule strategy (Gordon et al., 1982: 141–3). But occupational segregation has more commonly been associated with the sucking in of immigrant labour to replace indigenous workers who refuse to undertake the most arduous and poorly paid jobs. In some circumstances this almost leads to separated labour markets, for example the predominance of minority staff on the London Underground (Rex and Tomlinson, 1979). In other cases it is minority or immigrant workers who undertake specific tasks within enterprises, such as night work and shift work (Smith, 1974). But whatever the division, and however unwilling the white population appears to be to undertake certain jobs, this seldom appears to remove the resistance or discrimination of white workers (Ward, 1978).

Employers and racism

In Britain, employers' attitudes towards ethnic minorities even seem to relate to the recognition of trade unions. Recently, union recognition in enterprises where more than 10 per cent of employees are minority shows some degree of decline. Since 1980 even fewer such employers recognize trade unions, irrespective of the general decline in trade union membership and influence. Indeed, ethnic minority workers were employed in substantial numbers in fewer enterprises, primarily because of the collapse of staple industries which employed them and because of the selective shake-out of minority labour mentioned above (Millward and Stevens, 1986: 65–99). Thus, ethnic minorities started out from a position of structured subordination in the labour market, and the economic malaise of the early 1980s has merely served to compound the disadvantages (Smith, 1981; Thomas, 1984). But why should management be concerned about the ethnic content of their workforce when considering union recognition? Are unions, or rather union members and ordinary workers, responsible for the perpetuation of racism or the boosting of reward levels to undermine the economic rationale for employing workers from the ethnic minorities? Answers to this kind of question are developed in the final section of this chapter.

Trade unions, workers and racial discrimination

Trade unions and exclusionary theory

The assumption that class issues, or even just trade union issues, cut across, and are more important than, racial or ethnic issues has a long and ambiguous pedigree. The prioritizing of class above race and gender has already been discussed but it is important to note the continuing relevance of this outlook on the contemporary academic study of work. For example, both Kornblum (1974) and Burawoy (1979) insist that white workers' racism is subordinated to, and generated by, the imperatives of a specifically capitalist mode of production. Since minority wages are usually lower than white workers' wages it might seem paradoxical that capital should provide support for a form of discrimination that delimits the opportunity to maximize profits: if minority labour is cheaper then employers should not accept racism among their majority labour force. Three explanations for this paradox are possible. First, it may be that employers are unwilling to risk industrial action on the part of their majority workers by recruiting minority workers. Second, it has been argued that by encouraging racial discrimination within the workforce employers can actually persuade both majority and minority groups to accept rates of reward that are lower than those applicable where non-discriminatory practices operate (Perlo, 1953). Third, it may be taken as a management strategy of divide and rule to ensure that, irrespective of individual rewards, no collective action would occur. Such a strategy has been well documented in the USA over a long period of time (Piven and Cloward, 1977; Gordon et al., 1982).

Whether the exclusionary tactics that do exist, linked to the retention of demarcation boundaries, job allocation and recruitment controls, are beneficial to trade unions in the long run is questionable (Pagnamenta and Overy, 1984: 124–49; Guerin, 1979; Davis, 1985) but not the issue here. At the risk of repetition, what is important is to note how such exclusionary tactics become appropriated for use against specific groups of workers. That is to say that powerful groups of (usually) male, white and skilled workers operate discriminatory bans against (usually) women and ethnic minorities, but retain the camouflage of 'market-based', and therefore avowedly 'legitimate' exclusion. The implications of this for viewpoints on the relationship of class of work are covered in chapter 5; this section considers the impact it has on race and work, particularly with regard to Britain and America.

The British experience

Despite the frequent allocation of left-wing labels to British trade unions, their exclusionary strategies and tactics against ethnic minorities have a long history. Although Elizabeth I seems to have been responsible for the first attempt to repatriate black people from England in 1596, racism within the indigenous British workforce is nothing new (Fryer, 1988). Documented reports of racist attacks by British workers upon Irish workers in the nineteenth century, then Jewish workers at the turn of the century, long predate the disparagement of ethnic minorities from the Commonwealth (Miles and Phizacklea (eds), 1979). The TUC has, until very recently, also been prominent in acting against minority workers; for example, as early as 1892 it made a declaration in favour of controlling 'alien' labour. In fact, one of the first black British labour leaders appears to have been William Cuffay, a tailor and one of the Chartist leaders (Meade-King, 1986), but the last century and a half has not witnessed the universal 'brotherhood' for which they stood. Black workers had already reached a relatively high number in England by 1830, when a black community of between ten and fifteen thousand existed, and two black men, William Davidson and Robert Wedderburn, were actively involved in the working-class politics of the day (Fryer, 1984). But ethnic conflict was most easily generated where ethnic origin could be coupled with religion: a volatile mix that often disrupted unionism in Ireland, Scotland and the north-west of England as the Protestant orange tinge to trade unionism transformed it into political unionism (Foot, 1965; Neal, 1988).

One of of the earliest cases of official trade union hostility to their *own* minority members in Britain is that of the National Union of Seamen who were disinclined to support their minority members against the 1925 Special Restrictions (Coloured Alien Seamen) Order (Bhavnani and Bhavnani, 1985: 151–2). Even Ben Tillett, an avowed socialist and radical union leader of the London dockers at the turn of the nineteenth century, was equivocal about the arrival of Jewish immigrants: 'Yes, you are our brothers and we will stand by you. But we wish you had not come' (quoted in Meth, 1973: 5). Similarly, the population as a whole seems to have been at best ambiguous about the status of the Jews. The Anglo-Boer War was blamed by Keir Hardy and a substantial proportion of trade union leaders on the Army, composed as it allegedly was 'largely [of] Jews and foreigners' (Rhodes James, quoted in Fox, 1985: 210). Even during the Second World War indigenous anti-semitism was ever-present among the British working class, though they do not seem to have been as anti-semitic as the government feared or the gutter press assumed (Kushner, 1989).

With the influx of migrant labour to Britain at the end of the Second World War it might have been expected that competition for employment would provide the fertile ground for the construction of exclusionary strategies by indigenous workers. In fact, the persistent labour shortage, and funnelling of West Indian immigrants in particular into the unskilled jobs in the public and service sectors that were the most riven by shortages, ensured that there was little direct competition between white and minority workers. In the North and Midlands where many Asian workers found manufacturing jobs, particularly in textiles, the general pattern was one where white employees left, leaving vacancies for Asian workers, rather than one where cheaper Asian workers pushed white workers out of the labour market (Peach, 1968).

This did not deter the production and reproduction of racist attitudes by trade unionists and white workers alike, grounded in the putative threat to white jobs and indigenous culture (LATC, 1984; Mayhew and Addison, 1983: 333), and represented by the likes of Enoch Powell's 'rivers of blood' speech in 1968 on the political right. It should not be forgotten that he was supported by London dockers and (the alleged political left has argued) by the Labour Party – in and out of office – through their support for, and enactment of, various immigration controls based on racial origins (Joshi and Carter, 1984; Bhavnani and Bhavnani, 1985). Nor did it inhibit the General Council of the Trades Union Congress from adopting policy statements that explicitly linked the existence of immigrant workers to the issue of the 'coloured problem' (Phizacklea and Miles, 1987), despite condemning 'all manifestations of racial discrimination' three years earlier. Such racist attitudes were also made manifest in the TUC's support for both Conservative and Labour immigration legislation (Miles and

Phizacklea, 1977: 21–39). In fact, the first shift within the TUC from the 'problem of integration' to the 'problem of racism' did not occur until the 1973 Trades Union Congress, when the triple forces of anti-racist rank and file movements, the burgeoning number of strikes against trade union racism by ethnic minorities themselves (Commission for Industrial Relations, 1974; Moore, 1975), and the rise of the neo-fascist National Front coerced the TUC into belated reaction. Since then the TUC has instigated policy documents designed to undercut racism within its own ranks (Trades Union Congress, 1983a, 1983b), but not until the 1989 Trades Union Congress did the anti-racist resolution, originally agreed in 1984, acquire a rule providing for expulsion for 'deliberate acts of unlawful discrimination'. It remains to be seen whether this will have any major impact.

The apparent demise of labour solidarity and collectivism in Britain, most recently associated with the era of Thatcherism, has often been linked to the crumbling of social democratic and liberal 'morality'; in its place has arisen, it is alleged, a harsh Darwinian jungle bereft of morality and, therefore, ill-disposed towards social reforms of all kinds (Hobsbawm, 1981; Offe, 1984). This assumes the existence of prior forms of ideological solidarity that, in fact, seldom seem to have prevailed. Thus neither an entire society, nor the working-class elements of it, appear to have been held in place by unitary ideologies (Mann, 1970; Abercrombie et al., 1980; Held, 1987: 221–42; Marshall et al., 1987). This does not imply that trade unions in Britain or the USA are inherently and irrevocably sectionalist, exclusive and racist; the examples of the Knights of Labor and periods in the UAW's history in the USA (see below), and recent support by some British unions (most notably the National Association of Local Government Officers, NALGO) for anti-racist policies, suggest that a contradictory amalgam of sectionalism, exclusivity, solidarity and collectivism is a more accurate description of the historical role of the labour movement in most capitalist countries.

Such an amalgam also misrepresents the apparent solidarity of ethnic minorities. Although white assessments tend to assume a solidarity among heterogeneous groups like 'Asian' workers and 'black' workers, in reality they are often as disunited as any other apparently homogeneous group. For example, Asian workers are more likely to be organized through their regional and national loyalties than any putative supraethnic loyalty: the Indian Workers' Association, the Pakistani Workers' Association and the East Pakistani Welfare Association etc., rather than the Asian Workers Association (Brooks and Singh, 1978–9).

Much of the empirical research suggests that, despite members of ethnic minorities being favourably inclined towards trade unions (Lee, 1987: 145–7), white members of unions are generally less enthusiastic about anti-racist issues than their national officials (Radin, 1966; Commission for Racial Equality, 1981; Miles and Phizacklea, 1978), and, in many instances, racist themselves (CARF, 1981). An example of this appears to be the perpetuation of the 'black problem' attitude of trade union officials. That is to say, just as the early post-war union officials assumed that any problems arising out of racial conflict were 'coloured problems', rather than 'white problems', so it appears that the failure of anti-racist policies is blamed on the failure of minorities to participate in unions. Certainly Lee's (1987) evidence suggests that very few trade union officials regard the involvement of minority members as a union responsibility. Rather, minority workers are defined by their class not their colour; as Vic Feather, a former general secretary of the TUC, noted in 1968: 'If coloured immigrants are unwilling to integrate or are unable to secure acceptance as they are, we shall have, instead of integration, permanent and weakening division among workpeople' (quoted in Meth, 1973: 23). This is reflected in: the refusal of many white union officials to take issues of racial discrimination seriously; their hostility towards minority caucuses within unions (the most prominent exception to the rule here is NALGO: see Virdee and Grint, 1994); and the lack of interest which appears to prevail in support of minority officials. Individual minority workers who do make it into the union hierarchy at any level emerge despite, rather than because of, the 'support' from union officialdom (Lee, 1987: 150–3). This is not to disparage the activities of a minority of white shop stewards and union officials, but what evidence does exist suggests that anti-racism in practice is critically dependent upon the existence and actions of a caucus of minority activists, often operating in relative autonomy from the main union (Virdee, 1990).

A useful litmus test for the distinction between anti-racist rhetoric and reality is to compare official pronouncements with public policies. It may be easier for a full-time official to declare her or himself an anti-racist than for the local shop steward because the full-time official may not have to deal with the level of racism apparent within the British working class. It is, therefore, worth acknowledging the extent to which trade union bureaucracies are themselves staffed by white employees. While there is little systematic evidence on this, because very few unions have adopted ethnic monitoring, it is apparent that where studies do exist they disclose a depressingly conservative picture of grossly under-represented ethnic minorities (NUPE, 1985). The situation is worse than it appears at first sight because the level of union density among ethnic minorities is actually substantially higher than the equivalent figure for white workers (Lee, 1987: 145–6; Modad, 1997b). In 1986 only thirteen of the main thirty-three British unions had any minority officials, and many had only a token minority leader. There are exceptions of course, and Bill Morris, the General Secretary of the Transport and General Workers' Union, is the most senior minority union offical at the time of writing. But although 56 per cent of minority employees were unionized in 1986, compared with 47 per cent of white employees (the corresponding figures in 1997 were 40 and 33), only 4 per cent of minority men held elected posts within their unions, compared with 11 per cent of white men. The figures were identical for white and minority women at 2 per cent (Policy Studies Institute, 1986).

Majority group hostility to ethnic minorities in the 1980s was still very evident (Willmott, 1987). Not so much in official discrimination but in the disproportionate levels of material disadvantage experienced (Brown, 1984), and more personal, unofficial, tacit and even unconscious ways, such as the self-allocation of social class. Indeed, the TUC has made strenuous efforts to eliminate racism at work where it can – see, for example, the TUC's 2003 report *Black Voices at Work*' (available at <http://www.tuc.org.uk/equality/tuc-6519-f0.cfm>).

However, support for, and satisfaction with, trade unions in the 1990s remained high (Modood, 1997b: 136–7). In Lash's study of the USA the vast majority of white respondents placed themselves in an intermediate class above the 'poor', a label which they strongly associated with ethnic minorities (1984: 86), and a manifestation of the absence of labour solidarity. So is the general American experience any better?

The American experience

In the USA racial conflict between workers was evident through much of the nineteenth century, and while white workers seemed unwilling to support the slavery abolitionists' movement, abolitionists also appeared to denigrate the utility of any labour movement (Guerin, 1979: 144–6). As Du Bois noted: 'the abolitionists did not perceive the new subordination to which the worker was subjected by organized capital, while the workers did not understand that the exclusion from the working class program of four million workers was a fatal omission' (quoted in Guerin, 1979: 145). There were labour leaders who espoused progressive social policies on race, such as William H. Sylvis, leader of the National Labor Union in the 1860s, but the general practice of discrimination remained, buttressed by black support for the Republican 'liberators' from slavery, and white labour antagonism towards the same party perceived to be the representative of big business. This conflict, between the putative exploiters of class and the exploiters of race, is aptly captured by the dichotomous positions taken up by black and white employees of the Pullman Company in the 1894 strike. White workers struck, but their American Railway Union's (ARU) discriminatory policies, in sharp contrast to the more racially liberal policies of the Pullman Company, led black workers to resist the strikers. As Eugene Debs, the ARU's leader, so characteristically argued: 'there is no black question independently of the working class question . . . we have nothing special to offer the negro' (quoted in Guerin, 1979: 149).

The Knights of Labor, a progressive general union, did propose anti-racist programmes and recruited up to 60,000 black members by 1896, but they were quickly undermined by the sectionalist traditions of business unionism promulgated by the likes of Gompers and the American Federation of Labor (AFL). Not that the trade unions were sole repositories of racism of course, nor that the discrimination was restricted to blacks; the Irish, Catholics, Jews and women were commonly regarded by the English Protestant male hierarchy in America and England as legitimate scapegoats. Such exclusionary practices, in America particularly, merely fostered the strike-breaking activities that black workers were often recruited for by white employers, especially during the bitter steel disputes in the period immediately following the First World War. Yet greater levels of discrimination were practised against non-American-born workers; for example, the Arizona Legislature passed the Alien Labor Law which stipulated that 80 per cent of all workers in the state must be American born: a measure explicitly designed to stem the influx of Mexican and Chinese labourers (Hoefer, 1984: 39). Nor was racism restricted to the passing of legislation: in

1919 twenty-five major race riots took place in the USA as mass unemployment greeted many of the black war veterans. Among the more than seventy blacks lynched by white mobs during this time several were still wearing their army uniforms (Woodward, 1974).

The National Association for the Advancement of Colored People (NAACP) made several vain attempts to interest the AFL in a multi-racial movement, but the United Mine Workers were almost alone in carrying out such policies in some parts of the country. This progressive platform also framed the original structure of the Congress of Industrial Organization (CIO), set up in 1935 against the background of recruiting conflicts between the craft unions, represented by the leadership of the AFL, and the industrial unions, represented by the rebel CIO. Thus in CIO affiliates, like the United Automobile Workers (UAW), both black and white workers were involved in strike action and social struggles throughout the 1930s and 1940s. Inevitably, perhaps, some employers made attempts to undermine the incipient unity: first, by recruiting black workers instead of white workers because of the formers' traditional antipathy to trade unions; and second, when this failed, to promote the AFL instead of the CIO. Ford, in particular, was an exponent of this tactic.

The fusion of the AFL and CIO in 1957 did little to further the cause of black workers, and, while many unions eventually voiced support for the civil rights movement, only the UAW among the large unions pursued this with any vigour. Since US unions have never recruited a majority of white workers, let alone black workers, the continued discrimination against black workers represented by their disproportionate presence among the working class (Wright, 1985: 201) is clearly not the sole responsibility of the unions. Exactly how black workers should respond to this situation, which poses the interests of class and race as alternative rather than complementary forms of organization, is not self-evident. Neither integration nor separate organizations have proved overwhelmingly successful and while separate black sections of 'white' organizations may well be a prerequisite to any kind of substantive advance it is also the case that separate organizations can be, and have been, easy to isolate and ignore or have stimulated a white backlash (Wrench, 1985; Virdee, 1990; Virdee and Grint, 1994).

Of course, in the USA the great ethnic variety and wave-like periods of immigration brought favourable conditions for the pursuit of trade-union-organized sectionalism (Nelson, 1975), as indeed they have done across the capitalist world ever since (see Cohen, 1988), and the numbers involved were enormous: in 1852 over a thousand people a day were leaving from Britain alone for the USA (Armytage, 1981: 70), and Tranter (1973) estimates that between 1841 and 1939 8.6 million people emigrated from Britain – a third of the natural increase. The importance of the ethnic/family dimension to American patterns of work, particularly during the late nineteenth and early twentieth centuries, should not be underestimated: trade unions and business organizations were just as likely to be marshalled under their ethnic banners as their craft or class banners; thus the United German Trades and the Italian Chamber of Labor were commonplace during this period (Pelling, 1960: 213). Yet the ethnic mix which this generated in the USA, and the exclusionary reaction of American labour, have been considered, by Selig Perlman (1928) for example, as demonstrable proof of the 'maturity' of US unions. These strategies originated, according to Pelling (1960: 212), in attempts to restrict the competition of Chinese labour in California, and there were various methods involved, from constitutional bars on non-white workers to making US citizenship a pre-requisite for membership. In fact, the Chinese immigration into Hawaii's sugar plantations at the end of the nineteenth century is a useful example of the problems involved in banning particular groups while still requiring immigrant labour. With 50,000 Chinese labourers in Hawaii by 1898 and further immigration banned by an Exclusion Act of 1892, Japanese labourers were encouraged as replacements, at least until they outnumbered the Chinese and were deeply implicated in a rash of labour disputes, whereupon Koreans were sought out to supply the ever-expanding sugar plantations (Patterson, 1988). Where such groups have remained *in situ* and developed ethnic businesses, they have proved extraordinarily difficult recruiting ground for unions; not just because of the language problem but because ethnic businesses tend to be small, culturally homogeneous units where employer and employee often work side by side and where the class-based claims of union recruiters are devalued both by the ethnic allegiances and the general lack of interest of most unions in aspects of ethnic discrimination. A further problem for unions lies in the essentially ambiguous and often transient status of immigrant workers and those from established ethnic minorities: it is not merely geographic mobility that is common, but social mobility, between employer and employee, is also relatively widespread, a pattern that stretches across national boundaries (Morokvasic, 1987).

It can only be concluded that white workers, trade unions and trade unionists in the USA and the UK bear a major responsibility for not attacking – and by default, therefore, for the preservation of – racism at work, as Phizacklea and Miles argue: 'there remains very little real evidence that organized labour in Britain has seriously confronted the issue of racism within its own ranks and the reality of material disadvantage amongst those who have been the object of racism and discrimination' (1987: 117). Nevertheless, trade unions cannot be isolated from the environment within which they operate. If the environment is racist and the trade unions have to work within it but cannot transcend it, then the responsibility for the perpetuation of racism lies not just at the door of the union movement. Indeed, the most recent evidence suggests that workers with ethnic minority origins are better paid when they work within unionized enterprises than in non-unionized enterprises in so far as wage differentials based on race are narrower (Metcalfe, 1989). Trade unions may not have exerted themselves in the fight against racism at work until relatively recently but they have had a measure of success and, given the hostile environment within which they operate, must take at least some credit for positive action.

Summary

This chapter has attempted to demonstrate the interleaving of socially structured forces and the influence of agents in the labour market by highlighting several related features of race and ethnicity. It should be apparent that the material position of ethnic minorities, and the associated levels of racial discrimination, cannot be explained simply by reference to a neo-liberal market model where only individuals and the forces of supply and demand exist. Nor can the discriminatory practices of white employers or employees or trade unions be singled out. Rather, the practices of various agents need to be situated within their appropriate socially structured context to illustrate both the contingent openings appropriated by different work groups and the more permanent features of social exclusion that appear to persist in all market-based societies. Racial discrimination in the labour market is not a feature unique to capitalist economies nor to capitalists; nor, it has to be said, are trade unions unambiguous promoters of racial equality or inequality. It is this very fluidity that makes the apportioning of causation and responsibility so difficult. But undergirding the fluidity remains a stability based upon the principle of work as a social phenomenon: neither racism nor racial equality are simply the products of individual attitudes, instead they depend upon a complex web of socially constructed institutions and socially organized agents. And while racism remains a critical problem for society it is the case that patterns of inequality are changing in response to increased human capital by minorities (specifically educational qualifications) and to labour market restructuring (specifically the decline in unskilled jobs). The consequences of this are beneficial for some groups – Afro-Caribbeans, Indians and Chinese – but not for Pakistanis or Bangladeshis for whom the future remains bleak.

Exam/essay questions

1 Is racism at work inevitable?
2 To what extent are labour markets 'colour-blind'?
3 What are the advantages and disadvantages of black workers organizing independently of trade unions?
4 Class, race or gender – which aspect of identity is the most important for explaining the opportunities and constraints facing individuals at work?
5 'It doesn't matter which ethnic minority you belong to – you are discriminated against on the basis of being "black".' Discuss.
6 Why is institutionalized racism at work so difficult to eradicate and so pernicious in its effects?
7 'Scientifically speaking there are no homogeneous "races" and to continue to use the term "race" simply perpetuates the myth and foments prejudice and discrimination.' Discuss.
8 How can we best make sense of racism?
9 Is education or 'affirmative action' the best way of overcoming racial discrimination at work?
10 Historically, labour market restructuring, not the accumulation of human capital has provided the quickest route out of poverty for most ethnic minorities – what does this imply for the future?

Further reading

The most up-to-date compilation of data on ethnic minorities in Britain is Modood et al.'s *Ethnic Minorities in Britain* (1997). Fryer's *Staying Power* (1984) is a valuable history of black people in Britain, while the best comparative history of slavery is Segal's *The Black Diaspora* (1995). For an introduction to the complexities of the theoretical debate, readers could try Solomos's *Race and Racism in Contemporary Britain* (1989), Miles's *Racism* (1989), Banton's *Racial Theories* (1987) and Gilroy's *There Ain't No Black in the Union Jack* (1987). A review of racial violence and harassment is provided in Virdee's *Racial Violence and Harassment* (1995).

8
Working Technology

> People who experience themselves as automata, as robots, as bits of machinery . . . are rightly regarded as crazy. Yet why do we not regard a theory that seeks to transmute persons into automata . . . as equally crazy?
>
> R.D. Laing, *The Divided Self*

Introduction

The nature of the relationship between technology and work is as controversial as the definition of either. As has already been pointed out, 'work' has often been taken to be synonymous with paid labour, though this assumption embodies an enormous variety of evaluative baggage as to the importance of non-domestic labour and economic exchange. Similarly, the definition of technology tends to vary with author: from a delimited concern with machinery through to the entire corpus of organizational features, and all points in between (Winner, 1977: 8–12). Quite often the definition of technology remains implicit and therefore obscure. As a result, technology can become the reserve category which explains all aspects that cannot be explained by other factors, or the bewildering variety of definitions simply confounds any attempted comparisons (see Davis and Taylor, 1976: 390–1). Winner (1977: 8–12) makes an attempt to disentangle the knotty problem by differentiating between inanimate machinery which he calls 'apparatus', the technical activities of humans which he calls 'technique', and the social arrangements which fuse apparatus and technique, which he calls 'organization'. Ultimately his own analysis tends to conflate these terms and it is striking how difficult it is to separate social and technical aspects. Clearly, the fluidity of definition does inhibit comparative research but does it pose further problems? The critical issue is really one of the explanatory value of the concept. That is, if technology is defined so broadly that it encompasses almost all aspects of the work environment then its explanatory power as an independent variable is minimal: if everything explains everything then nothing can be explained. Relatedly, many sociologists would want to argue that technology, *qua* apparatus, cannot explain anything anyway since technology is itself socially constructed and the effect of technology depends upon the use made of it. Still others would want to deny the apparent neutrality afforded to technology here, for rather than technology being inert it is seen as inherently political in nature: it is not simply a means to any end but a means that already encapsulates particular preferences (Winner, 1985). All these arguments, of course, resurface within that most slippery of agendas, technological determinism versus social determinism. What are considered in the first part of this chapter are both these polar opposite approaches and a third approach which seeks to rescue a limited role for technology where technology does not determine the resultant phenomenon but does affect it as one of several independent variables. Finally, and very briefly because I have already discussed it in chapter 4, I raise again the Actor Network theory which rejects the division between human and non-human actors and conceptualizes the two apparently discrete phenomena as fused elements in a seamless web: a human–technology alloy. This alloy itself is perceived as unstable and inherently contingent – it is constructed through the interpretative processes of actors and does not, therefore, embody any definitive capabilities or 'effects'. This approach, then, denies the 'technicist' viewpoints where technology is regarded as an *independent* variable (of whatever significance) on the grounds that no objective account of technical capabilities can be constructed: such accounts are social constructions derived from, and subject to, the interpretative processes of actors. But this does not mean that technology is unimportant; it does mean that what counts as technology and how various rhetorics adopt particular forms of explanation are social constructions not concrete or objective 'facts'. In the second part of this chapter I consider arguments that information technology, among other things, has facilitated the construction of a radical new form of work organization: post-Fordism.

Technological determinism

At its simplest, **technological determinism** considers technology to be an exogenous and autonomous development which coerces and determines social and economic organizations and relationships; it appears to advance spontaneously and inevitably in a manner resemblant of Darwinian survival, in so far as only the most 'appropriate' innovations survive and only those nations and organizations that adapt to such innovations prosper. This is particularly prescient when information technology is considered, for the march of the microchip appears omnipotent and to deny this is to deny both reality and the future. Whether that future is to be one of Toffler's (1980) utopia or Burnham's (1983) Orwellian dystopia is secondary to the inescapable essence of the future. This approach also has a long history as well as an apparently radical future, from Saint-Simon and Comte (Kumar, 1978), to the arguments of Leavitt and Whisler (1958), Bell (1960, 1973) and Blauner (1964). While some of the more general discussions concerning technological determinism have sought to highlight the way technological advance tramples all before it, there are some rather more sophisticated résumés which leave a degree of freedom for social groups to manoeuvre (Pool, 1983; Freeman, 1987). Robey (1977), for example, argues that a more contingent relationship between technology and organizations exists in which organizations within unstable environments used computer technology to buttress a decentralized structure while organizations with stable environments used computers to centralize control.

However, technological determinism within the realms of the sociology of work is never quite what it appears to be. For example, although Woodward (1958) and Blauner (1964) are used here to illustrate the principle, neither is a cast-iron devotee of the approach: Woodward's later work (1965) certainly shifted away from this view towards the middle zone represented in her case by the **socio-technical systems** theorists (see below). Blauner's argument, despite his attempts to pursue the hard line, actually provides evidence against this and, indeed, he rolls out a disclaimer at the beginning of his book: 'modern factories vary considerably in technology, in division of labour, in economic structure, and in organizational character. These differences produce sociotechnical systems in which the objective conditions and the inner life of employees are strikingly variant' (1964: 5). Nevertheless, he still maintains that 'the most important single factor that gives an industry a distinctive character is its technology' (1964: 6). At the opposite end of the determinist spectrum, **social determinism**, Gallie similarly slides from a strong anti-technological determinist position into a much softer version. He reports that although technology may not be completely irrelevant 'it is improbable that the characteristics of advanced technology are of any substantial importance in explaining the degree of social integration of workers within the enterprise' (1978: 300). Yet contrast this with his comment earlier that 'There were clear signs in both countries that automation is *conducive* to a certain degree of team autonomy' (1978: 221, my emphasis; see Clark et al., 1988, on this). Accepting, then, that the allocation of author to viewpoint is a heuristic device not an objective typification, it is apparent that this kind of approach tends to produce 'impact studies' in which the exogenous and determining role of technology produces 'effects' upon work organization and/or worker attitude and behaviour. For example, Woodward's focus is upon the impact of technology on work organization and control structures.

Blauner

Blauner's intention is not to explain the impact of technology on work so much as to consider the extent to which feelings of alienation are associated with different types of work situation. In particular, Blauner is interested in operationalizing Marx's concept of alienation and examining the relationship between alienation and the patterning of technological and organizational trends through time. For Blauner alienation is:

> a general syndrome made up of a number of different objective conditions and subjective feelings and states which emerge from certain relationships between workers and the socio-technical settings of employment. Alienation exists when workers are unable to control their immediate work processes, to develop a sense of purpose and function which connects their job to the overall organization of production, to belong to integrated industrial communities and when they fail to become involved in the activity of work as a mode of personal self-expression. In modern, industrial employment, control, purpose, social integration and self-involvement are all problematic. (1964: 15)

Alienation, then, has four related facets: powerlessness, meaninglessness, isolation, and self-estrangement. Each facet expresses a principle of fragmentation; that is, each contributes to the prevention of workers' activities and experiences constituting a wholeness. Given this, Blauner argues that it is possible to locate different work groups on each dimension of alienation and thus to build corporate profiles of experience. The four facets of alienation link directly to technology, or indirectly to it through the division of labour, which he regards as a result of technology. On the basis of secondary survey data on industries in the USA Blauner argues that technology, 'more than any other factor, determines the nature of the job tasks performed by blue collar employees and has an important effect upon a number of aspects of alienation' (1964: 8). For example, technology is alleged to: delimit worker control and freedom; determine the level of interest in a job; affect the size of the plant and the nature of work groups, and thereby influence group cohesion; and finally it patterns the occupational structure and skill distribution. Moreover, since technology is inherently dynamic so too must be its effects upon alienation.

To map this differential and dynamic impact of technology Blauner focuses upon four organizations that he considers represent the basic phases of technological change over time, but which still persist in one form or another. Hence the original form of technology in the industrialization process was craft technology, represented by the printing industry, which, when the book was published in 1964, had little of the technology currently associated with it. Since the craft workers control much of the process of work directly, and have their considerable degree of freedom buttressed by powerful unions and labour market positions and integrating occupational communities, Blauner argues that this group's technology results in the highest levels of skill and lowest levels of alienation of all groups. In sharp contrast to this group are the textile workers, the machine tenders. Here the minute division of labour engenders a sense of powerlessness and meaninglessness, while the low status of the work is inimical to any occupational identity. The consequence is a high level of alienation correlated with a low level of skill. Yet Blauner implies that alienation would probably be higher but for the strong community bonds that exist beyond the confines of the factory. The highest levels of alienation exist, according to Blauner, among assembly line workers. The technology of the assembly line not only fragments the experience of work into an activity whose only relationship to meaning is through economic reward, it actively stimulates conflict and precludes social integration. Finally, Blauner considers the process work involved in the chemical industry, the technology of which marks the return of skill, autonomy and control to the worker and the related reduction in alienation. Thus Blauner's model of technological development represents an inverted 'U' curve: the early pattern of technology, requiring high levels of skill etc., induced low levels of alienation; the transitional phase where the levels of skill and alienation were inverted; and the final stage where technological developments returned the pattern to its initial formation.

Despite all his protestations to the contrary, then, Blauner certainly appeared to conclude that technological developments, however mediated, generated specific forms of work organization and worker experience. As he sums up his approach: 'the character of the machine system largely determines the degree of control the factory employee exerts over his sociotechnical environment and the range and limitations of his freedom in the work situation' (1964: 170). Yet his analysis has been subject to a cacophony of criticisms. First, his data sources are dubious: they were gathered for other purposes, were already dated, and involved questions of job satisfaction that are notoriously problematic. For example, not only do questions of satisfaction depend upon transient economic and social conditions, but they imply criteria of satisfaction that are seldom explicit and even less grounded in normative consensus. Second, although Blauner's explanations are mobilized through the technology, not all workers in any single industry are engaged in identical operations using equivalent technology. Blauner makes much of the alienation prevalent among all workers in automobile plants as a result of the assembly line technology, but admits that only 18 per cent are actually assembly line operatives. Third, although Blauner's conceptualization of alienation involves four facets relating to different areas of control, he argues that the issues of ownership and major decision-making powers are unimportant, not because the subjects of the research say they are unimportant but because Blauner assumes they are unimportant. Even if we accept that Blauner's subjective version of alienation is qualitatively distinct from Marx's objective notion of alienation (i.e., for Marx it is an inherent and undifferentiated element of all capitalist societies and therefore immune to the articulated attitudes of putatively unalienated individuals), Eldridge is surely right to claim that expressions of satisfaction 'are not a sufficient basis for making general statements about the extent to which workers are alienated in industrial societies' (1971: 191). Fourth, Blauner's model of textile workers involves several problems: despite having technology that allegedly induces powerlessness and meaninglessness, the textile workers are represented as having strong integrating tendencies produced in and through the local community – an exogenous feature that Blauner underplays, if not actually disavows, in his theoretical assumptions about the predominant explanatory power of technology. Fifth, one might want to question the ahistorical basis of Blauner's argument which persists despite his concern for the importance of technological developments over time. In particular, it could be argued that to focus upon the *operation* of technology in itself is to ignore the historical introduction of the technology. Thus, what Blauner appears to construe as the 'effects of the technology' might be considered as the effects of management's success in securing control through the technology. For example, although the technology of assembly line production does appear to be inimical to conventional conversations it *need* not be if noise proofing was improved, or workers were provided with radio headsets, or periods on the line were interspersed with jobs away from it.

Nor does assembly line technology mean that group cohesiveness is necessarily undermined (indeed the opposite might apply where the collective experience is one of alienation) and, moreover, the reduction in social interactions may have been one of the intentions anyway: certainly Taylor (1911) was well aware of the problems appertaining to group solidarity and explicitly designed his approach with this disintegrating effect in mind. Furthermore, the existence of assembly line facilities does not determine who controls its operation. Beynon recounts how workers could engage in all kinds of activity to reassert a measure of control, sanding the paint off trim lines to impress upon supervisors the folly of authoritarian line control or even organizing a 'rota': 'Eight of them contributed to a pool. Every eighth week one of them took the Friday shift off, and got paid a shift's money from the pool' (1975: 148). Nor are assembly lines themselves the only way to build mass production vehicles; the Volvo experiments in semi-autonomous work groups clearly deny such a deterministic account (Aguren et al., 1984; Berggren, 1989). Indeed, as mentioned at the beginning, Blauner's data actually tend to contradict the technologically determinist thrust to his argument, and this is particularly evident in his discusion of women workers. His assumption is conventionally patriarchal and simultaneously self-contradictory. Thus, for example, he argues that 'women have, on the average, less physical stamina than men' yet completes the same sentence '[since] working women often double as housewives and mothers, it is to be expected that they would be more fatigued by their work' (Blauner, 1964: 71). This is important not just because the double work of women inverts the stamina argument, but because the experiences of women within the textile mill can only be adequately explained by taking into account their domestic labour and relationships and by focusing upon the interpretation that women have of their jobs and technologies. In sum, technologies do not have determinate 'effects': how they are interpreted – and whether actors believe technologies to have determinate effects – is the upshot of contingent interpretations by the actors involved. Blauner actually admits as much, for as he notes: 'Objectively alienating conditions are more pronounced in women's jobs. Yet women are more protected from the self-estranging consequences of alienation because of their

more traditional attitudes, their alternative roles, and their secondary commitment to the labor force' (p. 59). The crucial point for the argument here is not
Blauner's unsubstantiated assumption that having domestic and non-domestic
labour makes alienation less critical but that it undermines any assumption about
technologically determined attitudes and behaviour. What needs to considered,
then, is how certain groups capture technologies and form an alloy of human
and non-human facets to further their own aims: management does not secure
control over car workers by dint of personality or role-based authority nor by
installing the technology of an assembly line; it secures (temporary) control by
secreting its own authority into the assembly line and persuading the workers
that managerial definitions of putative technical capabilities and limitations
are the only legitimate ones. It therefore becomes impossible to analyse the
position without focusing upon the human and technological facets simultaneously. The assembly line without management is as insecure, and indeed as
incoherent, as management without an assembly line.

Of course, Blauner's arguments do not fall perfectly into the technological
determinist category, and even if they did the weaknesses that undermine many
of his assumptions do not, in themselves, eliminate the case for technological
determinism; a poor example of a theory in action does not necessarily impover-
ish the theory, though if a theory consistently failed to provide the basis for
adequate empirical accounts we would be justified in resisting the utility of the
theory itself. Before we begin to cast further judgement on the theory let us
consider another classic account in the same genre: Ely Chinoy's *Automobile
Workers and the American Dream*.

Chinoy

Chinoy's account of car assembly workers in post-war America replicates the
kind of arguments used by Blauner: the detailed division of labour which is
inevitably associated with assembly line technology brings with it the dehu-
manizing consequences of all such technology. Ostensibly, skills are minimal,
social relations are almost non-existent, and the possibilities of self-realizing
experiences are written out of the work process by virtue of the technology.
The result is to create an entire blue-collar workforce without any intrinsic job
satisfaction whose reaction to the work is highly instrumental: work is, and
can only be in such circumstances, the means to an end. As a direct result the
workers focus upon material reward and the consumer products it can be
exchanged for; money becomes the only tenuous link between employees and
their work experience. In short, the technology prevents self-realization and forces
workers to substitute external consumption for intrinsic job satisfaction. There
are clear reflections of Marx's claims here about the alienating consequences
of work in capitalist society, and there are also ripples emanating from the general Hegelian tradition of work as *the* critical arena of life. Such implicit assumptions are, as has already been discussed in chapter 1, not unique to Chinoy

(Offe, 1985: 129–50); undoubtedly, they form the staple diet of most industrial sociology where work is the key category, such that those not in 'satisfying' paid labour are, in effect, prevented from realizing their true humanity. Chinoy, however, systematically fails to provide evidence that the actions of the assembly workers are manifestations of some distorted spirit, rather than the primary intentions of interpretative actors. That is to say, Chinoy just assumes that consumerism is the result of alienation at work, rather than examining whether alienation means the same thing to everyone or whether what counts as alienation might be the price individuals may be prepared to accept in order to pursue consumer durables or whatever else individuals prefer to do (see Du Gay, 1996). Thus cultural pursuits outside formal employment need not be regarded as a response to the shortcomings of work induced by technology or capitalism or whatever, but as a legitimate priority in their own right; in this perspective the search for identity, not the quest for meaningful paid labour, becomes the criteria of satisfaction (Moorhouse, 1984; see also Du Gay, 1996).

The significance of (non-)determinism

So what? one might very well ask. Does the possibility that work may be secondary to identity, or that identity can be constructed beyond work, make any difference to the implications of technological determinism? If the search for personal identity is not inherently focused upon paid labour, and reflects neither the technology of production in isolation, nor simply the social relations of work, then particular attitudes articulated during the experience of paid labour cannot be related directly and solely to the technology of work. Indeed, they may well be derived, to some extent at least, from sources external to the work situation. As far as this chapter is concerned, this means that we should be wary of assuming that the attitudes of employees in situations where specific forms of technology are present are technologically determined. Indeed, one might question why technology itself appears to reign so highly in research agendas: why do we appear to assume that technology *is* a critical facet of work but the climate or domestic concerns of employees are not?

This is not to say that work cannot be the focus of self-realization, nor that technology is irrelevant to the construction of attitudes; again, while social determinists would deny the latter, the fusion of social and non-social aspects poses inherent problems for either of these deterministic arguments. Neither attitudes, control structures, nor the form and use of technologies are determined, they are all elements in the negotiated order of work. As Woolgar (1989a) has demonstrated, the technologies themselves are not stable entities with fixed and determinate 'uses'. Rather the entire design and development process of a technological artefact is socially constructed to the extent that the point at which an artefact is completed is itself subject to stabilization rituals. Technological determinism is seriously flawed, then, but is social determinism, the opposite approach, flawless?

Social determinism

The opposite form of determinism is the social variety. This approach assumes that technological changes are themselves socially engineered and/or that work relationships are, in any case, derived from, and ultimately determined by, cultural and/or social aspects, rather than technological aspects (Gallie, 1978; Silverman, 1970; Goldthorpe et al., 1968, 1969). The problems of the technological determinist school were, for some authors at least, mere manifestations of a much deeper intellectual malaise. The issue at the heart of the debate was the social construction of knowledge: if the social world was qualitatively different from the natural world because of the essentially interpretative essence of social reality, then the methods and viewpoints of the natural sciences were inappropriate to examine the social world. Social reality was produced and reproduced in and through the meaningful actions of subjective individuals to the extent that there could be no direct connection between allegedly objective structures and human actions and attitudes. Rather, all social action was mediated by the subjective and interpretative understandings of individuals, and by the social relationships between individuals. In the context of technology, therefore, what was important was the mediating and subjectivist qualities of actors, not the particular form of technology – the nature of which was in any case the upshot of social constructions. In short, explaining patterns of work relationships and attitudes would be a case of examining individual interpretations and socio-cultural variables not technological variables. As Silverman, the leading authority in the action approach of the time, put it: ' "objective" factors, such as technology and market structure, are literally meaningful only in the sense that is attached by those who are concerned and the end to which they are related' (1970: 37). Ultimately, Silverman's approach moved from what may be called 'mainstream' action theory (for example, Goldthorpe et al., 1968; Bowey, 1976) towards the more radically oriented ethnomethodologists. But between conventional action theory and ethnomethodology lies the intermediate version of Berger and Luckmann (1966) for whom objective factors were socially constructed, but once constructed they became objective and therefore determining. The more radical implications of ethnomethodology, however, were first explored under the mantle of Garfinkel, and represented initially by the works of Bittner (1965) and more recently by the studies of 'scientists' at work (Latour and Woolgar, 1979; Woolgar, 1988). This relativist approach, which denies the intransitive nature of 'objects', focuses upon the shared 'accounting' procedures through which individuals attempt to make sense of the world. Thus technology itself has no objective existence independent of the accounts given to it by individuals. It is, therefore, the practical reasoning which participants engage in that is crucial; the issue of whether technology does or does not have any independent effect upon work and workers is deemed irrelevant since it implies the existence of entities that exist independently of participants' descriptions of them.

Most industrial sociology does not involve this kind of radical relativism and it has had little effective impact upon the mainstream, conventional versions of action theory. One of the most influential early studies was that of Goldthorpe et al.'s *The Affluent Worker* series, which was discussed at some length in chapter 4. The important point here is to note the limited role played by technology as an independent variable in the construction of the typical attitudes of the affluent worker. For Goldthorpe et al., technology influences the level of intrinsic job satisfaction and the patterning of social relationships, but the general attitudinal and behavioural patterns are uncontaminated by technological environments. Instead, they point to the importance of exogenous factors, of orientations and attitudes constructed outside the factory gates, for explaining action inside the factories. As they sum up their approach: 'the orientation which workers have to their employment and the manner, thus, in which they define their work situation can be regarded as *mediating* between features of the work situation objectively considered and the nature of workers' response' (1968: 182). This mediating, and externally created, set of orientations is self-evidently not the kind of argument put forward by the technological determinism of Blauner and Chinoy where attitudes directly reflect the technology of the labour process (see chapter 1 for further discussion of work orientations).

Gallie

Perhaps the most useful account based in the action tradition which focuses directly upon the plausibility of technologically determined actions and attitudes is Gallie's comparative study of French and British oil refineries (1978). Since all the refineries were owned by the same company and used technology that was comparable between the two nations (though internally differentiated), technological determinism would imply close parallels between the actions and attitudes of the two groups of employees. Yet as Gallie concludes:

> The principal conclusion of the research is that the nature of the technology per se has, at most, very little importance for the social integration of the workforce. . . . Advanced automation proved perfectly compatible with radically dissimilar levels of social integration and fundamentally different institutions of power. . . . Instead our evidence indicates the critical importance of the wider cultural and social structural patterns of specific societies for determining the nature of social interaction within the advanced sector. (1978: 295)

For example, Gallie's evidence suggests that while almost all the British workers expressed satisfaction with pay levels, two-thirds of the French workers expressed dissatisfaction; while only one strike had occurred in the British refineries between 1963 and 1972, the French refineries had been involved in twenty-four strikes; and while most of the British workers regarded their managers as technical experts, French employers were regarded as exploiters by their employees. How does Gallie explain the considerable divergences between French and British workers? Since the technology is similar, this, according to Gallie, rules itself out as an explanatory factor. In fact, Gallie argues that the difference results from three critical features: the more radical and egalitarian traditions of the French political left; the more autocratic and authoritarian approach of French management; and the more centralized and politicized essence of French wage bargaining.

This, on the face of it at least, seems to seal the fate of the determinist school and of the approach which rescues technology as an independent variable from oblivion. But are there any problems with Gallie's account? Some issues certainly seem worth considering. First, to argue that *national* cultural and political differences override any technologically determined similarities does not necessarily mean that technology is irrelevant, and, as Gallie admits: 'it may nonetheless be the case that technology has some influence within a specific national context' (1978: 300). Yet this still implies an underestimation of the significance of interpretative processes and assumes that the technological and human forces can be separated. But oil refineries are not composed of human-less oil-refining technologies any more than technology-less oil workers comprise an oil refinery. Thus, when we compare the oil refineries it is not the case that both British refineries are identical, irrespective of their different technologies, and the same applies to the French examples (the similarities are international rather than intranational, with the Kent and Dunkirk refineries having older technology and the Grangemouth and Lavera having newer technology). As an illustration we could consider the issues of satisfaction at work. Notwithstanding the conceptual and methodological terrors involved in measuring work satisfaction, it is the case that a smaller percentage of workers in the plants using old technology considered themselves 'rather happy at the idea of an interesting day in the refinery'. (The figures are: Laverna, 26 per cent; Dunkirk, 18 per cent; Kent, 34 per cent; and Grangemouth, 43 per cent: p. 86.) Now this is not to assume that technology is a determinant of attitudes because the evidence suggests that the national differences are more important than the ostensively technological. But the point here is that the levels of satisfaction are not identical within either country and, holding the country constant, they appear to correlate with technology. Since what counts as technology is an interpretative process the next step would not be to assume that technology has an independent effect but to investigate the way in which various employees adopt particular forms of explanation and description of the technology, and how such representations of the technology buttress or undermine other aspects of the Actor Network. Under this umbrella, since we ought not to distinguish between the social and the technical, it is problematic to argue that one or the other has a discrete impact. Instead we need to focus upon the way the Actor Network is brought into play and sustained.

A related case might be the printing industry. For many years this witnessed the capture and holding in place of a network of printing machines and printers, which secured their control over the labour process and provided relatively generous monetary rewards. While this is no longer the case, because the new network of new technology and management displaced the old network, it did exist alongside related machinery processes in other industries where management and 'old' technology prevailed. Without the technology neither side in either industry would have been able to maintain a network of control but neither the technology nor the social group in isolation determined the result.

In sum, I would actually concur with Gallie's assessment that technology does not *determine* organizational features or behaviour, and that social variables are important in explaining the differences between France and Britain; this does not, however, mean that technology is irrelevant.

Strategic choice

The final example of social determinism is that of 'strategic choice'. This originated in the criticism of contingency theory (see chapter 4) by Child (1972) for its determinist approach to organizational structure. Without going into detail here it will suffice to note that Child reproved contingency theory for ignoring the critical role played by powerful groups of managers who were in a position to manipulate their own environment. This political hue to the organizational process did much to bring people back in from the cold of structural variables and 'systems needs'. None the less, a stumbling block common to the action approach is the devaluation of socially constructed constraint: some actors may be more powerful than others but the choice of action is still limited by conditions and the power of others, particularly when these others have non-human and relatively intransitive form. That is to say, for example, that the explanation for particular decisions within organizations needs to extend beyond the political machinations of particular groups to encompass the way such groups appropriate and articulate forms of rhetoric about technologies. Whether management's arguments that an assembly line 'needs' to run at a particular speed or 'determines' the work organization, then, should not be discounted as irrelevant to the actual decision-making process because it actually underpins it: if workers can be persuaded by management that the technology determines the labour process, then in effect management control appears encased in steel. That it is actually contingent, that it could be otherwise, is a point of view delegitimated and suppressed by the power of managerial rhetoric.

Let us now turn to the middling theories that attempt 'to rescue the baby of technology without drowning in the technological determinists' bath water' (McLoughlin, 1990).

Socio-technical system theory

Somewhere between the polarities of technological determinism and social determinism lies a disparate amalgam of approaches that concede to both technology and socio-cultural forces variant degrees of consequence (Trist and Bamforth, 1951; Winner, 1977, 1985; Noble, 1979; Wilkinson, 1983; Rose et al., 1986; Clark et al., 1988; McLoughlin and Clark, 1988; Pfeffer, 1982). What we have, then, are a variety of different approaches to technology that suggest that 'the uses and consequences of . . . technology emerge unpredictably from complex social interactions' (Markus and Robey, 1988: 588).

One of the most significant practical advances towards this was the collaborative work of Rice (1963) and Trist and Bamforth (1951). The Tavistock approach or socio-technical system theory, as it became known, focused on the links between the technical system of production and the social system of work. The latter was essentially social not individual and, as such, technical production methods which undermined such social activity were necessarily problematic. Although a theoretical model of optimum efficiency could be construed from the technology of production, and a concomitant human model of social efficiency, the combination of social and technical systems inevitably produced a somewhat disjointed amalgam, and, equally significant, a system of disequilibrium. The trick, therefore, was to mesh the two in such a way as to develop an optimum socio-technical system that would, if separated into its component parts, not appear to be the most efficient use of resources, and not retain any long-term equilibrium. There was some disagreement about the significance of the economic system as a potential third leg of the theory, but the general position was that the economic system was a product of the functioning of the other two.

Armed with this composite approach, and an historical appreciation of the need for participatory groups, Trist and Bamforth began investigating the low levels of productivity then experienced by the National Coal Board (NCB). It had been assumed by the NCB that nationalization, new technology and the production methods familiar to assembly lines would generate huge advances in coal productivity after the war but the opposite appeared to occur. The traditional system of coal getting, the 'single place' or 'composite work role method', involved a small 'marra' group of miners (two to six) in a semi-autonomous relationship to the management: all the miners were multi-skilled, the division of labour was limited and they operated relatively independently of direct supervision. The groups themselves were self-selected and paid as a group, but to ensure the equal distribution of good coal-faces a 'cavil' or meeting of management and workers was held every three months to reorganize groups and redistribute coal-faces as necessary. Such an organization, in conjunction with the inherent dangers of mining, ensured that managerial control over the actual labour process was minimal; the system was, according to Trist and Bamforth, one of 'responsible autonomy'. However, the introduction of machine cutters and conveyers led to the reorganization of work: the 'single place' system was replaced by the 'longwall method' which, as the name implies, involved a continuous face of coal to be cut by up to fifty miners in a triple shift system: the division of labour was expanded, managerial control was increased and many miners were forced to specialize in one particular facet of mining. The result was not an enormous expansion in productivity but an explosion of wage bargaining, absenteeism and a collapse of morale.

However, one pit had been experimenting with ways of saving some of the benefits of the traditional system of coal getting in a 'composite longwall method' and Bamforth and Trist's research was conducted at the same pit. In the new system the self-selected group was reintroduced, albeit at a much larger level (around twenty-five members), and the division of labour, which was itself restricted, was also the subject of group decision. The result was not just the restoration of morale but the advance of productivity and evidence for the new theoretical approach: socio-technical systems. According to Trist and Bamforth the problems of the longwall system were the result of the disjunction between the technological system and the social system. It may have been the case that an assembly line method of production was *technically* the most efficient but the destruction of the traditional social system and the shaping of the new system to the determining mould of the technology induced severe social problems that became translated as productivity problems.

Two major theoretical conclusions were drawn. First, that the social and technical systems had to be jointly optimized, thereby eliminating at a stroke the pretensions of the technical determinists. Where organizational problems occurred was in the misfit between the characteristics and requirements of the technological system and those of the associated social system. Thus: 'the technological demands place limits on the type of work organization possible, but the work organization has social, psychological properties of its own that are independent of the technology' (quoted in Elliott, 1980). As Heller more recently argued, the problems occur when there is 'an improper application of the technological imperative' (1987: 23). In effect, the issue is that technology does not determine the social system but provides for 'options', that is 'choices based on particular contingencies' which may reconsider the 'impact of technology on people' (1987: 24–5). Given the significance of the interpretative approach to both social *and* technical issues it is evident that the socio-technical approach is gravely weakened by its assumption that technology still has certain determinate needs and objective 'effects' which necessarily constrain the appropriate social system. From the interpretative viewpoint it is the contingent interpretation of technologies and their putative constraints and capabilities which is crucial for explaining the relationships to humans. Not only does the technology not determine anything, but the entire system is permanently threatened by instability: no naturally equilibriating organizational systems exist. Heller is right to deny the determinism of technology but to retain the idea that technology still has independent effects is to underestimate the significance of the interpretative component of human–technology interaction.

This also has implications for critics of 'participationists' such as Beirne and Ramsay (1988), for whom even involvement in the (re)design of jobs is of marginal significance and: 'The further into the (design and implementation) process one gets, the more time, money and solidifying thought have already gone into rigidifying the system, and the more residual any participative influences must become' (p. 217). The implication, then, is that managerial control can be built into the technical system through the design and implementation process in an unproblematic way. The point is not that this is irrelevant but that the use of any technology is a contingent issue and is not determined by the design or implementation process. If managerial control could be achieved through monopolizing the design and implementation process (either overtly or through some deceptive scheme of putative participation) then management would be a considerably less equivocal and ambiguous task than it actually is. Moreover, if managerial control could be secured through a duplicitous but invisible mechanism such as semi-autonomous work groups (SAWGs), one wonders why many managers continue to operate the crude and mechanistic forms of control currently in service today.

The second major conclusion of Trist and Bamforth in particular and the Tavistock group in general was that semi-autonomous groups of workers provided the best structure for maintaining morale, defusing interpersonal frictions and therefore increasing productivity. The ultimate use of many of these ideas may have been overtly managerialist and productivist but it would seem fair to argue that the post-war reconstruction of *homo gregarious* was also an attempt to institutionalize the ideals of justice and equity at work that so many had just died for in the Second World War (see Rose, 1989: 92–3).

After the coal-mining study, which was not adopted by the National Coal Board nor supported by the miners' union after a switch to national pay bargaining, a sequence of others was undertaken by the Tavistock researchers. From the study of weaving sheds in Ahmadabad, India (Rice, 1958), it was argued that work ought to involve interdependent tasks and interdependent work groups. From the work in the Norwegian industrial democracy project (Emery and Thorsrud, 1964; Thorsrud et al., 1976), it was argued that optimum work organization would imply: job variety, group organization, worker involvement in decision-making, the potential for self-improvement, and some self-evident relationship between jobs and the outside world (see Kelly, 1982 for a useful review).

Whatever the intentions of the Tavistock theorists, their impact, at least in Britain, has been limited. Neither the NCB nor any other large industrial concern adopted the ideas. Yet they have had some success elsewhere, particularly in Sweden, Norway and Canada where the initial ideas have now merged into the Quality of Working Life movement that seeks to provide the kind of work experiences for all that are currently the property of the few (Sanderson and Stapenhurst, 1979; Witte, 1980; Zwerdling, 1978). Each have their own forms of participatory work organizations, and arguably the participatory form ranges from the most conservative, in terms of quality circles (Littler, 1985; Robson, 1982; Batstone, 1988a) which are primarily concerned with expanding forms of consultation, through to the radical end, probably the best-known examples of which are the semi-autonomous work groups, some of which have consciously attempted to redesign technology in line with the social aspects of production.

Designer technology

Winner's (1977, 1985) argument, that 'technical things have political qualities' is an interesting example of the '**designer technology**' approach. It starts out as an apparent emergent argument but is ultimately a form of technological determinism (1985: 26). What Winner is anxious to attack is the assumption that technology is neutral and, therefore, that the impact and importance of technology depend upon the use we put it to. In the context of this debate we could represent this argument, which Winner considers to be naive, as the assumption that the technology of the assembly line need not lead to repetitious and alienating work experiences. Part of the explanation for the rise of this naive view, in Winner's mind, is the distaste for technological determinism: since it is not the case that social developments are driven by technological developments, it has become a commonplace to assume that technology has no impact in and of itself. Rather, technology is socially constructed. Yet this underlines their inherently political nature, for if technology is not the product of auto-nomous creation then it must become entrammelled in the political ribbons of its designers and users; and it almost certainly carries with it the unintended consequences that so often manifest themselves. One of Winner's own examples (1985) relates how the New York architect Robert Moses designed bridges so low that buses, and therefore the black and poorer white sections of New York, could not gain access to Jones Beach on the south side of Long Island. What appears, therefore, to be the result of 'neutral' technological developments actually embodies the political preferences of the designer. Here, technological determinism reappears as 'designer determinism': control over the design and construction process of the artefact ensures the required result – or does it?

Contrary to the implications of 'designer determinism' – whether the poor are kept away from Jones Beach, and if they are whether that is determined by Moses's low bridges or something else – is also open to interpretation (Woolgar, 1990). At its most banal one might want to question *whether* the poor were deterred, and if they were *what* deterred them? Might it be that they had no desire to go there, or that the bridges were only interpreted as a minor impedi-ment in a whole system or network of human and non-human obstacles? I might not end up at the Queen's Garden Party this year but it will not be just because the gates will deter me. Contrary to Winner's assumption, and others of 'technicist' inclinations, the preferences of designers, makers and users do not lead in any unmediated way to particular outcomes, for the position and power of current users mediate between design and outcome and are channelled in part by the unintended consequences of social life. What is crucial, then, is to retain the ambiguity of technology in the sense that organizations and social relations are determined neither by technology nor by social agency; organ-izations are the contingent result of a permanently unstable network of human and non-human actors. Technology and its properties are not fixed or deter-minate but contingent.

Political technology

This is reflected in analyses that consider the relationship between gender and technology. Since this general approach incorporates the politics of tech-nology it also supports notions of gendered technology. Such concerns range from rescuing the role of women in the field of technological invention (Karpf, 1987) through to the links between technology and male domination on the shopfloor. Perhaps the clearest example of the latter is Cockburn's (1983a) study of the British printing industry where, for example, the creation and retention of 50 lb printing blocks was regarded as effective in preventing women from entering the hand compositors' craft. Even the linotype machine, introduced towards the end of the nineteenth century, which eliminated many of the skills of hand compositing, failed to open up the craft to women as shopfloor con-trol by male trade unionists prevented the entry of women. A similar pattern emerges in studies on new technology. In theory the expansion of keyboard skills through word processing and computer-based developments might be considered as providing an opportunity for women to break free from their subordinate position within offices and factories, but most of the case studies suggest that technological advance tends to buttress or even exacerbate gender-based discrimination (Barker and Downing, 1980; Liff, 1988; Webster, 1990; Grint and Gill, 1995). One area of overtly patriarchal dominance where women have made some headway, despite the predominance of technology normally associated with men, is engineering. Yet the efforts of the WISE campaign (Women into Science and Engineering) still face enormous difficulties in persuading women to take up such a challenge and persuading men to cease discriminating against women in general and female scientists and engineers in particular (Harding (ed.), 1986). In all these cases the crucial explanations illuminate the patriarchal, and therefore political, skin of technology. However, the texture of the skin is not a fixed feature: to continue the animal analogy, it is an unfortunate consequence for many animals that their skin can be reshaped to a variety of human-related forms.

Wilkinson's (1983) case studies, while not concerned with issues of gender, detail the introduction of new technology in a variety of work situations. He not only attacks the 'impacts of innovation' or determinist approaches for their failure to account for variable adoptions and effects of technology, but suggests that technical features constrain but do not determine the possible options open to management. Particularly relevant for this form of approach is the '**technicist**' notion that, irrespective of the social construction of technology, once the technology is constructed its technical capacity is to a large extent inscribed or encased into its fabric such that it operates as an independent variable. This, nevertheless, is still subject to two conditional assumptions: first, that the technology remains political; second, that its effects are still mediated by social action, structures and unintended consequences.

Among the recent attempts to articulate views bearing some resemblance to this ideal have been those of Rose et al. (1986), Clark et al. (1988), McLoughlin and Clark (1988) and McLoughlin (1997). Their studies of technological change in the telecommunications industry suggests that one form of exchange equipment facilitates individual working patterns while another lends itself more to team approaches, and that the relative impact of technological and social forces tends to alter the further away individuals are from the immediate work task. Technology in this framework becomes conceptualized as politically impregnated, as historically encumbered and as one among many potentially independent variables. But 'once the stages leading to the choice of a particular system are accomplished, then social choices become frozen in a given technology' (Clark et al., 1988: 32). This approach, I would suggest, which limits the social aspects of technology to the design process, underestimates the significance of the alloyed nature of technology. Inasmuch as technology embodies social aspects it is not a stable and determinate object (albeit one with political preferences inscribed into it), but an unstable and indeterminate artefact whose precise significance is negotiated but never settled. For example, telephone systems themselves were used originally to broadcast concert music and it was not axiomatic that the telephone would first be restricted primarily to a two-way personal communication system and now adopted to transmit digital communications between computers (Finnegan and Heap, 1988). Its use originally, and indeed its use now, was and is the result of negotiations, not determinations derived from the embodied politics of the artefact.

Actor networks and contingent technology

Finally, let me briefly run back through the actor network model (see chapter 4 for a longer review) which has been adopted principally as a way of explaining the development and stabilization of forms of technology. Fundamentally, the approach suggests that power depends upon the construction and maintenance of a network of actors; these networks involve both human and non-human 'actors' and we should not distinguish between human and non-human elements but should talk instead of the 'heterogeneous entities that constitute a network' (Bijker et al., 1987: 11). That is, we should consider the unity of human and non-human actors in terms of a 'seamless web' as Hughes (1979) calls it or 'heterogeneous engineering' in Law's (1986) case. Actor networks do not automatically maintain themselves, even though a viable method of extending the time span of a network is to inscribe it into material form. Rather, they, and their associated technologies, are inherently contingent and require constant reproduction and reaffirmation by the actors involved. For example, one of the ways the East German state managed to stem the haemorrhage of its population to the West in the 1950s was by building the Berlin Wall and persuading its citizens that the system was permanent and beyond challenge. This actor network linking the Communist Party, the armed forces, the Wall and associated border fences, and a proliferation of bureaucratic controls, was indeed interpreted by many as impermeable and its power appeared complete. The point that the actor network remained so solid for almost four decades but collapsed within a four-month spell in 1989–90 highlights the significance of the interpretative act: neither the political technology of the Wall nor the 'objective' power of the communist regime determined the state of East German society. When a large proportion of the population's interpretation of the power of that network altered so did the 'reality'.

In the next section I want to pursue the analysis of technology at work by considering one archetypal form, the assembly line, in some detail. I will also assess the current proclamations of its untimely death at the hands of new technologies represented in post-Fordism.

Flexible specialization, Fordism, neo-Fordism and post-Fordism

Fordism

Although the assembly line is probably most closely associated with Chaplin's film *Modern Times* (1936), its roots actually lie in the Chicago meat industry of the 1890s. But the first major assembly line production system was Ford's

Detroit plant, set up in 1913. As with the earliest factories (see chapter 2), the original assembly line technology was not innovative at all. What was new was the organizational development in which the work was brought by a conveyor belt to the worker so the speed of task completion could be controlled by management through the technology itself (Gartman, 1979). Note again that the Detroit plant would not have been viable without the juxtaposition of Ford's managerial style and the technology. In conjunction with these organizational changes the division of labour was radically expanded along the lines proposed by individuals like Taylor. Whatever the success of Taylorist assembly line production, there were three inherent, and in some ways ironic, limitations inscribed into the very system itself: variable consumer demand, the counter-productive effects upon employees, and declining improvements to marginal efficiency. As far as Taylor and Ford were concerned the system appeared to be a virtuous circle: first, as long as consumers wanted, or more probably could be persuaded, to buy invariant products, represented most typically by Ford's single-colour single-model mass-produced model T, then assembly lines were ideal. They took a long time to set up and were expensive in technological investment which took advantage of the very high division of labour and associated cheap labour, but once running they appeared to churn out identikit products *ad infinitum*. Second, the assumption was that since workers were only really motivated by high wages then providing startlingly high wages would solve all labour problems associated with the deskilling and degradation of jobs so clearly described by Braverman. Third, as long as a scientific approach to work organization was adopted gigantic improvements in technical efficiency were feasible.

However, Ford found to his own cost that the division of labour, and what his employees regarded as the alienating conditions associated with such a production method, took a heavy toll on employee morale: labour turnover rate rose to 380 per cent in 1913 and the revolutionary Industrial Workers of the World moved in to organize the workers. Ford's response was radical: wages leaped up to the magic 'five-dollar day' in 1914, though even this ultimately failed to provide a permanent solution to labour problems. A second problem was that if work processes could be scientifically assessed and improved then there was a finite limit to, or at least a declining return from, the extent to which time and motion studies etc. could increase productivity. Third, **'Fordism'**, as this method of mass production for a mass market became known, also had limitations in so far as consumer demand was concerned: it was all very well persuading everyone to buy a car or even two, but a saturated market would require some form of dehydration if it was not to choke off demand and hence production and profit.

One part of the solution was and still is to stimulate variable demand, but variable demand requires variable production systems – hence the adoption of new technology to provide a quicker response to consumer demand and to generate different consumer demands. This new technology also required a more flexible and probably, therefore, a more skilled workforce. Again, what we have is a technological and a social form which are interdependent: flexible technology with an inflexible workforce does not lead to flexible production.

Neo-Fordism

Neo-Fordism is often regarded as representing the alternative production system in which the stultifying rigidities of Fordism were eased apart to allow some degree of flexible production using new technologies to expand the range of products without modifying the tight managerial control structures (Sabel, 1982; Smith, 1989). However, this neo-Fordist solution to the problems of Fordism may be a transient one, or it may be a solution for particular forms of work in particular regions at particular times. After all, it is far from clear, and actually very doubtful, whether we can define all pre-neo-Fordist production methods as Fordist, hence it is not axiomatic either that neo-Fordism should be regarded as a solution to pre-existing problems or that it is prevalent in itself. Even where it does exist, and it is certainly the case that neo-Fordist calls for 'flexibility' and 'quality' are now vogue terms of the lexicon of business, there are many who doubt that neo-Fordism is the solution to the problem. For these people the problems lie much deeper than simply at the level of technology and reflect rather the very nature of Fordism as an organizational form, replete with its large-scale and cumbersome bureaucracies, its over-concentrated control structures and its over-centralized decision-making.

Post-Fordism and flexible specialization

The apparent long-term solution to the assembly line blues, **post-Fordism** or **flexible specialization,** implies that at the level of the organization it is necessary to decentralize, to become more flexible and to specialize. The solution at the level of the workplace is to do away with the assembly line, to increase the skill levels and flexibility of the workforce, to provide team work structures, and to seek out specialized niche markets for high quality, high value products and services. Flexibility, then, is a critical component of the new models of working technology, but flexibility itself tends to combine two rather different forms: numerical/external flexibility and functional/internal flexibility (Atkinson, 1985; Streek, 1987). The former couplet refers to a company's ability to adjust labour supply to product demand and relates to the use of internal and external labour markets in association with the polarizing of labour use, as critical, and thus privileged 'core', workers are divorced from non-critical and hence disadvantaged 'peripheral' workers. The latter couplet, of functional/internal flexibility, refers to the company's ability to assign work irrespective of the labour involved: the more multiskilled or polyvalent the workforce is, and the more it is itinerant, that is free from attachments to particular job, task or area territories, the more flexible labour is.

Post-Fordism or 'flexible specialization', which implies the use of new technologies to produce smaller batch, 'customized' products in contrast to the standardized products of the first two-thirds of the twentieth century, first made its physical appearance in the late 1960s and its academic debut at the hands of Piore and Sabel (1984), though the same argument had been made by Reich

(1983) slightly earlier under the term 'flexible system'. Whatever the term used, the notion marks the point of change both from 'Fordism' and 'neo-Fordism'. Post-Fordism or flexible specialization represents a rather ungainly mixture of craft-based work using new technologies within specific politico-industrial regions (such as the Tuscany region of Italy), combined with the more generalized adoption of new technologies within mass-production industries to tailor products much closer to particular niches within the market. Thus the ultimate destination of this apparent transition between production systems is one which combines the flexible worker (polyvalent and itinerant) and the flexible production method (computer assisted, robotized etc.), both geared towards the flexible demands of the modern consumer.

As ever, there is a considerable degree of confusion and overlap between different terms involved in the debates but I shall retain the distinctions set out above: Fordism represents the archetypal assembly line production system with extensive division of labour and isolated workers using limited skills; neo-Fordism represents a transitional form in which workers are required to become flexible through the use of multiple skills and multiple tasks; post-Fordism, or flexible specialization, occurs when these multiply-skilled and flexible workers are engaged in production systems which depend upon teamworking rather than isolated individuals, and involve a reduction in the division of labour and some flattening of hierarchical authority, that is, devolved responsibility for decision-making (e.g. semi-autonomous work groups). The division between neo-Fordism and post-Fordism extends beyond the workplace to encompass producer–customer relations, such that neo-Fordism is still premised upon Fordist mass production for international mass markets, whereas post-Fordism implies a large degree of product specialization for specialized, and often localized, markets.

Accounting for change

As so often appears to happen, the roots of these changes do not actually lie within the last decade but much deeper. For example, the quest to *develop* the consumption of manufactured artefacts, rather than rationalize the production process as Taylor suggested or simply *respond* to consumer demands, has a history that stretches back at least over fifty years just in the car manufacturing industry (Veblen, 1904; Sloan, 1965; Robins and Webster, 1989; Harvey, 1989: 126).

For example, just before the outbreak of the Second World War the British car producers (Morris, Austin, Ford, Vauxhall, Rootes and Standard) produced almost four times as many models as the American producers, but they exported twelve times less (Pagnamenta and Overy, 1984: 227). Unless we assume that British consumers were fifty years ahead of their time in terms of expanding consumer choice it is probably safer to assert that the market is actively created by producers rather than producers simply responding to consumer demand. That is not to deny the influence of the consumer but it is to rescue the significance of producer-generated consumer demand from the dustbin of preflexible production systems.

Relatedly, Smith et al.'s (1989) historical review of Cadbury's suggests that while flexibility of labour is a contemporary managerial ideal, there is little or no attempt to imbue labour with greater skills nor to extend the product range in line with apparently more sophisticated consumer demand. Yet Smith's own claim that the flexible specialization thesis is a variant of technological determinism is misplaced since Piore and Sabel (1984) are quite specific that product markets not technological determinism are at the centre of the paradigm shift. Nor does Smith's (1989) review of mass production in the food industry confirm that mass producers everywhere are cutting products and concentrating on a small number of items; they may be in food production but a glance through car magazines should be enough to persuade anyone that a multiplicity of options in body shape, engine size and performance, options packs, colours, ABS brakes, power steering, four wheel drive, four wheel steering etc., is the current trend. Perhaps the point is that different industries operate in quite different ways and a sectoral analysis is required. Similarly, Harvey (1989: 156) notes the declining half-life of products as neo-Fordist methods lock into rapidly changing fashions. Again, we have to be careful here. Motor cars have had their life expectancy increased considerably recently through the greater use of galvanized steel and plastics etc.: the era of the rust-bucket in five years is gradually being replaced by the 'lifetime guarantee' already provided by Volvo, for example, using post-Fordist production techniques associated with semi-autonomous work groups. What we have, then, is not the replacement of one form of production by another but the development of parallel and juxtaposed systems operating for different kinds of market. Diversity not uniformity is the more likely pattern because the market system is anarchic, because labour is recalcitrant and unpredictable, and because the Actor Network is unstable. Indeed, it is because capitalism is inherently unstable that such diversity is typical and it is this very diversity which makes attempts to straitjacket the entire corpus into one pattern, Fordist, neo-Fordist or whatever, such a dubious procedure: what appears to be happening in one place at a particular time need not be read off from alterations in another place at the same time.

The three models, in so far as they are discrete, are often assumed to be evolutionary in pattern, with Fordism predominating until the late 1960s and early 1970s since when neo-Fordist inroads have been made which are themselves now being challenged by the post-Fordist approaches. Yet it has never been adequately demonstrated that Fordist technologies and organizational methods were ever predominant, and some countries, such as Sweden and Japan in particular, have experimented with non-Fordist methods for many years. As argued in chapter 2 many British unions have a pre-Fordist tradition of single skills (monovalence) and demarcated territories (territoriality) which have protected them from the vicissitudes of managerial rationalization but tended to make British companies less flexible than, for example, the Japanese workforce. In fact, the Japanese system of sub-contracting adds another dimension to the flexible firm since sub-contracting allows fluctuations in demand to be displaced and dispersed away from the core firm towards its peripheral satellites.

As the economy and industrial organization become progressively less stable and more dynamic, so, it is alleged, firms which are more flexible in a variety of ways will be better placed to ride out the economic storm.

The displacing strategy also implies that Fordist, neo-Fordist and post-Fordist models of work may continue in parallel form. Thus, the core groups and processes may develop multiple skills and flexible non-assembly-line production methods, possible in semi-autonomous work groups, while the periphery continues with the Fordist system. Certainly a dualist approach combining core and periphery groups has some support (Goldthorpe, 1984a; Harrison and Bluestone, 1988). But what may appear to be a rational and strategic long-term plan at the level of the economy more probably involves individual firms in *ad hoc* and very variable approaches to such a dualist strategy, at least in Britain (Batstone and Gourlay, 1986; Batstone et al., 1987). Indeed, one might question the extent to which concern for flexibility in any form has been translated into effective procedures and practices: all enterprises may be interested in achieving a polyvalent, non-territorial and committed workforce producing high-quality products and services – but assertions of good intentions are not evidence of achievement.

The humanitarian implications of taking assembly lines out of commission and replacing them with more flexible, skill-oriented and computer-aided production systems are, however, supported by Piore and Sabel (1984), Reich (1983), Katz and Sabel (1985) and Piore (1986), who relate the changes directly to the fragmentation of the product market, and relate the work process changes to a wider decentralized and generally fragmenting socio-economic system. Of course the flexibility allegedly induced by neo-Fordism is not simply related to the freeing of labour restrictions in the form of demarcation disputes etc. Indeed, a complete corpus of literature has sprung up to contest the claims about the way firms have developed their labour market through expanding reliance upon peripheral labour in secondary labour markets (see chapters 7 and 9). Thus most of the recent growth in jobs in Britain has been in temporary or part-time work, primarily filled by women (see Hakim, 1990 for a review of core-periphery arguments).

It is worth noting just how such buzzwords as Fordism and 'managerial control' take on a life of their own within the pages of academic and business texts: for labour process theorists, managerial control appeared to be the quintessence of all capitalism to the extent that profits appeared to be subordinate to managerial control over the labour process. Chapter 5 argues that the opposite is the case, that is that control over the labour process is subordinate to profit-making, and the development of new working practices such as the semi-autonomous work groups in several Volvo plants could be taken as an example of both post-Fordism and the subordination of control to profit. For adherents to labour process approaches the critical question is: what do such technological and organizational developments imply for managerial control over labour and the labour process? By definition, since the exploitation of labour can only be increased by the securement of more effective mechanisms of labour control, all such developments must be simply more sophisticated versions of control, as indeed are all aspects of neo-human relations or neo-Fordism. This approach to human labour, what Doray (1988) calls 'a rational madness', axiomatically indicates that labour is inherently problematic and in consequent need of coercive control by management (Kern and Schumann, 1987).

It is not coincidental, as discussed in chapters 2 and 4, that where systems of labour regulation are enacted which are premised upon recalcitrant labour the end result is often to generate precisely this kind of reaction among the workforce. If one of the causes of factory development was the lack of control over homeworkers then the organization of the initial factory was likely to embody strict coercive routines. The disciplinary mechanisms of nineteenth-century factories are not, however, necessarily the most rational for a situation where employees do not have an alternative method of work, and have already become accustomed to, if not exactly compliant with, forms of hierarchical authority. Concomitantly, when competition increases and flexibility of demand in the product market requires an equivalent flexibility within the labour market, that is a co-operative rather than an obdurate workforce, such Fordist systems become increasingly ineffective and inefficient. The problem, however, is that switching from one form of production to another is not simply a question of replacing the technology and altering the organizational fabric. Technologies of production incorporate histories, and one such as Fordism embodies the very traces of coercion and distrust that the more flexible systems attempt to transcend. Thus any company which announces that 'as from tomorrow morning everything will be different' is unlikely to impress a workforce with generations of experience that suggests nothing changes expect the siren calls of management.

Alternatives and responsibilities

This does not mean that Taylorist or Fordist methods were the only ones appropriate for the first two-thirds of the twentieth century, but they are no longer. Instead there are always alternatives available, as the Japanese systems of flexible working have shown since their industrialization in the nineteenth century: a pre-Fordist post-Fordism, one might say. But once systems are in place they accumulate patterns of routine and institutional privilege that make it increasingly difficult to change them. As Olson (1982) has argued, the longer an organizational system survives, the more sclerotic it becomes as privileged agents and groups surround themselves with material and symbolic forms of protection. Only when such organizations or systems are shocked into re-organization, through war, revolution or plummeting membership or profits etc., are they in a position to change radically. In effect, then, Fordist technologies and their associated organizations of managers and trade unions grounded in the extreme divisions of labour are all locked together in the corporate system, and in such circumstances the intractable nature of Fordism becomes more understandable. Moreover, since trade unions, in Britain particularly, have conventionally tended to take a reactive stance towards management they have little experience or interest in work organization restructuring. The likely result therefore, at least where Fordist regimes exist and are being reconstructed, will be the construction of new working practices which further the objectives of capital without building in various practices to protect labour. If unions take no proactive role in designing work and its associated technology, no responsibility for ensuring the work practices operate properly, and are not the first point of reference for semi-autonomous work groups, it is not difficult to see that they may well find themselves, rather than their members, at the periphery of whatever post-Fordist developments might occur.

What semi-autonomous work groups and the like embody are methods of increasing profits and/or efficiency by increasing worker autonomy from management. Now self-evidently not all movements in this direction will be successful, nor will all enterprises want to go in this direction, but then neither are they forced into the opposite direction of decreased worker autonomy mirrored in Braverman's analysis. Nor, and this point is critical, need we assume that management is enamoured of production methods such as semi-autonomous work groups. Where worker autonomy is increased, albeit in the interests of, and dependent upon, higher productivity and profits, then we may well expect to discover resistance from line managers whose status, power and possibly even job security, are threatened by such developments. The crucial issue is that most first- and middle-level managers probably derive little direct material or symbolic benefits from this form of production but this may be considerably less important to senior managers, board members and shareholders than increased profitability. Some managers may be interested in managerial control, but they are a very heterogeneous group (Reed, 1989), and anyway, capitalism is driven by the quest for profits not the quest for managerial control.

The general argument also implies that flexibility is itself a disparate approach with some forms of work organization and their associated technologies, such as semi-autonomous work groups, considerably more autonomous and participative than others. Workers who are polyvalent can just as easily find themselves doing a number of different forms of work they regard as tedious without any increase in skill or rewards, as they may find themselves within jobs perceived as relatively meaningful, skilled and rewarded; the choices are constructed and executed through the Actor Network of human and non-human forms, they are not technically determined. This also implies that technical developments or social developments are unlikely, in and of themselves, to alter the nature of relations at work – in short, that class, gender and ethnic relations are, *ceteris paribus*, likely to remain and possibly even become strengthened under newer production systems (Walby, 1989; Jenson, 1989). Thus women may tend to make up the majority of any peripheralized work force while men continue to monopolize what counts as skilled work.

Defining 'reality'

The emphasis on definition should also alert us to the social construction of categories like neo-Fordism etc. For the current band of neologist disciples it would seem that the reverential repetition of 'neo-Fordism' or 'flexibility' is endowed with magical properties: since the terms are so prevalent among the academic and business literature surely this merely reflects the explosion of interest among business enterprise? I have severe reservations about this: most businesses appear to be much less coherently structured than such concepts imply and much more intractable than business consultants might admit. We cannot easily resolve the problems by reference to the empirical data since so little exists and since the criteria by which flexible specialization is deemed to exist are inherently flexible. No study has yet marshalled sufficient evidence to show that the movement towards flexibility is an inevitable and universal process but then there were few attempts to do the same for Fordism either. For example, even those forms of work which we might categorize as most clearly Fordist, such as the assembly of cars, seldom involves a majority of the workforce actually on the assembly line itself (Marsden et al., 1985: 68–70). It is quite plausible, then, to argue that within the archetypal Fordist organization, only a minority of the workforce is subject to Fordist systems of labour control. This is important because so much of the debate is constructed around the polarizing axis of Fordism – neo-Fordism and post-Fordism. Yet if the most Fordist of industries neither represents the typical industry of its time, nor do a majority of its own workers operate under Fordist conditions, then we have to ask whether the debate should remain constrained by an axis that is simply atypical. Once we reject the basis of the debate, that is once we move beyond such a simplistic and erroneous axis of work organizations, then we can begin to assess where new patterns of work fit in. If we do not have to situate them either as Fordist, neo-Fordist or post-Fordist then we have freed ourselves from the tyranny of what may turn out to be a false, or at least, partial, typology. It may be simpler to operate *as if* the history of production could be compressed into one of three moulds but if the excess extruding from the moulds is greater than the material within the moulds then we should think about changing their size and shape.

As far as industrial production is concerned the debate over flexibility tends to concentrate upon the impact of skills. Since Taylor the orthodoxy, promulgated by Braverman among others, has been that only through greater extension of the division of labour will the economies of scale, the cheapening and controlling of labour, and the specialization of skills be achieved. However, the advocates of flexible specialization (such as Sabel and Piore), which involves inverting the division of labour, decentralizing production and seeking higher value-added products, have argued not merely that Taylor and Braverman were wrong in their belief that production could not be organized in any other way, but that the flexible specialization path offered up the opportunity to restore dignity and control to the workforce. Thus the interpretative position on flexibility and Fordism often expresses more fundamental political paradigms. For those supporting the flexibility option it seems that new market forces, new technology and the self-limiting features of Fordism have offered up the opportunity to restructure work patterns in quite radical ways (Mathews, 1989). For those who disavow the appearance of flexibility and who retain the Fordist viewpoint, albeit with neo-Fordist trappings, the changes are either irrelevant or merely another sequence in capitalism's permanent quest for profits. Naturally, not all who accept the Fordist or flexibilist ideas are Marxists or pluralists, respectively; there are many radicals and conservatives in both camps but nevertheless the tendency has been for the debaters to split along the radical/pluralist divide. A rather different approach is encapsulated by the so-called regulation approach.

The regulation school

The 'regulation school' (Aglietta, 1979; De Vroey, 1984) sought out the links between various facets of capitalism, including norms, habits and laws etc. (Lipietz, 1987), in order to analyse its patterns of stability or regulation. Where the social relations of the labour process were deemed 'appropriate' for the technology involved, which, in turn, conformed to the consumption patterns and social institutions, then the fabric of the whole network was held secure through this symmetrical and symbiotic form of regulation or 'regimes of accumulation' (Lipietz, 1987).

> A regime of accumulation describes the stabilization over a long period of the allocation of the net product between consumption and accumulation; it implies some correspondence between the transformation of both the conditions of production and the conditions of reproduction of wage earners. A particular system of accumulation can exist because its schema of reproduction is coherent. (quoted in Harvey, 1989: 121)

Neo-Fordism was one such regime, deriving from the accumulating problems of Fordism in different levels of society. At the national economic level most capitalist countries ran into severe economic, and particularly monetary, problems in the early 1970s as inflation began to eat away at confidence and material wealth, and the various welfare systems looked increasingly precarious and deeply implicated in problems facing the capitalist states. At the level of the shop floor there were different manifestations of the same problem, especially increasing alienation among the workforce and the limitations of monovalent and territorial employees. These limitations are, under the regulation approach, derived not so much from the failings of the Fordist system as from the successes. Taylorist quests for the most systematic and scientific way of ensuring production have been followed to the extent that little more can be achieved by pursuit of such strategies: they are, so the theory goes, already as efficient as possible.

Harvey (1989) argues that Fordism failed to penetrate deeply into capitalism between the wars because it was so dependent upon the development of a new worker whose concerns were pecuniary and externally directed, and because Fordism was premised upon a level of stability and general affluence that did not arrive until the end of the Second World War. Certainly the New Deal, and the equivalent but radically reactionary policies in Germany and Italy, had been developed to transcend the problems of capitalist regulation during

the 1930s, but only the post-war boom provided the basis for the Fordist system of regulation, which also included a self-disciplining mechanism provided
by the trade unions (1989: 125–34). This, in itself, may seem paradoxical since
the capitalists of most nations had shown little enthusiasm for the regulatory
value of unions. Indeed, the argument bears more than a passing resemblance
to functionalist Marxist accounts through which all manner of phenomena that
appear to disrupt the system of accumulation within capitalism are apparently
essential to its long-term stability. Nevertheless, the significance of a regulation
approach is that it highlights the symmetry between production and consumption: mass production delivers and depends upon mass consumption.

Quite by what criteria we judge a culture or production system to be 'mass'
as opposed to 'individualist' is never clear. Certainly consumption patterns change,
but this is a necessary corollary of a successful capitalist system of production
and consumption and entails little about the direction in which it changes. After
all, to take a paltry but perhaps symbolic example, the arrival of the mobile
phone, the electronic organizer and its predecessor, the personal organizer, may
originally have been a mark of individualism but it is those without such con-
traptions that appear to be the individualists now. Products may be marketed
as individualizing but profits are generated by massaging the consumers' individualism so that it exactly replicates as many other individualists as possible.
Equally important, we have to question the assumption that the changes which
have occurred actually do represent a radical break with previous production
and consumption systems. As Kumar (1978) points out, the belief that a particular period marks out a radical discontinuity from the past is hardly new,
with the assumption that automation marked a qualitative new era in the early
1960s being just one in a long line.

The response to the problems of Fordism was also at different levels. States
began to cut back on their welfare systems and to introduce market forces into
all areas of public institutions. At the level of the firm and economic sector,
new products, new services and new methods of production were all attempted;
some of which involved relatively minor adaptations of the labour process to
suit the new technologies: job enrichment, quality circles and semi-autonomous
work groups became popular, though for the regulation schools' approach these
were merely attempts to patch up and reinvigorate the capitalist system of control rather than qualitative advances towards more humane conditions of work
(Palloix, 1976; Coriat, 1980). Also important were heavy and repeated doses
of market discipline for the labour force to induce some degree of flexibility
as well as shaking out labour itself through mass unemployment.

None of this means that nothing is new. The development of information
technologies and the closer integration of financial markets through the compression of time and space are self-evident alterations to the prior system, though
the undermining of national sovereignty and the ever-closer networking of
national economies, especially through integrated systems of financial credit,
are probably more significant than the generation of new forms of profitable
enterprise (Harvey, 1989; Held, 1989). What is important is to avoid the tidal
wave arguments of Sabel and Piore without resorting to the Canute-like position represented by Pollert (1988). The point is not that everything has changed

or that nothing has changed but that capitalism is inherently dynamic and fragmented in make-up. Thus Fordist, neo-Fordist, and even an occasional post-Fordist technique, exist side by side, sometimes within the same product market such as motor cars. This clearly poses problems for regulation theory, which suggests patterns of symmetry between production and consumption, labour control and public policy. But the reality is never likely to be one where symmetry exists and always more likely to manifest disharmony, tension and contradiction in conjunction with their opposites. Where these work patterns and problems have led to on a global scale is the focus of the final chapter.

Summary

This chapter has sought to illustrate two separate aspects of working technology: the theoretical problems of monistic accounts of technology at work and an explanation and critique of the current trend towards post-Fordism. I shall now summarize the theoretical approaches not by regurgitating the essence of each of the viewpoints considered but by linking the alternatives to the perennial debate on human agency reconstructed through a theatrical metaphor. The issue of technology and its importance for work and organizational change mirrors a much larger concern within social science on the importance that should be attached to human agency in any explanatory framework. In many ways the very essence of sociology is an attempt to grapple with this knotty conundrum: do people choose their circumstances or are they chosen for them? Are we simply players on a stage mechanically reproducing our various roles or is the performance really developed in a much more unpredictable manner through the interpretative skills of the actors? Relatedly, what part do the technical sets play – do they determine the production? do they just affect it? are they irrelevant? or is their importance again a result of the actors' interpretations and therefore a contingent issue?

The technological determinist school reflects the structural approaches that were prevalent during the 1950s and early 1960s, most notably in the guise of systems theories (Dunlop, 1958), and later the ideas of Blauner and Chinoy considered above. Here, humans simply reflect their structural position in some form or another, and the effect of autonomous humans is non-existent or minimal. Humans are merely role playing, and these roles are determined by the technologies of the stage. The reaction of many sociologists to this human automaton approach was first to push back the limits of structural determinism in all its forms and reconstruct a moral individualist approach to institutionalized individuals (Goffman, 1959), and then to draw the debate closer to organizational analysis through an alternative action approach (Silverman, 1970). Through the ideas of Goldthorpe, Gallie and Child this action approach not merely pulled humans back on stage to take their role among the structure of sets but actually began to suggest that the sets themselves were relatively unimportant given the significance of the performers. As such the technology itself tended to disappear from view into the proverbial black box. The third approach covered here, designer and political technology, is technicist in that it drags technology back on stage, but this time as one amongst a number of elements. It implies that although the sets on stage are socially constructed, once completed or frozen they have specific and identifiable effects upon the actors. The fourth approach, Actor Networks and contingent technologies, keeps the technical sets on stage but not as a determinant of organizations or change, rather as a critical element in an unstable and permanently negotiated network of human and non-human actors. For this approach what is important is not what the technology *is*, because this is always the subject of interpretations, but what difference such interpretations make to the eventual perfomance as a whole. In the post-Fordist debate I argued that however tempting such simplifying and reductionist models might appear to be, the world of work was and is considerably more complex than any of these models suggests. This is not just because the empirical data for verification is inadequate (though it most certainly is), but because the data are usually constructed through either of the monistic attitudes which I have already rejected as inadequate to the task. It is because we cannot read off developments at work through isolating the technological or social variables that the data are misconstructed. Only if we assume that the quintessence of the debate is the interpreted, negotiated, alloyed and contingent nature of social and technological elements can we even begin to account for the diversity of experiences of workers at work.

Exam/essay questions

1 'A sociology of machines is a contradiction in terms.' Discuss.
2 To what extent should we regard the links between technologies, people and organizations as a 'seamless web'?
3 Compare and contrast Marx's and Blauner's theories of alienation.
4 Is consumerism just a response to technologically derived alienation at work?
5 'The interpretative approaches to technology are fundamentally flawed because, in the end, machines are uninterpreted facts.' Discuss.
6 Has the era of Fordism passed or has it just moved to other countries?
7 What best explains the change in production methods over time?
8 It seems obvious that workers in interesting jobs make better workers – so why don't we make all jobs more interesting?
9 Does it matter whether we are in a Fordist, neo-Fordist or post-Fordist era?
10 Since Ford the history of work has seen the gradual displacement of humans by machines. To what extent is it possible to remove humans from work altogether?

Further reading

Four good collections of sociologically inspired analyses of technology are: Bijker, Hughes and Pinch, *The Social Construction of Technological Systems*

(1987); Law, *Power, Action and Belief* (1986); Law, *A Sociology of Monsters* (1991); and Elliott, *Technology and Social Process* (1988). There is a critical review of existing theories in Grint and Woolgar, *The Machine at Work* (1997), while McLoughlin and Harris, *Innovation, Organizational Change and Technology* (1997) provides a review of the state of play at the time of writing. A wider overview of the role of technology is the collection of work undertaken by the Programme on Information and Communication Technologies (PICT), available in Dutton, *Information and Communication Technologies* (1996); a similar text covering American material is published in Dunlop and Kling, *Computerization and Controversy* (1991). Finally, the relationships between gender and technology are covered in the collection edited by Grint and Gill, *The Technology-Gender Relation* (1995).

9

Present Work:
The Age of Employment

- Introduction
- Manufacturing, McDonaldization and migrants
- Living to work or working to live?
- Social class, wealth and health

- Work, productivity and pay: a fat cat or a dog's life?
- Summary
- Exam/essay questions
- Further reading

Introduction

Contemporary work, according to Peter Mandelson, 'is a moral duty . . . it offers the best conditions for genuine equality of opportunity' (quoted in Bunting, 2001a: 22). But, as Bunting suggests, whereas it used to be that poverty was associated with the absence of work, it is increasingly being associated with the presence of (low-paying) work (see also Toynbee, 2003c). Furthermore, despite the best efforts of Richard Reeves's book *Happy Monday* (2001c) – where work is described as 'a lifelong journey of discovery' – for most people a happy Monday is just as likely to be associated with not going to work. 'The Dissatisfaction Syndrome', a report on the state of work commissioned by Publicis, suggests that more than half (55 per cent) of British employees felt depressed or unhappy at work in 2000, while a report by Video Works in the same year suggested that only 25 per cent were 'happy in their jobs', compared to half of all Americans and Germans (Mills, 2000: 10) (though whether this implies happy *in* their job or happy *with* a job is always an interesting sub-question). Furthermore, the reports suggested that 'retail therapy' does not work anymore, despite the fact that the average British salary rose 57 per cent between 1990 and 2000 (Dhingra, 2001b: 7); this assumes that retail therapy did work as compensation for work at some point in time, or that work was always perceived by some as the necessary evil to facilitate fulfilment outside work. Even if work did satisfy personal fulfilment, there is a question to be asked about the level and the kind of commitment to work that is required of workers. When an application form for a casual summer job in a major retail store asks: 'Would you spend 100 per cent of your time thinking about satisfying the customer?', we might want to ask where the boundary between the world of private citizen and paid employee actually sits? Indeed, just like fundamentalist religions and political cults, some contemporary employing organizations seem hell-bent on converting employees into corporate zealots and organizational disciples.

Reeves puts the opposite spin on these figures, suggesting that since 40 per cent of the British are 'very satisfied' at work, and since 33 per cent say that 'work is the most important thing in our lives', then there must be a significant silver lining to work. Indeed, there probably is, but it seems to be a silver *lining*, not a silver *coat*. Curiously, Reeves suggests that work has recently shifted to become the centre of our identity construction, though there is no apparent date to this and it does seem unlikely. After all, many of our surnames are based upon our ancestors' occupation and there is precious little evidence that work was anything other than central during all our history: from the Ancient Greeks and beyond, what you do has been short-hand for what you are.

This does not mean that work has been the source of unending pleasure for most people most of the time; indeed, for some people work literally kills them: in 2002 the United Nations International Labour Organization noted that one person dies every fifteen seconds from work-related injury or disease – that's more than 2 million people and three times more people than were killed in war in 2002 (around 650,000 died from war that year). More people now die every day as a result of work-related disease or injury than were killed on 11 September 2001 in the terrorist attacks in the USA, and more people die from work than from drug or alcohol abuse combined. Globally, the most dangerous occupations are agriculture, construction and mining (Osborn, 2002: 13), and in the UK in 2002/3 construction accounted for 47 per cent of the total fatalities (36 in agriculture and 71 in construction); however, the most dangerous industry in terms of the proportion of injuries is recycling of waste, which was almost twice as dangerous as agriculture and construction combined (see <http://www.hse.gov.uk/statistics/overall/fatl0203.pdf>).

Zeldin's (2001) suggestion is to abandon the distinction between work and leisure on the assumption that it is the division and the promise of leisure time that persuades us to take awful jobs, and that the collapse of the division will eventually lead to individuals refusing to accept mind-numbing work. Possibly, there are certainly many moves afoot to bring work closer to home, either through providing crèches at work or allowing employees to work from home. But this transcendence does not necessarily mean that we will become liberated from mundane labour because most people are not in a strong position to refuse work, tedious or otherwise. Indeed, the contract for many is to put up with work so that they can live a little when they are not working. Thus rather than taking the initiative away from employers the dissolution of the work/leisure boundary is, for most people, just as likely to enthral them further by encouraging them to perceive crèches and such like not as necessary evils to accommodate contradictory demands on parents but as the manna provided by munificent corporations whose only interest is the welfare of employees.

Manufacturing, McDonaldization and migrants

One of the greatest myths of conventional industrial sociology in the 1970s related to the putative preponderance and typicality of factory workers. Thirty years later the opposite myth prevailed – that manufacturing jobs had ceased to exist. Moreover, all jobs are now, allegedly, being de-skilled – 'McDonaldized' – and migrants are taking these McDonaldized jobs that were previously the property of the indigenous population. This section looks at all three myths.

During the Victorian heyday of manufacturing, broadly the second half of the nineteenth century, not only did the percentage of the British population engaged in manufacturing actually fall (from 33 per cent in 1851 to 31 per cent in 1881), but also the fastest-growing income generator was not manufacturing and mining, or trade, but actually income from abroad (Best, 1979: 99–100). At the turn of the last century male occupations were widely distributed, with no single group comprising more than 5 per cent of the total. Figure 29 reproduces the proportions of the top five occupations at the time.

But for women a much greater concentration of occupations occurred. As figure 30 suggests, almost one-third (31 per cent) of working women were employed as domestic servants, while the greatest professional category was teaching with just 4 per cent. The overwhelming concentration of women,

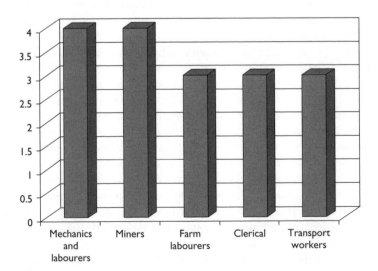

Figure 29 Top five men's occupations as percentage of total (UK), 1901
Total Male Employment, 1901: 10,160,000
Source: Labour Market Trends, January 2004

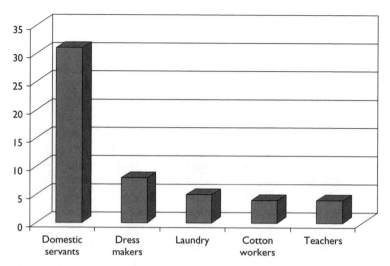

Figure 30 Top five women's occupations as percentage of total (UK), 1901
Total Female Employment 1901: 4,170,000
Source: Labour Market Trends, vol. 112, no. 1, January 2004

especially young women, in the domestic trades continued right into the 'golden age' of manufacturing. At the height of the manufacturing era, around 1911, for example, there were 2.1 million (female) domestic servants as opposed to 1.2 million (male) miners, 1.8 million in the 'metal-bashing industries', 1 million in clothing and textiles, 1.2 million in transport, 0.7 million in 'commercial occupations' and 0.4 million in the professions (Stevenson, 1984: 183). In short, no universal work experience ever channelled the working class into a homogeneous mass, and even if many were employed as manual workers in factories, their experience was never typical.

Yet it must be remembered that while employment may not have been the universal cohesive agent it has been claimed to be, neither should external factors that have combated the fragmentation of working-class experience be forgotten. In particular, this involved the role of community cultures and organizations: the co-operative movement, political parties, self-help groups, public houses, sporting associations, etc., all of which have acted as centripetal forces in a world of work where centrifugal powers of occupational differentiation were omnipresent. From the German working class during the imperial era (Geary, 1987), to eighteenth-century factory operatives in the British Industrial Revolution (Cunningham, 1980), working-class culture has spawned a web of supportive institutions and practices that have gone some way to compensate for the disjunctures in working-class experience induced through different forms of employment (Joyce, 1991).

This decline in the significance of manufacturing employment has continued apace, from about 7.5 million employees in the UK in the early 1970s to just over 5 million by 1990. In contrast, non-manufacturing employment has risen from 14.5 million to 17 million over the same period, with services employing

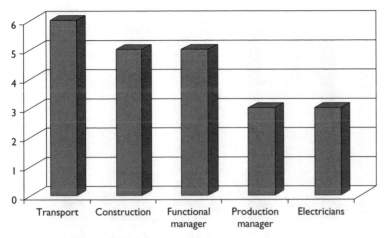

Figure 31 Top five men's occupations as percentage of total (UK), 2003
Total Male Employment 2003: 15,520,000
Source: Labour Market Trends, January 2004

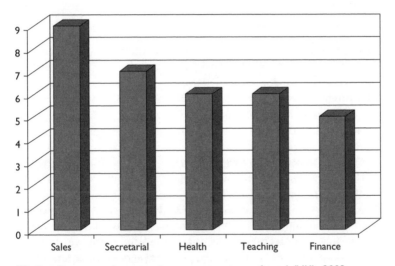

Figure 32 Top five women's occupations as percentage of total (UK), 2003
Total Female Employment 2003: 12,650,000
Source: Labour Market Trends, January 2004

more than 15.4 million *(Employment Gazette,* March 1989, April 1990; *Social Trends,* 1989). As figure 31 reveals, by 2003 the single largest male occupation was transport, followed by construction. But the greatest change over the century occurred for women with almost 10 per cent involved in sales, followed by secretarial and health (see figure 32). Overall, in 2003, 70 per cent of British women were economically active compared to 80 per cent of men. For women, 58 per cent worked full time and 42 per cent worked part time; the figures for men were 91 and 9 per cent respectively. And while 16 per cent of men were

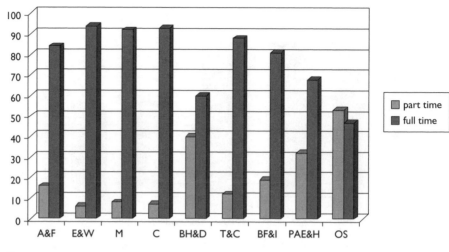

Key:

A&F	Agriculture and fishing
E&W	Energy and water
M	Manufacturing
C	Construction
BH&D	Building, hotels and distribution
T&C	Transport and communications
BF&I	Banking, finance and insurance
PAE&H	Public administration, education and health
OS	Other services

Figure 33 Distribution of full- and part-time labour (UK), 2003 (%)
Source: Labour Market Trends, January 2004

self-employed, the figure for women was only 7 per cent (*Labour Market Trends*, November 2003: 538). The industrial dispersion of full- and part-time labour is represented in figure 33.

In 2000 the British system of occupational classification was reshaped into nine categories (managers and senior officials; professional occupations; associate professional and technical occupations; administrative and secretarial occupations; skilled trades occupations; personal service occupations; sales and customer service occupations; process, plant and machine operatives; and elementary occupations: see <http://www.statistics.gov.uk/methods_quality/soc/structure.asp>) and the proportions for men and women in 2003 are reproduced in figure 34. As might have been expected, men dominate in three areas: managers and senior officials, skilled trades, and process and machine operatives; women dominate in administration and secretarial, personal services, and sales and customer services. In fact, the shift away from manufacturing towards services mirrors Foucault's (1975) general approach to discipline in society and suggests that we are moving – and have been for some time – away from a control system embedded in controlling bodies (explicitly so when considering slave societies), and towards a control system secreted within minds. We are shifting, then, from physical control through external disciplinary

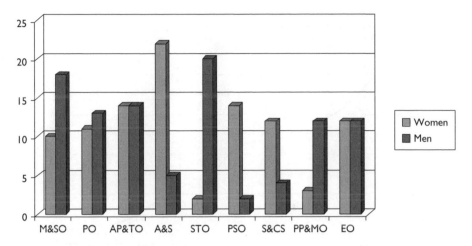

Key:
M&SO   Managers and senior officials
PO   Professional occupations
AP&TO   Associate professional and technical occupations
A&S   Administrative and secretarial
STO   Skilled trades occupations
PSO   Personal service occupations
S&CS   Sales and customer services
PP&MO   Process, plant and machine operatives
EO   Elementary occupations

Figure 34 Distribution of employees by occupation and sex (UK), 2003 (%)
Source: Labour Market Trends, October 2003: 506

systems (bind and lash) to ideological consent through internal disciplinary systems (mind and cash). Some might also argue that this parallels the move from manufacturing to services, from the factory to the restaurant, for the former requires physical labour and thus physical control over the labourer. The latter, however, requires symbolic labour and therefore symbolic control. And since services are now far more important than factories, we should, at last, be seeing the end of physical labour. But, as we shall see, this association and division are far from clear. Even a glance at figure 35 for US labour will suggest that such a scenario is doubtful, even on extrapolated data, for services have not only long been dominant, but also there has never really been a time when manufacturing was the dominant form of work. And with manufacturing jobs only accounting for 15 per cent of jobs in the USA at the beginning of the twenty-first century, the UK's 16 per cent appears to be following a similar track. Nevertheless, while it may be that Britain ends up as a nation of shopkeepers – or domestic workers – it remains the case that among the countries with the highest per capita income, the top group (Germany, Switzerland and Japan) maintain strong manufacturing sectors (Denny, 2000: 5).

But even a shrinking proportion of manufacturing camouflages an important contribution to national wealth. For example, many service industries are related to 'servicing' the manufacturing industry, either directly – for example

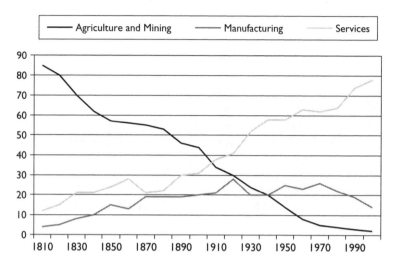

Figure 35 US employment, 1810–2000 (%)
Source: Reconstructed from US Bureau of Labor data

providing out-sourced or 'out-tasked' cleaning or payroll or IT services for car plants – or indirectly – providing employment for people who work in the local shops frequented by the same manufacturing workers. Certainly British car workers have difficulty competing with lowly paid car workers in Eastern Europe or Malaysia and so on. But the higher 'value-added' jobs in pharmaceuticals and internet companies *may* be the more important areas for job creation in the future (Atkinson, 2000: 23).

The word 'may' is important in the previous sentence. In May 2001 Forrester Research suggested that the age of the internet was over, and after the demise of 'e-business', manifest in Boo.com and e-toys, it might have seemed a self-evident case. Boo.com raised £80 million but crashed spectacularly. A large part of the problem seemed to lie in the traditional error of assuming that technology determines things (see Grint and Woolgar, 1997), thus the very existence of on-line shopping ostensibly overrides years of accumulated shopping cultures. Similarly, the requirement for conventional business skills and processes is rendered obsolete by the apparently self-evident fact that e-businesses are successful. Since neither of these truths is valid, it is also clear that the move has not been away from 'bricks and mortar' but towards 'clicks and mortar' (Scase, 2001: 13).

Even the giants of e-business, such as Yahoo and Amazon, had lost 65 per cent of their peak value by the middle of 2001, but by 2004 Amazon had at last begun to make money and Yahoo became the primary internet search engine. And, as Fingleton (2000: 25) has suggested, the products of manufacturing are often easier to export than the products of more culturally embodied products. For example, Microsoft's exports only account for 25 per cent of its sales because of the reconfiguration necessary for different languages. Yet 80 per cent of Japanese liquid crystal displays (LCDs) are exported. The link between services and manufacturing might best be represented by what happened when Delia Smith, Britain's most famous woman TV chef, recommended a particular omelette pan: annual sales of the Lune Metal Products pan rose from the usual 200 to 90,000: a 44,900 per cent increase (Wainwright, 1998: 7).

Despite all this, it remains the case that rising incomes and the growing number of working couples have generated an increased demand for service jobs, from entertainment to domestic cleaning. In 2000 around one-third of weekly spending in the UK was destined for leisure, personal and household goods and services (up from a quarter in 1970). Thus 900,000 people worked in restaurants, cafés and bars, and 350,000 worked in sports and recreation. By comparison only twice the number of the former group worked in engineering (1.8 million). These new jobs require 'soft skills' involving interpersonal relationships, and the evidence suggests that personal and physical appearance play a large part in the successful screening of employees (Philpot, 2000). Indeed, it is becoming increasingly apparent that 'style' – defined as embodying the image that the company is trying to portray through clothes, accent and appearance – is more important than skills. 'It is definitely more important', suggested Jerry Ford, Chair of Caffè Nero, 'that the employees reflect what Caffè Nero stands for than that they have experience . . . it's much easier to train someone to make a cup of coffee than to revamp their personalities' (quoted in Freeman, 2001: 10). What is also clear is that many employees today are expected to devote not just time and effort to their employers, but also an emotional commitment – or at least emotional labour; you may not have to love the customer, but you are expected to appear to do so. And the more we experience the 'trained smile' of the customer service 'rep' the more we expect it elsewhere and the less we are willing to put up with 'indifferent service' from 'unsmiling reps' (Bunting, 2004).

Anyway, have manufacturing jobs really disappeared or have they persisted in the same format under a different label? That is, are most of the new service jobs really little different from the factory jobs they allegedly displaced? In effect, we might consider a different link between manufacturing and services here, where the management control systems from the former are grafted onto the latter. Ritzer's (1997) McDonaldization thesis, for example, suggests that a growing proportion of jobs – in both manufacturing and service – have become Taylorized, in the sense that they are routinized, deskilled and devalued. Thus, just as McDonald's fast food 'restaurants' generate a rule-bound environment to remove discretion from the workforce in order to provide a perfectly replicable product and service delivery, so too, apparently, will other jobs gradually adopt a similar philosophy. Taylor's (1998) account of telephone sales agents in an airline suggests that many – though not all – of their telephone responses are scripted to ensure uniformity.

This, of course, runs directly counter to the assumption of, amongst others, Barley (1996), Drucker (1986), Hamel and Prahalad (1996) and Reich (1993), for whom the future is constructed by brain not brawn, by knowledge manipulation not physical dexterity and by autonomous agents not subordinate workers. Yet Reich's own analysis suggests that the majority of jobs in both manufacturing and service industries in the USA require only a limited degree of 'knowledge manipulation' and are very routinized. In contrast, only 7 per cent of jobs are predominantly 'symbolic analysts' (Henwood, 1996, quoted in Thompson and Warhurst, 1998). Indeed, Brown and Hesketh (2004) insist that few graduates end up in jobs that require graduate level skills.

One might go beyond this debate to question the degree to which a separation between symbolic and material manipulation actually exists. Zuboff (1988) certainly insisted that we were moving from sentient to symbolic knowledge manipulation – in her example, from feeling whether a pipe was hot enough to reading that temperature on a screen. But it is difficult to differentiate the two approaches in terms of sentient versus symbolic knowledge because both require acts of interpretation by the human agent and thus both are symbolic acts (see Grint and Woolgar, 1997: 130–8). In fact, one could argue that F. W. Taylor was amongst the first to recognize the role of symbolic knowledge in the most mundane task when he attempted to strip workers of precisely this knowledge and reconfigure it as management property.

Taylor was perhaps most famous for his experiments with a Dutch immigrant named Schmidt, and the reliance on 'foreign' labour remains a critical issue for all governments at the beginning of the twenty-first century. An OECD report published in 2001 confirmed that 'McJobs' were in a distinct minority when it came to examining new employment opportunities. On the contrary, the majority of new jobs are in the service sector; they are relatively well paid and highly skilled – hence the reason for many countries to encourage the immigration of such skilled foreign workers (see <www.oecd.org>).

But there is another reason to encourage immigration: when Taylor was undertaking his experiments in the USA at the beginning of the twentieth century, there were five employees for every pensioner in the UK; in 2004 there were 2.5 employees for every pensioner and by 2025 the ratio will be one for one. By 2004 – for the first time – there were more over 60-year-olds than under 16-year-olds in the UK. If we add these numbers to the current average age of people on different continents (Europe 37, Asia 26, and Africa 18), it should be clear that an 'Agequake' is set to threaten the welfare of British and many other European nations (McKie, 2004: 9–10).

One response would be to increase the age of retirement and/or reduce the value of state pensions. Another would be to consider whether the ratio of employed to non-employed needs to be the same throughout history: if every individual worker is now more productive than their equivalent in the nineteenth century, then future workers, presumably, will be more productive than we are – hence we need not assume that we have to retain the same ratios.

Another response would be to increase immigration, especially since most immigrants are young, and balance out the age and working ratio on that basis. Just prior to the expansion of the EU in May 2004, many of the original member states restricted entry from the ten new ones (Bowcott, 2004: 4; Wintour and Black, 2004: 1), though the UK was reluctant to impose any total ban, primarily because of the labour requirements in the future. But the dangers of a 'flood' of immigrants are often exaggerated: in 1989 the United Nations High Commission for Refugees (UNHCR) suggested that the collapse of communist states would generate a movement of 25 million people from East to West Europe in the 1990s; in the event, only 2.5 million moved (Black, 2004: 18).

In the USA in the 1990s more than 13.5 million immigrants arrived (a third of Silicon Valley's engineers and scientists were already – legal – immigrants in 1990), half of them illegally, mainly from Asia, Mexico and South America. Sum et al. (2003) have argued that this 'new blood' is the cause of America's economic growth, particularly since so few of the immigrants are elderly. It is also worth pointing out that perhaps as many as a third of the illegal immigrants to the USA arrived with few educational qualifications and tended to end up in low-paid service jobs. In any case, it is the 1990s rather than the 1890s that has seen the largest levels of immigration.

Certainly, economic migrants are a significant source of value for their original home: in 1989 the World Bank calculated that the developed world provided $45 billion in aid to the developing world, but emigrant workers in the developed world sent home $65 billion (L. Harding, 2001: 2–3). Of course the political aspects of immigration often conflict with the economic aspects and the hostility towards 'asylum seekers' in the UK has increased significantly since the turn of the century: in 2003 one-third of the British population thought that migration was the most important issue facing the country. In the same year net migration to the UK was about 172,000 a year and migrants contributed about £2.5 billion a year net to the British Treasury – that is *after* the £2 billion in costs associated with the asylum system (Spencer, 2003).

The British government's own Cabinet Office suggested in 2000 that a 1 per cent increase in the population through immigration would lead to an increase in Gross Domestic Product (GDP) of between 1.25 and 1.5 per cent (Stewart, 2001b: 19). However, that does not necessarily ensure a positive welcome on the part of the 'native' population. We might reconsider this hostility simply in terms of the proportion of the population – in almost any country – which is actually 'indigenous'. Britain, for example, has hosted many groups of immigrants and refugees in the past, from the Celts who themselves originally disposed of the 'small dark people' (as the Celts referred to the indigenous natives), to Romans, Anglo-Saxons, Scandinavians, Normans, French Huguenots, Dutch, Russian and European Jews, Belgians, Basques, Hungarians, Czechs, Ugandan Asians, Chileans, Vietnamese, Kurds, Romanians and Yugoslavians. Indeed, the hostility shown towards immigrants by 'the British' belies their own heterogeneous heritage: the first black people in England were not slaves in the time of Elizabeth I, but a division of north African troops in the Roman army, and geneticists have found links back to the Phoenicians amongst the contemporary inhabitants of Wales and Cornwall (Crace, 2000: 56). Few have put the image of this island's melting pot better than Daniel Defoe's 1701 assault on English chauvinism, *The True Born Englishman*, which spoke of 'this amphibious ill-born mob . . . Your Roman, Saxon, Danish, Norman, English. . . . A True-Born Englishman's a contradiction.'

The economic arguments for immigrant labour to the UK also relate to skills as well as to the proportion of employed to retired workers: the existing population simply cannot provide the necessary labour, even if older workers were (re)recruited. In 2000, 25 per cent of British employers could not fill vacancies, not because there was no unemployment but because applicants lacked necessary basic skills. Dickens et al. (2001) suggest that while unemployment has continued to drop in the 1990s (in January 2004 unemployment in Britain reached a 30-year low at 892,100 – that is, 2.9 per cent), for some groups the reverse is true. In particular, women with no qualifications in areas of high unemployment have seen their employment rate fall further, and the same, though less so, goes for men. Britain actually has one of the lowest levels of adult literacy in the industrialized world: one in three people leave school at 16 with inadequate basic skills (Woodward, 2001a: 9). Maths is especially prized by employers, but only 45 per cent of children left school in 1999 with GCSE grade C or above; 5 per cent achieved A-level maths, and just 1 per cent of all graduates were maths graduates. The problem is not restricted to school children – in 2003 a Department for Education and Skills survey revealed that 47 per cent of adults in England (15 million people) had poorer mathematical knowledge than was needed to achieve the lowest possible GCSE score – a grade G. Worse, over a fifth of the adult population (6.8 million people) were less numerate than the standard set for 11-year-olds in national tests. The equivalent figures for adult (il)literacy tests were 16 per cent at GCSE level and 5 per cent at the tests for 11-year-olds (see <http://news.bbc.co.uk/1/hi/education/3227263.stm>).

Beyond academic school qualifications, Britain also lags behind its main rivals: Germany had three times as many vocationally qualified staff as Britain in 2000 (Smithers, 2000: 6). A very large survey of skills in the UK in 2003 by the Learning and Skills Council suggested that 11 per cent of employees (2.4 million) were evaluated by their employers as 'incompetent' at their jobs, lacking either the basic skills or motivation or both; overall, 22 per cent were regarded as inadequately skilled. On the other hand, 40 per cent of employers provided no skills training in the previous 12 months, so a vicious circle is clearly evident (see <http://news.bbc.co.uk/1/hi/education/3446417.stm>). On the other hand, the British also produce proportionately more graduates than any other OECD country. Yet, as Reeves (2001b: 15) concludes: 'a quarter of British graduates are in posts where the qualification they need to *get* the job isn't needed to *do* the job' (also see the Social Mobility discussion paper from the cabinet office at <www.cabinet-office.gov.uk>). In effect, as figure 36 reveals,

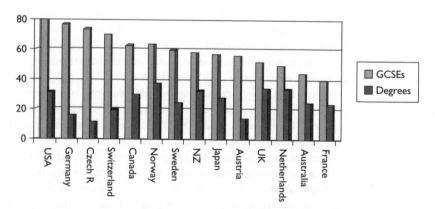

Figure 36 Comparative educational achievements (OECD), 1998 (%)
Source: OECD data

Britain has a notoriously inegalitarian educational system, with 7 million functionally illiterate adults (Van Reenan, 2000) – only Spain and Portugal are worse – but at the same time, at 35 per cent, nearly the highest proportion of graduates (Woodward, 2001b: 8).

We might summarize this section by suggesting that while the differentiation between manufacturing and service jobs is not always clear cut, it is the case that most newly created employment is in the service area, though not all are McDonaldized jobs and many require significant levels of skill. That said, the British workforce, while relatively well provisioned with graduates, remains extraordinarily bipolar in its skill levels, with a large minority being functionally illiterate and unable to acquire full-time or permanent employment. The age profile of many countries, particularly in Europe, is also heavily skewed against the young, to the point where either the old must work longer or accept poorer living standards, or immigration must be encouraged to take up the burden of taxation. It may be that manufacturing, McDonaldization and migration dominate the headlines of work, but it is actually the relative dearth of young skilled workers that ought to fix our collective focus. In the next section we consider what role working cultures play in working lives.

Living to work or working to live?

For some analysts, the end of the millennium should have witnessed a colossal change in patterns of work – or rather the lack of work – to the point where there would be no economic stimulus to immigration. As Jenkins and Sherman insisted in 1979: 'It is impossible to over-dramatize the forthcoming crisis. ... Now we have inflation, a slump and rising unemployment. In fifteen or twenty years time we shall have a boom, minimal inflation, high growth and the largest unemployment in our history ... a jobs holocaust' (1979: 182). According to Rifkin (1996: 24), 'The road to a near workerless economy is within sight: whether it leads to a safe haven or a terrible abyss will depend on how well civilization prepares for what is to come.'

Well we certainly have not reached the workerless economy – but have we instead arrived in a place where the kind of relationship we have to work has changed beyond all recognition? A survey by the research organization, Conference Board, confirmed such a scenario, for two-thirds of US companies and companies operating in the USA have already abandoned the concept of job security altogether (*Observer*, 11 May 1997). There used to be employment for all – or at least for most people for most of the time – jobs for life, a working day of 9–5 and a secure retirement through a state pension. Now the world has turned upside down yet again: we never know whether our employer will still be there tomorrow or whether our services will be required; we might be working 24/7 or not working at all, and the lives of pensioners are ever more precarious as national social services seek to cut benefits and displace responsibility on to the private individual and the private sector. On an equally pessimistic note, Beck (2000) proposes a related vision of the future where high unemployment in Europe coincides with the spread of temporary and insecure jobs.

While it is easy to scoff at the pessimism of Beck, Jenkins and Sherman, or even the polarized perspective embodied by Rifkin, it remains the case that the contemporary *perception* of job insecurity appears to be almost as high as the *unreality* of job insecurity they predicted. D. Smith (1997: 39), for instance, compared the relative insignificance of newspaper stories about insecurity in 1986 (when unemployment in Britain was much higher than a decade later) with its preponderant presence in 1996, by which time stories about job insecurity had increased 100-fold. According to the *Observer* (16 June 1996), 40 per cent of British employees feared for their jobs, while 60 per cent argued that insecurity had been rising. Figure 37 shows the rate of redundancy for different occupations in Britain from 1991 to 1996, and demonstrates that the perception of risk and actual risk are dissimilar things: for the highest risk occupations are craft workers and machine operators – not managers.

Yet, despite claims to the contrary (see Barley, 1996), job tenure in Britain only marginally decreased between 1975 and 2000 (from 6 to 5.5 years), with women's tenure actually increasing (Gregg and Wadsworth, 1999; Nolan, 2000: 3; Green (2000) suggests that in the 1970s the average job tenure was

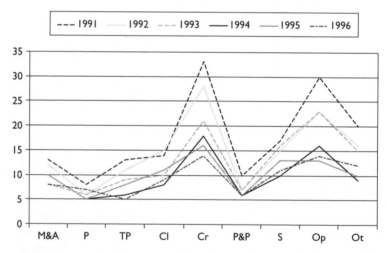

Key:
M&A   Managers and administrators
P   Professions
TP   Technical professions
Cl   Clerical
Cr   Craft
P&P   Person and protection
S   Sales
Op   Operatives
Ot   Others

Figure 37 British redundancy rates (per 1,000) by occupation, 1991–6
Source: Social Trends, 1997

10 years and it remained stuck at 9.5 in 2000). Indeed, in the allegedly worst period of the 'neurotic nineties', tenure actually increased over the rate of the 'erratic eighties'. Cappelli's (1995) review of the US data suggests that women's increased tenure was related to their decreasing habit of leaving work after having children rather than to any change in employment strategy by employers. On the other hand, men's job tenure was decreasing not only generally but also markedly in association with low levels of education or with age. Yet 80 per cent of British employees remain in permanent jobs, and 28 per cent of employees have remained with the same employer for more than ten years. Indeed, most people can probably look forward to staying with the same employer for, at the very least, four or five years.

It has also become common to insist that unprecedented levels of stress currently exist at work. For instance, 52 per cent of respondents in a *Guardian* newspaper survey (Brockes, 2000: 2–3) suggested that stress was a major factor in their working lives, and several aspects took precedence in explaining this:

- the quantity of work, especially unrealistic deadlines given by bosses and being unappreciated and underpaid by them;
- difficult colleagues;
- worries about the future;
- being in the wrong job.

In all, 75 per cent of respondents – who had never shouted at their boss, taken up smoking or shown signs of a nervous breakdown – wanted to swear at their boss and/or hit them. However, the universal politics and back-stabbing from colleagues seemed to cause more stress than the overt fights with bosses. What is worth considering here might not be so much about any argument concerning the cause or even existence of stress in itself, but more a concern for its apparent material consequences. For example, although the strike data given in chapter 5 clearly demonstrates a decline in collective industrial action, the data for absence through what is reported as 'stress' is significantly higher than it ever was. In 1995 there were 18 million days lost through 'stress'; this number increased to 33 million in 2002. In that year there were 60 times more days lost to stress than to industrial action (Bunting, 2003: 13).

What also appears consistently is that British workplaces are more stressful and less happy places to work in than their European or North American counterparts. Woudhuysen (2000) suggests there are several main reasons for British workplaces being such miserable places to work in:

1 The innate conservatism of British management.
2 'Churn': the apparent chaos of organizations that have downsized, re-engineered, merged, de-merged, relocated, contracted out, in-sourced, out-sourced and generally turned themselves inside-out to stay competitive – or at least do what the CEO thinks they ought to do.
3 Globalization: the critical issue here is working across time zones, which basically require people to stay late and arrive early in order to communicate directly with their counterparts across the world.

4 Size: big firms are alienating, but small firms are prone to collapse, poorer welfare standards and a lack of investment in people.
5 Long hours: both working and commuting.
6 Money-mad: everything must be sacrificed on the altar of shareholder value.
7 Political correctness: this relates to the apparent fear stalking the country that people can be disciplined and, if necessary, dismissed, subsequent to being 'denounced', Orwellian style, for allegedly harassing someone.
8 Home/work merger: the provision of crèches, shops, banks, gyms, manicurists and so on has left the typical employee not happier to be at work but hesitant to go home – since this may be seen as 'disloyalty'.
9 Bad management: only 33 per cent of British managers (compared to 80 per cent of American managers) feel they work in a corporate culture that promotes growth. Most significantly, there appears to be a general lack of direction – unless this means how to give the shareholders more 'value' (Brayfield, 2000: 3–4).

Robert Briner and Serge Doublet (quoted in Brayfield, 2000: 3), however, suggest that stress only becomes valid within the realms of those 'stress consultants' who peddle stress remedies. In effect, being miserable at work is, and always has been, a normal part of most people's experience. Nevertheless, we have to tread warily here – recall in the previous chapter that Roy's account of work implies that what occurs *at work* may have little to do with the *work* employees are supposed to be doing. Hence, workers may simultaneously dislike the work they are doing but enjoy the camaraderie that is often generated at work. *Going to work* may be stressful, but it is usually less stressful than being *out of work* – that is, unemployed, rather than retired. That in itself is worth reflecting on: having a surfeit of 'free time' on your hands may be great where you are on holiday, fine when you are retired, but very difficult if you are out of work or in prison.

Despite this, the Institute of Stress Management claim that 60 million days are lost to British industry each year through stress-related absence – at a cost of £7 billion. Perhaps more critical, there is an increasing number of compensatory payments being made to employees claiming stress-related illnesses at work. For example, in December 2000 Janice Howell received £254,000 after retiring early from her school teaching job following a nervous breakdown. The problem is not simply trying to measure stress but actually assessing the degree to which what counts as stress can be unequivocally related to aspects of work alone. One of these aspects might be working hours (see <http://www.bullyonline.org/media/nr13.htm>).

Working from 6 a.m. to 6 p.m. six days a week, with Sunday spent recovering in bed, might seem like a daunting prospect for those about to start a career in the city or with a firm of high-flying consultants – and this may be just the start of a long-term relationship where long hours drive the search for expensive compensatory leisure and consumption that, in turn, drives long hours and so on, ad infinitum. But the 72-hour week was the norm at the beginning of the twentieth century in British factories. There was a price to pay, not just in terms of lost time outside work, but also in time beyond work: the average

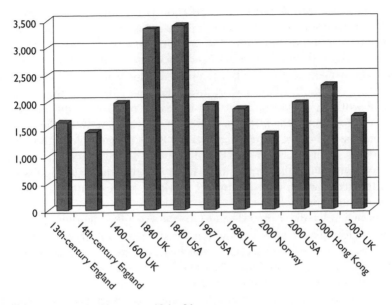

Figure 38 Hours worked per year, 13th–21st century
Source: Schor, 1992; *Labour Force Survey* (various)

male factory worker was dead by the age of 55, with women dying five years later. Indeed, it is worth just reconstructing a rough approximation of working hours across time simply to consider two contrary historical assumptions – both of which turn out to be wrong. First, that working hours have continuously decreased over time as technology has replaced human labour. Second, that we are now working more hours than ever before. As figure 38 suggests, working as an average peasant in medieval England involved markedly fewer hours than an average employee puts in today. Certainly, the former took more holidays than the latter, working perhaps as little as 150–75 days per year on their land and enjoying as much as a third of the entire year as official holidays, either as Sundays, saints' days or public holidays (Schor, 1992). In addition, since taxation rates were roughly three-quarters of today's during much of the medieval period, it would have needed significantly less effort to have accumulated the wherewithal to pay them.

By 1920 all children were banned from factories and by 1937 working hours for women and male youths (under 18) were limited to 48 a week. By 1959, as a result of industrial action not legislation, the average hours in industries like printing had been reduced to 40 and in 1980 these were further reduced to 37 hours a week. However, the first legislative limits on hours (and the first legal requirement for paid holidays) occurred 61 years after the last legal changes, with the 1998 Working Time Regulations in conjunction with regulated average weekly working time, holiday time and periods of rest while at work. In detail, the regulations limit the average working week to 48 hours, including overtime, over a 17-week period. A weekly rest of at least 24 hours is mandatory, as are daily rests of 11 hours and three weeks' holiday a year. About

10 per cent of the British working population (2.5 million) worked more than the 48-hour maximum in 1995 and Britain remains the only EU nation to make the 48-hour maximum 'voluntary' – in that you can sign away your rights (15 per cent work nights and 25 per cent work some hours between 6 a.m. and 6 p.m. (Summerskill, 2000: 6)). But the modal value was 31–40 hours, worked by two-thirds of the employed workforce. However, by 1998 the 10 per cent of people working above the limit had increased to 25 per cent, according to an Institute for Employment Services Report. Overall, between the end of the 1980s and the end of the 1990s, the average British household with two adults was working seven hours longer (Ezard, 2000: 7). And, since it is possible to sign away your own rights in this area, it may be that the legislation will make little difference. Indeed, British workers work far more hours than their main European counterparts.

In fact, when we dig a little deeper into the European working time figures, it becomes clear that the UK has the longest statutory weekly hours (48, along with Germany, Greece and Ireland), the highest agreed average hours (37.5, shared with Greece, Luxemburg, Portugal and Sweden), the least number of public holidays (8), the least amount of statutory annual leave (20 days, shared with Belgium, Germany, Ireland and Italy) and the lowest average agreed holidays (25 days, shared with Belgium, Greece, Ireland, Portugal and Sweden). All in all, as figure 39 suggests, amongst the larger members of the EU in 2003 British employees worked the longest hours.

The USA actually has the highest working hours in the 'Western' world: 1,966 per annum on average in 1997, in contrast to Norwegians who work 1,399 hours. However, workers in Hong Kong, Bangladesh, Sri Lanka, Malaysia, Singapore and Thailand all average 2,200–2,300 per annum (ABC News.com, 2000). By 2000 the average American undertook 256 hours more per year

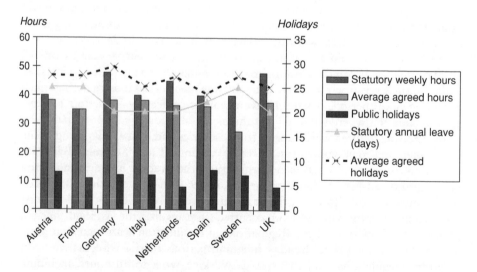

Figure 39 Working hours and holidays in Europe, 2003
Source: Incomes Data Services Ltd (<http://www.incomesdata.co.uk/infotime/eutable.pdf>)

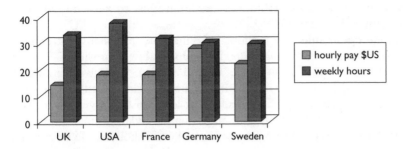

Figure 40 Comparative wages and hours
Source: Reconstructed from Reeves, 2000b
Note: the weekly hours are calculated as total annual hours divided by 52 – i.e., no account has been taken of the different holiday entitlements. The hourly pay rates are for factory work

(1,976 total) than the average Briton (1,720 total), and 400 hours more than the average German (1,556 total) (Stewart, 2001a: 23). It could be argued that this represents different cultural attitudes: Americans are fixated by the competitive spirit and ethic of self-advancement, Germans are not, while the British can't make up their minds. As figure 40 suggests, when it comes to the trade-off between hours and rewards, the Anglo-Saxon countries do worst. Indeed, around one-third of male American managers and professionals and about a fifth of female American managers and professionals regularly work more than 49 hours a week (see <http://www.bls.gov/opub/ils/pdf/opbils37.pdf>).

However, Bell and Freeman (1994) suggest that the underlying motivation is not cultural but economically rational: the USA has greater income inequality, less social support and a more ruthless approach to hiring and firing. As a consequence of this, Americans who work longer hours do so in the knowledge that this may help them achieve a well-rewarded promotion and should help protect them from redundancy. Germany, in contrast, has less inequality, so promotion does not bring such significant increases in salary, and a more generous social security system, so loss of employment is not as catastrophic as it is for Americans. Nevertheless, British managers and professionals, on average, work longer hours than their employees or staff: most managers work 8.5 hours a week beyond their contracted hours and most professionals work 9.5 hours beyond their contracted week. These groups are obviously paid more than their employees and staff, but it is very unusual for overtime payments to be made (<http://money.guardian.co.uk/work/story/0,1456,1092148,00.html>). Indeed, the American Bureau of Labor Statistics, which tracks American working hours, is notoriously problematic; it assumes, for example, that Wal-Mart managers work 35–40 hours a week when in reality a 60–70-hour week is the norm. The long hours in the USA also explain a productivity conundrum: the US economy grew by over 8 per cent in the third quarter of 2003 but employment only grew by 0.1 per cent. Why? In 1947 an American worker on average wages would have had to work for 62 weeks to earn the median family income. In 2001 that same average worker would have had to work 81 weeks. So although productivity increased threefold over that period, the average worker simply has to work longer and longer just to keep up with the average (Henwood, 2004: 23).

Despite the predilection for long working hours, British workers also show a marked inclination for watching TV and spending a considerable amount of time getting to work. Each week, around a third of the working population spends more than 36 hours at work, just under a third spend 36 hours watching TV and a similar proportion spend at least 26 hours getting to work and back (Saunders, 2000: 2–3). But these figures hide as much as they reveal: although the average British employee worked 37 hours in 1980 and in 2000, in the former period one person in six worked more than 48 hours; by the latter period that proportion had jumped to one in five. In effect, some were working longer hours, some were working shorter hours, but the average remained static. Overall, and per year, the average British worker works 4.5 weeks longer than a German worker and 2 weeks longer than a French worker (we have to exclude British MPs from this survey because they have 86 days 'summer holiday') (Riddell, 2001: 22).

There was also a stronger *perception* amongst British workers that they had been asked to work harder between 1991 and 1996 than had been the case for any other European country (the perception was ten times higher amongst British employees than among German employees) (Ezard, 2000: 7). There is some substance to this perception: only 20 per cent of British workers take more than five weeks' holiday a year, compared to 75 per cent of the French and 90 per cent of the Germans (Dhingra, 2001c: 7). But perhaps the real issue is not simply one of hours but, rather, one that relates effort to reward; this is the subject of the next section.

Social class, wealth and health

While working hours for the professional and managerial middle class are longer than those for the working class, the reward structure clearly compensates for this (the asymmetric rewards that relate to gender are discussed in chapter 6). Social class is not just a fixation of sociologists: it has both a subjective resonance with most of the population and – as we have already seen above – undeniable material consequences. The vast majority of the British population think that class is an inevitable feature of British society, can place themselves in the class structure, and have difficulty locating themselves within any other social category (Marshall et al., 1988). This in itself reinforces the imperative consequences of acknowledging the socially constructed nature of the categories: other categories can be devised (race, gender, age, religion, etc.), and each categorization results in a different view of the social structure. But social class does not exist independently of our attitudes to society – it is a means by which we develop such attitudes.

This is reflected in some of the academic developments in the field of employment which have been less directed by the class motif than is usual, though there has also been a resurgence of class-based studies that have generally taken a dual path. On the one hand, there are accounts, such as Gallie's (1989; see also Haralambos and Holborn, 1995), which consider the evidence for the growth of an underclass, below the conventional working class. On the other hand, there are orthodox Marxists (E. M. Wood, 1986) who have resisted the attacks of feminists and other radical non-Marxists, and have reasserted the central significance of class, and indeed employment, against the 'rainbow' alliance arguments of the new social movements (Mouffe, 1979). Let us first set out what contemporary empirical evidence there is for these arguments.

Perhaps the first thing to note is the significance of the split between inequalities constructed through earned income and those based upon the ownership of wealth. Wealth is generally more significant than earned income in so far as the basic patterning of inequalities is concerned, reflecting the significance of non-work factors in the construction of class structures and life experiences. These life experiences are also death experiences. As an illustration, using the conventional occupational division from A to E, it is currently the case that the bottom two categories visit their doctors almost twice as often as the top two categories. The Ds and Es are also more likely to suffer from breathing problems, digestive problems, high blood pressure, rheumatism and arthritis than any other group (Harris Poll, *Observer*, 18 February 1990). Similarly, the poor are more likely to develop cancer than the rich and less likely to survive once a diagnosis has been made (Kogevinas, 1990).

A similar myth pervades the area of corporate stress: it has long been assumed that today's executives work harder than any other group and suffer the highest levels of stress; but it is also the case that the most 'at risk' occupations in the stress tables are bus, lorry and taxi drivers, fishermen, bar workers and the unskilled (Kristiensen, 1995). Precisely which social group is most at risk, and from what, is probably better represented by figures 41 and 42, which reproduce the mortality rates for different social classes and occupations and clearly reveal that social class and occupation are strongly correlated with mortality rates. Of course, it may simply be that although the mortality rates are higher as you progress down the social classes, the level of work required does the opposite: thus those at the top work harder, even if they last longer. But the top of the British tree in corporate terms, whether public or private, is dominated by particular elites not entire social classes. For instance, more than half the appointments of judges and QCs (Queen's Counsel) are made from just seven barristers' chambers by 'secret soundings' taken by the Lord Chamberlain. A KPMG Consulting 1999 Survey on Business Leadership reported that the majority of the 200 senior directors of British and Irish large companies asserted that 'hard work' gained them their places. Yet the younger (under 45) members of this group were more aware than their elders that 'knowing the right people' (including the 'right' partner) and going to the right university were far more critical (Palmer, 2000: 18), and both these factors are directly related to social class.

Class is also directly related to a system of wealth distribution, though taxation policy is also critical, and from 1911 – and most particularly since 1946 – has been almost wholly progressive, at least until 1979. Whether employers, and any wage earners for that matter, have become personally richer or poorer has often been related more closely to taxation policy than to the level of

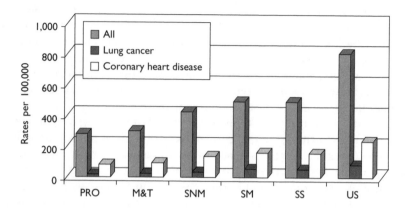

Key:
PRO   Professional
M&T   Managerial and technical
SNM   Skilled non-manual
SM   Skilled manual
SS   Semi-skilled
US   Unskilled

Figure 41 Social class and standardized mortality rates in men aged 20–64 (England and Wales), 1991–2

Source: Reconstructed from Acheson, 1999

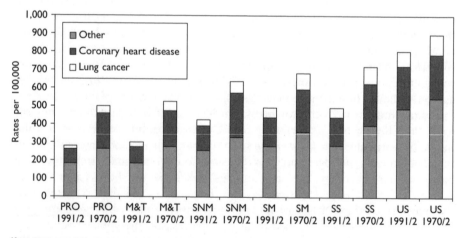

Key:
PRO   Professional
M&T   Managerial and technical
SNM   Skilled non-manual
SM   Skilled manual
SS   Semi-skilled
US   Unskilled

Figure 42 Social class and cause of death in men aged 20–64 (England and Wales), 1970–2 and 1991–2

Source: Reconstructed from Acheson, 1999

economic exploitation at the point of production. Indeed, it is not coincidental that by far the richest sector of the UK throughout the nineteenth century was not the factory capitalists of the north but the landowners and the commercial and financial capitalists of the south. Not until the collapse of land prices and the political developments of the late nineteenth century did industrial capitalism generate large numbers of overtly rich individuals (W. D. Rubinstein, 1988).

As mentioned above, one of the problems with arguments centred wholly on activities concerning employment is that although income from employment is clearly crucial to the life chances of most people, it is also the case that a large number of people at the bottom of the income pyramid depend on state support not earned income, while a small number at the top of the pyramid secure their life experiences through unearned income. Thus, while employment still remains significant for class structuration, some of the inequalities that underlie employment-related inequalities have little to do with employment themselves. For example, it is still the case that inherited wealth and class position play a significant role in deciding who controls the major industrial and business concerns not just of Britain but of Europe too (Marceau, 1989). And even though income derived from such control may be considerable, it is quite often dwarfed by the income and power generated by an inherited, and in this sense unearned, position (Shoard, 1987).

Estimates of British wealth ownership are notoriously difficult to verify, often very dated and not helped by the actions of the Conservative government between 1979 and 1997, which reduced the data-collection facilities concerning the distribution of wealth. Nevertheless, the best estimates available are reproduced in table 5. Between 1924 and 1972 in Britain the share of wealth owned by the richest 1 per cent and 5 per cent of adults fell by around 4 per cent each decade, a phenomenon common to most industrial nations (Wolff, 1987). After 1979 this trend ceased and, as a result of the 1988 budget, the trend went into reverse, thanks to 40 per cent of the tax handouts (£1,750 million) being channelled towards the richest 10 per cent, while a mere 10 per cent went to the poorest 50 per cent (G. Brown, 1988). In fact, the top 1 per cent got more than the bottom 70 per cent (Naughtie, 1988), and between 1979 and 1988, 24 per cent of income tax cuts went to the richest 1 per cent and 38 per cent went to the richest 5 per cent, leaving 17 per cent for the bottom half

Table 5 Distribution of wealth amongst the richest adults in Britain, 1938–2001 (%)

% of adults	Percentage of marketable wealth							
	1938	1966	1979	1985	1991	1996	2001	2001#
1	55	33	22	20	17	20	23	33
5	77	56	40	40	35	40	43	58
10	85	69	54	54	47	52	56	72
25	*	87	77	76	71	74	75	86
50	*	97	95	93	92	93	95	97

* Not available
# Less value of dwellings
Source: Inland Revenue statistics, 1988; *Social Trends 34*, 'Distribution of Wealth'

of the population (Huhne, 1988b). By 2001 the distribution of wealth – including the value of dwellings – had virtually returned to pre-1979 levels and if we exclude the value of dwellings then the distribution of wealth in the UK has returned to 1966 levels.

If pensions are included in the data, the top 5 per cent of the population own 25 per cent of the total, while the bottom 50 per cent of the population have seen their share drop from between 17 and 21 per cent in 1979 to between 15 and 19 per cent in 1985 (Stark, 1988; Huhne, 1988b). Despite the obvious decline in the wealth ownership of the top 10 per cent since the beginning of the twentieth century, the spread of wealth has tended to remain within the top 25 per cent of the population and provides a considerably distorted distribution figure, showing just how important income, rather than wealth, appears to be to the bottom 75 per cent of the population. The conventional outlook on employment, which is deflected away from the social elite, embodies two different facets: for the elite, employment-generated inequalities may well be secondary to wealth-generated inequalities, whereas for the vast majority of the population income is the crucial variable. Of course, there is also a very large pool of unpaid workers to consider: according to the 2001 Census, on average 10 per cent of people in England and Wales provide some form of unpaid care, and the proportions of the population who provide care for more than 50 hours a week range from the lowest – the London borough of Kensington with 1 per cent – to the highest – the Welsh district of Neath Port Talbot, at 4.2 per cent (*Guardian Society*, 19 February 2002, p. 111).

According to a report from the Institute of Fiscal Studies (quoted in the *Guardian*, 28 July 1997), incomes of the bottom 5 per cent remained stable at around £90 per week between 1983 and 1993, but the income of the top 5 per cent rose almost 50 per cent to £550 per week. Turning the numbers into images, in the 1990s about 60 per cent of the British population stood about 5 foot 9 inches in height. The elite group of entrepreneurs are as high as Nelson's Column in Trafalgar Square, while John Paul Getty clearly needs oxygen at a full 10 miles high. By 2004 there was a positive crowd in the stratosphere: the richest 1 per cent of Americans owned 40 per cent of their country's wealth, while in the UK the equivalent figure was between 18 and 23 per cent. If ever there was a new plutocracy it was George W. Bush's cabinet in 2004, in which every member was a millionaire and its total wealth was ten times that of Clinton's cabinet (Borger, 2003: 14; Foot, 2003: 25).

In the UK, income inequality grew steadily between 1991 and 1999: after tax, the poorest fifth of the population received 6 per cent of national income while the top fifth increased their proportion from 44 to 45 per cent. At the same time, the proportion of income taken in tax is higher for the poorest fifth (41.4 per cent) than for the richest fifth (36.5 per cent) (Ward, 2001: 5). Moreover, agricultural subsidies are often available to those who seem to need them least. In fact, Britain received £3 billion in farming subsidies from the EU but 80 per cent of this went to the richest 20 per cent of landowners. Five landowners recoup £1 million a year, though the government refuses to specify who these are on the dubious grounds of commercial confidentiality. The Earl of Iveagh, of the Guinness family, is a lowly 41st in the British League of the Rich, with a mere £700 million to his name, but he has in the past managed to secure £1 million in subsidies from the 'set aside' scheme on parts of his 23,000-acre Suffolk farm (Barnett, 2001: 5). In 2003 the Duke of Westminster – with estimated wealth in 2003 at £4.9 billion – received an annual farm subsidy of £326,144, while the largest single subsidy – £382,200 – went to the Duke of Bedford to support his 13,500-acre farm at Woburn Abbey. All of this is paid via Britain's taxpayers' annual subsidy of the CAP to the tune of £4 billion (Denny et al., 2004: 3). Besides the incongruity of paying subsidies at a time when Europe is already producing too much food, and the irony of that excess in the face of starvation elsewhere in the world, we should also compare the protection provided to agriculture with that provided elsewhere: the same government that provided subsidies to farmers because there was too much food around effectively closed down Britain's mining communities because there was too much coal around. That pit-closure programme had significant costs attached. First, the financial costs, estimated at £28 billion, which amounts to half the tax revenues collected from North Sea oil since 1985 (£10 billion incurred by the National Coal Board, the Central Electricity Generating Board, British Rail, British Steel and the police; £14 billion incurred in pit closures and redundancies; and £4 billion in unemployment costs calculated at 9 months' unemployment benefit for the 284,000 ex-miners). Second, the UK will no longer be self-sufficient in energy because of its reliance on imported gas (Feickert, 2004: 25). But then the closure of the pits never was a purely economic affair.

Work, productivity and pay: a fat cat or a dog's life?

Britain remains the least regulated nation amongst the OECD nations: it had the lowest corporation tax of all, and the lowest in its history in 2001; it has the lowest employment costs (social and labour insurance taxes average 24 per cent in Europe, 21 per cent in the USA and 13 per cent in the UK) (Toynbee, 2001: 19). As might be expected, the jobs in Britain that involve working with children or vulnerable adults – that is, care workers of various forms – are amongst the worst rewarded and the most difficult to recruit. This might also explain why the Germans seem to have adopted the term 'The English Patient' to refer to the parlous state of public services in the UK compared to Germany. Or, as the *Wall Street Journal* (2 March 2001) put it, analysing the British public sector: 'US-style taxes can't pay for German-style welfare.' Yet, despite claims to the contrary, organizations like the British NHS have not been brought to their knees by any recent explosion of management bureaucracy at the expense of doctors and nurses. Indeed, figure 43 suggests that costs have dropped significantly, and while the number of managers has risen, this is actually the result of a change in counting procedures to include the previously excluded managers within GP fundholders in the numbers. As the figure also suggests, British managers are often good at something: cost control. Indeed, the Foundation for Performance Measurement's *The Well Rounded Annual Report* (1998) concluded that 'Cost Control' was the best-reported measure in corporate annual reports,

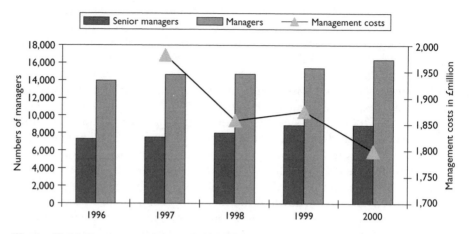

Figure 43 NHS management costs, 1996–2000

Source: Reconstructed from Health Authority and NHS Annual Trust Annual Accounts and from data in the *Guardian*, 2 May 2001, p. 119

with 80 per cent achieving an 'excellent' score. This should not be a surprise in a country with 250,000 accountants – proportionately more than in any other country. 'Excellence' in 'Staff Performance and Learning' was achieved by 36 per cent, while 'Excellence' in 'Management' was achieved by just 26 per cent. Only 21 per cent achieved 'Excellence' in 'Health and Safety'. As Sikka (2002: 18) suggests, company auditors have more powers than most police forces and a state-guaranteed monopoly of auditing, yet, despite the accounting scandals of Enron, Global Crossing and such like, 'No scandal has ever come to light because of audit forms or the professional accounting bodies.' (Of course, the $100 million legal fee for Weil, Gotshal & Manges for representing Enron during the legal hearings into the bankruptcy is not a scandal – see Berlins, 2004: 17.)

But the most significant point remains that British productivity is relatively poor. More than anything else, this appears to be the result of political and economic choices made since 1945. For in 2001 every German worker had 70 per cent more capital invested than every British worker, produced 29 per cent more per hour than their British counterparts and yet took 175 hours more off per year. Despite, or perhaps because of, this inequity, the ratio between British CEOs' pay to the average British workers' pay is twice that of their German counterparts, and the social benefits available to the British citizen, or rather the British 'subject', are just half those available to the German citizen (Hutton, 2001: 30). Yet there are examples where British workers out-perform their German colleagues. For example, workers at the Nissan plant in Sunderland in 2000 produced 101 cars per employee over the year, giving it the highest productivity in Europe. German workers at the Volkswagen plant in Emden, in contrast, produced just 27 cars per employee per year, less than half the European average of 58 cars and well behind the Toyota employees in Derby (86 cars per employee per year). However, the remaining British car workers are also a long way behind their Japanese-owned competitors, with Ford's Dagenham plant, at 62 cars, being only nineteenth in the European listing (Milner, 2001: 22). This may also explain the general shift towards out-sourcing jobs previously undertaken in Britain to cheaper areas abroad. For example, in October 2003 HSBC announced it was shedding 4,000 jobs in the UK (followed by Lloyds TSB) and moving them to India. The following year HSBC's chair, Sir John Bond, received a 24 per cent pay rise to £1.2 million (Connon, 2004b: 2).

The removal of HSBC's jobs is just one example of the 2 million European jobs in the financial services that are expected to transfer to India by 2008. Most of these jobs were originally in the UK because the out-sourcing market tends to be restricted to English-speaking countries. The US also out-sources many jobs to India – for example, in 2003 Dell employed 3,000 people at its Bangalore and Hyderabad facilities and altogether as many as 3 million jobs may move to India, the Philippines, China and Malaysia by 2018 (see <http://www.internetnews.com/ent-news/article.php/3113721>). Indeed, it has been claimed that the world's 100 largest financial services companies will out-source £220 billion of their operations and two million jobs out of the UK by 2008. The cheapness of labour and the relative equality of skills are critical to this movement – as represented in figure 44. However, out-sourcing to overseas call centres can come with a price both in terms of quality of service to existing clients – because the driving force is cheapness of labour not superior customer service – and quality of life of the new employees as well as those losing their jobs: many Indian employees are required to work 13-hour shifts, at times that suit the US or British customers and under enormous stress – the point where attrition rates (the rate at which employees leave the industry annually) can be

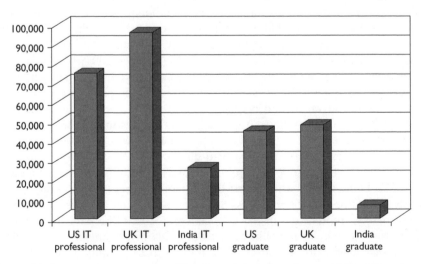

Figure 44 Comparative pay amongst IT professionals and graduates in USA, UK and India, 2003

Source: Reconstructed from National Association of Software Services Companies, India

as high as 30 per cent (Ramesh, 2004: 18; see also <www.union-network.org/Unisite/Events/Campaigns/call_centres.htm>).

It is not just 'high-tech' jobs that are moving: in 2003, for instance, the Northampton shoe factory, Dr Martens, closed, doing away with 1,000 jobs and transferring them to the Pou Chan factory in Guangdong, China, where wages are typically £70 per month (between five and twenty times lower than in the UK) plus board and lodging and where 15 per cent of the world's shoe production is based (Watts, 2003: 21). Of course, the 'loss' of jobs to low-cost competitors is hardly a novelty. Given that the UK in 2003 employed more people than ever before, it is difficult to conclude that the job loss is anything other than part of the process of longer-term relocation of labour to cheaper areas, which does not automatically result in long-term unemployment for those previously employed in the 'source' country, even if they do have to put up with short-term job loss and dislocation (Finch, 2003b: 26). Indeed, as Monbiot (2003b: 25) suggests, the flight of jobs to India is really a flight *back* to India: when that country was under the thrall of the British Empire, the British banned the import of Indian cotton cloth in 1700 and then systematically forced the Indians to supply Britain with cheap raw materials.

Even those with low wages are not immune from the drive to reduce costs. For example, between 2001 and 2003 more than 500 export assembly plants in Mexico were closed, leaving 218,000 workers unemployed. Since their average salary during employment was just US$1.26 per hour, they were clearly not displaced by European or American workers; but with Honduran wages at US59 cents per hour and Chinese wages at US27 cents per hour, it is not difficult to see where the competition lies. And that competition is often ruthless: in 2001, for example, the Disney Corporation abandoned its Shah Makhdum factory in Bangladesh, which had produced Disney shirts for eight years, after the female workforce asked for one day off per week (Roddick, 2003: 18; see also <http://www.nlcnet.org/campaigns/shahmakhdum/rsolidarite.pdf>). It may be recalled that Disney's CEO Michael Eisner received more than US$500 million in 1997 through a share option scheme (C. Walsh, 2002: 3).

Britain itself had 50,000 millionaires in 2000 (Fletcher, 2001: 14) and a growing proportion of these have achieved their wealth through business. In 1998, for example, forty-nine directors of Britain's top 350 companies were paid more than £1 million in salary and bonuses. The average salary of the leading directors of FTSE 100 companies (the *Financial Times* listing of the leading 100 companies on the London Stock Exchange) in 1998 was £800,000, excluding long-term incentives, while the best-paid director was Sam Chisholm, formerly of BSkyB, who earned £6.8 million in that year – £30,000 a day (Buckingham, 1998: 21). Philip Green, who owned British Home Stores (Bhs) and the Arcadia Group (Top Shop, Burton and Miss Selfridge) must rank amongst the wealthiest business entrepreneurs: in the financial year 2002/3 he paid himself £201 million for a year's work at Bhs after lending his own company £250 million (Bhs pre-tax profits dropped from £172 million to £123 million); in 2001/2 he was paid £160 million (Finch, 2003a). By contrast, the average annual salary of full-time British workers in 2000 was around £20,000. Within companies, the same pattern recurs: in March 2001 Barclays Bank paid £150 million in

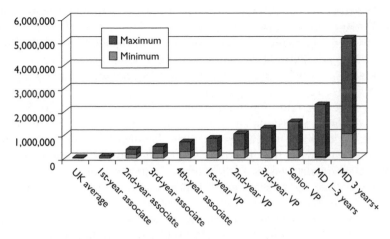

Figure 45 Annual average pay for UK investment bankers, 2001 (£)
Source: Reconstructed from data in Hart, 2001: 44–5

bonuses to its 6,300 staff at Barclays Capital and Barclays Global. The rest of the staff – all 50,000 of them – had to share £22 million between them (Farrelly, 2001: 1).

The UK's investment banking sector provides some of the richest rewards, and in the financial year ending April 2001 some £1 billion was distributed just in bonuses. The data given in figure 45 are averages and the point to note is the difference between minimum reward – which is primarily composed of salary – and maximum reward – which is almost wholly generated by the annual bonuses.

The size of the rewards awarded to those at the top of the work tree has stimulated an increasingly vocal group of dissidents. At one end of the scale of dissidents are the trade unions. For example, in September 1998, John Edmonds, a British trade union boss, in a speech to the Trades Union Congress, called such bosses 'greedy bastards' (*Guardian Editor*, 19 September 1998). But the workers are not alone in their growing contempt for the plutocrats of the business world: a survey of 1,500 students at eleven European universities and business schools in July 2001 (all members of the Community of European Management Schools) suggested that 'interesting work' was the most important criterion when looking for a job, followed by the 'social environment at work' and 'personal development'. The attraction of high salaries was only seventh on the list – but this did not translate into a sudden interest in serving the community: working in the public sector was the least popular option, attracting only 5 per cent of the respondents (Gooderham and Nordhaug, quoted in <www.ftdynamo.com> 20 July 2001).

Certainly, the PriceWaterhouseCoopers' 1998 report into executive pay found no linkage between executive pay and company results amongst the private sector boardrooms of the FTSE 500. The report suggested that the average company board executive bonus was 50 per cent of salary – though if rewards were linked to performance there would be a great deal more dispersal around the mean than there actually was. So, for example, Chris Gent, CEO of Vodafone, saw the share price of the company drop from £3.30 to £1.52 between July 2000 and July 2001 at the same time as picking up £8 million in share options (Treanor, 2001: 19). In fact, while profits dropped in the UK throughout 2000 and 2001, executive pay went in the opposite direction, and it did so at three times the rate of average earnings. Similarly, while a large proportion of British insurance companies have now admitted that their endowment policies linked to home purchases are unlikely to provide adequate sums at maturity, the rewards of the directors seem unaffected. For example, while the total bill to endowment policy-holders of the insurance industry was estimated at anything between £30 billion and £100 billion, the salary of David Prosser, CEO of Legal & General, increased by 56 per cent between 1999 and 2002, while Iain Lumsden, then CEO of Standard Life, saw a 71 per cent increase over the same period (Jones, 2004: 20). When Kate Swann became CEO of WH Smith's in 2004, her 'signing-on fee' was £475,000 in salary, an equivalent sum in bonus if targets were met, £500,000 in compensation for loss of earnings from her old company Argos and £1.4 million in share options – but the barrage of criticism was related to the sums that could be earned irrespective of performance. Admittedly, this was nowhere near the signing-on fee for William Aldinger, who joined HSBC with a reward package of £37.5 million (US$60m) that was unrelated to performance, but did include free medical and dental care for life for him and his wife should he lose his job (Doward, 2003a: 1). In the inimitable words of John Plender, chair of Pensions and Investment Research Consultants, '[executives] know a gravy train when [they] see one' (quoted in Denny, 2001b: 20). Indeed, even the shareholders seemed to be roused from their slumber: 20 per cent of HSBC shareholders voted against Aldinger's package, while 33 per cent voted against Swann's, though whether 'shareholder activism' would make a significant difference or even continue if the markets were to pick up is difficult to assess (Connon, 2004a: 5).

One of the reasons for the remarkably similar pattern of rewards may be that many of the directors sit on each others' remuneration committees – or 'enrichment committees', as Heller (2001: 9) calls them – proverbially scratching each others' backs. Thus in 2000, the remuneration committees of 98 out of the largest FTSE 100 companies were made up of 392 directors. In fact, between them, 30 of these directors sat on 67 committees. Equally significant, only 33 of these remunerating members (8 per cent) were women (Palmer, 2000: 18). The advice that these committees rely on is itself restricted primarily to that supplied by just four remuneration companies, like Towers Perrin which advises half of the FTSE 100 companies and nine of the ten largest companies (Connon, 2003a: 8).

Beyond remuneration committees, multiple directorships across different companies are common – or, rather, common to a relatively small number of people. In 2002, of the top 350 British companies, 80 directors held at least two other directorships, 6 held five directorships in total but most also have directorships at smaller companies. For example, Angus Crossart held seventeen, as did Bob Reid, while Allan Leighton and David Price held sixteen each;

in short, a rather small network of people controlled a very large number of companies (Morgan and Walsh, 2002: 3).

The gap between company directors and company employees has been increasing for some time. In the UK in 2000, for instance, the basic salary of directors rose 8 per cent on average – that is three times the rate of inflation and twice the rate of employees. On average the CEO of a top 30 company from the FTSE 100 earned £600,000 salary plus £200,000 in bonus, and most of these companies provided share options amounting to 81 per cent of the salary, in addition to a company car or cash equivalent worth £47,500; those in control of subsidiary companies earned about £150,000 (Elliot, 2001a: 19). By 2003 – and despite the introduction of a minimum wage – the average British worker was on less than average pay because the pay of executives had increased at such a rate. In fact, almost two-thirds of employees (65 per cent) were below average; in 1990, 60 per cent were on below average earnings (Denny, 2003: 24).

Of course, the reason for the rising inequalities between British employees and employers could be because British bosses are responsible for a huge surge in comparative productivity – but as we saw above this is not the case. Alternatively, it could be because the global market for executives is so competitive that British companies simply have to offer salary packages that are attractive enough to keep executives from crossing the Channel or the Atlantic. However, a glance at figure 46 suggests that this is not the case either: the pay gap between British executives and employees is higher than everywhere except the USA, where, in 2003, the average CEO of a Fortune 500 company was paid 400 times that of an ordinary worker (Caulkin, 2003a: 21). Such is the gap between the top and bottom in the USA that even Chris Gent suggested that 'the American level was a bridge too far' (quoted in Wray, 2003: 24). There is, however, one area where the British do pay themselves better than anyone else, and surprisingly enough it is in the area that the British appear to pride

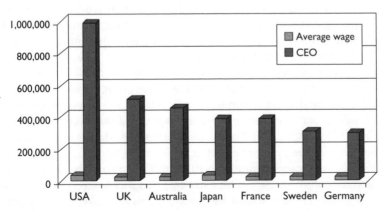

Figure 46 The international pay gap. Comparative rewards: CEOs and average wages, 2001 (£)

Source: Reconstructed from data in *Management Today*, 26 July 2001

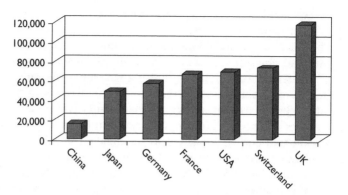

Figure 47 Comparative pay for accountants, 2001 (US$)
Source: Reconstructed from Clark, 2001: 28

themselves in, having the largest proportion of any country: accountancy (see figure 47).

A consequence of the increasing public concern at the rise of the executive 'fat cat' has been Long-Term Incentive Plans (LTIP), which measure executive performance against their peers; but this may still result in significant bonuses being paid to the directors of poorly performing firms, providing their competitors are doing even worse. For example, Anne Iverson, the ex-head of Laura Ashley, left the company with £450,000 after overseeing the company share price halved. Corus (ex-British Steel) managed to lose more than £1 billion in 2000, but it still managed to pay John Bryant and Fokko van Duyne, its two resigning co-CEOs, £2 million between them as golden goodbyes (*Guardian Notebook*, 23 April 2001). Similarly, Liam Strong, ex-head of Sears, left with £460,000 having led the company almost to the wall. And Lord Sainsbury's salary in 1998 rose by 37 per cent, despite his company losing out to Tesco. The board of the latter shared £11 million in bonuses and shares in 2004 – the same time that the company removed the right to paid sick leave for the first three days of any illness for some Tesco staff (Macalister, 2004: 17). But these sums remain small compared to the amount paid to Jim Fifield, who resigned from EMI in April 1998 with a useful sum of pocket money: £12.4 million (Barnett, 2001: 9), but still less than the £15 million that Michael Green received after the Carlton TV merger with Granada (Martinson, 2004: 21).

There is little evidence to suggest that the US is any different: an AFL-CIO study of US directors' remuneration systems concluded they were 'rigged to overpay CEOs. Cronyism, personal friendships and inter-relationships between top executives and corporate compensation committees and boards contribute to runaway executive salaries' (quoted in Palmer, 2000: 18). Some people just seem to have a knack of acquiring useful exit sums. Barclay Knapp, for instance, the former CEO of NTL, left with US$10 million, having already been criticized by American corporate governance experts in August 2003 for resigning from another company with a US$2.1 million pay-off after the company filed for bankruptcy under his leadership (Milmo, 2003: 19).

It is also important to note the pension benefits that accrue to the top executives. For instance, Jean Pierre Garnier, head of GlaxoSmithKline can currently expect a pension of £833,000 per annum – and that's after earning £7 million in 2002 supplemented by a £22 million pay-off while shares in GlaxoSmithKline fell (Toynbee, 2003a: 23). Geoff Mulcahy, head of the Kingfisher Group, can expect a pension of £660,000 – two-thirds of his £967,000 salary. The inequalities are not simply in terms of gross figures, but also in terms of the time necessary to acquire a full pension: Kingfisher employees, for example, must contribute for 40 years to take their top pension rights, but Kingfisher directors earn their full pension in just 20 years. Likewise, Telwest directors have an equivalent of 27.5 per cent of their salary paid into their pension scheme, compared to the 12 per cent secured for Telwest's staff. Only Marks and Spencer, amongst major British employers, offer pension rights to everyone on the same basis: 30 years (Inman, 2001: 2). Yet when Luc Vandevelde took over the ailing retailer, his reward package failed to reflect this pattern of equity: a £2 million golden hello, a salary of £650,000, stock options worth £10 million, and a free flat valued at £50,000 a year rental, all of which amounts to a significant investment. The public outcry against his £816,000 bonus in 2001 led him to waive his right to it, but he was still displaced in 2004.

The business response usually relates to the imperatives of the market and the importance of the shareholders' interests, but, of course, the canonization of the shareholders is simply the consequence of a choice made by business organizations – nowhere is it written in tablets of stone that shareholder interest (supplemented by executive rewards) is the only or even the most important aspect of all business organizations (Mickelthwaite and Wooldridge, 2003). Just because a market system seems to be the only viable way to organize an economy does not mean that shareholder value is the only goal in town. Whether those goals should be expanded to the Triple Bottom Line of economic prosperity, environmental protection and social equity (Elkington, 1999) or a more general Stakeholder Capitalism, or what Ellsworth (2002) refers to as 'Leading with a Purpose' – which is actually serving the customers – is less relevant than that shareholder value is not some immutable law of economics.

Indeed, despite the UK's excessive generosity towards its business leaders, the country's productivity consistently remains between 15 and 25 per cent behind that of the USA, Germany and France. The UK's 2003 Work Foundation report *The Missing Link: From Productivity to Performance* suggested that high-performing companies were those most likely to manage five related areas: customers and markets, shareholders, stakeholders, innovation and human resources. Any company that focuses on one of these (usually shareholders in the UK's case) was likely to fail because the system is just that – a system, not a device for enriching shareholders and/or executives. It is, therefore, the integration of all five elements that marks the difference between high and low performance. In the report's words: 'Managing the spaces in between can only be achieved by a workforce that sees the big picture and is enabled and motivated to act, with middle managers able to translate strategy into workforce goals' (quoted in Caulkin, 2003c: 11).

Perhaps an ancient Chinese story, retold by Phil Jackson (1995: 149–51), coach of the phenomenally successful Chicago Bulls basketball team, makes this point rather more emphatically. In the third century BC the Chinese Emperor Liu Bang celebrated his consolidation of China with a banquet, where he sat surrounded by his nobles and military and political experts. Since Liu Bang was neither noble by birth nor an expert in military or political affairs, some of the guests asked one of the military experts, Chen Cen, why Liu Bang was the Emperor. In a contemporary setting the question would probably have been: 'What added value does Liu Bang bring to the party?' Chen Cen's response was to ask the questioner a question in return: 'What determines the strength of a wheel?' One guest suggested the strength of the spokes, but Chen Cen countered that two sets of spokes of identical strength did not necessarily make wheels of identical strength. On the contrary, the strength was also affected by the spaces between the spokes, and determining the spaces was the true art of the wheelwright. In effect, holding together the diversity of talents was what distinguished a successful from an unsuccessful leader and the same can be said about an organization.

What makes it all the more difficult for low-paid British employees are the comparative living costs. In 2001 Britain's prices were the sixth highest in the world – which basically means that in a move from the USA to London, a family of three would need to double their expenditure to maintain the same standard of living. Given that British salary and tax rates are lower than most of its competitors, and that British manufacturing productivity in 2001 was 39 per cent behind American rates, one might wonder why this calamitous state of affairs has occurred. Caulkin (2001: 11) is sure that British management is the element most responsible for this complex problem: British plants run by American, German or Japanese management regularly outperform those run by British managers: take, for example, Mini, RR, Aston Martin, Bentley, Jaguar and Lotus (Caulkin, 2003c: 11). The consequence is that British managers are more likely to pass their inefficiencies on to the consumer through higher prices, than to resolve the underlying productivity problem.

Equally important, some executives seem either to misunderstand the nature of public concern, or simply not to care. For instance, in April 2000 Matthew Barrett, the CEO of Barclays Bank (basic salary £850,000 but existing annual income of £6 million), announced two developments. First, the closure of 172 branches, representing 10 per cent of the system, mainly located in rural areas; second, his own £30.5 million bonus in share options. Aside from the crass timing, the assumption that corporations are simply slaves to the market imperative is dubious. In the USA, for example, the Community Reinvestment Act (CRA) prevents such branch closures unless the bank can establish to the Federal Reserve or the courts that the banking needs of the community will continue to be met by the bank. No such legislation exists in the UK (Palast, 2000: 5; Treanor, 2000: 1). On the other hand, Guy McCracken probably 'earned' his £707,000 golden goodbye in conjunction with his £265,000 salary from Marks and Spencer after he closed down their overseas operations with the loss of 3,000 jobs (Finch, 2001c: 31).

In fact, in 1992 in the USA there was a correlation between the pay of the bosses and the level of redundancy: while the average CEO got a pay increase of 6 per cent, those who made the most staff redundant saw their pay increase by an average of 44 per cent. For example, Hewlett Packard 'lost' 25,700 employees, while their CEO, Carly Fiorina, had her pay increased by 231 per cent to US$4.1 million. Meanwhile at AOL Time Warner, 4,380 employees were dismissed, and the CEO, Gerald Levin, secured a 1,612 per cent pay increase to US$21.1 million. However, top of this league was Tyco's (ex-)boss Dennis Kozlowski, who was himself dismissed halfway through the year, having seen the dismissal of 11,300 other employees; it is doubtful that any of these received his reward package for that effort: US$71 million (Connon, 2003b: 2). Admittedly, at US$140 million Dick Grasso made twice Kozlowski's salary in 2003 as CEO of the New York Stock Exchange, but he did have to work the full twelve months for it – or he would have done if he hadn't been persuaded to resign shortly after the reward package was made public (*Business Week*, 15 September 2003). Grasso was replaced in September 2003 by the former Citigroup boss John Reed at a meagre US$1 – from the ridiculous to the sublime! (See <http://money.cnn.com/2003/09/21/markets/nyse_reed/>.) In fact the dismissal of 'under-performing' CEOs increased significantly in the late 1990s and into the twenty-first century. For example, in 2002, 39 per cent of all CEOs who left their positions were dismissed, compared to 25 per cent in 2001 and 10 per cent in 1995 (on average 10 per cent of all companies changed their CEO annually) (Skapinker, 2003: 1).

Strangely enough, the same kind of public opprobrium does not seem to be heaped upon sports personalities, who often earn far more than their 'business' counterparts. For example, more than 100 players in the English football's Premier League earned over £1 million in the 2000–1 season. Indeed, more than a third of that league's players (over 20-year-olds) earned over £500,000 a year. In effect, they earn more in one month just from football (ignoring sponsorship deals and endorsements) than the average Third Division player (lowest of the professional leagues) earns in a year (£37,000; the average Premier Division salary in 2000 was £128,000) (Brodkin, 2000: 32).

Beyond English football the rewards are significantly higher. For example, it is estimated that Michael Schumacher earned £41.8 million in 2002, while Tiger Woods received £37.5 million, Mike Tyson not far behind on £34 million and Michael Jordan on £26.2 million – all of which puts David Beckham's £10.87 million in the shade (see <http://news.bbc.co.uk/sport1/hi/football/1795385.stm>). Behind Beckham in 2003 in football rewards came Zinedin Zidane (£10.1 million) and Ronaldo (£8.5 million) from Real Madrid, while Michael Owen earned £6.45 million and Roy Keane earned £6.27 million (Thomas, 2003: 30).

Here may be a clue to the explosion of inequalities at work. In previous eras the greatest gap was between social classes, such that the aristocracy remained inordinately wealthy and the rest remained grindingly poor. This inequality was, at least according to the aristocracy, God's will, and the poor would receive compensation for their miserable lives, but only in heaven, and only if they accepted their fate on earth with equanimity. As such, the poor could blame their condition on their birth or look forward to death; either way, their position was beyond their control and responsibility. However, the rise of meritocracy, engendered by the beginning of compulsory education and competitive entry to the Civil Service, which encouraged all organizations to follow suit in their recruitment and promotion strategies, has now generated a different rationale for personal success. Whereas personal success could be explained by luck, or its absence, at birth, now personal success can be justified by reference to personal merit. Or to paraphrase certain television adverts in 2000, 'because you're worth it'. In effect, since merit now allegedly explains inequalities, there is no limit to how much inequality can be justified. Of course, there are significant problems with the claims that merit does indeed translate into, and justify, such inequalities, but these 'academic' problems can be ignored as the whining of the less successful rather than legitimate criticisms of the inequalities. Perhaps more important, the legitimations of the meritocrats (if accepted) undermine the accounts of the less successful: you are wholly responsible for your position in life (see Young, 1958). Runciman first enunciated this latter form of response in his 1966 work *Relative Deprivation and Social Justice*: 'The magnitude of a relative deprivation is the extent of the difference between the desired situation [e.g., the income of the richer] and that of the person desiring it' (p. 10), and it still holds good almost fifty years later: it isn't the (material) gap that matters; it's what we think about the (symbolic) gap that matters.

This is doubly ironic given that self-evident CEO failures in business are richly rewarded, or paid off. And since there is little downward mobility generally in the UK (the acquisition of middle-class jobs by the working class is more a consequence of the expanding market for professional workers rather than the replacement of the 'ordinary' middle class by the 'gifted' working class), the consequence generally is an ever-increasing chasm between the two main social classes. Even the movement from working-class background to middle-class occupation – which used to be relatively common in, say, the army, where soldiers could move through the ranks to acquire a commission – is less likely because, as Jonathan Gershuny has argued, the entry port to the middle class is now more or less restricted to university graduation. Indeed, it seems that even 'gifted' infants from the lowest socio-economic classes have trouble climbing the mobility ladder, for with every year that passes they are gradually overtaken by the 'average' children from more privileged backgrounds and this erosion and displacement is critical during the years between the ages of 5 and 10 (Feinstein, 2003). Work now offers much less of a second chance to those who fail to escape their working-class background through school. As the 2004 UK government's Strategy Unit report suggests, a middle-class child is 15 times more likely to remain middle class than a working-class child is to move up into the middle class, and a baby's fate is generally fixed by the age of 22 months (Aldridge, 2004).

This might also explain the sudden rush of business into ethics, values and corporate responsibility – a displacement activity by all those who have bought into the assumption that the (only) purpose of management is to maximize profit, whereas one could argue that the purpose of management is to make the aims of the organization possible – *one* of which might be profits. In effect, the nouveaux riches are now displacing not just the aristocracy in the wealth table but also taking over their social role: noblesse oblige. Here we have the ulti-mate justification for gross inequalities that protected the powerful from guilt for generations: the reason for my extraordinary wealth is my merit and hard work, but, fortunately for you, when I have accumulated enough wealth from your efforts, I will start to give some away to charities (and you can be sure that I will be a better judge of where the money should go than either leaving the money in your pocket or giving it the government to distribute). Even that would be a start: Children in Need (a British charity that takes over BBC One on one evening a year) raised around £27 million in 2002; in the same year the shopping magnate Philip Green earned more than five times that amount with an income of £157.7 million (Cohen, 2002: 31). Private charitable dona-tions are an interesting phenomenon in themselves: in 2002 the British public gave £13 million to Donkey Sanctuary, Devon, which looks after 75 per cent of the donkeys in the UK, and that is more money than is received by Mencap or Age Concern or the Samaritans. Donkey Sanctuary employs sixty welfare officers in the UK (Dowling, 2003: 1–3).

If it is the case that meritocracy is associated with growing inequalities (unless checked by government action), then we should expect to see the greatest inequal-ities in the country that is, at least ostensibly, the greatest meritocracy: the USA rather than the UK. In the UK in 2003 the average CEO of the FTSE 100 companies earned 80 times the average salaries of their employees (*Guardian*, 2 October, p. 27). But at the top end there were some significant increases on that ratio. At the very top is Rentokil's Sir Clive Thompson who, on £2,891,000 per annum, earned 247 times the average Rentokil salary of £11,696 in 2003 (see figure 48). The corresponding companies are reproduced in figure 49, and

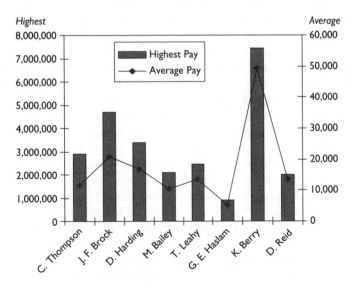

Figure 48 UK annual salary index, 2003 (£)
Source: Reconstructed from data in the *Guardian*, 2 October 2003, p. 27

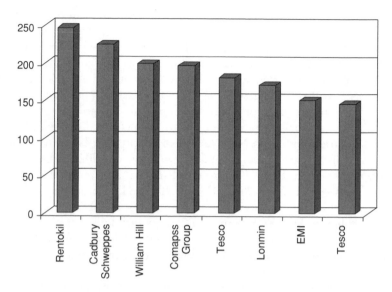

Figure 49 Ratio of top salary to average salary (UK), 2003
Source: Reconstructed from data in the *Guardian*, 2 October, p. 27

as this figure reveals, this is the case for the country where the average CEO's pay is the greatest multiple of the average wage: the USA (see <https://secure.payfinder.com/home.asp>). In 2000 the American minimum wage was approximately $10,712 – an increase of 36 per cent since 1990 (in 2003 the minimum wage in the UK was £4.50 an hour). The average wage of an auto-worker was about $50,044 (a 37 per cent increase over ten years). The average New York teacher might expect to make $49,030 (a 20 per cent increase), while the average Harvard Business School MBA graduate could expect a salary twice this rate ($105,000: a 50 per cent increase). A senior airline pilot could almost double this, with a salary of $193,656 (a 33 per cent increase), but only when we get to major sports players do we see the beginnings of an unbridgeable gap: the average player in the major league baseball teams got $1,895,631 (a 217 per cent increase). At this point we start accelerating to warp speeds: Richard Wagoner was paid $10,155,677 (a 288 per cent increase) by General Motors; Lee Raymond of Exxon-Mobil earned $33,207,948 (a 507 per cent increase); Douglas Daft took home $109,410,444 (a 1,997 per cent increase); General Electric's legendary Jack Welch received a little more at $125,340,263 (a 2,496 per cent increase); but top of the league came Sanford Weill, CEO of Citigroup, whose $150,688,160 annual salary for 2000 was 12,444 per cent higher than in 1990. In other words, Weill earns almost $3 million a week, or just over half a million dollars a day, or roughly $72,000 an hour. It would take an American on the minimum wage more than six years to earn what Weill earns in one hour. Now, of course we have not yet added in the other 'compensation schemes': the bonus, and stock options and so on. If we add these in, then Sanford Weill lives in relative poverty, because while Steve Jobs secured a $381 million package in 2000, even this was a pittance compared to

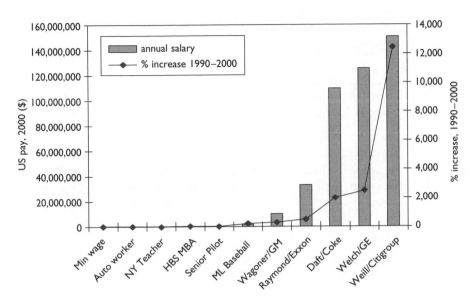

Figure 50 American work rewards, 1990–2000
Source: Reconstructed from Colvin, 2001 and Loomis, 2001

Charles Wang, whose 1999 reward package from Computer Associates topped $507 million (all data from Colvin, 2001). At this level it would take our minimum wage worker almost 23 years to catch Charles Wang's hourly rate of $243,750. Or to put it another way, Charles Wang is worth 47,330 people on the minimum wage: if we took the difference in terms of height, a minimum wage earner would be the equivalent of a mole hill to Charles Wang's Mount Everest. Figure 50 provides a visual representation of these inequalities.

It was not always thus. In the 1950s and 1960s CEO pay rose more slowly than the average wage, but since the early 1970s, partly as a result of CEOs finding more and more imaginative ways of paying themselves, two things have happened. First, CEO rewards have outrun all others; second, the rewards seldom reflect the performance of the company. In 1993 the US Congress passed section 162(m) of the tax code which inhibited companies from making a tax deduction for CEO salaries above $1 million per annum. The effect of this was not to impose a ceiling on inequalities but to raise many CEOs to that base line, and those already over it went hunting other options. Colvin (2001: 35) suggests several elements have combined to generate this extraordinary polarization:

1. Sacking CEOs means replacing them with new ones who demand compensation for forfeiting previous stock options – for instance, Gary Wendt took a $45 million signing-on bonus when he left GE Capital and joined Conseco in 2000.

↓

2. The new CEO obviously wants more than their miserably failing predecessors.

↓

3. The compensation committee provides a package that reflects the ever-rising median for CEOs.

↓

4. Poor performance hits the value of stock options and, to avoid further embarrassment with a hike in base salary, the CEOs secure even more stock options – allegedly to tie them to the fortunes of the company, but in reality the effect is to make them a fortune.

↓

5. The increasing reward now sets the new base for other new CEOs.

↓

6. The company underperforms, the CEO leaves (with a 'golden goodbye') and the whole process starts over.

↓

7. Return to 1.

The rise of stock options have led some shareholders to call their legitimacy into question. In February 2001, Hermes Investment Management, which managed £50 billion of pension fund cash for the Post Office and BT, proclaimed in a letter to the management of the NASDAQ (originally, the National Association of Securities Dealers Automated Quotation) that companies should be required to put their share option schemes to the shareholders: 'Many of the stock option plans in operation at Nasdaq listed companies, in particular, involve a considerable transfer of wealth from the existing shareholders to the directors and officers. This is more than just a capital allocation decision; in any other form of asset ownership such a transfer without the approval of the owners would be considered theft' (quoted in Finch, 2001a: 23).

Summary

This chapter has concerned the state and status of jobs in contemporary labour markets. It should be clear that while not all jobs are now McDonaldized, some are and many more are beginning to migrate beyond the West towards the cheaper labour zones, especially China and India. On the other hand, economic and political migrations continue into the West and, given the age structures of the latter nations, this is really just as well: it is probably not possible to maintain the health and welfare of most people beyond pensionable age by relying on the traditional relationship between the employed and retired.

Within this problem the continuing switch towards service jobs and away from manufacturing jobs continues apace, though it should be recalled that there probably never was a time for most countries when most employees were manufacturing workers, never mind factory workers. Certainly the likelihood is of a continuing relative decline in manufacturing jobs, but high value-added manufacturing will undoubtedly remain a significant employer and an even more significant source of revenue for governments. Indeed, a return to the model of the early twentieth century cannot be ruled out, as a minority of money-rich but time-poor people increasingly rely on domestic servants to service their houses and families. This will probably mirror the current class and status divisions, and although the perception of many will be that stress and exhaustion are increasingly their lot, a minority will be able to reap rich rewards from their efforts, while the majority simply maintain themselves at a very gradually increasing level of wealth. A further minority will, in all probability, remain at the margins of society – unskilled and unemployed.

Meanwhile at the opposite end of the spectrum the 'fat cats' will assuredly attract huge levels of rewards and, if the 'cats' are not of the pop, film or sports celebrity variety then the media will undoubtedly continue to lambast them for their 'unbridled greed' and 'despicable acquisitiveness'. On the other hand, if they happen to be Robbie Williams or David Beckham or Madonna or Catherine Zeta Jones then . . . well, they deserve every penny of our money don't they? In fact a poll in 2004 of British students suggested that looks and media exposure were far more influential than intellectual prowess: David Beckham, Brad Pitt and Justin Timberlake topped the poll with Tony Blair a mere 69th and George W. Bush 100th. Nelson Mandela was the only politician in the top 20 at 14th (Tysome, 2004: 3).

An interesting counter-wave of hostility developed in 2003, particularly against footballers, and it would seem against black footballers in particular. Take a comment from Brian Glanville – a noted British football commentator – on the trend to high football wages:

> I think many black players – in many cases, particularly with young West Indian players – they come from a society in which families are so often fatherless, mothers have to work, children are left all day in the care of minders. They have very little education and then suddenly these uneducated boys are projected into a world in which they are earning, say, £40,000 to £50,000 a week. There are no controls. (quoted in Toynbee, 2003b: 27)

So that's it, then: inequality is OK as long as it doesn't reach those who don't know how to spend it properly!

In fact the UK remains high in the inequality stakes within Europe but still a long way short of the USA, where only since the turn of the century have shareholders really begun to mobilize against what they regard as unjust executive reward packages. Perhaps the combination of long hours, low rewards and poor productivity that the typical British employee can expect to involve him- or herself in can be summarized in a single appropriate sentence that was the received wisdom in the first factory I worked in sometime in the summer of 1970: 'They don't pay us very much and we don't do very much.'

Exam/essay questions

1 'Wage inequalities are not immoral but simply the result of a market economy.' Discuss.
2 Does it matter if people are happy or unhappy at work as long as the work gets done?
3 To what extent is the McDonaldization thesis simply a consequence of a romantic notion of pre-contemporary labour?
4 Does it really matter whether jobs are categorized as 'manufacturing' or 'service'? Isn't a job still a job whatever is involved?
5 Do economic migrants pose a threat or a saving grace to host countries?
6 What do the correlations between illness and social class tell us about contemporary work?
7 If you are an employer faced with high labour costs in a call centre, are there any reasons why you should *not* out-source the work to a cheaper country?
8 Given the similarity in reward levels between business bosses, sports stars and rock, pop and film celebrities, to what extent is the 'fat cat' debate rooted in the antagonisms of social class rather than economic rationality?
9 'To some extent the real paradox of contemporary work is not the presence of radical inequalities but the absence of radical protest against them.' Discuss.
10 Which might be a better explanation for the persistence of poverty: the absence of work or the presence of low pay?

Further reading

Dickens, Gregg and Wadsworth's *The State of Working Britain* (2001) provides a valuable survey of contemporary work in the UK, while Bradley, Erickson, Stephenson and Williams's *Myths at Work* (2000) provides a vigorous and well-researched assault upon several related myths of and at work. Toynbee's *Hard Work: Life in Low Pay Britain* (2003) gives an account of her own experiment as a low-paid worker in the UK and is worth reading just to remind yourself how bad it can get. Across the water, Sum, Fogg and Harrington's *Immigrant Workers and the Great American Job Machine* (2003) is invaluable as a source for material on the USA and the role of immigrant workers in sustaining the American economy. George Ritzer's *McDonaldization of Society* was reissued in 2004 and remains the 'bible' of this approach.

10

Future Work: Globalization and the Age of Enthralment?

> I see in the near future a crisis approaching that unnerves me and causes me to tremble for the safety of my country . . . corporations have been enthroned and an era of corruption in high places will follow.
> President Abraham Lincoln to Colonel William F. Elkins,
> 21 November 1864 (quoted in Monbiot, 2000: 6)

Introduction

The future of work is regularly portrayed either as one of total novelty – the end of the post-war pattern, the end of the trade unions, the end of careers, the end of manufacturing, the end of male domination at work, the end of the working class, the end of the factory, the end of 'going to work', indeed, the end of work (Rifkin, 1996) – or as one of untold possibilities, as we exploit the potential of new technologies to create a long sought-after dream: the end of drudgery and the beginnings of global integration. This chapter addresses this index of possibilities by assessing what may be the most significant element: the rise of global capitalism. Despite the evidence to the contrary, global capitalism – that most plutocratic form of society – also embodies its opposite: planetocracy. By this I mean that the destruction of national borders and the gradual technical and economic integration of the major economies carries along with the manic accumulation of individual and national wealth – and poverty – the possibility of a system of global governance that also transcends national borders: a global democratic system – a planetocracy. We are self-evidently a long way from this, but the erosion of borders has been developing for generations, while the current public disquiet about global capitalism reaches a new level. The only long-term solution to the problems of the globe – and many of these are work-related – seems to be some form of global governance that constrains the actions of the market: just as capital is global, so too must be the democratic governance of capital by the world's population. However, this is a book concerned with work not global governance, and the former phenomenon will be investigated through two different lenses: in the first place we consider the claims and counter-claims appertaining to global capitalism as a general trend; in the second, we narrow the debate down to return to the issue that featured so heavily in the beginning of work: slavery.

That slavery still exists is an affront to us all, but there is another form of enslavement that probably does not affront us, mainly because it occurs metaphorically behind our backs: enthralment. According to the Collins English dictionary, 'enthralment' means:

1 'To hold spellbound, enchant, captivate'
2 'To hold as a thrall, to enslave':
    2(a) 'Thrall-dom' the state or condition of being in the power of another person;
    2(b) A person totally subject to some need, desire, appetite (from Old English '*thrael*' slave, from Old Norse '*thraell*')

The ambiguity of the word perfectly captures the problem here, because in sense 2(a) enthralment is simply another word for slavery: we are coerced against our will by another. But in sense (1) and 2(b), enthralment implies some degree of volitional behaviour: we either submit to our own passions through lack of self-discipline or we voluntarily submit ourselves to another person or thing; either way we remain responsible for our action even if we may proclaim our innocence and inability to resist temptation. The coercion of another will form the topic of the last section of this chapter but self-coercion forms the basis of the first section.

In some ways most of us have probably always been enthralled, if only by our own rituals. For instance, a 2001 survey by the business consultants Office Angels suggested that half the British workforce would rather wait for their favourite toilet cubicle at work to become free rather than use the next available one, and 46 per cent believed that if they failed to carry out their traditional daily routines (standing in the same spot on the station, sitting in the same chair and so on) then bad luck would befall them (Dhingra, 2001a: 7). More alarmingly, half the British population regularly consult a horoscope (though only 9 per cent admit to believing it), 33 per cent of British jobseekers apparently consult their stars before an interview and 6 per cent had seen an astrologer for advice before an interview (Dhingra, 2001a: 7). Even the 2001 winner of Wimbledon, Goran Ivanisevic, believed himself enthralled to luck – Tatjana Dragovic, his partner, was noticeably absent from the tournament because he thought she would bring bad luck (Coward, 2001: 9).

As shall be examined shortly, many of the attacks upon globalization imply that corporations have enslaved us, robbing citizens of their political rights and undermining the power of nation-states to constrain the unfettered freedom of the market. However, I want to suggest that this approach – while attractively removing us from responsibility for this state of affairs – is closer to slavery than enthralment, and it is the latter which both explains the phenomenon better and which poses more of a threat to the global corporations. But to understand this we first need to consider how the future is constructed, determined or modelled; for if we have no choice in the future – if we are slaves to the past – then all this is irrelevant.

Modelling the future or walking backwards into it?

Predicting the future is a risky business; even the prophet who reliably claims to fail to predict the future accurately can get it wrong, and thus be unwittingly right. The four most significant changes at the end of the twentieth and the beginning of the twenty-first centuries were probably:

- the fall of the Berlin Wall
- the rise of the internet
- the crisis of Asian economies
- 9/11

None of these was predicted. In 1956 Sir Richard Woolley, the British Astronomer Royal, regarded the possibility of space flight as 'bilge'. In 1957 *Sputnik 1* proved otherwise (Birch, 2001: 17). Perhaps the people least likely to get the future right are, ironically, the experts. It is regularly established, for example, that 'ordinary' investors outperform professional investment analysts (Saunders, 2001: 5), and in many other spheres of 'expertise' the level of arrogance, or at least over-confidence, associated with it leads to significant errors of judgement. This does not mean we should ask the ignorant for their opinion – though it is probable that the ignorant are likely to be more confident about their predictions than the experts. As MacKenzie's (1991) seminal work on missile accuracy suggested, the closer you are to the production of knowledge, the more uncertain you will probably be as to its reliability. Conversely, those at some distance from the production of knowledge are the most likely to be persuaded of the claims of the producers. This 'trough of ignorance' implies that expert forecasters are less confident than they appear to be in their predictions, while non-experts are more confident in the validity of these same predictions – a point that might account for the difference in confidence concerning the existence of weapons of mass destruction in Iraq between the Anglo-American secret services and their respective governments prior to the invasion of that country in 2003. That uncertainty, ironically, contrasts well with the surfeit of 'scientific' claims that regularly point out that eating a particular item is

(a) good for you, (b) certain to endanger your health, or (c) either (a) or (b). Baker (2001), for example, has suggested that the link between skin cancer and sun-tan lotions is, at best, unclear: maybe they work, maybe they encourage people to spend too long in the sun and maybe the chemicals they are composed of are, in and of themselves, dangerous. So perhaps the greatest caveat for what follows is to remember the following anonymous saying: 'Forecasting is very difficult – especially if it's about the future.'

Walter Benjamin probably came up with the best illustration of what we normally do in guessing what lies ahead – and why forecasting is so difficult: we walk backwards into the future. This image of stumbling into tomorrow, knowing only what happened yesterday as a guide, is both common and comforting; after all, if tomorrow simply replicates yesterday, we can rest assured that nothing untoward will happen. Indeed, many of these approaches are not simply 'linear' in their extrapolation of current trends to a future position; they also combine the straight line with an increasing degree of comfort. In other words, the future is both predictable, based on the past, and better than the past. Sometimes associated with 'Whig' approaches to historical explanation, such a future beckons us with less work, more leisure, less hunger, better health, less violence and so on. This kind of philosophy is also deeply rooted in the Enlightenment, from which stems an unerring belief in the utility of science and reason as the harbingers of peace and wisdom to the world. However, the issues raised below are all rooted in contentious debate: the future is debatable.

That said, if we look to California as the harbinger of the future, then – for the majority – it does not look enticing: the poorest 20 per cent have seen their real incomes drop for many years. At the top, however, the prospect of creating another 63 millionaires every day may seem exciting (Reeves, 2000a). Globally, 400 billionaires own more wealth than 45 per cent of the world's population (Brundtland, 2000). Britain alone had 50,000 millionaires in 2000 (Fletcher, 2001: 14). Indeed, in Britain real incomes doubled between 1975 and 2000 and are expected to double again by 2025. But this hides as much as it reveals: in 1979, 10 per cent of the British population lived in poverty (defined as the proportion of people receiving less than half the average income), but by 1995 this measure had doubled to 20 per cent of the population (Burgess and Propper, 1999). With the exception of sub-Saharan Africa, it would appear that most places and most people on earth will experience a rising standard of living in the foreseeable future. The World Bank even predicted a halving in world poverty by 2015, though it subsequently backtracked on this, suggesting that while urban poverty was decreasing, rural poverty was – as a direct consequence of diverted aid – now increasing (Fletcher, 2001: 14). Let us now consider the extent to which the future of work is ineradicably associated with the future of globalization

The context of globalization

The production of even relatively simple items is now quite commonly a global process. For example, Abrams and Astill (2001) traced an ordinary pair of Lee

Cooper jeans from the washers (using Turkish pumice stone) and final machine shops in Ras Jebel in Tunisia (where machinists earn 58p an hour) back to Milan where the material is spun and dyed using German colours made in Frankfurt. The cotton itself comes mainly from Benin where, typically, day labourers earn 60p and peasant farmers can earn £15 profit from 1.5 tonnes of cotton. These farmers may even get to spend the money if they can avoid being poisoned by the insecticides and fertilizers (100 people in Benin died in 2000 from insecticide poisoning). The cotton for the pockets of the jeans is grown in Pakistan. Beyond the cotton fabric itself, the strengthening threads are produced in Northern Ireland, Hungary and Turkey, though it was initially made in Japan, and while the zip tape comes from France, the zip teeth are again from Japan. The brass poppers are made in Germany from Namibian and Australian copper. In effect, it is most likely that the jeans you are wearing, or those in your wardrobe (or 'hanging' on your floor), are essentially global products. That global linkage which keeps the clothes you are wearing together also threatens to pull the metaphorical shirt from your back when one part of the network starts to fray. When the Asian economies started to crash, the entire world economy began to tremble, and in July 2001, as Argentina hovered on the precipice of defaulting over its £90 billion debt burden, the rest of South America was also gripped by financial fever (Elliott, 2001b: 23). So what, precisely, is this globalization that holds us all in its trance-like grip?

Well, as you might expect, the definition remains contested. Robins (1996: 345) defines globalization as a stage in the development of the world economy 'in which all aspects of the economy – raw materials, labour, information and transportation, finance, distribution, marketing – are integrated or interdependent on a global scale'. Castells (1994: 21), in contrast, is rather more concerned with the significance of temporal integration: 'By global economy we mean an economy that works as a unit in real time on a planetary basis.' Lovelock and Yip (1996: 65), however, probably capture the popular concern for the threat to local autonomy with their approach, in which 'a truly global company is one that not only does business in both the eastern and western hemispheres, but also in the northern and southern ones. The forces of globalization thereby tend to erode the integrity and autonomy of national economies.'

Just as globalization is a contested topic, so too are multinational corporations (MNCs). Schröter (quoted in G. Jones, 1994: 6) suggests an MNC is 'a firm which has at least two production facilities in two foreign countries or three production facilities in one foreign country; investments in colonies are excluded'. Nicholas's (1991) definition is rather simpler: 'any firm which has a production plant abroad'. However, 'production plant' limits MNCs to 'factories' and since 80 per cent of US employees now work in services, the umbilical cord between an MNC and a 'production plant' is increasingly tenuous. Dunning's (1993) approach is probably better, in which MNCs are 'enterprises involved in Foreign Direct Investment (FDI) and which own or control value-adding activities in more than one country'.

So what are the apparent causes of globalization? Again, the answers to that question are diverse, but the following list embodies many of the assumed causal agents:

- Profits: between 1981 and 1994, FDI in 'developing' nations rose from US$13 billion to US$80 billion. In the 1980s many American MNCs acquired between 25 and 40 per cent of their profits from overseas. In the 1990s many US commercial banks were reaping up to 60 per cent of their income from activities abroad.
- Access to raw materials: from iron, salt, slaves, cocoa, oil and beyond, though increasingly globalization is driven by access to knowledge.
- Costs of transport: which have encouraged the growth of food process plants etc., at the point of production.
- Access to new markets: thereby avoiding import restrictions and so on. It is also important to remember that access to the fastest growing markets is essentially linked to globalization too, because these tend to be within developing nations.
- Exploitation of cheap and skilled labour: for example, the Indian sub-continent for footballs and for computing (India's growth rate in 2003 was about 8 per cent); China overtook the USA in 2003 as the largest destination for FDI, which may explain why its economy grew by 8 or 9 per cent in that year. In 2003 China also imported a third of the world's coal, cement and steel output and was the second biggest importer of oil behind Japan (Collinson, 2004: 10). According to Deloitte, if the expansion rate of the Chinese economy continues, by 2020 it will have outstripped that of the USA (see <http://www.mbaworld.com/index.php?content=eventswelcome& mm=10&sm=3&>).
- Transplantation of factories: to countries with limited, or weakly enforced, health and safety legislation.
- Risk-spreading: complex products often use particular resources in specific countries to spread risk.
- Avoiding the 'burden' of the developed world's social welfare system.

Globalization, in the sense of a commercial movement across national boundaries has, of course, existed for centuries, and Moore and Lewis (1999) make a good case for suggesting that the first MNCs existed 4,000 years ago in Assyria. However, we can trace the development of contemporary globalization to the European companies of the sixteenth century: the Muscovy Company (1555), the Spanish Company (1577), the Senegal Adventurers (1588) and, most famously, the East India Company (1600). Within a couple of centuries, what started out as unusual trading organizations had become the norm, not just in a business sense but in a moral and ethical too. As a Select Committee of the House of Commons attested in 1811: 'No interference of the legislature with the freedom of trade, or with the perfect liberty of every individual to dispose of his time and his labour in the way and on the terms which he may judge most conducive to his own interest, can take place without violating general principles of the first importance to the prosperity and happiness of the community' (quoted in Fox, 1985: 71).

That moralizing tale would have found favour with Adam Smith but, as Lazonick remarks, Adam Smith – like the British House of Commons – had a penchant for ignoring history:

The political purpose of the *Wealth of Nations* was to attack the mercantilist institutions that the British economy had built up over the previous two hundred years. . . . In his assault on these institutions, Smith might have asked why the extent of the world market available to Britain in the late eighteenth century was *so uniquely under British control*. . . . In particular, Smith might have recognized the importance of the joint stock trading companies such as the East India Company and the Royal Africa Company . . . with their armed merchant fleets . . . Smith might then have mentioned Britain's use of its political power to stifle the growth of the textile industries of Portugal and Ireland in the eighteenth century. . . . How Britain's victorious wars against the Spanish in the sixteenth century, the Dutch in the seventeenth century, and the French in the eighteenth century helped to ensure that British ships would be free to trade where and when they pleased. . . . In short, Smith might have recognized the integral relation between economic and political power in the rise of Britain to economic dominance. (Lazonick, 1993: 2–3)

By the middle of the nineteenth century competitors to British MNCs began to emerge on the continent and in the USA, for example Singer and Siemens, and by the First World War manufacturing, extractive and service multinationals were significant elements of the global economy (in 1914, for example, the olive dye for British Army uniforms was imported from Germany, even as hostilities were opening up).

Before 1914, FDI was mainly channelled into the 'developing' world, with the UK being the largest investor, controlling about 40 per cent of the total. However, after 1914 FDI flowed back into the developed world and the USA displaced the UK with 50 per cent of the total by 1960. India and Russia had higher levels of foreign-owned companies before 1914 than for a long time after, and while Japan had little FDI but considerable economic growth in the late nineteenth century, the UK had the opposite combination: high FDI but low economic growth. In fact, Modelski (1972) is often credited with the contemporary invention of the word 'globalization', though Held et al. (1999: 1) suggest its origins lie in both French and American writings in the 1960s. Whatever the source of the word, most commentators agree that it comprises some or all of the following dimensions:

- the gradual connection between different societies;
- the compression, and increased consciousness, of the world;
- the growth of transnational and multinational corporations;
- the global presence of icons/brands like Coke and McDonald's;
- global production methods, such as: Just-in-Time (JIT), Total Quality Management (TQM), and Lean Production;
- global products, like Ford's 'Ka' and Western pop music;
- the pervasiveness of a global language: English;
- the development of universal computer standards: e.g., Microsoft Windows;
- the rapid increase in Foreign Direct Investment;
- the increasing domination of the world's capital and financial markets by 24-hour trading from New York, London and Tokyo.

As might be expected, there are many who suggest that globalization is either a figment of an over-active imagination, or that the current era does not mark its high point. Rugman (2000: 6–8), for example, has suggested, that 'globalization' is something of a misnomer since the vast majority of transactions occur within the three regional trading blocs: North America, Europe and Japan. Not only did 443 of the top 500 MNCs derive from these areas in 1996 (162 American, 155 European Union and 126 Japanese) but, taking automobiles as an example, 80 per cent of the trade occurs within, not across, these trading blocs (a similar story occurs in chemicals and steel). Rugman also suggests that within the regional triads, MNCs are more likely to observe the legal requirements of local countries than many other producers, and may be more concerned with competing with each other to worry too much about the local political issues.

Rodrik (1997: 34) accepts the globalization rather than regionalization argument, but insists that the timing is important. For instance, he suggests that global integration, as measured by the percentage of Gross Domestic Product (GDP) taken by exports, labour mobility across national boundaries and convergent commodity prices, was higher during the late nineteenth century than before or since. Blinder (ex-vice-chair of the US Federal Reserve) argues that the period between 1870 and 1914 marks the 'high water mark . . . "the golden age" of global integration'. Williamson (1995) divided globalization into three phases. Phase one was between 1850 and 1914, with converging living standards: in 1870 real wages in the USA were 72 per cent higher than in the UK, but by 1890 real wages in the USA were only 63 per cent higher than in the UK. A report of the American Immigration Commission (1911) concluded that immigration was damaging the economic interests of existing US workers and, as a result, there was a radical cut-back in immigration. During phase two (1914–50) convergence stopped because of 'deglobalization and implosion into anarchy'. Phase three marks the period since 1950 with the renewal of convergence. Even if we were to agree on this phasing, there is still a dispute concerning the substantive issues that are allegedly converging. Wallerstein (1983) and Fukuyama (1989), for example, insist that the world was converging upon a global culture – democratic capitalist – but both Whitley (1990) and Hofstede (1991) deny this, implying that the influence of national cultures is simply too strong for any kind of global 'norm' to prevail.

However, Letto-Gillies (2001: 18–19) has suggested a rather different triple phasing of globalization and 'normalization'. The 1960s and 1970s were the era of confrontation between governments and MNCs as the former sought to control the latter, if necessary by nationalization. The 1980s and 1990s witnessed the opposite trend – an era of co-operation between the two major players, often manifest in privatization of formerly nationalized industries. However, partly as a consequence of the growing gap between rich and poor and partly because of the apparent indifference of governments, the late 1990s and the first decade of the twenty-first century has seen a return to confrontation, only this time it is between MNCs and the citizens of nations who believe their political representatives are unwilling or unable to constrain the power of MNCs. But what is it about the power of MNCs and the effects of globalization that opponents find so concerning? Partly that concern mirrors the apparent polarization of rewards and future prospects, and partly it concerns the apparent aggrandizement of power by the MNCs to the point where MNC economics appears to have displaced the political power of national governments, the cultural independence of the host community and their environmental safety.

Global inequality

The first point of concern relates to the sheer economic scale of MNCs: by the early 1990s about 37,000 MNCs controlled over a third of the world's private assets (Kobrin, 1996: 13), and 359 MNCs accounted for 40 per cent of global trade, while of the largest 100 economies in the world, half were MNCs; indeed, 51 of the largest 100 economies in the world are corporations. Not all of the richest organizations are MNCs: for example, in 2001 Harvard University had £13.3 billion in assets alone, almost three times the wealth of Sainsbury plc (£4.8 billion) and more than ten times the wealth of GlaxoSmithKline (£1.6 billion). The richest educational establishments in the UK are Cambridge (£2.7 billion, including its colleges) and Oxford (£2.5 billion, including its colleges) (Sanders, 2001: 1).

The absolute wealth of MNCs should be of less significance than their impact upon the inequalities that prevail wherever they operate. The Stolper-Samuelson theorem, first developed in the 1940s, suggested that globalization would enhance the skills and rewards of whichever group dominated the national labour market; hence skill levels, wages and living standards should converge on a norm. But there are many critics of globalization who insist that it generates inequalities between and within nations, and that the only equality that results is one of misery for the majority. The United Nation's *Human Development Report* in 1997 certainly suggested an increasing gap between rich and poor – but this was a consequence of *selective* globalization by the West, rather than globalization in and of itself. In effect, help was being provided to increase the exports and financial services in the 'developing' world, but areas of less significance to the West, like agricultural reform and investment in textiles, were being left without investment. This polarizing effect essentially means that globalization can help developing countries to develop – but there have tended to be distinct winners and losers within the developing world itself.

John Berger (2001: 10), for example, has suggested that 'One in five of all people on the globe benefits from this system [globalization]. Four in five suffer in differing degrees from the new unnecessary poverty.' Since 1950 the world's trade has expanded 17-fold, but Latin America's proportion of that trade has dropped from 11 per cent in 1950 to 5 per cent in 2000. Over the same time span, Africa's proportion of world trade has dropped from 8 per cent (1950) to 2 per cent (2000). In 1977 the proportion of world trade of the poorest 48 countries was just 0.6 of the total. By 1997 even that had dropped to an almost invisible 0.3 per cent of the total. In 1960 the world's richest 20 per cent earned 30 times the world's poorest 20 per cent; in 1997 the world's richest 20 per cent earned 74 times the world's poorest 20 per cent; and in 2000 the world's richest 20 per cent earned 86 times the world's poorest 20 per cent. The richest 50 million people have the same income as the poorest 2.7 billion, or put another way the world's richest 1 per cent have as much as the world's poorest 57 per cent (Elliott, 2002: 19). In 2003 the wealthiest 5 per cent of the world's population earned 114 times the world's poorest 5 per cent, while the richest 500 people owned US$1.54 trillion – more than the gross domestic product of all of Africa and equal to the combined annual incomes of the poorest 50 per cent of the world's population (Monbiot, 2003a: 21). Ending absolute rather than relative poverty need not cost 'the earth' however. If the West gave up buying pet food, perfume and cosmetics (valued at US$37 billion per annum in 1998) the funds would provide education, food, healthcare, water and sanitation for all those people in the world who currently do not have them. There would still be US$9 billion left over (Elliott and Brittain, 1998: 18).

By 2000 the UN's *Human Development Report* suggested that sub-Saharan life expectancy was, at 49 years, barely two-thirds of the 'developed' world's life expectancy rate (75 years). But the growing gulf between rich and poor was not widening simply between the rich and the poor nations, but also within rich and poor nations – from the USA, Britain and Sweden to Russia, the gap was growing. And even when income per capita was roughly equal – as in Vietnam and Guinea for example – life expectancy rates were markedly different (65 years and 47 years respectively), as was adult literacy (94 per cent and 35 per cent respectively) (Brittain and Elliott, 2000: 14). As Frank (2001a: 6–14, 24) suggests, we have been here before: the Gini Coefficient – which measures inequality such that 0 would be total equality where all goods are divided equally, while 1 would be where all the goods were owned by one person – suggests that US inequality was rising rapidly at the beginning of the last century, only to collapse with the 1929 crash and the economic depression that followed during the 1930s. However, since the late 1970s that coefficient has risen remarkably and shows no sign of weakening in the early part of the twenty-first century.

The USA is also host to an institution ostensibly dedicated to the elimination of global poverty: the World Bank. Its inscription in Washington DC (51 per cent of its shares are held by the US Treasury) is 'Our Dream is a World Free of Poverty', and indeed, the bank was set up to provide capital for development. But there is still much to be done: 10 million children die each year from preventable diseases and half a million mothers die in childbirth from preventable complications; 113 million children do not even attend school at any point in their lives. Clearly the World Bank is not responsible for these failures, but its positive role is also limited: it is supposed to prevail where markets fail and where the state is inadequate to compensate for market failure. But the irony is that the bank lends 70 per cent of its funds to just 11 countries – and these are already the largest recipients of private investment, and where the local state is strong enough to guarantee economic and political stability and thus repayment (Gilbert and Vines, 2000). In 2002, for the first time, more money was sent by migrant workers working in the developed world

(US$80 billion) than by the states and bank aid of the developed world (US$16 billion). In 1995 the proportions were in reverse. India and Mexico each received US$19 billion, while the Philippines received US$5.8 billion. For places like Jamaica and Albania the income is critical – 10 per cent of both countries' income is derived from money sent home by migrant workers (Islam, 2003: 3). Indeed, in 2003 the largest source of foreign investment in Latin American was the money sent home by emigrant workers (Glaister, 2004: 15). The most dispro-portionate case appears to be the 1 million Indians working in the USA, who represent just 0.1 per cent of the Indian population but who earn 10 per cent of the latter's national income and send a large proportion home (Stuart, 2004: 23).

Outside sub-Saharan Africa, there are some internally driven successes (especially in East Asia): in 1991, 29 per cent of the world lived on less than US$1 a day (46 per cent in sub-Saharan Africa). In 2000 that proportion of the global population living on less than US$1 a day had dropped to 24 per cent, though half still lived on less than US$5 a day. The numbers living on £1 a day in China have dropped from 92 million in 1990 to 54 million in 1998, mainly because economic growth has been maintained at around 6.5 per cent per annum. In fact in 2001 – for the very first time – the UN's *Human Development Report* suggested that the majority of the globe now lived in a developed, rather than a developing, nation. Children born in 2001 can expect to live six years longer than those born in 1970 (from 60 to 66 years), adult literacy has risen from 47 per cent to 73 per cent, the proportion of rural fam-ilies with access to clean water had risen fivefold to 80 per cent and average incomes rose from £1,300 to £2,500. But the trend in sub-Saharan Africa is in the opposite direction, partly because the countries are too small to accumu-late the critical mass of population necessary to establish a significant market through economies of scale, but also because of the combination of debt, dictatorship and AIDS (Browne, 2001b: 23). That triangular cultural quagmire is also laid at the door of the world's rich nations and the MNCs, but are they responsible for such cultural imperialism?

Global cultural imperialism: branding

Of course, a lot of the debate around globalization assumes by default that it equates with US economic and cultural imperialism. But if we measure the extent of globalization by the flow of goods, services and capital, as well as the proportion of the population with access to the internet and so on, then we have quite different accounts of globalization. For example, Singapore has propor-tionately four times more outgoing telephone traffic than the USA, and the most global nations after Singapore are not the fundamentalist economic liberals, but social democratic Sweden, the Netherlands and Finland: in effect, free trade and social security are not logical contradictions (Walker, 2001: 15).

Some have clearly had enough of globalism, especially in its American colours. José Bové, for example, famously dismantled a McDonald's restaurant in Millau, France (and served nineteen days' imprisonment for doing so) in protest against the US government's 'arbitrary' import ban on Roquefort cheese (including that manufactured by Bové himself), which, in turn, related to the EU's ban on the import of US beef that had been injected with growth hormones (Bové and Dufour, 2001). Such dismantling is of little practical consequence for McDonald's: by 2001 there were already 23,300 McDonald's restaurants in the world and 29 new ones were being constructed every week. Such is the reach of the company that 33 per cent of all cows in the USA end up in McDonald's burgers and 12.5 per cent of all Americans end up working in the restaurants at some time in their lives (Borger, 2001: 3). (Before we turn our backs on 'fast food' in favour of 'fresh food', spare a thought for the work involved in providing us with 'fresh food'. After all, unless you live within a few miles of a fishing port, your 'fresh fish' is more likely to be 'fresh-frozen' at sea and then 'defrosted fish'. Similarly, 'fresh meat' is not really fresh – if it was fresh it would probably have been killed before our eyes, and would already be in the process of rigor mortis. As it is, much 'fresh' meat has to 'rot' to make it edible.) However, the scare over obesity and mad cow disease in the USA coincided with a turnaround in the company's fortunes: in December 2003 McDonald's posted its first ever quarterly loss after 47 years of growth (see <http://www.mcspotlight.org/media/press/mcds/usatoday1812021.html>).

The ethics of meat-eating is often something that meat-eaters prefer not to think about too much, and the same goes for the ethics of MNCs: if shareholders insist on the highest possible returns without concern for how these returns are achieved, then managers are likely 'to choose not to know'. Frank (2001b) has suggested that our current fascination with corporate brands is not coincidental but a method of controlling dissent and legitimizing the corporation, giving it a moral veneer that hides the activities undertaken to actually create the product – just at the time when the traditional restrainers of corporations (governments, trade unions and so on) appear to be in terminal decline. Thus we should have expected that corporate ethics even secured its own index on 10 July 2001 when the FTSE4Good index was launched, quoting only those companies that qualified as 'socially responsible' – which excludes all those engaged in tobacco, armaments and nuclear energy. The criteria for inclusion include:

- working towards environmental sustainability;
- developing positive relationships with stakeholders;
- upholding and supporting human rights.

Over a third of FTSE companies are ineligible under present conditions, though ethical investment funds grew from 0 to 40 between 1983 and 2001 when £3.5 billion was invested overall, but 'social responsibility' remains a minority interest for corporations: over half of British retailers do not have any socially responsible buying policy (Connon, 2001: 14). Indeed, it may well be that social responsibility is a minority interest for consumers too. True, 70 per cent of those polled in a *Guardian* survey suggested they would be prepared to 'pay a little more' for a product or service from a socially responsible company – but first, that means 30 per cent are not interested at all, and of the

70 per cent, we do not know whether they really would pay more, but were too embarrassed to say they wouldn't, and we do not know to what level they are concerned. The other problem is that companies only appear interested in social responsibility because their customers appear to care and thus profits may be deleteriously affected (Reeves, 2001b: 11). In a bizarre inversion of Kant, even ethics are given a monetary value – they become a means not an end in themselves.

The mercenary ethics of both MNCs and national governments have been scrutinized by the Zapatistas, who have defended the rights of the 10 million indigenous Mexicans more through words than through guns under their leader Subcomandante Marcos. But the Zapatistas' fight is not just with the Mexican government; it is also with what Marcos (2001: 117/147) calls 'the global dictatorship of the market. . . . The globalization of markets erases borders for speculation and crimes and multiplies them for human beings. Countries are obliged to erase their national borders for money to circulate, but to multiply their internal borders.'

This simultaneous creation and destruction of boundaries lies at the heart of the global project and global protest: on the one hand globalization appears to be a movement genuinely concerned to remove barriers between people – a force for good; on the other, the barriers that are removed have tended to benefit the rich and powerful at the expense of the poor and weak. This paradoxical movement underlies the work of Naomi Klein, who led the field in popular criticism of the current developments and future possibilities at the beginning of the twenty-first century. Klein's *No Logo* (2000) was a foundational assault on capitalism in the age of globalization, which she reconstructed as the age of the brand, the logo. The manifestations of corporate logos are everywhere: on billboards, in newspapers, on TV and radio, on clothes and in schools; indeed, a pivotal claim of Klein's is that 'private space' is rapidly diminishing under the onslaught of brands. And just as the lands of the American Indians shrank under the tracks of the railroads and the wagons of the white settlers, so too the space and rights of individual citizens are disappearing under the corporate and cultural imperialism of the likes of Nike, Coca-Cola and McDonald's (Coca-Cola was trademarked in 1887, having seen off its rivals, Koca-Nola and Mitch-o-Cola, with lawsuits; it failed to assault Brad's Drink, which became Pepsi-Cola: see Pavitt, 2001: 4). The generally accepted estimate in 2001 was that 25 per cent of the world's wealth was embodied by brands.

Klein's analysis suggests that we are now facing a new form of capitalism, dominated not by production but by marketing, or rather by branding. In effect, the brand itself has become separated from the product so that consumption is not based on brands, because brands represent quality; rather, consumption is of the brand itself.

Thus many successful corporations have deserted the factories for the factory outlets: Nike is not so much a running shoe as a cultural icon. That icon is often produced through a globally distributed network of factories, but the point of production is really irrelevant to the purpose of the corporation – which is to sell a lifestyle. As Walter Landor (President of Landor branding agency) suggests, 'products are made in the factory but brands are made in the mind' (quoted in Klein, 2000: 195). It is not at all clear that such a division is viable – for example, it is difficult to think of a 'product' such as Rolls Royce without thinking of the brand 'Rolls Royce', because to think otherwise is to suggest that the 'thing' that is obviously a car and looks remarkably like a Rolls Royce can somehow be considered as 'neutral' until we attach a label to it. But the important thing here is to transcend boundaries: the brand exists above and beyond the product, and the consumer's identity becomes lived in and through the brand. Thus the proposition is to persuade the consumer that only by embodying the lifestyle represented by the corporate logo will it be possible to maintain personal credibility: to wear unbranded trainers, unbranded jeans, unbranded shirts, and to drink own-label coke or 'unknown' coffee and eat 'unknown' burgers is to kiss goodbye to a life worth living.

Under the guidance of Nike's CEO Phil Knight, the company began promoting sports stars like Michael Jordan – himself now a 'brand' – and associating itself with US black youth to maintain its brand image as the essence of 'cool'. The parasitic relationship that Klein suggests exists between 'rebels' and brands ensures not only that anti-establishment movements become transformed into corporate brands (for example, the 'kidnapping' of Che Guevara's image), but that even anti-brand movements become branded. One might argue here that carrying a copy of Klein's *No Logo* (the 'Little Black Book') on an anti-capitalist demonstration is a brand manager's (in this case HarperCollins) ironic utopia: the new millennium's version of Mao's Little Red Book from the 1960s. Furthermore, one could suggest that Klein's account is itself a product of the branders' seduction. That is to say, that Klein provides an incisive critique of branding, but in doing so becomes enthralled by that very same process. After all, there is more to capitalism than Nike trainers, Manchester United shirts and Starbucks coffee and so on. For example, most people's largest purchase in the UK is probably their house, and, new or old, there does not seem to be the same desperate search for a branded house. Nor do many consumers really care that much which brand of computer they use at work – as long as it works. Nor do we necessarily have to assume that it is branding which is driving global capitalism, because it may simply be that branding is a response to the problem of surplus production and intensifying competition.

The power of the brand appears most visibly in areas where it is most necessary. For example, Orange claims to have developed a brand that locks not just customers but also employees into an emotional bond with the company. As Nicole Louise, head of brand communications suggests, that bond 'can't be bought with bonuses, it can't be incentivized, they fall in love with the brand. I did, it's a relationship' (quoted in Bunting, 2001b: 14). Thus the brand becomes the emotional glue that holds the organization together – and transcends the need for formal discipline-based systems. And if the organization is service-based then the employees are the front line: if they do not engage emotionally with the corporate brand then the customer service is less likely to be memorably good – at least that is the theory.

The *Guardian* newspaper ran an experiment on brands in July 2001 when full page adverts of a naked man in a large rubber ring accompanied by the words 'sing, laugh, drive, sleep, eat, breathe, cry . . . but do it with Joy' were accompanied by a free phone number and a website (www.withjoy.co.uk). There was no product or service mentioned, nor indeed was there one, but the adverts were intended to assess the extent to which people could be enthralled by a brand alone: 1,562 people responded either by phone or by visiting the website (Burkeman, 2001: 2–3). Perhaps we should not be surprised: in the last quarter of 1999 the dot.coms were spending on advertising as much as 95 cents of every dollar taken (Frank, 2001b: 7).

But the power of the brand is double-edged: it may be associated with significant sales, but its very power renders corporations vulnerable to an attack upon a brand. For example, in July 2000 the workers on Grand Marnier's orange plantations in Haiti (the poorest country in the Western hemisphere) won a 55 per cent increase in pay (from their legal minimum of £2 a day), the recognition of a trade union, as well as changes to their conditions which, until then, had provided no toilets, no running water (to wash off the orange acid that causes respiratory diseases and skin problems if left on the skin), no drinking water and no first-aid facilities. The campaign involved the charity War on Want, the Haiti Support Group, several local and international trade unions, and many people writing to Grand Marnier's HQ in France complaining about the company's (in)action (Tibbett, 2001: 12).

There is a double lesson in this. First, MNCs that operate unethically remain vulnerable where they are most powerful, i.e. in their brands; second, the brands do not operate autonomously: we, the consumers, have to engage with them for the brand to have any 'effect'. In other words, in the quest for blame for our current state of affairs, one major player seems to be missing: the consumer. Undoubtedly peer pressure and commercial selling techniques are powerful forces – but they are not determinate, for if they were we would all be wearing identical apparel and enacting identical cultural pursuits. In short, we would be what Garfinkle referred to as 'cultural dopes', or we would be 'over-socialized' to the point where individual freedom had been completely undermined. For example, Klein's (2000: 95) much-quoted example of a school pupil from Greenbriar, Georgia, who is suspended for wearing a Pepsi tee-shirt on the Coca-Cola-sponsored school sports day, is taken as a manifestation of an insidious corporate control over learning. If Coca-Cola officials had indeed demanded such a suspension, then Klein is absolutely right; but the culprit here is the teacher who suspended the pupil, not the company. The same goes for most of the other corporate sponsorship deals that litter Klein's account: they *are* very problematic – but only because the schools and colleges allow themselves to be outmanoeuvred by corporate negotiators, and even this is only because local governments and educational authorities have cut back on educational budgets to the point where schools are forced to go begging to the private sector. In sum, it is the derogation of duty by the state, and the poverty of negotiating skills on the part of those institutions that are sponsored, that are responsible for the corporate take-over of the public sector. Private companies are – by definition – in it for the money, but they can only dominate the world if we collectively let them do what comes naturally. In contrast, take the decision by Justice K. Balakrishnan Nair from the Indian state of Kerala's High Court, who ordered Coca-Cola to stop taking ground water for a bottling plant after

1,000 local families from Plachimada spent 20 months protesting about the desertification of their farm land (Brown, 2003: 15).

There are examples of where a more sophisticated approach to sponsorship on the part of the client can provide advantages that would otherwise not exist. For instance, IBM's £1 million engagement with 50 of the UK's so-called Beacon Schools funds a Reinventing Education programme which provides schools within the programme with laptops and software to network through IBM's Wired for Learning site with other schools and share best practice. Ironically, the programme is not about encouraging competition between schools – that is something which the government sees as its role – but rather about encouraging cooperation. The results from the UK experiment appear to be helping to raise standards, and IBM is praised for both funding and facilitating the project while maintaining a 'discreet distance' (Smithers, 2001: 12). Relatedly, the Ford Foundation supports several charities and organizations trying to inhibit the AIDS epidemic around the world and, for example, has provided $2.5 million to the University of Namibia to create a distance-learning project (Mather, 2001: 13). Even McDonald's seems to have learned a lesson: in 2002 it issued a 46-page *Social Responsibility Report* aimed at establishing a more community-oriented and environmentally friendly business face and has had some success in convincing sceptics (Maitland, 2002: 13).

In South Africa's Eastern Cape a rather different approach to the problems of development are being explored, though again the process is rooted directly in a corporate concern for the brand. Shell, with 20 million daily customers and 48,000 retail sites in 120 countries, was involved in 1994 in a potentially catastrophic dispute between the Nigerian military government and the Ogoni people who live around Shell's extraction plants. In an area of extreme poverty (six doctors for 600,000 people), the Ogoni people protested against the exploitation of their natural resources and suffered the assassination of four of their chiefs and the execution of their environmentalist leader Ken Saro-Wiwa. As a consequence, Nigeria was expelled from the Commonwealth, and Shell faced unprecedented public protests and boycotts. Those protests were not universally supported – Shell's own research suggested that 50 per cent of the population still regarded Shell as a 'good' company, and 40 per cent were 'indifferent', but a very active and very critical 10 per cent thought otherwise. The result was a reconsideration of Shell's social and ethical position. Sceptics might still maintain that any change is just cosmetic, but Shell was the first MNC to incorporate human rights into its business principles, it requires all its country CEOs to explain how these have been implemented, it publishes an annual report on its ethics, and it maintains a website that accepts vigorous criticisms. That said, Ken Saro-Wiwa's successor, Ledum Mittee, remained unimpressed: 'The change in rhetoric from Shell over the years has not been matched by a change in actions in Nigeria' (quoted in Vidal, 2001: 11).

One of the leading campaigners for ethical trading has actually been a large corporation: The Body Shop. Anita Roddick's home-grown empire, founded on its '5 pillars' of human rights (environment, anti-animal testing, community trading and social responsibility) also provides £1 million to various charities, including the Ruckus Society which was involved in the Seattle protests (Vidal,

2001: 28). The British Co-operative Bank has also pursued an overtly ethical investment policy since 1996, and in 2000 assessed the cost-benefits of the policy. Its report suggested that 105 of the 270 proposals referred to its ethical policy unit were turned down and this is estimated to have cost the bank £1.7 million in lost profits. However, since 25 per cent of current account holders claim that it was the bank's ethical policy that attracted them in the first place, between 15 and 18 per cent of the bank's overall profits (£96 million pre-tax) are estimated to have been derived from the ethical stance. In other words: ethics pay (Cowe, 2001: 19). (Since July 2000 all UK pension funds have had to include a statement on their social and environmental policy.)

The point, therefore, is not that branding is irrelevant or that brands do not 'enthral' some people some of the time; rather, the point is to be clear about the limits of branding power and to accept the complicity of the consumer in this apparent conspiracy. If humans really are held in enthralment by the sight of the Nike 'Swoosh' or a cup of Starbucks coffee – or anything else for that matter – then what chance do we really have of establishing a sophisticated and humanitarian global society?

In sum, if the corporations are in control, it is because we the public have not directly sought to corral them for the public good, or have failed to direct our political leaders to do the same: we have become entranced by our own apparent impotence – but that weakness is a reflection of the imperial corporation, and the corporate emperor really has no clothes. As Collins (2001) suggests, when things go wrong it is very tempting to look out of the metaphorical window to see who we can blame – and there is normally someone within range. However, the more honest approach is to look in the mirror and ask yourself: what have I done to 'stop the rot'? The enthralment that manifests itself in personal (ir)responsibility is often most apparent when we drive to the airport in our cars and fly off across the Atlantic – to complain about global pollution. Or when we complain about the strength of the sun on the beach in Spain thanks to global warming and the destruction of the ozone layer, having got there on a cheap flight.

Global exploitation: enthralment

A separate, but related, theme of Klein's *No Logo* is the impact that the new model of global capitalism is having upon the developing world. The subordinate role of manufacturing in her analysis also means that production activities have tended to shift to the cheapest source and the least regulated workplaces. In fact, some of the worst forms of exploitation are related to extractive work, such as mining, but the inevitable result, it would seem, has been the exploitation of cheap, and often child, labour in non-unionized sweatshop conditions in Asia. These are contracted to the corporate branders but provide the latter with a useful spatial and political gap should 'problems' occur. Hence, when it became apparent that Nike was employing children to sew its footballs for a pittance, Nike was able to deny immediate responsibility and to resolve such 'local problems' without too much political damage back home by deploying its enormous political and economic power. In fact, 80 per cent of the world's footballs are sewn in Sialkot, Pakistan, near the Indian border. In 1997 Nike and Reebok bowed to political pressure and banned child labourers under the age of 14 from making footballs for them. The downside is that what used to be a domestic industry where women could work with their children has now moved out of the home and into the factory. Some 6,000 children who once worked sewing footballs have enrolled into schools, but 1,760 have dropped out and returned to different jobs in the brick kilns or car workshops (McCarthy, 2001: 17).

Not all the protests are directed *against* the MNCs; some are directed at the anti-MNC protesters. For example, in February 2001 a protest in Managua, Nicaragua, urged the American Embassy there to take action against the protesters demanding an end to sweatshops, since this would mean an end to their employment. The ILO has claimed that the enforcement of minimum labour standards would ensure a level playing field, but some of those it is claimed to protect have suggested that this simply enables workers from the developed countries to compete. Hence in 1993, when US television showed Bangladeshi children making clothes for Wal-Mart, an American campaign forced the clothing companies to stop using children under the age of 14. The direct consequence was not to push them into school but to push many into more dangerous and less well-paid jobs. Ultimately, a local voluntary compromise was agreed: some children went to school and some returned to work (Denny, 2001a: 21). Here is a different aspect of enthralment, for the child workers are either exploited in one situation or exploited in another, and the consequence is that it becomes difficult to know what should or can be done about the situation. (The ILO's core Labour Standards, agreed by 176 member states, are: employees free to join a trade union; union freedom from interference from public authorities; freedom from forced or compulsory labour; freedom from discrimination on grounds of race, colour, sex, religion, political opinion, national extraction or social origins; ban on employment under the age at which compulsory education is completed; equal pay for men and women for work of equal value; ban on slavery, child prostitution, involvement of children in drugs.)

This problem of protests that damage the very people the protesters are trying to help has received an interesting inflection from the United Students Against Sweatshops movement, which is designed to end the sweatshop conditions of the workers employed to produce the sponsored clothing and sportswear at many American universities. The campaign, which gathered pace during the early part of 2000, was not a boycott of the producers but an attempt to persuade the universities to withdraw from the Fair Labor Association – on the grounds that it wasn't fair – and to join the Workers' Rights Consortium (WRC), an organization comprising students, trade unions, humanitarian organizations and universities. The effects were significant at a local level: Oregon, Michigan and Brown universities all joined the WRC and then cancelled their clothing deals with Nike (Birch, 2001: 12–13; see also <www.umich.edu/%7Esole/usas>).

Elsewhere, consumer boycotts have had significant affects upon MNCs. For example, Barclays Bank withdrew from South Africa in 1986 after a student campaign against Apartheid halved the number of student accounts held by

Barclays; the 'Burma Campaign' boycotted the Swiss-based lingerie manufacturer Triumph in 2002 for opening a factory in Burma in 2001 (average wages 70p a day) despite its military dictatorship; within two months of its advertising campaign – 'Support breasts not dictators' – Triumph withdrew (see <http://www.burmacampaign.org.uk/action_triumph.html>). On the other hand, the Baby Milk Action boycott of Nestlé has continued off and on since 1980 without deterring the company, even though 70 countries have introduced restrictive legislation on baby milk since that time. Moreover, in December 2002 Nestlé was forced to climb down from its demand that Ethiopia repay a US$6 million debt, which represented about an hour's turnover for the company at the time (the Ethiopian government – facing a famine that could affect 11 million people – had offered US$1.5 million) (Denny, 2002: 2). But it is often difficult to assess whether boycotts such as these actually work. For example; Exxon-Mobil has been targeted for some time because of its views on climate change, and although the company claims that its sales are unaffected, research by Mori suggests that perhaps 5 per cent of British motorists have ceased to buy Esso fuel (Pratley, 2003: 21).

It is the Free Trade Zones currently employing 27 million workers across 70 countries that particularly attract Klein's attention. For example, Cavite Export Processing Zone (one of 52 in the country), 90 miles south of Manila in the Philippines, is a 682-acre 'walled-in' site with armed guards protecting the 'miniature military state' of 207 'windowless' factories. Here, 50,000 mainly young women workers are paid pitifully small wages to make Nike trainers, IBM computer screens, Gap pyjamas, Old Navy Jeans and so on. Most of these factories operate on a tax-free basis for a five-year period, and Klein considers the corporations as economic tourists not investors, since the surrounding conditions bear precious little evidence of infrastructural improvement because so little tax is paid and because the wages of the employees are too low to stimulate significant demand and consequential improvements (Klein, 2000: 204–10).

(Part of) Nike's response to *No Logo* (the full text is available on Nike's official website) is reproduced below:

> Several times throughout the book, Klein references Nike's manufacturing operations in the Philippines. At one point, she alludes to the consolidation of manufacturing that Nike undertook in early 1999. As a result of the Asian crisis, the production of Nike apparel and footwear, like that of many other consumer goods, slowed down. This affected our production base in the Philippines, as well as in other countries, and resulted in a streamlining of manufacturing operations until the economy recovered from the crisis. Klein inaccurately states that Nike cut ties with higher-waged workers in the Philippines and moved into China. She claims that Nike made this decision because workers' rights are not as protected, monitoring is difficult and wages are lower in China. For years critics have tried to contend that Nike flees 'high-cost, unionized' countries for 'low-cost, repressive' countries like China and Indonesia. Over those years, Nike has repeatedly pointed out that we remain in Korea and Taiwan as a buyer,

despite higher wages and labor rights. In fact, Nike is the only branded athletic-footwear company still making shoes in Taiwan and South Korea. In addition to our presence there, we are still very active in the Philippines, with 20 factories. We have 1 footwear factory, 4 equipment factories and 15 apparel factories in the Philippines. In recent years, we have expanded our footwear sourcing country list to include countries like Vietnam, which boasts a recent record of promoting workers' rights through government labor bureaus; and Italy, which has a vibrant democracy and the highest wage base of any Nike footwear sourcing country.

In 2001 the San Francisco-based Global Exchange insisted that little progress had been made by Nike since the initial claims: workers were unable to make use of the company-provided education courses because their wages were so low they still had to work 70 hours a week to make ends meet. And despite Phil Knight's riposte to the report and denial of its claims, Nike's value fell 15 per cent between 1998 and 2000, while its main rival, Reebok, has seen its share price increase by 375 per cent over the same period (compare, for example, the review at <www.corpwatch.org/issues/sweatshops> with Nike's version at <www.nikebiz.com>).

Adidas, the German competitor to Nike, has also become embroiled in the sweatshop controversy, with claims that workers from two of its Indonesian suppliers, Nikomax-Gemiland and Tuntex, were forced to work 15-hour days, were paid less than $60 a month and had illegal amounts taken off their wages as a result of minor disciplinary problems. In Thailand, a woman employed as an Adidas sub-contractor claims that she and 23 others were sacked for trying to form a trade union. Adidas claimed that all the problems had been resolved since the claims were made (Burke, 2000d: 4). Even holding MNCs to ethical codes of conduct does not necessarily resolve the problem. Oxfam (2004) suggests, for example, that the level of sub-contracting and false documentation is so rife in many countries where production occurs that being able to comply with the ethical code fails to protect vast numbers of workers who produce the good for MNCs like Wal-Mart, Toys R Us and Tommy Hilfiger.

Yet, irrespective of these particular cases, it is not self-evident that global capitalism has generally made things universally and necessarily worse at a collective level, even if individual cases suggest otherwise and even though there are clearly winners and losers in this 'game'. Supporters of FDI generally suggest that it tends to raise wages and improve conditions rather than undermine both. And it is worth posing a familiar question here about the 'romance of labour'. It has become commonplace, following Braverman (1974), for example, to suggest that twentieth-century capitalism provided appalling conditions and exploitive wages for most factory workers who undertook mind-numbing repetitive tasks on alienating assembly lines. All this is very probably true, but the previous generations of workers probably suffered equivalent or more likely worse conditions in their working lives. In effect, there never was a 'golden age' when everyone had skilled, satisfying jobs in pleasant conditions for good wages. Thus, the issue is not *whether* workers in export zones are being grossly exploited – we can rest assured that most of them are; but that does not mean their lives were immeasurably better before global capitalism arrived on their doorstep. In other words, we do not have to assume that global capitalism is self-evidently munificent, but then neither do we have to accept that the alternative – whatever that is – would make life better. In short, probably like most workers under most conditions most of the time, work is something that is a necessary evil – and certainly preferable to not having work. The solution, then, might not be the atavistic demand for the end of global capitalism – a utopian call more likely to doom the very people it was intended to save – but, for example, to begin the global (labour) movement to restrict the levels and forms of exploitation.

Other approaches are also viable: at the level of local producers, there have been several attempts to constrain the power of multinationals. For example, while a 100g jar of Nescafé Goldblend cost £2.14 in Sainsburys in 2001, and although this same jar was £1.99 in 1994, the price paid to the coffee producers has dropped over the same period from 14 per cent of the retail price to 7 per cent of the retail price. Nestlé, who own Nescafé, made 33 per cent profit on the price of each such jar in 2001. Organizations like Fair Trade have been established to provide higher returns to the (small) producer by encouraging them to work in producer co-operatives and sell directly to Fair Trade. In turn, the retail outlets tend to sell the coffee at a higher price than conventional coffee but more of the profits are returned to the producer. This policy, when applied to bananas (the fifth most important global agricultural commodity, Britain's most popular fruit, and the third most valuable product to British supermarkets behind petrol and the national lottery), ensures that the local producers get 80 per cent more for a Fair Trade banana than for a conventional banana (Stuart, 2001: 2–3). As Purvis (2004) suggests: 'For every £1 spent on bananas at Tesco, for instance, only 1p goes back to the plantation growers in developing countries – far less than they need to feed their families. An estimated 40p goes to Tesco. Indeed, the company makes a profit of £1 million per week purely from the sale of bananas – enough to employ 30,000 plantation workers full-time and pay them a proper wage.'

At a global or regional scale the problem has often been associated with the subsidies provided to the richer nations at the expense of their more efficient but poorer neighbours. For example, the US pays a $4 billion subsidy to its own 25,000 cotton producers (three times the entire US aid package for the whole of Africa) that has led directly to the collapse of the West African cotton industry and its 10 million cotton farmers – despite the cheaper prices and greater efficiency of the latter (Williams, 2003: 15). Similarly, the World Bank notes that the average Japanese cow secures $7 a day in government subsidy and the average European Union cow receives $2.20 in daily subsidy – which is more than the amount that just under half the world's human population live on. Conversely, while the USA imposes tariffs on major imports from the EU and Japan of between 0 and 1 per cent, the tariff on goods from Bangladesh, Cambodia and Nepal are between 14 and 15 per cent (Monbiot, 2003a: 21). Mind you, the USA only gives about 0.1 per cent of GDP in foreign aid, while the UK gives 0.3 per cent: both are well below the UN target of 0.7 per cent. Yet intriguingly, most Americans believe their country gives around 20 per cent of GDP as foreign aid, and they would be much happier if the government gave away only between 5 and 10 per cent (Desai, 2003: 23).

Only in 2003, at the failed Cancun WTO talks, and after the emergence of bilateral trade agreements on a wide scale to replace the failing multilateral agreements, did some of the poorer countries eventually band together to form the G23 – representing 63 per cent of the world's farmers – to insist on the removal of agricultural subsidies by wealthier nations and trade organizations. In theory the justification for these subsidies often relates to the poverty of the recipients – for example, 40 per cent of agricultural income within the EU comes directly from its Common Agricultural Policy (CAP), but in reality the largest 2 per cent of European farms receive 24 per cent of the total CAP budget (Mathiason, 2003: 3).

But if consumer boycotts, selective buying, producers' co-operatives and trade unions are able to stem the gross exploitation of labour in developing countries, these strategies may not be sufficient to eliminate the real scourge of work in the twenty-first century, which is the same scourge it has always been: slavery.

Global exploitation: slavery

Slavery, if anything, is larger now than it ever was, at least in absolute terms (the 2004 UNICEF report on human trafficking in Africa can be found at <http://www.unicef.org/media/files/insight8e.pdf>). As Bales (2000a: 3) suggests:

> Across the world slaves work and sweat and build and suffer. Slaves in Pakistan may have made the shoes you are wearing and the carpet you stand on. [Unless, of course, you are standing on a Rugmark carpet, a symbol that the carpet was not manufactured using slave labour and a quality assurance system for improving the lives of carpet-makers by allocating 1 per cent of the wholesale price of the carpet to a fund to support child labourers. In 2000, about 30 per cent of handmade rugs and carpets sold in the UK had a Rugmark (Bales, 2000a: 241). B&Q and the Cooperative sell Rugmark carpets. For more information see <www.rugmark.net>.] Slaves in the Caribbean may have put sugar in your kitchen and toys in the hands of your children. In India they may have sewn the shirt on your back and polished the ring on your finger. They are paid nothing.

In effect, there are twice as many slaves now as crossed the Atlantic from Africa. The differences between contemporary slavery, which Bales estimates at involving 27 million people, and past slavery are several, but ultimately in the past it usually involved ownership, whereas today it is more concerned with control – what Bales (2000a: 5) refers to as 'Slaveholding' not 'Slaveowning'.

There is, of course, a difference between child labour and slavery: the former is based upon a free contract that either side can terminate, the latter is not. But there are forms of debt bondage that must make the difference between the two very obscure to those engaged in it – and in 2003 approximately 246 million children were involved in child labour (16 per cent of the population of children in the world). Contemporary slavery is more likely to be practised through bonded or indebted labour and perhaps as many as 20 million people are involved in India, Pakistan, Bangladesh and Nepal.

The increase in contemporary slavery appears to relate to two factors:

- a huge increase in the world's population – from 2 billion in 1945 to 5.7 billion in 2000 – which has left some countries with children comprising half the population but with few resources to sustain them;
- modernization and globalization, often associated with polarizing wealth between the elites and the mass.

There are very different forms of slavery, and at least five types still persist:

1 *Chattel slavery*: where an individual is captured, born or sold into slavery. This traditional and classical form of slavery is still found in North and West Africa and in some Arab countries.
2 *Debt bondage*: this is the most common contemporary form of slavery in which an individual borrows a specified sum for an unspecified form of repayment. That repayment is usually so high that the indebted labourers virtually enslave themselves to the loan provider; the debt may be inherited by the labourer's children. This is the most common form of slavery on the Indian sub-continent.
3 *Contract slavery*: here the workers are offered a contract but this merely lures them into a situation that is difficult to escape because of the intimidation that prevails. This is common in south-east Asia, Brazil, Africa and some Arab states.
4 *War slavery*: this is common in Burma and some parts of Africa (especially Sudan, Uganda and Sierre Leone), and involves enslavement of adults and children into the various armies that are usually involved in civil wars.
5 *Restavecs*: here, children are sold or given into domestic slavery, often through extended families. This remains common in West Africa and some parts of the Caribbean (Bales, 2000b: 5).

Contemporary slavery is also associated with a different relationship between slave and slave owner or controller. For example, a field slave in the American South in 1850 could exchange hands for as much as $1,800 ($100,000 in contemporary terms) and this was around six times the average wage at the time and would probably only give a 5 per cent return on investment. In short, slaves were expensive and thus slave owners had an incentive to keep them alive and well enough to work: slave owners could beat their slaves at will but killing them was – in theory – illegal and certainly counter-productive in economic terms. In contrast, the price of a bonded labourer in India in 2000 could be as little as US$12, and the bondholder might expect as much as a 50 per cent return on their investment per year. The estimated 35,000 girls in Thailand who are bonded into prostitution may cost significantly more initially – perhaps as much as US$2,000 – but the return on investment via the brothel within which they are held may also be much higher, at 800 per cent per annum.

The level of violence remains high in both past and present slavery, and since most contemporary forms are indebted, the historical markers of slavery – the chains and manacles – are no longer as apparent, even if the effects of the enslavement are very similar. And it should not be assumed that Europe or North America are immune to this new bacillus: examples of runaway domestic slaves and bonded prostitutes occur in every nation. For instance, Bales (2000a: 26) estimates that there are 1,000 domestic slaves in London, often brought to the UK as 'domestic staff' by British nationals returning, or foreigners moving, to the country. It is this change in relationship from outright ownership to control through an apparent legitimate 'contract' that prevents, or at least deters, many authorities from attempting to eliminate the problem. And even slaves in the most appalling conditions do not necessarily resist their controllers if they cannot see a solution to their conditions. Keshar Nankar, born into bonded labour in India but freed by anti-slavers, spoke of the problem after gaining his freedom in 1999:

> You people who are free, who were born free and have always lived free, you can never understand what it is to be a slave. When I was a slave I could not have dreamt that one day I would stand here and talk to you as a free man. My world was the farm where I was in bondage, and I simply could not imagine anything else. Because someone somewhere felt I should not be a slave, and then did something about that, I am now a free man. But I could never have freed myself. You must understand that if someone tells you year after year that you have no right to think, you stop thinking. If they say you must not cry, you stop crying. (Quoted in Bales, 2000b: 2)

One of the most common forms of contemporary slavery – human trafficking for the sex industry – is notoriously difficult to control and tempts between 1,400 and 2,000 impoverished young girls and women, especially from Eastern Europe and West Africa, into the UK to a life of degradation and enthralment that is slavery in all but name (Coward, 2003: 24). (Smuggling children into the UK for the purposes of prostitution is now punishable by up to 14 years' imprisonment.) In contrast, Mende Nazar, a Sudanese woman who was kidnapped by Arab slavers in the early 1990s, managed to escape from her eventual slave owner, a Sudanese diplomat, in London in 2001. Her appeal for political asylum was initially rejected by the government but was accepted in November 2002 (Leigh, 2002: 9). Mende was one of approximately 11,000 southern Sudanese kidnapped between 1980 and 2000 (Nazer and Lewis, 2004; see also <http://news.bbc.co.uk/1/hi/world/africa/3430305.stm>).

No European country seems immune from the problem of illegal immigrants who are enticed into paying extortionate sums (between US$5,000 from Egypt to US$25,000 from China) to be smuggled into Europe, where they are generally so heavily indebted and so poorly paid that they are essentially bonded labourers often working in appalling conditions in London, Paris and especially Italy, which operates as a staging post between Eastern and Western Europe. In 1993 there were an estimated 40,000 illegal immigrants in the EU; by 2000 that number had grown to 500,000, of whom about 100,000 are believed to be working as slaves, many within the garment industry (Edmondson et al., 2000: 56–68).

However, as the drowning of 19 Chinese cockle-pickers at Morecambe Bay in January 2004 demonstrated, economic hunger can drive people to do whatever is necessary. At around £8 a bag (after the 'gang master' deducts £3), filling four bags in a 8–12-hour day, the wages of an illegal cockle-picker seem hardly viable, but, as one of the survivors suggested, living four to a room keeps the costs down and since the wages remain six times higher than she could achieve back home in Northern China where she earned £66 a month in a factory, it still made economic sense to carry on the work – hence the exposure of illegal workers to levels of danger and exploitation that local workers would never contemplate (Pai, 2004: 4). It may be that these practices are simply unusual and extreme examples of gross exploitation by atypical, mendacious and rapacious employers. But it may also be that the competitive drive of globalization will inevitably drive more and more of these kinds of labour activities within apparently 'advanced' industrial societies (Lawrence, 2004). Indeed, Thompson (2004: 4) suggested that there may be as many as 100,000 illegal immigrants employed in 'slave' labour gangs in Britain, most of them working in agriculture.

The influx of nurses to the UK from abroad to fill the vacancies generated partly by the refusal of the state to fund public services adequately (since this would mean raising taxation) has also resulted in the growth of new forms of enthralment. The nurses are recruited by agencies and diverted from their promised destination of the NHS to end up in private nursing homes. Concomitantly, they are coerced into signing illegal contracts that allow their employers to exploit them to the point where an 'underground railway' (the name given to the escape system for runaway slaves in the American southern states) was in full service in 2001 to help such nurses 'escape' (Browne, 2001a: 5).

But most of the West's focus rests not on its own backyard but on the rest of the world, especially when the media uncover cases of child slavery. Child slavery recently came to the West's notice in the form of the *Etireno*, a 'slave ship' (whose name means 'end of story') that was allegedly carrying hundreds of child slaves somewhere off the coast of West Africa in April 2001. When the ship eventually docked in Benin it had only 23 children on board. In 1987 the *Croisière Atlantique* was discovered in Benin's Cotonou harbour with 400 children on board, but the captain was merely forbidden to call at the port again. Some estimates put the number of such children smuggled around this part of the world at 200,000 per annum, though the UN calculates that the region as a whole contains 200,000 child slaves (McGreal, 2001a: 13). Most come from Benin, Guinea, Mali, Senegal and Togo, where they are sold for around £10, and arrive in oil-rich Gabon or the Gold and Ivory Coasts' plantations and work as domestic or agricultural slaves at a cost of about £300. Gabon, for instance, has a per capita income of around £2,900, while that of Benin, Mali and Togo average about £150, and it has been the recent economic collapse of the poorer nations that has turned the previous movement of child labour into child slavery (Astill, 2001a: 17; 2001b: 19). Much of this form of slavery is related to the *Restavecs* system, called the *vidomégon* tradition in

Benin, the prime exporter of child slaves. Often the children are sent to distant relatives by their parents on the assumption that their economic futures are better there, but this pattern has a long history and a broad contemporary relevance running from Asia, Africa, Latin America and back into Europe.

The International Labour Organization (ILO) (a specialized UN agency) estimates that there are 250 million children between the ages of 5 and 14 working, 120 million of whom are full time with the largest employer being agriculture, while the single largest employer of girls is domestic service (not unlike Britain in the late nineteenth and very early twentieth centuries – indeed, according to the Better Regulation Task Force, there were still 1.7 million under-15-year-olds working part time in the UK, most of them without work permits and therefore mostly illegally: see <www.brtf.gov.uk>). The vast majority (70 per cent) work unpaid for their families, but the real problem lies with the 'worst forms of child labour' which involve 80 million children. These forms include: slavery, debt bondage, recruitment into military forces, prostitution, pornography, drug trafficking and all dangerous or immoral practices (Brown, 1999).

In Guatemala, one particular case exposed by the ILO (Brown, 1999: 22–3) was of 500 children between the ages of 5 and 15 who worked in Retalhuleu crushing rocks for the construction industry. With a 77 per cent illiteracy rate, low wages, long hours and very dangerous conditions, a project was carried out by Habitat, a non-governmental organization, funded by IPEC (International Programme for the Elimination of Child Labour, a subsidiary component of the ILO), to map and measure the problem, and to mobilize the local community and the local authorities. As a consequence, three developments occurred: 121 children stopped working and went to school, another 119 went to school instead of starting work, and families began to form cooperatives to purchase crushing machinery that would enhance their collective productivity and reduce their dependence on child labour. (Amongst the most useful website addresses concerned with child labour are the following: <www.globalmarch.org>, <www.ilo.org>, <www.cmt-wcl.org/pubs/>, <www.savethechildren.net>, <www.antislavery.org>, <www.child-soldiers.org>.)

More recently, young (some apparently just 4 years old) Pakistani boys appear to have been kidnapped (for a fee of about £2,100 each) or indentured by their parents at the rate of 30 boys a month, to work as camel jockeys in the United Arab Emirates, where the law forbids the employment of boys under the age of 14 or who weigh less than 45 kilograms in such work (Beaumont, 2001: 27). In July 2000 it was reported that a 4-year-old camel jockey from Bangladesh had his legs burnt by his employer in the United Emirates for 'underperforming' (*Anti-Slavery Reporter*, July 2000: 4).

In October 2003, 74 Benin children who had apparently been sold into slavery in Nigeria were rescued from a granite quarry by aid workers and the Nigerian police. Most had been sold by their parents for about £25, either as a way of making some desperately needed cash or in the hope that the children would send back remittances or even have a better life beyond Benin. Those who resisted the work were beaten and 13 died – though from malnutrition and illness rather than as a direct result of the beatings (Carroll, 2003: 21).

Such violence is notoriously present in one form of work that bears a marked resemblance to enthralment: child soldiers, or war slavery. According to the 'Coalition to Stop the Use of Child Soldiers', in 2001, 300,000 children (defined as under the age of 18) were employed in 41 countries as soldiers. Ironically, the UK ranks as one of the worst offenders, boasting the lowest recruiting age and the highest deployment of minors within Europe, though we might conventionally locate the problem more critically within places like Sierra Leone or Uganda, since young British soldiers are at least volunteers, while many of those in Sierra Leone and Uganda are not. In Uganda the Lord's Resistance Army abducted an estimated 5,000 children to fight in the war with the Dinka people (McGreal, 2001b: 13), while in Sierra Leone thousands of very young children were forced to join rebel gangs such as the notorious West Side Boys. As a result, the new Sierra Leone army being trained by the British Army prohibits anyone under the age of 18 from joining (none of Britain's 5,000 17-year-old soldiers is involved in the training) (Moszynski, 2001: 13).

But the UK is involved in child slavery (the first recognized case of child trafficking occurred in 1995) and Unicef estimates that 'a significant percentage' of the 10,000 children who enter the UK for 'fostering' every year from West Africa, Eastern Europe and Asia end up as slaves (often prostitutes) – hence the 2004 bill to outlaw child smugglers and provide up to 14 years' imprisonment for anyone caught engaging in it (Hill, 2003b).

Beyond childhood the major form of slavery is bonded or indebted labour. The UN suggests that there are as many as 20 million bonded labourers in the world, whose debts tie them to their 'owners/employers' (Monahan, 2001: 70). (The United Nations Convention on the Rights of the Child, 1989, 'guarantees' the following: the right to life; the right not to be separated from parents; the right to freedom from physical or mental violence, abuse, neglect or mistreatment; the right to health and good healthcare; the right to an education; the right to rest and leisure and the chance to engage in play. See <www.antislavery.org>, <www.globalmarch.org>, <www.unicef.org>.) Debt Bondage was prohibited by the International Labour Organization in 1930 (Convention 29 on Forced Labour) and by the United Nations in 1956 (Supplementary Convention on Slavery, the Slave Trade and Institutions and Practices Similar to Slavery). In fact, the UN's 1948 Universal Declaration of Human Rights suggested that 'no one shall be held in slavery and servitude: slavery and the slave trade shall be prohibited in all their forms'. Debt bondage usually involves someone promising themselves – or being promised by someone else – to work until a loan or debt is paid off. The work may be paid, but often it is not and the accumulated interest rates generally mean that the labourer can never complete the contract and is effectively enslaved for life. This tends to flourish in areas of extreme poverty where desperate individuals or desperate parents virtually sell themselves or their children in exchange for a loan. However, it is important to note that there is no unmediated causal relationship here: being in poverty does not force anyone to engage in slavery.

In India it is suggested that, despite the fact that indebted labour is illegal, perhaps between 10 and 40 million people work as indebted labourers (though the Indian government admits to only 251,000), mostly from the *Dalit* (untouchable) caste and the *Adivasi* (indigenous communities). An official commission in the state of Tamil Nadu categorized more than 100,000 individual cases of indebted labour and estimated that a further 1 million existed within the state boundaries alone. This area also has one of the largest concentrations of child labourers in the world: 45,000, many of whom leave for work at between 3 and 5 a.m. and do not return until 7 p.m. (Bales, 2000a: 200).

Slavery was made illegal in neighbouring Nepal in 1926, and debt bondage specifically prohibited in 1956 and again in 1991, but it still appears to affect many thousands of people. Both *Dalits* and the indigenous *Tharus* communities in western Nepal suffer from indebted labour. The latter were displaced from their traditional lands in the 1960s because little land was officially registered and many were forced to take loans to survive. Even a 14-hour day makes little impression on the loans because wages are as low as US$0.20 a day, hence the debt is often inherited by children from their parents, while women are also married into bondage (*Anti-Slavery Action Briefing*, July 2000).

In Pakistan, at partition, just 1 per cent of the population were indebted labourers; in 2000 the proportion is closer to 15 per cent, yet no single prosecution has ever been achieved for continuing this illegal activity. In 2001 a UN Sub-Commission on the Promotion and Protection of Human Rights suggested that between 80 and 90 per cent of all those involved in debt bondage in India, Nepal and the Sind province of Pakistan were *Dalits* and indigenous people, despite the fact that all countries outlaw debt bondage (Anti-Slavery, 2001). (Article 23 of the Indian Constitution forbids the use of forced labour; bonded labour is forbidden under the 1976 Bonded Labour System (Abolition) Act; the Bonded Labour System (Abolition) Rules (1995) prohibit it in Pakistan; Article 20 of the 1991 Constitution of the Kingdom of Nepal outlaw forced labour (Anti-Slavery, 2001). On 22 April 2000 the then military ruler of Pakistan, general Pervaiz Musharraf, proclaimed a crackdown on illegal forms of bonded and child labour.) *Dalits* tend to clean up after the rest of the community and are expected to work without payment, a system whose origins probably lie in the *begar* system of 'free labour'. The Pakistan brick-making industry is particularly associated with indebted families, making up perhaps 75,000 people in all (Bales, 2000a: 164). One such example was a 65-year-old man called Mano who escaped in 2000 along with 60 other bonded labourers from a farm in Sind during a funeral for a member of the landlord's family, when the armed guards were temporarily absent. He had worked on the farm for 36 years and could not remember how he came to owe the landlord the debt which had grown (at 10 per cent per month interest) over 36 years to 250,000 rupees (£3,125). Mano's earnings would mean he would have had to work for 20 years just to earn the money, never mind pay anything off the loan (McCarthy, 2000: 13).

At least the thousands of Brazilian contract slaves have a better possibility of release. There, unemployed men are enticed onto lorries with the promise of well-paid jobs only to be transported to remote areas of the Amazon where they work as labourers in the charcoal camps under armed guard for the two or three years it takes to exhaust the local timber supply, after which they are 'released' (Bales, 2000a: 128–9). Elsewhere, indebted labour is the backbone of Uzbekistan's cotton crop – a reflection of the old Soviet collective labour methods (Walsh, 2003: 18). But perhaps the most ironic example of contemporary slavery is that of the estimated 300,000 Haitian sugar-cane workers, whose ancestors were amongst the first to rid themselves of the scourge of slavery in the Caribbean, but who now find themselves enslaved on Dominican sugar estates (O'Grady, 2001). In some cases it appears that nothing has changed. (For contemporary developments in slavery and debt-bondage, see <http://www.antislavery.org/>.)

Summary

In conclusion, rather than reiterate the main points of this chapter, I want to reconsider two aspects of the links between the sections, especially between MNCs and contemporary slavery.

First, for all that many MNCs engage in exploiting cheap and unprotected labour, there is no evidence that they engage in slave labour. But, while MNCs and their supporting institutions, like the WTO and IMF, are keen to enforce discipline against those who infringe their right to trade, there is no equivalent concern for disciplining those who engage in slavery. For example, the tit-for-tat sanctions regularly imposed by the EU against the USA and vice versa only relate to those countries or companies that break the commercial regulations, but, unlike the British Navy's efforts in the middle of the nineteenth century, no institution of significant economic or political power enforces regulations against contemporary slavers (Bales, 2000a: 250). There is, in effect, one law for the rich and no law for the slaves.

Second, those who are enslaved – under whatever rubric of slavery – have markedly less degrees of freedom than most of the readers of this book. Of course, they can try and escape their bondage, but there may be severe penalties for attempts that fail; we only generally have to make a choice about which product to consume, which shares to buy, whether to question the possible use of slave labour in the rug we are standing on, whether to find out where our pension funds are being invested and so on. In short, someone else's enslavement may be the consequence of our enthralment, our indifference or our apathy. The MNCs, the WTO, the World Bank and our impotent governments may all be involved in the perpetuation of a grossly unequal global system of work – but we are not innocent bystanders in all this.

And the significance of protest is not simply in that it may overturn an odious act, but also that it reminds those who take such acts that they cannot rely upon, or proclaim the existence of, a political consensus or quiescence. If we are ever to rid ourselves of plutocracies and constrain plutocratic desires, we have to begin building a planetocracy. Slavery, the worst form of work, is not perpetuated by the acts of individual deviants who promote it, but by the passivity of those who could, collectively, stop it. Indeed, to adopt and adapt a remark allegedly made by Edmund Burke, it only requires the anti-slavers to do nothing for slavery to continue. Enslavement is essentially dependent upon enthralment: ridding others of the former requires us to escape the latter.

Exam/essay questions

1 To what extent do illegal workers prop up the lifestyles of most Western consumers?
2 'Globalization is neither good nor bad in itself, what's important is what kind of globalization.' Discuss.
3 Is it possible to eliminate slavery?
4 MNCs *may* exploit foreign labour and pollute host countries, but they are usually less exploitive and less polluting than local companies.' Discuss.
5 Are the problems of countries like Afghanistan, Iraq, North Korea and Libya the consequence of globalization or the consequence of its absence?
6 'The primary cause of exploitive labour conditions in developing countries is not the presence of MNCs but the absence of responsible consumers.' Discuss.
7 'If the West gave up buying pet food, perfume and cosmetics (valued at $37 billion per annum in 1998), the funds would provide education, food, healthcare, water and sanitation for all those people in the world who currently do not have them. There would still be $9 billion left over' (Elliott and Brittain, 1998: 18). So why doesn't the West give them up?
8 Since trade is primarily organized *within* the three trading blocs, rather than *across* the globe, should we continue to talk about 'globalization' when really we mean 'regionalization'?
9 Klein's critique of globalization is focused on branding. Is this to misunderstand the nature of the phenomenon?
10 Western subsidies to Western agriculture are high because Western agriculture is so inefficient. So should the West abandon most of its farming?

Further reading

Held and Mcgrew's (2002) *Globalization and Anti-globalization* is a useful short introduction to the field, as is Stiglitz's (2003) incisive review. Gray's *False Dawn* (2002) offers one of the bleakest outlooks on the phenomenon and perhaps might be contrasted with Anholt's (2002) account of the positive side of global branding.

Glossary

Affirmative action: a policy of positive discrimination to reflect and rectify the effects of accumulated discrimination by aligning recruitment and promotion requirements to the levels deemed appropriate to particular ethnic groups.

Alienation: for Marx (as opposed to virtually everyone else), an objective state that exists wherever capitalism exists. It is manifest by: (1) the absence of control of the producer over the product; (2) the production of goods for profit but not social need; (3) an ever-increasing division of labour which reduces work to a meaningless activity; (4) the continuing displacement of social relations by economic relations. Alienation, for Marx, is not related to unhappiness at work (a common interpretation of alienation) because people who express happiness at work under capitalism are so alienated that they don't even recognize their condition.

Anomie: Durkheim's argument that, under certain conditions of major and rapid change, the prevailing morality would temporarily disintegrate, leading society to become a jungle of selfishness until such time as a new collective morality prevailed.

Base-superstructure: a Marxist model of society in which the economic base determines the social-political superstructure.

Benchmarking: a method for improving standards and quality by comparative analysis with what are taken to be the market leaders.

'The British disease': a label applied to the common assumption in the 1960s that the apparently volatile industrial relations in some parts of British industry were both endemic within, and seriously damaging to, the British economy.

Bureaucracy: a system of administration in which the horizontal divisions between various elements or departments (bureaus) are complemented by vertical divisions of authority, and filled by professional career specialists.

Critical: an approach to organizational inquiry aimed at exploring the power relations underpinning organizations.

Designer technology: the assumption that the 'effects' of technology can be precisely predetermined by the design, and that once technological design has been finalized its effects become objective.

Determinists: those who assume that external structures override individual volition; in this context, that organizations can be assessed by examining the objective facts – which 'determine' the correct shape.

Dilution: the schemes agreed in Britain during both world wars between the government, employers and trade unions under which jobs traditionally restricted to skilled labour (i.e. men) could be undertaken by (unskilled) women and youths on three conditions: first, the agreement was for the duration of hostilities only; second, employers paid 'the going rate'; third, only war work would be affected.

Disembedded: the uprooting of local control over an organization and its reconstituting at a distance elsewhere.

Domestic labour: a blanket term often associated with 'housework', involving all unpaid activities related to the production and reproduction of a household.

Dual labour markets: a model of the labour markets which assumes a division between the primary sector where conditions are advantageous and a secondary sector where conditions are disadvantageous.

Economic long waves: the fifty-year cycle of economic and technological growth and decline that Kondratiev (1935) and Schumpeter (1976) suggested underlay capitalist development.

Embourgeoisement thesis: the assumption that the political and social habits of the working class become more middle class with rising affluence.

Equal value: a concept based on the assumption that rewards should be equal if the value of the job – as opposed to the content – is the same.

Ethnicity: the cultural, rather than physical or allegedly 'natural' differences between groups.

Ethnoscapes: representations of an environment which links land to the emotional roots of that land's current or former inhabitants.

Exclusionary action: the attempt by a superordinate group to exclude a subordinate group from the former's privileged position.

Exploitation: the disjunction between effort and reward.

External labour market: the general market for labour outside any particular organization.

Factory Acts: A series of Parliamentary Acts passed in the nineteenth century to outlaw or constrain certain industrial practices, typically processes, conditions and hours of labour involving women and children.

Factory politics: the relationships of power that exist between and within workers and managers.

False consciousness: the assumption that people misunderstand their 'true' interests.

Flexible specialization: see **Post-Fordism**.

Fordism: a term used loosely to describe either mass production and/or a phase of capitalism, dominant roughly between 1950 and 1974, in which large corporations using mass production methods operate in conjunction with the state to maintain high levels of production, consumption and employment.

Gender: since the 1970s, a term applied to culturally derived differences between men and women, as opposed to sex where the biological differences are normally considered.

Glass ceiling: the apparent limit on women's career progress.

Grapevine recruitment: a technique of recruitment based on familial or friendship associations.

Heterogeneous composites: the assumption that the identity of people at work cannot be reduced to any single social variable (class, gender, ethnic origin etc.) but is a composite construction.

Human capital theory: a theory that seeks to explain work rewards by reference to the quantity and quality of requisite qualifications, skills and experiences.

Human resource management (HRM): a method for organizing labour that, in its 'hard' form, seeks to align human resources (people) to the specific market sector of the organization. In its 'soft' form it implies that human resources are the critical resources for adding value and must therefore be nurtured and developed, rather than exploited and discarded.

Ideal type: Weber's methodological solution to the problem of comparing phenomena as complex as social organizations. Ideal types were neither typical in terms of their representing a norm, nor ideal in terms of representing the best form; rather, they were the artificial construction and exaggerations of the researcher intent on isolating those features of the phenomenon under examination which the researcher believed to be critical. This template was then used to compare real empirical cases.

Institutionalized racism: the indirect effect of policies and procedures which reproduce the status quo to the disadvantage of ethnic groups currently excluded or held in subordinate positions.

Internal labour market: a market, usually restricted to a particular organization, where promotion tends to be limited to existing employees.

Interpretativist: the approach that what we take to be the 'facts' – in this context of organizational existence/reality – are themselves constituted into existence through interpretative action; in short, the 'facts' are socially shaped.

Just-in-Time (JIT): a term applied to a method, originally of stock control, which seeks to minimize the level – and therefore the costs – of stock and only retain sufficient to maintain immediate production. The consequential fragility of work in progress implies that quality problems must be resolved immediately.

Labourism: the evolutionary reform-oriented policies of British trade unions.

Labour process: the production process at work, including the authority relations therein.

Laissez-faire (literally, 'let them act'): the principle of non-interference on the part of the government in business affairs; the opposite of mercantilism.

Mechanical solidarity: see **Solidarity.**

Mercantilism: an account of economic development, prevalent in Europe during the seventeenth and eighteenth centuries, which insisted that a country's wealth depended upon its stock of precious metals and state control over economic resources at all levels (the contrary of *laissez-faire*).

Militancy: industrial activity concerned with increasing the acquisition of economic rewards.

Moral economy: the pattern of work relationships that are rooted in social, moral and symbolic norms and traditions, in contrast to the 'market economy' where relationships are presumed to be based wholly in individual rational evaluations of effort, cost and reward.

Neo-classical labour market model: a model which presupposes that ethnic origin, class or gender are irrelevant to the allocation of labour to jobs.

Neo-Fordism: a production system which aims to remove some of the rigidities of Fordist assembly lines by introducing job-rotation, job-enlargement and greater worker-responsibility for quality.

Objectification: for Marx, the product of human labour on raw materials – the thing made – which under capitalism remained divorced from and opposed to the direct producer.

Oligarchical control: control of an organization by a small group or elite.

Organic solidarity: see **Solidarity.**

Orientation to work: an argument which suggests that satisfaction *from* work must be related to the expectations and attitudes people form *outside* work.

Paternalism: an employer's strategy for dealing with employees based on the assumption that the workers are unable to act independently of their 'masters' – at least in any civilized manner – and in which employers provide a package of 'privileges' (housing, education, health care etc.) to dissuade employees from taking any independent action.

Patriarchy: literally 'rule of the father'; an umbrella term for male domination. Hence the **patriarchal model** of work is based on a construction of work routines whereby the (female) partner of the (male) employee, or some other person, is assumed to be responsible for all domestic activities.

Pluralist: a model of power which assumes it is distributed relatively equally between representative groups over time.

Political technology: the assumption that technology is never neutral and always embodies political preferences of one sort or another.

Post-Fordism/Flexible specialization: a production system designed to invert Fordist approaches by decentralization, the adoption of flexible work practices, team-based procedures and responsibilities, and a shift in focus from mass to niche-based markets.

Problem of agency: the problem of relating the freedom of individuals to act independently of the constraints and supports constructed by social forces.

Productivism: the assumption that the producers of a product or service are more significant than the consumers and that social progress is primarily related to material progress.

Profession: an occupation requiring specialist training which is often overseen and maintained independently of the state.

Racism: any suggestion within which humans can be divided into discrete groups in order to legitimate inequality between these groups.

Radicalism: activity concerned with restructuring the reward system and or system of governance.

Re-engineering: also known as Business Process Re-engineering (BPR), this is a form of organizational design intended to replace vertical structures that support producers with horizontal structures that mirror customers' needs.

Regulation school: a school of thought which emphasizes the links between consumption, production and accumulation, as generated in conjunction with the state.

Reserve army of labour: the pool of unemployed workers alleged by Marxists, among others, to be essential to the smooth running of capitalism.

Social determinism: the assumption that technology plays no role in the construction of particular forms of society or organization.

Socio-technical systems: a set of theories based on the assumption that both the technological and the social system must be taken into account and reciprocally arranged in order to construct the most efficient and effective form of organization.

Solidarity: for Durkheim, the social glue which kept societies together. **Mechanical solidarity** was based on similarity and mutual independence while **organic solidarity** was based on difference and mutual interdependence.

Species being: Marx's argument that the essential uniqueness of humans relates to their ability to produce their own means of subsistence. Because 'work' was uniquely human it was only through work that humans could realize their true potential and a critical flaw in capitalism was that it made work into the source of alienation, rather than self-realization.

Sphere of necessity: those activities undertaken in order to survive – as opposed to the sphere of freedom.

Structuration: Giddens's model which explains the structure–action dichotomy as two sides of the same coin – the repeated action of individuals generates a structure which only exists in and through this 'structuration'.

Technicist: an approach to technology which asserts that it operates as an objective and independent variable – that is independent of human interpretation.

Technocratic: the assumption that organizational enquiry should be aimed at improving organizational efficiency and effectiveness.

Technological determinism: the assumption that technology determines – that is leads directly to – a particular form of society or organization.

Teleological: the belief that history has a particular pattern, plan, aim, end or intention.

Total quality management (TQM): a method for improving quality by insisting that responsibility for it lies at the lowest possible level – the operative making the product or delivering the service – and that improvements are continuous rather than one-off.

Underclass: the strata of society who are at the bottom of the hierarchy without access to employment and with a particular culture of poverty.

Usurpationary action: the attempt by a subordinate group to encroach upon or displace a superordinate group from the latter's privileged position.

Verstehen ('interpretative understanding'): Weber's methodological approach which included the assumption that only individuals, not collectivities, had intentions and interests and therefore all action, collective or individualistic, had to be understood (interpreted) as the result of individual action.

Vocabularies of motive: C. Wright Mills's term for the repertoire of language which legitimizes or delegitimizes certain actions.

Work: tends to be an activity that transforms nature and is usually undertaken in social situations, but exactly what counts as work depends upon the interpretation of powerful groups.

Bibliography

Abbott, P. and Sapsford, R. 1988: *Women and Social Class*. London: Tavistock.

Abercrombie, N., Hill, S. and Turner, B. S. 1980: *The Dominant Ideology Thesis*. London: Allen & Unwin.

Abercrombie, N. and Urry, J. 1983: *Capital, Labour and the New Middle Class*. London: Allen & Unwin.

Abercrombie, N., Warde, A., Soothill, K., Urry, J. and Walby, S. 1988: *Contemporary British Society*. Cambridge: Polity.

Abrams, F. and Astill, J. 2001: 'Story of the Blues', *Guardian*, 29 May.

Acheson, D. 1999: *Acheson Report*. London: Department of Health.

Adams, T. 2004: 'The Lesson Today . . .', *Observer Magazine*, 11 July.

Aglietta, M. 1979: *A Theory of Capitalist Regulation*. London: New Left Books.

Aguren, S., Bredbacka, C., Hansson, R., Ihregren, K. and Karlsson, K. G. 1984: *Volvo Kalmar Revisited: Ten Years of Experience*. Stockholm: Efficiency and Participation Development Council.

Ahmed, K. 2001: 'Asians Trail in Hunt for Health Jobs', *Observer*, June 17.

Alban-Metcalfe, B. and Nicholson, N. 1984: *The Career Development of British Managers*. London: British Institute of Management.

Albrow, M. 1970: *Bureaucracy*. London: Macmillan.

Aldridge, S. 2004: *Life Chances and Social Mobility: An Overview of the Evidence*. London: Cabinet Office publication, available at <http://www.strategy.gov.uk/files/pdf/lifechances_socialmobility.pdf>.

Alexander, S. 1976: 'Women's Work in Nineteenth Century London', in Open University (ed.), *The Changing Experience of Women*. Oxford: Martin Robertson.

Allen, I. 1988: *Doctors and their Careers*. London: PSI.

Allen, V. L. 1981: *The Militancy of the British Miners*. Shipley: Moor Press.

Alvesson, M. 1987: *Organization Theory and Technocratic Consciousness*. Berlin: De Gruyter.

Alvesson, M. and Willmott, H. (eds), 1992: *Critical Management Studies*. London: Sage.

Alvesson, M. and Willmott, H. 2002: 'Identity Regulation as Organizational Control: Producing the Appropriate Individual', *Journal of Management Studies*, vol. 39, no. 5, pp. 619–44.

Alvesson, M. and Willmott, H. (eds), 2003: *Studying Management Critically*. London: Sage.

Anderson, G. L. 1976: *Victorian Clerks*. Manchester: Manchester University Press.

Anderson, G. L. 1977: 'The Social Economy of Late Victorian Clerks', in Crossick, G. (ed.), *The Lower Middle Class in Britain 1870–1914*. London: Croom Helm.

Andrle, V. 1989: *Workers in Stalin's Russia: Industrialization and Social Change in a Planned Economy*. Brighton: Wheatsheaf.

Anholt, S. 2002: *Brand New Justice: The Upside of Global Branding*. London: Butterworth Heinemann.

Anthias, F. and Yuval-Davis, N. 1992: *Racialized Boundaries: Race, Nation, Gender, Colour, Class and the Anti-Racist Struggle*. London: Routledge.

Anthony, P. D. 1977: *The Ideology of Work*. London: Tavistock.

Anti-Slavery 2001: *Discrimination on the Basis of Work and Descent*. London: Anti-Slavery International.

Applebaum, H. 1992: *The Concept of Work: Ancient, Medieval and Modern*. New York: State University of New York Press.

Arber, S. and Gilbert, N. 1989: 'Men: the Forgotten Carers', *Sociology*, vol. 23, no. 1, pp. 111–18.

Archer, J. and Rhodes, V. 1987: 'Bereavement and Reactions to Job Loss: a Comparative Review', *British Journal of Social Psychology*, vol. 26, no. 3, pp. 211–24.

Arendt, H. 1958: *The Human Condition*. Chicago: University of Chicago Press.

Argyris, C. 1957: *Personality and Organization*. New York: Harper & Row.

Argyris, C. 1964: *Integrating the Individual and the Organization*. New York: Wiley.

Aries, P. 1973: *Centuries of Childhood*. Harmondsworth: Penguin.

Armytage, W. H. G. 1981: 'Population and Bio-social Background', in Roderick, G. and Stevens, M. (eds), *Where did we go Wrong?* Brighton: Falmer Press.

Arneson, R. J. 1987: 'Meaningful Work and Socialism', *Ethics*, vol. 97, no. 3, pp. 517–45.

Arnot, C. 2004: 'Where White Liberals Fear to Tread', *Guardian*, 30 March.

Arrow, K. 1972: 'Models of Job Discrimination', in Pascall, A. H. (ed.), *Racial Discrimination in the Labor Market*. Lexington, Mass.: D.C. Heath.

Ashley, J. 2002: 'We Really Can Have it All – With a Little Bit of Help', *Guardian*, 24 April.

Ashton, D. N. 1986: *Unemployment under Capitalism: the Sociology of British and American Labour Markets*. Brighton: Wheatsheaf.

Astill, J. 2001a: 'UN to Help Shipload of Child Slaves', *Guardian*, 14 April.

Astill, J. 2001b: 'Gabon's Oasis of Oil Lures Children into Slavery', *Observer*, 22 April.

Atkins, S. 1986: 'The Sex Discrimination Act 1975: the End of a Decade', *Feminist Review*, no. 24, pp. 57–70.

Atkinson, J. 1984: 'Manpower Strategies for Flexible Organizations,' *Personnel Management*, 16, pp. 28–31.

Atkinson, J. 1985: 'Flexibility: Planning for an Uncertain Future', *Manpower Policy and Practice*, vol. 1 (summer), pp. 26–9.

Atkinson, J. and Meager, N. 1986: 'Is Flexibility Just a Flash in the Pan?', *Personnel Management*, 18, pp. 26–9.

Atkinson, M. 1997: 'Black Footballers Are Less Well Paid,' *Observer*, 6 April.

Atkinson, M. 2000: 'Industrial Disease', *Guardian*, 14 December.

Avineri, S. 1968: *The Social and Political Thought of Karl Marx*. Cambridge: Cambridge University Press.

Ayres, G. E. 1988: *Social Conditions and Welfare Legislation 1800–1930*. London: Macmillan.

Babson, S. (ed.), 1995: *Lean Work: Empowerment and Exploitation in the Global Auto Industry*. Detroit: Western State University Press.

Badcock, C. 2000: *Evolutionary Psychology: A Critical Introduction*. Cambridge: Polity.

Bagwell, P. S. 1974: *Industrial Relations in 19th Century Britain*. Dublin: Irish University Press.

Bain, G. S. 1970: *The Growth of White Collar Unionism*. Oxford: Clarendon.

Bain, G. S. and Price, R. 1980: *Profiles of Union Growth*. Oxford: Blackwell.

Baker, R. 2001: *Fragile Science: The Reality Behind the Headlines*. London: Macmillan.

Baldamus, W. 1961: *Efficiency and Effort*. London: Tavistock.

Bales, K. 2000a: *Disposable People: New Slavery in the Global Economy*. Berkeley: University of California Press.

Bales, K. 2000b: *Slavery*. London: Channel 4.

Banton, M. 1983: *Racial and Ethnic Competition*. Cambridge: Cambridge University Press.

Banton, M. 1987: *Racial Theories*. Cambridge: Cambridge University Press.

Baran, P. A. and Sweezy, P. M. 1966: *Monopoly Capital*. New York: Monthly Review Press.

Barker, A. J. 1978: *The African Link: British Attitudes to the Negro in the Era of the Atlantic Slave Trade, 1550–1807*. London: Frank Cass.

Barker, J. and Downing, H. 1980: 'Word Processing and the Transformation of Patriarchal Relations of Control in the Office', *Capital and Class*, vol. 10, pp. 64–99.

Barkham, P. 2001b: 'As Good as it Gets', *Guardian*, 17 July.

Barley, S. 1996: *The New World of Work*. London: British-North American Committee.

Barnett, A. 2001: 'Things Can Only Get Fatter', *Observer*, 11 October.

Barrett, M. 1980: *Women's Oppression Today: Problems in Marxist Feminist Analysis*. London: Verso.

Barrett, M. and McIntosh, M. 1980: 'The "Family Wage": Some Problems for Socialists and Feminists', *Capital and Class*, no. 11, pp. 51–72.

Bartlett, C. and Ghoshal, S. 1989: *Managing across Borders: the Transnational Solution*. Boston, Mass.: Harvard Business School Press.

Bartos, J. 1989: *Marketing to Women: a Global Perspective*. London: Heinemann.

Basoux, J. L. 1987: 'Women's Intuition and the New Vogue', *Times Higher Education Supplement*, 17 July.

Batstone, E. 1979: 'Systems of Domination, Accommodation and Industrial Enterprise', in Burns, T. (ed.), *Work and Power*. London: Sage.

Batstone, E. 1985: 'International Variations in Strike Activity', *European Sociological Review*, vol. 1, no. 1, pp. 46–64.

Batstone, E. 1988a: *The Reform of Workplace Industrial Relations: Theory, Myth and Evidence*. Oxford: Clarendon.

Batstone, E. 1988b: 'The Frontier of Control', in Gallie, D. (ed.), *Employment in Britain*. Oxford: Blackwell.

Batstone, E., Boraston, I. and Frenkel, S. 1977: *Shop Stewards in Action*. Oxford: Blackwell.

Batstone, E., Boraston, I. and Frenkel, S. 1978: *The Social Organization of Strikes*. Oxford: Blackwell.

Batstone, E., Ferner, A. and Terry, M. 1983: *Unions on the Board*. Oxford: Blackwell.

Batstone, E., Ferner, A. and Terry, M. 1984: *Consent and Efficiency*. Oxford: Blackwell.

Batstone, E. and Gourlay, S. 1986: *Unions, Unemployment and Innovation*. Oxford: Blackwell.

Batstone, E., Gourlay, S., Levie, H. and Moore, R. 1987: *New Technology and the Process of Labour Regulation*. Oxford: Clarendon.

Baumgartner, T., Burns, T. R. and DeVille, P. 1979: 'Work, Politics and Social Structuring under Capitalism', in Burns, T., Karlsson, L. A. and Rus, V. (eds), *Work and Power*. London: Sage.

BBC, 1988: *Newsnight*, 21 September.

BBC, 1997: *East*, June 5.

Beaumont, P. 2001: 'Kidnapped Children Sold into Slavery as Camel Racers', *Observer*, 3 June.

Beavis, S. 1988: *Guardian*, 4 March.

Beavis, S. 1989: *Guardian*, 12 May.

Beck, U. 1992: *Rich Society*. London: Sage.

Beck, U. 2000: *The Brave New World of Work*. Cambridge: Polity.

Becker, G. S. 1976: *The Economic Approach to Human Behaviour*. Chicago: University of Chicago Press.

Becker, G. S. 1981: *A Treatise on the Family*. Cambridge, Mass.: Harvard University Press.

Becker, G. S. 1985: 'Human Capital, Effort, and the Sexual Division of Labour', *Journal of Labour Economics*, vol. 3, pp. 33–58.

Beechey, V. 1986: *Women and Employment*. Milton Keynes: Open University Press.

Beechey, V. 1987: *Unequal Work*. London: Verso.

Beechey, V. and Perkins, T. 1987: *A Matter of Hours: Women, Part-time Work and the Labour Market*. Cambridge: Polity.

Beetham, D. 1987: *Bureaucracy*. Milton Keynes: Open University Press.

Behagg, C. 1990: *Politics and Production in the Early Nineteenth Century*. London: Routledge.

Beirne, M. and Ramsay, H. 1988: 'Computer Redesign and Labour Process Theory', in Knights, D. and Willmott, H. (eds), *New Technology and the Labour Process*. London: Macmillan.

Belanger, J., Edwards, P. K. and Haivers, L. (eds), 1994: *Workplace Industrial Relations and the Global Challenge*. Ithaca, NY: ILR Press.

Bell, D. 1960: *The End of Ideology*. Glencoe, Ill.: The Free Press.

Bell, D. 1973: *The Coming of Post-industrial Society: A Venture in Social Forecasting*. New York: Basic Books.

Bell, L. and Freeman, R. 1994: 'Why Do Americans and Germans Work Different Hours?' New York: NBER Working Paper No. W4808 July.

Bennett, C. 1996: 'The Boys with the Wrong Stuff', *Guardian*, 6 November.

Bentham, J. 1977: 'Labour and Repose', in Clayre, A. (ed.), *Nature and Industrialization*. Oxford: Oxford University Press.

Berg, M. 1980: *The Machinery Question and the Making of Political Economy 1815–1848*. Cambridge: Cambridge University Press.

Berg, M. 1985: *The Age of Manufactures 1700–1820*. London: Fontana.

Berg, M. 1987: 'Women's Work and Mechanization', in Joyce, P. (ed.), *The Historical Meanings of Work*. Cambridge: Cambridge University Press.

Berg, M. 1988a: 'Workers and Machinery in Eighteenth Century England', in Rule, J. (ed.), *British Trade Unionism 1750–1850*. London: Longman.

Berg, M. 1988b: 'Women's Work, Mechanization and Early Industrialization', in Pahl, R. E. (ed.), *On Work*. Oxford: Blackwell.

Berger, J. 2001: 'A Tragedy the Size of the Planet', *Guardian Arts*, 28 May.

Berger, P. and Luckmann, T. 1966: *The Social Construction of Reality*. New York: Doubleday.

Berger, S. and Piore, M. 1980: *Dualism and Discontinuity in Industrial Societies*. Cambridge: Cambridge University Press.

Berggren, C. 1989: 'New Production Concepts in Final Assembly: the Swedish Experience', in Wood, S. (ed.), *The Transformation of Work?* London: Unwin Hyman.

Berggren, C. 1993: 'Lean Production: the End of History?', *Work, Employment and Society*, vol. 7, no. 2, pp. 163–88.

Berk, R. and Berk, S. F. 1979: *Labour and Leisure at Home*. London: Sage.

Berle, A. A. and Means, G. C. 1968: *The Modern Corporation and Private Property*. New York: Macmillan.

Berlins, M. 2004: 'So you think Inquiry Lawyers Get Paid a Lot?', *Guardian G2*, 24 February.

Bernstein, R. J. 1983: *Beyond Objectivism and Relativism*. Oxford: Blackwell.

Bertalanffy, L. 1981: 'General Systems Theory: a Critical Review', in Open Systems Group (eds), *Systems Behaviour*. London: Harper & Row.

Best, G. 1979: *Mid-Victorian Britain 1851–75*. London: Fontana.

Bevins, A. 1995: 'Powerless under the Pyramid', *Observer*, 12 March.

Beynon, H. 1975: *Working for Ford*. Wakefield: EP Publishing.

Beynon, H. and Blackburn, R. 1984: 'Unions: the Men's Affair?', in Siltanen, J. and Stanworth, M. (eds), *Women and the Public Sphere*. London: Hutchinson.

Bhavnani, K. K. and Bhavnani, R. 1985: 'Racism and Resistance in Britain', in Coates, D., Johnston, G. and Bush, R. (eds), *A Socialist Anatomy of Britain*. Cambridge: Polity.

Bijker, W. E., Hughes, T. P. and Pinch, T. (eds), 1987: *The Social Construction of Technological Systems*. Cambridge, Mass.: MIT Press.

Birch, D. 2001: 'Tomorrow Never Comes', *Guardian Online*, 4 January.

Bird, A. 2000: 'Parent Companies', *Guardian*, 21 August.

Bittner, E. 1965: 'The Concept of Organization', *Social Research*, vol. 32, no. 3, pp. 239–55.

Black, I. 2004: 'Sweden Acts to Stop Influx of EU Workers', *Guardian*, 31 January.

Blackburn, R. and Mann, M. 1979: *The Working Class in the Labour Market*. London: Macmillan.

Blauner, R. 1964: *Alienation and Freedom*. Chicago: Chicago University Press.

Blumberg, P. 1968: *Industrial Democracy*. London: Constable.

Blythe, R. 1969: *Akenfield*. Harmondsworth: Penguin.

BMRB (British Market Research Bureau), 1988: *Target Group Index Survey*. London: BMRB.

Bogdanor, V. 1990: *Women at the Top*. London: Hansard Society.

Bohning, W. 1972: *The Migration of Workers in the United Kingdom and the European Community*. Oxford: Oxford University Press/Institute of Race Relations.

Boje, D. M., Gephart, R. P. Jr. and Thatchenkery, T. J. (eds), 1996: *Postmodern Management and Organization Theory*. London: Sage.

Bonnell, V. E. 1984: *Roots of Rebellion: Workers' Politics and Organization in St. Petersburg and Moscow 1900–1914*. Berkeley: University of California Press.

Bonney, N. 1988: 'Dual Earning Couples: Trends of Change in Great Britain', *Work, Employment and Society*, vol. 2, no. 1, pp. 89–102.

Borger, J. 2001: 'Planet Mac', *Guardian G2*, 6 April.

Borger, J. 2003: 'Why America's Plutocrats Gobble Up $1,500 Hot Dogs', *Guardian*, 5 November.

Boseley, S. 1987: *Guardian*, 27 June.

Boseley, S. 1996: 'Men Losing Battle for Lowly Jobs', *The Guardian*, 25 June.

Boston, S. 1987: *Women Workers and the Trade Unions*. London: Lawrence & Wishart.

Boston, T. D. 1988: *Race, Class and Conservatism*. London: Unwin Hyman.

Bostyn, A. and Wight, D. 1987: 'Inside a Community: Values Associated with Money and Time', in Fineman, S. (ed.), *Unemployment: Personal and Social Consequences*. London: Tavistock.

Bott, E. 1971: *Family and Social Network*. London: Tavistock.

Bouchier, D. 1983: *The Feminist Challenge: the Movement for Women's Liberation in Britain and the United States*. London: Macmillan.

Bourdieu, P. 1979: *Algeria 1960*. Cambridge: Cambridge University Press.

Bové, J. and Dufour, F. 2001: *The World is not for Sale: Farmers Against Junk Food*. London: Verso.

Bowcott, O. 2004: 'Is this the Daily Mail Effect?', *Guardian*, 5 February.

Bowey, A. 1976: *The Sociology of Organizations*. London: Hodder & Stoughton.

Bowles, M. L. 1989: 'Myth, Meaning and Work Organization', *Organization Studies*, vol. 10, no. 3, pp. 405–21.

Bradley, H., Erickson, M., Stephenson, C. and Williams, S. 2000: *Myths at Work*. Cambridge: Polity.

Braham, P. 1980: *Class, Race and Immigration*. Milton Keynes: Open University Press.

Braham, P., Rhodes, E. and Pearn, M. (eds), 1981: *Discrimination and Disadvantage in Employment*. London: Harper & Row.

Branigan, T. 2001b: 'Women's Enjoyment of Careers Plummets', *Guardian*, 13 June.

Brannen, J. and Wilson, G. 1987: *Give and Take in Families*. London: Allen & Unwin.

Brannen, P., Batstone, E. V., Fatchett, D. and White, P. 1976: *The Worker Directors: a Sociology of Participation*. London: Hutchinson.

Braverman, H. 1974: *Labor and Monopoly Capital*. New York: Monthly Review Press.

Braybon, G. 1981: *Women Workers in the First World War*. London: Croom Helm.

Brayfield, C. 2000: 'Worked to Death', *The Times*, 26 June.

Brennan, J. and McGeevor, P. 1987: *Employment of Graduates from Ethnic Minorities*. London: CRE.

Briggs, A. 1955: *Victorian People*. Harmondsworth: Penguin.

Brighton Labour Process Group, 1977: 'The Capitalist Labour Process', *Capital and Class*, vol. 1, pp. 3–42.

Brittain, V. and Elliott, L. 2000: 'Rich Live Longer, Poor Die Younger in a Divided World', *Guardian*, 29 June.

Brittan, A. and Maynard, M. 1984: *Sexism, Racism and Oppression*. Oxford: Blackwell.

Brockes, E. 2000: 'Wound-up Over Work', *Guardian*, 8 May.

Brodkin, J. 2000: 'Hundred Premier Players Earn Over £1M Each', *Guardian*, 19 April.

Brooks, D. and Singh, K. 1978–9: 'Ethnic Commitment versus Structural Reality: South Asian Immigrant Workers in Britain', *New Community*, vol. 8, no. 1, pp. 19–30.

Brooks, D. and Singh, K. 1979: 'Pivots and Presents: Asian Brokers in British Foundries', in Wallman, S. (ed.), *Ethnicity of Work*. London: Macmillan.

Brown, C. 1984: *Black and White Britain: the Third PSI Survey*. London: Heinemann/PSI.

Brown, C. and Reich, M. 1997: ' "Developing" Skills and Pay through Career Ladders: Lessons from Japanese and US Companies', *California Management Review*, vol. 39, no. 2, pp. 124–44.

Brown, D. and Harrison, M. J. 1978: *A Sociology of Industrialization*. London: Macmillan.

Brown, G. 1988: *Guardian*, 17 March.

Brown, P. 1977: *Sabotage*. Nottingham: Spokesman.

Brown, P. 1999: *The New ILO Worst Forms of Child Labour 1999*. Geneva: NGO Group for the Convention on the Rights of the Child.

Brown, P. 2003: 'Coca-Cola Plant Must Stop Draining Water', *Guardian*, 19 December.

Brown, P. and Hesketh, A. 2004: *The Mismanagement of Talent: Employability and Jobs in the Knowledge Economy*. Oxford: Oxford University Press.

Brown, R. 1973: 'Sources of Objectives in Work and Employment', in Child, J. (ed.), *Man and Organization*. London: Allen & Unwin.

Brown, R. 1974: 'The Attitude to Work, Expectations and Social Perspectives of Shipbuilding Apprentices', in Leggatt, T. (ed.), *Sociological Theory and Survey Research*. London: Sage.

Brown, R. 1978: 'Work', in Abrams, P. (ed.), *Work, Urbanism and Inequality*. London: Weidenfeld & Nicolson.

Brown, R. 1982: 'Work Histories, Career Strategies and the Class Structure', in Giddens, A. and Mackenzie, G. (eds), *Social Class and the Division of Labour*. Cambridge: Cambridge University Press.

Brown, R. 1988: 'The Employment Relationship in Sociological Theory', in Gallie, D. (ed.), *Employment in Britain*. Oxford: Blackwell.

Brown, R. 1991: *Society and Economy in Modern Britain 1700–1850*. London: Routledge.

Brown, S. and Clayre, A. 1978: *Work, Morality and Human Nature*. Milton Keynes: Open University Press.

Brown, W. (ed.), 1981: *The Changing Contours of British Industrial Relations*. Oxford: Blackwell.

Brown, W. and Wadhwani, S. 1990: 'The Economic Effects of Industrial Relations Legislation since 1979', *National Institute Economic Review*, February, pp. 57–70.

Browne, A. 2001a: 'Britain's Foreign "Slave" Nurses', *Observer*, 27 May.

Browne, A. 2001b: 'Third World Boom Raises Hopes of End to Poverty', *Observer*, 8 July.

Brownmiller, S. 1976: *Against our Will: Men, Women and Rape*. Harmondsworth: Penguin.

Bruegel, I. 1983: 'Women's Employment, Legislation and the Labour Market', in Lewis, J. (ed.), *Women's Welfare, Women's Rights*. London: Croom Helm.

Bruegel, I. 1989: 'Sex and Race in the Labour Market', *Feminist Review*, no. 32 (summer), pp. 47–68.

Bruegel, I. 1996: 'Whose Myths are They Anyway?' *The British Journal of Sociology*, vol. 47, no. 1, pp. 175–77.

Bruland, T. 1982: 'Industrial Conflict as a Source of Technical Innovation', *Economy and Society*, vol. 11, pp. 91–121.

Brundtland, G. H. 2000: *Reith Lectures*. London: BBC.

Buchanan, D. A. and Boddy, D. 1983: *Organizations in the Computer Age: Technological Imperatives and Strategic Choice*. Aldershot: Gower.

Buchanan, D. A. and Huczynski, A. A. 1985: *Organizational Behaviour: an Introductory Text*. London: Prentice Hall.

Buckingham, L. 1998: '£1m-a-year Salary Club Swells to 49', *Guardian*, 6 August.

Buckland, S. and MacGregor, S. 1987: 'Discouraged Workers?: the Long Term Unemployed and the Search for Work', in Fineman, S. (ed.), *Unemployment: Personal and Social Consequences*. London: Tavistock.

Buick, A. and Crump, J. 1986: *State Capitalism: the Wages System under New Management*. London: Macmillan.

Bularzik, M. 1978: 'Sexual Harassment at the Workplace', *Radical America*, vol. 12, pp. 25–43.

Bunting, M. 2001a: 'Work is Turning Us into Emotional Pygmies', *Guardian*, 30 May.

Bunting, M. 2001b: 'A Nice Little Number', *Guardian*, 9 July.

Bunting, M. 2003: 'New Year: Same Grind', *Guardian*, 6 January.

Bunting, M. 2004: *Willing Slaves: How the Overwork Culture is Ruling our Lives*. London: HarperCollins.

Burawoy, M. 1979: *Manufacturing Consent*. Chicago: University of Chicago Press.

Burawoy, M. 1985: *The Politics of Production*. London: Verso.

Burawoy, M. and Lukács, J. 1989: 'What is Socialist about Socialist Production?: Autonomy and Control in a Hungarian Steel Mill', in Wood, S. (ed.), *The Transformation of Work?* London: Unwin Hyman.

Burgess, K. 1980: *The Challenge of Labour*. London: Croom Helm.

Burgess, R. G. 1986: *Sociology, Education and Schools*. London: Batsford.

Burgess, S. and Propper, C. 1999: 'Poverty in Britain', in Gregg, P. and Wadsworth, J. (eds), *The State of Working Britain*. Manchester: Manchester University Press.

Burke, J. 2000a: 'Army to Test Women for Combat Roles', *Observer*, 28 May, cited in <www.guardianlimited.co.uk>.

Burke, J. 2000b: 'Women to Fight on Front Line', *Observer*, 24 December, cited in <www.guardianlimited.co.uk>.

Burke, J. 2000c: 'Child Labour Scandal Hits Adidas', *Observer*, 19 November.

Burke, J. 2001: 'Record Numbers Desert the Army', *Observer*, 13 May.

Burkeman, O. 2001: 'A Hairy Naked Man in a Rubber Ring. Interested?', *Guardian*, 9 July.

Burkitt, N. 2001: *Workers' Rights and Wrongs*. London: Institute for Public Policy Research.

Burnett, J. (ed.), 1974: *Useful Toil: Autobiographies of Working People from the 1820s to the 1920s*. London: Allen Lane.

Burnett, J. 1990: Personal communication.

Burnham, D. 1983: *The Rise of the Computer State*. London: Wiedenfeld & Nicolson.

Burnham, J. 1962: *The Managerial Revolution*. London: Macmillan.

Burns, T. and Stalker, G. M. 1961: *The Management of Innovation*. London: Tavistock.

Burrell, G. 1988: 'Modernism, Postmodernism and Organizational Analysis 2: the Contribution of Michel Foucault', *Organization Studies*, vol. 9, no. 2, pp. 221–35.

Burrell, G. and Morgan, G. 1979: *Sociological Paradigms and Organizational Analysis*. Aldershot: Gower.

Callinicos, A. 1983: *The Revolutionary Ideas of Marx*. London: Bookmarks.

Callon, M. 1986: 'The Sociology of an Actor Network', in Callon, M., Law, J. and Rip, A. (eds), *Mapping the Dynamics of Science and Technology*. London: Macmillan.

Campbell, B. 1982a: 'Power not Pin Money', *New Socialist*, July–August.

Campbell, B. 1982b: 'Women: Not What they Bargained For', *Marxism Today*, March.

Campbell, D. 2001a: 'Flag Protest Aims to Get US Thinking', *Guardian*, 27 June.

Campbell, D. 2001b: 'LA Story', *Guardian*, 7 July.

Campbell, D. 2003a: 'Wal-Mart May Face Army of 1.5m in Class Suit', *Guardian*, 25 September.

Campbell, D. 2003b: 'Tribes Launch Headcount to Challenge US Census', <http://www.guardian.co.uk/international/story/0,3604,1107680,00.html>, 16 December.

Cappelli, P. 1995: 'Rethinking Employment', *British Journal of Industrial Relations*, vol. 33, no. 4, pp. 563–602.

CARF (Campaign Against Racism and Fascism), 1981: *Southall: the Birth of a Black Community*. London: Institute of Race Relations.

Carlyle, T. 1977: 'The Mechanical Age', in Clayre, A. (ed.), *Nature and Civilization*. Oxford: Oxford University Press.

Carroll, D. T. 1983: 'A Disappointing Search for Excellence', *Harvard Business Review*, November–December.

Carroll, R. 2003: 'Child Labourers Rescued From Nigerian Quarries', *Guardian*, 17 October.

Carvel, J. 2001a: 'Racism is Rife in NHS', *Guardian*, 19 June.

Carvel, J. 2001b: 'NHS Staff Tell of Morale-Sapping Racism', *Guardian*, 25 June.

Carvel, J. 2001c: 'Girl Power Generation Faces Work Place Shock', *Guardian*, 20 July.

Carvel, J. 2004a: 'Women Workers Earn £500 less a month than Men, says EOC', *Guardian*, January 14.

Carvel, J. 2004b: 'Divorced Women "Face Poverty at 65"', *Guardian*, 30 January.

Carvel, J. 2004c: 'NHS Racism: Long History, Little Change', *Guardian*, 13 February.

Castells, M. 1994: 'European Cities, the Information Society, and the Global Economy', *New Left Review*, 204.

Castells, M. and Aoyama, Y. 1994: 'Paths towards the Informational Society: Employment Structure in G-7 Countries, 1920–90', *International Labour Review*, vol. 133, no. 1, pp. 5–30.

Castles, S. and Kosack, G. 1973: *Immigrant Workers and Class Structure in Western Europe*. London: Oxford University Press.

Caudron, S. 1997: 'Don't Make Texaco's $175 Million Mistake', *Workforce*, March, pp. 58–66.

Caulkin, S. 1999: 'A Glass Ceiling Made of Lead', *Observer*, January 3.

Caulkin, S. 2001: 'The Price of Inefficiency', *Observer*, 24 June.

Caulkin, S. 2003a: 'Harder and Harder to Swallow', *Observer*, 4 May.

Caulkin, S. 2003b: 'Breaking out of the Budget Cycle', *Observer*. July 20.

Caulkin, S. 2003c: 'Best of British? You're Joking', *Guardian*, 19 December.

Caulkin, S. 2004: 'Evolving from a City of Fear', *Guardian*, 1 February.

Cavendish, R. 1982: *Women on the Line*. London: Routledge.

Central London Community Law Centre, 1987: *Organizing as Women Trade Unionists*. London: CLCLC.

Centre for Contemporary Cultural Studies, 1982: *The Empire Strikes Back*. London: Hutchinson.

Centre for Employment Research, 1990: *Ethnic Minority Businesses and Employment in Greater Manchester*. Manchester: Manchester Metropolitan University.

Cerny, P. 1997: 'Globalization and Strategies for Renewal', *Bulletin of the Centre for Industrial Policy and Performance*, no. 11, pp. 13–17.

Chadwick, E. 1842: 'Report on the Sanitary Condition of the Labouring Population', in Ward, J. T. (ed.), 1970: *The Factory System*. Newton Abbot: David & Charles.

Chadwick, N. 1970: *The Celts*. Harmondsworth: Penguin.

Chambers, M. 1995: *The Unplayable Lie: The Untold Story of Women and Discrimination in American Golf*. New York: Pocket Books.

Chandler, A. D. 1962: *Strategy and Structure: Chapters in the History of the American Industrial Enterprise*. Cambridge, Mass.: MIT Press.

Channon, D. 1973: *The Strategy and Structure of British Enterprise*. Cambridge, Mass.: Harvard University Press.

Chapman, S. D. 1972: *The Cotton Industry in the Industrial Revolution*. London: Macmillan.

Chatterjee, P. and Finger, M. 1994: *The Earth Brokers: Power, Politics and World Development*. London: Routledge.

Child, J. 1972: 'Organizational Structure, Environment and Performance', *Sociology*, vol. 6, no. 1, pp. 1–22.

Chinoy, E. 1955: *Automobile Workers and the American Dream*. New York: Doubleday.

Chiplin, B. and Grieg, N. 1986: *Equality of Opportunity for Women in the NHS*. London: DHSS mimeo.

Chiplin, B. and Sloane, P. J. 1974: 'Sexual Discrimination in the Labour Market', *British Journal of Industrial Relations*, vol. 12, no. 3, pp. 371–402.

Christie, I. R. 1984: *Stress and Stability in Late Eighteenth Century Britain*. Oxford: Clarendon.

Clark, A. 1982: *Working Life of Women in the Seventeenth Century*. London: Routledge.

Clark, A. 2001: 'British Pay Their Accountants Best', *Guardian*, 7 December.

Clark, D. Y. 1987: 'Families Facing Redundancy', in Fineman, S. (ed.), *Unemployment: Personal and Social Consequences*. London: Tavistock.

Clark, J., Mcloughlin, I., Rose, H. and King, R. 1988: *The Process of Technological Change: New Technology and Social Choice in the Workplace*. Cambridge: Cambridge University Press.

Clarke, L., Michielsens, E., Pedersen, F., Susman, B. and Wall, C. 2004: *Women in Construction*. London: Reed International/CLR Studies.

Clayre, A. (ed.), 1977: *Nature and Industrialization*. Oxford: Oxford University Press.

Clegg, H. A. 1976: *Trade Unionism under Collective Bargaining*. Oxford: Blackwell.

Clegg, H. A. 1979: *The Changing System of Industrial Relations in Great Britain*. Oxford: Blackwell.

Clegg, S. 1989: *Frameworks of Power*. London: Sage.

Clegg, S. and Dunkerley, D. 1980: *Organization, Class and Control*. London: Routledge.

Clegg, S. R. and Gray, J. T. 1996: 'Metaphors of Globalization', in Boje, D. M., Gephart, R. P. Jr. and Thatchenkery, T. J. (eds), *Postmodern Management and Organization Theory*. London: Sage.

Clement, B. 1995: 'Dinner Ladies Equal Pay Win Undermines Competitive Law', *Independent*, 7 July.

Clutterbuck, D. and Crainer, S. 1989: *Men and Women who Changed Management*. London: Macmillan.

Coates, D. 1984: *The Context of British Politics*. London: Hutchinson.

Coates, D. and Johnston, G. (eds), 1983: *Socialist Strategies*. Oxford: Martin Robertson.

Cockburn, C. 1983a: *Brothers: Male Dominance and Technological Change*. London: Pluto.

Cockburn, C. 1983b: 'Caught in the Wheels', *Marxism Today*, November, pp. 16–20.

Cockburn, C. 1986: *Training for Her Job and for His*. London: EOC.

Cockburn, C. 1987a: *Two-track Training: Sex Inequalities and the YTS*. London: Macmillan.

Cockburn, C. 1987b: *Women, Trade Unions and Political Parties*. London: Fabian Research Series, no. 349.

Cockburn, C. 1991: *In the Way of Women*. London: Macmillan.

Coe, T. 1992: *The Key to the Men's Club*. London: Institute of Management.

Cohen, A. P. 1979: 'The Whalsey Croft', in Wallman, S. (ed.), *Social Anthropology of Work*. Cambridge: Cambridge University Press.

Cohen, I. J. 1989: *Structuration Theory: Anthony Giddens and the Constitution of Social Life*. London: Macmillan.

Cohen, N. 2002: 'No Merit in Greed', *Observer*, 17 November.

Cohen, R. 1988: *The New Helots: Migrants in the International Division of Labour*. Aldershot: Gower.

Cohn, S. 1985: *The Process of Occupational Sex-typing*. Philadelphia: Temple University Press.

Cole, G. D. H. 1955: Miscellaneous documents on guild socialism, *The Cole Collection*, Nuffield College, Boxes B/3/3/E; B/3/5/B.

Cole, G. D. H. and Postgate, R. 1938: *The Common People*. London: Methuen.

Coleman, D. C. 1975: *Industry in Tudor and Stuart England*. London: Macmillan.

Collins, J. 2001: '5th Level Leadership', *Harvard Business Review*, January.

Collinson, D. 2002a: 'Revisiting the Shopfloor', *Organization*, vol. 9, no. 1, pp. 41–50.

Collinson, D. 2002b: 'Managing Humour', *Journal of Management Studies*, vol. 39, no. 2, pp. 269–88.

Collinson, D. L. 1987: *Barriers to Fair Selection*. London: EOC/HMSO.

Collinson, P. 2001: 'City Legend Goes with a Fortune: Will She Return?', *Guardian*, 29 March.

Collinson, P. 2004: 'Will China Make a Monkey out of You?', *Guardian: Jobs and Money*, 24 January.

Colvin, G. 2001: 'The Great CEO Pay Heist', *Fortune*, 25 June, pp. 30–6.

Commission for Industrial Relations, 1974: *Mansfield Hosiery Mills Ltd. Report no. 76*. London: HMSO.

Commission for Racial Equality, 1981: *BL Cars Ltd: Report of a Formal Investigation*. London: CRE.

Commission for Racial Equality, 1987: *Chartered Accountancy Training Contracts*. London: CRE.

Commission for Racial Equality, 1988a: *Ethnic Minority School Teachers*. London: CRE.

Commission for Racial Equality, 1988b: *Learning in Terror: a Survey of Racial Harassment in Schools and Colleges*. London: CRE.

Commission for Racial Equality, 1990: *From Cradle to Grave*. London: CRE.

Confederation of British Industry, 1970: *Race Relations in Employment: Advice to Employers*. London: CBI.

Confederation of British Industry, 1981: 'Statement and Guide on General Principles and Practice', in Braham, P. et al., *Discrimination and Disadvantage in Employment*. London: Harper & Row.

Connon, H. 2001: 'Footsie Takes a Walk on the Ethical Side', *Observer*, 8 July.

Connon, H. 2003a: 'Consultants Blamed for Fat Cat Frenzy', *Observer Business*, 4 May.

Connon, H. 2003b: 'Bosses Who Shed Most Staff Take Top Pay Packets', *Observer Business*, 31 August.

Connon, H. 2004a: 'Is it a Swann Song for Fat Cats?' *Guardian*, 1 February.

Connon, H. 2004b: 'Pay Bonanza Boosts HSBC Bosses' Pensions', *Observer*, 25 April.

Conway, O. 1987: *A Farewell To Marx*. Harmondsworth: Penguin.

Cooley, M. 1980: 'Computerization: Taylor's Latest Disguise', *Economic and Industrial Democracy*, vol. 1, pp. 523–39.

Cooper, R. 1986: 'Organization Disorganization', *Social Science Information*, vol. 25, no. 2, pp. 299–335.

Cooper, R. 1989: 'Modernism, Post Modernism and Organizational Analysis 3: the Contribution of Jacques Derrida', *Organization Studies*, vol. 10, no. 4, pp. 479–502.

Cooper, R. and Burrell, G. 1988: 'Modernism, Postmodernism and Organizational Analysis', *Organization Studies*, vol. 9, no. 1, pp. 91–112.

Cooperrider, D. and Pasmore, W. A. 1991: 'The Organization Dimension of Global Change', *Human Relations*, vol. 44, no. 8, pp. 763–88.

Coriat, B. 1980: 'The Restructuring of the Assembly Line', *Capital and Class*, no. 11, pp. 34–43.

Cornelius, A. 1987: *Guardian*, 27 October.

Cotgrove, S. and Box, S. 1970: *Science, Industry and Society*. London: Allen & Unwin.

Cowan, R. 2004: 'First Black Chief Constable Takes Helm' at <http://www.guardian.co.uk/race/story/0,11374,1116705,00.html>.

Cowan, R. S. 1983: *More Work for Mother: the Ironies of Household Technology from the Open Hearth to the Microwave*. New York: Basic Books.

Coward, R. 2001: 'The Evil Women Do', *Guardian*, 12 July.

Coward, R. 2003: 'Slaves in Soho', *Guardian*, 26 March.

Cowe, R. 2001: 'Why It's Time for Business to Give Something Back', *Observer*, 8 July.

Crace, J. 2000: 'Written in Black and White', *Guardian Education*, 17 October.

Craft, M. and Craft, A. 1983: 'The Participation of Ethnic Minority Pupils in Further and Higher Education', *Educational Review*, vol. 25, no. 1, pp. 10–19.

Crafts, N. F. R. 1985: *British Economic Growth during the Industrial Revolution*. Oxford: Oxford University Press.

Craib, I. 1984: *Modern Social Theory*. Brighton: Wheatsheaf.

Craig, C., Rubery, J., Tarling, R. and Wilkinson, F. 1982: *Labour Market Structure, Industrial Organization and Low Pay*. Cambridge: Cambridge University Press.

Crehan, K. 1986: 'How the Other Half Works', in Epstein, T. S., Crehan, K., Gerzer, A. and Sass, J. (eds), *Women Work and the Family in Britain and Germany*. London: Croom Helm.

Cressey, P. and McInnes, J. 1980: 'Voting for Ford: Industrial Democracy and the Control of Labour', *Capital and Class*, no. 11, pp. 5–33.

Crompton, R. 1989: 'Women in Banking: Continuity and Change since the Second World War', *Work, Employment and Society*, vol. 3, no. 2, pp. 141–56.

Crompton, R., Gallie, D. and Purcell, K. (eds), 1996: *Changing Forms of Employment: Organizations, Skills and Gender*. London: Routledge.

Crompton, R. and Jones, G. 1982: *White Collar Proletariat: Deskilling and Gender in Clerical Work*. London: Macmillan.

Crompton, R. and Sanderson, K. 1986: 'Credentials and Careers: Some Implications of the Increase in Professional Qualifications amongst Women', *Sociology*, vol. 20, no. 1, pp. 25–42.

Cronin, J. E. 1979: *Industrial Conflict in Modern Britain*. London: Croom Helm.

Cronin, J. E. 1984: *Labour and Society in Britain 1918–79*. London: Batsford.

Crouch, C. 1982: *Trade Unions: the Logic of Collective Action*. London: Fontana.

Croucher, R. 1986: *We Refuse to Starve in Silence: a History of the National Unemployed Workers' Movement 1920–46*. London: Lawrence & Wishart.

Crowley-Bainton, T. 1987: 'Discriminating Employers', *New Society*, 27 November.

Crozier, M. 1964: *The Bureaucratic Phenomenon*. London: Tavistock.

Crozier, M. 1983: 'Implications for the Organization', in Otway, H. J. and Peltu, M. (eds), *New Office Technology*. London: Ablex.

Cunningham, H. 1980: *Leisure in the Industrial Revolution*. London: Croom Helm.

Cunnison, S. 1984: 'Participation in Local Union Organization. School Meals Staff: a Case Study', in Garminikow, E., Morgan, D., Purvis, J. and Taylorson, D. (eds), *Gender, Class and Work*. London: Heinemann.

Curran, J. and Burrows, R. 1988: *Enterprise in Britain: a National Profile of Small Business Owners and the Self-employed*. London: Small Business Research Trust.

Currie, R. 1979: *Industrial Politics*. Oxford: Clarendon.

Curtin, P. D. 1972: 'British Images of Africans in the Nineteenth Century', in Baxter, P. and Sansom, B. (eds), *Race and Social Difference*. Harmondsworth: Penguin.

Cutler, A. 1978: 'The Romance of Labour', *Economy and Society*, vol. 7, no. 1, pp. 74–9.

Dabscheck, B. and Niland, J. 1981: *Industrial Relations in Australia*. London: Allen & Unwin.

Dahrendorf, R. 1959: *Class and Class Conflict in an Industrial Society*. London: Routledge.

Daito, E. 1979: 'Summary of Discussions of the 4th International Conference on Business History', in Nakagawa, K. (ed.), *Labor and Management*. Tokyo: University of Tokyo.

Dale, A. 1987: 'Occupational Inequality, Gender and Life Cycle', *Work, Employment and Society*, vol. 1, no. 3, pp. 326–51.

Daniel, M. 1975: *The Arabs and Medieval Europe*. London: Longman.

Daniel, W. L. 1968: *Racial Discrimination in England, Based on the PEP Report*. Harmondsworth: Penguin.

Davey, A. 2003: 'The Race to Judge', *Guardian Education*, 25 March.

Davidoff, L. and Hall, C. 1987: *Family Fortunes: Men and Women of the English Middle Class, 1780–1850*. London: Hutchinson.

Davies, C. and Rosser, J. 1987: 'Women's Career Paths: a Male Pathway unwilling to Bend', *The Health Service Journal*, 5 February.

Davies, R. J. 1979: 'Economic Activity, Incomes Policy and Strikes: a Quantitative Analysis', *British Journal of Industrial Relations*, vol. 17, pp. 205–23.

Davis, K. and Moore, W. E. 1945: 'Some Principles of Stratification', *American Sociological Review*, vol. 10, no. 2, pp. 242–9.

Davis, L. E. and Taylor, J. C. 1976: 'Technology, Organization and Job Structure', in Dubin, R. (ed.), *Handbook of Work, Organization and Society*. Chicago: McNally.

Davis, M. 1985: *Prisoners of the American Dream: Politics and Economy in the History of the US Working Class*. London: Verso.

Dawkins, R. 1976: *The Selfish Gene*. Oxford: Oxford University Press.

Deaton, D. 1983: 'Unemployment', in Bain, G. S. (ed.), *Industrial Relations in Britain*. Oxford: Blackwell.

Deem, R. 1985: 'Work and the Family', Unit 14 Part I, *Work and Society*. Milton Keynes: Open University Press.

Delmar, R. 1976: 'Looking again at Engels's "Origins of the Family, Private Property and the State"', in Mitchell, J. and Oakley, A. (eds), *The Rights and Wrongs of Women*. Harmondsworth: Penguin.

Delphy, C. 1977: *The Main Enemy*. London: Women's Research and Resources Centre.

De Lyon, H. and Migniolo, F. 1989: *Women Teachers*. Milton Keynes: Open University Press.

Denny, C. 2000: 'A Nation of Shop Keepers?' *Guardian*, 26 July.

Denny, C. 2001a: 'Cheap Labour, Ruined Lives', *Guardian*, 16 February.

Denny, C. 2001b: 'Profits Down, Top Pay Up', *Guardian*, 16 July.

Denny, C. 2002: 'Retreat by Nestle on Ethiopia's $6m debt', *Guardian*, 20 December.

Denny, C. 2003: 'Two-Thirds of Workers "On Less than Average Pay"', *Guardian*, 3 February.

Denny, C., Elliott, L. and Moore, C. 2004: 'If the CAP fits, Cash in: How the Wealthy Benefit', *Guardian*, 22 January.

Derrida, J. 1973: *Speech and Phenomena*. Evanston: Northwestern University Press.

Derrida, J. 1978: *Writing and Difference*. London: Tavistock.

Desai, M. 2003: 'With the Best Will in the World': Review of Peter Singer's *One World*, in *Times Higher Education Supplement*, 21 February.

De Vroey, M. 1984: 'A Regulation Approach Interpretation of the Contemporary Crisis', *Capital and Class*, vol. 23, pp. 45–66.

Dex, S. 1978–9: 'Job Search Methods and Ethnic Discrimination', *New Community*, vol. 7, no. 1, pp. 31–9.

Dex, S. 1985: *The Sexual Division of Work: Conceptual Revolutions in the Social Sciences*. Brighton: Wheatsheaf.

Dex, S. 1988: *Women's Attitudes towards Work*. London: Macmillan.

Dex, S. and Walters, P. 1989: 'Women's Occupational Status in Britain, France and the USA: Explaining the Difference', *Industrial Relations Journal*, vol. 20, no. 3, pp. 203–10.

Dhingra, D. 2001a: 'Can Astrologers Help you to Climb the Career Ladder?', *Guardian Office*, 23 April.

Dhingra, D. 2001b: 'Creatures of Habit', *Guardian Office*, 30 April.

Dhingra, D. 2001c: 'Another Day in Purgatory', *Guardian*, 4 June.

Dickens, L. 1989: 'Women: a Rediscovered Resource?', *Industrial Relations Journal*, vol. 20, no. 3, pp. 167–75.

Dickens, R., Gregg, P. and Wadsworth, J. 2001: *The State of Working Britain*. Manchester: Manchester University Press.

Diwan, R. 1997: 'Globalization: Myth vs. Reality', Internet paper on <http://genius.net/indolink/Analysis/globalization.html>.

Dobson, C. R. 1980: *Masters and Journeymen: a Prehistory of Industrial Relations 1717–1800*. London: Croom Helm.

DOE (Department of Employment), 1971: *British Labour Statistics*. London: HMSO.

Doeringer, P. and Piore, M. 1971: *Internal Labour Markets and Manpower Analysis*. Lexington, Mass.: D.C. Heath.

Dolby, N. 1987: *Norma Dolby's Diary*. London: Verso.

Donaldson, L. 1985a: *American Anti-management Theories of Organizations*. Cambridge: Cambridge University Press.

Donaldson, L. 1985b: *In Defence of Organization Theory*. Cambridge: Cambridge University Press.

Donegan, L. 2004: 'Club Culture', *Guardian 2*, 12 February.

Donoghue, H. 1988: 'University Statistical Records: Age Patterns', *AUT Woman*, no. 13, spring.

Donovan Commission, 1968: *Report of the Royal Commission on Trade Unions and Employers' Associations*. London: HMSO.

Doray, B. 1988: *From Taylorism to Fordism*. London: Free Association Books.

Dore, R. P. 1973: *British Factory–Japanese Factory*. London: Allen & Unwin.

Dore, R. P 1989: 'Where are we Now?: Musings of an Evolutionist', *Work, Employment and Society*, vol. 3, no. 4, pp. 425–46.

Dover, G. 2000: 'Anti-Dawkins', in Rose, H. and Rose, S. (eds), *Alas, Poor Darwin: Arguments Against Evolutionary Psychology*. London: Jonathan Cape.

Doward, J. 2003a: 'HSBC's New Man set to Make $60m', *Observer Business*, 27 April.

Doward, J. 2003b: 'Women Lose White Collar Pay Struggle', *Observer*, 19 October.

Doward, J. and Reilly, T. 2003: ' "Shameful" Pay Makes British Women Worst Off in Europe', *Observer*, 12 October.

Dowling, T. 2003: 'Pin the Cheque on the Donkey', *Guardian G2*, February 18.

Drucker, P. 1951: *The New Society*. London: Heinemann.

Drucker, P. 1986: 'The Changed World Economy', *Foreign Affairs*, vol. 64, no. 4, pp. 768–91.

Dubin, R. 1962: 'Industrial Workers' Worlds', in Rose, A. M. (ed.), *Human Behaviour and Social Processes*. London: Routledge.

Dubois, P. 1979: *Sabotage in Industry*. Harmondsworth: Penguin.

Duffy, D. 1997: 'Professional Jobs to Outnumber Manual in Decade', *Oxford Times*, October 31.

Du Gay, P. 1996: *Consumption and Identity at Work*. London: Sage.

Du Gay, P. and Salaman, G. 1992: 'The Cult(ure) of the Customer', *Journal of Management Studies*, vol. 29, pp. 615–33.

Dumont, L. 1977: *From Mandeville to Marx: the Genesis and Triumph of Economic Ideology*. Chicago: University of Chicago Press.

Dunlop, C. and Kling, R. (eds), 1991: *Computerization and Controversy*. New York: Academic Press.

Dunlop. J. T. 1958: *Industrial Relations Systems*. New York: Holt.

Dunning, J. 1993: *Multinational Enterprises and the Global Economy*. Wokingham: Addison-Wesley.

Durcan, J. W. and McCarthy, W. E. J. 1974: 'The State Subsidy Theory of Strikes', *British Journal of Industrial Relations*, March, pp. 26–47.

Durcan, J. W., McCarthy, W. E. J. and Redman, G. P. 1983: *Strikes in Post War Britain*. London: Allen & Unwin.

Durkheim, E. 1933: *The Division of Labour in Society*. New York: Free Press.

Durkheim, E. 1951: *Suicide*. Glencoe, Ill.: Free Press. French original, 1897.

Dustin, H. 2004: *Women and the Criminal Justice System*. London: Fawcett Society.

Dutton, W. H. (ed.), 1996: *Information and Communication Technologies*. Oxford: Oxford University Press.

Dworkin, A. 1981: *Pornography: Men Possessing Women*. London: Women's Press.

Dyer, C. 1988: *Guardian*, 10 October.

Dyer, C. 1995: 'Old Boy Network Stops Women Barristers being Judges', *Guardian*, 26 January.

Dyer, C. 2003: 'UK's First Woman Law Lord Appointed.' *Guardian Unlimited*, 24 October.

Earle, P. 1989: *The Making of the English Middle Classes: Business, Society and Family Life in London, 1660–1730*. London: Methuen.

The Economist, 1996: 'The End of Work', 28 September, pp. 19–23.

The Economist, 1996: 'Trade and Wages', 7 December, p. 122.

Edgell, S. 1980: *Middle Class Couples*. London: Allen & Unwin.

Edgeworth, F. Y. 1922: 'Equal Pay to Men and Women for Equal Work', *Economic Journal*, vol. 32, pp. 431–57.

Edmonds, D. 1995: 'A Negative Result', *Times Higher Education Supplement*, 21 April.

Edmondson, G., Carlisle, K., Resch, I., Anhalt, K. N. and Dawley, H. 2000: 'Workers in Bondage', *Business Week*, 27 November.

Edwards, I. 1983: 'The Art of Shovelling', in Richards, V. (ed.), *Why Work?* London: Free Press.

Edwards, P. K. 1978: 'Time-Series Regression Models of Strike Activity: a Reconsideration with American Data', *British Journal of Industrial Relations*, vol. 16, pp. 320–34.

Edwards, P. K. 1981: *Strikes in the United States 1881–1974*. Oxford: Blackwell.

Edwards, P. K. 1983a: 'The End of American Strike Statistics', *British Journal of Industrial Relations*, vol. 31, pp. 392–4.

Edwards, P. K. 1983b: 'The Pattern of Collective Industrial Action', in Bain, G. S. (ed.), *Industrial Relations in Britain*. Oxford: Blackwell.

Edwards, P. K. 1986: *Conflict at Work: a Materialist Analysis of Workplace Relations*. Oxford: Blackwell.

Edwards, P. K. and Scullion, H. 1982: *The Social Organization of Industrial Conflict*. Oxford: Blackwell.

Edwards, R. 1979: *Contested Terrain*. London: Heinemann.

Ehrenreich, B. and English, D. 1979: *For Her Own Good*. London: Pluto.

Ehrensal, K. N. 1995: 'Discourse of Global Competition: Obscuring the Changing Labor Processes of Managerial Work', *Journal of Organizational Change Management*, vol. 8, no. 5, pp. 5–16.

Eisenberg, P. and Lazarsfeld, P. F. 1938: 'The Psychological Effects of Unemployment', *Psychological Bulletin*, pp. 335–90.

Eisenstein, Z. R. 1979: 'Developing a Theory of Capitalist Patriarchy and Socialist Feminism', in Eisenstein, Z. R. (ed.), *Capitalist Patriarchy*. New York: Monthly Review Press.

Eisenstein, Z. R. 1984: *Feminism and Sexual Equality: Crisis in Liberal America*. New York: Monthly Review Press.

Elbaum, B. and Lazonick, W. (eds), 1986: *The Decline of the British Economy*. Oxford: Oxford University Press.

Eldridge, J. E. T. 1968: *Industrial Disputes*. London: Routledge.

Eldridge, J. E. T. 1971: *Sociology and Industrial Life*. London: Michael Joseph.

Elger, T. 1982: 'Braverman, Capital Accumulation and Deskilling', in Wood, S. (ed.), *The Degradation of Work?* London: Hutchinson.

Elkington, J. 1999: *Cannibals with Forks: The Triple Bottom Line of 21st Century Business*. Oxford: Capstone.

Elliott, B. (ed.), 1988: *Technology and Social Process*. Edinburgh: Edinburgh University Press.

Elliott, D. 1980: 'The Organization as a System', in Salaman, G. and Thompson, K. (eds), *Control and Ideology in Organizations*. Milton Keynes: Open University Press.

Elliott, L. 2001a: 'Bosses Pay Rises at Triple Inflation', *Guardian*, 8 May.

Elliott, L. 2001b: 'Argentine Debt Crisis Infects Markets', *Guardian*, 12 July.

Elliott, L. 2002: 'A Cure Worse than the Disease', *Guardian*, 21 January.

Elliott, L. and Brittain, V. 1998: 'The Rich and Poor Grow Further Apart', *Guardian*, 9 September.

Ellis, J. 1993: *The Social History of the Machine Gun*. London: Pimlico.

Ellison, J. 1989: *Guardian*, 2 March.

Ellsworth, R. R. 2002: *Leading With Purpose: The New Corporate Realities*. Stanford: Stanford University Press.

Elster, J. 1985: *Making Sense of Marx*. Cambridge: Cambridge University Press.

Elster, J. (ed.), 1986: *Rational Choice*. Oxford: Basil Blackwell.

Emery, E. F. and Thorsrud, E. 1964: *Form and Content in Industrial Democracy*. London: Tavistock.

Employment Gazette: December 1985; March and July 1988; March 1989; March and April 1990; August 1997. London: HMSO.

Engels, F. 1968: 'Origins of the Family, Private Property and the State', in Marx, K. and Engels, F., *Selected Works in One Volume*. London: Lawrence & Wishart.

Engels, F. 1969a: *The Condition of the Working Class in England*. London: Panther.

Engels, F. 1969b: 'Preface', in Marx's *Theories of Surplus Value*. London: Lawrence & Wishart.

Equal Opportunities Commission, 1987: *Sex Discrimination Decisions*, no. 16. Manchester: EOC.

Equal Opportunities Commission, 1989: *Women and Men in Britain 1989*. London: EOC.

Evans, M. 2001: 'Army Beefs Up Women's Pecs', *The Times*, 7 June.

Evans, M. D. R. 1987: 'Language Skill, Language Usage, and Opportunity: Immigrants in the Australian Labour Market', *Sociology*, vol. 21, no. 2, pp. 253–74.

Ezard, J. 2000: 'UK's Work Burden', *Guardian*, 21 June.

Fairbairns, Z. 1988: 'Wages for Housework', *New Internationalist*, March.

Falk, A. Fehr, E. and Fischbacher, U. 2003: 'On the Nature of Fair Behaviour', *Economic Enquiry*, vol. 41, no. 1, pp. 22–6.

Fallows, J. 1993: 'How the World Works', *Atlantic Monthly*, December, pp. 61–87.

Farkas, G. and England, P. (eds), 1994: *Industries, Firms and Jobs*. New York: Aldire de Gruyter.

Farrelly, P. 2001: 'Barclays Pays Out £150m in City Bonuses', *Observer Business*, 11 March.

Fawcett, M. G. 1918: 'Equal Pay for Equal Work', *Economic Journal*, vol. 28, pp. 1–6.

Feickert, D. 2004: 'Arthur was Right by Instinct', *Guardian*, 11 February.

Feinstein, L. 2003: 'Not Just the Early Years: The Need for a Developmental Perspective for Equality of Opportunity', *New Economy*, vol. 10, no. 4, pp. 213–18.

Feldberg, R. and Glenn, E. N. 1984: 'Male and Female: Job versus Gender Models in the Sociology of Work', in Siltanen, J. and Stanworth, M. (eds), *Women and the Public Sphere: a Critique of Sociology and Politics*. London: Hutchinson.

Feldman, D. 2002: 'Lessons About Letting in Outsiders', *Times Higher Education Supplement*, 1 March.

Ferguson, M. 1987: *The History of Mary Prince, a West Indian Slave*. London: Pandora.

Fevre, R. 2003: *The New Sociology of Economic Behaviour*. London: Sage.

Fildes, V. 1988: *Wet Nursing: a History from Antiquity to the Present*. Oxford: Blackwell.

Finch, J. 2001a: 'Stock Options "Are Theft"', *Guardian*, 7 February.

Finch, J. 2001b: 'Childcare Benefits Count for Nothing', *Guardian*, 1 March.

Finch, J. 2001c: 'Fresh Row Over M&S Payouts', *Guardian*, 9 June.

Finch, J. 2003a: 'Green Pays Himself Twice Bhs Profit', *Guardian*, 7 November.

Finch, J. 2003b: 'In India, it's Service with a Compulsory Smile', 17 November.

Fineman, S. 1983: *White Collar Unemployment: Impact and Stress*. London: John Wiley.

Fineman, S. 1987: 'The Middle Class: Unemployed and Underemployed', in Fineman, S. (ed.), *Unemployment: Personal and Social Consequences*. London: Tavistock.

Fingleton, E. 2000: *In Praise of Hard Industries*. London: Houghton Mifflin.

Finnegan, R. and Heap, N. 1988: *Information Technology and its Implications*. Milton Keynes: Open University Press.

Firestone, S. 1974: *The Dialectic of Sex: the Case for Feminist Revolution*. New York: Morrow.

Flanders, A. 1965: *Industrial Relations: What is Wrong with the System?* London: Faber.

Flanders, A. 1970: 'Industrial Relations: What is Wrong with the System?', in Flanders, A., *Management and Unions*. London: Faber.

Flanders, S. 1996: 'Life, Jobs and the Safety Zone', *Financial Times*, 29 April.

Fletcher, C. 1973: 'The End of Management', in Child, J. (ed.), *Man and Organization*. London: Allen & Unwin.

Fletcher, W. 2001: 'We've Never Had it So Good', *Guardian*, 2 January.

Foot, P. 1965: *Immigration and Race in British Politics*. Harmondsworth: Penguin.

Foot, P. 2003: 'Adding Up to Much Less', *Guardian*, 26 November.

Ford, R. 2004: 'EU Expansion Fails to Bring Migrant "Flood"', *Times*, 8 July.

Form, W. 1987: 'On the Degradation of Skills', *Annual Review of Sociology*, vol. 13, pp. 29–47.

Forrester, K. and Ward, K. 1986: 'Organising the Unemployed?: the TUC and the Unemployed Workers Centres', *Industrial Relations Journal*, vol. 17, no. 1, pp. 46–56.

Foster, A. 1987: 'The Invisible Men', *Management Today*, November.

Foster, J. 1974: *Class Struggles in the Industrial Revolution*. London: Weidenfeld & Nicolson.

Foucault, M. 1975: *Discipline and Punish*. London: Allen Lane.

Foucault, M. 1977: *Madness and Civilization*. New York: Vintage.

Foucault, M. 1979: *The History of Sexuality*, vol. 1. Harmondsworth: Penguin.

Foucault, M. 1980: *Power/Knowledge*. Brighton: Harvester.

Fox, A. 1971: *The Sociology of Work in Industry*. London: Collier Macmillan.

Fox, A. 1974: *Beyond Contract*. London: Faber.

Fox, A. 1976: 'The Meaning of Work', Unit 6, *People and Work*. Milton Keynes: Open University Press.

Fox, A. 1985: *History and Heritage: the Social Origins of the British Industrial Relations System*. London: Allen & Unwin.

Fox, A. and Flanders, A. 1969: 'The Reform of Collective Bargaining: from Donovan to Durkheim', *British Journal of Industrial Relations*, vol. 2, pp. 151–80.

Fox, R. 2001: 'Women Soldiers 8 Times More Prone to Injury in Training', *Evening Standard*, 16 February.

Frank, T. 2001a: *One Market Under God: Extreme Capitalism, Market Populism and the End of Economic Democracy*. London: Secker and Warburg.

Frank, T. 2001b: 'The Big Lie', *Guardian*, 9 July.

Franks, S. 1998: *Having None of It: Women, Men and the Future of Work*. London: Granta.

Fraser, A. 1988: *Boadicea's Chariot: the Warrior Queens*. London: Weidenfeld & Nicolson.

Fraser, R. (ed.), 1968: *Work: Twenty Personal Accounts*. Harmondsworth: Penguin.

Fraser, R. 1979: *Blood of Spain: the Experience of Civil War 1936–1939*. London: Allen Lane.

Freedman, M. 1984: 'The Search for Shelters', in Thompson, K. (ed.), *Work, Employment and Unemployment*. Milton Keynes: Open University Press.

Freely, M. 1996: 'Fem and Us', *The Guardian*, 7 May.

Freeman, C. 1987: 'The Case for Technological Determinism', in Finnegan, R. et al. (eds), *Information Technology: Social Issues*. Milton Keynes: Open University Press.

Freeman, H. 2001: 'Only the Young and Stylish Need Apply', *Guardian Work*, 13 February.

Freeman, R. and Katz, L. 1994: *Working under Different Rules*. New York: Russell Sage.

Frenkel, S. (ed.), 1980: *Industrial Action*. London: Allen & Unwin.

Friedman, A. L. 1977: *Industry and Labour: Class Struggle at Work and Monopoly Capitalism*. London: Macmillan.

Friedman, H. and Meredeen, S. 1980: *The Dynamics of Industrial Conflict*. London: Croom Helm.

Friedman, J. 1994: *Cultural Identity and Global Process*. London: Sage.

Fryer, D. and McKenna, S. 1987: 'The Laying Off of Hands: Unemployment and the Experience of Time', in Fineman, S. (ed.), *Unemployment: Personal and Social Consequences*. London: Tavistock.

Fryer, P. 1984: *Staying Power: the History of Black People in Britain*. London: Pluto.

Fryer, P. 1988: *Black People in the British Empire*. London: Pluto.

Fukuyama, F. 1989: 'The End of History?', *National Interest*, no. 16, pp. 3–18.

Gale, S. 1985: 'The Housewife', in Littler, C. R. (ed.), *The Experience of Work*. Aldershot: Gower.

Gallie, D. 1978: *In Search of the New Working Class*. Cambridge: Cambridge University Press.

Gallie, D. 1983: *Social Inequality and Class Radicalism in France and Britain*. Cambridge: Cambridge University Press.

Gallie, D. 1989: 'Employment, Unemployment and Social Stratification', in Gaillie, D. (ed.), *Employment in Britain*. Oxford: Blackwell.

Gapper, J. 1989: *Financial Times*, 20 February.

Garen, J. and Krislov, J. 1988: 'An Examination of the New American Strike Statistics in Analyzing Strike Incidence', *British Journal of Industrial Relations*, vol. 26, pp. 75–84.

Garfinkel, H. 1984: *Studies in Ethnomethodology*. Oxford: Blackwell.

Garnsey, E., Rubery, J. and Wilkinson, F. 1985: *Labour Market Structure and Workforce Divisions*. Milton Keynes: Open University Press.

Garrett, A. 2001: 'Still Begging Not to Differ', *Observer Work*, 24 June.

Gartman, D. 1979: 'Origins of the Assembly Line and Capitalist Control of Work at Ford', in Zimbalist, A. (ed.), *Case Studies on the Labor Process*. New York: Monthly Review.

Gavron, H. 1968: *The Captive Wife*. Harmondsworth: Penguin.

Geary, D. 1984: *European Labour Protest 1848–1939*. London: Methuen.

Geary, D. 1987: 'Working Class Culture in Imperial Germany', in Fietcher, R. (ed.), *Bernstein to Brandt: a Short History of German Social Democracy*. London: Edward Arnold.

Geertz, C. 1963: *Old Societies and New States: the Quest for Modernity in Asia and Africa*. Glencoe, Ill.: Free Press.

Gennard, J. 1977: *Financing Strikers*. London: Macmillan.

George, D. 1931: *England in Transition*. Harmondsworth: Penguin.

George, M. D. 1965: *London Life in the Eighteenth Century*. Harmondsworth: Penguin.

Gershuny, J. I. 1983: *Social Innovation and the Division of Labour*. Oxford: Oxford University Press.

Gershuny, J. I. and Thomas, G.S. 1980: *Changing Patterns of Time Use*. Brighton: SPRU.

Gerver, E. 1989: 'The Gender of Informatics', lecture quoted in *Times Higher Education Supplement*, 24 February.

Gibson, M. A. 1988: *Accommodation without Assimilation: Sikh Immigrants in an American High School*. Ithaca, NY: Cornell University Press.

Giddens, A. 1971: *Capitalism and Modern Social Theory*. Cambridge: Cambridge University Press.

Giddens, A. 1973: *The Class Structure of the Advanced Societies*. London: Hutchinson.

Giddens, A. 1977: 'Functionalism après la lutte', in Giddens, A., *Studies in Social and Political Theory*. London: Hutchinson.

Giddens, A. 1979: *Central Problems in Social Theory: Action, Structure and Contradictions in Social Analysis*. London: Macmillan.

Giddens, A. 1981: *A Contemporary Critique of Historical Materialism*. London: Macmillan.

Giddens, A. 1982a: *Profiles and Critiques in Social Theory*. London: Macmillan.

Giddens, A. 1982b: 'Labour and Interaction', in Thompson, J. B. and Held, D. (eds), *Habermas: Critical Debates*. London: Macmillan.

Giddens, A. 1984: *The Constitution of Society*. Cambridge: Polity.

Giddens, A. 1990: *The Consequences of Modernity*, Cambridge: Polity.

Gilbert, C. L. and Vines, D. (eds), 2000: *The World Bank: Structure and Policies*. Cambridge: Cambridge University Press.

Gilpin, R. 1987: *The Political Economy of International Relations*. Princeton: Princeton University Press.

Gilroy, P. 1987: *There Ain't No Black in the Union Jack*. London: Hutchinson.

Gimpel, J. 1992: *The Medieval Machine*. London: Pimlico.

Ginn, J., Arber, S., Brannen, J., Dale, A., Dex, S., Elias, P., Moss, P., Pahl, J., Roberts, C. and Rubery, J. 1996: 'Feminist Fallacies: a Reply to Hakim on Women's Employment', *British Journal of Sociology*, vol. 47, no. 1, pp. 167–74.

Glaister, D. 2004: 'Emigrants Provide Lifeline to Latin America', *Guardian*, 31 March.

Gleick, J. 1988: *Chaos: Making a New Science*, London: Abacus.

Glendinning, C. and Millar, J. (eds), 1988: *Women and Poverty in Britain*. Brighton: Wheatsheaf.

Gluckstein, D. 1985: *The Western Soviets: Workers' Councils versus Parliament 1915–1920*. London: Bookmarks.

Godelier, M. 1980: 'Work: the Words Used to Represent Work and Workers', *History Workshop*, no. 10, autumn, pp. 164–74.

Goffman, E. 1959: *The Presentation of Self in Everyday Life*. New York: Doubleday.

Goffman, E. 1961: *Asylums*. Harmondsworth: Penguin.

Goldberg, S. 1993: *Why Men Rule: A Theory of Dominance*. Chicago: Open Court Publishing Company.

Goldman, P. and Van Houten, D. R. 1980: 'Bureaucracy and Domination: Managerial Strategy in Turn-of-the-century American Industry', in Dunkerley, D. and Salaman, G. (eds), *The International Yearbook of Organizational Studies, 1979*. London: Routledge.

Goldschmidt-Clermont, L. 1987: *Unpaid Work in the Household*. Geneva: International Labour Office.

Goldthorpe, J. H. 1980: *Social Mobility and Class Structure in Modern Britain*. Oxford: Clarendon.

Goldthorpe, J. H. 1983: 'Women and Class Analysis: in Defence of the Conventional View', *Sociology*, vol. 17, pp. 465–88.

Goldthorpe, J. H. 1984a: 'The End of Convergence: Corporatist and Dualist Tendencies in Modern Western Societies', in Goldthorpe, J. (ed.), *Order and Conflict in Contemporary Capitalism*. Oxford: Clarendon.

Goldthorpe, J. H. 1984b: 'Women and Class Analysis: a Reply to the Critics', *Sociology*, vol. 18, pp. 491–9.

Goldthorpe, J. H., Lewellyn, C. and Payne, C. 1980: *Social Mobility and Class Structure in Modern Britain*. Oxford: Clarendon.

Goldthorpe, J. H., Lockwood, D., Bechhofer, F. and Platt, J. 1968: *The Affluent Worker: Industrial Attitudes and Behaviour*. London: Cambridge University Press.

Goldthorpe, J. H., Lockwood, D., Bechhofer, F. and Platt, J. 1969: *The Affluent Worker in the Class Structure*. London: Cambridge University Press.

Goldthorpe, J. H. and Payne, C. 1986: 'Trends in Intergenerational Class Mobility in England and Wales 1972–1983', *Sociology*, vol. 20, no. 1, pp. 1–24.

Goodman, G. 1985: *The Miners' Strike*. London: Pluto.

Gordon, D. M. 1972: *Theories of Poverty and Underdevelopment*. Lexington, Mass.: D.C. Heath.

Gordon, D. M., Edwards, R. and Reich, M. 1982: *Segmented Work, Divided Workers: the Historical Transformation of Labor in the United States*. Cambridge: Cambridge University Press.

Gordon, L. 1981: 'The Politics of Sexual Harassment', *Radical America*, vol. 15, pp. 7–14.

Gorz, A. 1970: 'Immigrant Labour', *New Left Review*, vol. I.

Gorz, A. 1982: *Farewell to the Working Class*. London: Pluto.

Gorz, A. 1985: *Paths to Paradise: On the Liberation from Work*. London: Pluto.

Gorz, A. 1989: *Critique of Economic Reason*. London: Verso.

Gospel, H. 1983: 'The Development of Management Organization in Industrial Relations: an Historical Perspective', in Thurley, K. and Wood, S. (eds), *Industrial Relations and Management Strategy*. Cambridge: Cambridge University Press.

Gouldner, A. W. 1954: *Patterns of Industrial Bureaucracy*. New York: Free Press.

Gow, D. 1987: *Guardian*, 3 September.

Gramsci, A. 1971: *Selections from Prison Notebooks*. London: Lawrence & Wishart.

Gramsci, A. 1978: *Selections from Political Writings 1921–1926*. London: Lawrence & Wishart.

Gray, A. M. and Robinson, G. 2004: 'What Women Want: Women and Gender Roles in Northern Ireland', available at <http://www.ark.ac.uk/publications/updates/update24.pdf>.

Gray, J. 2002: *False Dawn: The Delusions of Global Capitalism*. London: Granta.

Gray, R. 1981: *The Aristocracy of Labour in Nineteenth Century Britain*. London: Macmillan.

Gray, R. 1987: 'Languages of Factory Reform', in Joyce, P. (ed.), *The Historical Meanings of Work*. Cambridge: Cambridge University Press.

Green, F. 2000: 'It's Been a Hard Day's Night – But Why?'. Paper read at University of Kent at Canterbury, June.

Gregg, P. and Wadsworth, J. 1996: 'How Effective are State Employment Agencies?', *Oxford Bulletin of Economics and Statistics*, vol. 58, no. 3, pp. 443–67.

Gregg, P. and Wadsworth, J. 1999: 'Job Tenure, 1975–98', in Gregg, P. and Wadsworth, J. (eds), *The State of Working Britain*. Manchester: Manchester University Press.

Gregory, J. 1982: 'Some Cases that Never Reached the Tribunal', *Feminist Review*, no. 10, pp. 75–89.

Grieco, M. 1987: 'Family Networks and the Closure of Employment', in Lee, G. and Loveridge, R. (eds), *The Manufacture of Disadvantage: Stigma and Social Closure*. Milton Keynes: Open University Press.

Grint, K. 1986: *Bureaucracy and Democracy: the Quest for Industrial Control in the British Postal Business 1918–1939*. D.Phil Thesis. Oxford University.

Grint, K. 1988: 'Women and Equality: the Acquisition of Equal Pay in the Post Office 1870–1961', *Sociology*, vol. 22, no. 1, pp. 87–108.

Grint, K. 1993: 'Japanization?', *Industrial Relations Journal*, vol. 24, no. 1, pp. 14–27.

Grint, K. 1997: *Fuzzy Management*. Oxford: Oxford University Press.

Grint, K. 2000: *The Arts of Leadership*. Oxford: Oxford University Press.

Grint, K. 2001: 'Manpower', Unpublished case study, Oxford: Templeton College.

Grint, K. and Gill, R. (eds), 1995: *The Technology–Gender Relation*. London: Taylor & Francis.

Grint, K. and Willcocks, L. 1995: 'BPR in Theory and Practice: Business Paradise Regained?', *New Technology, Work and Employment*, vol. 10, no. 2, pp. 99–109.

Grint, K. and Woolgar, S. 1997: *The Machine at Work*. Cambridge: Polity Press.

Grint, Katy 2000: 'That Monstrous Regiment of Women: A Study of Violent Women'. Unpublished undergraduate thesis, LSE.

Grossman, D. 1998: *On Killing*. London: Back Bay Books.

Grusky, D. B. (ed.), 2000: *Social Stratification: Class, Race and Gender in Sociological Perspective*. Boulder, CO: Westview.

Guerin, D. 1979: *100 Years of Labor in the USA*. London: Ink Links.

Habermas, J. 1970: *Towards a Rational Society*. London: Heinemann.

Habermas, J. 1971: *Knowledge and Human Interests*. London: Heinemann.

Habermas, J. 1974: *Theory and Practice*. London: Heinemann.

Hadjifotiou, N. 1985: 'Rate for the Job', *Marxism Today*, June.

Hague, H. 1986: 'Women and Unions', *Marxism Today*, June.

Hain, P. 1986: *Political Strikes: the State and Trade Unionism in Britain*. Harmondsworth: Penguin.

Hakim, C. 1979: *Occupational Segregation: a Comparative Study of the Degree and Pattern of the Differentiation between Men and Women's Work in Britain, the United States, and Other Countries*. Research Paper, no. 9. London: Department of Employment.

Hakim, C. 1981: 'Job Segregation: Trends in the 1970s', *Employment Gazette*, December, pp. 521–9.

Hakim, C. 1990: 'Core and Periphery in Employers' Workforce Strategies: Evidence from the 1987 ELUS Survey', *Work, Employment and Society*, vol. 4, no. 2, pp. 157–88.

Hakim, C. 1995: 'Five Feminist Myths about Women's Employment', *British Journal of Sociology*, vol. 46, no. 3, pp. 429–56.

Hakim, C. 1996a: *Key Issues in Women's Work*. London: Athlone.

Hakim, C. 1996b: 'The Sexual Division of Labour and Women's Heterogeneity', *The British Journal of Sociology*, vol. 47, no. 1, pp. 178–88.

Hall, S. 1992: 'The West and the Rest: Discourse and Power', in Hall, S. and Gieben, B. (eds), *Formations of Modernity*. Cambridge: Polity Press.

Halsey, A. H. 1986: *Change in British Society*. Oxford: Oxford University Press.

Hambleton, R. 1988: 'The American Gender Gap', *Times Higher Education Supplement*, 12 August.

Hamel, G. and Prahalad, C. K. 1996: 'Competing in the New Economy', *Strategic Management Journal*, vol. 17, pp. 237–42.

Hammer, M. and Champy, J. 1993: *Reengineering the Corporation*, London: Nicholas Brealey.

Hammond, J. L. and Hammond, B. 1949: *The Town Labourer 1760–1832*, vol. II. London: Guild Books.

Hanami, T. 1979: *Labor Relations in Japan Today*. London: John Martin.

Handy, C. B. 1985: *Understanding Organizations*. Harmondsworth: Penguin.

Hannah, L. 1983: *The Rise of the Corporate Economy*. London: Methuen.

Haralambos, M. and Holborn, M. 1995: *Sociology*, 4th edn. London: Collins Educational.

Haraszti, M. 1977: *A Worker in a Worker's State*. Harmondsworth: Penguin.

Haraway, M. J. 1991: *Simians, Cyborgs and Women: the Reinvention of Nature*. London: Free Association Books.

Harding, J. (ed.). 1986: *Perspectives on Science and Gender*. Brighton: Falmer Press.

Harding, J. 2001: 'On the Move', *Guardian*, 23 May.

Harding, L. 2001: 'Delhi Calling', *Guardian G2*, 9 March.

Harding, P. and Jenkins, R. 1989: *The Myth of the Hidden Economy*. Milton Keynes: Open University Press.

Hardy, D. 1979: *Alternative Communities in Nineteenth Century England*. London: Longman.

Harman, C. 1982: *The Lost Revolution: Germany 1918–23*. London: Pluto.

Harper, K. 1990: *Guardian*, 8 June.

Harris, M. 1990: 'Working in the UK Voluntary Sector', *Work, Employment and Society*, vol. 4, no. 1, pp. 125–40.

Harris Poll, 1990: *Observer*, 18 February.

Harrison, A. E. and Eskeland, G. S. 1994: 'Multinationals and the Pollution Haven Hypothesis', *World Bank Occasional Paper*, May. Washington, DC: World Bank.

Harrison, B. and Bluestone, B. 1988: *The Great U-Turn*. New York: Basic Books.

Harrison, J. F. C. 1984: *The Common People: a History from the Norman Conquest to the Present*. London: Flamingo.

Harrison, M. 1979: 'Participation of Women in Trade Union Activities', *Industrial Relations Journal*, vol. 10, pp. 41–55.

Hart, J. 2001: 'Power of the Bonus Brigade', *Evening Standard*, 16 February.

Hartley-Brewer, J. 2000: 'Army Tests Women for Frontline', *Guardian*, 29 May, cited in <www.guardianlimited.co.uk>.

Hartley, J. 1987: 'Managerial Unemployment: the Wife's Perspective and Role', in Fineman, S. (ed.), *Unemployment: Personal and Social Consequences*. London: Tavistock.

Hartmann, H. 1982: 'Capitalism, Patriarchy, and Job Segregation by Sex', in Giddens, A. and Held, D. (eds), *Classes, Power and Conflict: Classical and Contemporary Debates*. London: Macmillan.

Harvey, D. 1989: *The Condition of Postmodernity*. Oxford: Blackwell.

Harvey, J. 1987: 'New Technology and the Gender Divisions of Labour', in Lee, G. and Loveridge, R. (eds), *The Manufacture of Disadvantage*. Milton Keynes: Open University Press.

Harvie, C. 1978: *The Experience of Industrialization*. Milton Keynes: Open University Press.

Hassard, J. and Sharifi, S. 1989: 'Corporate Culture and Strategic Change', *Journal of General Management*, vol. 15, no. 2, pp. 4–19.

Hatch, M. J. 1997: *Introduction to Organization Theory*. Oxford: Oxford University Press.

Hawkins, F. 1989: *Critical Years in Immigration*. Montreal: McGill-Queens University Press.

Haynes, M. 1988: 'Employers and Trade Unions, 1824–1850', in Rule, J. (ed.), *British Trade Unionism 1750–1850*. London: Longman.

Hearn, J. and Parkin, W. 1987: *'Sex' at 'Work': the Power and Paradox of Organization Sexuality*. Brighton: Wheatsheaf.

Hearst, D. 1988: *Guardian*, 25 May.

Heath, A. 1981: *Social Mobility*. London: Fontana.

Heery, E. and Kelly, J. 1988: 'Union Women: a Survey of Women Full Time Officials'. London: LSE, Department of Industrial Relations, mimeo.

Heery, E. and Kelly, J. 1989: ' "A Cracking Job for a Woman": a Profile of Women Trade Union Officers', *Industrial Relations Journal*, vol. 20, no. 3, pp. 192–202.

Held, D. 1980: *Introduction to Critical Theory*. London: Hutchinson.

Held, D. 1984: 'Power and Legitimacy in Contemporary Britain', in McLennan, G., Held, D. and Hall, S. (eds), *State and Society in Contemporary Britain*. Cambridge: Cambridge University Press.

Held, D. 1987: *Models of Democracy*. Cambridge: Polity.

Held, D. 1989: *Political Theory and the Modern State*. Cambridge: Polity.

Held, D. 1992: 'The Development of the Modern State', in Hall, S. and Gieben, B. (eds), *Formations of Modernity*. Cambridge: Polity.

Held, D. and McGrew, A. 2002: *Globalization and Anti-globalization*. Cambridge: Polity.

Held, D., McGrew, A., Goldblatt, D. and Perraton, J. 1999: *Global Transformations*. Cambridge: Polity.

Held, D. and Thompson, J. B. (eds), 1989: *Social Theory of Modern Societies: Anthony Giddens and his Critics*. Cambridge: Polity.

Heller, F. 1987: 'The Technological Imperative and the Quality of Employment', *New Technology, Work and Employment*, vol. 2, no. 1, pp. 19–26.

Heller, R. 2001: 'No Option but to Rake it in', *Observer*, 6 May.

Hencke, D. 1988: *Guardian*, 5 May.

Hencke, D. 1989: *Guardian*, 26 September.

Henley Centre of Forecasting, 1989: *The Women's Decade*. Henley.

Henwood, D. 1996: 'Work and its Future', *Left Business Observer*, 72.

Henwood, D. 2004: 'US Miracle is Based on Longer Hours for Less Pay', *Guardian*, 2 February.

Herding, R. 1972: *Job Control and Union Structure*. Rotterdam: Rotterdam University Press.

Hernandez, J. B. 1993: 'Dirty Growth', *New Internationalist*, 246, August.

Herzberg, F. 1966: *Work and the Nature of Man*. New York: Staples Press.

Hetherington, P. 2004: 'Unemployment Time Bomb is Ticking Inside List of Benefit Claimants', *Guardian*, 22 May.

Hewlett, S. A. 2003: *Baby Hunger: The New Battle for Motherhood*. London: Atlantic Books.

Hill, A. 2003a: 'Teenage Girls Just Want to Marry and Stay Home', *Observer*, 19 October.

Hill, A. 2003b: 'Child Slave Smugglers Will Face Jail at Last', *Observer*, 9 November.

Hill, B. 1989: *Women, Work and Sexual Politics in Eighteenth Century England*. Oxford: Blackwell.

Hill, C. 1969: *Reformation to Industrial Revolution*. Harmondsworth: Penguin.

Hill, J. 1978: 'The Psychological Impact of Unemployment', *New Society*, 19 January.

Himmelweit, S. and Mohun, S. 1977: 'Domestic Labour and Capital', *Cambridge Journal of Economics*, vol. 1, no. 1, pp. 15–31.

Hinton, J. 1973: *The First Shop Stewards' Movement*. London: Allen & Unwin.

Hinton, J. 1983: *Labour and Socialism: a History of the British Labour Movement*. Brighton: Wheatsheaf.

Hirst, P. and Thompson, G. 1992: 'The Problem of Globalization: International Economic Relations, National Economic Management and the Formation of Trading Blocs', *Economy and Society*, vol. 21, no. 4.

Hobsbawm, E. J. 1962: *The Age of Revolution 1789–1848*, London: Weidenfeld & Nicolson.

Hobsbawm, E. J. 1964a: *Labouring Men*. London: Weidenfeld & Nicolson.

Hobsbawm, E. J. 1964b: 'Custom, Wages and Work-load', in Hobsbawm, E.J., *Labouring Men: Studies in the History of Labour*. London: Weidenfeld & Nicolson.

Hobsbawm, E. J. 1969: *Industry and Empire*. Harmondsworth: Pelican.

Hobsbawm, E. 1975: *The Age of Capital 1848–1875*. London: Weidenfeld & Nicolson.

Hobsbawm, E. J. 1981: 'The Forward March of Labour Halted?', in Jacques, M. and Mulhearn, F. (eds), *The Forward March of Labour Halted?* London: New Left Books.

Hobsbawm, E. J. 1984: *Worlds of Labour Revisited*. London: Weidenfeld & Nicolson.

Hobsbawm, E. J. 1987: *The Age of Empire 1875–1914*. London: Weidenfeld & Nicolson.

Hobsbawm, E. J. 1994: *The Age of Extremes 1914–1991*. Harmondsworth: Penguin.

Hobsbawm, E. J. and Rudé, G. 1973: *Captain Swing*. Harmondsworth: Penguin.

Hochschild, A. 1989: *The Second Shift*. New York: Viking Press.

Hoefer, H. J. 1984: *American Southwest*. London: Harrap.

Hofstede, G. 1979: *Cultural Consequences*. Beverly Hills, CA: Sage.

Hofstede, G. 1991: *Cultures and Organizations: Software of the Mind*. London: McGraw-Hill.

Holland, J. H. 1998: *Emergence from Chaos to Order*. Oxford: Oxford University Press.

Holley, J. C. 1981: 'The Two Family Economies of Industrialism: Factory Workers in Victorian Scotland', *Journal of Family History*, vol. 6, no. 1.

Holton, B. 1976: *British Syndicalism 1910–1914*. London: Pluto.

Home Affairs Committee, 1989: *Racial Attacks and Harassment*. London: HMSO.

Home Office, 1989: *Domestic Violence: an Overview of the Literature*. London: HMSO.

Hopkins, E. 1979: *A Social History of the English Working Classes 1815–1945*. London: Edward Arnold.

Hopkins, E. 1988: *Birmingham: the First Manufacturing Town in the World, 1760–1840*. London: Weidenfeld & Nicolson.

Horne, J. 1987: *Work and Unemployment*. London: Longman.

Horner, M. 1976: 'Towards an Understanding of Achievement Related Conflict in Women', in Stacey, J., Beraud, S. and Daniels, J. (eds), *And Jill Came Tumbling After: Sexism in American Education*. New York: Dell Publishing.

Horrell, S., Rubery, J. and Burchell, B. 1989: 'Unequal Jobs or Unequal Pay?', *Industrial Relations Journal*, vol. 20, no. 3, pp. 176–91.

Horrie, C. 1989: *Observer*, 17 December.

Houghton, W. E. 1957: *The Victorian Frame of Mind 1820–1870*. New Haven, Conn.: Yale University Press.

Howkins, A. 1985: *Poor Labouring Men: Rural Radicalism in Norfolk 1870–1923*. London: Routledge.

Hudson, K. 1970: *Working to Rule: Railway Workshop Rules: a Study of Industrial Discipline*. Bath: Adams & Dart.

Hughes, P. 1989: 'Evaluating an Equal Opportunities Initiative', *Gender and Education*, vol. 1, no. 1, pp. 5–14.

Hughes, T. 1979: 'The Electrification of America: the Systems Builders', *Technology and Culture*, vol. 20, no. 1, pp. 124–62.

Huhne, C. 1988a: *Guardian*, 10 March.

Huhne, C. 1988b: *Guardian*, 30 June.

Humphries, J. 1988: 'Protective Law, the State, and Working Class Men', in Pahl, R. E. (ed.), *On Work*. Oxford: Blackwell.

Hunt, A. 1968: *A Survey of Women's Employment*, vol. 1. London: HMSO.

Hunt, E. 1981: 'Stamp out Women', extract from *British Labour History: 1815–1914*. London: Weidenfeld & Nicolson.

Hutson, S. and Jenkins, R. 1989: *Taking the Strain: Families, Unemployment and the Transition to Adulthood*. Milton Keynes: Open University Press.

Hutton, W. 2001: 'Why the Germans are Right About Us', *Observer*, 27 May.

Hyder, K. 1989: *Observer*, 21 May.

Hyman, R. 1971: *Marxism and the Sociology of Trade Unionism*. London: Pluto.

Hyman, R. 1972: *Strikes*. London: Fontana.

Hyman, R. 1989: *The Political Economy of Industrial Relations*. London: Macmillan.

Hyman, R. and Ferner, A. (eds), 1994: *New Frontiers in European Industrial Relations*. Oxford: Blackwell.

ICM, 1995: *Black in Britain*. London: ICM.

Imray, L. and Middleton, A. 1983: 'Public and Private: Marking the Boundaries', in Garminikow, E., Morgan, D., Purvis, J. and Taylorson, D. (eds), *The Public and the Private*. London: Heinemann.

IMS (Institute of Manpower Studies), 1990: *Good Practices in the Employment of Women Returners*. Report no. 183. Brighton: IMS.

Ingham, G. K. 1970: *Size of Industrial Organization and Worker Behaviour*. Cambridge: Cambridge University Press.

Ingham, G. K. 1974: *Strikes and Industrial Conflict*. London: Macmillan.

Inman, P. 2001: 'The Final Countdown', *Guardian*, 9 June.

Institute for Employment Services, 1998: *Breaking the Long Hours Culture*. London: Grantham.

Institute of Personnel Management, 1978: *Towards Fairer Selection: a Code for Non-discrimination*. London: IPM.

International Labour Office, 1997: 'The ILO, Standard Setting and Globalization', Report of the Director-General at the 85th Session of the International Labour Conference, Geneva.

IPPR (Institute for Public Policy Research), 1997: *Colour and Citizenship*. London: IPPR.

IRRU (Industrial Relations Review and Report), 1984: 'Part-time Work: a Survey', May.

Islam, F. 2003: 'How These People are Doing More for the Third World than Western Governments', *Observer Business*, 20 April.

Jackson, M. P. 1977: *Industrial Relations*. London: Croom Helm.

Jackson, M. P. 1987: *Strikes: Industrial Conflict in Britain, USA and Australia*. Brighton: Wheatsheaf.

Jackson, P. 1995: *Sacred Hoops: Spiritual Lessons of a Hardwood Warrior*. New York: Hyperion.

Jacobs, E., Orwell, S., Paterson, P. and Weltz, F. 1978: *The Approach to Industrial Change*. London: Anglo-German Foundation for the Study of Industrial Society.

Jacoby, S. M. 1988: 'Employee Attitude Surveys in Historical Perspective', *Industrial Relations*, vol. 27, no. 1, pp. 74–93.

Jacques, E. 1967: *Equitable Payment*. Harmondsworth: Penguin.

Jacques, M. and Mulhearn, F. (eds), 1981: *The Forward March of Labour Halted?* London: Verso.

Jacques, R. 1996: *Manufacturing the Employee: Management Knowledge from the 19th to the 20th Centuries*. London: Sage.

Jahoda, M. 1979: 'The Impact of Unemployment in the 1930s and 1970s', *Bulletin of the British Psychological Society*, vol. 32, pp. 309–14.

James, O. 1988: *Observer*, 17 July.

Jameson, F. 1991: *Postmodernism or the Cultural Logic of Late Capitalism*. London: Verso.

Jay, M. 1973: *The Dialectical Imagination: a History of the Frankfurt School and the Institute of Social Research, 1923–1950*. Boston, Mass.: Little Brown.

Jehoel-Gijsbers, G. and Groot, W. 1989: 'Unemployed Youth: a Lost Generation?', *Work, Employment and Society*, vol. 3, no. 4, pp. 491–508.

Jenkins, C. and Sherman, B. 1979: *The Collapse of Work*. London: Eyre Methuen.

Jenkins, R. 1985: 'Black Workers in the Labour Market: the Price of Recession', in Roberts, B., Finnegan, R. and Gallie, D. (eds), *New Approaches to Economic Life*. Manchester: Manchester University Press.

Jenkins, R. 1988: 'Discrimination and Equal Opportunity in Employment: Ethnicity and "Race" in the United Kingdom', in Gallie, D. (ed.), *Employment in Britain*. Oxford: Blackwell.

Jenkins, R. and Parker, G. 1987: 'Organizational Politics and the Recruitment of Black Workers', in Lee, G. and Loveridge, R. (eds), *The Manufacture of Disadvantage: Stigma and Social Closure*. Milton Keynes: Open University Press.

Jenson, J. 1989: 'The Talents of Women, the Skills of Men: Flexible Specialization and Women', in Wood, S. (ed.), *The Transformation of Work?* London: Unwin Hyman.

Jewson, N. and Mason, D. 1986: 'Modes of Discrimination in the Recruitment Process', *Sociology*, vol. 20, no. 1, pp. 43–63.

Johnson, T. 1972: *Professions and Power*. London: Macmillan.

Johnson, W. 1986: 'Worshipping Work', *New Internationalist*, no. 166, December.

Johnston, L. 1986: *Marxism, Class Analysis and Socialist Pluralism*. London: Allen & Unwin.

Joll, J. 1979: *The Anarchists*. London: Methuen.

Jones, G. 1994: 'The Making of Global Enterprise', *Business History*, vol. 36, no. 1, pp. 1–17.

Jones, G. S. 1983: *Languages of Class: Studies in English Working Class History 1832–1982*. Cambridge: Cambridge University Press.

Jones, R. 2004: 'MPs Slam Insurance Chiefs' Bumper Pay Rises', *Guardian*, 28 January.

Jones, T. and McEvoy, D. 1986: 'Ethnic Enterprise: the Popular Image', in Curran, J. et al. (eds), *The Survival of the Small Firm*, vol. 1. Aldershot: Gower.

Joseph, G. 1983: *Women at Work*. London: Philip Allan.

Joshi, H. 1986: 'Gender Inequality in the Labour Market and the Domestic Division of Labour', in Nolan, P. and Paine, S., *Rethinking Socialist Economics*. Cambridge: Polity.

Joshi, S. and Carter, B. 1984: 'The Role of Labour in the Creation of a Racist Britain', *Race and Class*, vol. 25, no. 3, pp. 53–70.

Jowell, R. and Prescott-Clarke, P. 1970: 'Discrimination against White Collar Workers in Britain', *Race*, vol. 11, no. 4, April.

Jowell, R., Witherspoon, S. and Brook, L. (eds), 1989: *British Social Attitudes Special International Report*. Aldershot: Gower.

Joyce, P. 1980: *Work, Society and Politics*. London: Methuen.

Joyce, P. 1987: 'The Historical Meanings of Work: an Introduction', in Joyce, P. (ed.), *The Historical Meaning of Work*. Cambridge: Cambridge University Press.

Joyce, P. 1991: *Visions of the People*. Cambridge: Cambridge University Press.

Judge, E. 2003: 'Women on Board: Help or Hindrance?' *The Times*, 11 November.

Judge, T. A. and Cable, D. M. 2004: 'The Effect of Physical Height on Work-place Success and Income', *Journal of Applied Psychology*, vol. 89, no. 3, pp. 428–41.

Kakabadsc, A. and McWilliam, G. 1987: 'Superpowers' Superwomen', *Management Today*, September.

Kamin, L. 1970: *The Science and Politics of IQ*. Harmondsworth: Penguin.

Kanter, R. M. 1995: 'Thriving Locally in the Global Economy', *Harvard Business Review*, vol. 73, no. 5, pp. 151–60.

Karier, C. J. 1976a: 'Business Values and the Educational State', in Dale, R. et al. (eds), *Schooling and Capitalism*. London: Routledge & Kegan Paul.

Karier, C. J. 1976b: 'Testing for Order and Control in the Corporate Liberal State', in Dale, R. et al. (eds), *Schooling and Capitalism*. London: Routledge & Kegan Paul.

Karlsen, C. F. 1988: *The Devil in the Shape of a Woman: Witchcraft in Colonial New England*. New York: W. W. Norton.

Karpf, A. 1987: 'Recent Feminist Approaches to Women and Technology', in McNeil, M. (ed.), *Gender and Expertise*. London: Free Association Books.

Katz, H. C. and Sabel, C. F. 1985: 'Industrial Relations and Industrial Adjustment in the Car Industry', *Industrial Relations*, vol. 24, no. 2, pp. 295–315.

Kelly, J. 1982: *Scientific Management, Job Redesign and Work Performance*. London: Academic Press.

Kelly, J. 1985: 'Management's Redesign of Work', in Knights, D., Willmott, H. and Collinson, D. (eds), *Job Redesign*. Aldershot: Gower.

Kelly, J. 1988: *Trade Unions and Socialist Politics*. London: Verso.

Kelly, M. 1993: 'Free Trade and the Politics of Toxic Waste', *Multinational Monitor*, October, pp. 13–20.

Kemp, R. 1989: 'How to Tame the Wildcats', *Management Today*, August.

Kendall, W. 1969: *The Revolutionary Movement in Britain 1900–21*. London: Weidenfeld & Nicolson.

Kern, H. and Schumann, M. 1987: 'Limits of the Division of Labour: New Production and Employment Concepts in West German Industry', *Economic and Industrial Democracy*, vol. 8, no. 2, pp. 151–70.

Kerr, C., Dunlop, J. T., Harbison, F. and Myers, C. A. 1960: *Industrialism and Industrial Man*. Cambridge, Mass.: Harvard University Press.

Kerr, C. and Siegei, A. J. 1954: 'The Inter-industry Propensity to Strike', in Kornhauser, A. et al. (eds), *Industrial Conflict*. New York: McGraw-Hill.

Kessler, S. and Bayliss, F. 1994: *Contemporary British Industrial Relations*. London: Macmillan.

Kieser, A. 1989: 'Organizational, Institutional and Social Evolution: Medieval Craft Guilds and the Genesis of Formal Organizations', *Administrative Science Quarterly*, vol. 34, pp. 540–64.

Kim, I. 1981: *The New Urban Immigrants: Korean Immigrants in New York City*. Princeton, NJ: Princeton University Press.

King, M. C. 1995: 'Human Capital and Black Women's Occupational Mobility', *Industrial Relations*, vol. 34, no. 2, pp. 282–98.

Kitching, G. 1983: *Rethinking Socialism*. London: Methuen.

Klein, N. 2000: *No Logo*. London: HarperCollins/Flamingo.

Knights, D. 1989: 'Culture, Control and Competition', paper presented at the PICT workshop on Culture and Information Technology, March, UMIST.

Knights, D. and Willmott, H. (eds), 1988: *New Technology and the Labour Process*. London: Macmillan.

Knights, D. and Willmott, H. 1989: 'Power and Subjectivity at Work', *Sociology*, vol. 23, no. 4, pp. 535–58.

Knights, D., Willmott, H. and Collinson, D. (eds), 1985: *Job Redesign*. Aldershot: Gower.

Knowles, K. G. J. C. 1952: *Strikes: a Study in Industrial Conflict*. Oxford: Blackwell.

Kobrin, S. J. 1996: 'Globalization and Multinationals', *Financial Times*, 8 March, pp. 13–14.

Kochan, T. A., Katz, H. C. and McKersie, R. B. 1986: *The Transformation of American Industrial Relations*. New York: Basic Books.

Kogevinas, E. 1990: *Sociodemographic Differences in Cancer Survival*. London: HMSO.

Kolakowski, L. 1978: *Main Currents of Marxism*, vol. 2. Oxford: Oxford University Press.

Kondratiev, N. D. 1935: 'The Long Waves in Economic Life', *Review of Economic Statistics*, vol. 17, pp. 105–15.

Kornblum, W. 1974: *Blue Collar Community*. Chicago: Chicago University Press.

Kornhauser, A. 1965: *The Mental Health of the Industrial Worker*. New York: John Wiley.

Korpi, W. and Shalev, M. 1979: 'Industrial Relations and Class Conflict in Capitalist Societies', *British Journal of Sociology*, vol. 30, pp. 164–87.

Korpi, W. and Shalev, M. 1980: 'Strikes, Power and Politics in Western Nations 1900–76', *Political Power and Social Theory*, vol. 1, pp. 301–34.

Kossler, R. and Muchic, M. 1990: 'American Dreams and Soviet Realities: Socialism and Taylorism', *Capital and Class*, no. 40, pp. 61–88.

Krechtig, M. 2001: 'First Women Join German Combat Units', *Guardian*, 3 January.

Krieger, J. 1984: *Undermining Capitalism: State Ownership and the Dialectic of Control in the British Coal Industry*. London: Pluto.

Kriegler, R. J. 1982: *Working for the Company*. Oxford: Oxford University Press.

Kristiensen, T. 1995: 'Executive Stress', Paper at the Congress of the European Society of Cardiology, Amsterdam, 22 August.

Kropotkin, P. 1983: 'The Wage System', in Richards, V. (ed.), *Why Work?* London: Aldgate.

Kumar, K. 1978: *Prophecy and Progress: the Sociology of Industrial and Post Industrial Society*. London: Penguin.

Kumar, K. 1984: 'The Social Culture of Work', in Thompson, K. (ed.), *Work, Employment and Unemployment*. Milton Keynes: Open University Press.

Kushner, T. 1989: *The Persistence of Prejudice: Anti-semitism in British Society during the Second World War*. Manchester: Manchester University Press.

Kussmaul, A. 1981: *Servants in Husbandry in Early Modern England*. Cambridge: Cambridge University Press.

Kusterer, K. C. 1978: *Know-How on the Job*. Boulder, CO: Westview Press.

Kynaston, D. 1976: *King Labour.* London: Allen & Unwin.

Labour Market Trends, 1997: London: HMSO.

Labour Market Trends, 2003: London: HMSO.

Labour Research Department, 1986: *Women's Pay: Claiming Equal Value.* London: LRD.

Labriola, A. 1931: *Beyond Capitalism and Socialism.* Paris.

Lal, D. 1989: *The Hindu Equilibrium,* vol. 2: *Aspects of Indian Labour.* Oxford: Oxford University Press.

Lambertz, J. 1985: 'Sexual Harassment in the Nineteenth Century English Cotton Industry', *History Workshop Journal,* vol. 19, pp. 29–61.

Landes, D. 1972: *The Unbound Prometheus.* Cambridge: Cambridge University Press.

Landes, D. 1986: 'What do Bosses Really Do?', *Journal of Economic History,* vol. 46, no. 3, pp. 585–623.

Lane, T. 1974: *The Union Makes Us Strong.* London: Arrow.

Lane, T. and Roberts, K. 1971: *Strike at Pilkingtons.* London: Fontana.

Larson, M. S. 1977: *The Rise of Professionalism.* Berkeley: University of California Press.

Lash, S. 1984: *The Militant Worker: Class and Radicalism in France and America.* London: Heinemann.

Lash, S. and Urry, J. 1987: *The End of Organized Capitalism.* Cambridge: Polity.

LATC (Lancashire Association of Trades Councils), 1984: *Lancashire United?* Report given at LATC conference.

Latour, B. 1986: 'The Powers of Association', in Law, J. (ed.), *Power, Action and Belief: a New Sociology of Knowledge?* London: Routledge.

Latour, B. 1987: *Science in Action.* Milton Keynes: Open University Press.

Latour, B. 1988: 'The Prince for Machines as well as for Machinations', in Elliott, B. (ed.), *Technology and Social Process.* Edinburgh: Edinburgh University Press.

Latour, B. and Woolgar, S. 1979: *Laboratory Life: The Social Construction of Scientific Facts.* London: Sage.

Law, J. 1986: 'On the Methods of Long Distance Control: Vessels, Navigation and the Portuguese Route to India', in Law, J. (ed.), *Power, Action and Belief: a New Sociology of Knowledge?* Keele: Sociological Review Monograph.

Law, J. (ed.), 1986: *Power, Action and Belief.* London: Routledge and Kegan Paul.

Law, J. 1988: 'The Anatomy of a Socio-technical Struggle', in Elliott, B. (ed.), *Technology and Social Process.* Edinburgh: Edinburgh University Press.

Law, J. (ed.), 1991: *A Sociology of Monsters.* London: Routledge.

Lawler, E. 1973: 'Satisfaction and Behaviour', in Straw, B. (ed.), *Psychological Foundations of Organizational Behaviour.* Santa Monica: Goodyear.

Lawrence, F. 2004: *Not on the Label.* London: Penguin.

Lawrence, P. R. and Lorsch, J. W. 1967: *Organization and Environment: Managing Differentiation and Integration.* Cambridge, Mass.: Harvard University Press.

Lazonick, W. H. 1979: 'Industrial Relations and Technical Change: the Case of the Self-acting Mule', *Cambridge Journal of Economics,* vol. 3, no. 3, pp. 231–62.

Lazonick, W. 1993: *Business Organization and the Myth of the Market Economy*. Cambridge: Cambridge University Press.

Leavitt, H. J. and Whisler, T. L. 1958: 'Management in the 1980s', *Harvard Business Review*, vol. 36, pp. 41–8.

Lee, D. 1980: 'Skill, Craft and Class: a Theoretical Critique and a Critical Case', *Sociology*, vol. 15, pp. 57–78.

Lee, D. 1982: 'Beyond Deskilling: Skill, Craft and Class', in Wood, S. (ed.), *The Degradation of Work?* London: Hutchinson.

Lee, D. 1996: 'Globalization and Employment: Is Anxiety Justified?', *International Labour Review*, vol. 135, no. 5, pp. 485–97.

Lee, G. 1987: 'Black Members and their Unions', in Lee, G. and Loveridge, R. (eds), *The Manufacture of Disadvantage: Stigma and Social Closure*. Milton Keynes: Open University Press.

Lee, R. and Lawrence, P. 1985: *Organizational Behaviour: Politics at Work*. London: Hutchinson.

Leeson, R. A. 1980: *Travelling Brothers*. St Albans: Paladin.

Legge, K. 1995: *Human Resource Management: Rhetoric and Realities*. London: Macmillan.

Leggett, J. 1968: *Class, Race and Labour*. New York: Cambridge University Press.

Leghorn, L. and Parker, K. 1981: *Woman's Worth*. London: Routledge.

Leigh, D. 2002: 'Diplomat's "Slave" Can Stay in UK', *Guardian*, 12 November.

Leiulfsrud, H. and Woodward, A. 1987: 'Women at Class Crossroads', *Sociology*, vol. 21, no. 3, pp. 393–412.

Lenin, V. I. 1968a: *Selected Works*. Moscow: Progress Publishers.

Lenin, V. I. 1968b: 'The State and Revolution', *Collected Works*. Moscow: Progress Publishers.

Lenin, V. I. 1968c: 'The Immediate Tasks of the Soviet Government', *Selected Works*. Moscow: Progress Publishers.

Lenin, V. I. 1970: *What Is To Be Done?* London: Panther.

Lenin, V. I. 1978: *Imperialism: the Highest Stage of Capitalism*. Moscow: Progress Publishers.

Leonard, A. 1987: *Pyrrhic Victories*. London: EOC/HMSO.

Lerner, S. 1994: 'The Future of Work in North America: Good Jobs, Bad Jobs, Beyond Jobs', *Futures*, vol. 26, no. 2, pp. 185–96.

Letto-Gillies, G. 2001: 'Wake Up and Smell the Fair Trade Coffee Mr President', *Times Higher*, 6 April.

Levy, D. L. 1997: 'Business and International Environmental Treaties', *California Management Review*, vol. 39, no. 3, pp. 54–71.

Lewenhak, S. 1977: *Women and Trade Unions: an Outline History of Women in the British Trade Union Movement*. London: Ernest Benn.

Liff, S. 1988: 'Gender, Office Work and Technological Change', paper delivered to the PICT/WICT workshop, Bath, 26 March.

Light, I. and Bonzicich, E. 1988: *Immigrant Entrepreneurs: Koreans in Los Angeles, 1965–1982*. Los Angeles: University of California Press.

Lindhert, P. H. 1980: 'English Occupations 1670–1811', *Journal of Economic History*, vol. 40, no. 4, 685–712.

Lindhert, P. H. and Williamson, J. G. 1982: 'Revising England's Social Tables *1688–1812*', *Explorations in Economic History*, vol. 19, pp. 94–109.

Linhart, R. 1981: *The Assembly Line*. London: John Calder.

Lipietz, A. 1987: *Mirages and Miracles: the Crisis of Global Fordism*. London: Verso.

Littler, C. R. 1982: *The Development of the Labour Process in Capitalist Societies*. London: Heinemann.

Littler, C. R. 1985: 'The Design of Jobs', in Littler, C. R. (ed.), *The Experience of Work*. Aldershot: Gower.

Locke, J. 1960: *Two Treatises of Government*. Cambridge: Cambridge University Press.

Lockwood, D. 1958: *The Blackcoated Worker*. London: Allen & Unwin.

Lockwood, D. 1966: 'Sources of Variation in Working Class Images of Society', *Sociological Review*, vol. 4, no. 2, pp. 249–67.

Lockwood, D. 1986: 'Class, Status and Gender', in Crompton, R. and Mann, M. (eds), *Gender and Stratification*. Cambridge: Polity.

Loomis, C. J. 2001: 'This Stuff is Wrong', *Fortune*, 25 June, pp. 37–42.

Lorsch, J. 1986: 'Managing Culture: the Invisible Barrier to Change', *California Management Review*, vol. 28, no. 2, pp. 95–109.

Loscocco, K. A. 1989: 'The Instrumentally Oriented Factory Worker: Myth or Reality?', *Work and Occupations*, vol. 16, no. 1, pp. 3–25.

Loudon, J. B. 1979: 'Workers, Lords and Masters', in Wallman, S. (ed.), *Social Anthropology of Work*. London: Academic Press.

Lovelock, C. H. and Yip, G. 1996: ' "Developing" Global Strategies for Service Businesses', *Californian Management Review*, vol. 38, no. 2, pp. 64–86.

Low Pay Unit. 1989: *Getting it Right for Women*. London: LPU.

Lukács, G. 1971: *History and Class Consciousness*. London: Merlin.

Lukes, S. 1973: *Emile Durkheim*. London: Peregrine.

Lukes, S. 1974: *Power: a Radical View*. London: Macmillan.

Luthra, M., Oakley, R., Austin, R. and Fitzgerald, M. 1988: *Racial Harassment*. London: Department of Environment.

Macalister, T. 2004: '£11m Bonus for Tesco Boardroom', *Guardian*, 18 May.

McCall, L. 2001: *Complex Inequality: Gender, Class and Race in the New Economy*. London: Routledge.

McCarthy, R. 2000: 'Bonded Workers Bid for Freedom', *Guardian*, 17 July.

McCarthy, R. 2001: 'Football Ban Sends Child Workers into Worse Jobs', *Guardian*, 25 April.

McClelland, K. 1987: 'Time to Work, Time to Live', in Joyce, P. (ed.), *The Historical Meanings of Work*. Cambridge: Cambridge University Press.

Mace, N. and Ross, M. J. 2002: *In the Company of Men: A Woman at the Citadel*. London: Simon Purse.

MacErlean, N. 1996: 'New Labour, New Unions', *Observer*, 16 June.

MacErlean, N. 1998: 'Employers Turn Clockwise over 48 Hours', *Observer*, 27 October.

McGeevor, P. and Brennan, J. 1990: *Ethnic Minorities and the Graduate Labour Market*. London: CRE.

McGreal, C. 2001a: 'Aboard the Slave Ship of Despair', *Guardian*, 16 April.

McGreal, C. 2001b: 'Misery of Children Enslaved by the Gun', *Guardian*, 10 July.

McGregor, D. 1960: *The Human Side of Enterprise*. New York: McGraw-Hill.

McGregor, D. 1984: 'Theory X and Theory Y', in Pugh, D. (ed.), *Organization Theory*. Harmondsworth: Penguin.

McGrew, A. 1992: 'A Global Society?', in Hall, S., Held, D. and McGrew, T. (eds), *Modernity and its Futures*, Cambridge: Polity.

McIlroy, J. 1988: *Trade Unions in Britain Today*. Manchester: Manchester University Press.

MacKenzie, D. 1991: *Inventing Accuracy: A Historical Sociology of Missile Guidance*. Cambridge, Mass.: MIT Press.

McKie, R. and Revill, J. 2003: 'Is Race only Skin-Deep?', *Observer*, 9 February.

McKie, R. 2004: 'Living with Britain's Population Timebomb', *Observer*, 25 January.

McLellan, D. 1974: *Karl Marx: His Life and Thought*. London: Macmillan.

McLellan, D. 1980: *Marxism after Marx*. London: Macmillan.

MacLeod, D. 1996: 'Men Still Dominate the Top Teaching Jobs', *Guardian*, 23 April.

MacLeod, D. 2000: 'Female Trouble', *Guardian Education*, 4 April.

McLoughlin, I. 1990: 'Technological Change at Work', paper presented at the Centre for Research into Innovation, Culture and Technology (CRICT), Brunel University, 2 May.

McLoughlin, I. 1997: 'Babies, Bathwater, Guns and Roses', in McLoughlin, I. and Harris, M. (eds), *Innovation, Organizational Change and Technology*. London: Thomson International Business Press.

McLoughlin, I. and Clark, J. 1988: *Technological Change at Work*. Milton Keynes: Open University Press.

McLoughlin, I. and Harris, M. (eds), 1997: *Innovation, Organizational Change and Technology*. London: Thomson International Business Press.

McLuhan, M. 1964: *Understanding Media: the Extension of Man*. London: Routledge.

Macnicol, J. 1988: 'Lumpen Proles', *Times Higher Education Supplement*, 11 March.

Macrae, C. 1988: *Observer*, 21 August.

Macrae, S. 1986: *Cross Class Families*. Oxford: Clarendon.

Maitland, A. 2002: 'McDonald's Responds to Anti-Capitalist Grilling', *Financial Times*, 15 April.

Maitland, A. 2004: 'What Women Want is to Change Things', *Financial Times*, 13 September.

Major, L. E. 1996: 'For She's a Jolly Good Fellow', *Guardian*, 1 October.

Major, L. E. 2001: 'Ladies First', *Guardian Education*, 16 January.

Malcomson, R. W. 1981: *Life and Labour in England 1700–1780*. London: Hutchinson.

Malcomson, R. W. 1988: 'Ways of Getting a Living in Eighteenth-Century England', in Pahl, R. E. (ed.), *On Work*. Oxford: Blackwell.

Malinowski, B. 1984: 'The Primitive Economics of the Trobriand Islanders', in Littler, C. R. (ed.), *The Experience of Work*. London: Heinemann.

Mallet, S. 1975: *The New Working Class*. Nottingham: Spokesman.

Mallier, A. T. and Rosser, M. J. 1987: 'Changes in the Industrial Distribution of Female Employment in Great Britain, 1951–1981', *Work, Employment and Society*, vol. 1, no. 4, pp. 463–86.

Mann, M. 1970: 'The Social Cohesion of Liberal Democracy', *American Sociological Review*, vol. 35, no. 3, pp. 423–39.

Mann, M. 1973a: *Consciousness and Action among the Western Working Class*. London: Macmillan.

Mann, M. 1973b: *Workers on the Move*. Cambridge: Cambridge University Press.

Mann, M. 1986: *The Sources of Social Power*, vol. 1. Cambridge: Cambridge University Press.

Mannheim, K. 1951: *Freedom, Power and Democratic Planning*. London: Routledge.

Manpower Services Commission, 1987: *Ethnic Minorities and Job Centres*. Sheffield: MSC.

Manwaring, T. 1984: 'The Extended Internal Labour Market', *Cambridge Journal of Economics*, vol. 8, no. 2, pp. 161–87.

Marceau, J. 1989: *A Family Business? The Making of an International Business Elite*. Cambridge: Cambridge University Press.

Marcos, 2001: *Our Word is our Weapon: Selected Writings*. London: Serpent's Tail.

Marcuse, H. 1964: *One Dimensional Man*. Boston, Mass.: Beacon Press.

Marcuse, H. 1969: *An Essay on Liberation*. Boston, Mass.: Beacon Press.

Marglin, S. 1982: 'What do the Bosses do? The Origins and Functions of Hierarchy in Capitalist Production', in Giddens, A. and Held, D. (eds), *Classes, Power and Conflict*. London: Macmillan.

Markus, M. L. and Robey, D. 1988: 'Information Technology and Organizational Change: Causal Structure in Theory and Research', *Management Science*, vol. 34, no. 5, pp. 583–98.

Marlow, J. 1985: *The Tolpuddle Martyrs*. London: Grafton.

Marsden, D. 1986: *The End of Economic Man: Custom and Competition in Labour Markets*. Brighton: Wheatsheaf.

Marsden, D., Morris, T., Willman, P. and Wood, S. 1985: *The Car Industry: Labour Relations and Industrial Adjustment*. London: Tavistock.

Marsh, A. I. 1982: *Employee Relations Policy and Decision Making*. Aldershot: Gower.

Marsh, A. and Ryan, V. 1989: *The Seamen: a History of the National Union of Seamen*. Oxford: Malthouse Press.

Marsh, C. 1988a: 'Unemployment in Britain', in Gallie, D. (ed.), *Employment in Britain*. Oxford: Blackwell.

Marsh, C. 1988b: *Exploring Data: an Introduction to Data Analysis for Social Scientists*. Cambridge: Polity.

Marshall, G. 1982: *In Search of the Spirit of Capitalism: an Essay on Max Weber's Protestant Ethic Thesis*. London: Hutchinson.

Marshall, G., Newby, H., Rose, D. and Vogler, C. 1988: *Social Class in Modern Britain*. London: Hutchinson.

Marshall, G., Vogler, C., Rose, D. and Newby, H. 1987: 'Distributional Struggle and Moral Order in a Market Society', *Sociology*, vol. 21, no. 1, pp. 55–74.

Marshall, J. 1987: 'Less Equal than Others', *Times Higher Education Supplement*, 17 April.

Martin, J. and Roberts, C. 1980: *Women and Employment*. London: HMSO.

Martin, J. and Roberts, C. 1984: *Women and Employment: a Lifetime Perspective*. London: Department of Employment.

Martin, P. 'The Concept of Class', in Anderson, R. J., Hughes, J. A. and Sharrock, W. W. (eds), 1987: *Classic Disputes in Sociology*. London: Allen & Unwin.

Martin, R. 1969: *Communism and British Trade Unionism 1924–1933*. Oxford: Clarendon.

Martinson, J. 2004: 'Pay Activists to Challenge ITV Directors', *Guardian*, 19 April.

Marx, K. 1954: *Capital*, vol. 1. London: Lawrence & Wishart.

Marx, K. 1968: 'The Eighteenth Brumaire of Louis Bonaparte', in *Selected Works in One Volume*. London: Lawrence & Wishart.

Marx, K. 1969: *Theories of Surplus Value*. London: Lawrence & Wishart.

Marx, K. 1970: *The German Ideology*. London: Lawrence & Wishart.

Marx, K. 1973a: *Selected Works in Three Volumes*, vol. 1. Moscow: Progress Publishers.

Marx, K. 1973b: *Grundrisse*. Harmondsworth: Penguin.

Marx, K. 1975: *Early Writings*. Harmondsworth: Penguin.

Marx, K. 1981: *Capital*, vol. 3. Harmondsworth: Penguin.

Marx, K. and Engels, F. 1968: 'The Communist Manifesto', in *Selected Works in One Volume*. London: Lawrence & Wishart.

Maslow, A. 1943: 'A Theory of Human Motivation', *Psychological Review*, vol. 50, pp. 370–96.

Mass Observation, 1943: *War Factory*. London: Hutchinson.

Mather, I. 2001: 'High-Tech Namibia Thrives Under Ford's Care', *Times Higher Education Supplement*, 29 June.

Mathews, J. 1989: *Tools of Change: New Technology and the Democratization of Work*. London: Pluto.

Mathias, P. 1969: *The First Industrial Nation: an Economic History of Britain 1700–1914*. London: Methuen.

Mathiason, N. 2003: 'Seeds of Anger Take Root', *Observer Business*, 14 December.

Matthews, D. 1996: 'Fat is a Relative Issue', *Management Today*, June, pp. 50–4.

Matthews, J. 1972: *Ford Strike*. London: Panther.

Mayhew, K. and Addison, J. 1983: 'Discrimination in the Labour Market', in Bain, G. S. (ed.), *Industrial Relations in Britain*. Oxford: Blackwell.

Maynard, M. 1985: 'Housework', Unit 3 part 2, *Work and Society*. Milton Keynes: Open University Press.

Maynard, M. 1988: 'Gender at Work', *Times Higher Education Supplement*, 26 August.

Meade-King, M. 1986: *Guardian*, 11 November.

Meade-King, M. 1988: *Guardian*, 8 September.

Meade-King, M. 1989: *Guardian*, 17 October.

Meikle, J. 1996: 'Through the Glass Ceiling', *Guardian*, 24 April.

Meikle, J. 2001: 'Inflexible NHS "holds back" Women Doctors', *Guardian*, 27 June.

Merton, R. K. 1957: *Social Theory and Social Structure*. New York: Free Press.

Metcalfe, D. 1989: 'Water Notes Dry Up', *British Journal of Industrial Relations*, vol. 27, no. 1, pp. 1–32.

Meth, M. 1973: *Brothers of All Men?* London: Runnymede Industrial Unit.

Meyer, J. W. and Rowan, B. 1977: 'Institutional Organizations', *American Journal of Sociology*, vol. 83, pp. 340–63.

Michels, R. 1949: *Political Parties*. New York: Free Press.

Mickelthwaite, J. and Wooldridge, A. 2003: *The Company: A Short History of a Revolutionary Idea*. London: Weidenfeld and Nicholson.

Middleton, C. 1981: 'Peasants, Patriarchy and the Feudal Mode of Production in England: a Marxist Appraisal', *Sociological Review*, vol. 29, no. 1, pp. 105–54.

Middleton, C. 1988: 'The Familiar Fate of the Famulae', in Pahl, R. E. (ed.), *On Work: Historical, Comparative and Theoretical Approaches*. Oxford: Blackwell.

Midgley, M. 2000: 'Why Memes?' in Rose, H. and Rose, S. (eds), *Alas, Poor Darwin: Arguments Against Evolutionary Psychology*. London: Jonathan Cape.

Miles, I. 1983: 'Adaptation to Unemployment?', Occasional Paper No. 20. Brighton: Science Policy Review Unit.

Miles, J. 1850: *Chapters in the Life of a Dundee Factory Boy*, in Ward, J. T. (ed.), 1970: *The Factory System*, vol. 2. Newton Abbot: David & Charles.

Miles, R. 1965: 'Human Relations or Human Resources?', *Harvard Business Review*, vol. 43, no. 4.

Miles, R. 1982: *Racism and Migrant Labour*. London: Routledge.

Miles, R. 1989: *Racism*. London: Routledge.

Miles, R. 1990: 'Whatever Happened to the Sociology of Migration?', *Work, Employment and Society*, vol. 4, no. 2, pp. 281–98.

Miles, R. and Phizacklea, A. 1977: 'The TUC, Black Workers and New Commonwealth Immigration, 1954–1973', CRER Working Papers. Coventry: University of Warwick.

Miles, R. and Phizacklea, A. 1978: 'The TUC and Black Workers, 1974–76', *British Journal of Industrial Relations*, vol. 16, pp. 195–207.

Miles, R. and Phizacklea, A. (eds), 1979: *Racism and Political Action in Britain*. London: Routledge.

Miliband, R. 1972: *Parliamentary Socialism*. London: Merlin.

Miller, D. 1984: *Anarchism*. London: Macmillan.

Mills, H. 1997: 'Why Our Jails Have No Black Governors', *Observer*, 10 August.

Mills, M. 2000: 'Making the Worst of a Good Job', *Guardian*, 4 October.

Millward, N. and Stevens, M. 1986: *British Workplace Industrial Relations 1980–1984*. Aldershot: Gower.

Milmo, D. 2003: 'Knapp to Net $10m from NTL Payoff', *Guardian*, 30 September.

Milne, S. 1989: *Guardian*, 9 September.

Milner, M. 2001: 'Lean Machine: UK Tops Productivity League', *Guardian*, 29 June.

Mincer, J. and Polachek, S. 1974: 'Family Investment in Human Capital: Earnings of Women', *Journal of Political Economy*, vol. 82, no. 2, pp. 76–108.

Mintel, 1995: *Leisure Time*. London: Mintel.

Mitchell, J. 1975: *Psychoanalysis and Feminism*. Harmondsworth: Penguin.

Mitchell, J. and Parris, H. 1983: *The Politics and Government of Britain*. Milton Keynes: Open University Press.

Modelski, G. 1972: *Principles of World Politics*. New York: Free Press.

Modood, T. 1997a: 'Qualifications and English Language', in Modood, T., Berthoud, R., Lakey, J., Nazroo, J., Smith, P., Virdee, S. and Beishon, S. (eds), *Ethnic Minorities in Britain*. London: PSI.

Modood, T. 1997b: 'Employment', in Modood, T., Berthoud, R., Lakey, J., Nazroo, J., Smith, P., Virdee, S. and Beishon, S. (eds), *Ethnic Minorities in Britain*. London: PSI.

Moher, J. 1988: 'From Suppression to Containment: Roots of Trade Union Law to 1825', in Rule, J. (ed.), *British Trade Unionism 1750–1850: the Formative Years*. London: Longman.

Monahan, J. 2001: 'Where Children Work as Slaves', *Guardian*, 8 May.

Monbiot, G. 2000: *Captive State: The Corporate Takeover of Britain*. London: Macmillan.

Monbiot, G. 2003a: 'The Worst of Times', *Guardian*, 2 September.

Monbiot, G. 2003b: 'The Flight to India', *Guardian*, 21 October.

Moore, B. Jr. 1967: *Social Origins of Dictatorship and Democracy*. Harmondsworth: Penguin.

Moore Campbell, B. 1988: *Successful Women, Angry Men*. London: Arrow.

Moore, K. and Lewis, D. 1996: 'The First MNEs: Assyria circa 2000 BC', *Templeton College Management Research Papers*, 96/3.

Moore, K. and Lewis, D. 1999: *Birth of the Multinational*. Copenhagen: Copenhagen Business School Press.

Moore, R. 1975: *Racism and Black Resistance in Britain*. London: Pluto Press.

Moorhouse, H. F. 1984: 'American Automobiles and Workers' Dreams', in Thompson, K. (ed.), *Work, Employment and Unemployment: Perspectives on Work and Society*. Milton Keynes: Open University Press.

Moorhouse, H. F. 1987: 'The "Work Ethic" and "Leisure" Activity: the Hot Rod in Post-war America', in Joyce, P. (ed.), *The Historical Meanings of Work*. Cambridge: Cambridge University Press.

More, C. 1980: *Skill and the English Working Class: 1870–1914*. London: Croom Helm.

Morgan, G. 1986: *Images of Organization*. London: Sage. Revised edition, 1996.

Morgan, O. and Walsh, C. 2002: 'The City's Magic Circle', *Observer*, 17 March.

Mormino, G. 1982: 'We Worked Hard and We Took Care of Our Own: Oral History and Italians in Tampa', *Labor History*, vol. 23, no. 3, pp. 395–415.

Morokvasic, M. 1987: 'Immigrants in the Parisian Garment Industry', *Work, Employment and Society*, vol. 1, no. 4, pp. 441–62.

Morris, L. 1987: 'Constraints on Gender: the Family Wage, Social Security and the Labour Market', *Work, Employment and Society*, vol. 1, no. 1, pp. 85–106.

Morris, L. 1990: *The Workings of the Household: a US–UK Comparison.* Cambridge: Polity.

Morris, W. 1983: 'Useful Work and Useless Toil', in Richards, V. (ed.), *Why Work?* London: Freedom Press.

Morton, A. L. 1962: *The Life and Ideas of Robert Owen.* London: Lawrence & Wishart.

Moszynski, P. 2001: '41 Countries Send Children Into War', *Guardian*, 13 June.

Mouffe, C. 1979: 'Hegemony and Ideology in Gramsci', in Mouffe, C. (ed.), *Gramsci and Marxist Theory.* London: Routledge.

Muir, H. 2004: 'Black Police to Tell Inquiry of Race Bias at Yard', *Guardian*, 22 January.

Musgrave, P. W. 1981: 'The Labour Force: Some Relevant Attitudes', in Roderick, G. and Stevens, M. (eds), *Where Did We Go Wrong?* Brighton: Falmer Press.

Nadworny, M. J. 1955: *Scientific Management and the Unions, 1900–32.* Cambridge, Mass.: Harvard University Press.

Nakase, T. 1979: 'The Introduction of Scientific Management in Japan and its Characteristics', in Nakagawa, K. (ed.), *Labor and Management.* Tokyo: University of Tokyo Press.

NALGO (National Association of Local Government Officers), 1981: *Sexual Harassment is a Trade Union Issue.* London: NALGO.

NAPO (National Association of Probation Officers), 1988: *Black People in the Criminal Justice System.* London: NAPO.

Naughtie, J. 1988: *Guardian*, 10 May.

Nazer, M. and Lewis, D. 2004: *Slave.* London: Virago.

NBPA (National Back Pain Association), 1989: BBC, Radio 3, 16 October.

Neal, F. 1988: *Sectarian Violence: the Liverpool Experience, 1819–1914.* Manchester: Manchester University Press.

Nelson, D. 1974: 'Scientific Management, Systematic Management and Labor, 1880–1915', *Business History Review*, vol. 28, pp. 479–500.

Nelson, D. 1975: *Managers and Workers: Origins of the New Factory System in the United States, 1880–1920.* Madison: University of Wisconsin Press.

New Earnings Survey, 1995. London: HMSO.

New Internationalist, 1988: 'Housework: the Facts', March.

New Internationalist, 1995: 'Unmasked: the East Asian Economic Miracle', January.

Newton, P. 1986: 'Female Engineers: Femininity Redefined?', in Harding, J. (ed.), *Perspectives on Gender and Science.* Brighton: Falmer Press.

Nicholas, J. 1991: 'British Multinational Investment before 1939', in Forman-Peck, J. (ed.), *New Perspectives on the Late Victorian Economy.* Cambridge: Cambridge University Press.

Nichols, T. 1969: *Ownership, Control and Ideology.* London: Allen & Unwin.

Nichols, T. and Armstrong, P. 1976: *Workers Divided*. London: Fontana.

Nicholson, N. 2000: *Managing the Human Animal*. London: Texere.

Nickell, S. and Bell, B. 1995: 'The Collapse in Demand for the Unskilled and Unemployment across the OECD', *Oxford Review of Economic Policy*, vol. 11, no. 1, pp. 40–62.

Nishikawa, S. (ed.), 1980: *The Labour Market in Japan: Selected Readings*. Tokyo: University of Tokyo Press.

Noble, D. F. 1974: *America by Design*. New York: Oxford University Press.

Noble, D. F. 1979: 'Social Choice in Machine Design: the Case of Automatically Controlled Machine Tools', in Zimbalist, A. (ed.), *Case Studies on the Labour Process*. New York: Monthly Review Press.

Nolan, P. 2000: 'Labouring Under an Illusion', *THES Millennium Magazine*, vol. 22, no. 29, December, p. 30.

North, D. C. and Thomas, R. P. 1973: *The Rise of the Western World*. Cambridge: Cambridge University Press.

Northcott, J. and Rogers, P. 1982: *Microelectronics in Industry*. London: Policy Studies Institute.

NUPE (National Union of Public Employees), 1985: *The Report of the Race Equality Working Party*. London: NUPE.

NUT (National Union of Teachers), 1988: *Women – What Does the NUT Offer You?* London: NUT.

Nyland, C. 1987: 'Scientific Planning and Management', *Capital and Class*, no. 33, pp. 55–83.

Oakley, A. 1974: *Housewife*. London: Allen Lane.

O'Brien, M. 1981: *The Politics of Reproduction*. London: Routledge.

O'Brien, M. 1982: 'The Working Father', in Beail, N. and McGuire, J. (eds), *Fathers: Psychological Perspectives*. London: Junction Books.

O'Donovan, K. and Szyszczak, E. 1988: *Equality and Sex Discrimination Law*. Oxford: Blackwell.

Offe, C. 1984: *Contradictions of the Welfare State*. London: Hutchinson.

Offe, C. 1985: *Disorganized Capitalism*. Cambridge: Polity.

Office of National Statistics, 1997: *Social Focus on Families*. London: ONS.

Office for National Statistics, 2001: *Social Focus on Men*. London: Office for National Statistics.

OFSTED (Office for Standards in Education), 1996: *Gender Divide*. London: HMSO.

O'Grady, M. (ed.), 2001: *Debt Bondage*. London: Anti-Slavery International.

Ohmae, K. 1990: *The Borderless World*. London: Collins.

Olson, M. 1965: *The Logic of Collective Action*. Cambridge, Mass.: Harvard University Press.

Olson, M. 1982: *The Rise and Decline of Nations: Economic Growth, Stagflation, and Social Rigidities*. New Haven, Conn.: Yale University Press.

Open Systems Group. 1981: *Systems Behaviour*. London: Harper & Row.

Open University, 1976: *Press, Papers and Print*. Milton Keynes: Open University Press.

Orwell, G. 1984: *The Penguin Essays of George Orwell*. Harmondsworth: Penguin.

Osborn, A. 2002: 'Work is Three Times as Deadly as War, says UN', *Guardian*, 2 May.

Ouchi, W. A. 1981: *Theory Z: How American Business can Meet the Japanese Challenge*. Reading, Mass.: Addison-Wesley.

Owen, S. J. 1987: 'Household Production and Economic Efficiency: Arguments for and against Domestic Specialization', *Work, Employment and Society*, vol. 1, no. 2, pp. 157–78.

Oxfam, 2004: *Trading Away Our Rights: Women Working in Global Supply Chains*, available at <http://www.oxfam.org.uk/what_we_do/issues/trade/trading_rights.htm>.

Ozanne, R. 1979: 'United States Labor-Management Relations 1860–1930', in Nakagawa, N. (ed.), *Labor and Management*. Tokyo: University of Tokyo Press.

Pagano, M. 1987: *Guardian*, 1 September.

Pagnamenta, R. and Overy, R. 1984: *All Our Working Lives*. London: BBC.

Pahl, R. E. 1984: *Divisions of Labour*. Oxford: Blackwell.

Pahl, R. E. (ed.), 1988: *On Work: Historical, Comparative and Theoretical Approaches*. Oxford: Blackwell.

Pai, H. 2004: 'I'm Illegal, So What Can I Do?', *Guardian*, 9 February.

Palast, G. 2000: 'US Would Run Barclay's Out of Town', *Observer*, 9 April.

Palloix, C. 1976: 'The Labour Process: From Fordism to Neo-Fordism', in Conference of Socialist Economists (eds), *The Labour Process and Class Strategies*. London: Stage One.

Palmer, C. 2000: 'A Job, Old Boy?', *Observer*, 11 June.

Pandya, N. 2003: 'Cutting a Deal? Not with Daggers Drawn', *Guardian Jobs*, 10 May.

Papworth, J. 2001: 'Lagging Behind in the Pregnant Pause', *Guardian*, 9 June.

Parker, S. R., Brown, R. K., Child, J. and Smith, M. A. 1967: *The Sociology of Industry*. London: Allen & Unwin.

Parkin, F. 1967: 'Working Class Conservatives', *British Journal of Sociology*, vol. 18, pp. 278–90.

Parkin, F. 1972: *Class Inequality and Political Order: Social Stratification in Capitalist and Communist Countries*. New York: Holt, Reinhart & Winston.

Parkin, F. 1979: *Marxism and Class Theory: a Bourgeois Critique*. London: Tavistock.

Parkin, F. 1982: *Max Weber*. London: Tavistock.

Paton Walsh, N. 2004: 'Russia Tops the Table for Women Managers', *Guardian*, 23 February.

Patterson, W. 1988: *The Korean Frontier in America: Immigration in Hawaii, 1896–1910*. Honolulu: University of Hawaii Press.

Pavitt, J. 2001: 'A History of Brands: Coca-Cola', *Guardian*, 9 July.

Payne, J. 1987: 'Does Unemployment Run in Families?', *Sociology*, vol. 21, no. 2, pp. 199–214.

Payne, J. 1989: 'Unemployment and Family Formation among Young Men', *Sociology*, vol. 23, no. 2, pp. 171–92.

Peach, C. 1968: *West Indian Migration to Britain*. Oxford: Oxford University Press.

Pearn, M. A., Kandola, R. S. and Mottram, R. D. 1987. *Selection Tests and Sex Bias*. London: EOC/HMSO.

Pelling, H. 1960: *American Labor*. Chicago: University of Chicago Press.

Pelling, H. 1968: 'The Concept of the Labour Aristocracy', in Pelling, H., *Popular Politics and Society in Late Victorian England*. London: Macmillan.

Pelling, H. 1976: *A History of British Trade Unionism*. Harmondsworth: Penguin.

Penn, R. 1982: 'Skilled Manual Workers in the Labour Process', in Wood, S. (ed.), *The Degradation of Work?* London: Hutchinson.

Perkin, H. 1969: *The Origins of Modern English Society 1780–1880*. London: Routledge.

Perkin, H. 1989: *The Rise of Professional Society: England since 1880*. London: Routledge.

Perlman, J. 1976: *The Myth of Marginality*. Berkeley: University of California Press.

Perlman, S. 1928: *A Theory of the Labor Movement*. New York: Kelley.

Perlo, V. 1953: *The Negro in Southern Agriculture*. New York: International Publishers.

Perri 6, 1997: *Chain Reaction: Tackling Network Poverty*. London: Demos.

Pfeffer, J. 1982: *Organizations and Organization Theory*. Marshfield, Mass.: Pitman.

Pfeffer, R. 1979: *Working for Capitalism*. New York: Columbia University Press.

Phillips, A. and Taylor, B. 1980: 'Sex and Skill: Notes towards a Feminist Economics', *Feminist Review*, no. 6, pp. 79–88.

Philpot, J. 2000: 'Face the Ugly Truth that "Lookism" is All the Rage', *Guardian*, 18 December.

Phizacklea, A. 1982: 'Migrant Women and Wage Labour: the Case of West Indian Women in Britain', in West, J. (ed.), *Work, Women and the Labour Market*. London: Routledge.

Phizacklea, A. 1987: 'Minority Women and Economic Restructuring: the Case of Britain and the Federal Republic of Germany', *Work, Employment and Society*, vol. 1, no. 3, pp. 309–25.

Phizacklea, A. and Miles, M. 1987: 'The British Trade Union Movement and Racism', in Lee, G. and Loveridge, R. (eds), *The Manufacture of Disadvantage*. Milton Keynes: Open University Press.

Pick, D. 1993: *War Machine*. New Haven and London: Yale University Press.

Piore, M. J. 1979: *Birds of Passage: Migrant Labor and Industrial Societies*. Cambridge: Cambridge University Press.

Piore, M. J. 1986: 'Perspectives on Labour Market Flexibility', *Industrial Relations*, vol. 25, no. 2, pp. 146–66.

Piore, M. J. and Sabel, C. F. 1984: *The Second Industrial Divide*. New York: Basic Books.

Piven, F. F. and Cloward, R. A. 1977: *Poor People's Movements: How they Succeed, How they Fail*. New York: Pantheon Books.

PLA (Provident Life Assurance), 1987: 'Life after Death: Putting a Price on your Wife', *Lifelines*, no. 3. London: PLA.

Polachek, S. 1975: 'Discontinuities in Labor Force Participation and its Effects on Women's Market Earnings', in Lloyd, C. B. (ed.), *Sex, Discrimination and the Division of Labor*. New York: Columbia University Press.

Polan, A. J. 1984: *Lenin and the End of Politics*. London: Methuen.

Polanyi, K. 1944: *The Great Transformation*. Boston: Beacon Press.

Policy Studies Institute (PSI), 1986: *Black and White Britain*. London: PSI.

Pollard, S. 1965: *The Genesis of Modern Management*. London: Edward Arnold.

Pollert, A. 1981: *Girls, Wives, Factory Lives*. London: Macmillan.

Pollert, A. 1988: 'The Flexible Firm: Fact or Fiction?', *Work, Employment and Society*, vol. 2, no. 3, pp. 281–316.

Pollitt, C. 1986: 'Democracy and Bureaucracy', in Held, D. and Pollitt, C. (eds), *New Forms of Democracy*. London: Sage.

Pool, I. de S. 1983: *Technologies of Freedom*. Cambridge, Mass: Belknap Press.

Porter, M. 1982: 'Standing on the Edge: Working Class Housewives and the World of Work', in West, J. (ed.), *Women, Work and the Labour Market*. London: Routledge.

Postan, M. M. 1972: *The Medieval Economy and Society*. Harmondsworth: Penguin.

Poulantzas, N. 1978: *Classes in Contemporary Capitalism*. London: Verso.

Power, J. and Hardman, A. 1978: *Western Europe's Migrant Workers*. London: Minority Rights Group.

Pratley, N. 2003: 'Kick Them Where it Hurts', *Guardian*, 19 December.

Prest, M. 1996: 'The Great Hole in the Wall Job Heist', *Observer*, 5 May.

Pretty, D. A. 1989: *The Rural Revolt that Failed: Farm Workers' Trade Unions in Wales, 1889–1950*. Cardiff: University of Wales Press.

Proceedings at York Special Commission, 1813: reprinted in *The Luddites: Three Pamphlets 1812–1839*; 1972: New York: Arno Press.

Procter, S., Rowlinson, M., McArdle, L., Hassard, J. and Forrester, P. 1994: 'Flexibility, Politics and Strategy: in Defence of the Model of the Flexible Firm', *Work, Employment and Society*, vol. 8, no. 2, pp. 221–42.

PSI, 1997: *The Impact of Public Job Placing Programmes*. London: PSI.

Pugh, D. S. and Hickson, D. J. 1976: *Organizational Structure in its Context*. Farnborough: Saxon House.

Purcell, J. 1989: 'The Impact of Corporate Strategy on HRM', in Storey, J. (ed.), *New Perspectives on Human Resource Management*. London: Routledge.

Purcell, K. 1984: 'Militancy and Acquiescence among Women Workers', in Siltanen, J. and Stanworth, M. (eds), *Women and the Public Sphere: a Critique of Sociology and Politics*. London: Hutchinson.

Purvis, A. 2004: 'Loaded! Why Supermarkets are Getting Richer and Richer', <http://observer.guardian.co.uk/foodmonthly/story/0,9950,1127912,00.html>.

Radford, J. 1993: 'Minister Aims to Crack Gender "Glass Ceiling" in the Sciences', *Guardian*, 4 March.

Radice, H. 1995: 'Global Myths and Realities', *Centre for Industrial Policy and Performance Bulletin*, no. 8, pp. 1–3.

Radin, B. 1966: 'Coloured Workers and British Trade Unions', *Race*, vol. 8, no. 2.

Rainnie, A. 1989: *Industrial Relations in Small Firms: Small Isn't Beautiful.* London: Routledge.

Ram, M. and Jones, T. 1998: *Ethnic Minorities in Business.* Milton Keynes: Open University Business School.

Ramazanoglou, C. 1989: *Feminism and the Contradictions of Oppression.* London: Routledge.

Ramesh, R. 2004: 'Cheap Phone Service Comes at a Price', *Guardian*, 6 February.

Randall, A. 1988: 'The Industrial Moral Economy of the Gloucestershire Weavers in the Eighteenth Century', in Rule, J. (ed.), *British Trade Unionism 1750–1850.* London: Longman.

Randall, V. 1988: 'In Whose Interest?', *Times Higher Education Supplement*, 12 August.

Rattansi, A. 1981: *Marx and the Division of Labour.* London: Macmillan.

Rattansi, A. 1982: 'Marx and the Abolition of the Division of Labour', in Giddens, A. and Mackenzie, G. (eds), *Social Class and the Division of Labour.* Cambridge: Cambridge University Press.

Ray, L. 1987: 'The Protestant Ethic Debate', in Anderson, R. J., Hughes, J. A. and Sharrock, W. W. (eds), *Classic Disputes in Sociology.* London: Allen & Unwin.

Redding, D. and Leydon, W. 1990: *Guardian*, 7 June.

Reddy, W. 1985: *The Rise of Market Culture.* Cambridge: Cambridge University Press.

Reed, M. 1985: *Redirections in Organizational Analysis.* London: Tavistock.

Reed, M. 1989: *The Sociology of Management.* Brighton: Harvester.

Reed, M. and Hughes, M. 1992: *Rethinking Organization.* London: Sage.

Rees, A. 1966: 'Information Networks in Labor Markets', *American Economic Review*, vol. 56, pp. 559–66.

Rees, B. A. 2003: *The Construction of Management: Competence and Gender Issues at Work.* London: Edward Elgar.

Reeves, R. 2000a: 'Working Late', *Guardian*, 4 April.

Reeves, R. 2000b: 'No More Nine to Five', *Observer Magazine*, 23 July.

Reeves, R. 2001a: 'The Way We Work', *Guardian*, 6 March.

Reeves, R. 2001b: 'The Way We Work', *Guardian*, 5 May.

Reeves, R. 2001c: *Happy Mondays: Putting the Pleasure Back into Work.* Harlow: Momentum.

Reich, R. B. 1983: *The Next American Frontier.* New York: Times Books.

Reich, R. 1993: *The Work of Nations.* London: Simon and Schuster.

Reich, R. 1997: 'New Deal and Fair Deal', *Guardian*, 14 July.

Reid, I. 1986: *The Sociology of School and Education.* London: Fontana.

Reid, R. 1986: *Land of Lost Content.* London: Cardinal.

Rex, J. 1970: *Race Relations in Sociological Theory.* London: Weidenfeld & Nicolson.

Rex, J. 1986: *Race and Ethnicity.* Milton Keynes: Open University Press.

Rex, J. and Tomlinson, S. 1979: *Colonial Immigrants in a British City: a Class Analysis.* London: Routledge.

Ricardo, D. 1951: *The Principles of Political Economy and Taxation.* Cambridge: Cambridge University Press.

Rice, A. K. 1958: *Productivity and Social Organization*. London: Tavistock.

Rice, A. K. 1963: *The Enterprise and its Environment*. London: Tavistock.

Riddell, M. 2001: 'All Work and No Play . . .', *Observer*, 1 July.

Rifkin, J. 1995: 'The End of Work?', *New Statesman and Society*, 9 June.

Rifkin, J. 1996: *The End of Work*. New York: Putnam Books.

Rimmer, M. 1972: *Race and Industrial Conflict*. London: Heinemann.

Ritzer, G. 1993: *The McDonaldization of Society*. New York: Pine Forge Press.

Ritzer, G. 1997: 'McJobs: McDonaldization and its Relationship to the Labour Process', in Ritzer, G. (ed.), *The McDonaldization Thesis*. London: Sage (2nd edn 2004).

Roberts, C. 1985: 'Research on Women in the Labour Market: the Context and Scope of the Women and Employment Survey', in Roberts, B., Finnegan, R. and Gallie, D. (eds), *New Approaches to Economic Life*. Manchester: Manchester University Press.

Roberts, D. 1979: *Paternalism in Early Victorian England*. London: Croom Helm.

Roberts, E. 1982: 'Working Wives and their Families', in Barker, T. and Drake, M. (eds), *Population and Society in Britain 1850–1980*. London: Batsford.

Roberts, M. 1979: 'Sickles and Scythes', *History Workshop Journal*, no. 7, pp. 3–28.

Roberts, Y. 2001: 'From Sex War to Sex Law', *Guardian*, 16 January.

Robertson, R. 1992: *Globalization, Social Theory and Global Culture*. London: Sage.

Robey, D. 1977: 'Computers and Management Structures: Some Empirical Findings Re-examined', *Human Relations*, vol. 30, pp. 963–76.

Robins, K. 1996: 'Globalization', in Kuper, A. and Kuper, J. (eds), *The Social Science Encyclopaedia*. London: Routledge.

Robins, K. and Webster, F. 1989: *The Technical Fix*. London: Macmillan.

Robinson, D. and Conboy, W. M. 1970: 'Wage Structures and Internal Labour Markets', in Robinson, D. (ed.), *Local Labour Markets and Wage Structures*. London: Gower.

Robinson Financial Corporation. 2001: *Labour Productivity Benchmarks and International Gap Analysis*. Icon Group Ltd.

Robinson, J. 1934: *The Economics of Imperfect Competition*. London: Macmillan.

Robinson, J. 2002: *Pandora's Daughters: The Secret History of Independent Women*. London: Constable.

Robson, M. 1982: *Quality Circles: a Practical Guide*. Aldershot: Gower.

Roche, W. 1983: 'Status, Economism and Wage Practices: Fox's Theory of Trust Dynamics', paper read to Nuffield College Industrial Sociology Workshop, 8 November.

Roche, W. K. 1986: 'Systems Analysis and Industrial Relations', *Economic and Industrial Democracy*, vol. 7, no. 3, pp. 3–28.

Roddick, A. 2003: 'The Price of Dignity', *Guardian*, 22 September.

Roderick, G. and Stephens, M. (eds), 1981: *Where Did We Go Wrong?* Brighton: Falmer Press.

Rodger, N. A. M. 1986: *The Wooden World: an Anatomy of the Georgian Navy*. London: Fontana.

Rodrik, D. 1997: 'Has Globalization Gone Too Far?', *Californian Management Review*, vol. 39, no. 3, pp. 29–53.

Roemer, J. (ed.), 1986: *Analytic Marxism*. Cambridge: Cambridge University Press.

Roethlisberger, F. J. and Dickson, W. J. 1939: *Management and the Worker*. Cambridge, Mass.: Harvard University Press.

Rogers, B. 1988: *Men Only*. London: Pandora.

Rose, H. 1986: 'Women's Work: Women's Knowledge', in Mitchell, J. and Oakley, A. (eds), *What is Feminism?* Oxford: Blackwell.

Rose, H., McLoughlin, I., King, R., Clark, J. 1986: 'Opening the Black Box: the Relation between Technology and Work', *New Technology, Work and Employment*, vol. 1, no. 1, pp. 18–26.

Rose, H. and Rose, S. (eds), 2000: *Alas, Poor Darwin: Arguments Against Evolutionary Psychology*. London: Jonathan Cape.

Rose, M. 1975: *Industrial Behaviour: Theoretical Developments since Taylor*. London: Allen Lane.

Rose, M. and Jones, R. 1985: 'Managerial Strategy and Trade Union Responses in Work Reorganization Schemes at Establishment Level', in Knights, D., Willmott, H. and Collinson, D. (eds), *Job Redesign: Critical Perspectives on the Labour Process*. Aldershot: Gower.

Rose, N. 1989: *The Productive Subject*. London: Routledge.

Rose, N. 1990: *Governing the Soul*. London: Routledge.

Rose, R. 1983: *Getting by in Three Economies*. Glasgow: Centre for the Study of Public Policy.

Rosenau, J. 1990: *Turbulence in World Politics*. Brighton: Harvester Wheatsheaf.

Rosenberg, H. 1986: *Surviving in the City*. Toronto: Oxfam.

Rosener, J. B. 1995: *America's Competitive Secret: Utilizing Women as a Management Strategy*. Oxford: Oxford University Press.

Ross, A. M. and Hartmann, P. T. 1960: *Changing Patterns of Industrial Conflict*. New York: Wiley.

Ross, K. 2000: *Women at the Top*. London: Hansard.

Routh, G. 1980: *Occupations and Pay in Great Britain 1906–1979*. London: Macmillan.

Rowbotham, S. 1997: *A Century of Women: the History of Women in Britain and the US*. London: Viking.

Roy, D. 1954: 'Efficiency and the Fix', *American Journal of Sociology*, vol. 60, pp. 427–42.

Roy, D. 1973: 'Banana Time', in Salaman, G. and Thompson, K. (eds), *People and Organizations*. London: Longman.

Rubery, J. 1980: 'Structured Labour Markets, Worker Organization and Low Pay', in Amsden, A. (ed.), *The Economics of Women and Work*. Harmondsworth: Penguin.

Rubinstein, M. 1989: 'Preventing Sexual Harassment at Work', *Industrial Relations Journal*, vol. 20, no. 3, pp. 226–36.

Rubinstein, W. D. 1988: *Elites and Wealthy in Modern British History*. Brighton: Harvester.

Rueschemeyer, D. 1986: *Power and the Division of Labour*. Cambridge: Polity.

Rugman, A. 2000: *The End of Globalization: What it Means for Business*. London: Random House.

Rule, J. 1987: 'The Property of Skill' in Joyce, P. (ed.), *The Historical Meanings of Work*. Cambridge: Cambridge University Press.

Rule, J. 1988: 'The Formative Years of British Trade Unionism', in Rule, J. (ed.), *British Trade Unionism 1750–1850*. London: Longman.

Runciman, W. G. 1966: *Relative Deprivation and Social Justice: A Study of Attitudes to Social Inequality in Twentieth-Century England*. London: Routledge and Kegan Paul.

Rushdie, S. 1988: *Observer*, 24 July.

Russell, B. 1984: 'In Praise of Idleness', in Richards, V. (ed.), *Why Work?* London: Freedom Press.

Russell, G. 1983: *The Changing Role of Fathers*. Milton Keynes: Open University Press.

Russell, M. 2001: 'Quotas are Good for Democracy', *Guardian*, 5 July.

Rustow, D. A. 1970: 'How Does a Democracy Come into Existence?', *Comparative Politics*, no. 2.

Ryan, M. and Haslam, A. 2004: 'Introducing . . . the Glass Cliff', at <http://news.bbc.co.uk/2/hi/uk_news/magazine/3755031.stm>.

Sabel, C. F. 1982: *Work and Politics: the Division of Labour in Industry*. Cambridge: Cambridge University Press.

Sahlins, M. 1972: *Stone Age Economics*. London: Tavistock.

Saint-Simon, H. 1964: *Social Organization, the Science of Man, and Other Writings*, ed. Markham, F. New York: Harper Torch Books.

Salaman, G. 1979: *Work Organizations, Resistance and Control*. London: Longman.

Salaman, G. 1984: *Working*. London: Ellis Horwood/Tavistock.

Salamon, M. 1987: *Industrial Relations: Theory and Practice*. London: Prentice Hall International.

Salway, P. 1981: *Roman Britain*. Oxford: Clarendon.

Samuel, R. 1983a: 'The Middle Class between the Wars: Part One', *New Socialist*, January–February.

Samuel, R. 1983b: 'The Middle Class between the Wars: Part Two', *New Socialist*, March–April.

Sanders, C. 2001: 'Cambridge is Worth 170 Guildhalls', *Times Higher Educational Supplement*, 20 July.

Sanderson, G. and Stapenhurst, F. (eds), 1979: *Industrial Democracy Today*. New York: McGraw-Hill.

Saunders, B. 2000: 'Working and Watching Hard', *Guardian*, 29 May.

Saunders, B. 2001: 'Don't Ask the Experts', *Guardian*, 29 January.

Saville, J. 1973: 'The Ideology of Labourism', in Benewick, R., Berki, R. N. and Parekh, B. (eds), *Knowledge and Belief in Politics*. London: Allen & Unwin.

Sayers, S. 1988: 'The Need to Work', in Pahl, R. (ed.), *On Work*. Oxford: Blackwell.

Scase, R. 2001: 'Tricks in Clicks and Mortar', *Observer Business*, 18 February.

Schor, J. B. 1992: *The Overworked American: The Unexpected Decline of Leisure*, New York: Basic Books.

Schumpeter, J. A. 1976: *Capitalism, Socialism and Democracy*. London: George Allen & Unwin.

Schwartz, F. N. 1989: 'Management Women and the New Facts of Life', *Harvard Business Review*, January–February.

Schwimmer, E. 1979: 'The Self and the Product', in Wallman, S. (ed.), *Social Anthropology of Work*. London: Academic Press.

Scott, J. 1979: *Corporations, Classes and Capitalism*. London: Macmillan.

Scott, J. F. and Homans, G. C. 1947: 'Reflections on the Wildcat Strikes', *American Sociological Review*, vol. 12, pp. 278–87.

Scott, W. R. and Meyer, J. W. 1994: *Institutional Environments and Organizations*. London: Sage.

Searle-Chatterjee, M. 1979: 'The Polluted Identity of Work: a Study of Benares Sweepers', in Wallman, S. (ed.), *Social Anthropology of Work*. Cambridge: Cambridge University Press.

Seccombe, W. 1974: 'The Housewife and her Labour under Capitalism', *New Left Review*, no. 83, pp. 3–24.

Seccombe, W. 1975: 'Domestic Labour: Reply to Critics', *New Left Review*, no. 94, pp. 84–96.

Seddon, V. 1983: 'Keeping Women in their Place', *Marxism Today*, July.

Segal, R. 1995: *The Black Diaspora*. London: Faber and Faber.

Segalen, M. 1983: *Love and Power in the Peasant Family*. Oxford: Blackwell.

Seglow, P. 1983: 'Organizational Survival as an Act of Faith: the Case of the BBC', in Thurley, K. and Wood, S. (eds), *Industrial Relations and Management Strategy*. Cambridge: Cambridge University Press.

Selbourne, D. 1985: *Against Socialist Illusion*. London: Macmillan.

Sennett, R. and Cobb, J. 1977: *The Hidden Injuries of Class*. Cambridge: Cambridge University Press.

Sharpe, S. 1976: *Just like a Girl*. London: Penguin.

Sharrock, W. and Anderson, B. 1986: *The Ethnomethodologists*. London: Tavistock.

Sheldrake, J. 1996: *Management Theory*. London: International Thomson Business Press.

Sheridan, A. 1980: *Michel Foucault: the Will to Power*. London: Tavistock.

Shields, A. 1986: *On the Battle Lines 1919–1939*. New York: International Publishers.

Shoard, M. 1987: 'Pursuit of the Gentry', *Times Higher Education Supplement*, 7 July.

Shorter, E. and Tilly, C. 1974: *Strikes in France 1830–1968*. Cambridge: Cambridge University Press.

Sianne, G. and Wilkinson, H. 1995: *Gender, Feminism and the Future*. London: Demos.

Sievers, B. 1984: 'Motivation as a Surrogate for Meaning', Arbeitspapiere des Fachbereichs Wirtschaftswissenschaft, no. 81. Wuppertal Bergische Universität. Quoted in Alvesson, M. 1987: *Organization Theory and Technocratic Consciousness*. Berlin: De Gruyter.

Sikka, P. 2002: 'We Are a Nation of Accountants', *Guardian*, 20 February.

Silver, M. 1973: 'Recent British Strike Trends: a Factual Analysis', *British Journal of Industrial Relations*, vol. 11, pp. 66–104.

Silverman, D. 1970: *The Theory of Organizations*. London: Heinemann.

Simmel, G. 1971: 'The Metropolis and Mental Life', in Thompson, K. and Tunstall, J. (eds), *Sociological Perspectives*. Harmondsworth: Penguin.

Sinfield, A. 1981: *What Unemployment Means*. Oxford: Martin Robertson.

Sinfield, A. 1985: 'Being out of Work', in Littler, C. R. (ed.), *The Experience of Work*. Aldershot: Gower.

Singh, A. 1994: 'Global Economic Changes, Skills and International Competitiveness', *International Labour Review*, vol. 133, no. 2, pp. 167–83.

Sirianni, C. 1982: *Workers' Control and Socialist Democracy: the Soviet Experience*. London: Verso.

Sisson, K. 1975: *Industrial Relations in Fleet Street*. Oxford: Blackwell.

Sivanandan, A. 1982: *A Different Hunger: Writings on Black Resistance*. London: Pluto.

Skapinker, M. 2003: 'CEOs Pay Price for Poor Performance', *Financial Times*, 12 May.

Skeels, J. W. 1971: 'Measures of US Strike Activity', *Industrial and Labour Relation Review*, vol. 24, pp. 515–25.

Sklair, L. 1991: *Sociology of the Global System*. Brighton: Harvester Wheatsheaf.

Sloan, A. P. 1965: *My Years with General Motors*. London: Sidgwick & Jackson.

Sloan, P .J. (ed.), 1980: *Women and Low Pay*. London: Macmillan.

Sloan, R. P., Gruman, J. C. and Allegrante, J. P. 1987: *Investing in Employee Healthcare: a Guide to Effective Health Promotion in the Workplace*. San Francisco: Jossey Bass.

Smith, A. D. 1997: 'Nations and Ethnoscapes', *Oxford International Review*, vol. 8, no. 2, pp. 11–18.

Smith, C. 1987: *Technical Workers: Class, Labour and Trade Unionism*. London: Macmillan.

Smith, C. 1989: 'Flexible Specialization, Automation and Mass Production', *Work, Employment and Society*, vol. 3, no. 2, pp. 203–20.

Smith, C., Child, J. and Rowlinson, M. 1989: *Innovation in Work Organization: Cadbury Ltd. 1900–1985*. Cambridge: Cambridge University Press.

Smith, D. 1997: 'Job Insecurity and Other Myths', *Management Today*, May, pp. 39–41.

Smith, D. J. 1974: *Racial Disadvantage in Employment*. London: Political and Economic Policy/Social Science Institute.

Smith, D. J. 1977: *Racial Disadvantage in Britain: the PEP Report*. Harmondsworth: Penguin.

Smith, D. J. 1981: *Unemployment and Racial Minorities*. London: Policy Studies Institute.

Smith, H. L. 1984: 'The Womenpower Problem in Britain during the Second World War', *The Historical Journal*, vol. 27, no. 4, pp. 925–45.

Smith, J. H. 1987: 'Elton Mayo and the Hidden Hawthorne', *Work, Employment and Society*, vol. 1, no. 1, pp. 107–20.

Smith, S. 1981: 'Craft Consciousness and Class Consciousness', *History Workshop*, no. 11, pp. 33–56.

Smith, S. 1988: *Observer*, 20 March.

Smithers, R. 2000: 'Firms say 2M not up to the Job', *Guardian*, 27 June.

Smithers, R. 2001: 'Wired for Co-operation', *Guardian Education*, 12 June.

Smithers, R. 2004: 'More Women Move into Academia Despite the Glass Ceiling', *Guardian*, 1 October.

Snell, K. D. M. 1985: *Annals of the Labouring Poor: Social Change and Agrarian England 1660–1900*. Cambridge: Cambridge University Press.

Snooks, G. 1996: *The Dynamic Society*. London: Routledge.

Snowden, F. M. 1983: *Before Colour Prejudice: the Ancient View of Blacks*. Cambridge, Mass.: Harvard University Press.

Social Trends. 1986. 1988. 1989. 1990. 1997. London: HMSO.

Solomos, J. 1989: *Race and Racism in Contemporary Britain*. London: Macmillan.

Sonenscher, M. 1989: *Work and Wages: Natural Law, Politics and the Eighteenth Century French Trades*. Cambridge: Cambridge University Press.

Sousa, E. de 1988: *The Firms that Like to Say No!* Birmingham: BTURC Publishing.

Spence, R. 2000: 'Truth Behind the Window Dressing', *Guardian*, 25 November.

Spencer, A. and Podmore, D. 1986: *In a Man's World: Essays on Women in Male Dominated Professions*. London: Tavistock.

Spencer, S. (ed.), 2003: *The Politics of Migration*. Oxford: Blackwell.

Spretnak, C. and Capra, F. 1985: *Green Politics: the Global Promise*. London: Paladin.

Spriano, D. 1975: *The Occupation of the Factories: Italy 1920*. London: Pluto.

Stalker, P. 1986: 'Street Wise', *New Internationalist*, December.

Standing, G. 1997: 'Globalization, Labour Flexibility and Insecurity: the Era of Market Regulation', *European Journal of Industrial Relations*, vol. 3, no. 1, pp. 7–37.

Stanworth, M. 1984: 'Women and Class Analysis: a Reply to John Goldthorpe', *Sociology*, vol. 18, no. 2, pp. 159–70.

Stark, T. 1988: *Income and Wealth in the 1980's*. London: Fabian Society Papers.

Stead, J. 1987: *Never the Same Again: Women and the Miners' Strike*. London: Women's Press.

Stearns, P. 1993: *The Industrial Revolution in World History*. Oxford: West View Press.

Steingard, D. S. and Fitzgibbons, D. E. 1997: 'Challenging the Juggernaut of Globalization: a Manifesto for Academic Praxis', Internet paper on <http://weatherhead.cwru.edu/amjdc/papers/85.html>.

Stevenson, J. 1984: *British Society 1914–45*. Harmondsworth: Pelican.

Stewart, H. 2001a: 'Why it Pays for Hank to Chain Himself to a Desk', *Guardian*, 18 June.

Stewart, H. 2001b: 'Migration May Be Moving off the Hush-Hush List', *Guardian*, 25 June.

Stewart, M. L. 1989: *Women, Work and the French State*. Montreal. McGill-Queens University Press.

Stewart, S. 1993: *Ramlin Rose*. Oxford: Oxford University Press.

Stiglitz, J. E. 2003: *Globalization and its Discontents*. London: Penguin.

Stinchcombe, A. L. 1965: 'Social Structure and Organizations', in March, J. G. (ed.), *Hand Book of Organizations*. Chicago: McNally.

Stone, K. 1974: 'The Origin of the Structures in the Steel Industry', in Edwards, R., Reich, M. and Gordon, D. (eds), *Labor Market Segmentation*. Lexington, Mass.: D. C. Heath.

Storey, J. 1992: *Developments in the Management of Human Resources*. Oxford: Blackwell.

Strauss, A., Murray, D. J. and Potter, D. C. 1963: 'The Hospital and its Negotiated Order', in Freidson, E. (ed.), *The Hospital in Modern Society*. New York: Free Press.

Streek, W. 1987: 'The Uncertainties of Management in the Management of Uncertainty', *Work, Employment and Society*, vol. 1, no. 3, pp. 281–308.

Stringer, C. and McKie, R. 1997: *African Exodus*. London: Pimlico.

Stuart, L. 1998: 'Women are Still Not Welcome to the Club', *Guardian*, 7 November.

Stuart, L. 2001: 'Change the World with Your Shopping Trolley', *Guardian Jobs and Money*, 23 June.

Stuart, L. 2004: 'Monthly Cheques Home from Migrant Workers are Building Prosperity', *Guardian*, 12 April.

Sum, A., Fogg, N. and Harrington, P. 2003: *Immigrant Workers and the Great American Job Machine*, Washington, DC: Diane Publishers Co.

Summerfield, P. 1985: *Women Workers in the Second World War: Production and Patriarchy in Conflict*. London: Croom Helm.

Summerskill, B. 2000: 'One in Four Britons Now Work Nights', *Guardian*, 10 September.

Sweezy, P. M. 1942: *The Theory of Capitalist Development*. New York: Monthly Review Press.

Sykes, R. 1988: 'Trade Unions and Class Consciousness: the Revolutionary Period of General Unionism, 1829–1834', in Rule, J. (ed.), *British Trade Unionism 1750–1850*. London: Longman.

Taylor, A. J. 1972: *Laissez Faire and State Intervention in Nineteenth Century Britain*. London: Macmillan.

Taylor, C. 1979: *Hegel and Modern Society*. Cambridge: Cambridge University Press.

Taylor, D. 1988: 'Life Sentence: the Politics of Housework', *New Internationalist*, March.

Taylor, F. W. 1903: 'Shop Management', reprinted in Taylor, F. W. 1964: *Scientific Management*. New York: Harper & Row.

Taylor, F. W. 1911: *The Principles of Scientific Management*. New York: Harper & Row.

Taylor, R. 1982: *Workers and the New Depression*. London: Macmillan.

Taylor, S. 1998: 'Emotional Labour and the New Workplace', in Thompson, P. and Warhurst, C. (eds), *Workplaces of the Future*. Basingstoke: Macmillan.

Thayer, C. 1987: 'Retraining Women', *Health Service Journal*, 5 February.

Therborn, G. 1977: 'The Rule of Capital and the Rise of Democracy', *New Left Review*, 103.

Therborn, G. 1986: *Why Some People are More Unemployed than Others*. London: Verso.

THES (*Times Higher Education Supplement*), 1996: 'Women Storm Male Citadel', 4 October.

Thomas, D. N. 1984: *White Bolts, Black Locks: Participation in the Inner City*. London: Allen & Unwin.

Thomas, K. 1997: 'So, if it's Software you Want, then Send to India', *Guardian*, 1 March.

Thomas, R. 2003: ' "Showbiz" Beckham Tops Earners' League', *Guardian*, 7 May.

Thompson, E. P. 1968: *The Making of the English Working Class*. Harmondsworth: Penguin.

Thompson, E. P. 1971: 'The Moral Economy of the English Crowd in the Eighteenth Century', *Past and Present*, vol. 50, pp. 76–136.

Thompson, E. P. 1982: 'Time, Work Discipline and Industrial Capitalism', in Giddens, A. and Held, D. (eds), *Classes, Power and Conflict*. London: Macmillan.

Thompson, F. 1973: *Lark Rise to Candleford*. Harmondsworth: Penguin.

Thompson, G. 1984: 'Economic Intervention in the Post-war Economy', in Mclennan, G., Held, D. and Hall, S. (eds), *State and Society in Contemporary Britain: a Critical Introduction*. Cambridge: Polity.

Thompson, J. D. 1977: *Organizations in Action*. New York: McGraw-Hill.

Thompson, K. 1982: *Émile Durkheim*. London: Tavistock.

Thompson, K. 1988: *Under Siege: Racism and Violence in Britain*. Harmondsworth: Penguin.

Thompson, P. 1984: *The Nature of Work: an Introduction to Debates on the Labour Process*. London: Macmillan.

Thompson, P. and Warhurst, C. (eds), 1998: *Workplaces of the Future*. Basingstoke: Macmillan.

Thompson, T. 2004: 'UK Gangmasters Control 100,000 "Slave" Labourers', *Observer*, 15 February.

Thorsrud, E., Sorenson, B. A. and Gustavsen, B. 1976: 'Sociotechnical Approaches to Industrial Democracy in Norway', in Dubin, R. (ed.), *Handbook of Work, Organization and Society*. Chicago: Rand McNally.

Tibbett, S. 2001: 'Curbing the Abuses of Global Capitalism', *Observer*, 8 July.

Toffler, A. 1980: *The Third Wave*. London: Collins.

Tomlinson, J. 1982: *The Unequal Struggle: British Socialism and the Capitalist Enterprise*. London: Methuen.

Tönnies, F. 1955: *Community and Society*. London: Routledge. German original, 1897.

Toynbee, P. 2001: 'Bullying Bosses', *Guardian*, 23 March.

Toynbee, P. 2003a: 'Starve the Fat Cats', *Guardian*, 16 May.

Toynbee, P. 2003b: 'Daylight Snobbery', *Guardian*, 10 October.

Toynbee, P. 2003c: *Hard Work: Life in Low Wage Britain*. London: Bloomsbury.

Trades Union Congress. 1983a: *Race Relations at Work*. London: TUC.

Trades Union Congress. 1983b: *TUC Workbook on Racism*. London: TUC.

Trades Union Congress. 1986: *Statistical Statement and List of Delegates.* London: TUC.

Tranter, N. L. 1973: *Population since the Industrial Revolution.* London: Croom Helm.

Traub, R. 1978: 'Lenin and Taylor: the Fate of "Scientific Management" in the early Soviet Union', *Telos*, vol. 37, pp. 82–92.

Travis, A. 1997: 'Blacks Losing Out in Blair's New Britain', *Guardian*, 22 July.

Treanor, J. 2000: 'Barclays Closes 172 Branches', *Guardian*, 6 April.

Treanor, J. 2001: ' "Mr Vodafone" Under Fire', *Guardian*, 10 July.

Treas, J. 1987: 'The Effect of Women's Labour Force Participation on the Distribution of Income in the United States', *Annual Review of Sociology*, vol. 13, pp. 259–88.

Trist, E. L. and Bamforth, K. W. 1951: 'Some Social and Psychological Consequences of the Longwall Method of Coal Getting', *Human Relations*, vol. 4, no. 1, pp. 3–38.

Truman, C. and Keating, J. 1988: 'Technology, Markets and the Design of Women's Jobs', *New Technology, Work and Employment*, vol. 3, no. 1, pp. 21–9.

Turnbull, P. J. 1988: 'Leaner and Possibly Fitter: the Management of Redundancy in Britain', *Industrial Relations Journal*, vol. 19, no. 3, pp. 201–13.

Turner, B. S. 1986: *Citizenship and Capitalism: the Debate over Reformism.* London: Allen & Unwin.

Turner, D. 2002: 'Equality Watchdog Attacks Fire Service Policies on Women', *Financial Times*, 30 October.

Turner, H. A. 1962: *Trade Union Growth, Structure and Policy: a Comparative Study of the Cotton Unions.* London: Allen & Unwin.

Turner, H. A. 1963: *The Trend of Strikes.* Leeds: Leeds University Press.

Turner, H. A. 1969: *Is Britain Really Strike Prone?* London: Cambridge University Press.

TURU (Trade Union Research Unit), 1986: *Women and Trade Unions*, Technical Note no. 100. Oxford: Ruskin College.

Tusa, J. 1997: 'The Agony and the Ecstasy', *Guardian*, 19 July.

Tysome, T. 2004: 'Youth Drool at Cool', *Times Higher Education Supplement*, 30 January.

UNCTAD (United Nations Conference on Trade and Development), 1995: *Recent Trends in International Investment and Transnational Corporations.* Geneva: UN.

United Nations, 1995: *The Human Development Report.* Oxford: Oxford University Press.

United Nations, 1997: *The Human Development Report.* Oxford: Oxford University Press.

Vanek, J. 1974: 'Time spent in Housework', *Scientific American*, November.

Van Reenan, J. 2000: 'Technological Change and the Labour Market'. Paper read at 'The Future of Work' Conference, 1 June, Templeton College, Oxford University.

Vasager, J. 2001: 'Men Still Leave the Housework to Women', *Guardian*, 6 July.

Veblen, T. 1899: *The Theory of the Leisure Class.* London: Macmillan.

Veblen, T. 1904: *The Theory of Business Enterprise*. New York: Viking Press.

Veblen, T. 1921: *The Engineers and the Price System*. New York: Viking Press.

Vidal, J. 1996: 'Be Very Afraid', *Guardian*, 29 May.

Vidal, J. 2001: 'When Disaster Strikes', *Guardian*, 9 July.

Vinnicombe, S. and Singh, V. 2003: *Women Pass A Milestone: 101 Directorships on the FTSE 100 Boards*. Available at <http://www.som.cranfield.ac.uk/som/research/centres/cdwbl/projects.asp>.

Virdee, S. 1990: 'Trade Unions and Racism: the Case of Independent Black Caucuses', Unpublished Master's Thesis, Brunel University.

Virdee, S. 1995: *Racial Violence and Harassment*. London: PSI.

Virdee, S. and Grint, K. 1994: 'Black Self-organization in Trade Unions', *Sociological Review*, vol. 42, no. 2, pp. 202–25.

Wainwright, M. 1998: 'Delia Causes a Stir', *Guardian*, 6 November.

Wajcman, J. 1983: *Women in Control: Dilemmas of a Workers' Cooperative*. Milton Keynes: Open University Press.

Walby, S. 1986a: *Patriarchy at Work: Patriarchal and Capitalist Relations in Employment*. Cambridge: Polity.

Walby, S. 1986b: 'Gender, Class and Stratification', in Crompton, R. and Mann, M. (eds), *Gender and Stratification*. Cambridge: Polity.

Walby, S. 1988: 'Gender Politics and Social Theory', *Sociology*, vol. 22, no. 2, pp. 215–32.

Walby, S. 1989: 'Flexibility and the Changing Sexual Division of Labour', in Wood, S. (ed.), *The Transformation of Work?* London: Unwin Hyman.

Walby, S. 1990: *Theorizing Patriarchy*. Oxford: Blackwell.

Waldinger, R. 1985: 'Immigrant Enterprise and the Structure of the Labour Market', in Roberts, B., Finnegan, R. and Gailie, D. (eds), *New Perspectives on Economic Life*. Manchester: Manchester University Press.

Walker, C. R. and Guest, R. H. 1952: *The Man on the Assembly Line*. Cambridge, Mass.: Harvard University Press.

Walker, C. R., Guest, R. H. and Turner, A. N. 1956: *The Foreman on the Assembly Line*. Cambridge, Mass.: Harvard University Press.

Walker, D. 2001: 'Global's Good Side', *Guardian*, 2 May.

Walker, K. E. and Woods, M. 1976: *Time Use: a Measure of Household Production of Family Goods and Services*. New York: American Home Economics Association.

Walker, M. 1989: *Guardian*, 14 June.

Walker, M. 1995: 'All the King's Men', *Guardian*, 16 January.

Walker, M. 1997: 'God Bless (White) America', *Guardian*, 17 May.

Wallace, A. 1978: *Rockdale: the Growth of an American Village in the Early Industrial Revolution*. New York: Knopf.

Wallace, J. 1997: *Overdrive: Bill Gates and the Race to Control Cyberspace*. London: Wiley.

Wallerstein, I. 1974: *The Modern World System*. New York: Academic Press.

Wallerstein, I. 1979: *The Capitalist World Economy*. Cambridge: Cambridge University Press.

Wallerstein, I. 1983: *Historical Capitalism*. London: Verso.

Wallman, S. (ed.), 1979: *Social Anthropology of Work*. Cambridge: Cambridge University Press.

Walsh, C. 2002: 'Corporate Meltdown Finally Ends Supremos' Licence to Print Money', *Observer Business*, 24 November.

Walsh, N. P. 2003: 'Child Cotton Slaves of an Asian Tyranny', *Observer*, 18 May.

Walsh, N. P. 2004: 'City Pays Women 43 per cent less than Men', *Observer Business*, 25 January.

Ward, D. and Beavis, S. 1996: 'Bosses Quash Pay Revolt', *Guardian*, 27 July.

Ward, L. 2001: 'Record Income Gap Between Rich and Poor', *Guardian*, 18 April.

Ward, L. 2004: 'Barriers to Girls in "Male" Jobs must go, says Report', *Guardian*, 6 May.

Ward, R. 1978: 'Race Relations in Britain', *British Journal of Sociology*, vol. 29, no. 4.

Ward, R. 1985: 'Minority Settlement and the Local Economy', in Roberts, B., Finnegan, R. and Gallie, D. (eds), *New Perspectives on Economic Life*. Manchester: Manchester University Press.

Ward, T. (ed.), 1970: *The Factory System*, 2 vols. Newton Abott: David & Charles.

Warhurst, J. 1994: *Environmental Degradation from Mining and Mineral Processing in 'Developing' Countries*. Paris: OECD.

Warner, J. 2003: 'Wild Women', *BBC History Magazine*, vol. 4, no. 10, pp. 13–15.

Warner, W. L. and Low, J. O. 1947: *The Social System of the Modern Factory*. New Haven, Conn.: Yale University Press.

Warr, P. 1983: 'Work and Unemployment', in Drenth, P. J. D., Thierry, H., Willems, D. J. and de Wolff, C. J. (eds), *Handbook of Work and Organizational Psychology*. London: John Wiley.

Warr, P. B. 1987: *Work, Unemployment and Mental Health*. Oxford: Clarendon.

WASH. 1987: 'Women Against Sexual Harassment'. London: WASH.

Watson, T. J. 1986: *Management, Organization and Employment Strategy*. London: Routledge.

Watts, I. 1984: 'Industrial Radicalism and the Domestic Division of Labour', in Siltanen, J. and Stanworth, M. (eds), *Women and the Public Sphere*. London: Hutchinson.

Watts, J. 2003: 'Go East or Go Bust', *Guardian*, 19 November.

Webb, S. and Webb, B. 1919: *The History of Trade Unionism, 1666–1920*. London: Webb & Webb.

Webb, S. and Webb, B. 1920: *Industrial Democracy*. London: Longman.

Weber, M. 1948: *From Max Weber*, ed. Gerth. H. H. and Mills, C. W. London: Routledge.

Weber, M. 1976: *The Protestant Ethic and the Spirit of Capitalism*. London: Allen & Unwin.

Weber, M. 1978: *Economy and Society*. Berkeley: University of California Press.

Webster, J. 1990: *Office Automation: the Labour Process and Women's Work in Britain*. London: Harvester Wheatsheaf.

Wennerås, C. and Wold, A. 1997: 'Nepotism and Sexism in Peer-Review', *Nature*, vol. 387, pp. 341–3.

Westwood, R. and Clegg, S. 2003: *Debating Organizations*. Oxford: Blackwell.

Westwood, S. and Bhachu, P. (eds), 1989: *Enterprising Women: Ethnicity, Economy and Gender Relations*. London: Routledge.

Whipp, R. 1987: 'A Time to Every Purpose: an Essay on Time and Work', in Joyce, P. (ed.), *The Historical Meanings of Work*. Cambridge: Cambridge University Press.

Whipp, R. and Grieco, M. 1983: 'Family and Workplace: the Social Organization of Work', paper given at the SSRC workshop on 'Work Organization', July.

White, M. 1983: *Long Term Unemployment and Labour Markets*. London: Policy Studies Institute.

Whitebloom, S. 1995: 'Computers May Wipe Out 50pc of Bank Branches', *Guardian*, 9 June.

Whitley, R. D. 1990: 'The Social Construction of Business Systems in East Asia', *Organization Studies*, vol. 12, no. 1, pp. 1–28.

Wiener, M. J. 1981: *English Culture and the Decline of the Industrial Spirit 1850–1980*. Cambridge: Cambridge University Press.

Wilkins, M. 1994: 'Comparative Costs', *Business History*, vol. 36, no. 1, pp. 18–50.

Wilkinson, B. 1983: *The Shopfloor Politics of New Technology*. London: Heinemann.

Williams, F. 2003: 'Talks Unravel Over Cotton', *Financial Times*, 16 September.

Williamson, J. G. 1995: 'Globalization, Convergence and History', Presidential Address to the Economic History Association, Chicago, 9 September.

Willis, P. 1977: *Learning to Labour: How Working Class Kids Get Working Class Jobs*. Aldershot: Gower.

Willmott, H. 1987: 'Racism, Politics and Employment Relations', in Lee, G. and Loveridge, R. (eds), *The Manufacture of Disadvantage: Stigma and Social Closure*. Milton Keynes: Open University Press.

Willmott, H. 1997: 'Rethinking Management and Management Work: Capitalism, Control and Subjectivity', *Human Relations*, vol. 50, no. 11, pp. 1329–59.

Wilson, E. O. 1975: *Socio-Biology: The New Synthesis*. Boston. Mass.: Harvard University Press.

Wilson, P. and Stanworth, J. 1988: 'Growth Strategies in Small Asian and Caribbean Businesses', *Employment Gazette*, January.

Wilson, W. J. 1987: *The Truly Disadvantaged: the Inner City, the Underclass and Public Policy*. Chicago: Chicago University Press.

Winn, M. 1983: *Children without Childhood*. New York: Pantheon.

Winner, L. 1977: *Autonomous Technology*. Cambridge, Mass.: MIT Press.

Winner, L. 1985: 'Do Artefacts have Politics?', in Mackenzie, D. and Wajcman, J. (eds), *The Social Shaping of Technology*. Milton Keynes: Open University Press.

Wintour, P. and Black, I. 2004: 'UK May Tighten Benefit Controls to Deter New EU Immigrants', *Guardian*, 5 February.

Wintour, P. and Tirbutt, S. 1988: *Guardian*, 26 October.

Witte, J. F. 1980: *Democracy, Authority and Alienation in Work*. Chicago: Chicago University Press.

Wojtas, O. 1989: 'Forced off Career Ladder', *Times Higher Education Supplement*, 10 March.

Wolff, E. N. (ed.), 1987: *International Comparisons of the Distribution of Household Wealth*. Oxford: Clarendon.

Wolff, J. 1977: 'Women in Organizations', in Clegg, S. and Dunkerley, D. (eds), *Critical Issues in Organizations*. London: Routledge.

Womack, J. P., Jones, D. T. and Roos, D. 1990: *The Machine that Changed the World*. New York: Rawson and Collier/Macmillan.

Wood, E. 1981: 'Marxism and Ancient Greece', *History Workshop*, no. 11, pp. 3–22.

Wood, E. M. 1986: *The Retreat from Class: a New True Socialism*. London: Verso.

Wood, S. (ed.), 1982: *The Degradation of Work*. London: Hutchinson.

Woodburn, J. 1980: 'Hunters and Gatherers Today and Reconstruction of the Past', in Gellner, E. (ed.), *Soviet and Western Anthropology*. London: Duckworth.

Woods, G. 2001: 'When the Going gets Tough', *Guardian*, 5 July.

Woodward, C. Vann. 1974: *The Strange Career of Jim Crow*. New York: Oxford University Press.

Woodward, J. 1958: *Management and Technology*. London: HMSO.

Woodward, J. 1965: *Industrial Organization*. Oxford: Oxford University Press.

Woodward, J. (ed.), 1970: *Industrial Organization: Behaviour and Control*. Oxford: Oxford University Press.

Woodward, W. 2001a: 'Britain Near Bottom for Adult Literacy', *Guardian*, 29 March.

Woodward, W. 2001b: 'UK Spending on Education Lags Behind Rivals', *Guardian*, 14 June.

Woolgar, J. 1989: Personal communication.

Woolgar, S. 1988: *Science: the Very Idea*. London: Ellis Horwood/Tavistock.

Woolgar, S. 1989a: 'Stabilization Rituals: Steps in the Socialization of a New Machine', paper presented at the PICT conference, Brunel University, May.

Woolgar, S. 1989b: 'Designing Users and Selling Futures', paper presented at the PICT conference, CRICT, Brunel University, May.

Woolgar, S. 1990: Personal communication.

Wootton, B. 1955: *The Social Foundations of Wage Policy*. London: Allen & Unwin.

Wray, R. 2003: 'Gent Regrets Accepting £15m Options Package', *Guardian*, 20 February.

Wrench, J. 1985: 'Unequal Comrades: Trade Unions, Equal Opportunity and Anti-Racism', mimeo, RUER. Coventry: University of Warwick.

Wright, E. O. 1978: *Class, Crisis and the State*. London: New Left Books.

Wright, E. O. 1985: *Classes*. London: Verso.

Wright, P. 1968: *The Coloured Worker in British Industry*. Oxford: Oxford University Press/Institute for Race Relations.

Wright, T. 1867: *Some Habits and Customs of the Working Classes by a Journeyman Engineer*. London: Tinsley Brothers. Republished 1967 by Augustus M. Kelley Publishers.

Wright Mills, C. 1951: *White Collar*. Oxford: Oxford University Press.

Wright Mills, C. 1970: *The Sociological Imagination*. Harmondsworth: Penguin.

Wrong, D. 1961: 'The Oversocialized Conception of Man in Modern Sociology', *American Sociological Review*, vol. 26, pp. 183–93.

Wylie, I. and Papworth, J. 1996: 'Are Women Still Being Squeezed?', *Guardian*, 26 October.

Yeandle, S. 1984: *Women's Working Lives: Patterns and Strategies*. London: Tavistock.

Yearley, S. 1996: *Sociology, Environmentalism, Globalization: Reinventing the Globe*. London: Sage.

Young, J.A. 1990: 'An American Giant Rethinks Globalization', *Information Strategy*, vol. 6, no. 3, pp. 5–19.

Young, M. 1958: *The Rise of the Meritocracy*. Harmondsworth: Penguin.

YWCA (Young Women's Christian Association), 1987: *Girls in 'Male' Jobs: a Research Report*. London: YWCA.

Zabalza, A. and Tzannatos, Z. 1985: *Women and Equal Pay*. Cambridge: Cambridge University Press.

Zaleznik, A. 1989: 'Real Work', *Harvard Business Review*, January–February.

Zaretsky, E. 1976: *Capitalism, the Family and Personal Life*. London: Pluto.

Zeitlin, J. 1982: 'Trade Unions and Job Control: a Critique of Rank and Filism', paper to the Society for the Study of Labour History at Birkbeck College, London, 27 November.

Zeitlin, J. 1983: 'Social Theory and the History of Work', *Social History*, vol. 8, pp. 365–74.

Zeitlin, J. 1985: 'Engineers and Compositors: a Comparison', in Harrison, R. and Zeitlin, J. (eds), *Divisions of Labour: Skilled Workers and Technological Change in Nineteenth Century England*. Brighton: Harvester.

Zeldin, T. 2001: 'Conversation', Presentation at Templeton College, Oxford, 20 May.

Zobel, G. 1997: 'Horsemen of an Apocalypse', *Guardian*, 13 August.

Zuboff, S. 1988: *In the Age of the Smart Machine: The Future of Work and Power*. Oxford: Heinemann.

Zwerdling, D. 1978: *Democracy at Work*. Washington, DC: Association for Self Management.

Index